The Master of Seventh Avenue

David Dubinsky at Local 89 installation at the Hippodrome, New York City, 1934. *ILGWU, UNITE Archives, Kheel Center, Cornell University.*

The Master of Seventh Avenue

David Dubinsky and the
American Labor Movement

Robert D. Parmet

NEW YORK UNIVERSITY PRESS
New York and London

NEW YORK UNIVERSITY PRESS
New York and London
www.nyupress.org

© 2005 by New York University
All rights reserved

Library of Congress Cataloging-in-Publication Data
Parmet, Robert D., 1938–
The master of Seventh Avenue : David Dubinsky and the American
labor movement / Robert D. Parmet.
p. cm.
Includes bibliographical references and index.
ISBN 0–8147–6711–7 (cloth : alk. paper)
1. Dubinsky, David, 1892– 2. Clothing workers—Labor unions—
United States—History. 3. Labor unions—United States—Officials
and employees—Biography. 4. Labor leaders—United States—
Biography. I. Title.
HD6509.D8P37   2005
331.88'187'092—dc22   2004029212

New York University Press books are printed on acid-free paper,
and their binding materials are chosen for strength and durability.

Manufactured in the United States of America

10 9 8 7 6 5 4 3 2 1

For Joanie

Contents

All illustrations appear as an insert following p. 212.

Preface

It was around 1950, and I was with my mother at Unity House, the summer vacation resort operated by the International Ladies' Garment Workers' Union (ILGWU) in the Pocono Mountains of Pennsylvania. There at last I caught a glimpse of David Dubinsky, playing cards with his friends on the terrace of the Administration Building while his English racer bicycle rested alongside the outer wall. Growing up in an ILGWU household, as a member's son, I had often heard about Dubinsky and read about him in the union newspaper, *Justice*.

In 1983, a year after his death, I discovered his correspondence at the ILGWU Archives, then located on Seventh Avenue in Manhattan. In appreciation of the value of these papers, I used them as the major resource for a biography of Dubinsky. Now I offer what I hope will be regarded as an honest, accurate, and insightful study.

In preparing this work, I received much help, for which I am extremely grateful. At the ILGWU Archives, archivist Bob Lazar provided outstanding assistance. Similarly, after four years, when the Archives moved to Ithaca, Richard Strassberg, the director of what is now the Kheel Center for Labor-Management Documentation at Cornell University, gave my work invaluable support.

I found the gracious, professional assistance of librarians and archivists to be indeed universal. My special thanks go to the many dedicated professionals at such other institutions as the York College Library, Tamiment Library and Robert F. Wagner Labor Archives, George Meany Memorial Archives, Queens College Library, La Guardia and Wagner Archives at La Guardia Community College, Archives of Labor and Urban Affairs at Wayne State University, New York Public Library, John F. Kennedy Library, Library of Congress, Arthur and Elizabeth Schlesinger Library at Radcliffe College, YIVO Institute for Jewish Research, Yale University Library, Columbia University Libraries, Jewish

Labor Bund Archives, University of Rochester Library, Seeley G. Mudd
Manuscript Library at Princeton University, National Archives, Hoover
Institution Archives, Franklin D. Roosevelt Library, New York Munici-
pal Archives, and Great Neck Public Library.

In addition to directing me to research materials, archival personnel
provided assistance in the selection of photographs to be used in this vol-
ume. In this regard I am appreciative of the help provided by Remy
Squires of the Hoover Institution, Barbara Morley of the Kheel Center,
and E. Philip Scott of the Lyndon B. Johnson Library.

I would also like to thank the Research Foundation–CUNY for two
PSC-CUNY Research Awards that facilitated travel to archives and the
transcribing of recorded interviews. Thanks, too, to Jitka Salaquarda for
her transcriptions. For research assistance at the Hoover Institution, I
thank Robert Feigin. Special thanks are also in order for B and R Computer Services of San Diego for updating the computer format of my text,
and to Vanessa Grande and Stephen Yu of York College for invaluable
administrative and technical assistance. For translating text from Yiddish
to English, my thanks go to Rabbi Herbert Kavon and the late Rabbi
Judah Mayefsky. Perceptive and knowledgeable, Gail Malmgreen provided indispensable copyediting assistance.

Over the past two decades, and in various ways, numerous other individuals, some of whom have passed away, provided support to help make
this book possible. They include Roza Alexander, Joseph Gotteiner, Benjamin A. Gebiner, Meyer Miller, Edward Schneider, Samuel Weiss, Harry
Goldberg, Bernard Bellush, Ira Leonard, Michele Briones, Barry Gewen,
Dwight Burton, Patrick Giagnacova, Burton Hall, Herman Benson,
Philoine Fried, David Melman, Morris Weisz, Dr. Edwin C. Weiss,
Howard Presant, Elisabeth Burger, Alonzo Hamby, Allen Breslow, Herbert Rose, Herbert Hill, Walter Mankoff, Marvin Rogoff, Joseph
Kissane, David A. Rush, and Janet Willen. Thanks, too, to the members
of the Dubinsky family, union associates, and friends whose personal in-
terviews are cited in the text

As this work evolved, I was able to present portions at conferences,
which produced helpful suggestions. In this regard, I thank Dominic
Capeci, Kitty Krupat, Irwin Yellowitz, Philip Napoli, and Ellen Schrecker.
Additional suggestions included those made by my brother, Herbert S.
Parmet, who read the manuscript and provided steadfast counsel.

My wife, Joan B. Parmet, often served as my "silent partner." In many
ways, from providing research assistance to reading the manuscript,

chapter by chapter over several years, to offering sound advice at every stage of the book's development, she contributed to its successful completion.

For his counsel, too, I thank my son, Andrew. As a participant in the roller-coaster ride that the preparation of this book entailed, he was an important source of stability as the years wore on.

Finally, thanks to Stephen Magro and Debbie Gershenowitz of NYU Press. It was their enthusiastic support for this project that made the book a reality.

Introduction

Only five feet, four inches in height but a giant in the American labor movement, David Dubinsky has not been the subject of a serious biography. Such was my discovery in 1983, a year after his death at age ninety, when I commenced work on this book. It amazed me that the story of this man, who had been the president of a major trade union for thirty-four years, a founder of two political parties, and an active enemy of Nazism and Communism, had been told only in a brief "pictorial biography" by the philosopher John Dewey; a longer work by Max Danish, the editor of his union's newspaper; and a taped autobiography edited by his close friend, journalist A. H. Raskin. Believing that Dubinsky deserves better, I decided to provide an honest and accurate view of his exceptionally productive, and often controversial, life.

As a youth Dubinsky combined pragmatism and ideology to become a center of attention. Influenced by the Jewish Labor Bund, he was twice arrested in czarist Poland for union activity. Fleeing the police in his homeland, he arrived in New York City in January 1911, became a garment cutter, and joined the International Ladies' Garment Workers' Union and the Socialist Party. Energetic and ambitious, he became a leader of the Cutters' Union and ILGWU, only to find Communists vying for control of both. Opposed to a radical takeover, he engaged in a civil war that threatened the existence of the International in the 1920s. Though a sturdy survivor of that bitter conflict, Dubinsky emerged permanently scarred. His enmity toward Communism would remain.

As he would often note, 1932 saw the election of two presidents, Franklin D. Roosevelt and David Dubinsky. The ILGWU president greatly admired FDR and identified with New Deal liberalism, eventually leaving the Socialists. Within the International, he continued and greatly expanded a vision known as "social unionism," offering workers benefits ranging from health care to housing. Within the national labor movement, he championed industrial unionism but characteristically avoided radicalism. He helped found the Committee for Industrial Organization within the American Federation of Labor (AFL) but later rejected the committee's conversion into a separate labor federation, favoring reconciliation. Averse to the major political parties, Dubinsky also created the American Labor Party (ALP) in New York State. After protracted conflict with the left wing of the ALP, headed by fellow needle-trade union leader Sidney Hillman, he abandoned that organization and founded a new Liberal Party. Relying on the ILGWU for financial support, Dubinsky and the Liberals played balance-of-power politics in New York City and State into the 1970s. Liberal endorsement contributed to the election of Governor W. Averell Harriman in 1954, President John F. Kennedy in 1960, and Mayor John V. Lindsay in 1965.

Dubinsky fought Fascism and Nazism as well as Communism. With family in Poland, and aware of the plight of Europe's Jews, in the 1930s he mobilized organized labor in America against Nazi Germany. When the Second World War began, he undertook activities to rescue democratic Socialists from Hitler and afterward engaged in refugee relief efforts. Shaken by the destruction of European Jewry, he abandoned his aversion to Zionism and supported the creation of the State of Israel.

During the war, Dubinsky also exported his anti-Communism. In conjunction with the American Federation of Labor, he initiated efforts to check Communist influence over organized labor in Western Europe, most notable in France, Germany, and Italy. A founder of the AFL's Free Trade Union Committee and then the International Confederation of Free Trade Unions, he waged war on international Communism, relying on the expertise of former Communist Jay Lovestone.

A household name as early as the 1930s, Dubinsky, though very conscious of his Jewish immigrant origins and Yiddish accent, held his own in the company of politicians such as Franklin Roosevelt, John Kennedy, and Lyndon Johnson and labor leaders such as William Green, John L. Lewis, Sidney Hillman, Alex Rose, George Meany, and Walter Reuther. Along with Hillman and Rose, he was a Jew in a gentile world.

During the 1950s things went awry. A "labor statesman" to some observers, he took pride in the 1955 merger of the American Federation of Labor and the Congress of Industrial Organization (CIO) and the new organization's adoption of a "Code of Ethical Practices." On excellent terms with AFL-CIO president George Meany, Dubinsky appeared to epitomize the successful labor leader. But times were changing, and Dubinsky's response to them appeared to reflect complacency and advancing age. As the ILGWU was "Dubinsky's union," cracks in its foundation were his responsibility. Criticism of Dubinsky and the ILGWU came from both conservatives and liberals. In 1957 a U.S. Senate investigation into labor racketeering compelled him to address allegations of corruption within his own union, despite his long-standing reputation as a foe of such practices. As a union founded and run by Jewish and Italian immigrants, the ILGWU had long supported racial justice, but complaints coming from the respected National Association for the Advancement of Colored People (NAACP) that the union itself was guilty of racial discrimination caused considerable embarrassment. In addition, when admittedly underpaid members of the International's own staff created a union of their own, Dubinsky vehemently resisted recognizing it. Finally, in 1965 senior ILGWU officers publicly questioned his support of the Republican Lindsay for mayor. With age and health concerns bearing down on him, this dissent was especially difficult for Dubinsky to endure. The next year Dubinsky retired without having solved another problem: increasing competition from garment imports.

Combative, both adored and despised, David Dubinsky contributed significantly to the labor movement. Based largely on archival sources, including his personal correspondence and personal interviews, this book tells his story, independent of union or family authorization or approval. A biography that respects the humanity of its subject, it is an account of an immigrant's rise to prominence that places him where he properly belongs, at the center of the history of American labor in the twentieth century.

1

Escape from Czarism

On the 160th anniversary of George Washington's birthday, February 2, 1892, David Isaac Dobnievski, the youngest of five boys and three girls of Bezalel and Shaine Wishingrad Dobnievski, was born in the city of Brest-Litovsk near the Russian border in eastern Poland, then part of the Russian Empire.[1]

The Dobnievski family resided in Brest-Litovsk until 1895, when Bezalel moved it to Lodz, the leading textile center in the western part of the Russian Empire.[2] In 1815 the Russians had succeeded the Prussians as rulers of the city. Under Russian direction the textile industry developed, attracting Jewish weavers, and the Jewish population grew considerably. The city's more than 98,000 Jews in 1897 comprised almost 32 percent of the general population.[3] By the turn of the twentieth century, most of the Jewish industrial workers in Lodz were in textiles,[4] and by 1910 Jews owned 159 of the city's 305 "larger factories."[5]

The concentration of industry made the city ugly, and worse than Lodz's filth was its contrast between rich and poor. It was a city of mansions alongside slums and streets discolored by the textile waste dyes because there was no sewage system.[6] As late as 1903 its factory workers labored from "sixteen to eighteen hours a day."[7]

As might be expected, Lodz was a place of much industrial unrest. On May 1, 1892, 70,000 workers participated in a general strike, but an anti-Jewish riot, or pogrom, followed. In 1897, a Jewish socialist party, the General Jewish Labor Bund, was founded at Vilna, but Lodz was one of its leading centers of activity, resulting in repression of the city's workers' movement. In March 1901, 2,000 workers gathered for the funeral of a popular Bundist but were dispersed by Cossacks.[8]

The Dobnievski family arrived in Lodz shortly before David's third birthday. Initially they lived in the basement of an old house at 1 Kamienna Street,[9] where David recalled feeling little parental affection. As the youngest of eight children, he evidently felt it necessary to use his wits to gain attention or simply hold his own among his older brothers and sisters. Bezalel Dobnievski was a religious man. He prayed in the synagogue three times each day but had little interest in the bakery he owned or in anything other than religion. As David would later recall, "All he did was keep the books and order the flour. He knew very little else about the bakery or even about baking." "The real boss" of the business and the family was Shaina, David's mother.[10] David was eight when she died, and a year and a half later Bezalel returned to his native Brest-Litovsk and brought back to Lodz a stepmother named Rayzel for his eight children.

Rayzel Dobnievski gave her husband two sons and a daughter,[11] but her stepchildren, including David, despised her. She was "a stranger" in the house who allegedly dominated Bezalel even more than Shaina had. The stepchildren believed that she feigned fainting spells in order to be revived with a favorite cordial. During one such spell, one of David's brothers checked to see if it was real by sticking her with a pin, only to be in turn smacked by his father who had entered the room."[12] With David's older siblings playing an important part in running the bakery after Shaina's death, business had improved and the family moved to better surroundings, from the basement on Kamienna Street to ground-floor rooms at 27 Srednia Street, behind the bakery. In warm weather, David's usual "bed" was a delivery wagon in the backyard, but when the temperature dropped he moved into the kitchen. Near the head of his bed, in the kitchen, was a board on which the bakers who worked in the evening left bread and rolls to cool. David could not have had a more direct introduction to baking.[13]

However, education came before a career in baking. David first attended a Hebrew school, where he studied Polish, Russian, and Yiddish, and then the semi-private Poznansky School. Named for the leading textile manufacturer in Lodz, it was on the level of an American high school and was, along with the Kunstadt School, the best of only four such schools in the city. Because of Bezalel's preoccupation with prayer and Rayzel's dislike of him, David had to rely on his own devices to gain admission. Therefore, he took the trolley, registered at four schools, and luckily was chosen by Poznansky.

Even while attending the primary school, however, David began each day by delivering freshly baked bread and rolls to stores supplied by his father. At 6 a.m. he was a delivery boy and at 8 a.m. a student. One day as he neared his fourteenth birthday, and after he had already spent two years at the Poznansky School, Bezalel insisted that he leave school and replace his older brother in the bakery. Lazer, a master baker, had gone to play cards and not returned.[14]

David entered an industry that was singularly unattractive. Among Jewish workers in Poland, bakers endured some of the worst working conditions, with employer-employee relations regarded as extremely paternalistic. In 1901 the bakers of Bialystock had called a strike and won several demands, including a twelve-hour day and the regular payment of wages. In Lodz there was less sense of class consciousness. As of 1903, bakers there had not yet participated in the labor movement and were working as many as fifteen hours a day, six days a week.[15]

By 1905 the possibility that bakers and other workers within the Russian Empire might have a better life suddenly appeared realistic. Russia was in revolution. Agitation for reform and unrest had been on the rise since 1904, when a disastrous war began with Japan over control of Manchuria and Korea and a terrorist bomb took the life of Minister of the Interior Vyacheslav Plehve. On January 9, 1905, Father Georgy Gapon, a Russian Orthodox priest, led a group of workers to the Winter Palace of Czar Nicholas II in St. Petersburg for a peaceful protest. The military fired on them, killing about two hundred and staining the white snow on the ground red. "Bloody Sunday," as the day was called, led to additional agitation for reform, which was expressed via strikes, terrorist bombings, and a naval mutiny by the crew of the battleship *Potemkin* at Odessa.

For Russia's Jews, the revolution meant new waves of government-supported oppression. Feared and despised by Russian Christians, Jews had been residentially segregated within the empire since the 1790s, in southern and western provinces known as the Pale of Settlement. Blamed for the assassination of Czar Alexander II in 1881, Jews became the targets of violent pogroms and of laws designed to isolate them. Widespread anti-Semitic violence continued through 1905. Government officials blamed the revolution on the Jews and incited new pogroms in the Pale of Settlement.[16] Primarily under the leadership of revolutionary socialist organizations, the Jewish workers fought back, especially the Jewish Labor Bund.[17] Immediately after Bloody Sunday, the Bund, as it was known, issued a leaflet, *To Arms!* which proclaimed that "The Revolution" had arrived and urged workers to seize weapons from arsenals. A wave of demonstrations and general strikes followed, and casualties mounted.

Lodz experienced "open rebellion."[18] In June, Cossacks attacked Jewish and Polish demonstrators, leading to a huge protest rally. A few days later there was a second rally, twice the size of the first, and another attack on the demonstrators. The result of these assaults was a full-scale uprising, "the battle of Lodz," on June 22 and 23. Lodz's proletariat rose up and the streets were filled with barricades and human casualties.[19]

In October 1905, revolutionary events reached a climax. Less than two months after a negotiated settlement ended the war with Japan, Russia was paralyzed by a general strike. In response to the latter, Nicholas II signed the October Manifesto, granting a constitution that guaranteed civil liberties, broadened suffrage, and granted legislative powers to the Duma, a national congress that had been established in August. It seemed that Russia was on the road to democracy, but for her Jews there was renewed despair. As the manifesto was made public, Russia plunged into the most severe pogroms in her history.[20]

The persecution continued into the middle of 1906. By this time fourteen-year-old David was a unionist as well as a baker. At a mass meeting he had attended in 1905, he had been greatly impressed by several Bund speakers, notably Ephraim Loozer Zelmanowicz, the leader of the hosiery union. This gathering evidently began his gradual involvement with the Bund. He joined the bakers' union, which was controlled by the Bund, and, owing to his superior education, soon became assistant secretary of the union. As he later recalled with regard to the Bund, "I was not a member of the party but I considered myself already a Bundist without being a member of the party." Furthermore, he said he "began reading" Bund literature only after he joined the union.[21]

The Bund had been founded in September 1897 at a conference in Vilna during the Jewish High Holy Days so that outsiders, the police in particular, would view the movement of the delegates as the ordinary travel of friends. Their goal was to organize the Jewish working class throughout the western part of the Russian Empire, represent Jewish interests, and become part of the larger revolutionary movement.[22] As the creation of Jewish Socialists, the Bund was more Socialist than Jewish, but Jews would be recognized as a nationality within a workers' state and the Yiddish language and cultural expressions fostered and respected. As Bernard Johnpoll has written, the Bund was not "interested specifically in the welfare of the Jewish workers as Jews, but rather as a working-class party interested in the Jewish workers as part of the working class."[23] Approaching adulthood in an era of repression and revolution, David Dobnievski embraced democratic socialism as the path to a better world and accepted the Bundist vision of a utopia where Jews could thrive as a nation by being granted cultural freedom, and where one could be proudly Jewish without being religious.

As early as age fifteen, David moved in the direction of the Bund and away from his father. As assistant secretary of the bakers' union, it was David's first task to draw up a call for a strike demanding a pay increase. Bezalel Dobnievski's bakery was among those to be struck. Moreover, David enlisted his young stepsister, Gita, to the cause. To avoid being caught by the police with strike flyers in his possession, he had Gita carry them in her basket from the printers to a union meeting. The bakers won an increase, but immediately afterward the police arrested the strike organizers, including David. They came for him in the middle of the night, at 3 a.m., but before he left the house Bezalel gave him something to take to the police station: coins to buy favors from the jailers. David was placed "in a big cell with more than sixty other strikers" but freed after three days, before he could be docketed, on the condition that he leave town and not return. Bezalel had bought his release from the chief of police for twenty-five rubles.[24]

He left for his birthplace, Brest-Litovsk, and then traveled to Kobrin, thirty miles east. There he worked as a baker, earning very little—and yearned for Lodz. Knowing he could not be seen in Lodz as David Dobnievski, he first returned to Brest-Litovsk, where he obtained a passport under a pseudonym. By claiming he had lost his original passport and then advertising the loss for three days in a newspaper, he was able to secure a replacement from authorities who knew nothing of his political activities. Even with the new document, David was fearful. A policeman in Lodz could recognize him by sight. So he went back but also hid, living in turn with various friends and relatives.[25]

David had no scruples about rejoining the union and was pleased to carry out various assignments, including one concerning his father, to whom he had also returned. David was responsible for learning from Bezalel and then reporting to the union the plans of the bakery owners. Simply stated, he informed on his father, the man whose money had recently secured his release from jail. But it was also David's task to put an end to the bakery workers' practice of stealing from their employers.[26]

This activity was short-lived. On January 8, 1908, six weeks before his sixteenth birthday, David was arrested again at a union election meeting, which was held with a police permit. Permits were required to hold all meetings, but this particular one was issued for a special purpose, as afterward became obvious. In attendance was a government official. Also present was Shmul Domshevski, known as "Noach," a Bund representative and union leader. During the open voting by shows of hands, the nominees awaited the results in the nearby hosiery workers' union office. The first nominee was Noach, who was waiting in that office when a Bund member warned him that the police had surrounded the meeting and urged him to escape through a rear door. Instead of leaving, Noach returned to the meeting room and informed David of the police presence. Noach would not leave but offered to nominate David for secretary, which would give him a chance to get out. The fact that Noach, a well-known Socialist with a police record, stood his ground, impressed David, who likewise refused to run. The meeting ended with the arrest of everyone.

His son's second arrest was too much for Bezalel Dobnievski to tolerate. This time, as David later said, "my father disowned me and would not help me. As a result of it, I spent 18 months in jail and was sent to Siberia."[27] In any case, Bezalel probably could not have done much to help. David had returned to Lodz without permission and was now regarded as a political prisoner, a revolutionary, just like Noach; still only sixteen years old, David was sentenced to exile in Siberia.[28]

Thus proceeded his prison odyssey, which began in Lodz. It was followed by Warsaw's Paviak and Moscow's Butyrki. The year and a half he spent in prison put him in physical contact with bedbugs and intellectual contact with both hardened criminals and political offenders. The criminals thought kindly of the "politicals," whom they saw as idealists sacrificing themselves for the downtrodden. David, perhaps for the first time, began to think seriously about the contrasting fates of rich and poor in society.

From Moscow, David journeyed to Samara, where he spent time in yet another jail en route to Chelyabinsk in Siberia. He made the trip to Samara in handcuffs that kept slipping off because his hands were so small. Stymied, his guards told him that in the presence of their superior he should act as though he were chained to the prisoner alongside him.[29]

Chelyabinsk was the last stop on the train, but it was not where David was being sent. He had hoped to remain there with some exiled friends, Yussel and Esther Rosenberg, but his request to the local governor received no reply. Hence, he was compelled to march with other exiles to some remote Siberian village. It was summer and hot, and the marchers covered between twenty and thirty miles per day beginning at 8 a.m. and ending at 6 p.m. As David had left Lodz with only heavy clothes, he found the heat hard to bear. Some of the clothes he carried in a sack, and some he sold to a guard. His food was "black bread and hot water."

After the tenth day he made up his mind to escape. His plan was to place himself at the end of the prisoner convoy and then just disappear. Before it could be tested, however, a guard, who observed how David was lagging behind and guessed what he aimed to do, suggested another escape route. He advised David to meet a Polish Socialist medical aide who was an exile in a village in which they were to sleep. The guard would even arrange the meeting with this man, who could tell David how to escape. With the guard's help, David found the aide, who told him to go on foot through the woods to a railway station twenty miles from the village, not the station nearest it. After his departure, the police would be sure to watch the nearby station, not the more distant one.

Unable to carry excess weight, David gave those clothes he could not wear on the run to another exile, a criminal named Krynin. While the guards had breakfast in their hut, David just walked out, then ran. Exhausted, he rested in a haystack and fell asleep. A few hours later he resumed his flight and soon encountered a peasant on horseback. The peasant concluded that he was a fugitive. "If you weren't a fugitive, why would you be sleeping in a stack of straw?" he asked. Hearing of the escape and obviously sympathetic, the peasant took him to his village and the house of a friend.

After he was introduced, David told the villager of his problem. The man then walked over to an icon hanging on a wall, knelt before it, and said a prayer for him. David's new protector advised him to sleep, because his escape would be carried out long after dark. When he awoke, the man offered a deal. He would give David his old-fashioned gun. David, once he returned home, would as a revolutionary naturally have access to a more modern rifle, which he would then send back to complete the swap. David then confessed that he knew nothing about and had no interest in firearms. Nevertheless, the escape plan was set, and in the middle of the night the villager took him in his wagon to an out-of-the-way stop along the railroad line. He gave David train fare plus two extra rubles and then, after praying again, placed him aboard a train bound for Chelyabinsk.

That city was still dark when David arrived, but he was determined to go immediately to the Rosenbergs. He hired a droshky to take him to their address, but the driver could not find it in the darkness and instead left David "in a dark alley" around where he thought it might be. With nowhere else to go and nobody around to ask for help, David spent the rest of the night sleeping in the alley "between two piles of stones." He was awakened at daybreak by the foot of the town crier, who was making his rounds. The crier told him to move on before the police arrested him "as a beggar." However, before he could leave the alley, a woman came out the front door of a house. David asked her where Yussel Rosenberg lived. She replied that the Rosenberg family had just moved from "that very house." To David's astonishment she asked, "You're David Dobnievski, aren't you? We've been expecting you." A letter he had sent from prison four weeks back had arrived the day before he did.

In the company of other exiles, David made himself comfortable in Chelyabinsk. Yussel's friends suggested he seek the assistance of a shamus, or caretaker, of a synagogue, who regularly advised the exiles. The shamus was from Brest-Litovsk and knew Bezalel Dobnievski, whom he telegraphed without delay with news of his son's freedom. Ignoring the Sabbath injunction against handling money, Bezalel immediately wired twenty-five rubles, explaining to his family that the Bible permitted it "to save a life."

The money arrived within hours, but it was the exile community that "saved" David. He lived with a butcher's family, worked as a baker, and even considered becoming a tailor. For relaxation, David had plenty of friends, especially girls, with whom he attended concerts and went swimming and bicycle riding—reviving one of the relatively few pleasant memories of his childhood in Lodz.

After six months in Chelyabinsk, David decided to risk the danger of being caught and return home. Unable to afford a train ticket, he sneaked aboard. Lodz had not become any more beautiful during David's absence, and for him, as a fugitive, it was more perilous than before. He slept where he could, changing places nightly to avoid arrest. Yet he was able to find employment. During the day he worked "for an express company loading and unloading textiles," and on Friday nights, using a pseudonym, he "worked as a master baker on challahs." His aim was to save enough money to emigrate to the United States.[30] Here the Bund could help. The local Bund organization could help arrange his departure and provide some funds; a weaver and underground textile industry activist known as Laezer Ber had primary responsibility for this operation.[31]

There was family help as well. Brother Godel, who was already in America, sent steamship tickets for David and brother Chaim. The two

Dobnievskis then paid to be smuggled across the Polish border into Germany. From there they went to the port city of Antwerp, Belgium.[32] On December 24, 1910, they sailed in steerage on the Red Star liner *Lapland* for New York. As their ship entered New York Harbor on New Year's Day 1911, they could not immediately disembark. Two days later, on January 3, they were officially in America.[33]

Having tasted social and political injustice, David could recognize and combat it in his new land. He would never forget his origins or dismiss them as inconsequential. If anything, he took pride in them and tended, as was not unusual among refugees from the world of Czar Nicholas II, to exaggerate their significance.

2

East Side Socialist

Nineteen-year-old David Dubinsky, as he renamed himself after arriving in America, brought with him mixed baggage to his new country. The traditional Yiddish culture of East European Jewry had imparted a sense of ethnic identity and helped shape sexual and familial attitudes. Yet the skills required for survival in a youth he would remember as "full of misery, poverty, and inconvenience"[1] had included cleverness and pragmatism rather than intellectuality and traditionalism. His Bundist socialism would remind him of his revolutionary youth in Europe and provide the scaffolding of a secular Jewish faith in America.

Dubinsky's introduction to New York was through that intense concentration of humanity known as the Lower East Side. Jewish immigrants from the various corners of Russia, Poland, and Austria-Hungary found their way to that part of Manhattan Island. There David's brother Godel and sister-in-law Ruchska occupied a tenement apartment where he and Chaim could stay until they found their own lodgings. The apartment was located at 14 Clinton Street, a few blocks from the Manhattan Bridge, and consisted of "two rooms and a kitchen" with a single toilet shared by "all the tenants on the floor." Godel was a business agent for the bakery workers' union. David and Godel enjoyed the distinction of being the only literate family members, and the older brother thought his younger sibling might pursue a career more lucrative than baking.

Godel suggested David become a physician, but David had other ideas. Without his brother's knowledge, he found a job as a dishwasher and busboy in a basement restaurant on Clinton Street. However, he soon moved on. Through brother Chaim, David became a kneepants operator in a nonunion shop in Brooklyn. Up at five and at work by seven each morning, David paid three cents fare for the trolley that took him across the Williamsburg Bridge. After work, he saved the fare by walking home.

This new job paid him nothing for his first two weeks as a "learner," and afterward only three dollars per week.[2]

Rather than follow Godel's advice and study medicine, which would have been expensive, Dubinsky went into garment cutting. Cutters, especially of coats and suits, were the well-paid aristocrats of the needle trades. Full membership in this elite group was restricted. It required, first, the necessary skills and, second, admission to their prestigious organization, the Amalgamated Ladies' Garment Cutters' Union.

With both luck and deception, Dubinsky accomplished the feat. The good fortune was that sister-in-law Ruchska knew a landsman at the Boston Cloak Company on Twenty-fourth Street who would train him for a fee of twenty-five dollars. The money was supposed to cover the cost of materials that he might ruin because of his lack of expertise, but when he saw the cutter, Danziger, pocket the money, Dubinsky realized it would never be used to pay expenses.[3]

Once in the shop David learned quickly, laboring without pay with the help of a Russian designer who sat behind him. The next hurdle was the task of joining the exclusive Amalgamated Ladies' Garment Cutters' Union. Its origins lay in the Gotham Knife Cutters' Association of 1884, which came into being when the invention of a heavy, long-handled cutting knife made garment cutting a male occupation. More recently, the cutters had been organized as Local 6 of the International Ladies' Garment Workers' Union. In 1900 immigrant Jewish Socialists had founded the ILGWU, but Local 6 was largely native-born, Irish, and German. Monopolistic and conservative, the leaders of Local 6 feared an influx of immigrant labor radicals.

Conflict between the native-born and immigrant cutters flared after the turn of the century. In 1906, President Samuel Gompers of the American Federation of Labor stepped in and cutters were placed under the jurisdiction of a new Local 10, the Amalgamated Ladies' Garment Cutters' Union of Greater New York. But feuding between the cutters and other garment workers continued, becoming so bitter that Local 10's charter was revoked in 1907. Even after the local was reinstated two years later, the conservative attitudes of its leaders persisted.[4]

It was to this kind of club that David Dubinsky sought admission. As opportunistic as ever, he did what was necessary. In the United States only four months, he would have to convince the cutters' union that he had served an apprenticeship of three years in the trade. As a union business agent, Godel Dubinsky knew Sol Metz, who headed the cloakmakers' union. Metz approached Jesse P. Cohen, the manager of the cutters' union, who asked for some documentary evidence of experience. Ruchska Dubinsky then fabricated, on a tailor's letterhead she had customprinted, a letter stating that David had a year's experience. David then gave the letter to Cohen. Then, on June 1, David Dubinsky appeared before the Executive Board of Local 10. He told the ten board members that he had three years' experience, which included two years' employment on Walnut Street in Philadelphia and one year on Essex Street in New York. Not persuaded by his testimony, the board set aside his application pending further investigation.[5] Ten days later, at a Local 10 membership meeting held at Arlington Hall on St. Mark's Place, he was rejected.[6]

On June 29 he was back before the Executive Board. This time he had with him a "reference from Philadelphia" and "an affidavit stating that he worked for the firm of Jos. Cohen in Philadelphia for two years." Dubinsky also presented Local 10 manager Jesse Cohen with a letter of recommendation signed by three ILGWU notables: Cloak joint manager Sol Metz, President Abraham Rosenberg, and former president Benjamin Schlesinger. Dubinsky's admission to the cutters' union was moved and seconded, but there was continuing reluctance to admit him; for a second time, his case was to be investigated.[7] This inquiry, if it ever actually occurred, could not have been very thorough, possibly because of Godel's efforts on his behalf. On July 3, 1911, six months after his arrival in America, David Dubinsky was one of six new members elected to Local 10.[8]

Dubinsky joined Local 10 just as the International Ladies' Garment Workers' Union was beginning to attract attention as a significant force in New York City. Since its birth in 1900, the ILGWU had remained alive by somehow overcoming an uneven national economy and its own internal conflicts. Though sweatshop conditions cried out for amelioration, the union could not compel management to negotiate—not until November 1909. Then, demanding improved working conditions, the mainly Jewish immigrant women of Local 25, the shirtwaist workers, startled the garment industry and the city with a general strike. Though the ILGWU's entire membership numbered only two thousand, more than fifteen thousand waist- and dressmakers walked out of over five hundred factories. This "Uprising of the Twenty Thousand," as it was called, continued until February 1910. It ended without union recognition, but 339 of the 353 firms in the manufacturers' association, the target of the strike, signed agreements with the union, whose ranks now exceeded ten thousand.[9]

Five months later, more than fifty thousand cloakmakers went on strike for union recognition and improvements in wages and hours. They also won, and the strike settlement included the Protocol of Peace, an agreement with management that embodied the principle of impartial arbitration. Among the ILG-ers it drew bitter criticism from economist Dr. Isaac A. Hourwich and his supporters, who wanted to redefine and broaden employers' obligations. This "Hourwich Affair" divided the union until 1914 when Hourwich resigned and President Abraham Rosenberg was compelled to decline nomination for another term.[10] Observing this schism, David Dubinsky, who favored the dissidents, had his first real taste of American trade-union realism.[11]

Tragedy as well as victory advanced the cause of the ILGWU. On March 25, 1911, fire destroyed the three factory-loft floors of the Triangle Shirtwaist Company, a block east of Washington Square Park in lower Manhattan, taking the lives of 146 ladies' garment workers, most of them young Jewish and Italian immigrant women. Victims of blocked and inadequate emergency exits, these people gave vivid meaning to the word *sweatshop*.[12]

Reading of the Triangle Fire in a special edition of the *Jewish Daily Forward*, Dubinsky was deeply moved. With "tens of thousands" of other mourners, he marched in the funeral parade.[13] The fire, Dubinsky said, converted him from "a listener" at political rallies to an activist.[14]

In 1912, Dubinsky became a member of the Socialist Party.[15] He joined Branch Number One, the Jewish Branch, located on East Broadway. This Yiddish-speaking unit was known as a place where factional fights were frequent and from which future union leaders emerged. It was the "main" Socialist hotbed, fueled by the local bible of socialism, the *Jewish Daily Forward,* under the extraordinary editorship of Abraham Cahan.[16]

Under the leadership of Indiana's Eugene V. Debs, the nation's Socialists in 1912 were among the progressives who believed the time had come to reform U.S. governmental and economic institutions. Debs, in his fourth presidential bid, headed the national Socialist ticket, while on the Lower East Side there was special concern for Socialist attorney Meyer London, who was making his second consecutive race for Congress.

Along with many other Jewish Socialists, including the ILGWU's Cloak Joint Board, Dubinsky jumped into that campaign. He made speeches and chaired meetings. When a scheduled speaker failed to arrive on time, Dubinsky made his own debut as a political orator, speaking in

Yiddish. In supporting London, Dubinsky defied his own union's leaders, including manager Jesse Cohen, a staunch supporter of the Democratic machine, whom the Socialists derided as a "Tammanyhallnik." Dubinsky and thousands of others awaited the returns at the Forward Building on East Broadway. On their arrival at the *Forward*'s office, he transmitted the results to the crowd outside, reporting Woodrow Wilson's victory and London's defeat.[17]

Second Avenue within the Eighth Assembly District, considered "uptown," was the center of a thriving Yiddish theater world and of East Side socialism. Its district's Socialists were generally "English-speaking" and "youthful, a mixture of intellectuals and workers from various trades" who met regularly to discuss their common concerns. Their political leader and perennial candidate, Louis Waldman, was finally elected to the State Assembly in 1917, only to be one of five Socialist assemblymen expelled in 1920 because of their party membership.[18]

The famous Cafe Royal on Second Avenue and Twelfth Street was a gathering place for Yiddish actors and writers. First introduced to the restaurant by brother Godel, Dubinsky would later make it his "hangout" and eat there on an almost daily basis. However, shortly after becoming a cutter, he and nine Socialist friends each contributed ten dollars to open their own restaurant, a cooperative establishment that they initially located on Tenth Street, east of Second Avenue, but then moved onto Second. It was a place to get twenty-five-cent meals and participate in a literary discussion club that met on the premises. Among its more notable patrons was a revolutionary named Leon Trotsky, who resided in New York in early 1917.[19]

The cooperative venture was not a success, and Dubinsky soon extricated himself from it. But it was there he met his future wife in 1914.[20] One day at the restaurant, dressmaker and literary club member Abe Rottenberg noticed two attractive girls and called them to David's attention. They were Emma Goldberg, an eighteen-year-old brunette from Lithuania, and Molly Farbyash. Both were ladies' garment workers, operators on underclothes. "I was always a faker," David would later reminisce as he explained that he preferred Emma to Molly but did not want anyone to know. "So it cost me double," he said, noting that he dated both girls together, "but always as part of a larger group" of as many as eight people. On one occasion, when David took Emma alone to vaudeville at the

Palace Theater on Broadway, he told her he was returning to Europe because he had to serve in the Russian army. She became alarmed, and he
was delighted.

As their romance ripened, David and Emma became "very intimate."
According to his account, "as a Socialist without interest in religious rit-
ual," he could easily have bypassed a religious ceremony, but Emma
wanted one. So they were married by a rabbi, in 1914 or 1915, in a dry-
goods store owned by Emma's aunt on Pitkin Avenue in Brooklyn. Her
family, but not his, was present at the very modest affair. The newlyweds
moved to an apartment on Bay Twenty-second Street in Brooklyn's Bath
Beach area. Emma would later give birth to their daughter, Jeannette,
who would also be known as Jean.[21]

The conservatism of Local 10 was consistent with that of the parent International Ladies' Garment Workers' Union. Though Socialists had
founded the ILGWU, from its inception it combined radical ideas with
conservative trade-union practices. It regularly adopted resolutions in
favor of socialism and independent labor politics but was wary of strikes,
fearing that the loss of a general strike might be ruinous. During the
union's difficult first decade, its problems included a challenge from the
Industrial Workers of the World (IWW), which established rival unions
among cloak- and dressmakers and pressers. Not only was the IWW
guilty of the cardinal sin of engaging in "dual unionism," it was also in
competition with the ILGWU's patron, Samuel Gompers.

Twenty days after its founding, the ILGWU received a charter from
Gompers's American Federation of Labor.[22] Though one of the AFL's
largest affiliates, the ILGWU was not a major force within it. The pre-
dominantly Jewish organization was not represented on the Executive
Council of the Federation, whose membership was largely native-born or
of "old immigrant" ancestry. Additionally, there were ideological differences between the two trade organizations. The Garment Workers embraced socialism, which remained an anathema to Gompers, and strongly
opposed immigration restriction, which he vehemently advocated. In
1914 they supported the creation of the Amalgamated Clothing Workers
of America, which Gompers denounced as a dual union in opposition to
the AFL's United Garment Workers of America.

Despite these differences, the ILGWU's leaders cultivated friendly relations with Gompers. The reason for this amity was practical; in organizational and strike activity they often needed his assistance. Between

1903 and 1917 the AFL helped the ILGWU in such places as Cleveland, Chicago, Philadelphia, and New York. By 1920, after two decades of AFL support, the direction of the ILGWU was far from radical.[23]

Young but shrewd, and a veteran of union politics in Poland, Dubinsky began his career in Local 10. Probably feeling grateful for his admission to the local and indebted to Jesse Cohen for making it possible, he was not inclined to challenge the conservative leadership. Considering his Bundist background, this inactivity was difficult for others to understand.[24]

Elmer Rosenberg had no such inhibitions. A Hungarian-born Socialist who had joined Local 10 in 1909,[25] he spearheaded a movement to break the conservative grip.[26] His initial victory came in December 1913, when he won election as secretary of the union. Rosenberg's group, the Committee of Fifty, then reorganized as the Good and Welfare League.[27]

The irony of David Dubinsky's early labor activism is that it was inspired more by opposition to his union than to his employers. Upset at the arrogance of Local 10's old guard leadership, he joined the Good and Welfare League at its founding. However, as he had both reformist and conciliatory instincts, he was supportive but cautious about the League and would not become a League activist until 1916.[28]

The Good and Welfare League, which never had more than eighty members,[29] served the interests of Local 10's "newcomers," who "outnumbered the old-timers by almost four to one." Though the local's membership was mainly Jewish, the leadership was predominately gentile, "and even the few who were Jewish were more gentile than the gentiles." The leadership's loyalty to Tammany Hall irked the majority, who were Socialists, and other radicals of virtually all varieties. However, the most unpopular aspect of the union was its system of "favoritism and discrimination in employment."[30]

In 1917 the immediate task for Dubinsky and other East Side Socialists was to elect Morris Hillquit mayor of New York. Hillquit was a well-known lawyer for the ILGWU and an opponent of America's entry into the European war. In April 1917, the United States entered the conflict by declaring war on Germany. The November election in New York City would become America's "only referendum" on the wisdom of that action.[31] Hillquit ran well but in November lost to Tammany's John F. Hylan.

As New Yorkers elected a mayor, Bolsheviks in Russia seized power. Led by V. I. Lenin, these revolutionaries overthrew the liberal provisional government that had been established in March when an upheaval precipitated by wartime hardship toppled Czar Nicholas II and the Romanov dynasty. Many American Jews were thrilled; the Bolshevik revolution had some Jewish leadership and appeared to offer the benefits of freedom and security to Jews.[32] Dubinsky, though, was not pleased. He identified himself with the moderate Menshevik wing of the Russian revolutionary movement, sometime allies of the Bundists.

In a fight over Meyer London, Dubinsky lined up with the right wing of the Socialist movement in New York. In 1914, London had at last been elected to Congress. However, in 1918 many Socialists opposed his bid for a third term. At issue was London's support for America's involvement in the European conflict. Before April 1917, during the period of American neutrality, London had opposed such a step. With America at war he shifted and in Congress could not vote against war appropriations. Elsewhere he participated in rallies promoting the sale of war bonds.

Another issue of concern was London's failure to introduce a congressional resolution endorsing the Balfour Declaration of November 1917 in which the British government recognized Jewish claims to a national home in Palestine. Labor Zionists and left-wing socialists welcomed the declaration, but anti-Zionist Bundists opposed it. Accordingly, its supporters sought to block London's renomination.

Dubinsky "became the spokesman" for the pro-London faction. As the two sides in the dispute were of approximately equal strength, the battle was not easily decided. At tumultuous meetings votes were taken, but the outcome kept changing. At last "the Dubinsky group" of East Side Socialists won the contest and London was renominated, only to lose his seat in the general election.[33]

Hillquit and London were defeated, but Dubinsky was back. With the Good and Welfare League of Local 10 and the Socialist Party as his two bases, he was ready for new and more complex encounters. In 1917 his insurgent group had gained control of the union, thus paving the way for his election to its Executive Board in 1918 and to the vice presidency in the following year.[34]

Soon afterward he was in another kind of fight. The issue was the full affiliation of Local 10 with the Joint Board of the cloak and suit industry, which he strongly opposed. As 1920 began, the local enjoyed partial affiliation, which involved cooperation in such areas as strike action and shop control but no unified command or direction. In 1920 the question of full affiliation returned, supported by Israel Feinberg, chairman of the

Joint Board, and Manager Morris Sigman of Local 10. Dubinsky, Isidore Nagler, Samuel Perlmutter, and other cutters opposed it. They feared such a move would limit the local's freedom of action. However, that consideration was now secondary in view of an economic slowdown affecting the cutters. They needed help, which the proposal promised to provide. Putting that priority first, the opposition yielded.[35]

Though Dubinsky was defeated on the affiliation issue, his political progress lost no momentum. In March 1920 he was elected a delegate to the ILGWU's convention to be held in Chicago in May, and in December he won the presidency of Local 10, defeating John C. Ryan, a veteran of the Gotham Knife Cutters of the 1880s and the local's first president.[36]

Paralleling Dubinsky's ascendancy was the rise of a left wing within the ILGWU. In 1917, stirred by revolution in Russia, shirtwaist- and dressmakers of Local 25 had organized a Current Events Committee to spread the word. These women, many of whom had left Russia after the failed Revolution of 1905, hoped for a better world in America and particularly in their immediate sphere, the ILGWU. They cast critical eyes on the administration of President Benjamin Schlesinger, which they regarded as excessively bureaucratic. The Current Events Committee was gone by 1919, but the criticism was taken up by cloakmakers in Locals 1 and 9. The International's leadership had real cause for concern.[37]

In 1919, a year when radicalism seemed rampant, the Shop Delegates League was born. Inspired by the British shop-steward system and the Bolshevik revolution, this organization was at first called the Workers Council, a translation of the Russian word *soviet*. Its premise was that workers organized according to shops could shift union power from the hands of entrenched officials to those of the rank and file. In an effort to weaken the radicals by dividing them, the ILGWU's General Executive Board (GEB) in 1920 received convention approval to remove the dressmakers from Local 25 and place them in a new Dressmakers' Union, Local 22. The GEB accomplished the maneuver but succeeded only in spreading the dissidence and adding members to a new radical group, the Trade Union Educational League (TUEL).[38]

Founded in Chicago in November 1920, the TUEL was a consequence of the great steel strike of 1919. Beginning in Gary, Indiana, as a strike against United States Steel, the walkout, aimed at gaining a wage increase and an eight-hour day, spread to include 350,000 workers in nine states. However, the industrial giant refused to yield, and in January 1920 the strike ended in failure.[39]

Syndicalist William Z. Foster, who had led the strike, now headed a new combination of radicals that would serve as an educational agency and a rallying ground for militants within the American Federation of Labor. Though Communists initially held Foster's group in contempt for its policy of "boring from within" the established trade unions, the TUEL soon became acceptable to them. In July the initial congress of the Red International of Labor Unions, meeting in Moscow, endorsed the new direction, which opened the door for Foster and other TUEL militants to join the Communist Party. Moreover, American Communists could now organize their own version of Russian-type "fractions." Called "party nuclei" in America, they were clusters of party members organized to take over and control nonparty organizations, such as trade unions.[40] By 1922, TUEL members were on ILGWU executive boards or joint boards in four cities, setting the stage for a confrontation with the Schlesinger administration at the International's Cleveland convention in May.[41]

The appeal of radicalism even attracted some members of the prestigious cutters' union. Within Local 10, left-wingers soon emerged as a new insurgent group, succeeding the Good and Welfare League, which now held power. As a leader of both the League and the local, Dubinsky felt threatened and intensified his anti-Communism.

At the end of May 1919, five months after his election to Local 10's executive board, Dubinsky represented the union as a delegate to the fourth convention of the Jewish Socialist Federation of the Socialist Party. Meeting in Boston's Labor Lyceum, 136 delegates from twenty-six states and forty-eight cities divided into left and right, Communist and anti-Communist. Russian Communism and the recognition of Russia were the only issues. The Left urged the Federation to sever ties with the Socialist Party and accept Bolshevism. Dubinsky and the Right opposed such a step, which was rejected by a vote of almost two to one. Defeated, left leader Alexander Bittelman declared that his group was leaving the Federation. He and his followers then walked out and held their own convention in another room.[42]

Dubinsky viewed the left-wingers as representatives of an ideology and foreign dictatorship, the Soviet Union, that he could and would not abide.[43] Moreover, he expected that the fight with the Left, which began within the Socialist Party, would "ultimately . . . go to the trade union movement." In preparation for a confrontation, he increased his own trade-union activity.[44]

Temporarily, the Left appeared to be more concerned with its own internal divisions. In May and June 1919, the Socialist Party had suspended or expelled 70,000 of its nearly 110,000 members for their adherence to Bolshevism. In September the outcasts formed two organizations, the Communist Party of America and the Communist Labor Party of America. The former consisted mainly of foreign-born federations and the latter mainly of native-born Americans. Both initially operated openly and democratically, but not for long. Many Americans feared infection by the Bolshevik virus and reacted with a "Red scare," subjecting radicals to both official and private persecution in the form of arrests, deportations, and physical attacks. Government suppression drove the Communists to underground and conspiratorial methods and to reorganize and create new groups. The Communist International, which had been founded in Moscow in March 1919, viewed this internecine conflict with alarm and ordered it ended. In 1923 a new Workers' Party would finally emerge as the sole Communist party in America, but with a membership of only 15,400.[45]

By June 1919, evidence existed of a left-wing faction within Local 10. The Soviet-style Workers' Council, created earlier in the year within Local 25, began to function as an independent body. It was also attracting workers from Local 10, arousing the wrath of the local's executive board. On June 30 the board urged the expulsion of cutters' union members who refused to sever connections with the radical group. The cutters' membership then "unanimously" endorsed the recommendation, as the few leftists in their ranks abstained from voting. Local 10 subsequently fined and expelled others for alleged "offenses against union solidarity."[46]

Nevertheless, the left opposition in Local 10 remained and regrouped. In 1921 it created Dress and Progressive Leagues within the local. As the Left became entrenched, the ILGWU found itself in crisis. An industrial depression had hit the economy in mid-1920 and was taking its toll of business failures and jobs. For the employers, this downturn was an ideal opportunity for an assault on organized labor. Genuine trade unions and the "closed shop," they argued, were contrary to American traditions and thus unpatriotic. Management-run company unions, by contrast, were just fine. Under this "American Plan," business leaders successfully undermined labor organizations across the country.

Their attack on the ILGWU began in October 1920. Cloak manufacturers in Cleveland, Chicago, and Philadelphia; embroidery manufacturers in New York; and dress manufacturers in Philadelphia demanded wage reductions and other changes to existing agreements. In New York, Boston, Toronto, and Toledo, manufacturers unilaterally reneged on collective bargaining agreements. In February 1921, workers in Boston began a general strike that failed to restore a contractual agreement guaranteeing forty-two weeks of employment per year. A strike of dress- and waistmakers in New York at the same time did, however, result in union shop agreements with some independent employers.

This success was the exception rather than the rule. In April and October 1921, the New York Cloak and Suit Manufacturers' Protective Association waged war with astonishing fury. Employers insisted on a "general readjustment of working conditions," including wage cuts, restored piecework, and expanded rights of hiring and firing. Such demands spread to Chicago, Philadelphia, and several small towns. The ILGWU was clearly on the defensive, and in August, Philadelphia's dress- and waistmakers lost a bitter strike. In October the offensive was stepped up. The manufacturers' Protective Association decided that all members would operate on a piecework basis under Association-determined working conditions. Some 55,000 New York cloakmakers walked out in November. Cloakmakers in Philadelphia, Chicago, Montreal, Los Angeles, Baltimore, and Cleveland followed.

Morris Hillquit, the ILGWU's attorney, proposed that the union obtain a court injunction against the Protective Association for having violated its agreement of May 1919. Such injunctions had traditionally been powerful strike-breaking weapons in the hands of management, but now it was labor's turn to use the courts. With the assistance of noted lawyer Samuel Untermyer, Hillquit and the ILGWU won a temporary injunction in November, which was made permanent in January. In making the injunction permanent, New York Supreme Court justice Robert F. Wagner demanded that management unconditionally comply with the 1919 agreement. The Protective Association yielded, and the strike ended.[47]

Local 10 had been prepared for this strike by making its administration leaner and more efficient. In August 1921 the membership had agreed to create the office of general manager, to replace the three managers that had previously served the 3,000 male cutters. Evidently the changes were made just in time. During the strike, Local 10 maintained remarkable discipline; 1,800 members struck and only 18 "scabbed."[48]

Before the strike ended, the cutters also elected their new general manager. Dubinsky ran against Max Gorenstein, a vice president of the local and a fellow member of the Good and Welfare League who had some left-wing support. By running against Dubinsky, the League's choice, he seemed to violate the principle of union solidarity. When the votes were finally cast, Dubinsky received 616 to 399 for Gorenstein, with decisive majorities in both the cloak and dress branches of the local, but Local 10 remained divided.[49]

A challenge to the administration of the International began less than five months after David Dubinsky's election as general manager of Local 10. Twice elected to the presidency (in 1903 and 1914), Benjamin Schlesinger had impeccable radical credentials. A rabbi's son from Lithuania, in 1891 he came to Chicago. After briefly peddling matches, he found employment in a cloakmaking shop and became an operator. Discovering the misery of sweatshop labor, he led a strike at age seventeen. Schlesinger's activism in behalf of Chicago's cloak and dress union led to his becoming its manager. Politically he leaned toward Daniel DeLeon's Socialist Labor Party (SLP). In the mid-nineties he moved to New York City, where he briefly edited the SLP's Yiddish-language daily newspaper, *Abendblatt,* but soon joined anti-DeLeon Socialists associated with the new *Jewish Daily Forward* and later the Socialist Party. In 1903 he was elected president of the ILGWU, a position he held for a year before becoming the *Forward*'s business manager and then the New York Cloak Joint Board's general manager. In 1914, he returned to the ILGWU presidency.[50]

As president in the early 1920s, Schlesinger headed a union whose social composition was changing but whose leadership had remained essentially unchanged for two decades. The ILGWU was still dominated by Jewish males of the same group that had founded the union twenty years earlier.[51] In 1910 more than 80 percent of the workers in New York City's cloak trade were Jewish. Of the women workers in the dress and waist trade, in 1913 more than 56 percent were Jewish.[52]

Italians had followed the Jews into the needle trades. As the Italians were organized, the number of Jews in the unions also grew, but at a reduced rate. The children of Jewish workers sought careers outside factory work, which made their replenishment dependent on immigration. However, war in Europe and discriminatory U.S. immigration legislation curtailed immigration, and the proportion of Jews relative to others in the needle trades declined. During the 1920s Italian women became the largest single group in the needle trades, with Jewish men and women constituting less than 20 percent of the labor force. As Jews continued to lead the needle-trades unions, there was "fruitful ground for antagonism."[53]

In May 1922 civil war broke out. The occasion was the ILGWU's sixteenth biennial convention, which met in Cleveland. Dubinsky, though only thirty years of age, had thus far succeeded in keeping the left wing in his own local under control. Now he would attempt to do the same in the International. The battle between left and right would at last be joined.

President Schlesinger opened the gathering with a plea for unity. Samuel Gompers then followed with praise for Schlesinger's "wonderful leadership" but warned the delegates against injecting "anything that is calculated to create bitterness, hostility or division" into the International.[54] B. Charney Vladeck, the manager of the *Jewish Daily Forward*; Morris Hillquit, the revered ILGWU attorney; and *Forward* editor Abraham Cahan sounded the same theme in their speeches.[55]

Despite these appeals there was controversy rather than peace, and David Dubinsky played a prominent role. He was secretary of the credentials committee, which refused to seat several left-wingers because of their allegedly disruptive and disloyal behavior. With Chairman Joseph Breslaw of the pressers' union, Dubinsky defended the committee's action.[56] The left-wingers protested their unseating, but the convention's appeal committee was unsympathetic. The committee's recommendation, which was adopted by a vote of 138 to 51, expressed the convention's "wholehearted indignation and resentment against these malicious intermeddlers and disrupters" and warned against "these sinister influences which . . . are seeking to destroy what has been built up at much cost and sacrifice."[57]

On the side of the administration and the convention majority, Dubinsky continued his climb up the ILGWU ladder. He was elected a vice president, which entailed membership on the General Executive Board. Max Gorenstein, whom Dubinsky had defeated in the contest for the Local 10 general managership, was also chosen. In fact, Gorenstein owed his election to Dubinsky, who had shrewdly moved to heal wounds by nominating him for a vice presidency.[58]

Despite its discipline, the left wing made no headway against the administration and its defenders. By emphasizing the ILGWU's success in improving wages and cutting hours, as well as the insurgents' abject loyalty to Soviet Russia, the right wing prevailed.[59] Benjamin Schlesinger won another term as president without challenge, as his critics were defeated but not silenced. The "shop delegates" idea was still alive, as were demands that joint boards and convention delegates be elected by locals. At the same time, the employers were putting new energy into the efforts to undo labor's hard-won gains. In the spirit of the postwar Red Scare, the National Association of Manufacturers and its allies aimed to destroy American trade unionism by associating it with foreign radicalism, and to replace collective bargaining with the open shop and the company union.[60]

The goal of the Communists was to take over the needle trades in New York City. The industry had a workforce that was preponderantly Jewish, significantly radical, and sufficiently sympathetic to the Soviet Union to make the idea of Communist dominance very plausible. The left wing that rose to challenge the Schlesinger administration was, in actuality, a combination of radical elements, encompassing Communists, anarchists, and Socialists of varying degrees of intensity. Yet the Communists were the only ones of significance to Dubinsky. As the general manager of Local 10, he regularly engaged them in battle during meetings and elections. Each time he won handily, as he would explain, "because of the support that I received from the old timers, the former conservatives—the so-called Tammany [people]. They supported me because they had faith in me, not because I was a socialist." In short, Dubinsky now was the darling of the traditionalists he had toppled from power.[61]

He believed the leftists' sole concern was the welfare of Russia.[62] Benjamin Schlesinger and the General Executive Board of the ILGWU shared that view and refused to entertain suggestions for change. How could those who followed the orders of the Communist International in Moscow not be misguided, dangerous, or both?

When the growing strength of the Left began to cause concern, attention was focused not on the structure of the union but on the man at the top. Schlesinger, by 1923, had been in office nearly a decade, which many of his colleagues on the General Executive Board felt was too long. Perhaps a stronger leader was necessary to deal with the Communists. Such a person, Morris Sigman, had forsaken ILGWU activity in favor of farm life at Storm Lake, Iowa. A Bessarabian-born anarchist who came to New York by way of London, Sigman was a cloak presser by trade and a labor militant by temperament. In 1903, Sigman organized an Independent Cloak Pressers' Union, which charged ten cents for workers to join. Soon he took his union into Daniel DeLeon's Socialist Trade and Labor Alliance, which in 1905 helped found the Industrial Workers of the World, a bastion of syndicalism. Quickly losing faith in the IWW, in 1907 he abandoned it for the ILGWU. In 1914 he was elected secretary-treasurer of the International, but unable to endure the relatively inactive position under President Schlesinger, he resigned after a year and resumed his factory work. From 1917 to 1920 he was back in a leadership role, managing the Cloak Joint Board. In 1920 he became first vice president of the International, but a dispute resulted in his resignation from both positions and retirement to his farm.[63]

Though physically distant from New York, Sigman had many sympathizers around ILGWU headquarters, especially among those who had complaints about Schlesinger. A classic Socialist intellectual as well as labor leader, Schlesinger was devoted to the International but also in chronic poor health and tended to keep himself aloof from his colleagues. "Locked in his own shell," wearing an "armor of gloom," he felt unappreciated and often threatened to resign.[64]

In January 1923 he actually carried out his threat. The occasion was a General Executive Board meeting at Montreal. Schlesinger, at home with influenza, had sought to have the meeting postponed on account of his illness. However, the other board members denied his request[65] and convened with First Vice President Salvatore Ninfo of Local 48, the Italian cloakmakers' union, serving as acting president. Arriving late, President Schlesinger chaired the tenth session and told the GEB that "he had decided to retire" from the presidency. He said he would not be returning to his New York office. "I am very tired, very tired, and cannot have any heart in the work."[66]

The GEB members listened in silence, understandably skeptical since Schlesinger had often threatened to resign only to be persuaded to remain. Joseph Breslaw, the sturdy leader of the pressers, then handed the president a sheet of paper, insisting he should "put it in writing." Stunned and unable to turn back, Schlesinger wrote out a resignation for reasons of "poor health."[67] At its next session, the GEB considered a motion to accept Schlesinger's resignation. Ostensibly because Schlesinger merited "respect rather than rejection," David Dubinsky opposed the motion.[68] Secretary-Treasurer Baroff then moved, without success, to have the matter considered at a special convention. The GEB then accepted the resignation, with only Dubinsky and Baroff dissenting. Everyone agreed that a special convention would be called to elect a successor to Schlesinger.[69]

Dubinsky's actions at this meeting reflected his characteristic shrewdness and superb political instincts. Here was a freshman board member, just approaching his thirty-first birthday, who was deciding the fate of an elder statesman. Perhaps, as he later asserted, the GEB wanted Schlesinger removed because "almost half the members . . . wanted to be president themselves."[70] This allegation cites the ambition of others but ignores Dubinsky's own. With only seven months of GEB service under his belt, and obviously too young to move up, Dubinsky was not yet in the running for the job. His moves in support of Schlesinger gained attention but could not be seen as self-serving.

Dubinsky felt the presidential breeze that was blowing from Iowa. He was interested in a no-nonsense strongman to combat the Communists, and such a person ran a farm at Storm Lake. Taking the initiative, Dubinsky sent Morris Sigman a telegram asking whether he would be interested in becoming president.[71] On Thursday, February 15, the special ILGWU convention opened at Baltimore. With Local 10 in the forefront of his supporters, Sigman appeared the obvious choice. On the seventeenth, the convention elected him.[72]

The tough, former IWW-er was now president, and he would have to deal with a leftist presence that was of continuing concern to the International's executive board. Salvatore Ninfo complained that a dissident faction within his Italian cloakmakers' union was threatening to wreck the organization by accusing it of financial impropriety. Joseph Breslaw charged that the shop delegates' "business will absolutely ruin all the locals." Though his own cloak pressers' Local 35 was not yet affected, he feared that it would "gradually be menaced." As for Dubinsky, he felt his situation was presently under control. Local 10's finances were "excellent," its membership was increasing, and its "few left-wingers . . . for the last few months" had "not opened their mouths."[73]

Sigman was determined to "eliminate" the "evil" insurgency from the International. He claimed that the problem persisted because the GEB "never tried to agree on a uniform policy of action." A plan was needed, Sigman said, to explain the International's rules and penalties to the entire membership. The GEB's first response was a decree that ILG-ers who belonged to insurgent groups were subject "to trial and discipline by the local union" to which they belonged.[74]

On August 16, Sigman directed the ILGWU locals "to order all their members" of Shop Delegate Leagues "to immediately cease all activities in the 'Leagues' in any shape or form." Those persisting in League activities were to be "brought to trial on the charge of conduct detrimental to the organization."

On September 25 the GEB acted on the Local 22 complaint and disqualified the left-wingers from serving on the dressmakers' executive board. Their membership in an outside "league" had violated the ILGWU's constitution. "It is my sincere conviction," Sigman told the GEB in October, "that no local with a left executive board takes any action without first consulting the leaders and advisers of the Trade Union Educational League, which represents the Workers' Party and perhaps the Communist movement in general."[75]

Sigman's purge succeeded; the leftists resisted but were overwhelmed. Within Local 1, the New York Cloak and Suit Operators' Union, and Local 9, the New York Cloak Finishers' and Tailors' Union, there was especially strong defiance. However, under pressure to comply with the order, the Local 1 membership accepted it by a vote of 437 to 12. Local 9 capitulated in November, though six executive board members chose to retain their TUEL membership rather than comply. Among the Italian cloakmakers of Local 48 there was a fight, but Salvatore Ninfo's right wing predominated. Similarly, within Local 10, TUEL members urged rejection of the Sigman order, but the cutters "voted to do away with the leagues and remain loyal to the International." Four TUEL members chose to resign. In Chicago, Philadelphia, Boston, and several smaller areas, leftists were removed from office.[76]

As 1923 ended, the left-wingers appeared to be losing the war. Socialist elder statesman Eugene V. Debs, attempting to mediate, urged TUEL secretary-treasurer William Z. Foster to hold a conference with the ILGWU leadership to thrash out their differences. Foster was willing, but not Sigman. The latter issued a warning to the TUEL leader to keep his organization out of ILGWU affairs.[77] Sigman interpreted Foster's overture as a sign of Communist weakness, and there would be no negotiations. "From all indications the leagues were beaten by the International," Sigman told his executive board.[78]

But Sigman underestimated his enemies' resiliency and determination. As 1923 ended, they were regrouping and preparing new challenges to his direction of the ILGWU. A crisis was developing that would tear apart the International and produce a new leader—David Dubinsky.

3

At War within the ILGWU

Local 10 was Dubinsky's political home and base of power. It admitted him to membership when he was a mere "greenhorn," gave him the opportunity to earn a respectable living, and provided a union base. As the Good and Welfare League took over Local 10, he also realized he was no longer a union insurgent. With the traditionalists, his former adversaries, now on his side, he could now meet the challenge of those on his left.

Sigman's purge meant that the entire International must be cleansed of the left-wingers, including those in Local 10. As 1924 began, Dubinsky seemed in complete agreement and was doing his best to keep the cutters in line. His mood was optimistic, and he was planning to organize nonunion shops in the waist and dress industry.[1] In January he told the General Executive Board that the left-wingers in Local 10 were in disarray.[2]

At the ILGWU's seventeenth convention, which opened in Boston on May 5, Dubinsky remained on the offensive. Sixteen radical delegates, allegedly members of the "dual organization," the Trade Union Educational League, were accused of disloyalty and denied seats by the credentials committee. They protested but were easily overcome by Chairman Joseph Breslaw, supported by Dubinsky and President Sigman, and were excluded from the convention.[3] During these hearings, Dubinsky championed orthodoxy and stood by the ILGWU hierarchy of which he was now an increasingly important part.[4] In a blistering statement, he accused the eight radicals from Local 9 of defying the GEB's orders to withdraw from the TUEL, regularly disregarding GEB orders and financially supporting the Yiddish-language Communist newspaper, the *Freiheit*.[5]

The radicals had suffered only a temporary setback. Though the convention excluded those opposed by the credentials committee, some forty others, several of whom were Workers' Party members, were seated. The left-wingers had fought well. On the horizon, a new test of strength between the Right and the Left was clearly looming.[6] Dubinsky's activities and visibility were definitely increasing. On the eve of the convention, he sat on the ILGWU committee that was negotiating with cloak and suit industry employers over renewing agreements nearing expiration on June 30. However, the talks reached an impasse and the union prepared for a strike.[7] In need of additional funds,[8] President Sigman called on Dubinsky for a loan of five thousand dollars from Local 10.[9]

When a strike seemed unavoidable, Governor Alfred E. Smith intervened to prevent it. He appointed an Advisory Commission headed by lawyer George Gordon Battle. The Battle Commission recommended that subcontractors pay union wages and employ only union labor, but also recommended a consolidation of submanufacturers and contractors to reduce "the number of shops in the industry from 3,000 to nearer 1,500."

Not surprisingly, the ILGWU approved the Commission's report, and to supervise the reorganization process, established a committee headed by Dubinsky.[10] The Left, however, regarded the settlement the ILGWU produced as "class collaboration." In fact, conditions in the industry seemed to warrant suspicion that something was awry. Overall the industry was shrinking, and the dress sector was growing to the detriment of cloaks. Uncertainty in retail ordering compelled manufacturers to reduce their overhead by becoming jobbers, which in turn meant increased unemployment and insecurity for workers. Yet the GEB, which had "remained virtually unchanged" since 1920, seemed ineffective to growing numbers of dissident ILGWU members.[11] When Sigman and the New York Joint Board then pressured locals for dues increases, the TUEL mobilized its forces in opposition.[12]

Only thirty-two years old, Dubinsky was the rising star in the ILGWU and the first manager to attempt to implement the Sigman administration's dues policy. Without delay he passed the bad news on to his fellow cutters.[13]

On August 18, Dubinsky and the cutters' executive board recommended a fifteen-cent increase in the dues to fifty cents per week.[14] A few hours later he submitted the proposal to a special meeting of his membership, but following heated debate, with opposition led by the Left, "a decided majority" rejected it.[15]

Dubinsky was stunned. In shock and fury he announced his resignation as manager. Highly combative and emotional, he was a tenacious fighter. It is difficult therefore to regard this "resignation" as anything more than a ploy to rally his troops for future skirmishes.

Nevertheless, the morning after the dues rejection, Dubinsky contacted the firm of Henry Rosenzweig and arranged to report to work the next week. He also obtained a working card from Local 10. On August 21 he submitted his resignation to the local's executive board and "insisted that it be accepted." With the ILGWU in crisis, President Morris Sigman appeared in person before the executive board and "practically ordered" Dubinsky not to leave. After this plea, the board "decided not to consider the resignation."

Dubinsky then called a "special meeting" of the membership to reconsider an increase. On August 25, at the meeting, Sigman not only urged but also ordered Dubinsky to withdraw his resignation. In response, Dubinsky complained that the members' failure to support him on the eighteenth "had stripped him of the prestige necessary" to manage the union's affairs. Overwhelmingly the membership first voted not to consider Dubinsky's resignation and then to raise their dues to fifty cents.[16]

With local elections approaching in December, the radicals next sought to defeat Dubinsky's bid for reelection. Their chief complaint was that wages had not improved during his tenure in office. At a membership meeting, Dubinsky denied these allegations. By quoting from the working cards of six opposition candidates, he demonstrated that they had received five to ten dollars per week in wage increases since 1922. On December 20, he polled 1,230 votes, as opposed to 419 for leftist Jacob Lukin.[17]

Such success in collective bargaining did not come as readily in Dubinsky's homeland, Poland. Resurrected as a state in 1918 as a result of the defeat in the First World War of its three partitioning powers—Germany, Austria-Hungary, and Russia—by 1931 Poland would have a higher percentage of Jews than any land other than Palestine. However, in a land where anti-Semitism and pogroms were customary, Jews were regarded as a lower caste and as foreigners. Jews tended to reside in cities; though they made up only 10 percent of Poland's overall population, they were 25 percent of its urban dwellers and increasingly impoverished, in large part a result of deliberate government policies.[18]

Dubinsky had not seen his parents since 1910. Possibly influenced by the reports of economic distress back home, as well as by the fact that one of his brothers was going there, he decided on a visit.[19] He did more than visit relatives, touring for more than ten weeks and spending time in Germany, France, Italy, Austria, and England, as well as Poland. In Warsaw he met with European unionists and was appalled at the misery and unemployment he found. It was a chaotic situation exacerbated, he thought, by Communists.[20]

While Dubinsky was abroad, the civil war within the ILGWU had intensified. His cutters were mainly on the right, but most ILG-ers were moving to the left. The purges of 1923 and 1924 had convinced many garment workers of the validity of the left-wing charge that the International's leadership was oligarchic, resulting in new demands for union democracy. Moreover, TUEL members routinely signed the loyalty pledge required by the revised ILGWU constitution to run for local offices. In elections that followed, the radicals won handsomely. They gained control of 70 percent of New York City's ILGWU members by taking over the executive boards of three locals: 2, 9, and 22.[21]

The Workers' (Communist) Party was thrilled and called for May Day demonstrations of garment-worker solidarity. A rally at the Metropolitan Opera House, held under the auspices of Locals 2, 9 and 22, featured a speech by Dr. Moissaye J. Olgin, the editor of the Communist *Freiheit*. Olgin offered standard Communist rhetoric, ending with "Long live a soviet America!"[22]

This affair attracted little attention except on the part of Morris Sigman. The ILGWU president cited it as evidence that the leadership of the three left-wing locals had violated the International's constitution by collaborating with the Communists.[23] On June 11, 1925, Vice President Israel Feinberg, a member of Local 2, formally brought charges before the Joint Board of the Cloak and Dress Makers' Unions of New York. The Joint Board appointed an investigating committee, ordered a temporary suspension of the locals' managers and executive boards pending the outcome of a trial, and asked the International's officers "to attach the treasuries of the three locals in order to prevent a raid on their funds by the Communists."[24]

Under siege, the locals acted to retain their property. They changed the locks on the doors of their offices and "organized a system of watchers, some of them hired," but "they could not prevent the offices of Locals 2 and 9 from being broken into at night and having their treasuries taken." "Local 22 was another story." The building of the dressmakers' union on

West Twenty-first Street was patrolled by men and women around the clock and was untouchable. Further mobilizing their forces, the radicals organized a Joint Action Committee, chaired by Louis Hyman, manager of Local 9, which urged noncooperation with the officers of the International.[25]

On June 25, the eve of Dubinsky's return, the trial began at the Hotel Cadillac, Forty-third Street and Broadway.[26] In the meantime, the Joint Action Committee was functioning as a union, even to the extent of collecting dues and adjusting grievances. It enjoyed widespread support because the bulk of New York's ladies' garment workers saw its fight as their fight for democracy within the union. Communism was not their concern.[27] Nevertheless, with Dubinsky back, the cutters met and voted overwhelmingly to endorse the suspensions.[28]

In question was Morris Sigman's ability to hold the ILGWU together. The Battle Commission, unable to achieve a breakthrough in conflicts with the employers, recommended a one-year extension of existing contracts. Reluctantly, Dubinsky, the Joint Board, and the rank and file accepted its report.[29] More satisfactory to the administration, the trial committee of the Joint Board found the suspended officials of Locals 2, 9, and 22 guilty of radical activities and expelled them.[30]

On July 27, with the ILGWU obviously in jeopardy, the General Executive Board met to save it. Though Dubinsky remained steadfast in his opposition to the Communists, the GEB session ended with an agreement. Morris Sigman would take charge of the Joint Board, from which militant right-wingers Meyer Perlstein and Israel Feinberg would resign. In addition, Breslaw would head its finance department, Dubinsky its protective division, and tailor Jacob Halperin its legal operation.[31] Dubinsky did not object.[32]

As the anti-Communist fight intensified, Local 10 became a bulwark of the Right. The number of left-wingers among the cutters was relatively few, but Dubinsky would not tolerate them.[33] On August 1 three members were suspended for slanderous statements and disruptive activity.[34] Not taking anything for granted, Dubinsky warned Local 10 members "against the conspiracy on the part of the Communists to disrupt and destroy our Union."[35]

Sigman, the nemesis of the Communists, bore primary responsibility for their suppression. The expulsions and suspensions of the past two years were his doing and gained the Communists numerous fellow travelers who were easily attracted by the rhetoric of free speech and democracy. Low-paid immigrant garment workers, accustomed to religious and political oppression in the Old World and economic insecurity in New York, found plausible the argument that their union leaders were also their enemies. In the belief they were being betrayed, many workers inadvertently served the interests of the Workers' Party, which indeed had its own agenda. As adopted by the party's secretariat in Chicago, the eleven-point program included the repudiation of the Joint Board suspensions and the Governor's Commission's recommendations, a demand and preparation for a strike to protest the recommendations, insistence on another convention of the International, and promotion of Louis Hyman of Local 9 for its presidency.[36]

The intervention of the Workers' Party in ILGWU affairs was undeniable,[37] but Sigman's counterproductive tactics would soon compel him to retreat. In a display of strength, the Joint Action Committee called for a two-hour work stoppage in the cloak industry at 3 p.m. on August 20, 1925. Sigman, trying to abort the walkout, denounced it as "a fake, an advertising stunt," and a device to compel ILGWU officers to resign and the Joint Board to be reorganized.[38] When the walkout finally occurred, with as many as fifteen thousand participants, nobody was surprised, but Sigman proclaimed it "a fizzle."[39]

Before the month was over Sigman knew he had been defeated. The pressure was on him to relent before the ILGWU was destroyed. Morris Hillquit, the esteemed Socialist Party chairman and ILGWU attorney; Abraham Cahan, the staunchly anti-Communist editor of the *Jewish Daily Forward*; and the Forward Association all called for a truce.

On August 28, before a special meeting of the GEB, Sigman presented a "Plan for Peace." Declaring that the ILGWU had "won completely" the anti-Communist fight and that the main issue was the Communist Party's intervention in union affairs, he called for "reconstructing the Union on the basis of greater democracy and more efficient administration."[40] Dubinsky, supporting the plan, took it to his local, emphasizing that it was only the Communist Party he opposed and warning against a new left-wing cutters' league that had just been organized.[41]

Both sides wanted peace. On August 29, 1925, shop chairmen and cloak- and dressmakers meeting at the Manhattan Lyceum adopted resolutions reflecting the dissidents' point of view.[42] Four days later, at a meeting of shop chairmen at Cooper Union, Dubinsky and Sigman presented the conservatives' plan.[43]

On September 10, the chairmen met again at Cooper Union and, in hopes of resolving the crisis, agreed that the date of the next ILGWU convention should be advanced five months, from May 1926 to November 30, 1925, in Philadelphia. The next day the GEB issued a call for it.[44] Perhaps, somehow, the ILGWU would save itself from destruction.

As Sigman's lieutenant in the struggle with the Left, Dubinsky supported his decision to pursue peace, though it must have been with misgivings. Dubinsky's local had repeatedly endorsed both him and his anti-Communism, rendering the left-wing cutters more of an annoyance than a serious threat to his leadership. His personal position was one of strength, which meant that outright victory was more attractive than a negotiated settlement.

Though Local 10 remained vigilant in its war against its dissidents, peace did seem to have arrived. In late September 1925, a committee of fifteen shop chairmen, elected on the eleventh, negotiated a settlement to be submitted to a meeting of chairmen at Cooper Union on the twenty-fourth.[45] The meeting was a great success. Shop chairmen and members of Locals 2, 9, and 22 packed Cooper Union and two overflow halls to hear the agreement, which met with no objections.

The Joint Action Committee won what it had sought. It was agreed that "all discrimination for political opinion be abolished." A design for proportional representation would be drawn up at the next convention. The suspended executive boards would be reinstated via an appeal process. In fact, all political suspensions would be lifted. Dues would be decided by referendum. The members in each of the three meeting halls gave their approval.[46] Now Dubinsky was free to resume full-time work at Local 10 headquarters.

With peace apparently achieved, the ILGWU sent a delegation to the convention of the American Federation of Labor at Atlantic City, New Jersey. Headed by Morris Sigman, the International's AFL convention contingent for the first time included David Dubinsky.[47]

On his return, Dubinsky discovered that the truce brought about by the peace agreement was only temporary. At Arlington Hall on October 12, more than a thousand Local 10 members clearly welcomed an end to the warfare. They were pleased when Dubinsky suggested that recently disciplined Local 10 radicals could avoid suspension by using the appeals process.[48]

But the New York Cloak and Dress Joint Board had decided to hold a general election on October 29 for the business agents that sat on it, instead of allowing them to be elected by individual locals, as in the past. Dubinsky and the other right-wingers were appalled, realizing that candidates of the Communists in the largest locals could dominate such a contest.[49]

The left-wing argument was that business agents on the Joint Board would represent all crafts, not just cutters. Rejecting this position, the cutters chose local elections, thus becoming the only union not represented in the general election, which, as expected, the left wing won. Louis Hyman was elected general manager of the new Joint Board, which would name Charles Zimmerman to head its dress division.[50]

While the matter of representation on the Joint Board was being resolved, Local 10 approached another of its annual elections. To Dubinsky's dismay, the radicals, who called themselves the "Progressive Cutters of Local 10," were still active and vitriolic. Still intent on demonstrating the extent of his popularity, Dubinsky threatened for the second time in two years to leave office. On November 9, with two weeks left before nominations, he startled a membership meeting by announcing his retirement. "I shall not accept office any more," he said. He blamed his retirement on the Left.[51] Dubinsky, of course, had never intended to retire, and the left-wingers' campaign could only have reinforced his determination to remain in office. On the twenty-fourth, he accepted nomination for election to another term.[52]

When the special convention convened in Philadelphia, David Dubinsky was prepared for it. The attacks of the Progressive Cutters had offended him personally, and he viewed them and their allies as a menace to the ILGWU's future. Not yet thirty-two, he was too young to concede defeat and face political oblivion.

Committed both ideologically and emotionally to the Right, he viewed with growing alarm the failure and apparent surrender of its standard bearer, Morris Sigman. Now, in 1925, two years after Dubinsky had helped maneuver Sigman into the presidency, the Communists were stronger than ever. Moreover, instead of urging their expulsion, Sigman was negotiating with them.

Even before the convention opened, the Joint Action Committee had entered into negotiations with Sigman in hopes of forging an alliance against the supposedly tougher right-wingers. Charles Zimmerman and

Louis Hyman thought they reached agreement with Sigman on proportional representation at ILGWU conventions and on joint boards, but there was no accord on left-wing representation on the General Executive Board or on the formation of a labor party. The Workers' Party wanted the latter very much, but Sigman was adamantly opposed.[53]

What was advertised as the ILGWU's "harmony convention" began as scheduled on November 30, but discord soon surfaced when delegates bearing placards demanding proportional representation, recognition of Soviet Russia, and "general amnesty" interrupted one of the opening speeches.[54] On the second day, the credentials committee declined to seat delegates from five locals, representing 70 percent of the membership. In this situation the body to entertain appeals was the one that ruled on charges against locals, namely, the General Executive Board. Louis Hyman immediately declared that he and the questioned delegates did not recognize, and would not appear before, any appeal committee, which was to meet on the last day of the convention. Hyman's defiance threw the convention into an uproar, compelling Sigman to adjourn the session. When business resumed the next morning, Dubinsky was the first to respond, accusing Hyman of threatening the convention with "firecracker oratory."[55]

The debate intensified. Zimmerman and Julius Portnoy of Local 22 came to Hyman's defense, while Sigman and Julius Hochman, former general manager of the New York Dress Joint Board, backed Dubinsky. "We are all acquainted with the bulldozing methods of Delegate Dubinsky. He is nothing but a cheap actor," Zimmerman said. After further exchanges, the delegates finally voted on the report of the credentials committee and accepted it by a vote count of 158 to 107.[56]

The "harmony" convention continued as a struggle between the Left and the Right, with the opposing sides staying at separate hotels. Though Dubinsky acted as though all he wanted was to rid the ILGWU of the Communists, he was also undermining Morris Sigman, who sought the peace that he opposed. Dubinsky had been a member of a preconvention committee established to negotiate with Zimmerman and the Left on an understanding that the radicals would receive "four seats on the General Executive Board." The two sides met, but Dubinsky, demonstrating complete intransigence, napped in the meeting room. By subverting Sigman's peacemaking, Dubinsky hastened the advent of a more staunchly anti-Communist ILGWU president: Benjamin Schlesinger.[57]

On the morning of the fifteenth day, the report of the law committee was read. In accordance with the preconvention peace agreement, provision was made for proportional representation at conventions. As the discussion progressed, the Left became nervous. Dubinsky, as chairman, held that any design for proportional representation would be decided on by the convention. Zimmerman demanded a membership referendum. Sigman endorsed Dubinsky's position, denying that the peace agreement put the convention under any obligation or that he even favored proportional representation.

The Left was furious. Challenging Dubinsky, Hyman said the Right was breaking a treaty and "disregarding the membership," and called on supporters of the Joint Action Committee to walk out of the convention, which they did. Charles Zimmerman afterward returned, only to be told by Julius Hoffman that he knew he would come back because he had read in the *Daily Worker* that his policy was "to stay within."[58] The next morning the convention voted to submit the proportional representation questions to a referendum six months later.[59]

On the sixteenth and final day of the convention, the somewhat pacified delegates held elections for officers of the International. The ostensibly loyal vice president Dubinsky nominated Sigman for another term as president, praising his virtuous judgment, "excellent ability," and "courage and conviction to go through with . . . reforms." The Left picked Hyman to oppose Sigman, and Zimmerman to run against incumbent secretary-treasurer Abraham Baroff. As expected, the radicals lost these contests, but reflecting their newfound respectability and strength, they afterward elected Hyman, Portnoy, Joseph Boruchowitz of Local 2, and David Gingold of Local 20 to the General Executive Board. Zimmerman, the acknowledged mastermind of the Left, was evidently regarded to be too dangerous. Dubinsky was reelected as a stalwart of the Right, but the Left now had the four board members they had been promised. So, despite Hyman's embarrassing walkout, the convention significantly enhanced the role of the left wing.[60]

As Local 10's elections were scheduled for December 19 in New York, Dubinsky had a convenient excuse to miss the GEB meeting in Philadelphia on the eighteenth at which the four left-wingers made their debut.[61] Home again, he won handily, defeating Max Bernstein by a vote of 1,106 to 242.[62]

The year 1925 ended with the right wing in clear retreat. The Left had successfully defied the expulsion policy and won control of the New York

Joint Board, which also gave it, except for the Sigman administration, control of the International. Sigman and Dubinsky stood together as allies against a common enemy, the Communists, but the ILGWU president understood much better than the Local 10 manager that the so-called rotten borough system, by which small locals were disproportionately represented at ILGWU conventions, was undemocratic and that much of the criticism of the administration was well founded.

Dubinsky the hard-liner was defending his machine and in effect preserving the conservative tradition of Local 10. Outside Local 10 he did not have many allies, but among those he had were the ILGWU's two Italian-language locals, 48 and 89, the cloak- and dressmakers' unions, respectively, and their able leaders, Salvatore Ninfo and Luigi Antonini. The Italian locals had their own interests to protect. They, too, had opposed the at-large election of business agents, on grounds of autonomy and ethnicity. They were suspicious of the Communists and wanted continued Italian representation of their own kind within the Jewish-controlled ILGWU. Despite some resentment over the use by some Jews of Yiddish in their speeches and discussions and feelings that they were treated as second-class citizens within the International, the Italians were proud of their locals and would defend them. More sensitive than the Communists to these considerations, Dubinsky and his faction sought and secured Italian support.[63]

The Philadelphia convention had been an extraordinary event. For nearly three weeks the delegates publicly aired their soiled linen in an uninhibited and painful display of union democracy.[64] There were 110 radical delegates in attendance.[65] The convention reformed the ILGWU's internal political structure and offered the prospect of increased labor militancy as a solution to the economic problems of the membership and the ladies' garment industry.

Morris Sigman's failures and concessions had left him with greatly reduced presidential power. David Dubinsky defended his own interests, which were intertwined with those of his power base, Local 10. Approaching his thirty-fourth birthday, the pugnacious manager and ILGWU vice president was not about to concede defeat and face political oblivion because of the hated Communists.

In early January, at the first General Executive Board meeting of 1926, Sigman reported that the ILGWU in New York had "been absolutely smashed and destroyed," with finances exhausted and members demoralized, defiant, and distrustful. In response, Louis Hyman and others suggested that a successful strike could "overcome their present indifference." A walkout in the middle of the season, February, would surprise the employers and defeat them. However, it could occur only if management were to reject a Governor's Advisory Commission report favorable to the union, and if the union raised $300,000 by taxing its members to finance it.[66] Three days later Hyman repeated his suggestion but, as before, received no support. Dubinsky and Sigman remained unconvinced, the latter contending that with union money in short supply a strike would be "a dangerous move."[67]

Another element of danger was gangsterism. It was not unusual for employers to hire gangsters to attack union organizers or break up strikes, or for unions to make use of them. Once threatened with violence, David Dubinsky obtained a gun permit and then kept a pistol in a desk at his Local 10 office.[68]

The Advisory Commission's second report, issued on May 20, was on balance sympathetic to labor. In particular, it supported the union in identifying the jobbers, who should be held accountable for transgressions by their subcontractors, as the real force behind management. Of special satisfaction to Dubinsky was a recommended increase in the cutters' minimum wage scale.[69] Sigman and the inside manufacturers were ready to negotiate on the basis of this report, but not the jobbers or the ILGWU left-wingers, who were deeply divided. Louis Hyman was an independent left-winger who "resented" Workers' Party use of the Joint Board for its own purposes and, accordingly, threatened to resign as the board's general manager.[70] For its part, the party was displeased with actual members, including Charles Zimmerman, who were, like Hyman, too independent.[71]

But the Workers' Party leaders, Charles Ruthenberg and William Z. Foster, were determined to have a garment strike. Under the leadership of Communist Ben Gold, furriers had walked out in February and would gain the garment industry's first forty-hour week and a wage increase of 10 percent.[72] In contrast, in Passaic, New Jersey, a Communist-led walkout of textile workers in January had resulted in middle-class ire and law enforcement officers breaking up picket lines with guns and clubs.[73] Despite the fact that both the party and the New York Joint Board were broke, and that Hyman was reluctant, the Communists were determined to have a garment strike. Behind the scenes and aware of the party's internal division, Moscow wanted proof of their militancy.[74]

The walkout was foreordained. In anticipation of the report of the Governor's Commission, the Workers' Party had selected the personnel for the Joint Board to place on the strike committees. Zimmerman and fellow left-winger Joseph Boruchowitz had been in favor of Sigman for chairman of the general strike committee, but the party leadership gave the position to Hyman. Thus, for the first time in the history of the ILGWU, someone other than the president would occupy that seat. Sigman was aggrieved as Hyman took the post and Zimmerman was made his secretary. So that the right-wingers would share responsibility for the strike, Dubinsky and his allies also received some appointments. Dubinsky became secretary of the settlement committee, chaired by Salvatore Ninfo, the manager of Local 48. The settlement committee would deal with employers who wished to operate during the strike independent of their trade association.[75]

Primarily because the commission's report gave management the right to reorganize shops, the Joint Board rejected its report. A subsequent meeting of ILGWU shop chairmen concurred in the rejection, as did Local 10's executive board and membership. Dubinsky called the reorganization plan "a dangerous weapon" in the hands of the manufacturers.[76]

Despite the poor prospects for success, by the middle of June, Sigman conceded that a cloakmakers' strike was "inevitable" and would be "hard-fought."[77] Sigman reminded the General Executive Board that the International's coffers were already being drained to sustain walkouts in Mount Vernon and White Plains, New York.[78]

Toward the end of June, with the expiration of the contract and the beginning of the strike only a few days away, the fragile, unofficial truce between Dubinsky and the Joint Board began to unravel over where the cutters would meet during the strike. Traditionally the cutters had conducted their strikes from a separate meeting hall, apart from members of other locals. Hyman had agreed to respect this tradition. Consequently, the cutters chose Isidore Nagler as their hall chairman, and it was understood that they would register and meet at Arlington Hall.

Then came word that the cutters had been denied the separate hall. Dubinsky was incensed, believing the purpose was to spread his followers over the other halls in order to weaken their collective influence and pave the way for a takeover of Local 10 by "those who have long sought to capture it." The cutters then adopted a resolution reaffirming their loyalty to their leaders and appointed a committee to help persuade the Joint Board to grant them the hall.[79]

Before the cutters adjourned their meeting, Dubinsky instructed them to stop working at 4 p.m. the next day, Tuesday, June 29, as the Joint Board had decided, and make their way to Madison Square Garden to attend a mass meeting on the imminent strike.[80] Twenty thousand cloakmakers heard speeches by numerous dignitaries, including Sidney Hillman, president of the Amalgamated Clothing Workers of America, and Hugh Frayne, organizer for the American Federation of Labor, who brought greetings from AFL president William Green. Though Sigman had originally counseled the Joint Board not to strike, he and other right-wingers pledged their public support to demonstrate union solidarity versus the employers. Hyman told the throng that they had to stand and fight to force the jobbers to meet their responsibilities. In response, the cloakmakers authorized their leaders to call a general strike. The strike committee then met and called for a walkout on July 1.[81]

At 10 a.m. the cutters responded to the strike call by leaving their shops and marching to Arlington Hall on St. Mark's Place. By noon, 95 percent of the members had registered for strike duty. By the end of the day their participation was complete.[82] However, the question of a regular meeting hall was as yet unresolved. On the afternoon of July 2, cutters packed Arlington Hall in a great outpouring of enthusiasm for the strike. At Dubinsky's invitation, Hyman came and addressed them and found their spirit impressive. Dubinsky thought this might be sufficient to make the Joint Board abandon its notion of scattering the cutters. He was mistaken. That same day the Joint Board withdrew Arlington Hall from them.[83]

The cutters were stunned but not defeated. The main threat to Local 10 seemed to be from the Joint Board rather than management. Dubinsky knew that a membership scattered in various halls would be difficult to defend against Communist ideology and tactics. Nevertheless, the strike could not be ignored, and the future of the ILGWU was at stake.

Hyman and the general strike committee devised a compromise. Meeting on July 6, they produced a solution acceptable to Dubinsky, pending the approval of his union. It called for a weekly rather than daily meeting of cutters in Arlington Hall and gave Local 10 the right to designate a vice chairman to be present in each hall where cutters were assembled in order to assist them.

The next day, July 7, Dubinsky presented this plan to nearly 2,000 cloakmakers at Cooper Union. Special guest Morris Sigman told them to "cast aside" their political differences and focus on the strike, but Dubinsky then took the floor and accused the Joint Board of attempting to "weaken" and "demoralize" Local 10 and create hardships for the individual cutters.

In the name of unity, cutter Arthur Weinstein introduced a resolution to accept the verdict of the general strike committee, be loyal to the Local 10 leadership, and fully support the strike leadership. Put to a vote, Weinstein's resolution failed. Determined to rescue it, Dubinsky made a fervent plea for its unanimous adoption in view of the much greater issues of the strike. The cutters took a second vote. This time the resolution passed "almost unanimously." After the voting, Dubinsky made a final statement. He told the cutters they must no longer talk about a separate hall. "You must talk strike, strike, strike."[84]

Dubinsky's plea for unity made no impression on those who were directing the strike; they continued to distrust and denounce him and the right wing. The *Freiheit* vilified "the Dubinsky gang," accusing "the pigmy leaders of Local 10" of having defied the orders of the strike committee in their efforts to obtain a separate hall, and of having hired "hoodlums of the underworld" to beat up four cutters who were independent of "their strike-breaking gang."[85]

As the strike continued, Morris Sigman kept his promise to speak in support of it. In early August, Commission chairman George Gordon Battle announced that the time was ripe for labor and management to reach an understanding. Sigman responded that his people would stay out until the ILGWU's "entire program of demands" was met.[86]

Along with Louis Hyman, Sigman rejected a suggestion by Governor Al Smith that the dispute be submitted to arbitration for settlement. "Arbitration would serve no useful purpose in our present condition," they said.[87] Smith urged them to reconsider.[88] With both pain and pressure building, at the end of August the ILGWU and the Industrial Council agreed to confer.[89]

Negotiations were necessary because the strike was faring poorly. Union funds were rapidly vanishing, and the Joint Board was settling with individual firms on terms much less favorable than the recommendations of the Battle Commission. The picket committee alone spent close to $250,000 but could account only for half; the rest probably went for police bribery and other illegal activities. The Joint Board would misappropriate some $800,000 of employer funds left with it as contract security. As for ILGWU money, $3,500,000 would be spent, with less than half, $1,500,000, paid as strike benefits. As the costs mounted, thousands of cloakmakers returned to their shops under poor terms, further under-mining the strike.[90]

By the eighth week of the strike a tentative settlement was drafted on the basis of terms favorable to the ILGWU. It was understood that the cloakmakers would receive an average wage hike of 10 percent, a forty-hour work week, and a guaranteed thirty-two week employment year, while manufacturers could reorganize by discharging 5 percent of their employees. Formal negotiations were to follow, but the left-wing leaders of the Joint Board dared not begin them without the prior consent of the Workers' Party.[91]

Zimmerman, Hyman, Boruchowitz, Julius Portnoy, and Rose Wortis of Local 22 took the terms of the tentative settlement to the needle trades committee of the party. At the Communists' Fourteenth Street headquar-ters, the ILG-ers met with Benjamin Gitlow, William Weinstone, Charles Krumbein, and Joseph Zack. Zimmerman argued that the terms were the best obtainable and that the time was ripe to end the strike. The commit-tee approved, but now the party's "leading fraction," its "most active people," had to concur. "A couple of hundred" of these party dignitaries had been in another room awaiting the committee's decision and were ready to act on it. Zimmerman spoke first and reported on the settlement and the committee's approval. Joseph Boruchowitz also recommended the settlement but remarked, in his characteristic way, that "maybe we could have gotten more." No sooner was Boruchowitz's speech over than Weinstone rose and said that if it was possible to get a better deal, the party should attempt it. Unwilling to appear less aggressive than Wein-stone, the Ruthenberg and Foster people opposed the settlement. Forced by this unexpected development to meet again, the committee reversed its position. The leading fraction then endorsed the reversal. Zimmerman and the other unionists left party headquarters instructed not to end the strike until victory was won.[92]

These instructions made it almost impossible to negotiate a compro-mise. Conferences held September 2 and 3 between the ILGWU and the Industrial Council ended with the latter again insisting on the right to re-organize by dismissing 10 percent of their employees. On the heels of that failure, the Industrial Council complained to Justice Charles L. Guy of the New York State Supreme Court that the striking garment workers had re-sorted to violence, and the Council obtained an injunction that virtually outlawed the strike. This writ kept the ILGWU from legally picketing or even holding meetings in the halls to discuss the strike as it related to the Industrial Council's members.[93]

As the strike progressed, Dubinsky continued to negotiate settlements with individual shops and monitor employment at them. Dubinsky told his striking cutters to carry on as usual and remember the glory days of 1910. He also reported to them that more than 10,000 strikers had returned to work, according to the ILGWU's demands, by way of deals hammered out by the settlement committee of which he was secretary.[94]

Supporters of the general strike committee remained convinced that Dubinsky was out to embarrass the Left by subverting the strike. In late September, the general strike committee authorized work on Saturday, September 25, so that the day's earnings could be donated to the ILGWU's strike fund, but Dubinsky, saying such employment threatened the forty-hour principle, took exception.[95] The Left also alleged that Dubinsky and other right-wing officers refused to abide by a Joint Board decision and go unpaid during the strike. They received full pay, even though most cloakmakers were enduring great hardship and those who returned to work or found temporary work in other trades had to turn over a portion of their earnings to the strike fund. To refute the hostile rumors, a mass meeting of cutters at Arlington Hall voted unanimous support of Local 10 and its officers and the ILGWU and the Joint Board.[96]

To continue the walkout, the ILGWU's leaders sought the support of other unions. They appealed to the conservative American Federation of Labor but did not receive much more than a sympathetic resolution passed by its convention in Detroit. On the other hand, the Amalgamated Clothing Workers helped out with $25,000, while the *Daily Forward* gave $15,000.[97]

The failure to settle the ILGWU strike in its eighth week left it more discordant than ever, and directionless. Out of the confusion came a suggestion, not from an actual participant but from William Z. Foster. With negotiations going nowhere, the Communist leader proposed to rescue the strike by amalgamating all the needle trades. Zimmerman and the ILGWU Communists thought the idea ridiculous and voiced their opposition. Then, at a meeting of the general strike committee, Ben Gold appeared. The Communist furrier, on behalf of his party, made a speech in support of amalgamation. The idea still made no sense to the ILG-ers, and the strike continued.[98]

Progress came in mid-October. Negotiating from weakness, the ILGWU yielded on the reorganization issue and offered other concessions. On November 12, 1926, an unfavorable accord came about with fewer restrictions on reorganization than recommended by the Governor's Commission and loss of the workers' protection against discharge. The ILGWU did, however, gain a slight reduction in the work week. Three days after the settlement, the leaders of the general strike committee and of the International endorsed the settlement as the best obtainable under the circumstances. However, the right-wing position, which Dubinsky articulated, was that the International would have been better off negotiating on the basis of the Governor's Commission's report than undergoing the misery of the strike. That distress and the failure to settle sooner he blamed on the left-wing Joint Board. The Left, he noted, after having rejected traditional collective bargaining as "class collaboration," later accepted the intervention of outsiders, capitalist "meddlers." On November 16, 78 percent of 12,733 cloakmakers who cast secret ballots voted to ratify the agreement with the inside manufacturers.[99]

After twenty weeks of picket lines and the expenditure of more than three million dollars, the ILGWU in effect accepted defeat. With agreements with the other employers' groups yet to be concluded, recriminations between the Right and the Left flared anew over who was responsible for the debacle. Dubinsky defended his work on the settlement committee and denied charges that he had ordered his cutters not to work for single pay on a Saturday, thereby sabotaging the strike fund. On the contrary, by committing its resources to the strike, Local 10 had become "penniless."[100]

With failure apparent, and the strike not yet completely ended, the GEB moved to oust the left-wing strike leadership. Its statement of December 1 called on the cloakmakers to cleanse their own ranks. On December 2, though the GEB meetings were still continuing, Sigman and Dubinsky addressed a meeting of cloakmakers at Cooper Union and assured them of a change in leaders if such was their desire. The cloakmakers enthusiastically received their visitors, raising Sigman to their shoulders and suggesting that the International take control over the Joint Board. With the stage thus set, the GEB took action. On the thirteenth, Dubinsky moved the adoption of a resolution to wrest control of the strike and the Joint Board from the left-wingers. Opposed by only two votes, the measure passed with ease.[101]

Throughout the long strike, David Dubinsky was second to none as the target of left-wing criticism. Even President Morris Sigman, nominal leader of the right wing, commanded a certain measure of respect. Despite his frequent anti-Communist pronouncements, he had accommodated the Left both before and during the walkout, most dramatically by permitting Hyman to serve as chairman of the general strike committee. By contrast, Dubinsky was younger and more outspoken, a foe whose career was still ahead of him. Supported by the powerful, conservative cutters, he had little reason to compromise.

As December began, the civil war again showed signs of life even within Local 10. Rising again for their annual challenge to the Dubinsky machine, the left-wing cutters reorganized themselves as the Welfare League. Their purpose, they said, was "to build and strengthen the union and not to split our union." "A union is organized," they proclaimed, to protect workers in their "daily struggles with the bosses and not for the sake of a few job holders and their clique." The latter, of course, referred to "Dubinsky and his group," whom they accused of "maintaining their control by pursuing a policy of terrorism, intimidation, suppression of minority opinion, denial of freedom of speech, partiality and favoritism."[102]

In the annual cutters' elections, Dubinsky's steamroller again crushed the opposition. He defeated Falk Cooper by 1,890 votes to 155, receiving 92.4 percent of the votes cast. At Local 10's installation meeting nine days later, he called the victory part of the greater "fight against the communist disruptors in the labor movement," to which the cutters pledged their "full support."[103]

The house of cards that was the ILGWU's bargaining position collapsed in the aftermath of the November 12 agreement with the Industrial Council. The submanufacturers demanded the same terms, and the jobbers declined even to discuss a settlement. Sigman finally settled with the contractors, on terms like those received by the inside manufacturers. Regarding the primary enemy, the jobbers, the International came full circle. On January 12, 1927, it in effect renewed the agreement that had been rejected on its expiration in July 1926.

Thus, twenty-eight weeks after it began, and at a cost of $3,500,000, the cloakmakers' strike ended with the International in ruins, the Communists momentarily set back, Sigman exhausted, and Dubinsky more firmly than ever in command of Local 10. A victorious strike in 1926 would have been miraculous.[104] The ILGWU's left wing, directed by the

Workers' Party, began and continued the strike for political motives and as a demonstration of its brand of militant unionism. The right wing provided perfunctory support. Each side when possible blamed failures on the other, exacerbating the disunity, which made winning the strike all the more improbable. Unscathed by the Left's attacks, Dubinsky was on the rise in an ILGWU perhaps already too weak to survive.

The general strike concluded with cloakmakers in jail on assault charges and a rekindling of the flames of the civil war between the Left and the Right.[105] When the General Executive Board took control of the New York Joint Board in December 1926, it reorganized that body and its four left-wing locals. The GEB packed what became known as the Provisional Joint Board with rightist officers led by Sigman, who became general manager. Concurrently, it appointed conservatives to head the four leftist locals and revamped the various strike committees. Dubinsky became co-chair of the organization committee. To complete this counterrevolution, Local 35 would again elect conservative Joseph Breslaw manager.

The choice for the members of New York Joint Board locals was simple: ratify the changes or leave the International. All members of reorganized Joint Board locals were required to register with the revamped Joint Board and receive new union books. Dubinsky's own Local 10, which he and the Right controlled, was not reorganized, making its members uniquely exempt from the registration requirement. But even in Local 10 a remnant of the Left persisted in its assault on the leadership. Small but vocal, the left-wing Welfare League regularly attacked Dubinsky in its newsletter, *The Cutter*. The radical sheet sought to unmask "the little clown," Dubinsky, and "his policies of favoritism and supplementary agreements," which allegedly undermined both the Local and the cloakmakers' strike. The ousted radicals of the left-wing locals condemned the GEB takeover as unconstitutional. As the left-wing board retained considerable rank-and-file support, it continued to function and even collected dues.

For the moment there were rival boards, but this situation would not last very long. The International had the upper hand. It aggressively recruited the cloakmakers and issued new charters to the reorganized locals, which in turn dropped members for nonpayment of dues. The employers were delighted to deal with the right-wingers, whom they chose to regard as the sole representatives of the workers, thus further weakening the Left.[106]

On January 3, 1927, the Provisional Joint Board was installed. Within the next six weeks, 32,000 workers responded to its call. By May, 90 percent of the cloakmakers had registered. The ILGWU had not died, but the years of civil war and the disastrous strike had left it extremely feeble. With the International no longer an effective watchdog, working conditions deteriorated throughout the ladies' garment industry. Manufacturers, jobbers, and submanufacturers felt free to do as they pleased.[107]

Dubinsky's goal, as ever, was to crush the stubborn internal faction. The deposed left wing of the Joint Board, he complained, was even trying to find jobs for cutters as a means of weaning them from Local 10. Their efforts in that regard were not very successful, but he knew that it would be folly to let down his guard.

"It seems that you are not aware," he wrote to a journalist in Chicago, "that the Communists in New York are licked and admit so themselves."[108] In fact, the Communists were conceding nothing of the sort. Ever defiant, Charles Zimmerman was still counseling cutters to forsake Local 10. In the face of such a threat, Dubinsky invoked broad disciplinary powers authorized by the members of Local 10 back on December 26, 1926, and ordered all cutters to secure or renew working cards from the Local. Noncompliance would result in automatic suspension, with reinstatement to be treated as though there had been expulsion.[109] By the end of February, twenty-six cutters had been suspended, and Dubinsky announced that even Communist sympathizers were adhering to the discipline of the local.[110]

The suppression of dissent within Local 10 only mirrored the continuing crackdown by the General Executive Board. Following counsel Morris Hillquit's opinion that it could constitutionally suspend locals and individuals without trial for nonpayment of dues after thirty days' notice, the Board moved to suspend and reorganize Locals 2, 9, 22, and 35. As he was visiting Philadelphia's cloakmakers at the time, Dubinsky was absent from the crucial February 13 session. Louis Hyman, Julius Portnoy, and Joseph Boruchowitz, the three left-wing GEB members, also were missing. In their absence, the resolution passed unanimously.[111]

Fines, suspensions and verbal brickbats all poisoned the atmosphere of Local 10, but on the weekend of March 26 and 27, 1927, warfare was suspended while the union held its twenty-fifth anniversary Jubilee Celebration in grand style at Mecca Temple on West Fifty-sixth Street. Among those on hand to praise the cutters were William Green and Matthew Woll of the AFL, Abraham Cahan of the *Jewish Daily Forward,* and, as a sharp rebuke to the Communists, Alexander Kerensky, exiled former premier of Russia. With 4,000 in attendance at the concert and almost 1,200 at the banquet, Dubinsky had good reason to feel that the Jubilee was a complete success.[112]

Conditions in the cloak and dress trade were something else. Business was slow, and the number of nonunion shops in operation had doubled since 1925.[113] Permitted under the new agreement in the cloak industry to "reorganize," or discharge, up to 10 percent of their employees on June 1, members of the Industrial Council began to eliminate cutters.[114] The Joint Board promised to remedy that situation with a vigorous organization campaign.[115] The Cutter's Welfare League questioned the sincerity of the campaign, calling it "nothing else but a new method by Sigman and his henchmen to sell Company union books." Reviled by the Left as Sigman's "partner," Dubinsky was accused of participating in this "fake" organization drive.[116]

The Left also accused Sigman and Dubinsky of stealing $400,000 from the Unemployment Insurance Fund of the Cloak, Suit and Dress Industries.[117] Created in 1924 after demands by the ILGWU, the fund provided a maximum benefit of $120 per year in unemployment benefits and was to be administered by trustees representing the union, management, and the public. Both the workers and employers made contributions, which began in November 1924 and continued smoothly until the general strike of 1926.

In the aftermath of the November 1926 settlement with the Industrial Council, numerous employers ceased making payments, thereby jeopardizing the future of the fund. In March 1927, the ILGWU suspended the fund until July 1, 1928, and appointed Morris Sigman, David Dubinsky, and Julius Hochman as trustees to put the fund back in order and collect the overdue payments. At the time of its suspension, the fund had a balance of "somewhat less than $400,000," which would be needed to meet various operating expenses.[118] This was the sum the Left claimed Dubinsky and Sigman had stolen.

In September, the Left held a mass meeting at Madison Square Garden. Somewhat sparsely attended, it nevertheless served to rally the forces on the Left and again shout defiance at the Right. The left-wing leaders correctly understood that prolonging the civil war could stir up latent right-wing impatience with Sigman and might cause a rift within the General Executive Board, where several ambitious vice presidents were becoming restless. Despite his public support of Sigman, Dubinsky was again growing critical of the president. His doubt that Sigman would ever prevail over the Communists was shared by such other powers on the GEB as Joseph Breslaw and Salvatore Ninfo.[119]

At this juncture, the question of proportional representation, the most frequently debated individual issue since the start of the civil war, again arose. Dubinsky, with a majority of the 1925 convention, had favored a modified version of proportional representation. The Left called for a system of direct proportional representation. Preoccupied with the 1926 general strike, the GEB did not act on the matter until June 1927, when it established a committee chaired by Dubinsky to plan a referendum in the fall. The committee reported in September, with balloting to take place by November 15.[120]

As the referendum neared, the issue again was debated. Endorsed by the executive board of Local 10, the indirect plan was urged upon the cutters. Isidore Nagler presented the recommendation to the cutters, arguing that it would be suicidal to permit certain locals to dominate conventions because of large membership. Eleven hundred cutters, voting unanimously, agreed. So did the great majority of the ILGWU membership.[121] Altogether, 93.2 percent chose the majority report, thereby handing the Left a significant defeat.[122]

His power consolidated and secure, Dubinsky was elected to an uncontested seventh consecutive term as manager of Local 10. All nine other officers were also elected without opposition.[123] Dubinsky had taken command of Local 10 and converted it into his personal machine. With the International still divided and beset by problems, the question now was when he would make his bid for the presidency.

4

Second in Command

Dubinsky's unopposed reelection in 1927 was stunning even by Local 10's customary standards.[1] More securely in power than ever before, Dubinsky sought to expand benefits for his constituents. The closing of several large shops had cost the jobs of veteran cutters. Dubinsky felt that Local 10 ought to provide its members "some measure of protection for old age," but he stopped short of advocating a union pension. In lieu of a permanent pension fund, Dubinsky suggested a fund of "a few thousand dollars" to help the elderly cope with "depression and . . . acute need." On his recommendation, Local 10 took a step in that direction. It agreed that the proceeds of a souvenir of a union affair in April would be earmarked for the new fund.[2]

How could labor standards be defended when the International could claim the membership of only about 40 percent of the workers in the ladies' garment industry? Undeterred by the hard times, Locals 10, 22, 35, and 89 planned to launch a major organizing drive in the dress industry, and the Joint Board tried to persuade employers to enforce previously negotiated agreements in the cloak industry.[3] The relatively strong Local 10 had shrunk to 2,700 members from its longtime average of 4,000. The greatest losses had occurred in the dress trade, but cloakmakers, too, were hard pressed for employment. They increasingly found it in nonunion shops, thereby setting an example for organized workers to stop paying dues and drop out of the union. Preying on weakness, management tried to restore Saturday work without overtime. Dubinsky would only remind the General Executive Board that the union could do nothing unless its members paid their dues.[4]

This weakness also aided the Communists. Direct confrontation having failed, the left-wingers continued their outward support for the "peace movement" in the guise of the Tolerance Group, while gauging their chances to exploit what they called a "confusion of forces," or factional discord, under the ILGWU leadership.[5]

Their perception of a split was accurate. Sigman had won the war, but Dubinsky and Breslaw, among others, thought someone else should make the peace. Dubinsky, the pragmatist, regarded Sigman as ideologically inflexible. Indeed, the strong-willed president had contempt for those he saw as opportunistic bureaucrats and was, to Dubinsky, "a poor angel of peace."[6]

Although conceding defeat in the civil war, William Z. Foster had rallied the Trade Union Educational League against the ILGWU president, focusing on the theme "Sigman must go!"[7] The Communist change of heart originated in Moscow. Signs of a shift in policy were evident as early as 1924, when V. I. Lenin died.[8] In 1928, Stalin was still consolidating his power. On the road to vanquishing his actual and imagined rivals, he altered the trade-union policy of the Comintern and its labor arm, the Profintern. Meeting in Moscow in February, the Comintern urged American Communists to forsake "boring from within" established unions in favor of establishing competing organizations where workers were poorly or not yet organized. In practical terms, Communist garment workers in the United States were free to create new garment unions instead of vying for control of the ILGWU and other organizations.[9]

When Moscow changed course, Dubinsky sensed that the time was ripe to make a peace gesture to the Left. Such a move would win him plaudits as a peacemaker and a personal identity clearly distinct from that of Morris Sigman. With the next ILGWU convention still three months away, Dubinsky therefore suggested to Sigman that former president Benjamin Schlesinger be brought back and handed a leadership role in the International.[10]

Nevertheless, the convention opened with peace still out of sight. For the first time in nearly a decade, an ILGWU convention began without a significant radical delegate representation. With left-wingers seemingly excluded from the scene at Musicians' Hall, Boston, Louis Hyman and Joseph Levin of the New York and Chicago Joint Boards, respectively, demanded the Left's inclusion and denounced "the ruthless war against the workers" waged against them by Dubinsky, Sigman, and others on the General Executive Board for the past eighteen months.[11] Dubinsky said that the complainants included people who pretended "to have been elected as delegates of fictitious locals" and who "were suspended from their local unions for non-payment of dues." The convention unanimously concurred in the exclusions.

Though the convention opened on this exclusionist note, several delegates introduced conciliatory resolutions. Dubinsky rejected unconditional reinstatement, but peace was in the air and irresistible, even to the resolutions committee that he chaired. The result was a committee recommendation that former ILG-ers be reinstated "with full rights and privileges," with those who belonged to the Communist Party or Trade Union Educational League and accepted the party's "leadership" to be denied union office. This recommendation prevailed by a vote of 111 to 5.[12]

Both peace and personalities were at stake in the process of electing a president. The 204 delegates listened to several guest speakers, including Abraham Cahan, the bête noire of Jewish Communism, who boasted that Sigman, Dubinsky, and Breslaw came to consult with him: "Dubinsky and I are like old chums." On the presidency, though, Cahan observed that Dubinsky and he differed. Cahan backed Sigman, while Dubinsky was behind Schlesinger. Most important, Dubinsky and Cahan "were together day and night" in the "fight against that terrible monster—'Communism.'" Alluding to the "misunderstanding between Sigman and Dubinsky," Cahan was tactful. "Dubinsky is no fool. He is only human, and this man [Sigman] is also human. Dubinsky is a civilized enemy."

In the name of democracy, Breslaw and Dubinsky made it known that they wanted a referendum whereby all members of the ILGWU, not just convention delegates, would be eligible to vote for president, and Sigman might be toppled. Cahan denounced this move as a device to override the convention and place the presidency in the hands of the New York membership, who would dominate it by their numbers. Stripping the convention of power this way would be "one of the greatest crimes in history." Breslaw, backed by Dubinsky, replied that Cahan's speech was "not at all for peace." Meanwhile, virtually ignored in this exchange was Morris Sigman, who was chairing the session.[13]

Sigman could sound militant because he still had the support of many anti-Communist veterans of the civil war. The Italian cloakmakers and dressmakers, Locals 48 and 89, respectively, sided with him, as did the locals that had been reorganized during the war—2, 9, and 22—and the locals outside New York City. This coalition also included such union power brokers as Julius Hochman and the two Italian leaders, Salvatore Ninfo of Local 48 and Luigi Antonini of Local 89. Altogether, Sigman commanded the allegiance of most of the convention's delegates.[14]

Dubinsky realized that Sigman's strength was formidable and that an open floor fight would bloody both sides and benefit only the Communists. According to Dubinsky, Abraham Cahan approached him with a compromise settlement: reelect Sigman and make Dubinsky "secretary-treasurer and heir apparent." Dubinsky declined the offer, claiming a lack of personal ambition and a desire to avoid additional hard feelings within the International.

Respected ILGWU general counsel Morris Hillquit, however, might be persuaded to serve as mediator. Approached by Dubinsky, Hillquit suggested that the convention unite behind Sigman but also bring back Schlesinger by giving him a new, specially created position: he would hold the title of executive vice president until such time as Sigman would resign as president. Sigman yielded to the Hillquit compromise.[15] Two days later the delegates unanimously reelected Sigman. Next they turned to Schlesinger. Dubinsky nominated the former president to serve as an additional vice president, who would, in Hillquit's words, "direct and supervise and organize" New York's cloak and suit and dress industry. The convention rubber-stamped the scheme.[16]

The manipulators of this convention achieved their results in an atmosphere of intense bitterness. Sigman resented the maneuvering to remove him from office. Schlesinger, too, was displeased with what was happening. In failing health, he had been visited privately by Dubinsky at a vacation resort in Belmar, New Jersey, prior to the convention. It is clear that Schlesinger abhorred the idea of working for or with Sigman, who had taken the presidency from him five years before. Dubinsky may well have approached him to become a candidate for president. Even after he accepted the less prestigious title of executive vice president, it is by no means clear that Schlesinger expected Sigman to retire in his favor.

Benjamin Schlesinger would soon regret his course. At some point during the convention, Sigman had a "talk" with him, which was a humiliating experience. Schlesinger felt he "should have left the convention." "I made an unpardonable mistake in accepting as vice president. It should have been president." Apparently Schlesinger accepted for two reasons. First, the compromise depended on him, and second, he was led to believe that his title would be executive vice president, not just vice president.[17]

His relations with Sigman in the aftermath of the convention were extremely strained. Nominally in charge of the New York cloak and dress situation, he faced monumental problems. The International was close to bankruptcy. When the convention ended, only a third of New York's cloakmakers were organized, and substandard employment conditions continued to be rampant in the industry.[18] The situation in dressmaking was even worse. At Boston the delegates had endorsed a resolution introduced by Local 22 authorizing a general strike in the New York dress industry.[19]

Acting on that resolution, the General Executive Board "instructed and authorized" Schlesinger to prepare for such a strike. Next it discussed another idea that had surfaced at the convention, the establishment of a trade board within the New York Joint Board to make recommendations regarding the dress trade. Schlesinger said the new body would be "a board within a board" and proposed that the GEB would do better if it created a committee to prepare for the general strike authorized by the convention. Dubinsky agreed, as did Sigman, but the committee the GEB then set up was to "take up the matter of a dress trade board with the Joint Board."[20]

The sensitive Schlesinger could only have been personally offended by talk of a trade board. As supervisor of New York's dress trade, it was now his responsibility to protect that area; creating a board could do nothing but undermine his authority. Sensitive to slights, Schlesinger considered walking out of the Philadelphia meeting and probably thought of resigning. But he did neither and instead "offered to stay [at his job] another four weeks." He stayed on when that period ended, an unhappy man who felt unappreciated and did not expect to be called to the presidency.[21]

Morris Sigman had even greater cause for bitterness than Schlesinger. His taste of victory had turned sour with his growing awareness of enemies within his own camp. The same Schlesinger whose poor health had kept him from continuing as president and standing up to the Communists in 1923 was back as a vice president. With Dubinsky and others promoting his return to the presidency, Schlesinger seemed to be in position for that eventuality despite the fact that his health had continued to decline. No fool, Sigman knew his presidency was about to end, but it had to be done gracefully. With luck he would return with his dignity intact to Storm Lake, Iowa.

The opportunity for his escape arose in October, at a meeting of the General Executive Board. A firm believer in industrial unionism, Sigman in 1924 had merged the reefermakers, who made children's coats, and the cloakmakers into a new Local 2. Unfortunately, the marriage failed, and the reefermakers sought a divorce. At the Boston convention Dubinsky and Breslaw had led a group of delegates from several locals in introducing a resolution to give the reefermakers their independence. The convention appointed a committee, which reported in October in favor of separation. Without delay the GEB then moved to create a new reefermakers' local, which would be headed by an old nemesis, Jacob Heller. His work undone and industrial unionism repudiated, Morris Sigman resigned as president.[22]

Issued two days after the GEB action, while the Board was still meeting, Sigman's statement was characteristically blunt. Most of his remarks pertained to the decision to separate the reefermakers, which he said was "basically wrong," but he also had some choice words for his enemies. He denounced the "unwholesome pre-Convention campaign" against him by certain "New York local leaders."

Dubinsky the next day won adoption of a motion to establish a committee to determine how Sigman's successor would be chosen. This committee, which included Dubinsky, reported on October 29 that it had asked Benjamin Schlesinger to take the job, but that he insisted it be through a membership referendum that would give him "at least a three-quarter majority." Dubinsky, Luigi Antonini, and others dismissed that idea as sure to give the Communists new life. A special presidential election convention was another possibility but too expensive. The most expeditious solution was for the GEB to elect him, which it did, unanimously, after first obtaining his acceptance.[23]

Defeated but not dead, the Left hoped to benefit from demoralization on the Right. Back in May, delegates barred from the ILGWU convention in Boston had met to regroup and reshape their strategy. They held a three-day conference to create a new needle-trades union. After electing a National Organization Committee (NOC) as the foundation for such a structure, the conference issued a call for all ILG-ers to join their revitalized crusade. They claimed an attendance of 15,000 at a rally held at the Bronx Stadium in August.[24]

Contrary to Dubinsky's expectation, Sigman's resignation did not advance the cause of left–right peace. The National Organization Committee concluded that the right-wing leadership was "on the point of financial bankruptcy" and "divided into hostile cliques that are in a desperate struggle with each other."[25] To demonstrate its grip on the needle trades, the NOC planned a general strike in the depressed dress industry.[26]

As president of the International once again, Benjamin Schlesinger bore the burden of obtaining immediate financial relief for his organization. One possible source was the American Federation of Labor, which in November was holding its annual convention in New Orleans. Schlesinger went to the Crescent City, where sympathetic "representatives of about ten international unions" suggested that their organizations might make loans to the ILGWU. However, when he requested the help in writing, he was turned down. With the International's "financial condition . . . at its lowest point," Schlesinger persuaded the GEB to approve the issuance of three-year bonds that would pay 5 percent interest.[27] These bonds, which were intended to gain a quarter of a million dollars, were crucial to the ILGWU's survival. Members were expected to buy most of the bonds, and they had never before been asked for such a loan.

Their response was enthusiastic, thanks in good measure to Dubinsky. Seizing the initiative, he became a super-salesman. "Within two months," according to the union, the rank and file and organizational and individual friends of the ILGWU bought $135,000 of the issue. Local 10 "bought over $30,000 worth of bonds, which placed it easily in the lead of all other locals." Dubinsky himself purchased two hundred dollars' worth, double the amount bought by any other New York cutter.[28]

Dubinsky's dynamism was a factor in the success of the International's "open door policy" as well as its bond sales. The decision of the Boston convention to readmit expelled members, implemented by the GEB, proved popular, and Dubinsky was in the forefront of those urging a return to the fold. On December 30, at Pythian Temple in Coney Island, he spoke for an hour and a half on the subject. Nevertheless, he warned that the Communists could not "and would not conclude peace" with the ILGWU because they had been ordered to "destroy the labor movement, and form Communist unions in their place."[29]

By this time, the Communists had already formed three such unions to compete directly with existing AFL unions. In September 1928, they had established the National Miners Union and the National Textile Workers Union. At the end of December and beginning of January they created the Needle Trades Workers Industrial Union. The NTWIU was to represent all needle trades, with Louis Hyman and Rose Wortis as its chairman and secretary, respectively; but its dominant personality was Ben Gold, the leader of the furriers.

In September 1929 the Communists created the Trade Union Unity League, an umbrella group for the new Communist unions. Dual unionism was back in fashion.[30] While the Communist forces regrouped, the ILGWU struggled to survive, but now with a leader who was gravely ill.

Benjamin Schlesinger was suffering from Hodgkin's disease.[31] Sadly, though, many ILG-ers tended to discount the seriousness of his plight.[32] Morris Sigman was among the unsympathetic. In exile in Iowa, with a mortgage and business debts to be paid and with physical ailments of his own, the displaced and disgruntled Sigman was not overly concerned about the health of Schlesinger, whom he considered an "irresponsible crank."[33]

At the end of January 1929, the Communists at last voted to strike the dress trade, ostensibly "to organize the unorganized dressmakers." They regarded this walkout as "the first big task" of the Needle Trades Workers Industrial Union and "a revolt against the company unions formed by Schlesinger."[34] Special care would be taken for Communist Party members to be "in the thick of the struggle" and for the party's interests to be advanced.[35]

On February 6 the long-awaited event took place, but it proved to be less than overwhelming. Not more than 2,500 of New York City's 40,000 dressmakers walked out. When the strike ended twelve days later, the leaders refused to concede defeat. Ignoring their obvious failure, they claimed victory.[36]

The ILGWU leadership took great delight in the Communists' misadventure but still had to resolve its own problems with management. With the International's contract with the Industrial Council of Cloak, Suit and Dress Manufacturers due to expire on May 31, Schlesinger initiated negotiations. His demands included an increase in the minimum-wage scale, the reestablishment of the unemployment insurance fund, and the establishment of a joint committee to eradicate industrial evils.

On the other side, management had a different kind of shopping list. Though admitting that sweatshop conditions had returned, the Industrial Council insisted its members required greater rather than less control of the workplace and sought a return of piecework and Saturday work, for "at least three months each season."[37] As an impasse developed, Schlesinger's health deteriorated. In February, *Justice* reported that his ailment was mainly the result of "a neglected cold complicated by overwork" and that he was also troubled by a "gland disorder" that had required surgery.

Despite his illness, Schlesinger was not a figurehead president. His remaining energy went into saving the organization. To Dubinsky's surprise, Schlesinger upset the rules of financial orthodoxy. He persuaded the nearly broke ILGWU to contribute $5,000 to Jewish charities. In the past,

Schlesinger explained, the International had "scored its greatest gains" because of its reputation for responsibility to the community. His action generated enough goodwill for him to approach several pillars of the Jewish community for interest-free loans to the ILGWU. Through Schlesinger's efforts the International would obtain loans of $50,000 from Julius Rosenwald of Sears, Roebuck and $25,000 apiece from Herbert H. Lehman and Felix M. Warburg. The Workmen's Circle led a number of community labor and fraternal groups in buying reconstruction bonds.[38]

On March 15, Schlesinger advised the GEB that on doctor's orders he would be leaving the next day for "a rest" in Atlantic City. When the Board met again, on April 10, Schlesinger was present, but at the end of his presidential report he announced that his physician had again suggested that he leave town to convalesce. So that the ILGWU would not be left leaderless in his absence, he asked the GEB to select an acting head or committee. On the sixteenth, with no decision yet made by the GEB, Schlesinger appointed David Dubinsky to act as president in his absence.[39]

Now the former fugitive from czarist justice was acting president of the International. Dubinsky's tenure in his new position depended on the health and temperament of Benjamin Schlesinger, and he was responsible for directing a union that was close to both bankruptcy and a major strike. As sensitive as ever to personal slights, the deliberate, contemplative Schlesinger was suspicious of him. Seriously ill and privately desirous of retiring, Schlesinger nevertheless clung to his office, possibly out of a fear of a Dubinsky succession.

Relations between the ailing and acting presidents remained rather formal. Dubinsky sent Schlesinger detailed, written accounts of his attempts to raise money and negotiate with management. For advice in both areas the acting president leaned on Morris Hillquit. As it alternated between begging and bargaining, the ILGWU stumbled along toward another strike. In view of the International's poor condition, Hillquit was not favorably disposed to such a prospect. The New York Joint Board, which would be at the heart of any walkout, was having trouble meeting its financial obligations, as were its affiliated locals, which owed it $10,000.[40]

Neither the Industrial Council nor the other employers' associations would make concessions to the weak International, but Dubinsky was not disappointed. As he revealed much later, he conspired with the executive director and president of the Industrial Council to bring about a strike to strengthen the ILGWU and thus weaken the NTWIU. The plan was for the International to walk out and the employers to refrain from strong-arm, strike-breaking tactics. The union would then win the fight but gain better enforcement of labor standards rather than higher wages. Management would have freedom from strikes during the life of the contract. The major losers would be the Communists.[41]

In mid-May, more than a thousand shop chairmen crowded into Webster Hall vowing to fight a return to the sweatshop. Benjamin Schlesinger, still convalescing, sent a message of support, but it was Acting President Dubinsky who stirred the throng, sounding very much like a union president. The strike would be called, he said, at the union's convenience, not "as the Communists did [in 1926], at the behest of Moscow, but only after . . . a referendum vote" by the cloakmakers.[42]

In late June, union–management talks broke down. Even before they collapsed, Dubinsky had called a strike "inevitable." He explained to William Green that it would serve to organize the significant part of the ladies' garment industry that had become "infested with scab nests and sweat-shops" because of the 1926 strike. Green cautioned that lingering Communist elements in the ILGWU would welcome a walkout to advance the cause of "world revolution." In the aftermath of the NTWIU's recent strike debacle, Dubinsky discounted the Communists' influence. "They do not figure at all in the labor movement," he wrote to an English trade unionist.[43]

With the strike in sight, Dubinsky rallied his troops at Manhattan's Seventy-first Regiment Armory. On June 20 an estimated 10,000 cloakmakers heard him, Schlesinger, and Green send them into battle. On July 2, 28,000 cloakmakers walked out, drawing workers from 250 nonunion shops and eliciting an invitation the next day from Governor Franklin D. Roosevelt for the interested parties to meet with him in Albany. On July 15, only thirteen days after the strike began, a peace settlement was ratified by the cloakmakers; 16,094, or 97.8 percent, of the 16,452 who voted approved, with only 265 casting blank ballots. The formal signing took place the next day at New York's City Hall. The result was a victory for the union, which had ostensibly adopted a successful strategy to undercut the employer associations. In the agreement the ILGWU gained, among other things, the establishment of a state-supervised commission to eliminate substandard and sweatshop conditions from the garment industry. Moreover, the employers' right to dismiss by reorganizing was greatly curtailed, but, as prearranged, there was no wage increase.

The International seemed to have rebounded brilliantly. It now represented more than twice the number of cloakmakers it had before the strike. Local 10 alone gained three hundred shops and four hundred members. At City Hall a euphoric Benjamin Schlesinger told Mayor Jimmy Walker, "The time will come when the workers will run the government of this city."[44]

Success was a tonic. Schlesinger and Dubinsky immediately announced plans to drive the sweatshop from the dress industry.[45] Continuing an approach to the major department stores begun during the strike, Schlesinger asked fourteen of them to deal only with reputable union cloak and suit shops. Several, including R. H. Macy, Gimbel Brothers, and Abraham and Straus, responded sympathetically. Dubinsky and Joseph Breslaw met with officials of J. C. Penney to enlist that chain of 1,400 stores.[46] In September, Dubinsky and Isidore Nagler would reach agreement with Sears Roebuck.[47] The ILGWU announced plans to unionize "the entire American women's wear industry." This feat would be accomplished by initial strikes in Toronto, Chicago, Boston, Cleveland, Toledo, Baltimore, and Kansas City, followed by a massive walkout of 45,000 dressmakers in New York in December. To finance these strikes, the union would issue bonds. Never before had the ILGWU paid for a walkout in this manner.[48]

After the cloak strike, Dubinsky swung into action with astonishing energy. He visited Boston several times to rescue that city's cloak- and dressmakers from the Needle Trades Workers Industrial Union. In Toronto he helped initiate a cloakmakers' organization drive, and in Montreal he formed a new cloakmakers' union. His travels ended with visits to Chicago, where he met with union and management leaders, and Cleveland, where he helped formulate cloak and dress industry demands. In New York, a successful embroiderers' strike, masterminded by Dubinsky and vice president Jacob Halpern, resulted in the creation of an impartial chairman to aid in settling disputes and eliminating the sweatshop from the trimming trades.[49] On October 22, at a testimonial dinner held by the New York Joint Board in Dubinsky's honor, speaker after speaker attributed the International's recovery to him, but he graciously credited Benjamin Schlesinger.[50]

Two days after the banquet, prices fell sharply on the New York Stock Exchange. It was not yet evident that this collapse marked the onset of the Great Depression, and in December the ILGWU convention in Cleveland could still open on a note of optimism.[51] Though controversial at the 1928 convention, the idea of a referendum to elect officers now was acceptable to most delegates. Assured that the election for president would be uncontested, even Dubinsky could advocate an election by the membership instead of the convention, and the convention made the necessary amendment to the ILGWU constitution.[52]

Despite his poor health, Schlesinger accepted renomination for president but again lauded Dubinsky. He "would never have undertaken" the bond issue without Dubinsky's approval and called Dubinsky "the only man qualified" to succeed him. The president then insisted that only with Dubinsky as secretary-treasurer "to share the work" could he serve another term.

As the ailing Abraham Baroff was retiring, the secretary-treasurership was available, but Dubinsky really did not want it. He preferred to remain in charge of Local 10, but his mentor, Morris Hillquit, advised him to take the job as a matter of duty.[53] As Dubinsky's election was uncontested, he resigned as manager-secretary of Local 10. On January 7, 1930, the membership of the ILGWU reelected Schlesinger, with Dubinsky as secretary-treasurer.[54]

After surviving its civil war, the International had to contend with the Great Depression. Though the conflict had debilitated Morris Sigman and Benjamin Schlesinger, it strengthened David Dubinsky. Steadfast in his opposition to the Left and in his efforts to repair the ILGWU's fiscal foundation, he provided needed energy and emerged as the hands-down personal winner of the war.

5

Acting President

The struggles of the 1920s were fought against a backdrop of economic expansion. Despite occasional recessions, prosperity was the norm, and the ILGWU and other labor organizations sought a share of it for their members. With the stock market booming and unemployment low, the nation's mood was indifferent to those who sought advancement through collective bargaining. Businessmen touted the "American Plan" as the golden path for their workers. This scheme eschewed independent unions and the closed shop for employer paternalism, often expressed through company unions. In this atmosphere, organized labor lost millions of members. Under the bland leadership of William Green, the American Federation of Labor seemed incapable of reversing the trend, leaving many workers, especially in the mass-production industries, unorganized.

Capitalist dreams of indefinite prosperity ended abruptly when in a few days, from October 24 to 29, 1929, a devastating crash of the stock exchange wiped out everything it had gained in the preceding twelve months.[1] The number of unemployed in the United States, 1.8 million in 1929, would jump to 4.9 million in 1930 and peak at 13.2 million, or 24.9 percent of the workforce, in 1933.[2]

The slump affected the garment trades, particularly the dress industry, and the ILGWU soon felt its effects. In hard times, fewer firms manufactured better-quality dresses and more turned out the $3.75 and $6.75 lines that came to dominate output. Contractors, who had traditionally produced cheaper lines, proliferated, while inside manufacturers declined. In the cloak and suit industry the trend was similar. By 1932 the New York cloak industry would employ only 27,000 workers, slightly more than half of the 50,000 working 1912.[3] The membership of the ILGWU, which had advanced to 39,148 in 1930, slid to 23,876 by 1932.[4]

The 1920s had also witnessed a change in the ethnic composition of the union. Initially an almost entirely Jewish organization, it now showed signs of diversification beyond the Italians of Locals 48 and 89. First blacks and then Hispanics, mainly Puerto Ricans, entered the needle trades and the International. Blacks had worked in New York's garment industry at least since the beginning of the century, but not until 1928 did the ILGWU move decisively to organize them. In September 1929, as part of their drive to rid the dress industry of the sweatshop, Benjamin Schlesinger and David Dubinsky mounted a campaign to organize the 3,000 to 4,000 black women dressmakers in New York.[5]

What was happening to the *Jewish* unions of the *Jewish* labor movement? The old process of heavy immigration to supply and then replenish Jewish workers for the garment industry was no longer operational. The First World War, followed by restrictive, discriminatory quota legislation in 1921 and 1924, drastically reduced the flow of Jews to America. In the years that followed, the number of Jews in the garment unions began to decline and the average age of Jews in those organizations steadily rose.

The Jewish decline resulted from several factors. First, during this period the garment trades became decentralized, spreading to new production centers across America, including areas with small or no Jewish populations. Second, the garment industry divided its labor into "section work," which meant that many functions could be performed by workers with few skills or limited training. Third, and "the main factor" according to Will Herberg in 1952, was the combination of the reduced flow of immigrants in the 1920s and "the deep-seated reluctance of Jewish workers to have their children follow them into manual occupations instead of rising in the social scale to professional or white-collar status."[6]

In 1932 the General Executive Board noted the recent changes in the ILGWU's membership. The GEB cited a fifteen-year decline in the cloak industry, attributing some of it to the Great Depression and various changes in manufacturing techniques, but also observing that "thousands of cloakmakers" had retired because of old age and that there had been "comparatively few" replacements. "Except for the cutter branch," it said, "the American-born children of the older generation of cloakmakers have kept out of the cloak shops preferring to seek means of a livelihood in other trades or professions."[7]

. . .

With both the stock market and the national economy depressed, the Schlesinger-Dubinsky administration entered the thirties determined to keep the ILGWU on the upswing. For Schlesinger, weakened by terminal illness, that goal was particularly grueling. Coast-to-coast conflicts demanding his and Dubinsky's personal attention taxed his diminished energy to its limit. Of immediate concern were New York's dressmakers as they prepared for a major strike and California organizers who encountered Communist competition.

On February 4, 1930, the long-awaited dress strike began. On February 12, it ended. Following the lead of the cloakmakers the previous summer, the dressmakers won a settlement to maintain standards in their trade. Among their many gains were reestablished relations with the employer associations; a renewed commitment to the five-day, forty-hour week; and the creation of a commission to adjust disputes. The victory was significant, but the lackluster economy and strike expenses had kept the International from raising sufficient funds to erase its operating deficit.[8]

Though money was tight, Schlesinger and Dubinsky could not ignore the International's many trouble spots. San Francisco's Industrial Council, with whom the ILGWU was dealing, had engaged in a mass lockout of left-wingers, who in turn called six shop strikes and were threatening a general strike. In the meantime, thugs attempted to beat up organizer Abraham Plotkin, who suffered only torn clothing but "was ordered to get out of town immediately." As he was then negotiating an agreement with the employers, he had to stay.[9]

Though Plotkin and Local 8, San Francisco obtained a settlement with the Industrial Council, Dubinsky had another matter on his mind. As the watchdog for a depleted treasury, Dubinsky pinched pennies, questioning the bills Plotkin submitted for reimbursement of expenses.[10]

Dubinsky's hand seemed to touch virtually everything of substance in the International, such as the establishment of a separate dress joint board. In recognition of the growth of the dress industry and the divergence of interests between the dress and cloak trades since 1923, the Cleveland convention had decided in favor of such a board. Under Dubinsky's leadership, a committee swiftly made it a reality.[11]

In 1930 ,Dubinsky traveled extensively, prompted by continuing problems on the West Coast and in the Midwest and by Schlesinger's poor health. What he found most appalling were sweatshop conditions in Los Angeles, especially in the dress trade. By early May, Dubinsky was back in New York, but in June he was away again, this time on a brief Canadian organization tour.[12]

The nation's stagnant economy was beginning to exert a downward pressure on the ILGWU. By July 1930 it still had not made good on a loan of $15,000 from the International Association of Machinists (IAM) that had come due on March 1, 1929. The IAM cooperated with the ILGWU by canceling the original note and issuing a new one for the initial loan amount plus the $2,250 in accumulated interest, but a year later the second note would not be paid. In the deepening general economic crisis, the New York State Banking Department closed two banks that had lent to the ILGWU and was demanding debt repayment without delay.[13]

As these and other debts went unpaid, Schlesinger and Dubinsky strove to maintain the ILGWU's normal functions. Both officers remained on the move, Dubinsky to Baltimore and Boston, Schlesinger to Philadelphia and Chicago, but neither could cope with a resurgence of gangsterism. Labor racketeering was spreading through the dress industry in particular because, unlike the cloak trade, it was not concentrated in Manhattan. Scattered throughout New York, including upstate and Long Island, and into New Jersey, dress employers were more isolated and thus more vulnerable than their cloak counterparts to racketeers who offered them protection from union agreements. David Fruhling, the assistant manager of Local 10, tried to keep track of these criminals, but on Monday morning, July 16, en route to his office, he was attacked by five men who slashed his neck and face with knives and left him lying in his blood in the street.[14]

The police could not apprehend Fruhling's assailants, but in October they did manage to arrest Dubinsky. The ladies' tailors of Local 38 were on strike against Milgrim Brothers in New York. In the strike, which was two weeks old, hired company guards joined policemen in controlling the picketing strikers, often resorting to violence. On the scene, Dubinsky protested to a police captain when a patrolman arrested a striker who had been beaten rather that the guard who had attacked him. The guard even struck Dubinsky. The same patrolman arrested Dubinsky "for attempting to assault the captain." In person and in writing, Dubinsky protested the brutality of the police to their commissioner, but he gained only a dismissal of the charges against himself.[15]

By the end of September 1930, the indebtedness of the ILGWU had climbed beyond one million dollars.[16] Yet, as Dubinsky dealt with this deficit, he again had the management of the ILGWU thrust into his hands.

Schlesinger left for a hotel in upstate Parksville, New York, to recuperate from a sore throat.[17] While he was in the Catskills, weekend visitors, especially Dubinsky, kept him abreast of union affairs.[18] On December 29, Dubinsky informed the GEB that Schlesinger had "been ordered to leave the city again for three or four months."[19] At last, in February the GEB gave him a leave for three months and placed Dubinsky in charge of the general office.[20]

At this difficult juncture, Dubinsky's personal affairs demanded attention. From Lodz, Poland, came a request from Bezalel Dobnievski, who had received only one letter from David during the past year and now begged to be visited. Adding urgency to the situation, brother Lazer also asked David to write his "old sick father" and expressed "doubt" that David would "ever see him again."[21]

Dubinsky prepared to leave New York for Poland on May 29, accompanied by veteran Bundist writer and editor Dr. Bencil Hoffman, who was known as Zivion.[22] Hoffman, a veteran Bundist, wrote for the *Forward* and edited *Gerechtigheit,* the Yiddish-language edition of *Justice.* As the soul of the International's lingering sense of socialism resided within the Bund and the Jewish workers of Poland, the union was sensitive to their current condition. In May, the GEB pledged one thousand dollars to the Bund and sent nine hundred dollars to the Warsaw section of the Clothing Workers' Union of Poland.[23]

On the twenty-ninth, Dubinsky and Hoffman sailed on the White Star steamship *Majestic.* After first stopping at London, they went to Antwerp and then Lodz, where Dubinsky saw his ailing father and other relatives, who regarded him as a celebrity. Acting the part, he gave out dollar bills to his admirers.[24]

At Lodz, Dubinsky also met with the leaders of the Jewish trade unions and the Bund, who celebrated his visit with a large, festive gathering that featured drinks, cakes, and speeches.[25] At Warsaw, more than five hundred clothing workers attended a meeting at which Dubinsky spoke for an hour and a half. An evening banquet in his honor lasted until dawn.[26]

His sojourn in Poland a success, Dubinsky then crossed the Russian border. In two weeks he would go to Leningrad, Moscow, and Kharkov and at each stop would visit the largest women's coat factory. The factory at Leningrad employed four thousand women but produced only six thousand garments per day, or one and one-half per worker. An American worker would turn out "at least nine coats" in the same time. In

Kharkov they made three garments per day. "The favorite slogan for these workers," Dubinsky observed, was "Catch up and beat America." With surprising fairness Dubinsky observed: "I cannot frankly say that I noticed anywhere any outspoken dissatisfaction with the Communist regime, though suffering and want are widespread."[27]

Emma Dubinsky's mother resided in Kharkov, and Dubinsky found her, as he had his father, in ill health. The evidence of family trouble, or *tsuris* as he called it in Yiddish, continued as he visited relatives in Vienna, who were living in shocking poverty. They reminded Dubinsky "of the Jews in the Balmut section of Lodz, where several families live in one or two rooms."

Dubinsky was at Karlsbad, Czechoslovakia, when he received the news of Morris Sigman's death on July 19 of "heart failure" at his Iowa farm.[28] Three weeks later, on August 12, Dubinsky returned to New York.[29] His excursion had only added to his personal financial woes. He could still afford to send his father ten dollars a month, but Emma could not visit her sick mother in Kharkov.[30]

The International's economic state verged on disaster. A union debt of $153,000 to the International-Madison Bank had to be cleared up in ninety days to permit the New York State Banking Department to liquidate the institution. Moreover, $135,000 in ILGWU bonds was due to mature at the end of the year. These obligations would be met, as usual, by assessing the membership. Twenty-two dollars per member, payable in two installments, was Dubinsky's suggested levy.[31] However, following President Schlesinger's recommendation, the GEB voted for a much smaller assessment, $3.75 per person. As notes were soon due and the ILGWU's income was half what it had been the previous year, "the officers and some of the clerical staff" took a voluntary 15 percent wage cut.[32]

Indeed, the situation was critical, especially as December 31 approached. The three-year bonds that had played a vital part in rescuing the ILGWU in 1928, many of which were held by ILG-ers, would not be honored by that due date. The GEB announced that the bonds would not be paid off before May, when the ILGWU's next convention would "undoubtedly provide for the necessary funds."[33]

There was also resistance to the $3.75 assessment. Locals 1, 9, and 22, where left-wing sentiment was concentrated, voted not to pay, and Dubinsky fumed. The power of the General Executive Board and the fiscal integrity of the ILGWU were at stake. He and Schlesinger had even proposed calling a special convention for as early as January or February to deal with the crisis, but the idea went nowhere, as critics said a meeting at that time would interfere with other functions of the ILGWU.[34]

As the May convention came closer, the ILGWU's prognosis again was gloomy. Desperate employers were resorting to cutthroat competition, making for chaotic working conditions. All the ILGWU could do in response was strike, but its efforts in that and every other direction were limited by the lack of funds. The opposition of three large locals to the $3.75 assessment reopened old factional wounds and stirred fears of a second civil war.

Additional trepidation centered on Schlesinger, whose health was declining and term of office ending. An unlikely candidate for reelection at the forthcoming convention, his withdrawal might spark a scramble for succession that could only further weaken an already debilitated ILGWU.[35]

In February, the ILGWU survived a two-week dress strike. At an impasse with three management associations over the renewal of agreements, dressmakers walked out even though the International could not offer financial support. By moderating their demands, the workers gained a relatively quick settlement.[36]

Several ILG-ers, notably Luigi Antonini, felt that this strike should not have been called because the International was not prepared financially to support it, in part because the dressmakers' union had not paid the $3.75 assessment. However, Local 22 also attracted attention because its ranks again included a significant left-wing element, among whom was Charles Zimmerman. Since 1929, Zimmerman had been controversial among Communists, largely through his association with Jay Lovestone, executive secretary of the Workers' (Communist) Party in America. A friend and supporter of Nikolai Bukharin, head of the Communist International, Lovestone shared Bukharin's forecast of a prosperous rather than revolutionary future for capitalism, which placed him in opposition to Joseph Stalin. Reviled as a "right-wing" dissenter, Bukharin lost his position in April 1929.

Within the next six months, Lovestone and Zimmerman were both expelled from the party. In defiance, the brilliant, combative Lovestone organized the Communist Party of the USA (Majority Group) with its own weekly newspaper, *Revolutionary Age*. A prominent "Lovestoneite," Zimmerman returned to dressmaking but had trouble finding steady work, ostracized by his former left-wing friends as well as right-wing enemies.[37]

Estranged from the Communist Party but still tied to the Needle Trade Workers Industrial Union, Zimmerman thought of reapplying for membership in Local 22. It was consistent with Dubinsky's character and certainly in his interest to exploit the rift in the Communist camp by welcoming back Lovestone's ally.[38] In May 1931, Zimmerman and others in his group rejoined the ILGWU[39] with the blessing of his old adversary, David Dubinsky. A bridge had been built to the anti-Stalinist, Lovestoneite Left.

On May 2, 1932, some 2,500 ladies' garment workers packed the ballroom of the Elks Hotel in Philadelphia.[40] Beyond the customary greetings and ovations were serious issues, including the question of Zimmerman, whom the dressmakers had elected to their executive board in April. Alarmed at his rapid reemergence as a power in the local, right-wing elements appealed to the General Executive Board to nullify his election, contending that the Local 22 constitution required a year's good standing for a member to run for office. However, when the GEB rejected their plea, they brought the issue before the Philadelphia convention.[41]

Charles, who was also known as Sasha, Zimmerman had few friends in Philadelphia. The Communist Party USA (Majority Group) sent a seven-person delegation to observe, but within Locals 1, 9, and 22 there was only one Lovestone Group member in a "Progressive bloc" of fourteen delegates. Therefore, as the convention began, Zimmerman, who was not a delegate, did not expect positive results.[42] He was wrong, because David Dubinsky was in his corner.

Eight days later the convention turned to his case. Though Zimmerman was the celebrity, Louis Nelson also was involved, having been elected to Local 22's executive board despite less than two years' membership in the Local. Zimmerman wanted to speak for himself, but the delegates voted down his request. Dubinsky, a brilliant defense attorney, ripped into the prosecution. "You are the very people who are capable of rendering what you call justice only to those who bear your label," he charged. "You are, on the other hand, ready to knife and to destroy anyone else, who is not of your faction, no matter how deserving his case may be." Dubinsky added he did not "deny anyone the right to join" the ILGWU, "to become active, to become leaders, to have their say," and to help the union achieve its "destiny." Those who had erred in the past "are welcome to our ranks as long as they are union people and behave like union people." Dubinsky did not, he said, stand on technicality, nor did the convention, which accepted his position with only one vote in dissent.[43]

Never inclined to hold his tongue, Zimmerman called the convention "one of the blackest and most reactionary" in the ILGWU's history. Instead of reforming or restructuring the organization, he said, it strengthened the machine that controlled it. The favorable decision in his own case, he said, was due not to any spirit of generosity but rather to counterbalance the leniency Dubinsky and the convention had just extended to two troublesome right-wingers, Israel Feinberg and Louis Langer.[44] "Your intentions," Zimmerman charged, "were to fool the membership with your so-called impartiality and generosity."[45]

He was not very wrong. More was involved than the spirit of fair play and dedicated unionism, and even-handedness was an important element, especially to Dubinsky. The secretary-treasurer was fighting Communists with Communists by welcoming people like Zimmerman and Nelson.[46] He was also placing the prodigal sons in debt to him. By reaching out to the Lovestone Group, he made it feasible to find common cause against enemies they both abhorred. By seating Feinberg, who had not paid dues, he made it easier for conservatives to stomach Zimmerman, and by restoring rights to Langer, who had been accused of mismanagement as secretary of the New York Cloak Joint Board, he avoided a fight with Joseph Breslaw, the ILGWU vice president who had emerged as the union's staunchest figure on the right. Fellow members of the pressers' union, both Langer and Breslaw had elective office in mind. In Breslaw's case it was the presidency of the International.[47]

Before they could act on the presidency and other offices, the delegates had to dispose of two other matters: the mode of election and the controversial assessment. The Cleveland convention of 1929 had taken the elections for general officers of the ILGWU out of the hands of convention delegates and established a system of election by national referendum. Initially a cause of the Left, in December 1929 it had the endorsement of Dubinsky and Local 10 and led to the election of the Schlesinger-Dubinsky team the next month.

Now, two years later the circumstances were different. Schlesinger was reluctant to run for reelection, and a line to succeed him already was forming. The hopefuls included Julius Hochman, general manager of the New York Dress Joint Board, and Jacob Heller and Joseph Breslaw, the managers of the children's dressmakers and the pressers, respectively. Dubinsky believed that a Breslaw presidency would accomplish three things: it would move the ILGWU backward at a time when reconciliation with the Left was desirable, put the union in the hands of criminals, and, finally, forestall any presidential notions that he, Dubinsky, might be entertaining.

Breslaw could be kept at bay if there were a suitable alternative. With that goal in mind, Dubinsky thought the previously unthinkable: collaboration with the Left. As a convention force, the left-wing "Progressive bloc" was weak, meeting defeat on many issues.[48] On the other hand, a question that might go its way was the choice of president.

When Dubinsky heard of Breslaw's candidacy, he moved to counteract it, quickly lining up his moderate rightists, including his own cutters of Local 10, against the wishes of Sam Perlmutter, their manager.[49] In addition, he had the unexpected counsel of the revered "M.H.," Morris Hillquit. Soon after the convention opened, Benjamin Schlesinger placed a call to his son, Emil, in New York. The elder Schlesinger wanted Emil to come to Philadelphia "because he was being pressured to run again." Without delay Emil took a train to the City of Brotherly Love. On entering the convention hall, he was spotted by Dubinsky, who immediately asked him if he had come "to make trouble." The younger Schlesinger replied that he was unaware of what Dubinsky had in mind; he had come only because of his father's request. As soon as Benjamin saw Emil, he took him into an anteroom at the rear of the convention hall and proceeded to tell of the pressures applied to him to run and of his own determination to step down. He said he needed Emil's "help" to resist the pressure and asked him to call Hillquit to the convention. Hillquit, Schlesinger believed, could persuade those who were on his back to leave him alone.

Emil then left his father and found a public telephone. Again Dubinsky saw him, but his time the secretary-treasurer did not approach. Curious as to what Emil was up to, Dubinsky entered the adjoining booth, not to make a call but to listen in on Emil's conversation with Hillquit. Emil apprised the noted Socialist of the situation confronting his father. Hillquit said he would come if he could find a substitute for a speaking engagement in New Jersey and asked Schlesinger to call back in an hour. Schlesinger made the second call, with Dubinsky again nearby. Hillquit reported that he had found another speaker and would therefore "take the six o'clock train" to Philadelphia. As Schlesinger left the telephone booth, Dubinsky asked to whom he had been speaking. Schlesinger said that he had spoken to Hillquit, who would be arriving shortly.

When Hillquit stepped off the train, he was greeted by a delegation headed by Dubinsky, who whisked him off in a taxicab to the hotel. "Madder than hell," Emil Schlesinger returned to the hotel alone. The next morning the younger Schlesinger finally saw Hillquit, who told him it was agreed that his father would not seek reelection.

Both Emil Schlesinger and Morris Hillquit returned to New York, as the Dubinsky group began to look for a successor. Having no luck, the searchers called Hillquit back to Philadelphia, and at last they decided on Julius Hochman. "The thing is settled," Hillquit telephoned Emil Schlesinger. "Hochman is going to be president. Dubinsky is going to be secretary-treasurer."[50]

Dubinsky made contact with the left-wingers of Locals 1, 9, and 22 and apparently not only warned them of Breslaw but also suggested they consider Hochman. When Reuben Zuckerman of Local 1 then advised the Progressive caucus of the Breslaw bid, the news came as a shock. But when Zuckerman went on to suggest Julius Hochman as "the lesser evil," that name was likewise greeted with bitter opposition.[51]

The Hochman suggestion was dead. The Progressives would not buy it; nor would Breslaw, who possessed the power to break up the convention. But with the convention nearing nomination time, something had to be done. On Saturday morning, May 14, Hillquit presided over a breakfast conference. In attendance were both Schlesingers; Dubinsky; Max Danish, the editor of *Justice*; and Hannah Haskel, Dubinsky's secretary. Hillquit urged Benjamin Schlesinger to accept the nomination. "Ben, take it because the Union will fall apart. There will be a terrible scene here at this convention. A political fight." But the seriously ill president still had his pride. "I don't want to be a rubber stamp for anybody," Schlesinger said. "There will be no decision taken by the Union, I give you my word, unless I approve of it." Hillquit announced an agreement. Benjamin Schlesinger would write the convention and ask not to be nominated, at the same time agreeing to accept the decision of the convention. It was also understood that after the convention Schlesinger would visit a sanitarium in Colorado Springs to try to improve his health. By acquiescing in this manner, though he knew death was not distant, Schlesinger engaged in an act of unprecedented self-sacrifice for the ILGWU.

At 10:30 a.m., when the convention session opened, Dubinsky announced that Danish would read a statement from Schlesinger, who was not present. The letter cited "ill health" and the insistence of his "physicians, . . . family and . . . friends" as reasons for Schlesinger's retirement. It did not seem to matter that this man, who could be seen spitting blood into bits of paper at the convention, did not want to be nominated. As soon as Danish completed his reading, Isidore Nagler spoke. Nagler acknowledged that Schlesinger's health "has been seriously endangered, so much so that his very life is perhaps at stake." "Nevertheless," he continued, "I cannot, for one moment, forget that we must have him as our President," and he placed Schlesinger's name in nomination. Hochman and Breslaw then seconded the motion, and Dubinsky moved that Schlesinger be elected by acclamation. The delegates responded accordingly, "amidst tremendous enthusiasm and applause." Only the votes of six Communist delegates prevented unanimity.[52]

That a greater number of left-wingers did not oppose Schlesinger was due to behind-the-scenes arrangements. After the Progressive caucus rejected a Hochman candidacy, Louis Levy of Local 1 and Nicholas Kirtzman of Local 9 negotiated on their own with Dubinsky and his followers. The result was an agreement for Schlesinger's reelection as president and Levy and Kirtzman's election as vice presidents. This deal directly contradicted a decision of the Progressive caucus *not* to bargain for vice presidencies. Issues, not seats, were worth bargaining for, according to the caucus majority. However, once the commitment to Dubinsky was made, it was difficult to repudiate their own representatives, and the weak and divided left-wingers had little choice other than to accept it.[53] They, did, however, gain one other concession. Dubinsky, who would later claim to have been opposed to it all along as not collectible, killed the controversial $3.75 assessment.[54]

As an accomplice to Schlesinger's sacrifice, Dubinsky steadfastly denied having presidential aspirations of his own. Chances were that a Dubinsky candidacy at this point would result in an unseemly fight with Breslaw, and maybe a compromise choice. Conceivably, the whole matter could go beyond Dubinsky's control. Why chance it? Dubinsky had come too far in the union to permit Breslaw or anyone else to take the presidency by default through either Schlesinger's retirement or his own noncandidacy. So Dubinsky played the role of loyal lieutenant. Dubinsky's purpose, it is clear, was to hold the presidency until the time, which would be soon, that Schlesinger would die and he could take it.[55]

Benjamin Schlesinger was in his hotel room, accompanied by his son, when he was nominated. When both Schlesinger and Dubinsky had been reelected, the delegates asked Hillquit to accompany a committee to bring Schlesinger to the convention hall.

Hillquit gladly accepted the assignment, remarking that he would do his "very best to induce" the president "to change his resolution" not to run. Soon afterward, Schlesinger made his entrance. The delegates gave him a tumultuous welcome and then listened to him speak. What they heard were the bitter words of a man who told them he had wanted to leave office because he was ill and that they had "no right" to elect him to another term. "You have decided upon a certain course," he said. "I don't know whether you have the right to take such an action out of consideration to me, but you have taken it and I stand by it." With these words, "pandemonium broke loose in the convention hall and there was a deluge of wild applause and cheers that lasted for several minutes."[56]

The convention behind him, Benjamin Schlesinger went without delay to his physicians. They told him to abandon his union activity temporarily and go to Colorado Springs for medical treatment. Short of funds because the ILGWU had been unable to pay him for eighteen weeks, he had to borrow. At his request, Emil took him to Morris Hillquit's office on Forty-fourth Street. Hillquit told him his health would improve and the International would be in good hands in his absence. He advised Schlesinger that Dubinsky, who often seemed to take matters into his own hands, would be on good behavior: "Don't worry about anything. I have Dubinsky's promise that he will do nothing, he will do absolutely nothing, take no action of any kind, or permit the General Executive Board to take any action, unless it's first cleared with me and I agree." On receiving that assurance, Schlesinger replied, "Okay, I'm ready to go."

On June 6, Benjamin Schlesinger died at Cragmore Sanitarium in Colorado Springs at age fifty-five.[57] At his bier, David Dubinsky and Salvatore Ninfo eulogized him. Dubinsky called him "a symbol of strength and hope" to the members of the ILGWU and a person who "died the death he always wished to die—as captain at the helm of our ship, at his post as President of our International Union."[58]

With a cloakmakers' strike imminent, the General Executive Board felt it imperative to move quickly to fill the vacancy caused by

Schlesinger's death. On June 14, exactly a month after Schlesinger's election, a five-person selection committee unanimously recommended David Dubinsky, whom it "then asked . . . to accept the presidency." In response, Dubinsky again said he did not want the job. Morris Hillquit, as usual, had a solution. He asked the committee to come up with the name of a candidate to succeed Dubinsky as secretary-treasurer. With a suitable assistant, Dubinsky might be induced to become president.

The committee met again and reported to Hillquit that its choice for secretary-treasurer was Jacob Heller. Though the Dubinsky-Heller team was still subject to GEB approval, Hillquit said he would discuss it with Dubinsky. The group had also considered Breslaw and Ninfo but had rejected both for fear of creating "dissension in the ranks of the Union." The discussion continued into the afternoon session, when Antonini proposed to make Dubinsky the unanimous choice for president and defer the other election until the conclusion of the cloak walkout. Nagler accepted Antonini's suggestion, as did the GEB, and the committee then took it up with Dubinsky. When Nagler reported back to the GEB on the morning of the fifteenth, he gave the group Dubinsky's conditions for his becoming president. The committee had acted with unanimity to assure him that he had the support of the entire General Executive Board, that no secretary-treasurer would be elected until there would be "substantial unanimity" regarding a choice, and that, for the time being, he would hold that position.

Those were Dubinsky's terms. Unanimously, the body accepted them and elected him president. In accepting the honor, he told the GEB that his only program was "welfare" of the ILGWU, which, in a cooperative spirit, should "try to enlist" the services of "all elements of the progressive and radical Labor movement if necessary."[59]

Though Dubinsky was elected president, he would also serve as secretary-treasurer until yielding that position to Louis Stulberg in 1959, twenty-seven years later.[60] By donning two hats in June 1932, Dubinsky spared the GEB a destructive fight over the secretary-treasurership at a critical time for the ILGWU. Such a struggle might have created a presidential line of succession that included a personality independent of, and therefore unacceptable to, Dubinsky. One has to agree with Emil Schlesinger's assessment that a desire for power rather than harmony was Dubinsky's primary reason for retaining his old position. He kept it by design because he wanted no opposition.[61]

A new era in ILGWU history, the Dubinsky era, thus began. The union under Sigman and Schlesinger had been wedded to socialist and anarchist traditions. In the future, pragmatism would outweigh ideology, but personality would often overwhelm both. Though many ILG-ers would resent it, in the mind of the public their organization would be known as "Dubinsky's union."[62]

6

Dubinsky's Union

America's business was business, President Calvin Coolidge had proclaimed in 1925, but seven years later the industrial giant that had seemingly discovered the secret of prosperity was a land of despair. The urban landscape now included tar-paper "Hoovervilles" for the homeless, soup kitchens for the hungry, and street-corner sales of apples and pencils to sustain some of the thirteen million unemployed. In May 1932, as Congress and the president grappled with the problems of the Great Depression, 17,000 veterans of the First World War descended on the nation's capital in quest of a bonus that had been promised them for their service. Though peaceful and apolitical, their encampment at Anacostia Flats was destroyed by U.S. Army troops commanded by Chief of Staff Douglas MacArthur, who regarded it as a threat to the government.

As the economic crisis wore on, President Hoover reluctantly modified his belief that private voluntarism and the efforts of state and local agencies could adequately deal with it. Congress acceded to his request to establish a Reconstruction Finance Corporation that could stimulate the economy by lending funds to major economic institutions, such as banks and insurance companies. Responding to pleas by organized labor for relief from labor injunctions, Congress also passed the Norris–La Guardia Act. Washington became more involved with the nation's plight, but public sentiment demanded new presidential leadership to restore confidence and the economy.

In November the voters repudiated Hoover by electing Governor Franklin Delano Roosevelt of New York president. Roosevelt had waged a campaign that was distinguished more for merciless attacks on Hoover than fresh ideas. Opting for change, but not too much, the American people gave Socialist Norman Thomas and Communist William Z. Foster a combined total of 988,000 votes, as opposed to more than 22.8 million for FDR and nearly 15.8 million for Hoover. Yet, in accepting the nomination of the Democratic Party at its Chicago convention, Roosevelt had said, "I pledge you, I pledge myself, a new deal for the American people." The "new deal" became an instant campaign motto, and it helped produce a landslide victory. Thus, as David Dubinsky would recall, in 1932 "two new presidents were elected in the United States—Franklin D. Roosevelt and me; only, I beat him by a few months."[1]

Those months were among the worst in ILGWU history. When Dubinsky became president the ILGWU, reduced to fewer than 40,000 members, had liabilities in excess of one million dollars. It was an organization, he said, of "inactivity, pessimism and apathy."[2] Moreover, it "was bankrupt in every respect, financially, morally, [and] organizationally." The minimal general office staff consisted of the president-secretary-treasurer, a bookkeeper, an accountant, and a clerk.[3] So scarce were funds that the elevator was shut off to reduce the cost of electricity.[4]

Citing "financial stringency," Dubinsky had a GEB meeting scheduled for October in Montreal moved closer to New York, to Unity House, the ILGWU's vacation resort in Forest Park, Pennsylvania. In November, Dubinsky was the only ILGWU delegate sent to the convention of the American Federation of Labor in Cincinnati, but he was denied a seat because the International was behind in its per capita payments to the AFL by four months. Despite its past history of good standing and common causes, AFL secretary Frank Morrison refused to accept a postdated check to cover the debt.[5]

Two factors, however, would prevent the demise of the International. The first was Dubinsky's personality. He was a classic survivor. Active, able, and aggressive, but nondoctrinaire, he was a fighter who preferred to bargain with management rather than walk the picket line. The second was FDR, who would emerge as both the savior of American capital and the benefactor of American labor. During Roosevelt's presidency, organized labor would gain unprecedented prominence and power, with the flourishing ILGWU known as "Dubinsky's union." Inevitably this phrase would cause resentment, particularly in ILGWU locals that had become virtual fiefdoms but were now witnessing a centralization of power in the hands of a five-foot, four-inch garment cutter.[6]

As he took office, Dubinsky's relatives in Europe continued to suffer. Aged and poor, Emma's parents in Russia needed help, which he tried to provide. He planned for Emma to visit them by way of London. There she would pick up Russian rubles purchased on the black market in Warsaw by his brother-in-law Moshe. As was the case in 1931, and again possibly for financial reasons, she was forced to delay her trip. Though she stayed at home, during the summer of 1932 two Dubinsky associates visited Europe and assisted in the transfer of money.[7]

In New York, Dubinsky served as his union's financial agent and cheerleader. Elevated to the presidency of the ILGWU in good part because of his financial skill,[8] he now had to demonstrate it on a larger scale. Dubinsky understood that in order to keep the ILGWU functioning he had to satisfy its creditors. Especially when they were banks, they could not be put off indefinitely. Pressed by the Manufacturers' Trust Company for payment of $10,000, Dubinsky insisted that the International raise the bulk of that amount mainly from locals indebted to the general office or face "serious and embarrassing consequences."[9] Some debts would never be repaid in full. Settlements with amenable creditors, such as the United Mine Workers of America, the International Madison Bank, and the International Association of Machinists, saved more than $150,000 through April 1934.[10]

Other savings could be achieved by internal retrenchment. At Dubinsky's suggestion, the General Executive Board agreed to call all New York City locals together for a conference on reducing expenses. Additionally, the GEB authorized its finance committee and Dubinsky "to look into the finances of each and every local and sub-division and to direct them how and when to make necessary economies."[11]

For the ILGWU to cut costs, it was inadvisable to go on strike, but when circumstances dictated, it used that weapon. In February 1932, New York's dressmakers had walked out despite a virtually nonexistent strike fund, but within three weeks they returned with directly negotiated agreements.[12] After the dressmakers' dispute was settled, attention shifted to the cloakmakers. In May, while the ILGWU met in Philadelphia, the ladies' garment industry's three employer associations decided to press for fundamental changes in contracts due to expire on June 1. On the pretext that they wished to end chaos and demoralization in the cloak industry, they sought to revive the piecework system, which week work had long since supplanted. The union rejected that demand and offered a counterproposal that the industry's "auction block system" be eliminated. By this system, contractors engaged in intense competition with one another for work offered by manufacturers and jobbers. The solution to this problem, the union argued, was to permit jobbers to deal with only as many contractors as their production warranted.

Negotiations between the two sides began during the spring of 1932 and continued beyond the contract expiration. The death of Benjamin Schlesinger on June 6 caused a delay as pressure built for a settlement because of the fast-approaching new season. With no accord in sight, Vice President Isidore Nagler, the head of the New York Cloak Joint Board, began to mobilize his forces for a strike, which they approved in a referendum held on July 12 and 13. At the behest of the union leadership, Lieutenant Governor Herbert H. Lehman intervened in the dispute. He then mediated a settlement that retained the week-work system and placed some limitations on contractors but also reduced wages by five dollars per week, or about 10 percent. On July 25, Dubinsky and Nagler addressed a meeting of shop chairmen and endorsed the accord, as did the membership afterward in a referendum.

The general weakness of the ILGWU was so apparent that the Joint Board decided to go ahead with a strike regardless of the outcome of the talks. On July 27 the cloakmakers walked out, their purpose being to enhance whatever market control they already possessed and to organize some new shops. They returned on August 18, three weeks later.[13] What the walkout achieved is highly questionable. Perhaps it made some workers momentarily forget that their leaders had negotiated a wage decrease. Occurring as Dubinsky's presidency began, this episode indicated that his conception of labor–management relations included "give" as well as "take" and realism more than idealism. The capitalist was not his enemy during the Great Depression and never would be afterward. In the back of Dubinsky's mind, perhaps, were recollections of Bezalel Dobnievski in Lodz. Like Bezalel, the proprietor of a small family business, struggling entrepreneurs in New York were entitled to earn a living.

America hit rock bottom in 1933. On March 4, Franklin D. Roosevelt was inaugurated as joblessness in the nation reached an unprecedented 29.2 percent.[14] Under gray clouds, Chief Justice Charles Evans Hughes administered the oath of office. Roosevelt then addressed his audience of thousands of spectators and millions of radio listeners, announcing at the very beginning of his speech that he would speak candidly and truthfully about the nation's problems. He then gave reassurance that the nation would endure and again be prosperous, and that "our greatest possible task is to put people to work."[15]

Along with the rest of America, the ILGWU needed that leadership and action without delay. In a gesture that Dubinsky regarded as inadequate, the GEB ordered all paid officers of the ILGWU to "contribute one week's salary out of every five" to the unit of the International that employed him; five weeks' salary would be contributed in that manner. Even more pathetically, the board empowered Dubinsky to raise "a mortgage on the furniture, fixtures, typewriters, etc." possessed by the ILGWU.[16]

Resurfacing most visibly, the Communists made their presence felt. During the fall of 1932, the Left in New York was split within itself, but out of town it was allied against the International. The schism in New York threatened to bring chaos to Local 22 and the Dress Joint Board. Trouble began in September, when Max Bluestein announced his resignation as manager. He took this action against the advice of Dubinsky, who feared a struggle for succession. Dubinsky was correct, and a contest ensued between Lovestoneite Zimmerman and Communist Max Stempler. The struggle extended into 1933, and Zimmerman won, but aided by the continuing hard times the Communists remained a presence in Local 22.[17]

In fact, their presence extended from coast to coast. In San Francisco the "United Front Movement" posed a threat to Local 8, the cloak- and dressmakers' union. The Communists were attempting to wean workers from the destitute ILGWU local by both demeaning and pretending to cooperate with it. Management, observing the spectacle of competitive dual unionism, exploited the situation by cutting wages and increasing hours. From New York, Dubinsky could only order Local 8's leaders to have nothing to do with the Communists.[18]

As Dubinsky had previously welcomed some Communists, notably Zimmerman and Nelson, back into the International and upheld their right to hold office, this new challenge from the Left posed another problem. How could he keep those Communists who were a threat to the International from subverting it? In December 1932, before the New York members of the GEB, Dubinsky moved to rather uncertain middle ground. ILGWU members, he said, should not be prevented from running for office because of their Communist opinions or party membership, but Communists who were tried and convicted of "definite complaints" should be kept from office.[19]

The union needed immediate help, possibly from Washington, to hold off both the creditors and the Communists. When FDR became president, he promised executive and legislative action. How David Dubinsky and the ILGWU would be affected remained to be seen.

How Roosevelt hoped to cure America's ailments took more definite shape immediately after his inauguration. On March 5 he called the Seventy-third Congress into special session and declared a national bank holiday. Much more would follow between March 9 and June 16, a period that would be known as the "Hundred Days." Bill after bill aimed at relief and recovery would come from the White House and pass through two legislative houses with hardly a hesitation. They addressed emergency banking relief, economy in government, revenue, the abandonment of the gold standard, and, most important for labor, the National Industrial Recovery Act (NIRA).

At first glance revolutionary, the NIRA was in fact quite the opposite. With roots reaching as far back as the New Nationalism of Theodore Roosevelt, this legislation made partners of government and business in the task of raising employment. Supervised by a new National Recovery Administration (NRA), representatives of business and labor would devise codes to govern the operation of the nation's major industries. Under Section 7(a) of the law, labor gained the right of collective bargaining and organization, and through its role in making codes it could ensure decent working conditions. In exchange for its cooperation, business gained exemption from the antitrust laws. Along with Title I, which contained the provisions for industrial recovery, the law's Title II provided for public construction projects directed by a Public Works Administration. General Hugh S. Johnson, whom Roosevelt appointed to head the NRA, devised a Blue Eagle symbol with the motto "We Do Our Part" to be displayed by those Americans who were proud to proclaim that they were pulling together for the common good.[20]

David Dubinsky's world had changed for the better even before FDR's inauguration. Between June 1932 and March 1933 he had established himself firmly as president of the ILGWU, and on January 2, 1933, he was an invited guest at the inauguration of Governor Herbert H. Lehman in Albany. Lehman had already come to know Dubinsky personally, having helped rescue the International with a loan. Dubinsky not only accepted Lehman's invitation but also offered to begin immediate discussions with him on garment industry matters.[21]

By including representatives of organized labor in the preparation of recovery legislation, the Roosevelt administration at its very outset served notice to the Socialists that it was tough competition. At the suggestion of President Sidney Hillman of the Amalgamated Clothing Workers of America (ACWA), Secretary of Labor Frances Perkins called a conference of labor leaders as a means of demonstrating the administration's concern for workers.

Such a conference, in which the Department of Labor and organized labor joined forces, was unprecedented. Hillman, the senior garment union president, was there, as were John L. Lewis of the United Mine Workers of America, Alexander F. Whitney of the Brotherhood of Railroad Trainmen, Rose Schneiderman of the Women's Trade Union League, and William Green. Green was in the company of Hillman, whose ACWA he had kept from AFL affiliation for reasons of "dual unionism"; Dubinsky, whose ILGWU embodied principles of industrial unionism; and Lewis, who was being denied a place on the AFL's Executive Council. In other words, the AFL president was not entirely surrounded by friends. Beneath the surface cordiality, Green and the AFL people were hostile to Lewis and, according to Secretary of Labor Frances Perkins, viewed Dubinsky and Hillman with "a big pickle eye." Kept on track by Miss Perkins, the leaders produced a list of legislative requests, including relief for the unemployed, a ban on child labor, minimum wages in some industries, and a right of workers to organize collectively. On March 31, Hillman presented the group's recommendations to the president. In response, Section 7(a), guaranteeing collective bargaining rights, would go into the recovery bill.[22] When the National Industrial Recovery Act became law, labor rushed to take advantage of those rights.

In April and May 1933, Dubinsky took issue with Green over proposed labor legislation that sought to outlaw the transport of goods produced by firms with employees who worked more than thirty hours per week. Dubinsky, Hillman, and John L. Lewis agreed with Green and the AFL on the maximum hour provision, but differed with him over a minimum-wage section. The three presidents demanded the inclusion of a wage floor, but Green and the AFL Executive Council vehemently opposed it, Green voicing a traditional fear of skilled workers that minimum wages actually depressed earnings.

Dubinsky tried to make Green understand that minimum-wage legislation was essential to the garment workers. He pointed out that runaway employers were abandoning major production centers, where workers were organized, for "small towns in States where protective labor and factory laws barely exist" and that were virtually beyond the reach of the unions. A minimum wage in such places, Dubinsky said, "would not only at once check the merciless competition" of the sweatshop employer but also "protect the better paid, organized worker from the demoralization of wage scales and work standards emanating from the sub-standard shop." Demonstrating an independent spirit, Dubinsky took his case for a minimum wage to the sympathetic Frances Perkins. The proposed legislation failed, but the advent of the New Deal had brought Dubinsky onto the national scene, where his voice would continue to be heard.[23]

Similarly destined for prominence was Sidney Hillman, whose early years were not very different from Dubinsky's. Born in 1887, five years before Dubinsky, under Russian rule in Zagare, Lithuania, he also had a Bundist background that led to arrest, imprisonment, and flight to freedom. In 1906 he found refuge with an uncle and brother in London before journeying to America the next year. He landed in New York but then went on to Chicago, where he entered the garment industry as a pants cutter. He became a member of the AFL-affiliated United Garment Workers of America and emerged as an able spokesman and negotiator for his fellow workers.

Led by Thomas Rickert, the native American or Americanized immigrant–controlled United Garment Workers (UGW) represented nativism and elitism. Those who, like Hillman, were of East European ancestry and whose first tongue was Yiddish felt excluded from power. In January 1914, Hillman accepted an invitation from the ILGWU to return to New York to represent its members before the conciliation board established in 1910 under the "Protocol of Peace." That job lasted until December, when Hillman received and accepted another invitation. His friends had seceded from the UGW to form a new union, the Amalgamated Clothing Workers of America, and they wanted him to serve as its president.

The ACWA was unwelcome in the house of the AFL. President Samuel Gompers denounced it as an outlaw "dual union," in competition with the UGW. Rejecting pleas by the ILGWU for its inclusion, Gompers and then his successor, William Green, kept it out until 1933. The Amalgamated nevertheless established itself as a major force in the men's clothing industry, and its president pioneered the "new unionism." Influenced by progressive thinkers, Hillman favored the application of scientific thought to boost manufacturing efficiency. In addition, "Hillman became the leading spokesman and the ACWA the leading laboratory for experiments in industrial democracy." During the 1920s, cooperative housing and banking and unemployment insurance all came to be identified with the Amalgamated, and by 1933, Hillman was an ideal choice to represent the garment unions before the NRA.[24]

As a recovery bill took shape, Hillman became ever more prominent. To seek benefits from the pending legislation, Hillman, Dubinsky, and two other presidents—Max Zaritsky of the cloth hat, cap, and millinery workers and Emil Rieve of the hosiery workers—announced they had joined forces. Ben Gold, the Communist leader of the fur workers, was conspicuously missing. As chairman of the needle-trades union bloc, Hillman said its leaders would try to cooperate with government to establish a way for their industries to have equal working conditions while they maintained a respectable level of production.[25] Within a year of its formation, however, it was already understood that the bloc had no future. An alternate plan, amalgamation, had been suggested during the 1920s but became intertwined with the Communist question and was shelved.

Hillman, who led the informal group and was the person most likely to head an amalgamated union, was politically and personally unacceptable to Dubinsky. In 1922, Hillman had drawn fire from right-wing elements when he helped organize the Russian-American Industrial Corporation to provide technical assistance to the Soviet clothing industry. Two years later, he came under attack from the Left when Communists tried to take over the Amalgamated. Hillman defeated them by 1927. He survived not only the Communists but also the exclusion of his organization by the AFL and, by 1933, was, in Dubinsky's words, "the dean of needle trade presidents." In May 1934, Dubinsky would address the Amalgamated's convention and publicly acknowledge "the splendid aid, the splendid assistance and cooperation" its "great leader, President Hillman" had given to the ILGWU. However, this public friendship would not be able to contain Dubinsky's private emotions. The Communist question, which was literally the red flag before his eyes, would in due time be the catalyst to transform those feelings into a public feud.

The distrust exacerbated other differences. While Dubinsky was very close to Abraham Cahan and the *Forward*, Hillman remained aloof, preferring other advisers. In addition, in March 1933, it was Hillman, not Dubinsky, who was close to Franklin D. Roosevelt. To assist General Johnson in running the NRA and offset a board of business advisers, Frances Perkins appointed Hillman and the ACWA's statistician Leo Wolman to a five-member Labor Advisory Board, thus confirming his closeness to the administration and status in the needle trades.[26]

For the moment, in the spring of 1933, Dubinsky was concerned most about the cloak trade, where management was again campaigning to legalize piecework. In April, the GEB advised the New York Cloak Joint Board and its affiliates to prepare for "every possible emergency that might arise out of negotiations with the employers."[27] As they prepared, they knew they might also encounter rank-and-file resistance, as many cloakmakers were already doing piecework, even in collusion with employers. To those workers, piecework was preferable to no work at all.

The International, trying to overcome this handicap, negotiated with the cloak employers from April through June. On June 29 it held a referendum, and 66 percent of the cloakmakers voted to reject piecework. With neither side yielding, a strike now seemed inevitable, unless the NRA could be utilized to resolve the stalemate. Hoping to avert a walkout, management moved to have Johnson's agency consider the cloak situation before all others. On June 13, three employer associations submitted a code proposal to him.

On the defensive, the ILGWU rejected the management initiative and prepared one of its own. Yet Dubinsky needed help, as he had so many times in the past, from Morris Hillquit. The eminent attorney was gravely ill, suffering from a recurrence of chronic tuberculosis. As Dubinsky later recalled, "nothing was done without Hillquit," but at this crucial time he was in a sickbed in Avon, New Jersey. Now he was being asked to go to Washington to represent the ILGWU. Though thin and weak, Hillquit disobeyed doctor's orders and accepted the assignment. On July 20 he met Dubinsky and presented the International's proposal. Unable to stand, the pallid Hillquit was seated as he brilliantly proposed the terms that had been devised "under his direction." Calling for a thirty-hour week, ten hours shorter than the management plan, and no piecework, the ILGWU code was "the first to be presented by a labor organization under the National Industrial Recovery Act."[28]

The hearings in Washington took two days and marked the final public appearance of Morris Hillquit, who would die in three months. Conferences and hard bargaining under NRA auspices followed, and a compromise agreement and code for the coat and suit industry finally took shape. Management obtained some piecework concessions, but the cloakmakers won a thirty-five-hour week. An ecstatic Dubinsky went on the radio to extol both the Recovery Act and the code. Speaking from Washington, he declared, "The atmosphere of hopelessness that has hung over the heads of the garment and other workers for the past four years is clearing. The time of complaining and crying over bad conditions is past—the hour of action has arrived!" Approved by the NRA, the code went to FDR, who signed it on August 4. On the ninth, two days after it had taken effect, the cloakmakers gave two-to-one approval by referendum, but instead of accepting their settlement quietly, they went on strike to organize unorganized shops and tighten union control where it was weak, establish proper price settlement machinery for piecework, and ensure enforcement of code agreements.

Dubinsky was riding high. The cloak code applied nationwide, and he became acting chairman of an NRA Coat and Suit Authority established in August to administer it. Impartial chairman George W. Alger soon succeeded him and became its permanent director. Dubinsky's identification with the National Recovery Administration, symbolized by a Blue Eagle, had become complete, and all coats and suits manufactured under the code bore an NRA label.[29]

"Rising from the dead." In those words the GEB would describe what happened to Local 50, the Philadelphia dressmakers' union, in 1933. A woefully weak organization that had not struck since 1921, the Philadelphia union faced determined opposition from manufacturers who were accustomed to controlling their labor market. Only a massive walkout, Local 50 and the GEB believed, could break their grip. On May 9 the walkout at last took place, and it was a huge success, with more than 4,000 unified workers representing numerous ethnicities. Dubinsky took charge of the negotiations, which required only one day, and on May 11 it was settled. The dressmakers gained a 10 percent wage increase, a forty-hour week beginning January 1, 1934, and union recognition, and the ILGWU acquired renewed self-assurance to take into other battles in other cities. The newly confident ILGWU waged campaigns "simultaneously in nearly 60 cities."[30]

New York was one of those places. Its dressmakers hoped to imitate the success of their brethren and sisters in Philadelphia, but they, too, had to wait for the right time. Their problems were political as well as economic. First they had to end the struggle between the Lovestoneites and the Communists for control of Local 22. It lingered on through March 1933. During this internecine contest, the dressmakers nevertheless waged an organizing campaign, making a special effort to sign up the black dressmakers of Harlem. In April, the political dust finally settled; Zimmerman was elected manager. When he took office, the dressmakers of New York were so broke their joint board could not afford to make outgoing telephone calls.

Despite this poverty, they felt they had to strike. Nonunion jobbers had organized into an association to have the new National Recovery Administration adopt a wage and hours code entirely to their own design, without reference to labor's wishes. The dressmakers then took a strike vote, which Dubinsky endorsed, but they desperately needed funds. One finance company, the Morris Plan, would help with a loan of five thousand dollars, provided the ILGWU leadership guaranteed it personally. Presented with that condition, Charles Zimmerman, Luigi Antonini, Julius Hochman, and David Dubinsky combined as underwriters. With the money in hand, the next question was whether the rank and file would actually go out. Planning its own strike, the Needle Trade Workers International Union urged them to stay put and reviled the ILG-ers' organization as a company union.[31]

The dressmakers ignored the NTWIU. On August 16, following the example of the cloakmakers two days earlier and excited over the cloakmakers' code, 60,000 dressmakers walked out. Dubinsky, as always, rallied his troops. It took only a day for both sides to accept mediation under NRA auspices by former New York City police commissioner Grover A. Whalen. "The great general strike of 1933," as Zimmerman called it, gained a thirty-five-hour week and rejuvenated both his union and Local 89, Luigi Antonini's Italian dressmakers. By 1934, the latter went from around 1,500 members before the strike "to nearly 40,000," while Local 22 was transformed from a virtually all-Jewish organization of 2,500 to an ethnically diverse body of 28,000.[32] The ecstatic New York dressmakers could credit this success to their own determination and the protective presence of the NRA. Its advent had placed the federal government on the side of collective bargaining, and from initial appearances it was a boon to organized labor.

Shortly thereafter, Dubinsky headed for Washington and a regular quarterly meeting of the General Executive Board with much to report, including the news that the ILGWU's membership was now "about 165,000," raising it from twenty-third to third place in size within the American Federation of Labor. Since May, he also reported, the International had conducted "11 strikes in New York City and 15 in other markets, as well as individual shop strikes conducted by the Out-of-Town Department." Utilizing the National Recovery Administration to its fullest, the ILGWU "took part in the preparation of and participated in hearings on 17 codes." The expansion of the International encompassed new locals in fifty-six localities and ongoing organizing campaigns in another fourteen. To deal adequately with this wave of unionization, Dubinsky said the International would establish a research department and widen its educational activities. In an indication that times were indeed changing, he proposed that the union produce a "Spanish publication for members speaking that language." *Justicia,* in Spanish, then appeared and took its place alongside *Gerechtigkeit, Giustizia,* and *Justice,* the ILGWU's Yiddish, Italian, and English journals.[33]

Though the International seemed to have been borne aloft by the Blue Eagle, the Needle Trades Workers Industrial Union refused to concede that the NRA was beneficial to the rank and file.[34] Trying to chip away at what had suddenly become a much sturdier ILGWU facade, the Industrial Union established contact with the officials of Local 9, the cloak tailors' and finishers' union. That approach resulted in a vehement protest to the GEB by right-wing members of the union. The board agreed to investigate the charges and, in a related move, took a swipe at the bothersome NTWIU, ruling that applicants for membership in the ILGWU who had "participated in dual unions" would be "admitted with working privileges" but would have to wait six months for admission "as full fledged members."[35]

The early stages of New Deal and the NRA did not miraculously cure the American economy. Unemployment and underproduction remained serious problems, and by permitting industrialists to operate without fear of antitrust prosecution, the Blue Eagle seemed to magnify rather than reduce problems of monopoly. Global in its impact, the depression fed the ambitions of ascendant totalitarians in Europe and Asia. Though geographically distant from the United States, those dictators could not be ignored by millions of Americans who had migrated from their lands and still had relatives or friends there, or who simply valued freedom. For now, though, most eyes were on the undeniably charming and popular FDR. David Dubinsky, seeing in the New Deal a life preserver, seized it and identified himself and the International with it. No longer was there danger of drowning. The question now was how to make the most of the new opportunities and lead nearly 200,000 ladies' garment workers to a better life.

7

A World of Conflict

As the ILGWU's health improved, the condition of world politics deteriorated. A new age of conflict dawned in international relations, and the emerging barbarism made victims of millions of ordinary people. Democratic socialism, trade unionism, and Jewish culture lay apparently defenseless as powerful forces menaced them. Incapable of witnessing this oppression in silence, Dubinsky and the Jewish labor movement mobilized their forces as best they could.

The huge membership increase of 1933 significantly altered the International's ethnic character. ILG-ers in 1934 were more diverse than before, and most were not Jewish. The recent recruits, dubbed "NRA babies," were mainly female, immigrants or their children, and newcomers to trade unionism. Most were young Italian American women, who "poured into the dressmaking trade on the Eastern seaboard."[1] By February 1934 one-fifth of the ILGWU's members belonged to Luigi Antonini's Italian dressmakers' union of New York. Next in size, with 30,366 members, or just over 15 percent of the total, was Charles Zimmerman's multiethnic Local 22.[2]

By virtue of its greatly increased size, the ILGWU was now a major component of the American Federation of Labor. Nevertheless, it could not seriously think of challenging its administration. Gompers had on occasion lent a helping hand to the ILGWU, but he also differed with it on key issues, especially immigration restriction, and respected the reality of a largely gentile Federation with its sometimes overt strains of anti-Semitism.[3] A supreme realist like Gompers, Dubinsky respected the racial and religious tone of the AFL and the power of its president. Nevertheless, the rush of events, Dubinsky's irrepressible personality, and the size of the organization behind him would combine to give the ILGWU a voice it had not previously possessed in the councils of organized labor.

By drawing from coffers containing the dues of 160,000 new members, between September 1933 and March 1934 the International liquidated $414,000 of its $664,000 in debts and returned to good standing within the American Federation of Labor. Its per capita payments met, the ILGWU sent Dubinsky and three other delegates to the Federation's October 1933 convention,[4] which seemed to go out of its way to mollify the Jewish-led needle-trades unions. Two actions were exceptional. First, President Green announced that the Executive Council had decided to grant a charter to the Amalgamated Clothing Workers. The Amalgamated and the rival United Garment Workers had resolved a jurisdictional dispute clearing the way for it to enter the labor federation, and the convention acted accordingly. As the ILGWU had fought for ACWA's admission since its founding in 1914, this decision was very gratifying.

Second, in response to a vehement plea by William Green, the delegates voted to "join with other public-spirited organizations in officially adopting a boycott against German-made goods and services."[5] The situation in Germany was both dramatic and frightening. As leader of the defeated Central Powers in the First World War, Germany had been compelled in the Treaty of Versailles of 1919 to accept harsh terms of surrender. Preaching an intense nationalism and blaming the nation's problems on Jews and Social Democrats, Adolf Hitler and the Nazi Party gained many admirers. Then the depression brought an additional measure of extreme economic hardship. As banks failed and unemployment mounted, it became virtually impossible to maintain a viable governing coalition. Desperate for order, Germany's semi-senile, eighty-five-year-old president, Paul von Hindenburg, acquiesced in a deal to make Hitler chancellor and appointed him on January 30, 1933. This perfectly constitutional act sounded the death knell for democracy. Germany became a one-party state as the Nazis either outlawed or forced the dissolution of rival political parties. Assuming complete control, they also destroyed free trade unions, for which they substituted a state-run "labor front," and initiated the most virulent persecution of Jews the world had yet known.

For Jews and others who wished to leave Germany for the safety of America, the timing was terrible. America had withdrawn her welcome to eastern and southern Europeans when, in 1924, the Johnson-Reed Act established a permanent set of "national origins" quotas designed to reduce their flow to a trickle. The immigration restriction movement enjoyed the long-standing support of the American Federation of Labor.

In 1930, at President Hoover's request, the State Department found an administrative way to curb immigration. Previous policy had been to admit almost all healthy immigrants who had the money to come to the United States, on the assumption that they would be able to find work after their arrival. The recommended change questioned whether those jobs were still available and required immigrants to demonstrate that they were not "likely to become a public charge." Zealously enforcing the new policy, American consulates denied visas and cut European immigration by 90 percent in five months. In 1933, despite the growing numbers seeking to flee Hitler's regime, neither Congress nor the AFL wanted to relax the quota system or the new rule.[6]

As the standard-bearer of the AFL's restrictionism, William Green reiterated his organization's position but also became a staunch critic of Hitlerism and joined a drive to persuade Germany to cease its persecution of Jews. On March 27, 1933, he and 20,000 others in Madison Square Garden protested against that treatment. Though the rally was called by the American Jewish Congress and its honorary president, Rabbi Stephen S. Wise, participants included representatives of numerous Christian, nonsectarian, and secular groups. Green said he was protesting "the atrocities which are being perpetrated upon the Jewish population of Germany" and pledged to "render every assistance possible."[7]

Within a month of the rally, a group eventually known as the Non-Sectarian Anti-Nazi League to Champion Human Rights was formed to institute a boycott of German goods. By 1934, 288 diverse groups had joined in supporting it.[8]

With developments in Europe coming into sharper and more frightening focus, Dubinsky and other Jewish trade unionists felt an organization should be established to consolidate the anti-Nazi activities of the Jewish labor movement. Consequently, on February 25 a meeting of 1,039 delegates, representing the ILGWU, ACWA, United Hatters Cap and Millinery Workers' International Union, United Hebrew Trades, Workmen's Circle, Jewish Socialist Farband, Forward Association, and Jewish National Workers' Alliance (Poale Zion), founded the Jewish Labor Committee (JLC). B. C. Vladeck, Dubinsky, and Joseph Baskin of the Workmen's Circle became chairman, treasurer, and secretary, respectively.[9]

In April the JLC defined its goals, making clear that it aimed to function independent of other Jewish organizations, including the American Jewish Congress and the American Jewish Committee. As the creation of labor groups, the JLC would wage war against Nazism from its unique trade union perspective, thereby avoiding conflicts of interest with the other bodies.[10]

No doubt in deference to the Bundist background of several of its founders, including Dubinsky, the JLC rejected Zionist emigration from Europe to Palestine as a solution to the problem of persecution. Most Jewish workers in America, the committee said, were "of the opinion that the Jewish question must be solved in the countries in which the Jews live." Understandably, the representatives of the Poale Zion, the Labor Zionists, added a loud, discordant note to the founding meeting.[11]

If the European Jews were not going to leave home, they at least needed money from America to fight for survival. In June, the Jewish Labor Committee addressed that necessity at a rally of "more than 600 delegates" at Town Hall. The assembled unionists reaffirmed their support for the anti-German boycott and "voted to raise a $150,000 fund" to combat Hitler and fascism.[12]

A city of tragedy and revival, Chicago was an appropriate place for the ILGWU to hold a convention. Not since 1920 had the ILGWU met there, but now, fourteen years later, the union was back in rejuvenated condition, with 200,000 members.[13] On Monday, May 28, 8,000 garment workers from Chicago's eight ILGWU locals paraded with pennants and flags to the opening ceremonies at Carmen's Hall, where Morris Bialis, manager of the city's Cloak and Dress Joint Board, greeted them.[14]

In April, Bialis had said he hoped "to be able to give the delegates the right sort of welcome" when they arrived,[15] but there was a problem. Most members of Chicago's Hotelmen's Association barred blacks, several of whom would be in the ILGWU delegations. Therefore, a hotel that was an exception had to be found. The Medinah Michigan Avenue Club represented itself as such a place and promised not to discriminate against black and Hispanic delegates. Dubinsky and the local leaders then booked it.[16]

Of the 368 delegates at the convention, 6 were black, coming from New York, Chicago, and Kansas City.[17] As soon as they appeared, the hotel made it clear that they were not welcome. On Sunday, May 27, two black women, Eldica Riley and Edith Ransom, were among the arriving

Local 22 delegates, but the Medinah Club refused to admit them. Unwilling to abide this insult to their sisters, the dressmakers as a bloc said they would enter the hotel only as an entire delegation. All twenty of them then stood defiantly outside the Medinah Club "on the sidewalk for hours." Finally, the hotel yielded and admitted everyone.[18]

The next day Dubinsky spoke at the opening ceremonies. His address included a warning about "the growing danger of Fascism in America" and an attack on domestic bigots. He said those who a decade ago had promoted "the Ku Klux Klan and similar organizations based on race hatred, labor hatred and the hatred of all democratic institutions" were again active, calling "themselves Black Shirts, silver Shirts, and all other kinds of Shirts. . . . They would incite race against race, color against color," but their main objective was to destroy "the Labor movement, which stands as a tower of strength in defense of all democratic institutions in our country."[19] On the third day, a delegation of Local 22 introduced a resolution against racial discrimination in the American labor movement.

On Thursday, May 31, the dressmakers made a stirring gesture. "In the name of the 4,000 Negro dressmakers of Local 22," Eldica Riley presented a bouquet of roses to the convention and then spoke glowingly of the economic benefits and "complete [racial] equality in the shops" provided by the ILGWU. She concluded by reading a resolution for the Chicago Federation of Labor to demolish "Jim Crow" in Chicago's hotels and for labor unions from outside the city not to hold meetings there "until the Hotelmen's Association will withdraw its rule barring Negro workers from its hotels."

Dubinsky's remarks in support of this resolution ignited a lengthy demonstration, after which he extolled the convention's and ILGWU's racial policy as a model of human rights. "It is the first time" he said, "that our parliament is attended by so many of this exploited and oppressed race . . . and we are glad and able to open our doors and arms and say to them, 'Here is a place in this world where you are equal. . . . Both of us can work together. We can give the proper resistance against our common enemy.'"[20]

Sadly, the antagonist immediately at hand was the Medinah Club. On June 1 the hotel tried to deny black delegates the use of the regular guest elevators to reach the convention on the seventh floor. White guests, the hotel said, were refusing to ride in the cars with the blacks. The ILG-ers insisted that the blacks had the same right as anyone else to use the elevators. "Virtual flying formations of white delegates" then surrounded the blacks and escorted them into the cars and up to the convention.[21]

The hotel's actions violated the civil rights of the black delegates and threatened to disrupt the convention. Therefore, the International had to move immediately to support its members and salvage its remaining business. On Sunday, June 3, the GEB met and heard Charles Zimmerman, who, as head of the Local 22 delegation, urged the convention to uphold its professed principles and abandon the Medinah Club for another hotel. With the board's unanimous endorsement, Dubinsky told the Medinah Club's managers that their discrimination against black ILG-ers was unacceptable, "and on the same day the entire convention moved out."

On Monday morning, June 4, the ILGWU meeting convened at the Morrison Hotel, which did not discriminate. Dubinsky explained to the delegates that the move would "serve as evidence to those who suffer from race persecution everywhere" that the labor movement was "ready to act in their behalf, not merely with words but by deed." Speaking the next day, Harlem labor leader Frank R. Crosswaith commended the ILGWU for its "very civilized, outstanding attitude . . . with respect to race discrimination during the course of this convention." A native of the Virgin Islands, Crosswaith closely cooperated with the ILGWU, which soon afterward appointed him as a general organizer. Dubinsky offered Crosswaith's services to Zimmerman. For eighteen months representatives of the more than 5,000 black dressmakers in Local 22 had been requesting the appointment of "one of our race as an Organizer for the interest of the colored members" in the union.[22]

A primary purpose of the ILGWU convention was to further the protest against fascism. During its two weeks of sessions, the ILGWU meeting often resembled an anti-Fascist rally, as the delegates warmly greeted appearances by Dr. Max Winter, a Socialist who had formerly been vice mayor of Vienna, and Martin Plettl, a labor leader who had escaped from Germany.[23]

In the belief that "resolutions alone" could not combat fascism, the resolutions committee proposed a "program of action." Included in the proposal were a continuation of the boycott of German-made goods, the active participation by the ILGWU in anti-Fascist underground movements, the appointment by Dubinsky of a committee of fifteen representatives of New York organizations to fight fascism, and the creation of an "anti-Fascist Fund" to "raise a minimum of $50,000." The idea of B. Charney Vladeck, the manager of the *Jewish Daily Forward,* who had addressed the convention, the fund was set so high because his presentation was so effective. In October, 2,000 workers appeared at an ILGWU rally to raise the money.[24]

Behind the brave talk of the ILGWU meeting was fear for the welfare of relatives in the troubled Old World. Fascism, anti-Semitism, or both threatened most of them, including the Dobnievski family in Poland. Shortly before the Chicago convention, David Dubinsky cabled Lodz. He was concerned because he had not recently received any news of his family. For reasons unknown, not until August was he told what had happened in May. Bezalel Dobnievski had died at age eighty-six. Perhaps now more determined than ever to preserve his personal roots, Dubinsky remained in contact with his family, continuing to send modest amounts of money.[25]

Dubinsky and the convention did not overlook the Blue Eagle, which seemed much less attractive in mid-1934 than it had during its "honeymoon" period less than a year before. In his opening address, Dubinsky noted the emergence of concerted management resistance to decent labor standards and the guarantees of Section 7(a). One result of the changed climate, Dubinsky said, was that while living costs had risen since the NRA's inception, worker purchasing power was "hardly above what it was a year ago." Another consequence was "the return of the sweat shop."[26]

Despite the NRA's imperfections, as the committee on the president's report noted, the coat and suit industry was now "completely organized." Reflecting Dubinsky's attitude, which had been made clear even before the convention, the report amounted to qualified endorsement of the NRA.

Charles Zimmerman was appalled. As spokesman for the Communist anti-Stalinists of the Lovestone group, he regarded not only the NRA but the New Deal in general as "a Fascist idea" and hastened to tell the world. Zimmerman spoke at length on how the NRA was "a very grave challenge to trade unionism." Suggesting that within NRA "circles" talk favored the conversion of "unions into government agencies," Zimmerman detected "a tendency which bears within itself the seeds of Fascism."

As Zimmerman spoke, Dubinsky was taken aback. He had not expected such a speech, but during its delivery he took notes in preparation for a reply. Speaking with characteristic passion, Dubinsky at length defended the NRA, citing the gains made by the International during its existence. His main point, though, was that the NRA was but "one step forward," and that the ILGWU wanted it improved. It was "because of the NRA," he reminded Zimmerman, that Local 22 and other ILGWU unions could approach workers to organize them: "We are not hated any more. The word 'union' is not a curse. The government spoke of it; it said that labor has a right to organize."

The convention considered both viewpoints. Zimmerman's was submitted as a minority report. Dubinsky was angered afterward when Zimmerman had his dissent printed in pamphlet form. The convention had spoken, Dubinsky felt, and it was thus improper for Zimmerman to persist in his views, obeying the discipline of his group rather than the wishes of the International. To make matters worse, Zimmerman's pamphlet did not include the convention's rejection of its argument.[27]

As the meeting drew to the end of its twelfth and last day, the delegates elected their officers. For the first time, Dubinsky was a convention's choice for president. Next came the office of secretary-treasurer. Re-elected to this office by the 1932 convention, Dubinsky had continued to hold it during his term as president. Clearly happy to be wearing two hats, he was not inclined to shed one.

In an organization where political suspicion and manipulation were ways of life, it was necessary to orchestrate Dubinsky's retention of the second hat. In 1934 there was no pressing reason for one person to hold the ILGWU's two leading offices. The convention was prepared to exercise its constitutional responsibility and elect a secretary-treasurer to serve alongside the president. But Dubinsky could not permit such an election to occur. As the unanimously reelected president, it was unseemly for him to seek the second office. He had to appear to be the popular choice of others. Accordingly, a groundswell of support for him suddenly materialized. Delegations from seven locals—1, 9, 10, 35, 48, 60, and 89 —said they wanted Dubinsky to remain as secretary-treasurer. Citing his "astounding success" in that role, they proposed that the convention waive the requirement to hold an election. Obediently, most delegates voted to continue his dual office holding. By so doing they in effect legitimized and made permanent one-man rule over the ILGWU. With no successor in waiting as secretary-treasurer, Dubinsky's power was virtually absolute.

As Dubinsky consolidated his power, Charles Zimmerman and Luigi Antonini did their own share of rising within the ILGWU hierarchy. Though still a Communist and too independent-minded, Zimmerman was no longer a threat to Dubinsky's rule. Therefore, despite his thrusting forward the minority report, there was no controversy when the convention elected him to a vice presidency. Antonini had reached that level in 1925 and thrived as the leader of Local 89 and an anti-Communist ally of Dubinsky. More than anyone else, Antonini held the Italian bloc in line for Dubinsky. In recognition of his influence, Julius Hochman nominated him for first vice president, lauding him as an "outstanding fighter against Fascism." Salvatore Ninfo, the first vice president since 1922, knew it was time to step aside. He declined nomination, leaving Antonini unopposed. The next day Dubinsky announced Ninfo's appointment as general organizer.[28]

As 1934 progressed, criticism of the NRA mounted. Increasingly, employers ignored labor standards and promoted company unions; the year would witness 1,470,000 workers out on strike. Four of the walkouts, in Irving Bernstein's words, were "social upheavals," namely, those of automobile parts workers in Toledo, truckers in Minneapolis, dock workers in San Francisco, and cotton–textile mill workers in the South and New England.[29]

The Dutch-born A. J. Muste, whose American Workers Party became involved in the automobile-parts workers' dispute with the Auto-Lite company in Toledo, and the Australian-born Harry Bridges, whose Marine Workers Industrial Union was at the center of the conflict in San Francisco, were not William Green's kind of labor leaders. The San Francisco affair began in May with a walkout of longshoremen but soon became a general strike throughout the city. On July 17, the General Executive Board of the ILGWU endorsed the general strike, thereby joining San Francisco's ILGWU organization and other AFL unions. Repudiating the unauthorized conflict, Green said that "the strikers, if they win, win a moral victory, but, if they lose, they lose all."[30]

Dubinsky, whose relations with Green were thus far excellent, refrained from public criticism of the AFL president. However, Zimmerman publicly condemned Green's statement, characterizing it as "a powerful instrument in the hands of the bitter union-hating, open-shop employers of San Francisco."[31]

On reading Zimmerman's remarks in the *New York Times,* Dubinsky became livid. Zimmerman had unilaterally and needlessly antagonized Green, thereby embarrassing Dubinsky and the ILGWU. "Evidently you have not changed," Dubinsky wrote Zimmerman. "You were reported to be an avowed Communist then and your statements, your utterances and your notions lead to the belief that you are a Communist now."[32]

If Dubinsky thought he had silenced Zimmerman, he was mistaken. Backed by 30,000 dressmakers, Zimmerman had dramatically returned to public prominence, and Green was a perfect foil for him. Shortly before the opening of the AFL's annual convention in San Francisco on October 1, he offered Green some gratuitous advice. Zimmerman suggested that the convention should support "a nation-wide strike movement to achieve union recognition, a rise in wages to meet the cost of living and to increase buying power, and the shortening of hours to allow for real reemployment." In addition, it was time "for labor to declare its political independence by breaking with the two old parties." Here was the Lovestoneite program, and again Dubinsky felt compelled to draw a line between ILGWU policy and Zimmerman, who, he said, was not an authorized ILGWU spokesman or convention delegate. Therefore, the International regarded his "uninvited intrusion . . . merely as his personal views and as a bid for publicity for his 'political group.' "[33] Having drawn the line, Dubinsky was ready for San Francisco.

As the International was getting things done, it approached the AFL meeting with confidence. Carrying out the mandate of the Chicago convention, in July the GEB approved plans for the anti-Fascist campaign. Officially known as the "Anti-Nazism–Anti-Fascism $50,000 Fund," it was launched on August 15.[34] As treasurer of the Jewish Labor Committee, Dubinsky made certain that ILGWU locals also filled the coffers of that organization.[35] In August, the International had struck the knitgoods industry in New York for ten days and gained a thirty-five-hour week and earnings increases.[36] Discontented with the wage and hour provisions of the cotton garment code under the NRA, the ILGWU demanded modifications. On August 21, President Roosevelt issued an executive order cutting the work week in the cotton garment industry from forty hours to thirty-six, with no reduction in pay. The White House's demonstration of support for those who made cotton garments was a tremendous morale booster.[37]

In August, William Green invited Walter M. Citrine, the secretary of the British Trades Union Congress and president of the International Federation of Trade Unions, to speak against European Fascism at the forthcoming convention of the AFL in October. Citrine immediately accepted, and in late September he was in New York. According to Dubinsky, en route to California from New York, Citrine, B. Charney Vladeck, and he "thought up the idea of organizing a central fund-raising agency to muster all of labor's resources in support of the forces fighting Fascism in Europe. We even thought up a splendiferous name, the Labor Chest for Aid of the Oppressed Peoples of Europe."[38]

At San Francisco the plan worked to perfection. After describing conditions in Germany, Austria, and Italy, Citrine told his American audience that the European struggle was their struggle, and "that the battle of democracy" was "being fought in Europe" where it might "be decided." Vladeck passionately condemned Fascism and anti-Semitism. Concurring, Green said that "the persecution of the Jew is simply the forerunner to the persecution of Labor." The convention agreed to continue the German boycott and fully support what was now called the Chest for Liberation of the Workers of Europe. On November 15, Dubinsky would accept William Green's invitation to serve on a committee of labor federationists to cooperate with the Chest.[39]

Also with an eye on Europe, the ILGWU submitted a resolution calling on the AFL to reaffiliate with Citrine's International Federation of Trade Unions (IFTU). Citing differences with the IFTU over autonomy, ideology, and dues, in 1921 the Executive Council had withdrawn the AFL from membership. By returning to the fold at this time, the ILGers argued, the AFL would "immensely" strengthen the already weakened international trade union movement, shoring up democratic unions not yet controlled by Nazis or Fascists. The convention agreed and therefore instructed the "Executive Council to take steps for affiliation." In 1937, after three years of negotiation, the AFL would be back.[40]

While the AFL moved to reestablish ties with the IFTU, it became embroiled in internal dissension over its basic principles. From its founding in 1886, the Federation had consisted mostly of skilled workers who belonged to craft rather than industrial unions. The United Mine Workers of America (UMWA) and the International Ladies' Garment Workers' Union were notable exceptions. An elitist federation, it was inhospitable to the unskilled and often discriminatory against women, blacks, and some ethnic minorities. Under the presidencies of Samuel Gompers and William Green, it also tended to be politically conservative, eschewing radicalism.

In the 1920s, bolstered by an interlude of national economic prosperity, this patriotic welfare capitalism wrested millions of workers from traditional unions. Gompers and Green seemed incapable of arresting the tide or even of comprehending that its character had changed. Moreover, they could not prevent runaway New England cotton textile manufacturers from finding refuge in the nonunion South or provide medicine for a coal industry sickened by technology's love affair with petroleum or miners in competition with labor-saving power machinery. Perhaps worst of all, they could not organize the workers in such new mass-production industries as automobiles, steel, and rubber.

John Llewellyn Lewis was disgusted with this inertia. A coal miner's son, Lewis had been born in Lucas, Iowa, in 1880 and worked in the mines at age sixteen. After a decade of mining metal as well as coal and a move to Illinois, he was elected president of a local of the United Mine Workers of America. Thereafter he rose rapidly within the UMWA, becoming acting president in 1919 and president the next year. Lewis presided over the miners during the industry-wide decline of the 1920s, when the UMWA overcame competition from three rival miners' unions. As with the ladies' garment workers, the birth of the Blue Eagle added much-needed bodies to the union. UMWA membership rose sharply, adding to Lewis's power. In the 1930s he found a new foe: the craft unionists of the AFL Executive Council.

Beginning in 1932, Lewis tried to convert the AFL to the idea of industrial unionism. A huge influx of unskilled industrial unionists might end nearly four decades of craft union control, an eventuality that Green and his cohorts were unwilling to contemplate. At the 1932 AFL convention, and again in 1933, Lewis failed in a bid to enlarge the AFL Executive Council by allotting seats to industrial unionists.

A year later, in San Francisco, compromise was in the air. The industrial unionists reduced their requested number of new vice presidents from seventeen to seven. The Council would now have eighteen places, with only three of the new slots to be occupied by progressives. John L. Lewis would lead the incoming progressives, accompanied by the printing pressmen's George Berry and David Dubinsky.[41]

The garment cutter from Lodz made no speeches but openly supported Lewis. Industrial unionism was the very foundation of the ILGWU structure; it was the principle behind the International's joint boards. The union had even gone on record in favor of organizing automobile and steel workers into industrial unions. Along with Dubinsky's attitude, his power was no secret. He was a force within the "needle trades bloc," and by virtue of the ILGWU's 200,000 members, its six-man delegation could cast 1,500 of the convention's 25,305 votes.

As such a prominent actor on the AFL stage, Dubinsky merited a seat on the Executive Council, where his presence would offset that of the conservative Thomas Rickert of the United Garment Workers of America. The convention unanimously elected him thirteenth vice president.

The enlargement of the Council brought the craft-versus-industrial question within its ranks but settled nothing. Communist William Dunne had a premonition of what would follow. "Keep this for the historical record," he wrote at the top of a note to Dubinsky. "They have just signed their own political death warrant—but they don't know it."[42]

A man in the middle, Dubinsky was caught between practical concerns and principle. At age forty-two, he enjoyed both the power of his ILGWU presidency and the prestige of his new AFL vice presidency, but the schism over industrial unionism threatened to drive a wedge between the two. Despite occasional differences with AFL policy, the ILGWU still treasured its affiliation. In 1934, Dubinsky was not about to sever that connection. Too much was at stake on both the national and international fronts. Deeply worried about Europe, Dubinsky recognized the importance of the labor federation to the anti-Fascist fight. As an industrial unionist, he wondered how he could remain at peace with the craft unionists who ran the Federation.

8

Fast Company

David Dubinsky's elevated status within the AFL depended on his presidency of the International, which provided him with both power and security. His world, in essence, remained that of the Jewish labor movement in New York City. Self-conscious because of his Yiddish accent and Lodz–Lower East Side background, he cautiously traversed the gentile realm of William Green and John L. Lewis, aware that the Jewish Samuel Gompers had trod through anti-Semitic minefields that still existed. Whatever his national or international achievements, Dubinsky would always be most comfortable on and around Seventh Avenue. He was the quintessential New York Jew of the thirties.

Much of Dubinsky's strength derived from the ILGWU treasury, which time and again funded causes close to his heart. A penny pincher in the daily operation of the International, he somehow found generous amounts of money to finance social, political, and economic projects. Labor's boycott of German goods generated considerable initial optimism. At the ILGWU fund-raising rally in October 1934, Walter Citrine predicted it would topple Hitlerism by the spring of 1935.[1] Hoping for that result, by the beginning of November ILG-ers donated $50,780 to the general anti-Nazi effort, prompting Dubinsky to raise the quota to $75,000.[2]

Dubinsky's anti-Fascist activities did not cause him to forget about the Communists. The Chicago convention had suggested that the GEB call "all needle trades unions" together to confer on their amalgamation. Dubinsky made it clear that "all" did not include Needle Trade Workers Industrial Union affiliates. He listed five unions with which the GEB would talk, all of which belonged to the AFL. Three months later, Ben Gold, the general secretary-treasurer of the struggling NTWIU, proposed amalgamation for his left-wing furriers' union, but Dubinsky was not interested. When Dubinsky returned home from San Francisco, he found another proposal. Gold was offering to transfer the Dressmakers Industrial Union of the NTWIU to the ILGWU as an "honest and sincere" gesture in order to combat "the attacks of the bosses." Dubinsky rejected the offer, calling it "insincere, hypocritical and brazen as all . . . former attempts were."[3]

While Dubinsky displayed continued contempt for the left-wing "dual union," his anti-Communist rhetoric was modest compared to that of the American Federation of Labor. In August, meeting in Atlantic City, the Executive Council had approved a statement to all Federation members and organizations calling on them "to expel from membership . . . every known proven communist and communistic propagandist," and had noted that the AFL had already urged the "Department of Labor to deport all alien Communists" who were "in this country illegally and deportable."[4]

This declaration disturbed the ILGWU leadership because it appeared to imply that AFL organizations should assist in such deportations by ferreting out the undesirables. In agreement with Charles Zimmerman, who said implementation "would discourage union activity and would set a dangerous precedent," Dubinsky and the GEB conveyed their misgivings to Green.[5]

Dubinsky's action is further evidence that since 1932 some of his hard-line anti-Communism had eroded. It was good ILGWU politics to share the planet with some Communists, notably the Lovestoneites. At mid-century, Dubinsky would still distrust left-wingers but again oppose extreme measures to combat them. Inevitably, Dubinsky's relations with the Socialist Party also changed. He was too close to the New Deal and the American political mainstream to play more than a nominal role in Socialist affairs. Beholden to Franklin Roosevelt, he was also proud of his traditional independence of the Democrats, especially of New York's Tammany Hall machine.

Though Dubinsky and other leaders of the ILGWU continued to profess a belief in socialism, their actions seemed to indicate an even greater faith in collective bargaining and capitalism. Bread and butter preceded ideology, but the good life the union hoped to gain for its members went beyond hours and wages. It also covered several concerns that had first been addressed before the 1920s, including health care, education, and recreation.

After the catastrophe of the Triangle Shirtwaist Fire, two separate investigations revealed that garment worker health, as well as safety, was a serious problem. In 1913, the New York State Factory Investigating Commission found an alarming incidence of pulmonary tuberculosis.

The next year the U.S. Public Health Service confirmed that finding and noted other health problems. Consequently, in 1914 three New York locals cooperated with the Board of Sanitary Control to open a medical center in two rooms at 31 Union Square; in 1917 the Board added a dental clinic. In 1919 the sponsoring locals assumed sole control of the center, and they reopened it as the Union Health Center (UHC) in a newly acquired building at 131 East Seventeenth Street in December 1920. By 1924 it was run by nine unions with a total membership of 45,000. Concurrently, more than a dozen locals outside New York were offering their members health plans.

The Union Health Center was the first of its kind to be established by a trade union. Commemorating the achievement fifty years later, in 1963, Congress authorized the striking of a medal.[6]

Few ILGWU members would have bet in 1927 that the UHC would even live to age fifty. The civil war in the International had created a serious deficit, but an aggressive fund-raising campaign restored some of the funds. Also important was the successful dental department, which, at least until 1929, generated profits great enough to offset losses by the medical department.[7] The Great Depression brought annual deficits, resulting in significant staff and salary reductions.[8]

To save the Union Health Center, in May 1934 the GEB placed it under complete ILGWU control. It then gained a solid foundation, thanks mainly to Pauline Newman, UHC educational director since 1918. After emigrating as a child from Lithuania, she worked for eight years at the Triangle Shirtwaist Company, leaving after the 1909 shirtwaist strike to become the ILGWU's first woman organizer. A feminist and suffragist, she was also active with the Women's Trade Union League and the Socialist Party. It was she, more than anyone else, as an ILG-er wrote anonymously to Dubinsky in 1934, who persuaded locals to contribute to the center and workers to use it.

Under direct ILGWU control, the Union Health Center served far more people than in the past. Before the ILGWU takeover, the average number of examinations per year had been 18,000. By 1935 the number had risen to 51,997, and the center moved its headquarters from East Seventeenth Street to a skyscraper at 275 Seventh Avenue.[9]

Along with inexpensive health care, ILGWU membership offered the possibility of an affordable summer vacation at a resort in the Pocono Mountains of Pennsylvania. The origins of the idea went back to 1915 and the

Catskill Mountains of New York. Juliet Stuart Poyntz, a Barnard College history instructor whom the waist- and dressmakers' union, Local 25, had just hired as its educational director, believed that the members of the local should have a pleasant country place for low-cost summer vacations. The union then found such a place, a rented vacation home that could hold fifty guests, at Pine Hill, New York; they called it Unity House.[10]

The Catskill venture touched off a "Unity House" movement within the ILGWU, with several locals setting up similar retreats. The most popular and durable was the original Unity House, owned and run by Local 25. In 1919 it moved to a 750-acre property with a 70-acre lake at Forest Park, Pennsylvania, where it became profitable but too burdensome for the dressmakers to manage. At their request, the ILGWU took it over at the end of 1924.[11]

Management by the ILGWU general office meant immediate renovation and expansion of facilities. ILG-ers now paid seventeen dollars per week, which was about half the rate charged by other vacation hotels.[12] Under ILGWU ownership Unity House had indeed become a major resort, comparable to the more expensive places. It increasingly entertained the adult children of ILGWU members; usually native-born and often professionals, they had risen above factory work but could share their parents' pride in what had become the summer showplace of the union.[13]

In June 1935, Unity House opened its seventeenth season. Featuring a new main building with a huge dining room, new cottages and dormitory, and lakeside facilities and landscaping improvements, it was, Dubinsky said at the opening ceremony, a symbol of "the creativeness and initiative of the working class."[14]

Dubinsky took special delight in Unity House as a symbol of progressive unionism. It was a place where he would be able to entertain Eleanor Roosevelt, play gin rummy with George Meany, swim each morning across a large lake, or ride an English racer bicycle. Unity House was heaven in Pennsylvania.

On March 28, 1935, a telephone call from William Green reminded Dubinsky that his membership on the AFL Executive Council entailed responsibilities beyond ILGWU affairs. Green informed Dubinsky that he had been "conscripted and ordered" by the American Federation of Labor to represent it at a meeting of the Governing Body of the International Labor Organization (ILO) of the League of Nations in Geneva,

Switzerland. Dubinsky would substitute for Green, who could not attend, and be "the first representative of the American labor movement to attend" such a session. Though the ILO had been founded in 1919, the United States had not joined until 1934.[15]

As he crossed the Atlantic, accompanied by his wife, Dubinsky had much more on his mind than what promised to be a largely ceremonial appearance. Given Dubinsky's leadership role in the Chest for Liberation of Workers in Europe, Green may also have sent him to confer with anti-Fascist trade unionists. On February 28, the American Federation of Labor president had issued a strong appeal to organized labor for contributions. In response the ILGWU was second to none, having pledged $50,000 of the $250,000 sought.[16]

On a more personal level, Dubinsky's trip coincided with efforts to help his nephew come to America from Poland. Mates Szejnwald was the twenty-year-old son of Dubinsky's oldest sister, Yenta. A resident of Lodz, Mates had applied to the American consul in Warsaw for a visa to immigrate to the United States. To sponsor him, Dubinsky solicited character references. On March 27, one day before Green's call, he requested one, which came without delay, from Sidney Hillman.[17]

The delegates at Geneva convened on April 10 and spent three days discussing the maintenance and improvement of labor standards. On April 12, the final day of the gathering, Dubinsky addressed them, pleading strongly that they consider the idea of reducing the hours of textile workers in order to lessen unemployment in industry. As the conference concluded, Dubinsky made a second speech. In a transatlantic radio broadcast, he reviewed the work of the ILO, taking care to mention the position of the American Federation of Labor that the protection of foreign labor also benefited America's workers.[18]

After the conference, Dubinsky went to Poland. Stopping first in Warsaw, he visited the American consulate regarding the visa for his nephew. Afterward, he visited his family in Lodz. On May 1 he was back in New York aboard the liner *Champlain*. Szejnwald, who would be known as Matthew Schoenwald, arrived in America later in the year.[19]

Homeward bound on the Atlantic, Dubinsky sent a message to the ILGWU membership to commemorate the First of May. He was not optimistic. "The only positive force for peace and orderly human co-living still remaining in the world today," he said, was "the organized force of the working class." The crushing weight of a towering armament race," he continued, appeared to be moving Europe toward another cataclysmic conflict. "Tyranny, dictatorship and arrogant denial of human rights stalk the highways and byways of the Old World." In the New World, he observed, America still had ten million who were unemployed, and another "twenty million on relief rolls." The New Deal had begun with good intentions but had "thus far resulted in swelling the profits of business without improving substantially the lot of workers."[20]

The little man with the Yiddish accent was traveling in very fast company. Within six months he had made his presence felt from San Francisco to Geneva, and from Unity House and the Union Health Center to the International Labor Organization. The troubles he identified in his May Day message were genuine, and his own part in dealing with them was destined to gain in significance as social and political turbulence intensified at home and abroad.

9

Beyond the Blue Eagle

Labor's revitalization since 1933 had in good part resulted from the National Industrial Recovery Act. In defending it at the 1934 ILGWU convention, Dubinsky simply acknowledged the NIRA's contribution to the revival of his union, especially the extraordinary addition of 125,000 members in a single year.

Unusual, too, was an agreement with the Printz-Biederman Cloak Company of Cleveland. A leading manufacturer of women's coats and suits, Printz-Biederman had stubbornly resisted ILGWU organizational efforts for two decades. However, relentless pressure from the ILGWU and its Cleveland Joint Board at last resulted in the workforce's unionization, which a delighted Dubinsky attributed to "the general spirit of the times."[1]

Though the breakthrough at Printz-Biederman gave Dubinsky a good excuse for hyperbole, it was not indicative of a nationwide rush toward unionization. Since 1933 efforts at industry-wide organizing had resulted in significant but uneven gains. The International Ladies' Garment Workers, Amalgamated Clothing Workers, United Textile Workers, and United Mine Workers together had added about 700,000 of the 913,000 new members added by all unions since 1933. These four industrial affiliates of the AFL grew by 132 percent, compared to 13 percent growth by AFL craft unions.[2]

The National Industrial Recovery Act was not the answer to labor organizers' dreams. Section 7(a) declared that workers had the right to be organized and be represented by unions of their own choosing, but nothing in the law enforced or protected that right. Employers' resistance was stubborn, even violent, and included company unions, labor spies, and blacklists.[3]

When employers violated NRA codes, virtually nothing was done to compel that the codes be honored. Practically, punishment meant removal of the compliance emblem, the Blue Eagle. NRA officials, too few in number to pursue violators and hostile to unionists, had little sympathy for the cause of labor, which was perceived as self-interested and inimical to general economic recovery.[4]

Dissatisfaction with the NRA even included the needle-trades unions, despite their growth. Codes of fair competition had stabilized industry labor costs nationwide, but geography caused headaches, and supposedly temporary wage differentials somehow became entrenched. When the unions later sought to equalize labor costs by modifying the codes, Washington posed both bureaucratic and political obstacles. The lax code enforcement contrasted with tight enforcement of collective bargaining agreements. Impatient with the slow compliance procedure, culminating in court action, the ILGWU set up its own watchdog bureau to take direct action, only to find itself, as well as the fur workers' union, accused of resorting to coercion and violence to achieve its goals.[5]

If the NIRA's imperfections were undeniable, its value was also clear. On February 1, 1935, Dubinsky testified before the National Industrial Recovery Board in a public hearing on employment policy. He noted that there had been "tens of thousands of unemployed" cloak- and dressmakers in major women's wear markets in the summer of 1933. Garment workers who were employed at that time had a work week ranging from forty hours for the organized and fifty-five to sixty for others. "The reduction of these work hours to 35 per week," he added, "resulted at once in a wider spread of employment, giving jobs to thousands of workers who until then could not obtain any work in the shops." Yet unemployment in the women's garment trades persisted. With the NIRA due to expire on June 16, Dubinsky urged Congress to remedy its defects as far as labor was concerned. Reflecting AFL as well as ILGWU policy, he called for legislation to mandate labor representation on all code authorities, tighten code compliance procedures and enforcement, and establish a thirty-hour work week.[6]

At an ILGWU-sponsored symposium two weeks later, Dubinsky repeated his disappointment with the results of the industrial codes but added that he would not yet scuttle the NRA. To ensure greater respect for labor as future codes were negotiated, he suggested that workers might go on strike. Julius Hochman, general manager of the Dress and Waist Makers Union's joint board, said there would probably "be an effort made to organize a third political party, to be called a labor party, or otherwise, but in any event with the backing of labor."[7]

With the NIRA's expiration date fast approaching, labor's interest was in legislation rather than independent politics. Several measures were before Congress. Senator Robert F. Wagner of New York had introduced a bill to protect the rights of organization and collective bargaining that the NIRA had purported to guarantee. In addition, Senator Hugo L. Black's thirty-hour bill was back for consideration. As for the NIRA itself, the Senate Finance Committee was debating its extension, with modifications. Yielding to pressure from business interests, the Senate Finance Committee voted to extend the NIRA for only ten months. Reacting swiftly, the AFL demanded a two-year extension, as well as passage of the Wagner and Black bills.

Dubinsky also moved quickly, proposing to a special meeting of the ILGWU's General Executive Board that the New York City needle-trades unions cooperate with the Central Trades and Labor Council of Greater New York to hold a huge rally to support the AFL's legislative aims. On the afternoon of May 23, 18,000 unionists at Madison Square Garden heard William Green, John L. Lewis, David Dubinsky, Sidney Hillman, and Max Zaritsky demand the two-year extension.[8]

May 27, 1935, came to be known as Black Monday. The U.S. Supreme Court, in *Schechter Poultry Corp. v. United States,* invalidated the National Industrial Recovery Act. That evening Dubinsky issued a statement to the press. "We are disappointed and distressed by the decision of the Supreme Court," he said, and he expressed the hope that new legislation could "overcome the technical objections" to the old. The Court's decision, he then concluded, was "a great victory for big business and the reactionary forces of America" and was "the strongest argument for independent political action by labor," which would "be able to designate Senators and Congressmen as well as have a voice in passing upon nominees for the Supreme Court."[9]

Dubinsky's reaction did not go unchallenged. Charles Zimmerman, as he had done at the Chicago convention, expressed sharply different sentiments relative to the NIRA. Introducing a discussion at the GEB's session on May 28, Zimmerman shed no tears for the invalidated legislation. He argued that unions did not have to rely on the NIRA to maintain conditions; unionists should be taught to rely on their own organizations. Moreover, what the labor movement should campaign for was genuine labor legislation, not the type that was "friendly to labor only superficially."

As the Blue Eagle passed into history, those who had hoped the NIRA would be succeeded by legislation more directly supportive of labor had their wishes soon fulfilled. In June, Senator Wagner's bill overcame determined employer opposition and cleared Congress with surprising ease. On July 5, it became the National Labor Relations Act (NLRA), affording labor the protection it had previously lacked. Section 7 declared that employees had the right to organize and bargain collectively through representatives of their own choosing. To protect these rights, the law listed specific "unfair labor practices" on the part of management and created a National Labor Relations Board with power to issue cease-and-desist orders.[10]

The *Schechter* decision had been handed down five days before the expiration of the cloak and suit industry agreements entered into in 1933. Negotiations to renew them had not fared well before the decision, and now, lacking the protection of the NIRA, the ILGWU faced an employers' association with a strengthened bargaining hand. Management seemed intent on repudiating the union's hard-won victory stipulating that the number of contractors or submanufacturers in the industry be limited in order to reduce competition and maintain wages. As neither side would yield on the issue, a strike of 40,000 workers appeared likely.[11]

On June 27, Governor Herbert H. Lehman acted to prevent a walkout by inviting both sides to meet with him in Albany the next day. Dubinsky and Isidore Nagler represented the ILGWU during a three-hour session. On July 1, Lehman urged the parties to negotiate new collective bargaining agreements in which provisions pertaining to "the designation of contractors," hours, and wages would "continue unchanged and be renewed." The ILGWU and the employers reached agreement within a week. Consummating their marriage, they established a voluntary National Coat and Suit Recovery Board to succeed the NRA Code Authority. A Consumer's Protection Label to be used by all employers would take the place of the NRA label on union-made garments. The Blue Eagle was gone, but both the passage of Wagner Act and the creation of the Recovery Board gave the ILGWU reason to celebrate.[12]

As promisingly as the transition to the post-NRA era began, racketeering in the garment industry persisted. David Dubinsky in 1930 and Sidney Hillman the next year complained about corruption to New York City officials, but neither received much help.[13] In 1935 jobbers had to hold off a bid to control them by Louis "Lepke" Buchalter's gang in order to conclude negotiations with the ILGWU over contractor limitation.[14] Finally, at the behest of Governor Herbert Lehman, District Attorney William Copeland Dodge appointed attorney Thomas E. Dewey special prosecutor to investigate the overall situation.[15] Dewey's crusade extended to the American Federation of Labor, where a committee that included Dubinsky asked him to prosecute criminals who had entered and exploited certain unions.[16] As ILGWU attorney Emil Schlesinger, a son of Benjamin Schlesinger, would later acknowledge, one union in which racketeering was prevalent was the ILGWU.[17]

Consider the case of Luigi Antonini, the head of the largest local in the AFL as well as the ILGWU, who was both ambitious and powerful. Dubinsky and the officers of Local 89 likewise knew about Antonini's association with an underworld figure named Joe Amoruso, alias "Strawberry." At Local 89 headquarters, Strawberry was a familiar sight, announcing his arrival by banging on the door of Antonini's office with a large cane.[18] In 1936, questions concerning Strawberry's activities would come to Dubinsky's attention.

Dewey, not Dubinsky, was Antonini's problem. The special prosecutor's eyes were firmly fixed on unions. Dubinsky, Hillman, and George Meany and met privately with him to determine his intentions. Dubinsky and Hillman committed themselves to his cause and steadfastly denied having personal knowledge of corruption within their industry. Dewey was not persuaded.[19]

Early in 1936, Dewey subpoenaed the records and books of the Cloak Joint Board. After first consulting with criminal attorneys, Dubinsky agreed to cooperate. Emil Schlesinger, with Dubinsky's approval, met with Dewey's assistant, Murray Gurfein, who was noncommittal. Then Dewey met regularly and directly with Dubinsky.[20] The union lawyer fielded questions regarding several ILGWU operations, most notably Local 102, the Cloak and Dress Truck Drivers. Dewey, according to Schlesinger, "had positive proof that [local manager Saul] Metz had borrowed monies from employers in the industry in the thousands and thousands of dollars, and there was an agreement that these loans would never be repaid. And they never were."[21]

Dubinsky knew that "the leadership of that local could not be trusted" and nearly approved an "arrangement" to transfer the entire trucking operation to the Teamsters' Union. However, he "refused to go through" with it when the Teamsters "demanded that the jobs which were held by the Local 102 members would be turned over to the Teamsters Union." He felt the safest place for the rank and file was under his own wing.[22]

Dewey's curiosity about the Cloak Joint Board stemmed from a suspiciously large bank account held by one of its members, Abe Etkin. Dubinsky explained that the problem was the Joint Board's bankruptcy, not its corruption. Etkin held the funds because Morris J. Ashbes, its secretary-treasurer, "didn't have a bank account." Schlesinger described this arrangement to Gurfein, who took no further action."[23]

In 1936, Dubinsky met with Dewey on a "weekly" basis. On one especially hot day, Dubinsky and Schlesinger met with Murray Gurfein at the Brevoort Hotel. Dewey's assistant told the ILG-ers "that he planned to indict seven members of the union," including Antonini, Metz, and officers of Locals 10, 48, and 60. "The charge against Luigi Antonini was that he was paying off Joe Strawberry." Dubinsky pleaded in Antonini's behalf, noting that he was an important figure in the Italian community, a leader in the anti-Fascist fight, "a man who took nothing for himself," and someone who "was completely honest."[24]

Gurfein refused to listen to the arguments, and "Dubinsky left with his shirt wringing wet," but somehow "none of the seven men were indicted." Eventually, Joe Strawberry was convicted of racketeering. While Strawberry was in jail, Antonini "continued to pay his wife a weekly sum [of fifty dollars] from union funds for her support and maintenance."[25]

At one point during his discussions with Dubinsky, Dewey had told him what he thought of him: "I think you're a very honest man but I don't think you're very frank with me."[26] Dubinsky knew at least as well as anyone else that racketeering was endemic to the garment industry, and to the International. In his autobiography he would recall that the problem "was entrenched in the craft unions." "Autonomy was so sacred," he explained, "that the worst crooks could wrap themselves into a union charter and use it as a license for industrial piracy." Claiming that corruption was more prevalent among the AFL's craft than industrial unions, he contended that the withdrawal from the Federation by the latter, beginning in 1935, left it in a position where its otherwise "untainted" leadership "preferred to look the other way" rather than confront wrongdoing.[27] As Dubinsky's dealings with Antonini and others within the ILGWU indicate, he, too, avoided confrontation.

Dubinsky had a different kind of problem with the Socialists. A Socialist since his youth in Poland and a member of the American party since soon after his arrival in New York, he had been drifting rightward as he ascended to the top of Local 10 and the International. A defender and beneficiary of the New Deal and of cooperation with business through the NRA, he outgrew his allergy to capitalism. Concurrent developments within the Socialist Party were fast making his affiliation with that organization more sentimental and less active.

A new breed of Socialists, younger, less Jewish and immigrant, and more radical, now controlled the party. Eugene V. Debs was gone, having died in October 1926. Norman Mattoon Thomas, a Presbyterian minister, succeeded him as party leader. However, for David Dubinsky and the Jewish labor movement a more personal loss occurred in October 1933, when Morris Hillquit died. Hillquit had advised the garment unions through their early years of struggle and had been a genuine mentor to Dubinsky.

Though Dubinsky and other needle-trades Socialists revered Hillquit, in 1932 the party's convention had repudiated him. Marxist militants and non-Marxist Progressives in the party regarded Hillquit and his followers as the archaic old guard and tended to support Thomas, whose sympathies lay with the militants and Progressives. In the fall, Thomas ran for president and Hillquit for mayor of New York. They supported each other, but both lost. With the advent of the New Deal and Hillquit's death seven months later, the factional split became wider than ever.[28]

The breach grew over attitudes toward two capitals, Washington and Moscow. The old-guard coalition of Jewish garment union leaders and their journalistic tribune, Abraham Cahan of the *Forward,* appreciatively followed Franklin Roosevelt as he appeared to carry out much of the Socialist program. The generally younger Thomas faction was less impressed, viewing the New Deal as an expedient to save American capitalism. On a more emotional level, the rival factions debated the wisdom of collaboration with Communists. In 1933, Hitler's coming to power had shocked the Communist Party of the Soviet Union (CPSU) into a tactical shift. In a reluctant move born of fear of the German dictator, the CPSU refrained for the moment from denouncing democratic socialists and other non-Communist advocates of worker rights and urged common cause against both Hitler and Franklin D. Roosevelt. This "United Front," as the Communists called their campaign, meant a truce between traditionally bitter enemies. Socialist militants and Progressives responded positively. In contrast, remembering the garment industry civil warfare of the twenties, the old guard responded firmly in the negative, dubbing Norman Thomas "the conscious or unconscious tool of the Communist Party."[29]

As the split continued, Dubinsky distanced himself from the Socialist Party leadership while quietly siding with the old guard. In May 1935, Dubinsky was more openly belligerent. In a newspaper column, Norman Thomas commented on the AFL's anti-Fascist Labor Chest. Though the Federation's Executive Council was "really pushing this drive," Thomas wrote, "[m]ost of the credit for initiating it goes to our friend and comrade, B. C. Vladeck." Annoyed that Thomas seemed to be taking some of the credit for the fund from the AFL, Dubinsky charged that Thomas's remarks might have even undermined "the success and usefulness of the 'Labor Chest.'" Finally, Dubinsky called it "poor ethics to create in the public press the impression that" a non–trade union person such as Vladeck "had 'put the job over'" on the leaders of the AFL.[30]

Dubinsky was no friendlier to Thomas in the fall of 1935 than he had been in the spring. On the eve of the AFL's annual convention, Thomas suggested to Dubinsky that he use his influence to have the Federation "set up some kind of central machinery for strike relief, strike strategy and legal defense" and assist the biracial Southern Tenant Farmers' Union (STFU), which was in the midst of a strike in the cotton fields, to gain AFL affiliation. Dubinsky curtly replied that the STFU matter should be discussed directly with William Green, calling himself "a 'rooky' [*sic*] in the [AFL] Executive Council."[31]

As Dubinsky completed his first quarter of a century in America, he tested old affiliations and discovered new alliances. The garment industry rescued its internal labor standards by forming the National Coat and Suit Recovery Board, and Congress gave organized labor unprecedented protection by passing the Wagner Act. Other developments were not as positive. Racketeering was back and not entirely controllable, and the Socialist Party was waltzing with the Communists. Moreover, the American Federation of Labor had not yet resolved the issue of industrial unionism.

10

Industrial Unionism and Labor Politics

The industrial unionists had emerged from the 1934 AFL convention with a partial victory. They had won a concession from the craft unionists on organizing the mass-production industries; it would be done on "a different basis," and the Federation was obligated to charter industrial-type unions in those industries according to need as perceived by the Executive Council (EC). Regarding iron and steel, the charge was explicit: organize. To protect the jurisdictional interests of existing unions, the convention had placed the establishment of new unions in the hands of an enlarged Executive Council. Such direction meant that while the AFL in principle endorsed industrial unionism, in effect it left implementation to the discretion of craft unionists, fifteen of whom sat on the seventeen-man body.

At the EC's first meeting, from January 29 to February 14, the majority made clear their distaste for industrial unionism. John L. Lewis was offended. Supported by Dubinsky, Lewis pressed the issue of organizing the mass-production industries, beginning with auto and steel. Only Dubinsky voted with him as a dozen Council members defeated his resolution to postpone jurisdictional questions in the auto industry until after the workers were organized.[1]

The opportunity to resolve the industrial unionism issue came in October, when the American Federation of Labor's Fifty-fifth Annual Convention opened in Atlantic City. Lewis was there, and Dubinsky, his ally on the Executive Council, was present as head of a seven-man ILGWU delegation. On the afternoon of October 16, the convention reached its climax when two reports came from the resolutions committee. An unsigned majority report accused the industrial unionists of either misunderstanding or seeking to abandon the position of the previous year's convention to the effect that new charters in the "mass production industries . . . would include all of the mass production workers employed in such industries" but not injure the existing AFL unions.

Six committee members, including Dubinsky and Lewis, had signed a minority report, which Charles P. Howard of the International Typographical Union introduced. They declared that that the AFL had not kept pace with changing technology and job categories. The report denied that its intent was to take members from the craft unions, but it did ask the AFL "to issue unrestricted charters" to industrial unions and "to enter upon an aggressive organization campaign" in the mass-production industries.

Dubinsky made an appeal for industrial unionism on the radio. At 8 p.m., during the debate, he broadcast a report on the convention from Atlantic City over stations WEVD and WPG. He told his listeners that "legitimate interest" was "clearly visible" on the convention floor. Representative of "a new spirit," this movement reflected "the voice of a younger element" that was "making itself heard . . . stronger and clearer than at any previous gathering of the American Federation of Labor." "We want the unorganized workers to be organized no matter whether it is attained through craft unions or through industrial unions," he declared, to bring them "into the fold of the American labor movement." Industrial unionism, he added, was "a logical development" that would someday add enormous strength to organized labor.

The convention debated the reports through the late afternoon and evening, concluding just before midnight. The weary delegates voted first on the minority report and rejected it by a vote of 18,024 to 10,933. By voice vote they approved the majority report.[2]

At the outset of the convention, when a committee of seven left-wingers appeared before the Council to protest William Green's recent appointment of the officers of a recently chartered auto workers' union, the Communist issue arose. Speaking for the committee, Wyndham Mortimer called for elections of officers to offset the "undemocratic" appointments. Turning to face Mortimer, Dubinsky asked him, "How many of your committee are Communists?" "I don't know and I don't care a damn," he replied. "Every member of this committee is a member of our international union in good standing and duly elected by the [auto workers'] convention to appear here before you. Such a question is irrelevant and out of order!" The Executive Council received but took no action on the committee's protest.[3]

On October 19, the final day of the convention, William Hutcheson discovered that John L. Lewis of the mine workers' union was much more dangerous than Wyndham Mortimer. As they were when delegate William Thompson requested an industrial charter for the rubber workers, Hutcheson raised a point of order, contending that the discussion of industrial union issues had already ended. Lewis interjected, calling his complaint "small potatoes." "I was raised on small potatoes. That is why I am so small," the heavily built Hutcheson replied.

Angry words continued until, finally, Lewis heard Hutcheson call him a "bastard." Like a big cat, Lewis pounced upon Hutcheson and then smashed his right fist into the carpenter's jaw, leaving him with a bloodied face and swollen lip. Lewis emerged unscathed and, after adjusting his tie and collar and relighting his cigar, casually strolled toward the rostrum.[4]

Though the AFL convention had adjourned Saturday night, by late Sunday morning John L. Lewis had not yet left his hotel. At 11 a.m. he was in the hotel dining room seated at a table with eight industrial unionists he had invited to breakfast. David Dubinsky, Sidney Hillman, and Max Zaritsky of the garment unions were there, as were Philip Murray, Thomas Kennedy, and John Brophy of the mine workers; Charles P. Howard of the typographers; and Thomas McMahon of the textile workers. Lewis spoke of many thousands of workers who wanted to be unionized. Their hopes, Lewis said, depended on the men seated at the table who had the power to transform America into a land where the labor movement embraced almost every worker. The group agreed that this vision could best be realized by authorizing Lewis to create a committee.[5]

Only three weeks later, a larger group of industrial unionists met in the Tower Building, the Washington, D.C., headquarters of the United Mine Workers of America. Lewis and Howard served, respectively, as temporary chairman and secretary. Others present were Dubinsky, Hillman, Zaritsky, and McMahon, and two newcomers, Harvey C. Fremming of the oil, gas, and refinery workers and Thomas H. Brown of the mine, mill, and smelter workers. Unanimously, these eight union presidents agreed to form a permanent Committee for Industrial Organization (CIO) to organize the unorganized and "to bring them under the banner and in affiliation with the American Federation of Labor." They appointed Lewis to chair the committee, Howard to serve as secretary, and John Brophy of the mine workers to be director. For financial sustenance, Lewis, Hillman, and Dubinsky each pledged donations of $5,000 from their respective unions.[6]

The CIO thus came into being. Dubinsky was a charter member but, according to Harvey Fremming, "a most uncertain quantity" who "was never definite upon any subject" and "never certain upon any program of the Committee for Industrial Organization."[7] "I have to confess that I had some reservations from the start," Dubinsky would say three decades later. "I knew we could not count on the A.F.L. to organize the unorganized, but I smelled a rat. I was not sure everyone at the meeting had the same desire that I did to act as a pressure group within the Federation, not as a dual-union movement outside it."[8] Dubinsky nevertheless honored his pledge; in December, he sent his check.[9]

Dutifully the ILGWU president embarked on the CIO venture. On November 12, Dubinsky presented the matter of CIO affiliation to the International's General Executive Board.[10] Then came William Green's reaction to the recent creation. On November 23 he wrote to those who had met in Washington. After warning that "bitterness and strife" would develop between advocates of "different forms of organization," Green advised against going ahead with the committee.[11]

Though the Federation president had sent separate letters to all the committee members, John L. Lewis knew that he was the primary target. Lewis, whose copy of the letter had arrived by special delivery, replied the same day, November 23, without advising the other CIO-ers. He wrote: "Effective this date, I resign as a Vice President of the American Federation of Labor."[12] By departing so suddenly, Lewis irritated Dubinsky as well as Green. As the only other Executive Council member on the CIO, Dubinsky believed that Lewis should have consulted him before taking his step. "He gave me no inkling, much less notice, that he was going to quit, . . . and his unexplained action left me to hold the fort alone." Lewis did explain his move to Dubinsky, two days after he made it. On November 25, Lewis wrote that he had resigned because he "personally felt that further membership would avail nothing in the form of constructive action from the Executive Council."[13]

Only little more than a year had passed since both Dubinsky and Lewis were elected to the Council. By virtue of his thunderous presence and forceful leadership, Lewis increasingly became the symbol of industrial unionism.[14] Dubinsky, his quiet partner, was now the lone dissenter. In Lewis's absence, the spotlight would shift to the Jewish Socialist from the Lower East Side.

There were advantages to being at the center of attention. Here was an excellent opportunity for Dubinsky to reestablish his identity as a radical. Though left-wingers no longer seriously challenged his control of the ILGWU, they remained annoying gadflies. As a CIO activist, Dubinsky might not win their affection, but he could quiet them.[15] The boy Bundist had become the middle-aged old guardsman. Had his youthful fire burned out? Had it ever existed? Fervor on behalf of industrial unionism was an ideal way to dispel such doubts.

But Dubinsky did not seek a rebellion. When the CIO first met following Lewis's resignation, Dubinsky quipped, "If you'd told me that you were going to do it, John, maybe I'd have joined you."[16] In truth, he never would have taken such a step. An open break with Green was something he had hoped to avoid. His purpose was to strengthen the American Federation of Labor, not to weaken it.[17] For the moment, at least, the Lewis resignation seemed to make it even less likely than before that the Federation would come to terms with the new committee. For Dubinsky, this could only jeopardize the cordial relations he had enjoyed over many years with men such as Green and Woll, and which the ILGWU had established with the AFL.[18] For the general labor movement, its effects could be catastrophic.

Three days after the birth of the CIO, Dubinsky announced it to a special meeting of the New York members of the General Executive Board of the ILGWU. The question was whether the ILGWU should be affiliated with the new committee, and the New Yorkers decided that the entire board should consider this crucial matter at its next meeting on December 2 in Cleveland.[19] There Dubinsky reported fully on the genesis of the CIO, and noting Green's negative response, Dubinsky asserted that both the CIO and "the right of unions in a group to organize for the purpose of propagating their ideas for a change of either policy or tactics" within the labor Federation were indisputably legal. "If it [the CIO] should travel on the road originally set for it," he said, it "should accomplish its objectives which are of great importance to the future progress of the trade union movement in the United States." However, he stressed, the CIO should not stray from that course and engage in "oppositional or dual union tactics." Having had bitter experience with dual unionism, the ILGWU would oppose any step by the CIO in that direction. With that warning, Dubinsky presented the question of CIO affiliation to the GEB.

The board members' responses ranged from full support for the CIO to strong opposition. Dubinsky pressed forward with a carefully worded policy statement for its approval. The text called for ILGWU cooperation with the CIO, which would function as an "educational and advisory" body "to encourage and promote organization of the workers in the mass production and unorganized industries." Six board members—Harry Wander, Jacob Heller, Samuel Perlmutter, Isidore Nagler, Israel Feinberg, and Joseph Breslaw—called for the International to leave the Committee. They argued that the CIO was destined to lead to "dual union agitation," could not be strictly educational in nature, might foster "personal grudges and ambitions," and could lead to a movement to secede from the Federation. Four vice presidents—Charles Zimmerman, Julius Hochman, Morris Bialis, and Basilio Desti—argued for remaining within the Committee, on the grounds that continuation was in the best interest of unorganized labor, industrial unionism, and the ILGWU. Dubinsky summed up for this group, emphasizing continued backing of the CIO only if it avoided "oppositional or dual union trends." The GEB voted twelve to nine in favor of CIO affiliation.[20]

The ILGWU statement is revealing; it endorsed the CIO while reaffirming the union's faith in the AFL. Personally, Dubinsky was more comfortable with Green and Woll than with Lewis and Hillman. While Lewis was relatively remote, Hillman was close—too close—a highly visible and esteemed needle-trades union president and an obvious rival.[21] Hillman's prominence during the NRA era had been galling. It is clear, therefore, that Dubinsky was prepared to jump ship, but appearances dictated that policy differences rather than personalities would be the official reason for any future break.

Dual unionism could be such an issue. As ILGWU organizer Jennie Matyas later recalled, Dubinsky believed that if the CIO became "a permanent body, dual in character" to the Federation, the International could leave it. Dubinsky's feet may have been in John L. Lewis's camp, Matyas said, but they were not very firmly planted.[22]

With the GEB's endorsement in hand, Dubinsky went to Washington for the December 9 meeting of the Committee for Industrial Organization, the first since its birth. Each of the founding presidents was in attendance, but only Dubinsky's executive board had approved the committee. At Sidney Hillman's suggestion, the industrial unionists decided to begin their organizational promotion with the automobile workers.[23]

On December 11, David Dubinsky assured William Green of the ILGWU's "continued loyalty to the American Federation of Labor" and its "devotion" to him "as its President."[24] Acutely uncomfortable "as the sole representative of the minority on the question of industrial unionism on the Executive Council" of the AFL, Dubinsky reiterated his absolute rejection of dual unionism.[25] Two weeks later the Executive Council met at Miami, where Dubinsky argued that the evidence thus far did not prove a drift toward dual unionism. Ignoring him, the Council voted twice to condemn the CIO, the first time by eleven to six. On January 23 a second and stronger motion, that the CIO "should be immediately dissolved," passed unanimously in Dubinsky's absence. The prospect of a strike in the New York dress industry had given Dubinsky an excuse to leave the meeting and escape from what John L. Lewis called "a trying situation." However, on returning to New York, Dubinsky immediately professed his loyalty to the AFL, assuring the craft unionist majority that any movement toward dualism by the CIO would be "promptly corrected" or the Committee would be "dissolved without the Executive Council having to make decisions about it."[26]

Despite its undoubted importance, the CIO question was not Dubinsky's top priority. As always, ILGWU concerns came first. Consequently, he plunged into conferences with representatives of the dress industry to reach an agreement and avert a general strike of "more than 105,000 workers."[27] In preparation for a walkout, the dressmakers rallied at Madison Square Garden, and Dubinsky and Julius Hochman, general manager of the Dressmakers' Joint Board, issued strike bulletins; but, prodded by Mayor Fiorello H. La Guardia, the International and the employers bargained and the strike was averted when the workers won a favorable settlement.[28]

Not forgotten by Dubinsky was the support of William Green, which had been steadfast throughout the negotiations. When three of five anticipated agreements were concluded, Dubinsky reported the news directly to the AFL president.[29] The two leaders still appeared to be the best of brothers.

If left undisturbed, this fraternal harmony would have remained intact; but others were destroying it by broadening the gap between the craft and industrial unionists. Within the AFL's United Automobile Workers of America, dissidents led by Vice-President Homer S. Martin took control of the organization and appealed to Sidney Hillman and the CIO for support.[30] In opposition to an AFL-approved takeover of their union by the International Brotherhood of Electrical Workers, radio industry workers formed an independent United Electrical and Radio Workers.[31] On February 20, William Green warned all AFL unions not to ally themselves with the CIO, but the next day Dubinsky joined other committee members in denying that their group was dualistic and refusing to dissolve it.[32] Lewis then sent Green a plan to organize the steel industry with a CIO contribution of $500,000.[33]

Another of Dubinsky's major concerns in 1936 was national politics. On the eve of the presidential election campaign, he regarded assistance to Franklin D. Roosevelt as an urgent consideration. On the strength of his exuberant, confidence-restoring personality and popular New Deal programs, Roosevelt and his Democrats had trounced the Republicans in the 1934 congressional elections.

But the Depression persisted, driving many Americans to seek nontraditional political ideas and leaders offering extremist solutions. From Royal Oak, Michigan, came Father Charles E. Coughlin, the "Radio Priest," who attributed the ills of the economy to the machinations of Communists on the left and bankers on the right. Louisiana produced Reverend Gerald L. K. Smith, the successor to Senator Huey P. Long (who was assassinated in September 1935), as the head of the "Share Our Wealth" movement. Long, the "Kingfish" of Louisiana, had proposed that the federal government grant each family an initial allowance of five thousand dollars and guarantee an annual income of two to five thousand dollars. The plan would be financed by confiscatory property, inheritance, and income taxes on millionaires. Dr. Francis E. Townsend was a California physician who thought all persons over age sixty should receive a pension of two hundred dollars per month, provided they spent it immediately. A national tax on business transactions would provide the funding. In recognition of the overlapping nature of their constituencies, Coughlin, Smith and Townsend formed a coalition, aiming at the creation of a political party and the nomination of candidate for president in 1936.[34]

Conservatives who resented Roosevelt's leadership and regarded governmental intervention in the economy as a threat to freedom rallied around the American Liberty League. Organized in 1934 by prominent Democrats Jouett Shouse and John J. Raskob, the League recruited conservatives in the worlds of finance and industry to defend capitalism and oppose what they regarded as the excesses of the New Deal.[35]

The Communists and Norman Thomas's Socialists had never accepted Roosevelt, and in 1935 they appeared closer than ever to accepting one another. Norman Thomas suggested that his party had room for those on his left: "We don't have to agree on everything in order to work together for the cooperative commonwealth," he said. Following his lead, the Socialists' executive committee opened the party rolls to wayward radicals.[36]

More troublesome to old guarders such as Dubinsky was that Thomas and the militants were simply too cozy with the mainstream Communists, now led by Earl Browder. Aware that the Socialists' national treasury was empty, Browder proposed to replenish it with proceeds from a debate between himself and Thomas at Madison Square Garden. Over bitter old guard opposition, Thomas accepted the offer, and in late November the two men filled the Garden, where only eighteen months earlier Socialists and Communists had come to blows. This time there was a rather mild verbal exchange, which included praise by Thomas for Soviet achievements and Communists and Socialists singing revolutionary songs together. Some old guarders were on hand to spy on the gathering, but most boycotted it.[37]

In January 1936, with the New York State organization coming apart, the Socialist Party's National Executive Committee revoked its charter and placed party control in the hands of a new committee. On April 3, an election to choose New York's delegates to the Socialist Party's national convention revealed the new party sentiment. Socialist voters elected thirty militants, six old guarders, and seven independents.[38] This contest decided the issue. The party faithful had handed the legacy of Eugene V. Debs and Morris Hillquit to Norman Thomas and other advocates of a "united front" with the Communists. Moreover, Thomas was a potential spoiler in the forthcoming presidential election. In the New York City municipal elections of 1935, the Socialists had polled nearly 200,000 votes. That electoral strength might enable Thomas, as Socialist candidate for president in 1936, to throw New York State into the Republican column.[39]

Roosevelt needed help, and the leaders of the CIO rushed to offer it. On April 1, Sidney Hillman, John L. Lewis, and George L. Berry of the Printing Pressmen's Union announced that they had formed Labor's Non-Partisan League (LNPL), which would strive to unite the various AFL and CIO unions behind FDR. The CIO, especially Lewis's United Mine Workers, would supply money and manpower. On April 9, Sidney Hillman kicked off LNPL's campaign for Roosevelt with an address in which he charged that labor's enemies were "'ganging up' against the President's re-election."[40]

After having belonged to the Socialist Party for nearly a quarter of a century, Dubinsky now resolved to leave it and work for Roosevelt's re-election. On April 10, he sent the Cloakmakers' Branch of the Socialist Party a letter of resignation. Owing to his ILGWU position and AFL Executive Council membership, he explained, he found it "necessary . . . to resign from the party." "What Dubinsky is doing is the logical outcome of the policy of the 'Old Guard' of the Socialist Party with whom he has been associated," said the *Daily Worker*.[41]

With his resignation public knowledge, Dubinsky openly endorsed Roosevelt. On April 22, he said a Roosevelt defeat in November would also be one for organized labor. Addressing the schism among the Socialists, Dubinsky assailed the party leadership for aligning with labor's "eternal enemies," the Communists. "I can no longer be identified with a party which is making alliances with Communists."[42]

When Dubinsky resigned from the Socialist Party, he went to Labor's Non-Partisan League. In late May, he asked the GEB to endorse Labor's Non-Partisan League's campaign for Roosevelt. Three board members, Luigi Antonini, Joseph Breslaw, and Isidore Nagler, readily agreed, but six vice presidents, including Julius Hochman and Charles Zimmerman, dissented, contending that a Roosevelt endorsement would violate the International's "traditional policy" of not "endorsing candidates of capitalist parties."

Then Dubinsky spoke, explaining that he had resigned from the Socialist Party in order to help the man who had sponsored social legislation that had made possible "the growth and expansion" of the International, and to oppose those reactionary forces that were against FDR "primarily because of his great aid to the laboring masses." Aware that a resolution for outright endorsement would fail, Dubinsky introduced a compromise statement: the GEB would concede that it had "no authority officially" to endorse Roosevelt but nevertheless express strong "sympathy" with LNPL's movement for him and the hope that it would ultimately lead to "independent labor political action." The resolution carried by three votes.[43]

Despite the resolution, in the summer of 1936 the New York State organization of Labor's Non-Partisan League transformed itself into an independent labor party to provide President Roosevelt with a second ballot line in New York State. FDR felt he needed such a line in view of nearly 200,000 votes cast in the state for Socialist Norman Thomas in 1932.[44] As Bronx Democratic Party boss Edward J. Flynn later recalled,

"President Roosevelt, with [Postmaster General] Jim Farley and myself, brought the American Labor Party into being. It was entirely Roosevelt's suggestion," to gain voters "who would not join the Democratic Party."[45]

According to Flynn, Sidney Hillman and David Dubinsky were the creators of what would very soon be known as the American Labor Party (ALP). "They were the nucleus. . . . the voting strength was from the [garment] unions."[46]

Frances Perkins recalled the political attitudes of the many workers in these unions. She described them as people who "couldn't bring themselves to vote for Roosevelt under the Democratic star because they were *bona fide* Socialists, or more than that, and they had always regarded Tammany as their enemy."[47] More specifically, the new party promised independence from such people as Flynn, Farley, and Joseph P. Ryan. The last of these, who headed both the International Longshoremen's Association and the Central Trades and Labor Council, regularly supplied Tammany with the labor vote in exchange for "private rewards." Indifferent to the ideals of the garment unions' leaders, the Tammany machine had little understanding of progressive politics and social thought. Opposed to that organization, Republican-Fusion mayor La Guardia, up for re-election in 1937, could also use a line from the ALP.[48]

In the spring of 1936 the movement to form a labor party began. Sidney Hillman was the key figure. With White House approval, Hillman presented a plan at a meeting of New York Socialist and needle-trades leaders at Greenwich Village's Hotel Brevoort. Those present included the ILGWU's David Dubinsky and Luigi Antonini, the *Jewish Daily Forward*'s Alex Kahn and B. Charney Vladeck, and the United Hat, Cap and Millinery Workers Union's Max Zaritsky and Alex Rose.[49]

Roosevelt's support assured the organizers of the new party of a ballot line. State law required petitions signed by 12,000 voters who resided in all sixty-two counties, at least 50 from each. FDR instructed Farley to assist by keeping Democratic Party chairmen from interfering with the petition process. Unhindered, and with invaluable statewide help from Arthur F. Whitney's Brotherhood of Railroad Trainmen, the necessary signatures were obtained.[50]

Lest the party be perceived as a narrow combination of Socialists and unionists, it also enjoyed the backing of noted intellectuals such as Adolph A. Berle Jr., Dorothy Thompson, and John Dewey.[51] By contrast, several important unionists kept out of the alliance, preferring to remain with the Socialist Party and its presidential hopeful, Norman Thomas.

This group included Charles Zimmerman and Julius Hochman of the ILGWU and Joseph Schlossberg of the ACWA, as well as the Brotherhood of Sleeping Car Porters' A. Philip Randolph and the American Federation of Teachers' Jerome Davis.[52]

On July 16 a conference to establish a branch of the LNPL for New York State was held at the Hotel New Yorker. Fifty delegates committed themselves to the reelection of President Roosevelt and Governor Lehman and elected Antonini and Rose state chairman and secretary. At this time no distinctive name for the new organization was selected, but the board soon afterward adopted the designation American Labor Party, as proposed by Isidore Nagler.[53] Dubinsky participated in the early planning of the ALP and in August became finance chairman.

During the spring and early summer of 1936, Dubinsky faced a dilemma. His industrial unionism had placed him at odds with his friends among the AFL hierarchy, but he could not abandon the CIO. Though uncomfortable with John L. Lewis and Sidney Hillman, he had traveled too far to make leaving them a viable option.

The San Francisco convention of the AFL in 1934 had directed the Executive Council to organize the iron and steel industry, but no action resulted. At a January 1936 meeting of the Executive Council in Miami, the issue was again raised. With no concrete action taken by February, John L. Lewis lost patience and devised his own plan, much to the chagrin of William Green. Lewis's offer of $500,000 from CIO funds carried conditions: AFL unions would add $1 million, and an industrial union would result. Some AFL Executive Council members doubted that $1.5 million could be raised or that the steel workers were even organizable, but Green regarded the offer as a challenge and in March announced his own plan, costing $750,000. He then polled 110 unions, including the CIO affiliates, on his scheme, but received only five favorable responses and pledges totaling a mere $8,625.

Handicapped by this embarrassing lack of enthusiasm, Green could do little but observe as Lewis swung into action and took his offer of $1.5 million and a proposal for a joint campaign with the CIO to Michael Tighe, president of the Amalgamated Association of Iron, Steel and Tin Workers. Despite reservations about organizing the unskilled, joining with Lewis, and antagonizing the Executive Council, Tighe accepted the offer, and on June 4 the Association affiliated with the CIO and a new Steel Workers Organizing Committee (SWOC). Lewis basked in victory as an irate Green suffered humiliation. Philip Murray, vice president of the United Mine Workers, became Lewis's handpicked chairman of the SWOC. To represent the ILGWU on the committee, Dubinsky chose Julius Hochman.[54]

The steel-worker controversy placed David Dubinsky once again between old friends and new allies. When William Green solicited a pledge for his own steel-worker organizing campaign, Dubinsky responded that only the General Executive Board of the ILGWU, scheduled to meet on May 20, could address such a request. However, in view of the urgency of the matter, he might consider convening a meeting of the board's New York members to do it. In any event, he wanted Green to advise him of the amounts pledged by other unions. The New York members met on April 17, but as Dubinsky had not yet received the requested information, they deferred consideration of Green's solicitation.[55]

At this meeting Dubinsky only described Lewis's plan. The board did not even discuss a contribution toward the $500,000 he sought to raise. However, on April 23, Dubinsky pledged $100,000 to Lewis on behalf of the ILGWU. "We should not lose any time," he said in a letter to Lewis. "The Communists are very active in efforts to horn in on the steel field. . . . The best way to fight the Communists and their Left Wing allies, . . . is to begin a wide campaign of organization among the unorganized."[56] On August 28 the GEB would ratify the pledge Dubinsky had made unilaterally in April by voting to assess ILGWU members one dollar each. By the following spring, the pledge would be honored.[57]

Dubinsky's offer appears to have resulted mainly from his deep-seated hatred of Communism. Emotion overcame reason, and he ignored his own argument that the CIO was an educational rather than organizational body. But he soon acted to mend his AFL fences. In a rather obvious bid to regain favor within the AFL, Dubinsky reaffirmed his aversion to dual unionism. Before the Executive Council in May 1936, he supported the Green plan, agreeing that only the AFL had jurisdiction over the steel workers.[58] Soon afterward, he told his own General Executive Board that a CIO campaign in the steel industry would fail without AFL cooperation.[59]

The idea that Dubinsky and the International could maintain good terms with both the AFL and the CIO came to a swift end. Created in January to consult with the CIO, the AFL's committee of three vice presidents, headed by George M. Harrison, remained dormant for four months. In May it came to life and requested a meeting on the nineteenth with the CIO leadership. Dubinsky, on his way to Los Angeles for the beginning of a GEB meeting to be held in two cities, could not be present. Of ten CIO unions, only three were represented, but the AFL committee nonetheless drafted a letter of condemnation. On May 20 the Federation vice presidents advised the CIO presidents that theirs was "a rival organization" and called upon it "to dissolve immediately." The industrial unionists had two weeks in which to reply.

At the continuation of the GEB meeting in San Francisco, the ILG-ers weighed an appropriate answer. Luigi Antonini upheld the GEB's six-month-old resolution in support of the CIO but urged the board to proceed cautiously in order to prevent a "dangerous fight which might not be helpful to the cause." If the situation became critical, Julius Hochman said, it should be turned over to the New York Board of the GEB for possible action. Hochman insisted that the ILGWU had to retain its CIO membership no matter what happened. Summing up, Dubinsky said it was important to "avert a split in the labor movement." He and the GEB then endorsed a proposal by Isidore Nagler to send Harrison a letter advising him that the "ILGWU had not been given an opportunity to appear and be heard, and that under the circumstances, the Executive Council had no right to make any decision in the matter."[60]

None of the CIO unions complied with the ultimatum. Infuriated, William Green demanded that each president explain this noncompliance in person before the Executive Council. Due to depart for London on July 1, Dubinsky could not keep an appointment Green had scheduled for the tenth, but on June 30 he stated his views in a letter to the Federation head. The Harrison committee, Dubinsky wrote, "did not even make an attempt at conciliation," and any move to suspend the noncomplying unions would be divisive, unwise, and illegal. Only ninety days before an AFL convention, the labor movement would be split by an action for which the Executive Council lacked authority.[61]

This warning went unheeded. Two weeks after its issuance, the Executive Council acted on charges prepared by John Frey, president of the AFL's Metal Trades Department, against what were now twelve CIO member unions. Directed by the EC, Green "requested and invited" the president of each union to attend a hearing on August 3 to respond to the charges, which accused the CIO of being both a "dual" and "rival organization" of the AFL.[62]

On July 21, with Antonini on hand as acting president of the ILGWU, the CIO met and prepared a reply. In his remarks, Antonini said that the

International favored "unity in every honorable way" but was "not going to desert" the Committee. Accordingly, he added his signature to a Committee-approved letter from Lewis to Green. Lewis said that only an AFL convention had the power to suspend a union or revoke its charter, which meant that the action of the Executive Council was unconstitutional. "The Committee for Industrial Organization will carry on," the letter concluded.[63]

Dubinsky advised the GEB that it was imperative to hold the CIO together to demonstrate to the Executive Council that extreme measures on its part could not dissolve it. In addition, he said he would request the Council delay sanctions against the CIO unions until the next AFL convention, three months away. If the convention decided the CIO was an unlawful dual organization, he would even abide by a majority rather than the two-thirds vote required by the Federation constitution. Dubinsky said he would also urge the appointment of an Executive Council committee to enter into negotiations with the CIO before the November convention.[64]

Dubinsky had enormous responsibility. The CIO made up 40 percent of the AFL membership, the 225,000-member ILGWU was the largest CIO union, and he was the only CIO-er on the AFL's Executive Council. "We are against a split; we are for unity in the American labor movement," he said as he headed for Washington. "The future of the American labor movement is at stake in this controversy."[65]

It was too late. On August 3, in Washington, John Frey and the Electrical Workers' Edward Bieretz had already recited the charges against the CIO to the Executive Council. Dubinsky pleaded for the matter to be left to the forthcoming convention, but the other Council members were in no mood to delay. On August 5, with only Dubinsky dissenting, the Executive Council voted thirteen to one that unless ten unions severed their connections with the CIO "on or before September 5th, 1936," they would "automatically stand suspended from the American Federation of Labor." Dubinsky denounced this action as "undemocratic" and "calculated obviously to disfranchise in advance a large minority of unions" from participating in the AFL's November convention. Though Dubinsky's was the lone dissenting vote, George Harrison and William D. Mahon, two other members of the Executive Council, shared some of his sentiments. Harrison, who had not attended the meeting, questioned the EC's authority to suspend without direction by a convention. Mahon regarded the EC itself as partly responsible for the controversy.[66]

When Green officially notified the CIO unions of the EC's suspension, the industrial unionists met and decided to stand rather than yield. Consistent with what he had told the GEB of the ILGWU, Dubinsky made his approval of the CIO position subject to ratification by the board, which was not a pro forma step.[67] On August 28, Dubinsky laid everything out before the GEB. As he had anticipated, there was unhappiness. Three vice presidents, Joseph Breslaw, Charles Kreindler, and Isidore Nagler, called for the International to abandon the CIO and thus avoid suspension. Nagler contended that the CIO had "usurped the powers of the Executive Council" and embarked on a campaign, "dual in character," to organize the steel workers. "This straying from the original policies of the CIO," Nagler reminded his colleagues, was what the GEB said it would oppose when it voted to endorse the CIO. By remaining with the Committee, he warned, the International would isolate itself from the main body of the labor movement.

The debate was both heated and lengthy. When the GEB at last put the question to a vote, only Breslaw, Kreindler, and Nagler supported dissociation. Dubinsky and thirteen others opted to remain with the CIO. Three abstained. As if to reaffirm their decision, the board members also matched a recent step taken by the Amalgamated Clothing Workers and ratified the pledge Dubinsky had made in April to contribute $100,000 to the steel workers.

The GEB thus took its stand, which made certain the suspension of the ILGWU on September 5. In anticipation of that action, Dubinsky announced that he planned to resign his AFL vice presidency before the October meeting of the Executive Council, where his right to be present would be challenged.[68] On September 1, he resigned. In his letter of resignation, Dubinsky again said that the forthcoming convention would have resolved the current controversy and accused the Executive Council of deciding "on an obdurate course."[69] The next day he informed the rank and file of the ILG's $100,000 pledge to the steel workers.[70]

Green insisted on attributing the schism to "the creation of . . . a rival organization."[71] Defiantly, he rejected a last-minute appeal by Zimmerman. Dubinsky, rather than display contrition, continued to accuse: "The Executive Council must be ready to assume and cannot escape full responsibility for whatever deplorable effects its course of rule-or-ruin have upon the unity and integrity of the organized labor movement at a period when such unity and indivisibility are most urgent and imperative."[72] On September 5 the ILGWU and nine other unions affiliated with the CIO were automatically suspended from membership in the AFL. "We Are Still in the A. F. of L.," an editorial in *Justice* insisted on the fifteenth, denying that the Executive Council had acted lawfully.[73]

In early August 1934, Walter M. Citrine and Walter Schevenels, president and secretary, respectively, of the International Federation of Trade Unions, appealed to Dubinsky for funds for the relief of workers in Spain. The civil war in Spain was between Fascist army officers who were attempting to overthrow the democratic Spanish Republic and Loyalists who were trying to save it. To alleviate shortages of food, medicine, and clothing during the conflict, the IFTU had established a Labor Solidarity Fund.

Citrine and Schevenels asked Dubinsky to raise $100,000 from the American labor movement to help sustain that operation. Responding immediately, he cabled the International's General Office to contribute $5,000. The GEB also issued an appeal to organized labor in the United States "to help the Spanish workers because a victory for reaction and autocracy in Spain would mean a victory for the forces of reaction and oppression of labor in every country including our own." "The defeat of the Spanish Fascists is considered to be absolutely essential to the preservation of democracy and peace," Dubinsky told the press.[74]

Led by the International, the Jewish labor movement endorsed the Loyalist cause. To collect the needed funds, the ILGWU set up the Trade Union Red Cross for Spain, with Charles Zimmerman as chairman, Alex Rose as secretary, and Dubinsky as treasurer. Within two weeks of the start of the campaign, Dubinsky sent Citrine $20,000 raised by the unionists and another $8,000 collected by the Communists. By May 1937, the Trade Union Red Cross, popularly known as "Labor's Red Cross," would collect more than $125,000.[75]

In the heat of national party politics, the campaign to help Spanish workers became enmeshed in the 1936 presidential race. Dubinsky's resignation from the Socialist Party and role in the formation of the American Labor Party had unmistakably placed him within the Roosevelt camp. In identifying with the Spanish Loyalists, he flirted with controversy. Though the Roosevelt administration avoided direct involvement in the Spanish affair, the public quickly took sides. Conservatives, including the leaders of the Republican Party, regarded the Fascists and their leader, General Francisco Franco, as defenders of the Catholic Church who were fighting to save their land from atheistic Communism.

In contrast, those on the left saw the Loyalists as Spain's only hope to avoid following Italy and Germany, who were directly aiding the rebels, down the path to Fascist dictatorship.[76]

Publishing magnate William Randolph Hearst, a one-time supporter of Franklin D. Roosevelt, had come to loathe Roosevelt for his labor and tax legislation of 1935 and his advocacy of U.S. membership in the World Court.[77] Seeking ammunition against Roosevelt, Hearst's aides discovered Dubinsky, whom, along with Roosevelt, they sought to associate with the Communists. The $5,000 Dubinsky had ordered committed to Labor's Red Cross was their evidence of his connection. They began their campaign on an isolationist note, claiming that the contribution was a form of interference in European affairs. "Most Americans, except Mr. Dubinsky and a few others . . . are content to let Europe stew in its own juice," the *New York American* observed.[78]

In late August the attack intensified. Through an arrangement between the Democratic and American Labor Parties, Dubinsky, Hillman, Max Zaritsky, and three other ALP unionists became Roosevelt electors in New York State. Their designation attracted the attention of Melvin C. Eaton, New York State's Republican chairman, who expressed profound dismay. He was alarmed because they had sent assistance to the "Anarchist-Communist-Socialist Government in Spain."[79]

Republican national chairman John D. M. Hamilton joined the attack, demanding that Roosevelt drop Dubinsky as an elector. "How long, Mr. Roosevelt," Hamilton asked, "do you intend to affront the voters of America by retaining as one of your presidential electors on the Democratic ballot a man who has rendered financial aid to the Communists in Spain so that they might continue to horrify the civilized world with their murders of clergymen?"[80] To anti-Communism the Republicans added a touch of anti-Semitism. A Republican newspaper advertisement spotlighted FDR's Jewish unionist backers. It proclaimed, "Dubinsky, Zaritsky and Hillman Are for Roosevelt," explaining that they were James "Farley's hand-picked candidates for presidential electors in the State of New York." The advertisement explained:

> Dubinsky was born in Poland, grew to manhood in Russia. After serving two jail sentences, his parents shipped him to America. It was Dubinsky who raised money in this country to aid the communist cause in Spain where such shocking atrocities have been committed.[81]

The ILGWU president made a tempting target, even attracting the attention of Father Charles E. Coughlin. On September 11, the Radio Priest addressed a rally at Ebbets Field in Brooklyn, denouncing the $5,000 contribution to the Loyalists. Coughlin continued the attack into October, calling Dubinsky a "Communist supporter" and alleging "on good authority" that if FDR were reelected, the ILGWU president would be appointed ambassador to Russia.[82]

The attacks from Coughlin, Hamilton, and Hearst could not go unanswered. "It is deplorable that in the heat of the campaign Father Coughlin permits his fervor to carry him away from facts," Dubinsky said of the priest. With regard to a diplomatic appointment, Dubinsky revealed that he could not even obtain a visa to visit Russia, having been denied one in July, evidently in retribution for the conditions he described after his 1931 trip. Of the publisher Dubinsky said, "Mr. Hearst's attempt to paste the Communist label upon me and my colleagues in the trade-union movement is an outrageous piece of slander and character assassination."[83]

Other critics contributed to the defense. Norman Thomas alleged that by demanding Dubinsky's withdrawal as an elector John Hamilton had "brought the Fascist issue into American politics in a left-handed fashion," and he noted that the International Federation of Trade Unions was "not a Communist body." Samuel Klein, executive director of the Industrial Council of Cloak, Suit and Skirt Manufacturers, said that "were it not for Mr. Dubinsky and certain of his associates, Communist factions might now be in control of the ladies' garment unions."[84]

If Dubinsky was indeed a liability to Roosevelt, he could resign as elector. In his autobiography, Dubinsky says that he actually contemplated stepping down and asked Mayor La Guardia to present the idea to Roosevelt. La Guardia then served as "messenger" to FDR, who replied, "Tell that little son-of-a-bitch to mind his own business. This is my business; I'll take care of it. Let him stay where he is."[85]

Roosevelt took excellent care of his business, and Dubinsky got out the vote for him through the American Labor Party. Though Hamilton had vowed to demand Dubinsky's ouster up to Election Day, in early October he abruptly terminated his campaign, probably because of the storm of public and private criticism it had created.[86]

During the election campaign, Dubinsky urged ILGWU members to vote, organized lists of speakers in English and Yiddish, raised money, and addressed rallies. On October 27, before an ALP rally at Madison

Square Garden, he praised FDR as the "President that saved our country from chaos and total demoralization," denounced the Republicans' "red bogey," and predicted that Roosevelt would receive "the greatest majority an American president has ever received in all history."[87]

On Election Day, November 3, the American voters bore out Dubinsky's forecast. Roosevelt won a smashing 523-to-8 majority in the Electoral College. "The election indicates that the undiscriminating Republican attack on all President Roosevelt's supporters as being either 'Reds' or lunatics was a boomerang," observed Hamilton Fish Armstrong, editor of *Foreign Affairs*.[88]

The results also revealed that the American Labor Party helped Roosevelt but was not essential to his success in the Empire State. On the Democratic line alone he polled 53.9 percent of the statewide vote and 64.9 percent of the total in New York City. Nevertheless, the ALP did emerge suddenly as the state's third strongest political party. With 274,925 votes, or 4.9 percent, it drew more than double the total of the Socialists and the Communists combined.[89]

Roosevelt's friends had pulled together to defeat the Republicans, but after the election those in organized labor in particular remained as divided as ever among themselves. The AFL–CIO rift appeared to be widening. With regard to the American Labor Party, the question was its direction now that its primary goal had been accomplished. Dubinsky's prominence in national labor and political controversies had transformed him into more than just a local labor leader. Though not as Americanized or politically well-connected in Washington as the Amalgamated Clothing Workers' Sidney Hillman, he had become a household name.

11

An Independent Spirit

The momentous changes of 1936 took place within six short months and in the heat of a presidential election campaign. With the American Labor Party the new force in New York State politics and with unions in conflict over industrial unionism, John L. Lewis, William Green, Sidney Hillman, and David Dubinsky competed with Franklin D. Roosevelt for headline space. Wary of Lewis and Hillman and eager to mend fences with Green, Dubinsky began to question the wisdom of his recent marriages of necessity.

The ILGWU was Dubinsky's home, where he reigned supreme, with Luigi Antonini as his commissioner of Italian American affairs and Charles Zimmerman as his loyal left-winger. Resurgent, dynamic, and at the center of national controversies in labor and politics, the International attracted to its ranks a new generation of intellectuals and idealists who regarded it as an instrument to create a new and better world for working people.

No radical alien enterprise intent on class warfare, the immigrant-led union was as patriotic as its friends, the Roosevelts. Somehow this message failed to reach the Donnelly Garment Company of Kansas City. In 1933, Dubinsky assigned Abraham Plotkin to organize workers in Kansas City to eliminate sweatshop conditions. Plotkin formed Local 117 and organized "about half" of the city's cloak and dress firms, but two large firms remained resistant: Donnelly and the Stern, Stagman and Prinz Company cloak concern.[1]

Nell Donnelly, who employed about 1,200 workers, especially irked the ILG-ers, who felt she was blatantly evading National Recovery Administration code rates. She allegedly paid workers on ready-to-wear silk dresses according to the lower cotton dress rate.[2] In November 1933, the NRA had granted Donnelly and several other firms permission to manufacture under the cotton dress code. This decision followed a hearing in Washington at which the former isolationist senator James A. Reed of Missouri served as their counsel. Dubinsky attended the hearing as labor adviser, but the day belonged to Reed. In December, within weeks of their victory, Reed married Nell Donnelly.[3]

Recognizing that the Southwest needed organizing, the ILGWU's General Executive Board held its March 1934 meeting first in Kansas City and then in St. Louis. Kansas City's anti-union employers were prepared in advance. As the ILGWU leaders spoke, company-planted private detectives and a stenotypist recorded their statements. The next morning the GEB authorized Dubinsky to negotiate with the Kansas City cloak and dress manufacturers, call a general strike if necessary, and add an organizer to the market.[4]

The International organized a Donnelly local, but management intimidated those who wished to join it. Workers who indicated interest or enrolled in it were dismissed or assigned to work apart from nonunionists in a separate, isolated shop. At last the ILGWU took legal action, in December 1934 filing a complaint that Donnelly had violated its workers' right to organize and bargain collectively, as guaranteed by Section 7(a) of the National Industrial Recovery Act. The next month ILGWU regional director Meyer Perlstein advised the company that the International had chartered the organization of its employees. Challenged by these moves, in February 1935 the firm established a de facto company union known as the Nelly Don Loyalty League, in which membership was compulsory, as was the wearing of its button. "We protest against and will resist all attempts of outside interference with the business of said company, or with our relations to the company as employees," members pledged. The ILGWU complaint led to hearings before the National Labor Relations Board, but before the matter could be decided, the Supreme Court declared the NIRA unconstitutional, killing the case as well as the Blue Eagle. Encouraged by its victory, the Donnelly Garment Company then closed the separate shop, causing most of those who had worked there to leave Kansas City to find other employment. Local 117 ceased to exist.

The ILGWU refused to abandon Donnelly. During the 1936 presidential campaign, James Reed added a personal note by joining William Randolph Hearst and Father Coughlin in questioning Dubinsky's patriotism. In February 1937 the Kansas City press reported that the ILGWU was about to embark on a renewed campaign to organize Donnelly. In anticipation, on March 2 the company circulated a loyalty pledge to "refuse to acknowledge any union labor organization"; about 1,125 Donnelly employees signed. Four days later, Dubinsky appeared in town to renew the campaign. Before some seven hundred members in the Little Theater of the Municipal Auditorium, he announced he would ignore the "many harsh things" Reed had said about him and "deal with him only as a maker of dresses."

Donnelly ILG-ers were more concerned that they were working under substandard conditions. On March 9, they sent the company an invitation to bargain collectively. Infuriated and fearing a strike, Nell Donnelly Reed called a mass meeting at her factory. She read the ILGWU letter to her employees, ignoring wage and hours grievances included in it, and threatened to "fire anyone in the plant that joined the Union." According to some witnesses, Mrs. Reed said she would close her plant rather than have it unionized, and never permit "Dubinsky or any other 'ski' to tell her how to run her business." She and other witnesses would deny she ever made such remarks. They claimed that what she actually said was that "neither Dubinsky or any other buttinsky is going to intimidate me or the company into forcing you to join the International Union (ILGWU) against your will." Whatever her exact words, it is clear that she vowed never to tolerate the ILGWU. On April 27, as if to underscore her point on the International, the company jettisoned the Loyalty League and unveiled its latest creation, the Donnelly Garment Workers' Union.[5]

Though Donnelly remained unalterably hostile, other Kansas City employers softened their stance and reached agreement with the union. Still unhappy with their own situation, several Donnelly workers suggested to Meyer Perlstein that they appeal for help at the forthcoming union convention at Atlantic City, New Jersey. At that gathering in May, Sylvia Hull, a delegate of Local 118, the Kansas City Dressmakers' Union, requested financial aid and a publicity campaign in order to improve conditions at Donnelly, where, she declared, the company paid wages "at least 40 percent lower" than in other shops, "completely ignored" human rights, and "brutally suppressed" "the right of the worker to join a labor organization."

Hull received strong support, first from Joseph Breslaw and then from Dubinsky, who revived his feud with James Reed, calling him "an exploiter of labor" who fired "American workers who want American conditions in their shops." The convention then authorized $100,000 for a publicity campaign and possible strike.[6]

On reading Dubinsky's remarks in the press, Reed erupted. "He has the nerve to talk about Americanism although he was born in Russia and has only been in this country a few years." With regard to the Donnelly Company, Reed said it was his wife's. "I have not a dollar invested and moreover I have nothing to do with its management or control." He also denied that he had attacked the union during the election campaign but admitted criticizing Dubinsky as an elector because he "was a Socialist, if not a Communist," and his presence "was an affront to the Democratic Party and to all decent American citizens."[7]

Dubinsky used the convention as his forum to respond. He began by addressing Reed's complaint that the foreign-born union president had challenged his Americanism. "On the basis of this test of Americanism," Dubinsky said, "we must be permitted to believe that James Reed, when about to be born, decided to choose America as the place of his birth, while I, given the same free selection, picked Russia." On Reed's denial of control over the Donnelly Company, Dubinsky observed that it was well known in Kansas City that Donnelly employment policy was made with his "advice and approval." As for Dubinsky's role as an elector in 1936, the claim that the ILGWU's current $100,000 organizing campaign was being waged in retaliation for Reed's comments at that time was "childish."[8]

This rhetoric may have delighted the convention delegates, but all it accomplished was to call attention to the personal and cultural aspects of the Donnelly matter. The Reeds' anti-unionism was indeed intensified by a fear of alien invaders from New York City with Jewish names like Dubinsky, Plotkin, and Perlstein. Always conscious of his Jewishness and sensitive to anti-Semitism, Dubinsky might publicly ridicule slurs directed his way, but privately he would take them to heart. No ordinary adversary, the Donnelly Company had to be defeated.

Yet, even as the union delegates met at Atlantic City, the Reeds were constructing their fortifications. Having dismissed all ILG-ers, Nell Donnelly Reed enrolled her entire nonsupervisory workforce in the Donnelly Garment Workers' Union (DGWU). As her workers' sole bargaining agent, the DGWU pretended to negotiate with the company and on May 27 and June 22 signed contracts with it.[9] Nevertheless, the ILGWU's organizing campaign, managed by Perlstein, proved so bothersome that the company went to federal court and obtained a restraining order to abort it. Dubinsky hired noted attorney Frank P. Walsh, former chairman of the National Labor Relations Board, to fight the order. Walsh was delighted to be working for Dubinsky but was pessimistic about the outcome of the union's case.[10]

On July 5, Judge Merrill E. Otis issued a preliminary injunction against the ILGWU. Five days later he held a hearing on it. Walsh, who had flown in from New York the night before, led the defense team. James Reed listened as company attorneys argued that the Donnelly employees had formed a "union of their own." They charged the ILGWU with harassment and Dubinsky with "hoodlumism." "Mr. Dubinsky," Walsh retorted, "for honesty, courage, culture and citizenship is the peer of any man in this courtroom." Looking at Reed, Walsh added, "as a gentleman he is superior of the man who penned . . . and who conceived these charges." With regard to the injunction, Walsh contended that a "labor dispute" was at issue, and that under Norris–La Guardia it could be issued only in certain specified situations, none of which had now occurred.[11] Donnelly's lawyers contended that the law was unconstitutional and on that basis alone could not shield the union from an injunction. In October, the case came to the attention of U.S. Attorney General Homer S. Cummings because it involved recently passed congressional legislation, the "Compromise Act" enacted in lieu of FDR's plan to reorganize the federal courts. Where the constitutionality of an act of Congress was involved, the new law required a decision by a three-judge court. On Walsh's motion, Judge Otis ruled that this legislation applied to the Donnelly case, and he appealed to the senior judge of his circuit to appoint two additional judges to render a verdict.[12] As it turned out, Otis favored the ILGWU position on Norris–La Guardia and the injunction, but his colleagues thought otherwise and the union lost a two-to-one decision.[13]

The organizing campaign that had begun in 1933 was the first phase of a war that would continue for more than three decades. Ugly and personal, the opening skirmishes through 1937 merely set the stage. From 1938 to 1940, the two sides engaged in endless litigation and appeals. In July 1938, Federal Judge John C. Collet ended the injunction by accepting the applicability of Norris–La Guardia, but three months later he called for a full trial for a final resolution of the conflict. Dubinsky, Perlstein and other ILGWU leaders testified, but the company, claiming that the union was now conducting a "malicious secondary boycott," succeeded in obtaining a broad injunction. After the trial, Walsh died. Dubinsky replaced him with Washington attorney Dean Acheson, who led the ILGWU legal team in taking their case before the National Labor Relations Board, which found that Donnelly had engaged in unfair labor practices and therefore had violated the Wagner Act. On March 6, 1940, the NLRB ordered the company union and its contracts with Donnelly dissolved, checked-off employee dues reimbursed, and a dismissed employee reinstated.[14]

James Reed died in 1944 and David Dubinsky retired in 1966, but the struggle to organize Donnelly continued until July 18, 1968, when the ILGWU won a representation election. After overcoming yet another company appeal to the NLRB, the union negotiated a contract that established a work week of thirty-five hours with a wage increase of 25 percent. The International finally won, thirty-five years after Dubinsky assigned Abraham Plotkin to Kansas City.[15]

The suspension of the ILGWU by the Executive Council of the AFL, which became effective September 5, 1936, was a personal as well as institutional tragedy. The International had been thrust out of the Federation that had chartered it at birth and supported it through the turmoil of the twenties. Dubinsky rejected the AFL Executive Council's allegations that the CIO engaged in dual unionism. An AFL loyalist who viewed industrial unionism as a means of strengthening the Federation, he did not relish friction with his old allies. Sensitive to sentiments within the General Executive Board of the ILGWU, he also understood the potential for internal schism should there be external strife. Unlike John L. Lewis, Dubinsky had no personal quarrel with Green, and unlike Sidney Hillman, he had not experienced independent unionism.

Dubinsky was the sole representative of the "new immigrants" on the AFL's Executive Council in 1936. Among the "trade union elite," he was respected and more influential than his fellow needle-trades union president Sidney Hillman. Among the CIO-ers, the more assimilated and widely influential Hillman stood tall; "Dubinsky moved in Hillman's shadow."[16]

Moreover, Dubinsky could not renege on his own words. After having argued that the CIO was only an educational committee, he did not understand by what authority it could issue charters. Accordingly, he "seriously opposed" an application by the United Electrical and Radio Workers for such a document. Prior to the suspension of the CIO unions, the only practical obstacle had been their tenuous status within the AFL. With the Executive Council having resolved that question, the CIO approved the request over Dubinsky's opposition.[17]

Max Zaritsky shared a background and sentiments similar to Dubinsky's. A fellow immigrant, the Russian-born Zaritsky had joined the Cloth Hat, Cap and Millinery Workers' International Union in 1907, overcome Communists in the union in the 1920s, and co-founded the Committee for Industrial Organization in 1935. Unlike the ILGWU, the cap makers had a conflict with the AFL over dual unionism. For allegedly competing with the hatters' union, the AFL had expelled them for sixteen years until 1934, when they amalgamated with the hatters. As president of the Cap and Millinery Department of the merged union, Zaritsky wanted to retain the recently reestablished AFL affiliation. Very much his own person, he formed a loose alliance with Dubinsky to prevent a final break with the Federation.[18]

Zaritsky managed to keep a foot in the Federation's door. Although his department was affiliated with the CIO, the hatters' section and the union as a whole were not. In the absence of direct affiliation, the United Hatters, Cap and Millinery Workers' International Union (UHCMWIU) avoided suspension, and Zaritsky was free to attend the upcoming AFL convention at Tampa.[19]

Before heading for Florida, he made news at his own union's convention at the Hotel Pennsylvania in New York. On October 4, Zaritsky, aided by Dubinsky, launched a peace campaign. In an address to the convention, Dubinsky laid out terms of reconciliation:

> We are ready to give up the CIO; we are ready to comply with every decision of the AFL; we are ready to submit to any decision of the convention of the AFL. Let them, together with us, work out a plan of organizing the steel workers and the other workers in the mass production industries on an industrial basis and there will be no division, there will be united power.

Instead of promoting unity, Dubinsky's speech created the impression that he was ready to abandon the CIO. The *New York Times* printed his remarks but mistakenly reported him as saying that the ILGWU would consider leaving the CIO "if [the AFL's] organization work in the steel industry would be continued effectively." Speaking after Dubinsky, Zaritsky appealed for harmony within the Federation "at all costs." When told what the two men had said, William Green expressed delight. He called their statements "most significant and most helpful" and representative of "the spirit of reconciliation, which is precisely what is needed in this very deplorable situation." Furthermore, Green said he would address the Cap and Milliners' convention and confer with Dubinsky and Zaritsky.[20]

Neither needle-trades president had cleared his convention statement in advance with John L. Lewis, which would have been appropriate if CIO unity had been deemed essential. However, Dubinsky and Zaritsky had clearly decided that peace came first, and that they were its best proponents. Even so, Dubinsky was reluctant to offend Lewis and was embarrassed by the *Times*'s version of his remarks. To repair the damage, he reassured Sidney Hillman and Lewis that though the ILGWU was interested in peace, the AFL still had to embrace industrial unionism. The ILGWU was not prepared to abandon the CIO if the AFL simply launched a campaign to organize steel. Though he must have fumed privately, Lewis publicly announced that he was convinced that Dubinsky had not attempted to alter CIO policy. "Mr. Green can have peace if he rescinds the suspension order," Lewis said, adding that the CIO intended "to go ahead to assist in organizing the mass production industries." Correctly sensing that CIO unity was fragile, Green observed, "Some one must have got hold of Dubinsky since he made the speech."[21]

With an opportunity to split the CIO leadership having presented itself, Green swiftly exploited it. He hastened to the cap makers' and hatters' convention, where he "delivered an impassioned appeal for amity." That night, after the convention session, Green conferred at length with Dubinsky and Zaritsky on a peace formula.[22] The next day the convention adopted resolutions calling for the AFL Executive Council to allow CIO representatives to attend the Tampa convention to resolve the suspension issue, and to appoint subcommittees of the Executive Council and CIO to settle the dispute over industrial unionism.[23]

Unable to criticize the peace initiatives, John L. Lewis gave them his blessing, declaring that he would negotiate with the Executive Council following reinstatement of the suspended unions. Hillman also sounded cooperative, applauding "any efforts to bring about unity in the labor movement." Cautiously optimistic, Dubinsky expressed fervent "hope for a united labor movement."[24]

Green reported to the Executive Council that for the first time Zaritsky and Dubinsky had said a settlement "was necessary by all means," but the means of achieving it were "not discussed." When Green asked Dubinsky about his reported willingness to see the CIO dissolved, the latter "said that was not exactly what he said." Green pressed him on this point because he regarded dissolution as "basic and fundamental because the Council dealt with it and decided the CIO was dual." The AFL chieftain had declined to discuss the steel campaign.

Zaritsky then appeared before the Council as a self-styled "angel of peace." The teamsters' Dan Tobin asked him if he belonged to the CIO. "I was a member of the CIO when I was head of the Cloth Hat, Cap and Millinery Workers," he replied, but then he noted that "that Department does not exist any more, it died Wednesday night." The United Hatters, he said, had "never been affiliated with the CIO." After listening to Zaritsky, Green said the Council would confer with CIO representatives. Then he appointed a committee of vice presidents chaired by George M. Harrison and including Felix H. Knight and Matthew Woll to serve as the Federation's negotiators.[25]

The Council's response electrified Dubinsky, who acted quickly to arrange negotiations. He asked Lewis to convene the CIO "as early as possible" to consider the Executive Council's action and the selection of a negotiating committee. The CIO chairman was perturbed; the situation appeared to be careening out of control. Green had made no substantive concessions but was nonetheless able to crack the facade of CIO unity and undermine Lewis's leadership.

Dubinsky had written to Lewis, but CIO director John Brophy replied. The CIO would meet November 9 and 10 in Pittsburgh, when the ILGWU's GEB was scheduled to meet in Washington and only a week before the AFL convention in Tampa, allowing little time for compromise. In separate appeals, Dubinsky and Zaritsky implored Hillman and Lewis for a date in advance of Election Day, November 3. Lewis contended that he could not pull together a majority of the CIO before November 2, but suspicion was rife that he was holding out for a late meeting in order to delay negotiations with the AFL committee until after FDR's anticipated reelection, which would greatly benefit the strongly supportive CIO. Lewis finally relented, but only slightly; he agreed to November 7 and 8.[26]

Dubinsky had reason to believe Lewis would go ahead with the negotiations. In late October, at a Roosevelt campaign rally, Lewis and Hillman told Dubinsky and Zaritsky that they supported them. However, at the CIO meeting in Pittsburgh, everything unraveled. Dubinsky, who was accompanied by Charles Zimmerman and Julius Hochman, discovered that Lewis was in opposition. The CIO chairman rejected the idea of subcommittee meetings. Negotiations should be directly between himself and William Green. In an attempt at compromise, Hochman joined Dubinsky in proposing that a CIO subcommittee be created to negotiate with the AFL if a meeting between Lewis and Green failed to reach an accord. Siding with Lewis, Hillman said no agreement would be reached prior to the AFL convention and asked for faith in Lewis as "the leader of the CIO." With the meeting at an impasse, Hillman and Lewis left the room, but returned shortly afterward with a telegram they proposed to send to Green. According to Zimmerman, the message "was an invitation to continue the suspension . . . it wasn't a peace move." After two hours of debate, the CIO-ers agreed upon a "drastically revised" document, informing Green that Lewis had been "authorized . . . to confer" with him.

Green replied positively, saying he was not authorized to change Executive Council policy but would nevertheless "gladly meet and confer" with Lewis. The CIO received this telegram during a joint meeting with the Steel Workers' Organizing Committee. It was an open session, with "about 150 persons" present. Private on-the-spot discussion of Green's reply was thus impossible. Rather than delay a CIO response, which would have followed closed debate, Lewis exploited the public setting and had the CIO approve a sharp rejection. With Dubinsky voting "present," Lewis called it "futile" to negotiate with Green, as he could not alter EC policy, and denounced the suspensions under his "leadership" as "intemperate and violent." Outmaneuvered and outnumbered, Dubinsky could only say was that though he personally favored fighting the suspensions on the floor of the AFL convention, his GEB would decide whether to send an ILGWU delegation.

Convinced that his CIO associates "were not anxious for, and would do nothing to help bring about a reconciliation with the AFL," Dubinsky met with the ILGWU's General Executive Board. With regard to the AFL convention, in the absence of credentials to participate, the GEB decided "not to send delegates." However, it did urge a reconciliation of the "grave differences in the labor movement." Most significantly, anger surfaced, directed not at Green but at Lewis. Joseph Breslaw and Charles Kreindler suggested withdrawal from the CIO, and Isidore Nagler and Morris Bialis accused Lewis of obstructionism, but Charles Zimmerman and Basilio Desti called for calm and continuation with the CIO. Sensitive to his vice presidents, Dubinsky urged patience and proposed that the GEB take no action until after the AFL convention. The resolution carried by a vote of thirteen to three. Never completely committed to the CIO, the GEB now entertained the possibility of an exit. At least for the moment, Dubinsky blocked the way out.[27]

John L. Lewis's apparent opposition to peace had no doubt shaken the ILGWU contingent at Pittsburgh. Lewis perceived that Green was attempting to divide the CIO. He understood that the AFL subcommittee would be unable to move the hostile Executive Council majority, and the CIO unions would be handicapped by the illegal suspensions that had placed them in an inferior and unequal bargaining position.[28]

More surprising about Lewis was his attitude toward the just-reelected Franklin D. Roosevelt. Despite a Republican background, Lewis had helped found Labor's Non-Partisan League, committed CIO and United Mine Workers personnel, and traveled through five states to ensure that victory. Moreover, his UMW had handed FDR's campaign an astonishing $600,000. At a Madison Square Garden rally on October 27, Lewis had driven home the message that the labor movement depended on Roosevelt in the White House.[29] At the Pittsburgh meeting of the CIO, less than two weeks afterward, Lewis expressed doubt that FDR was indeed the godsend for whom he had fought. Hinting that his alliance with Roosevelt was not as firm as it appeared on the surface, Lewis said, "Roosevelt is not the answer to my maiden prayer."[30]

As the Tampa convention approached, Dubinsky kept his physical distance but worked quietly to effect reconciliation. His efforts, however, were largely in vain. Without supportive delegates from the suspended unions, resounding defeat was a foregone conclusion. By a vote of 21,679 to 2,043, the convention sustained, and thus legalized, the actions of the Executive Council. To keep alive chances for reconciliation, it also agreed to continue the Harrison committee.

As the awkward and ill-conceived suspension process unfolded, it revealed a trace of bigotry. The resolutions committee's report on the CIO unions accused several of ingratitude for past assistance by the Federation. Organizations thus cited were the United Mine Workers, the Textile Workers, the Ladies' Garment Workers, and others "composed largely of Jewish workers." The injection of "the Jewish question" into the CIO controversy was too much for Zaritsky, who attacked Matthew Woll, the committee's "prophet of despair," who publicly raised it. John Frey, the committee secretary, responded to Zaritsky by announcing the withdrawal of the offensive language, and Woll expressed regrets. In an editorial after the convention, *Gerechtigkeit,* the Yiddish-language edition of *Justice,* said the slur "stands out as an example of crass tactlessness." The ILGWU then sent an English translation to all EC members and CIO unions.[31]

The reference to Jewish unions added a bitter aftertaste to an already ugly convention, which officially divided the labor movement. Nevertheless, with determined optimism, the ILGWU's newspaper, *Justice,* observed mildly that the AFL leadership had kept open the door to peace and might yet "discover an effective and working compromise."[32]

Additional encouragement to heal the rift was provided by George Berry of the Pressmen's Union. An AFL vice president since 1935 and founder of Labor's Non-Partisan League the next year, Berry enjoyed good relations with the key figures in the CIO dispute. Labor's division, he advised George Harrison in December, "will be harmful not only to all of us in the labor movement but to the nation itself." He suggested that the Federation give "power and authority" to the Harrison committee to bring about a settlement. Both Harrison and Dubinsky doubted that the AFL would confer such rights, and Dubinsky reminded the ILGWU GEB that at the AFL convention in Tampa, Berry had voted to ratify the action of the Executive Council.[33] Committed to industrial but not dual unionism, Dubinsky continued to have faith in the possibility of rapprochement with Green and Woll. Careful not to forget the sentiment for the AFL within his General Executive Board, Dubinsky had little choice but to remain on a course that was becoming ever more independent of his ostensible industrial union allies, Lewis and Hillman.

12

Allies and Adversaries

Rather than heal the rift between the AFL and CIO, the passage of time seemed to aggravate it. Officially suspended, and with no peace in sight, the CIO unions came under renewed pressure. In February 1937, Green demanded that all AFL affiliates "renew their pledge of loyalty and devotion" to the Federation. As far as Dubinsky was concerned, ILG-ers should do just that, "because we are loyal . . . despite the fact that we disagree with their [organizing] methods."[1]

While still refusing to concede that the CIO was a dual union, he prepared the report of his General Executive Board to the forthcoming ILGWU convention. The document's chapter on Lewis's committee recited its history, without criticism, reserving blame for the "rule-or-ruin" attitude of the AFL Executive Council. As a CIO founder, Dubinsky hoped for unanimous GEB approval of his account, but when it was put to a vote, Cloak Joint Board chairman Isidore Nagler and the pressers' Joseph Breslaw refused to ratify it. That doubts about the CIO persisted among ILGWU vice presidents became even more evident when a resolution to ask the convention to maintain the ILGWU's affiliation and fully support its organizational activities failed by a vote of six to seven.[2]

Among the shadows over the CIO were those cast by its relations with Communists. In 1937 it was already very apparent that the once rabidly anti-Communist John L. Lewis was amenable to cooperating with his former foes as a means of building the CIO.[3] American Communists were moving into the mainstream of American politics and trade unionism. The party's adoption of a "Popular Front" position in 1934 had led, two years later, to de facto support for Roosevelt. Directed by Moscow, Communist Party leader Earl Browder ran for president. His rhetoric lambasted primary target Republican Alf Landon but spared the Democratic incumbent.[4]

The Communists' rightward movement also led them to embrace the CIO. By 1934, after several ineffective ventures into dual unionism, they declared it necessary to work inside the AFL in order to make inroads in basic industries. They moved aggressively into the dock, textile, iron and steel, and automobile trades.[5] The advent of the CIO presented dangers as well as opportunities. John L. Lewis, its driving force, had been at war with Communists within the United Mine Workers of America and the labor movement since the 1920s. But by October 1935, signs abounded that Lewis was no longer an adversary. Immediately following the AFL convention's rejection of industrial unionism he approached the Communists, first by granting an exclusive interview to the *Daily Worker.* Talks with party leaders produced an agreement that opened the CIO to the Communists. Brophy hired the British-born Len De Caux to be the CIO's publicity director, and Lewis made Lee Pressman the legal counsel to the Steel Workers Organizing Committee and the CIO. In exchange, the Communists gave Lewis organizers—loads of them. Despite these ties, some Communists, notably William Z. Foster, continued to distrust Lewis and feared that their association with him would impede a peace settlement between the AFL and CIO.[6]

The legitimization of the Communists by John L. Lewis did not signal their across-the-board acceptance by all CIO-ers. Present tactical needs could not erase years of rivalry and conflict. As early as 1935, Dubinsky had warned the AFL Executive Council about Communist influence in the automobile workers' union. Late in December 1936 the United Automobile Workers of America went on strike against General Motors. Led by President Homer S. Martin, the UAW, which had been founded the previous year and was a member of the CIO, sought to negotiate improvements in working conditions through collective bargaining. However, when the company began to decentralize parts manufacturing in order to dilute concentrations of troublesome employees, it took direct action. Workers in Flint, Michigan, and Cleveland occupied Fisher Body buildings in a sit-down strike, which kept replacement laborers, or "scabs," from entering. In January, in what they called the "Battle of the Running Bulls," the sit-downers successfully withstood an invasion by policemen who sought to enforce a court injunction for them to vacate the premises. With strikers behind barricades and under threat of fines and imprisonment, John L. Lewis negotiated a peace agreement that was signed on February 11 and authorized the United Automobile Workers to bargain for its GM-employee members.[7]

The GM settlement revolutionized collective bargaining in the auto-mobile industry. Momentum from its victory propelled the UAW to quick accords at smaller automobile manufacturers Packard, Studebaker, and Hudson; numerous parts producers; and another industry giant, Chrysler Corporation. A sit-down strike in May closed nine Chrysler plants before achieving a settlement that virtually duplicated the victory at GM.[8]

"Mr. Lewis," Walter Chrysler said to the CIO chairman at the con-clusion of negotiations, "I do not worry about dealing with you, but it is the Communists in these unions that worry me a great deal." UAW pres-ident Homer Martin and David Dubinsky shared this concern. Martin, Dubinsky would later recall, was a person "who did not know his right foot from his left when it came to organization." After having been kept from the negotiations by John L. Lewis, who sent him on a trip, Martin, feeling insecure, feared a Communist takeover of the UAW. To prevent such a coup, he approached Dubinsky, who recommended Jay Love-stone.

The ILGWU president and Communist opposition leader had known each other since 1918, when Lovestone attended a Lower East Side So-cialist meeting in quest of converts to Communism. Bitterly anti-Stalinist after his narrow escape from Moscow in 1929, Lovestone reestablished contact with Dubinsky and a few years later helped facilitate Charles Zimmerman's return to the ILGWU. Though Dubinsky regarded Love-stone as "an S. O. B.," he continued to collaborate with him.[9]

With Lovestone and Dubinsky in the background, Homer Martin purged the leadership of the UAW and brought in a host of Lovestoneites, including Alex Bail, Irving Brown, William Munger, and Francis Henson. Martin's campaign even included an accusation that the three Socialist Reuther brothers, Victor, Walter, and Roy, were Communists. Soon there would be "almost open warfare" between the Martin and anti-Martin factions. In April 1939, Martin would lead his followers into the AFL, but a year later his enemies, known as the UAW-CIO, would win repre-sentation elections in forty-eight General Motors plants and soon after-ward become the sole bargaining agency in GM and even add the Ford Motor Company, the third and last of the industry giants to be orga-nized.[10]

How could Dubinsky conspire to cleanse the UAW of Communists while remaining loyal to the CIO that appeared to welcome them? In August 1937, at the UAW convention at Milwaukee, he boasted to the auto workers of his anti-Communist record but claimed that while he disagreed with the Communists' principles and "fought their tactics," he accepted their "right to disagree" with him.[11]

The delegates were Midwesterners who found it "a little bit strange" to be listening to the Jewish-accented Dubinsky from New York. "So you want democracy, eh?" he asked. "Well, let me tell you. In my union we've got lots of democracy, and I want you to know I'm the boss." According to Victor Reuther, "the convention roared. . . . [Dubinsky] made a great hit because he didn't bullshit them. . . . Of course, they didn't believe a damn word of what he said about their having democracy."[12]

In 1937, lingering questions compelled Dubinsky to complement his candor with serious analysis. Unresolved matters included future relations with the American Labor Party, which had fared well in the 1936 election campaign. As Herbert Lehman had garnered more than 50,000 votes on the ALP line, by New York State law the party was entitled to register members and conduct primary elections. Its constitution explicitly barred Communists, but with no enforcement of this provision, they flocked into it. Many came from Communist-led unions, such as the United Electrical Workers, Transport Workers, and State, County, and Municipal Workers.[13]

Communists gained entry into the ALP, but actual power still resided with the anti-Communist needle-trades unionists who had founded it. Dubinsky himself was not involved in the daily operation of the party. Luigi Antonini served as state chairman, while ILGWU executive secretary Fred Umhey shared ALP decision making with the Amalgamated's Jacob S. Potofsky and the Milliners' Alex Rose. According to Potofsky, Antonini was a "platform man," while Rose was the "politician."[14] Behind them was Dubinsky, wielding the "power of the purse." At the end of the 1936 campaign the ALP had a $50,000 deficit, of which the ILGWU covered $27,500. Altogether, the International's campaign contribution totaled $141,673.28.[15]

Though the ALP was founded primarily to assist FDR in 1936, its initial success seemed to ensure that it would not disband after the elections. Dubinsky favored continuation, as did Luigi Antonini. Hillman felt otherwise but found himself overridden by the state executive committee. Having tasted politics and liked it, Antonini and fellow vice president Harry Greenberg anticipated even greater union involvement.[16] However, the GEB would rule some months later that ILG-ers in the ALP must not act as individuals on policy matters.[17]

As a bona fide party, the ALP could not ignore an old friend, Fiorello La Guardia, who was seeking reelection as mayor of New York. A Republican who was on good terms with the needle-trades unions and who had been "a leading spirit" in the ALP's founding, he was its "natural candidate" for the mayoralty in 1937.[18] He also needed the Republicans, several of whose chieftains were reluctant to forgive his backing of Roosevelt the previous year. Greatly outnumbered by the Democrats in party registrations, the Republicans really had little choice but to nominate the Little Flower.[19]

Jeremiah T. Mahoney, a state supreme court justice who appealed to the same ethnic and economic constituencies as La Guardia, was the Democrat's nominee. In place of an issue, he resorted to smear tactics. He called the ALP an "active adjunct of the Communist party" and accused La Guardia of coddling Communists.[20] On October 28, he attacked Antonini, Hillman, and La Guardia for past associations with Communists, which he said were "consistent with the Mayor's whole record."[21]

Mahoney's Red-baiting irked Dubinsky, still smarting from the Republican attacks on his own patriotism during the presidential campaign. On the twenty-eighth, while Tammany rallied at the Hippodrome, the American Labor Party packed Madison Square Garden with an outpouring for La Guardia. An overflow crowd heard La Guardia endorse the ILGWU's Isidore Nagler, the ALP nominee for Bronx Borough President.[22]

In 1937, Hillman, Dubinsky, and the ALP also reached into the Republican Party to nominate special prosecutor Thomas E. Dewey for New York district attorney. By July, at age thirty-five, the politically ambitious Dewey had already made a name for himself as a first-rate crime fighter.[23] But he was reluctant to run for district attorney, having been offered a lucrative law position and seriously considering a run for the U.S. Senate in 1938. Aware that the Democrats enjoyed a nearly five-to-one voter registration edge, Dewey anticipated a probable loss and premature end to his career and therefore resisted pleas of Republican county chairman Kenneth Simpson, Judge Samuel Seabury, Fiorello La Guardia, and Dubinsky and Hillman. La Guardia's adviser, former FDR "Brain Truster" Adolf A. Berle, and the milliners' Alex Rose supplied additional pressure. At last, just before the legal filing deadline, Dewey agreed to run.[24]

On Election Day, La Guardia, Dewey, and the American Labor Party triumphed. The Little Flower received more than 1,344,000 votes, nearly 483,000 of them, 21.6 percent of the total cast, on the ALP line. Dewey was elected district attorney with 60 percent of the vote. Isidore Nagler, who ran for Bronx borough president, was narrowly defeated, but the ALP sent five members each to the city council and the state assembly. "New York has a Labor Party!" cheered the ILGWU's *Justice*.[25]

Among the other winners in 1937 were the Communists. Loyal ALP-ers and hard workers, they and their sympathizers had been on their best behavior for the common cause. Anathema to right-wing Socialists in the ALP, they nevertheless avoided open competition and conflict and pulled together a broad spectrum of pro- and anti-Communist unionists. Along for the ride, and hoping to transform the ALP into a true labor party, were Lovestoneites, notably Charles Zimmerman and Will Herberg of the ILGWU's dressmakers. Dubinsky, Rose, and Hillman were under no illusions about the Communists' conversion to democracy. They just thought the leftists could be controlled.[26]

In preparation for the ILGWU's May 1937 convention in Atlantic City, the General Executive Board drafted a report to the delegates in which the CIO controversy was the subject of a twenty-five-page chapter. Predictably, the account condemned the actions of the AFL's Executive Council, declaring that its "arrogance of power" and "attitude of rule-or-ruin" rendered it "overwhelmingly responsible for the present turmoil, rancor and division."[27] But the GEB steered clear of personal denunciation of the AFL leadership or praise of Lewis and his lieutenants. Significantly, the document did not endorse the CIO.

Even without such an endorsement, the draft report ran into opposition on the GEB. In April, the board approved it by a thirteen-to-two vote, with Joseph Breslaw and Isidore Nagler dissenting. At the same time, and even more revealing of affinity for the AFL, the GEB rejected by a six-to-seven vote a resolution to recommend to the convention that the International remain affiliated with the CIO and fully support its organizing campaign.[28] With GEB support for the CIO so lukewarm, the ILGWU's future within it appeared cloudy.

Dubinsky, the ultimate publicist, would never permit this disaffection to interfere with the extravaganza he planned for Atlantic City in May. The twenty-third ILGWU convention took place as scheduled and did in public what the GEB had declined to do privately, that is, unequivocally commit to the CIO while simultaneously promoting peace.[29] As a peacemaker, Dubinsky had invited both sides to present their arguments. John L. Lewis and Sidney Hillman appeared on separate days on behalf of the

CIO. Matthew Woll also came, defended the AFL, and pleaded for peace. Uninvited and absent, William Green telegraphed similar sentiments.

It was Emma Dubinsky who uttered the most memorable words of the convention. After her husband's unanimous reelection to the presidency of the ILGWU, he asked her to speak. "I can't say very much right now," she began, "but I think that you and I have the right man." The delegates applauded and laughed.[30] When the laughter subsided, the convention returned to the serious CIO–AFL conflict. The statement it adopted, Dubinsky afterward explained to Woll, was "a compromise resolution which satisfied both extremes" among the delegates.[31] Seemingly uninterested in compromising with the CIO unions, Green and the AFL Executive Council pressed forward with their effort to divide them. In October, the AFL convention empowered the EC to revoke the charters of the CIO unions, while also authorizing continuation of the Federation's negotiating committee.[32]

Sidney Hillman's appearance at the Atlantic City convention was more than just a demonstration of labor unity. It signified the apparent settlement of a jurisdictional dispute between his union and Dubinsky's. Through the years such matters rarely amounted to much, but this time the CIO was involved, placing the International in conflict with it as well as the Amalgamated.

At issue were the "sick" textile industry and the failure of attempts by the United Textile Workers to organize it. In early 1937, the CIO decided on a campaign to unionize 1.25 million underpaid textile workers. During the NRA era the United Textile Workers had gained about 400,000 members, but after two years the number was down to 60,000. In March 1937, the CIO created the Textile Workers' Organizing Committee, chaired by Hillman, to revitalize organizational activities.[33] The ILGWU, represented by Charles Zimmerman, was to play a leading role in directing the committee and, along with the ACWA, made a substantial financial contribution to it.[34]

On the surface the ILGWU was a full partner and willing partner in this venture, but behind the scenes Dubinsky was miffed. He had been in the Midwest on ILGWU business when the TWOC was founded in Washington and was unhappy that the action was taken in his absence.[35] If Lewis had appointed a chairman other than Hillman, Dubinsky probably would have been less critical of the means by which the TWOC was founded.

This complaint appears to have predisposed Dubinsky to believe that Hillman and the ACWA would exploit the TWOC for their own benefit. As the ILGWU was preparing to convene at Atlantic City, Dubinsky received reports that such a situation had already arisen. The TWOC was allegedly organizing the knitwear industry regardless of ILGWU claims in that area. In 1933 the International and the United Textile Workers had fought a prolonged jurisdictional battle over knitwear, which ended the next summer with a settlement brokered by the American Federation of Labor. Though the ILGWU's organizational efforts under the agreement were not especially successful, they were nevertheless pursued intensively across the country, in such states as Pennsylvania, Massachusetts, Ohio, and California.[36]

Now, three years after that settlement, the TWOC under Hillman's direction appeared to be invading the ILGWU's jurisdiction in Minnesota. The Amalgamated's manager in the Twin Cities was "secretly negotiating an agreement" with the Munsingwear Corporation, which the ILGWU had been attempting to organize for nine months. With organizers on the scene and a chartered local with two hundred members, the International was ready to do business, but the employer was quoted as saying he would have nothing to do with it because "Dubinsky is a Communist and an Anarchist."

Asked to step aside by ILGWU organizer Meyer Perlstein, ACWA representative Sander Genis refused, whereupon Dubinsky confronted Hillman, who declined to waive any jurisdiction in the knitwear field. The ACWA president and TWOC chairman claimed that knitwear belonged under the "textiles" heading and "therefore refused to recognize the agreement between the ILGWU and the UTW."

Dubinsky warned Hillman that the TWOC's "intrusion" in Minneapolis was "bound seriously to affect the relations between our unions and to discredit the work of the CIO." On April 29, he told his GEB that it might "seriously affect the affiliation of the ILGWU with the CIO."[37]

Perhaps reluctant to risk such consequences, John L. Lewis and Sidney Hillman backed off. At the ILGWU convention, Lewis revealed that the CIO had already yielded jurisdiction. From the same platform, Hillman declared the next morning that "nothing" would "ever be permitted to make a rift, to create any disagreements between" the International and the Amalgamated.[38] Five days later, Dubinsky announced that he and Hillman had indeed reached a settlement, with the Amalgamated yielding to the International.[39]

Privately, the ILGWU president remained cautious. He told Matthew Woll he would "watch developments for the next two, three weeks" to see if the International really would be permitted to organize the industry.[40] For the time being the ILGWU continued to honor its own pledge of $20,000 per month financial support for the TWOC but also to seek a guarantee of jurisdictional rights.[41]

By late August it was evident that Dubinsky's reservations were justified. The Munsingwear matter was unresolved, the TWOC was signing up additional knitwear shops, and the Amalgamated was permitting the manufacture of "mannish" style women's suits in men's clothing shops it had organized in Pennsylvania. Again the ILGWU claimed jurisdictional rights. On September 2 the GEB of the ILGWU suspended further payments to the TWOC. Only $60,000 of the $250,000 pledged had thus far been paid. In response to this step, Hillman moved to make peace, but through surrogates, assigning the task to Emil Rieve of the Hosiery Workers. It was Rieve and a "very friendly" Jacob Potofsky who then conferred with Dubinsky. The TWOC and ACWA generally acceded to the ILGWU, which then resumed payments to the TWOC.[42]

Just as it was forced to defend its jurisdiction within the TWOC, the ILGWU found itself in conflict over knitwear with the AFL in Cleveland. Using the ILGWU's suspended status as a pretext, the AFL ignored jurisdictional rights it had granted the International in 1934 and aggressively attempted to organize workers in that city, making it a dangerous place. In March 1937 thugs severely beat and nearly killed ILGWU vice president Abraham Katofsky outside his home, but not until the TWOC had withdrawn from Cleveland did the full extent of the AFL threat become clear. With the TWOC gone, Dubinsky ordered increased ILGWU activity, only to discover that AFL organizers had moved in "and were negotiating with the employers."

A furious Dubinsky protested to William Green.[43] Green's response, addressed to Nathan Solomon of the ILGWU's Cleveland Joint Board, who had likewise protested, indicated that most of Cleveland's knitgoods workers had signed AFL petitions and thus demanded affiliation with the Federation. Once again he blamed any ill feelings that had ensued on the "setting up of a dual movement," which the ILGWU supported.[44]

The jurisdictional strife along Lake Erie precipitated an ILGWU strike of four shops beginning in June and ending in September, following plant elections, two of which were won by the International. A lost season left the Cleveland knitwear industry in a shambles. Consequently, three large shops closed their doors while others hired ILGWU members only with great reluctance. Many ILG-ers had to abandon their union for the AFL in order to gain employment.[45]

What Dubinsky must have found especially disheartening during this dispute was his inability to resolve it amicably through Green, who seemed determined to punish him and the ILGWU for their insubordination. When Dubinsky complained of "outright scabbery" by the Cleveland Federation of Labor, Green sarcastically replied that "his sincere friend during a period of many years" was influenced by "anger and feeling, rather than by judgment, balance and self-control." The AFL president reveled in Dubinsky's discomfort, displaying a talent for psychological warfare that pushed friendship to its outer limit.[46]

In June and July 1937, the AFL's jurisdictional offensive against the International extended beyond Ohio. It also included nine other sites in five states: Pennsylvania, Maryland, Kentucky, Illinois, and Texas.[47]

As it suffered these consequences, the International kept alive the dream of 1935, preferring it to the reality of 1937. The trouble with the CIO was not its growth, which was phenomenal, but its direction. Within two years, according to Benjamin Stolberg, the CIO's membership rose to 3,300,000 as "in the mass production industries it . . . raised wages by $1,000,000,000 a year, cut hours by some 2,000,000 a week, and improved working conditions everywhere." Its organizers captured "75 per cent of the steel industry, 70 per cent of the automobile industry, 65 per cent of the rubber industry, and about one-third of the maritime and textile industries."[48] Despite these successes, Dubinsky and the ILGWU were uneasy.

One reason for concern was the prominence of Communists. Alarmed that the left-wingers were again visible within the International, at the Atlantic City convention of the International, Dubinsky endorsed a resolution mandating the dissolution of all groups or clubs whose existence was not approved by the General Executive Board. Charles Zimmerman, an almost legendary veteran of past battles, spoke at length in opposition. The convention then adopted the resolution by voice vote.[49]

By welcoming Communists into the CIO, John L. Lewis seemed to be reopening the gates of labor to an unrelenting enemy. In a scurrilous folder entitled *Does the CIO Seek to Promote Red Revolution?* the Industrial Defense Association, Inc., of Boston presented portraits of Dubinsky, Hillman, and Lewis alongside that of Joseph Stalin. "Remember that the CIO is led by Communists," the circular warned.[50] The *Chicago Tribune* misquoted Dubinsky's remarks at the convention of the United Automobile Workers at Milwaukee, saying he told the gathering that provided the Communists served his union and despite his disagreement with their principles, he was "for them." In reply, Dubinsky noted that all he had said was that Communists were "entitled to participate" in ILGWU activities provided they placed "the interests of their fellow members above the interests of a political party."[51]

Against this backdrop of tension and schism, the movement for peace suddenly revived. In early September 1937, a month before the start of the AFL's annual convention, William Green adopted a beneficent pose. The Federation, he said, would extend a welcome to the ten suspended unions if they agreed to an unconditional return. "Men big enough on each side," such as "John Lewis, Sidney Hillman, Matthew Woll and Dan Tobin," might then resolve outstanding differences.[52] An "olive branch" was thus proffered, but Lewis snubbed it, using a radio address the next evening to boast of the growth of the CIO rather than offer a response.[53]

As Lewis had called a CIO conference for Atlantic City on October 11, a week after the start of the AFL affair, a sense of urgency prevailed. Dubinsky suspected that at Atlantic City "the question will come up of calling a convention for the purpose of organizing the CIO on a permanent basis and as a national movement in opposition to the AFL."[54]

William Green opened the AFL convention without a trace of conciliation. For ninety minutes he spoke of war against the CIO. With regard to the suspended unions, he urged the delegates to authorize the Executive Council to revoke their charters.[55]

On October 11, the convention gave Green the expulsion authorization he had requested by a vote of 25,616 to 1,227. Included within the resolution on the CIO were sharp personal attacks, on John L. Lewis as his committee's "dominating and fulminating Caesar" and on Sidney Hillman as its "Machiavelli." In a heavy-handed bid to separate Dubinsky from such egregious leadership, the resolution directly addressed the ILGWU, suggesting that its democratic heritage and ideals would compel it to "revolt against dictatorship, selfish grasping for power and its ruthless exercise."[56]

The CIO conference bore out Dubinsky's fears by authorizing a call for a convention to found a permanent organization, but it also seized the initiative for peace. He along with Philip Murray spoke strongly in favor of a peace resolution, which the CIO-ers unanimously adopted, calling for unity conferences to be undertaken by committees of one hundred members from each side. Accepting the idea of conferences but rejecting "mass conferences" as unproductive, the Federation suggested that its "special committee" meet with "a like representative committee" from the CIO. With the door to peace open again, the two sides exchanged additional telegrams resulting in an agreement that the Federation's three-member committee confer with ten CIO representatives in Washington on October 25.[57]

The CIO's Committee of Ten, headed by Philip Murray, met eleven times with George M. Harrison, Matthew Woll, and Gustave M. Bugniazet of the AFL from October 25 to December 21, 1937. Both Dubinsky and Hillman were in the CIO group, but illness soon ended the latter's participation. Dubinsky remained a force for reconciliation. Yet it was evident from the beginning that the two sides were far apart. The CIO proposed immediate, simultaneous AFL acceptance of all its unions, which would be placed in a new AFL department called the Committee for Industrial Organization. The AFL proposed a two-stage return: first, the dissolution of the CIO, and then the reinstatement of the ten suspended unions. Other CIO unions would join after resolving their jurisdictional differences with AFL affiliates. Philip Murray understood that acceptance of this offer would be tantamount to total capitulation. Not only would the CIO cease to exist; without its protection, the twenty unions presently affiliated with it could not possibly ward off AFL raids.[58]

Though Dubinsky was not usually prone to wishful thinking, he now expressed what appears to have been excessive optimism. On November 23 he reported to the General Executive Board of the ILGWU "that an excellent basis for peace had practically been agreed upon." The AFL, he said, had yielded on industrial unionism, conceding its appropriateness to at least eight industries, and was prepared to rescind the ten suspensions. What remained to be done was "simply a matter of adjustment." Dubinsky said he firmly believed that peace would come, "in spite of certain leaders."[59]

A week later his dream appeared to come true. The conferees discussed a "basis for agreement" to extend AFL admission to all CIO unions, thirty-two altogether, "concurrently." Moreover, the AFL would consider limiting the power of the Executive Council to suspend unions, and a special AFL convention would determine representation of unions at conventions.[60] "In the end we reached an understanding that would have totally guaranteed the integrity of the C.I.O. unions," Dubinsky later recalled.[61]

He made the assertion, for which there is no convincing evidence, that an accord had indeed been reached, and that Philip Murray took it to John L. Lewis for approval. Lewis "read it, tore it into pieces and threw it out the window," leaving Murray "standing there, hypnotized" and speechless. "It was like a cemetery in the room. All our efforts were dead."[62]

The talks failed because the leaders of both sides did not really want them to succeed. That the disputants afterward blamed one another was predictable. By blaming the collapse of the conference on the CIO chairman, Dubinsky in effect endorsed the AFL position. Never large, the gap between the ILGWU and the AFL now seemed rather small.

On January 3, 1938, Dubinsky told the General Executive Board of the ILGWU "it was his definite conviction that John Lewis did not want peace."[63] The AFL, Dubinsky stressed, did not expect any CIO union to return prior to a general settlement covering all thirty-two unions, but Lewis prevented further negotiations. As for ILGWU relations with the CIO, Dubinsky declared, "the ILGWU must not withdraw from the CIO lest it place itself in the position of being blamed for any disintegration of this movement."

Zimmerman also opposed withdrawal. He contended that ILGWU expressions of opinions "on the outside" would jeopardize the CIO.[64] But Dubinsky resented the criticism by Lewis and the Communists and was determined to respond to it in public. And what better forum might he have than a gathering of his own lieutenants, the executive boards of New York ILGWU unions?

On January 11 about 1,200 ILG-ers filled the Manhattan Opera House to hear him speak on "The CIO, AFL and PEACE." Without delay Dubinsky decried the absence of labor unity and "the collapse of the peace negotiations," denying that the International had distorted facts or created confusion in its accounts of the situation and denouncing extremists on both sides. With obvious reference to Lewis, he added that the labor movement was "not the property of any individual or group," and that "no one" had "a mortgage" on it.[65]

In his address Dubinsky also said he would remain in the CIO. Seizing on that point when informed of his remarks, Lewis challenged Dubinsky to take a definite position for or against the committee. "Mr. Dubinsky, whom I esteem highly, seems to be giving an imitation of Eliza crossing the ice and looking backward like Lot's wife," Lewis observed. "I think he ought to finally decide whether he is flesh or fowl or good red herring." Dubinsky accused Lewis of making a "flippant" response to important matters. Labor peace, he declared, was fervently desired by American workers and would not be denied them much longer, despite Lewis's "wisecracking."[66]

A major salvo in the undeclared war within the CIO, Dubinsky's speech brought it to the public attention as never before. It delighted the growing body of those who feared and hated Lewis and the Communists around him. "It required courage, but that you have always had. Communism has been severely scorched by your address," an admirer wrote to Dubinsky. "Will Lewis continue to insist upon war and thus play into the Communists' hands or will he go American?" asked the *New York Herald Tribune*.[67]

By speaking out from within the CIO against Communist influence, Dubinsky established a clear line of division between himself and Lewis and gave credence to the argument that the problem with the CIO was more serious than dual unionism. Lewis stood charged with consorting with the devil, whom he could not repudiate. With such an alliance in control of the CIO, how could Dubinsky keep his word and remain within the organization?

Not all observers shared the ILG-er's views. The *Daily Worker* blamed the AFL Executive Council, alleging it had planned "to pit worker against worker and union against union in bloody, destructive warfare."[68] More to the center of the political spectrum, the January 26, 1938 issue of the *New Republic* included no fewer than three separate pieces critical of Dubinsky's position. Columnist Heywood Broun accused him of timing his attack in order to injure the CIO and engaging in "histrionics" aimed at making headlines.[69] Similarly, an editorial charged that Dubinsky's criticism, combined with that of other foes of the CIO, was giving "popular currency to the charge that the CIO is a stalking-horse for revolutionaries and disrupters."[70] In the third piece, columnist "T.R.B." thought Lewis acted with sound judgment in refusing to continue the peace conference with no more than "verbal assurance" of an eventual written agreement from the AFL negotiators."[71]

With Lewis alienated and the reviews of his January 11 speech somewhat mixed, Dubinsky extended a hand to Sidney Hillman. In early 1938,

Dubinsky still maintained at least a working relationship with his counterpart at the Amalgamated. As Jewish immigrant leaders of needle-trades unions, the American Labor Party, and the CIO, they had strong common denominators. However, Hillman had greater influence than Dubinsky with President Roosevelt, and his union occasionally trespassed on ILGWU jurisdictional turf. For the moment, though, these considerations were secondary, because it was Lewis whom Dubinsky regarded as the obstacle to labor peace and the collaborator with Communists. In May, Dubinsky addressed the Amalgamated convention at Atlantic City. He used the occasion to promote peace with the AFL and praise Hillman, whose absence from the conference due to illness he said he regretted.[72]

Labor leaders who longed for peace could only have been dismayed by the course of events after the conference. The AFL Executive Council moved to banish CIO unions and fellow travelers from state and city centrals, and AFL unions combatively competed for members with CIO affiliates, disregarding traditional jurisdictional and craft distinctions. In the political world, Federation officials called the CIO Communist-dominated, lobbied for federal legislation to inhibit industrial unionism, and opposed CIO-endorsed candidates.[73] In the face of this onslaught, Dubinsky now sought to make peace. But principles of unionism became even less important to what was left of the debate as the Communist issue emerged. By attacking the Communists' role in the CIO, he in effect confirmed the AFL charges of their influence. Once again, he was an anti-Communist hero.[74]

From Los Angeles came a warning for Dubinsky to protect his own organization. J. W. Buzzell, secretary-treasurer of the AFL-affiliated Central Labor Council of that city, reported to him that there was "a well laid out program in operation for the Communists to seize control of your International Union, and of the local branch of it here in Los Angeles." In reply, Dubinsky informed Buzzell that the ILGWU had "close to 300 locals functioning in 120 cities" and "in only about a dozen of them" were there Communists, whose influence was "negligible."[75]

Despite these assurances, in New York City, Communists were visibly active in several locals, including Local 9, the Finishers' and Tailors' Local; Local 10, the Cutters' Union; and Local 117, the Cloak Operators' Union. In March 1937, Communist cloak operators led by ILGWU civil war veteran Joseph Boruchowitz had entered into a United Front alliance with right-wingers to direct their union. In April 1938, Communists in

Local 9 passed a measure in favor of the union's participation in New York's May Day parade; the International, the Amalgamated, and the New York Socialist Party had already opted to boycott the event. Expressing their dissent, an estimated "several hundred" ILG-ers from Locals 9 and 117 marched in the parade, sponsored by the Communists' United May Day Committee. Jay Lovestone, who at this time was telling Dubinsky about Communists in the United Automobile Workers, also warned of subversion within the ILGWU.[76]

As the leader of the Communist opposition since his break with Stalin in 1929, Lovestone had initially assumed that his movement was a Communist faction at odds with the Communist International (CI). When the CI's policies changed, the faction would return to the fold. Eight years later it was apparent that reform would not occur. Stalin's control was more absolute than ever, strengthened by purges and executions, and Stalinists were attempting to create a dictatorship in Spain out of the tragedy of the civil war. Among the casualties there were Spain's Communist oppositionists. On the basis of such evidence, Lovestone jettisoned his identity as a dissident Communist and instead sought to create a new, international body of anti-Stalinist "revolutionary socialists."[77]

Lee Pressman, the Communist general counsel of the CIO, would later reminisce that a "common denominator" existed between Lovestone and Dubinsky: their "very strong anti-Communist, anti-Soviet Union position."[78] In 1937 this meeting of minds facilitated the forging of an alliance between Lovestone, who was then editor of the weekly newspaper *Workers Age,* and Dubinsky. Moreover, Lovestone's followers, such as Charles Zimmerman and Louis Nelson of Locals 22 and 155, respectively, were among the most effective deterrents to the rise of Stalinist influence within the International.[79]

The Communists' problems within the ILGWU began with Dubinsky. As Socialist intellectual Gus Tyler, who came to the International in 1934 by way of Local 91, the Children's Dressmakers, would recall, "Dubinsky understood Communists . . . he really understood them." He could identify with those who toppled the czar.[80] "He fought the Communists like crazy. He was the ultimate Communist-hater in the labor movement."[81]

Another obstacle and concern the Communists faced was the racial and ethnic makeup of the International. The left-wingers concluded that the ILGWU's "many nationalities" had "specific problems" and tailored their appeals accordingly. By 1935, Communists were exceptionally visible in Harlem. In March a riot erupted on 125th Street, fueled by an erroneous report that a young black shoplifter had been beaten to death. The mayhem cost four blacks their lives and $350,000 in property damage. Turning the tragedy to their advantage, Communist Party officials called attention to the dreadful living conditions in Harlem and gained black recruits for their organization.[82]

In contrast, black ILG-ers were not generally attracted to Communism. By organizing blacks during the 1920s and regularly taking public positions in support of civil rights, the International effectively blunted the appeal of the Communists. In 1934 the ILGWU had made headlines by changing convention hotels in protest against racial discrimination in Chicago, and the next year the union assisted in the founding of the Negro Labor Committee (NLC) in Harlem. The brainchild of ILGWU organizer Frank Crosswaith, the NLC encouraged blacks to unionize. Typical of the public attitudes of the International were four resolutions adopted by its 1937 convention. One pledged "full co-operation" with the NLC and moral and financial support for it, and the other three called for action against racial exclusion and discrimination in the labor movement and elsewhere in society. On behalf of the convention's black delegates, Winifred Gittens of Local 22 expressed "appreciation" to Dubinsky and the ILGWU for the "opportunity" they were given "to find our place in the ranks of our class and to share in the benefits, duties and responsibilities of trade union life in America."[83]

Black and Puerto Rican garment workers who had been organized in recent years were pleased to be laboring under decent conditions and regarded as full-fledged unionists. Nevertheless, it was evident that black labor was not equally distributed among the various crafts. As Maida Springer Kemp, who began a long ILGWU career by joining Local 22 in 1933, would recall, blacks were concentrated at the lower levels of the garment trade. "There were very few cutters and there was exclusion. . . . If you were white, you got a chance. But if you were Negro, you didn't get a chance, it was very hard." Furthermore, the International was not inclined to remedy this situation. "The union . . . was a closed corporation."[84]

There was no shortage of black labor. By 1930, New York City's population was 4.7 percent black, but that of Manhattan was 12 percent.[85] Among the ILGWU locals were significant discrepancies. Of 128,275 ILGWU members in Manhattan in 1935, 6,260, or 4.9 percent, were black. There were only two blacks among the 8,500 cutters of Local 10, less than 1 percent, but five hundred among the 1,500 truck drivers and helpers of Local 102, or 33.3 percent, and seven hundred among the 4,500 dress and waist pressers of Local 60, or 15.6 percent. Of the 30,000 dressmakers in Zimmerman's Local 22, 3,000, or 10 percent, were black.[86]

If black members of the ILGWU tended to be indifferent to Communism, the union's much larger Italian American population was even hostile. Italian anti-Communism within the ILGWU dated back to the 1920s, long before the Dubinsky era. Though Jewish domination of the International had long irked Italians, they had built locals of their own and allied with their top officers against what they perceived as their common Communist enemy. In the 1920s, Italian ILG-ers also developed a strong sense of loyalty to Local 48's Salvatore Ninfo and Local 89's Luigi Antonini. As Charles A. Zappia has written, "it was not simply that Antonini and Ninfo were union leaders, they were also community leaders —*uomi rispettati,*" to whom was accorded Old World–style "honor, respect, and deference."[87]

Though Ninfo would remain on the GEB of the ILGWU until 1945, Antonini had succeeded him as first vice president in 1934 and emerged as a force in the ILGWU as well as a leading anti-Fascist. Interested in preserving his place in the International, Antonini kept his ethnic constituents in check, and, respecting Dubinsky's power, he never vied for the presidency.[88]

Nothing, it seemed, could close the breach between Dubinsky and Lewis, which greatly exacerbated the already delicate relationship between the ILGWU and the CIO. For the International to continue to deny it planned to withdraw, it had to present some evidence of cooperation. With Dubinsky seen as siding with the AFL on the cause of the conference failure, he was compelled to occupy the high ground of principle, lest he be drowned in a flood of accusations of treason.

Even before the breakdown, the CIO had moved forward and established state and local governing bodies known as Industrial Union Councils. Organized parallel to already existing AFL bodies, these councils were formed to deal with such matters as labor legislation, unemployment, and the enforcement of the labor laws. In addition, they would coordinate union activities and educate and counsel the rank and file. On January 3, 1938, CIO regional director Allan S. Haywood asked Dubinsky to endorse the creation of a council in New York City.

Dubinsky replied coyly, suggesting "considerable discussion" was necessary before he could decide. Avoiding conflict, Dubinsky finally acquiesced but kept his personal distance as two ILGWU vice presidents, Zimmerman and Hochman, appeared to help Haywood. On January 21 representatives of thirty-four CIO organizations met at ILGWU Joint Board headquarters and reportedly agreed to set up a New York council.[89]

The news did not thrill William Green. He called the CIO venture in New York a "splitting matter," designed to embarrass Dubinsky by contradicting his peacemaking efforts. Rebutting the criticism, Zimmerman said that Green was the divisive party, having previously ordered the unions represented at the meeting expelled from the AFL's Central Trades and Labor Council in New York City.[90]

On February 8 the ILGWU seemed to reverse itself during a meeting of its General Executive Board. No doubt wary of Green, none of the three ILG-ers involved in the council planning—Dubinsky, Zimmerman, and Hochman—wanted the council established at the moment. Furthermore, they had actually been attempting to delay its formation. The next day Dubinsky instructed the managers of all ILGWU locals in New York City "to take no action" on a call by Haywood to organize it.[91]

This delaying tactic only added to the ILGWU–CIO friction. Moreover, instead of being free to promote conciliation, Dubinsky was mired in endless controversy over the failed conference. That none of the other CIO peace negotiators shared his interpretation caused obvious stress. Transport Workers Union president Michael J. Quill cautioned "certain leaders" who were "making advances without consulting their membership" to cease immediately "because the CIO will remain one body."[92]

By April 1938 the International Ladies' Garment Workers' Union, less than three years earlier a proud co-founder of the Committee for Industrial Organization, was on the verge of withdrawing from it. As the CIO was moving toward becoming an independent federation, the ILGWU was left with two choices: continued affiliation or independence. Reconciliation with the AFL was not yet politically viable; it would have been viewed as tangible evidence of the ILGWU's consorting with the enemy. John L. Lewis began the month by calling for a meeting of the CIO in Washington on the twelfth. Apprehensive that the meeting would lead to a convention to form a permanent organization, Dubinsky made it known that he would not attend. Hochman would take his place, and the International would not "go along" with a decision for the CIO to become permanent.[93] The meeting began by establishing vice presidencies, to be held by Hillman and Murray, and four standing committees, including one on housing to be chaired by the absent Dubinsky.[94]

Meanwhile, back in New York, Dubinsky denied that the ILGWU was about to bolt the CIO but again decried the failure of peace negotiations. The next day the heads of thirty-eight unions voted to meet in convention to create a permanent organization. Hochman abstained.[95] Dubinsky then commented that the decision had created "a new situation" that his GEB would consider and declined the honor of chairing the housing committee. Such a committee, he told Lewis, could not function effectively without representation by the AFL building-trades unions, and he could not "presume to represent them."[96]

Dubinsky's independent attitude irked Lewis but encouraged the AFL leaders, who hoped he would return with his union. Accordingly, the Executive Council made an exception of the ILGWU as it revoked the charters of all other CIO affiliates.[97] Perhaps embarrassed by this special treatment, ILG leaders again asked for labor peace. On May 27, the GEB appointed a committee of three, Antonini, Nagler, and Hochman, to explore opportunities to resume the peace conference at the point where it had ended. At the same time, the ILG-ers avoided a decision on participating in a convention to make the CIO permanent. They said they would wait until such a meeting was "actually called."[98]

At long last, Allan Haywood called a convention for September 15 to set up a CIO Industrial Council in New York State. He even invited Dubinsky to address it.[99] Haywood's call arrived at a terrible time to enlist ILGWU cooperation. The International and three other major unions had just announced their withdrawal from the Los Angeles Industrial Union Council.[100] Led by CIO Pacific Coast director Harry Bridges, Communists allegedly committed numerous misdeeds, which included the selection of organizers who "were not appointed on merit but on Party affiliation."[101] Breaking away from Bridges but not from the CIO, the Ladies' Garment Workers, United Rubber Workers, United Automobile Workers, and United Shoe Workers afterward created an anti-Communist Los Angeles Trade Union Conference.[102]

In New York, Dubinsky responded to Haywood with silence. Dubinsky's lack of cooperation had already helped prevent the founding of a CIO council for the city. Now he was not about to welcome a state council, which would compete directly with the AFL's New York State Federation of Labor. On August 31 the New York members of the GEB decided that the state locals should not participate on September 15.[103] Though the Communist question was troublesome, the primary factor separating the ILGWU from the CIO was Dubinsky's break with Lewis. On August 12, Dubinsky sent letters to William Green and John L. Lewis to make appointments for them to meet individually with the ILGWU peacemaking committee of Luigi Antonini, Isidore Nagler, and Julius Hochman. On August 22, at Atlantic City, the committee met with Green, who reaffirmed his (and Dubinsky's) understanding of the December failure and said "the Executive Council would be ready to resume conferences with the CIO at the point where they left off." In Washington the next day, accompanied by Dubinsky, the committee met with Lewis, who had requested his presence. Accompanying Lewis were four other CIO-ers, including director John Brophy and counsel Lee Pressman. Lewis, like Green, refused to give ground, and the committee would eventually report "that it had failed in its mission." Columnists Drew Pearson and Robert S. Allen reported that Lewis had "told Dubinsky he was welcome to jump the C.I.O. reservation at any time."[104]

In retrospect, the separation of Dubinsky from Lewis appears to have been inevitable. What might have reconciled at least some of their differences was an intermediary with the ability and desire to serve as peacemaker. Sidney Hillman was potentially such a person, but in mid-1938 he, too, angered Dubinsky. The American Labor Party as well as the CIO would suffer as the Dubinsky-Hillman relationship deteriorated.

On June 17, Senator Royal S. Copeland of New York suddenly died. Hours after Copeland's funeral, Governor Herbert Lehman announced his candidacy for the now vacant Senate seat. Lehman's statement alarmed supporters of Mayor La Guardia. Already antagonistic to the governor for allegedly shortchanging New York City financially, they wanted La Guardia to run for the Senate. Tied to both potential rivals, the American Labor Party was in the middle and conceivably could decide the fall election with its endorsement. Speculation on its choice reached across the country and included Sidney Hillman and David Dubinsky.[105]

Always controversial, the Labor Party was subject to numerous influences. Like the CIO, it welcomed Communists, of the Lovestoneite as well as the Stalinist variety. Lovestoneites and Socialists hoped to separate the Labor Party from the Stalinists, while the latter sought to retain its Popular Front complexion. As these groups feuded with one another, Alex Rose, the party's executive secretary and chief tactician, whose goal was to support the New Deal while remaining independent of the Democrats, increasingly determined its direction.

The ALP was pro-CIO as well as left-wing, a combination sure to provoke a hostile reaction by the AFL. In March 1938, William Green asked all AFL affiliates to cut their connections with it. The following month President George Meany asked the same of the unions in the New York State Federation of Labor. Under such strong attack, the ALP appeared to be on the wane.[106]

On June 20 the ALP's leaders met to plan the fall campaign. At stake besides the Copeland vacancy were Robert F. Wagner's full senatorial term and Lehman's seat in Albany. When Lehman said he wanted to serve the final two years of Copeland's term, some Democrats as well as Labor Party people had reservations. In 1937 the governor had opposed President Roosevelt's proposal to reform the U.S. Supreme Court by enlarging it.[107] Now it was just possible that FDR did not want him in the Senate.

What raised eyebrows was a story in the *New York World-Telegram* that Hillman, backed by the White House, was the tentative Labor Party choice for the two-year Senate term. Alex Rose would later recall this story as a product of the imagination of a reporter whom he had "jokingly" told that Hillman would be a Senate candidate. When that information appeared in print, Rose said, Hillman called and offered to meet him for lunch at the Plaza Hotel. Rose welcomed the meeting as an opportunity to tell Hillman the truth about the story, but when the two met the latter revealed that he actually was interested in the seat, and he claimed to have Roosevelt's support. At the Plaza, Hillman then asked Rose to be his campaign manager. As Rose would later recall, he replied that he would do what he could. Regarding "the whole thing," which had begun "as a little joke," as "so ludicrous," Rose "couldn't wait" to run over to tell Dubinsky "the comedy."

Recuperating from hemorrhoidal surgery, Dubinsky was at Mt. Sinai Hospital when Rose told him. Dubinsky "laughed so hard," according to Rose, that a nurse had to caution him to restrain himself lest he break his stitches. After his visit, Rose told the press Hillman was well qualified but declined to commit himself on his candidacy. When reporters asked Dubinsky's opinion, he offered none. He said the policy committee of the ALP would make a decision on the nomination.

The developing story was no laughing matter to Hillman, who requested a meeting of the policy committee while trying, unsuccessfully, to contact FDR, who was away from Washington. At the meeting, Hillman charged that Dubinsky and Antonini had spoken out against him and in favor of Lehman. Schlesinger denied the allegation, insisting that the nomination was up to the policy committee but failing to persuade Hillman.[108] Pressing for representation on a coalition ticket with the Democrats, Rose and the ALP-ers kept his name alive, suggesting it along with several others, including Dubinsky's. "I am not a candidate for any office," Dubinsky said.[109]

As the head of the largest union behind the American Labor Party, Dubinsky commanded respect, but a senatorial candidacy was extremely improbable. Regarding the Hillman "boom," Dubinsky's ally Abraham Cahan was an ideal person to neutralize it. Cahan declared that Hillman's candidacy would wreck the Labor Party by appearing to justify the charge that the party was a tool of the CIO. Stepping into deeper water, Cahan charged that Hillman was too close to the Communists. Dubinsky himself adopted a statesman-like pose, refraining from criticism of Hillman. He attacked the ALP's snub of Lehman, calling it "very regrettable" that this "stanch and sincere friend of labor, with an admirable labor record" was overlooked. On the AFL side, George Meany exploited the situation by endorsing the governor, to whom he said the New York State Federation of Labor had "always been very friendly."[110]

Two developments finally ended Hillman's candidacy. On July 5 he conferred with Roosevelt and Farley, resulting in a decision to withdraw, and the next day Luigi Antonini publicly called for a Labor Party endorsement of Lehman for senator. The stage was now set for the ALP to join with the Democrats on a state ticket of Representative James Mead of Buffalo for the Copeland Senate term, Robert F. Wagner for reelection to the Senate, and Lehman for reelection as governor.[111]

When Sidney Hillman actually considered making a Senate race, he stirred the fires of envy in David Dubinsky, who no longer regarded the idea as humorous. Thanks to Abraham Cahan, Dubinsky rediscovered an old weapon, anti-Communism, that could be aimed at his needle-trades rival. Already displeased by Lewis's intimacy with Communists in the CIO, Dubinsky found Hillman similarly engaged in the ALP, which would provide the basis for a permanent breach in the Labor Party. Hillman's relationship with FDR, too close for Dubinsky's comfort, translated into influence. In September 1938, a word from Hillman would result in Roosevelt canceling a White House appointment with Dubinsky.[112] During Dubinsky's hospitalization, Hillman sent flowers,[113] but when the CIO was about to lose the ILGWU, he did not stand in the way. Neither did anyone else.

The conspicuous absence of a delegation from the International Ladies' Garment Workers' Union could not keep the New York State CIO-ers from holding their convention. Meeting at Manhattan's Hotel Center, eight hundred delegates endorsed the American Labor Party, the New Deal, and the senatorial candidacy of Governor Lehman and established an Industrial Union Council. Lest they forget about the ILGWU, they heard a telegram from Charles Zimmerman, who echoed David Dubinsky and called for labor unity.[114]

Within the next few weeks, both the political and labor landscapes underwent dramatic change. New York Republicans nominated District Attorney Thomas E. Dewey for governor. An effective, hard-hitting campaigner against racketeering, corruption, and Tammany Hall, Dewey seemed a sure winner unless the Democrats fielded a strong candidate to oppose him. State Democratic leaders Ed Flynn and Jim Farley pressured Lehman to abandon his quest for a seat in the Senate. Lehman yielded, explaining that he wanted to return to Albany in order to "protect our social gains." The Democrats then nominated him, as did the American Labor Party, the latter following a stirring speech by David Dubinsky. In November, Lehman went on to defeat Dewey by fewer than 65,000 votes. Deciding the election were the nearly 420,000 votes he received as the candidate of the ALP. At the same time, Democrat James Mead won the two-year Senate seat and Democrat Robert F. Wagner reelection to a regular Senate term, both with ALP backing.[115]

The change in the labor scene would come by way of John L. Lewis. The long-awaited convention to make the CIO permanent would be held on November 14 in Pittsburgh. To decide on participation, the ILGWU's General Executive Board would meet in advance.[116] On October 25, invitations went out for a preliminary meeting of CIO presidents on November 11. As the GEB meeting had already been set for November 10 in Washington, Dubinsky said it would "not be possible" for him to attend the Pittsburgh meeting.[117] Jay Lovestone expected the GEB to vote "20–1 against going to the CIO convention."[118]

Lovestone's prediction was almost completely correct. When the GEB considered the matter, it first received the report of its three-member subcommittee on peace conferences. As expected, Antonini, Hochman, and Nagler reported failure. Then the board heatedly discussed the CIO convention. Only Zimmerman suggested sending delegates. Dubinsky said the ILGWU must state that it "would remain independent until unity is achieved" in order to demonstrate that it was not "merely awaiting the first opportunity to get back into the AFL." A resolution to that effect passed unanimously, with even Zimmerman voting for it. On November 16 the Pittsburgh convention adopted a constitution for a new federation to be called the Congress of Industrial Organizations.[119] The ILGWU and the Cloth, Hat and Cap Makers had declined to participate. Though committed to industrial unionism, Dubinsky could not accept the leadership of Lewis and Hillman and their allies on the left. He also felt discomfort with the American Labor Party, which was no longer the solid coalition that had helped reelect Franklin Roosevelt in 1936. As controversy surrounded Dubinsky, the future direction of the ILGWU, the organization for which he had primary responsibility, remained to be determined.

13

Home at Last

The experiment in industrial unionism that had begun in the fall of 1935 ended for the International Ladies' Garment Workers' Union three years later. It would have been unbearable for David Dubinsky to witness the premiere of John L. Lewis's production in Pittsburgh. ILGWU warnings against dual unionism had gone unheeded.

The ILGWU's isolation from the heart of the labor movement came at a time of increasing turmoil at home and abroad. Americans were struggling with an economic downturn that New Deal critics gleefully called the "Roosevelt recession." As the New Deal seemingly waned, it was all the more disconcerting for Dubinsky to observe Communists tied to Lewis in the CIO and Hillman in the American Labor Party.

The outlook overseas was terrifying. Fascism, Nazism, and militarism were tightening their grip on Europe and Asia. Mussolini and Hitler had helped push General Franco to victory in Spain. In Central Europe, Germany annexed Austria and the Sudetenland, a portion of Czechoslovakia. In Asia, war had already begun. Having invaded northern China the previous year, Japan appeared ready to plunge southward in 1938. In Palestine, governed by Britain under a League of Nations mandate, a Jewish population swelled by refugees from Nazi Germany was subject to outbreaks of Arab hostility. In an effort to appease Arab forces, the British issued a White Paper in 1939 that decreed a virtual end to the lawful immigration of Jews to mandate territory.

As news of these events reached the United States, friends of democracy feared the worst, and Jews felt particularly vulnerable. As a founder of the Jewish Labor Committee and an American Jew with a deep, personal concern for Jews abroad, David Dubinsky sought to assist the imperiled. But in his present situation, independent of both labor federations, he lacked the influence that accompanies affiliation.

· · ·

Understandably the ILGWU deferred reconciliation with the AFL. A return immediately after the creation of the permanent CIO would have been humiliating.[1] To explain its hesitation, the International introduced a moral factor: blatant, unchecked corruption within the Federation. "Despicable thugs" had so dirtied the AFL, David Dubinsky would allege, that the International could not identify or associate with it until it agreed to reform—all rather implausible, since the ILGWU long suffered from similar problems.

In a November 13, 1938 radio address, Dubinsky expressed friendship toward both sides, and a readiness "to assist" the cause of labor peace."[2] Lest his intentions be questioned, in December the ILGWU published a documentary record of its positions since 1934 in the controversy over industrial unionism. The first "white paper" ever published by a trade union, it revealed, as one editorial observed, a "lonely and uncomfortable" situation.[3]

Beginning in December 1938, the Roosevelt administration orchestrated its own campaign for reconciliation, directing Secretary of Labor Frances Perkins to initiate efforts to resume CIO-AFL negotiations. The potential benefits for the president were several: inject life into a waning New Deal, demonstrate a united America in the face of war threats from abroad, and unite the Democrats on the eve of the 1940 elections, when FDR might just run for an unprecedented third presidential term.

There were private talks between FDR, William Green, and John L. Lewis, meetings of other CIO and AFL representatives, and well-publicized presidential letters to Green and Lewis. On March 7, with Roosevelt looking on, negotiations resumed in the White House, but on April 5, after a month of renewed deadlock, they collapsed. For several months afterward, FDR would attempt without success to revive them.[4]

The alienation of the ILGWU from the CIO deepened, and without the common bond of CIO membership, not much remained to reconcile the personal differences between Dubinsky and Sidney Hillman. The two presidents and their organizations still sustained the American Labor Party, but with only a fraction of the unity they had displayed in founding it. In 1939 the ILGWU became entangled in a nasty jurisdictional dispute with the Amalgamated Clothing Workers, and Dubinsky saw the specter of Communism rising in the ALP, UAW, and even his own Local 10.[5] By May 1939, several ILGWU locals and joint boards from the East Coast to as far west as Winnipeg had complained that the Amalgamated had taken shops from the International by offering employers longer work weeks and lower wages.[6]

The rash of ILGWU-ACWA jurisdictional disputes eventually produced open conflict. Local 91, angered by the loss of shops to the ACWA, called a strike against William I. Nathan, a New York City manufacturer of mannish women's clothing, which it then retook from the ACWA.[7] Protesting a loss of twenty-five shops in the bathrobe industry, Local 91 members picketed in front of the Amalgamated's general offices at Union Square.

Both Dubinsky and Hillman initially distanced themselves from direct, public involvement in this dispute.[8] But *New York Herald Tribune* reporter Paul Tobenkin predicted that "a growing friction" between the International and the Amalgamated "would lead to the disruption of the American Labor Party and the return of the ILGWU to the AFL, the latter to occur in 1940. Tobenkin expected "a resounding break in the long silence" maintained by Dubinsky and Hillman over their differences.[9]

Harry Greenberg, manager-secretary of ILGWU Local 91, took his campaign against the Amalgamated directly to Hillman. In an open letter, he charged the ACWA with "flagrant violation of trade union jurisdiction."[10] Before the conflict erupted, Greenberg had unsuccessfully attempted to persuade Jacob Potofsky and Hillman to arrange a meeting of the latter with Dubinsky to reconcile differences.[11]

Convinced of Hillman and Potofsky's culpability, Dubinsky entered the controversy. In a speech on August 17, he endorsed Greenberg's letter to Hillman. Four days later ILG-ers again picketed the ACWA.[12]

If indeed the Amalgamated had declared war, Hillman was reluctant to acknowledge it. Publicly silent on Dubinsky's remarks, he let an official statement in the ACWA's newspaper, *The Advance*, explain the union's position, which was that it had "no quarrel" with the ILGWU in the bathrobe trade.[13]

Though the Amalgamated's statement maintained a civil tone, the conflict between the sister unions was genuine and occurring at a perilous point in time. In New York the two most important components of the Jewish labor movement were fighting over jurisdiction, while in Europe war with Nazi Germany appeared imminent. Adolph Held, the president of the Amalgamated Bank and chairman of the Jewish Labor Committee, invited the ACWA and ILGWU to meet to settle their differences.[14] The two unions conferred in September but failed to reach an accord. In November, the ILGWU's GEB declared that the Amalgamated was "waging open warfare."[15]

Hillman declined comment,[16] and negotiations resumed in December. In March the unions at last agreed "to respect" existing jurisdictions and to resolve between themselves future problems of overlapping.[17] Calm was restored, but the illusion of needle-trades unity had been shattered.

The diplomatic marriage of Hitler and Stalin occurred in 1939 when, on August 23, Germany and the Soviet Union signed a ten-year nonaggression treaty. On September 1, German troops invaded Poland. On the sixteenth of the month, Soviet forces seized the rest of that country.

The destruction of Poland and threat to East European Jewry struck at the heart of David Dubinsky. With much of his family in that land, Dubinsky had continued to worry about them and other Jews. Intense anti-Semitism in Poland had made life extremely difficult even before the Nazi invasion. As early as February 1937, Dubinsky had lamented that the Labor Chest concerned itself with problems in Germany and Spain but neglected Poland. And differences within the American labor movement prevented the Labor Chest from functioning as effectively as it should have.[18]

The American Labor Party already was experiencing turbulence as it tried to deal with the European situation. The ALP refrained from taking action until President Roosevelt introduced legislation to repeal the embargo on munitions to belligerents. When FDR acted, the State Executive Committee gave its complete support through a resolution denouncing the Nazi-Soviet pact and calling the American Communist Party "betrayers of the labor movement, antagonists of democracy and protagonists of dictatorship." A vote of 605 to 94 by a citywide conference of the ALP then ratified the resolution. In addition, it moved to expel the Communists from its ranks. The State Executive Committee made endorsement of the resolution the "acid test," as Alex Rose described it, for running on the ALP ticket.

Though the right wing of the ALP seemed in control, as the April 1940 primary approached the Left seemed unbowed. Organized as the Progressive Committee to Rebuild the American Labor Party, the left-wingers remained cause for considerable right-wing consternation. This committee included the heads of the Newspaper Guild, Printers Union, and National Maritime Union, none of which had affiliated with the ALP. Yet, as Alex Rose reported in January, the group wanted to rid the Labor Party of all its non-Communist unions.[19]

An active participant in the primary campaign, Dubinsky rallied anti-Communist support. He argued that a left-wing victory might result in the ALP becoming "a Communist sideshow." The alternative was up to those voters who wanted "to maintain the ALP as an instrument for carrying on the New Deal." On the radio just before the election, Dubinsky vividly described his enemies as a "band of Stalinists" who wanted to make the ALP "another Communist front, another tail to the bloody Moscow kite."[20]

The conservative ALP forces won the primary, running strongly upstate and in Brooklyn and the Bronx and retaining control of the State Executive Committee. But the future direction of the ALP was not yet certain. Furthermore, the party was $25,000 in debt.[21]

Within the Labor Party's left wing were many ILG-ers, who remained concentrated in a few unions. Locals 9 and 117, the Ladies' Tailors' and Finishers' Union, and the Cloak and Suit Finishers' Union, respectively, were under Stalinist direction, while Locals 22 and 155, the Dressmakers' Union and Knitgoods Workers Union, were Lovestoneite-led. A left-wing presence surfaced even in Local 10, the Cutters' Union.

After heading the Cloak Joint Board for a decade, Isidore Nagler sought to replace Samuel Perlmutter as manager of the cutters. In the election campaign that followed, the radical Cutters Rank and File Committee participated, choosing their own ticket but also endorsing Nagler and Louis Stulberg, who ran for general business manager. Nagler and Stulberg repudiated the committee's endorsement and, in February 1939, won election. Though the radicals lost the four major races, their candidates for president and vice president both finished second.[22]

Sharing Dubinsky's aversion to Stalinists, Charles Zimmerman increasingly found himself in alignment with his president. The Nazi-Soviet pact brought the two leaders even closer. When Zimmerman joined Dubinsky, Abraham Cahan, Louis Waldman, Norman Thomas, and others in condemning it, Stalinist patience ended. The Tenth Assembly District of the Communist Party denounced them as "reactionaries."[23]

With Franklin Roosevelt's possible third presidential race ever closer, labor unity became a more serious White House priority. At the end of February 1939, FDR publicly wrote to Green and Lewis to "end the breach" and negotiate "peace with honor." Dubinsky, however, believed the labor split was "far too big for any one individual to solve."[24]

For a while the presidential initiative seemed to be ineffective. Green quickly rejected Lewis's proposal for a new federation, the American Congress of Labor, in which neither he or Green would be an officer. Nor would Green give a direct answer to Lewis's question of whether the AFL would welcome back the CIO unions as they were presently structured. Lewis broke off the talks, which even FDR could not afterward revive. Exacerbating the situation, on July 31, Lewis proclaimed that the CIO would challenge the AFL's monopoly over the building trades with a newly created Construction Workers Organizing Committee (CWOC). By the fall of 1939, the outlook for peace had dimmed again.[25]

While observing the peace process from afar, Dubinsky interpreted it for the ILGWU's General Executive Board, declaring that a settlement depended on Lewis.[26] Later that month the GEB met in Washington and unanimously adopted a resolution Dubinsky had prepared for its approval. In anticipation of the ILGWU's May 1940 convention, the GEB resolved that if peace were "not accomplished by that time," the triennial meeting would determine the question of the International's "continued independence or affiliation with the AFL."[27] Having hinted broadly at a return, the International planned its fortieth anniversary convention in New York.[28]

Before the ILGWU's meeting, Dubinsky arranged the conditions of its return to the AFL. He first met with William Green and then Matthew Woll, advising them of "the three chief obstacles . . . in the way." Each was a problem because it violated a basic principle. The first was a one-cent per capita assessment the Federation had levied in May 1937 in order to finance its struggle with the CIO. Long on record in favor of labor peace, the ILGWU would not finance warfare and hence demanded the revocation of the assessment. The second obstacle concerned the continuing constitutional question over the Executive Council's suspension of unions between conventions. Dubinsky and the CIO had argued since 1936 that the EC had no power to suspend. Now Dubinsky insisted that his objection be accepted. The final question related to racketeering. The immigrants who built the ILGWU had fought czarism, capitalism, and gangsterism; they now asked the Federation to take steps to depose corrupt leaders within its affiliates.[29]

Though Green and Dubinsky had discussed racketeering in advance of the ILGWU convention, the latter's report to the AFL Executive Council was silent on the matter. If he had brought it before the EC, the furor it would have created might have jeopardized the ILGWU's homecoming. What Green did say was that Dubinsky and the International were very favorably disposed to reconciliation. Dubinsky presented to the EC only two conditions for the ILGWU's return, the abolition of both the one-cent assessment and the power of the Executive Council to suspend affiliates between conventions. He proposed converting the assessment into a tax. Added to the AFL's existing one-cent tax, the second penny would provide the Federation with sufficient operating funds and could not be accused of being "for the purpose of making war on the CIO." EC action on the suspension of unions, Dubinsky said, "would have a good psychological effect and remove a lot of criticism." Without debate the Executive Council gave Green "such authority as is necessary to be helpful" to bring back the ILGWU.[30]

With a huge crowd expected, the International chose Madison Square Garden for its opening-day sessions, which began on May 27. Dubinsky delivered a lengthy address touching upon the ILGWU's achievements and place in the labor movement. After frankly stating that "isolation" was not a "permanent solution for our Union," he acknowledged the "strong sentiment in our ranks to rejoin the American Federation of Labor." Then he listed the three obstacles to reaffiliation: the one-cent assessment, the right of suspension, and the AFL's permissiveness toward disreputable individuals within its unions. These hurdles, he said, kept the International, "at least for the present," from returning.[31]

On Tuesday, June 4, the GEB met to consider reaffiliation. After first describing the three prerequisites, Dubinsky produced a letter he had arranged for Green to send him in response. The Federation president compromised on two of the points but omitted mention of the question of local autonomy. The power to suspend, Green said, would be presented to the next AFL convention to be granted "exclusively" to conventions. On a motion to reaffiliate, the twenty-two board members split virtually down the center, with Isidore Nagler casting the deciding vote in favor. For the record, the vote was made unanimous.

The next day the resolutions committee reported to the convention that it had received forty-two resolutions on the question of reaffiliation. Twenty-five favored reaffiliation with the AFL, sixteen called for continued independence, and one requested CIO affiliation. Then the committee dropped its bombshell, the letter from Green to Dubinsky, which resulted in a recommendation "that the ILGWU rejoin the AFL."

The vote was 640 in favor of reaffiliation and 12 opposed. The vote, Dubinsky said, demonstrated a "conflict between the Communist party and the interest of our Union."

One item of unfinished business remained—the question of labor racketeering. Annoyed at the AFL's still cavalier attitude, and believing the ILGWU should take a stronger position on the subject, Emil Schlesinger approached Dubinsky with a suggestion that ILGWU delegates to the next AFL convention be armed with a "meaningful" resolution on racketeering. Dubinsky approved the suggestion and asked Schlesinger to draft a resolution.

His statement cut directly to the heart of the AFL's impotence. It asked that the Executive Council, "or any other authorized agency, have summary power to order" unions to remove "any person or persons convicted for any offense involving moral turpitude or convicted of using their official positions in their unions for personal gain." In addition, the resolution required the constitutions of AFL unions to "contain appropriate provisions for adequate disciplinary action against" crooked officers, and the AFL to "use its full moral force to compel the filing of charges and the holding of a hearing." On June 5 the convention unanimously adopted the resolution.

Along with arranging to send a letter to the ILGWU convention, William Green had agreed to address the convention once it approved reaffiliation.[32] Green arrived on June 6. "It was pandemonium in that hall. But it was a joyous occasion," Leon Stein would recall, as Green returned to Dubinsky the original charter the ILGWU had received in 1900.[33]

The homecoming to the Federation, though cloaked in principle, was also facilitated by extraordinary events at home and abroad. In April 1940, Germany invaded Norway and Denmark, and then Belgium, Luxembourg, and the Netherlands in May. German troops advanced on several fronts, but the greatest shock to the United States occurred on June 14 and 22, when Paris and then much of France fell to them. The Battle of Britain soon followed, with the Royal Air Force dueling the German *Luftwaffe* over the English Channel.

As the 1940 presidential election approached, President Roosevelt broke with tradition and opted for a third term. Overriding all putative issues was the potential involvement of the United States in the foreign conflict. FDR's new running mate was Secretary of Agriculture Henry A.

Wallace, replacing the more conservative incumbent vice president, John Nance Garner. Also passed over for the second spot was John L. Lewis. Though a Republican and an isolationist, Lewis wanted the vice presidency, regarding it as due recognition of labor support he had mustered for FDR in 1936. It was a slight he bitterly resented. As Lewis watched his relations with Roosevelt deteriorate, he saw Hillman's grow closer. In May 1940, FDR appointed the ACWA president to a new, seven-member National Defense Advisory Commission to overview defense production. At odds with both Roosevelt and Hillman, Lewis endorsed Wendell Willkie for president and pledged to resign as head of the CIO if he lost.

In 1940, Lewis's view on Roosevelt's foreign policy coincided closely with the Communists'. Seizing the opportunity to exploit this harmony of opinion, Dubinsky said the CIO chieftains who supported Lewis were themselves Communists or connected to Communists. To rid the labor movement of Lewis, Dubinsky urged a redoubling of unionists' efforts on behalf of FDR. On November 5, Roosevelt won a third term by five million votes. Afterward the ILGWU president gloated over the failure of Lewis's attempted "betrayal" of the American worker.[34]

The delegates who assembled at New Orleans for the AFL's sixtieth convention were pleased with FDR's victory but unsure of what to expect at their own affair. Dubinsky and his ILGWU delegation were present to submit their resolution on racketeering, with friction between them and Federation traditionalists a certainty.[35] Expecting the confrontation, the Executive Council addressed the question. Its report to the convention conceded that the Federation had been "penetrated" by individuals who had "been influenced by criminal instincts." However, the EC condemned "racketeering, gangsterism and disregard for law" and observed that "the millions" of AFL members were "honest, sincere, law-abiding citizens." The Federation's unions were "autonomous organizations," and their members should choose leaders of "character, . . . honesty and integrity" and reject "those with criminal records."[36]

Although the ILGWU resolution got a strong hearing at the convention, it failed to pass. Deftly diluting the proposal, the resolutions committee kept it from empowering the AFL to remove corrupt officials. The EC now would be authorized to use "all of its influence" to act against wrongdoers, with local unions asked to revise their constitutions to make such action possible. The defeated ILGWU had little choice but to accept this compromise. However, in one last gesture of defiance, when the convention voted to reelect George E. Browne as twelfth vice president,

Charles Zimmerman rose to announce that the ILGWU was abstaining. Browne, whose indictment and conviction for extortion would soon occur, was unanimously reelected to the Executive Council.[37]

Despite having to accept a compromise, the International returned home with its head held high. Even the weak antiracketeering resolution moved the Federation in the right direction. By mending fences with William Green, Dubinsky further antagonized John L. Lewis, whose ire flared at the CIO convention in Atlantic City, also in November. Lewis alleged that Dubinsky, who had sworn "he would never waver" from the CIO, "crept back into" the AFL "on his adversary's terms. He is crying out now and his voice laments like that of Rachel in the wilderness, against the racketeers and the panderers and the crooks in that organization."[38]

The failure of movements to draft Lewis for the CIO presidency or organize an opposition group around Hillman resulted in the unanimous election of Lewis's handpicked successor, Philip Murray.[39] Beyond the reach of Lewis, Dubinsky was back with Green and Woll, his past allies in foreign as well as domestic causes. Late in 1940, with Hitler's shadow spread across Western Europe, Dubinsky could gain satisfaction from his renewed relationship with friends who seemed to share his concerns, especially the plight of Europe's Jews.

14

War on Two Fronts

The prosperous ILGWU of the early 1940s bore little resemblance to the virtually bankrupt organization that David Dubinsky had come to lead in 1932. With close to a quarter of a million members and a solvent treasury, it commanded respect and wielded influence. At work from early morning to late at night—just about married to the union—Dubinsky kept it all under control. Without losing face the International had returned to the Federation, and he had become the face of independent, progressive unionism.

The ILGWU's expansion also meant continued ethnic change, especially since proportionately fewer women's clothing jobs were created in New York during the 1930s. By 1941 "only 39 percent of all garment workers" were employed in the city as numerous employers had moved to lower-wage sites. Not far from New York there was a plentiful labor supply, a consequence of declines in the anthracite coal industry of northeast Pennsylvania and the cotton textile industry of southeast Massachusetts.[1]

By 1940 about 75 percent of the garment workers in New York were Jewish, but Jews accounted for only 25 percent of the total membership of the International. About 70 percent of the 25,000 members of Local 22 were Jewish, but the 33,000 members of Local 89 made the majority of the dressmakers of Italian ethnicity.[2]

As the thirties ended, the ILGWU continued to have a small but significant black and Spanish-speaking membership. Nearly 10 percent of Local 22's dressmakers were black and 7 percent Latin American.[3] Will Herberg, the local's educational director, would later note that though race prejudice was "regarded as a high crime" in the union, it was "by no means absent from the shops."[4]

At the International's 1937 convention, it adopted three resolutions against discrimination. The first two condemned discrimination in the labor movement in general, both attacking "jim-crowism" and calling for "complete equality" of the races. The third mandated that the ILGWU instruct all its locals "to actively participate in the struggle against Negro discrimination."[5] Again, in 1940, the convention condemned the broad pattern of racial discrimination in the South, covering such areas as employment, housing, legal protection, and suffrage and demanding the abolition of segregation laws, lynchings, and poll taxes.[6]

Even in the North, reality sometimes failed to live up to the ideal of equality. In Chicago there were complaints that racial bias impeded organizing efforts. In 1933 the Chicago branch of the National Urban League had begun to organize the black women who worked in the Sopkin housedress factory "and sought to have the ILGWU accept them as members." But an ILGWU local rejected them, the Urban League felt, for "patently anti-Negro" reasons. By 1937 the ILGWU wanted the women, but the civil rights group was now opposed. Nevertheless, the International signed them up, and in March they went on strike. While they picketed they sang spirituals with labor lyrics and were visited by Dubinsky. Three months later they won. Subsequently, the ILGWU had to mend fences with the Urban League, which organizer Abraham Plotkin had accused of attempted strike-breaking.[7]

Despite this affair, the International's relations with blacks remained, at least on the surface, exceptional. At its 1940 convention, Frank Crosswaith showered praise. "Here is one organization of labor," he said, "in which the color of a man's skin, or the religion he professes, or his sex, mean but very little." "Coming from an abused and exploited race," David Dubinsky commented, "he [Crosswaith] knows that in our ranks we all enjoy equality."[8]

In 1940 the American Labor Party again assisted Roosevelt's reelection. The 417,418 votes cast in New York State on the ALP line gave him a margin of 224,440 over Willkie. The campaign concluded with the right-wingers still in command of the party, but not by much.[9] As Kenneth Waltzer has written, the leftists, based mainly in New York City and tied to the CIO, "usually, if not always, took their lead from the Communist line."[10]

Dissension resurfaced at the beginning of the 1941 New York City mayoral race. Early in June, Communists threatened to challenge Fiorello La Guardia in the party primary scheduled for September.[11] La Guardia strongly believed that the United States should aid the anti-Nazi cause in

Europe, but on June 22 that ceased to be a problem, because Nazi troops invaded the Soviet Union. Eager to save Mother Russia, American Communists now agreed that the United States should mobilize its resources against Hitler.[12]

Overnight, Communist opposition to La Guardia evaporated, and at an ALP conference in New York, the right-wingers booed the leftists and drafted him for a third term. Dubinsky, a spokesman for the rightists, explained, "We want to support those fighting Hitler, but this does not mean that we will stop fighting the Communist line in America."[13]

Though the right wing of the Labor Party had its way with the major nominations during the campaign of 1941, leftists continued to control the New York county committee. After a bitter altercation in early October, the right-wingers bolted a meeting, calling the committee "an outlaw organization." After the right-wingers departed, the meeting chose City Council candidates and a new chairman, Representative Vito Marcantonio.[14] A product of East Harlem, Marcantonio was passionately committed to protecting the interests of the downtrodden, and very close to La Guardia. On La Guardia's election as mayor, Marcantonio found himself in possession of both a political machine and Republican affiliation with which to gain election to Congress in 1934.[15]

Though politically Marcantonio swung to the left of his mentor, on election night 1941 the mayor was at his side. ALP right-wing leaders who attempted to speak with La Guardia at that time were unable to make contact with him. Two weeks after the election, the press reported that the ILGWU, in cooperation with rightists in the ACWA, was threatening to quit the American Labor Party. The International did not want to bestow a "cloak of respectability" on the Communists in the party and was piqued at La Guardia for failing to assume an active role in the war against them.[16]

The International, the Amalgamated, and the Millinery Workers did indeed plan to discuss withdrawal among themselves, but a departure from the ALP would involve foreign as well as domestic considerations. Since Germany had invaded Russia, American Communists were "the most ardent supporters" of Roosevelt's defense policies, Dubinsky explained to the GEB of the ILGWU. "Undoubtedly," he reasoned, the shift of the Communists in the CIO would cause them to abandon the isolationism of John L. Lewis and align themselves with Sidney Hillman's faction. Regardless of the ILGWU's wishes, it then would "most likely be drawn into another united front position within the [American Labor]

Party." Future Labor Party membership, Dubinsky concluded, would depend on whether the International would want to join this new alignment. The GEB agreed to talk with the other needle-trades unions before making a "definite decision."[17]

On December 7, 1941, Japanese aircraft destroyed the Pacific Fleet of the United States in a surprise attack on its base at Pearl Harbor, Hawaii. The next day President Roosevelt asked Congress to declare war, which it did. On December 11, Germany and Italy declared war on the United States. Japan's attack deferred many decisions. For the ILGWU, an immediate concern was its impact on the women's clothing industry, especially the future availability of textile materials. In response to a request by Sidney Hillman, now associate director general of the Office of Production Management in Washington, Dubinsky released ILGWU Executive Secretary Fred Umhey for service in that agency. Umhey's presence might help to assure that the women's wear industries would receive an equitable share of the textile allocations. In a direct move to aid the war effort, the GEB approved a campaign for ILGWU members to "pledge and undertake the investing of $25 million in government defense bonds."[18]

Perhaps inevitably, reports soon surfaced that the U.S. Government was discriminating in favor of men's and against women's clothing manufacturers in the awarding of contracts to produce military uniforms. The International complained to Donald M. Nelson, the chairman of the War Production Board, who promised to remedy the situation. Dubinsky first met with Nelson and then with Hillman and finally accepted the assurances of Nelson and a committee headed by Boston department store head Louis E. Kirstein that discrimination where it existed would end, and that ILGWU shops would receive 20 percent of the production allocations for uniforms.[19]

In May 1942, Herbert Lehman announced without advance indication or consultation with other Democratic Party leaders that he would retire after four terms as governor. With the Democratic nomination now up for grabs, State Attorney General John J. Bennett Jr. and U.S. Senator James M. Mead declared their candidacy for it. Bennett, capable but colorless, had antagonized the political left by past association with the American Legion, which had supported strike-breaking, and those who supplied medical relief to the Fascist side in the Spanish Civil War. Nevertheless, he had served four terms and accumulated numerous allies, including former postmaster general James A. Farley, who had opposed a third term for Roosevelt and thus come to be bitterly at odds with the president. Mead was a Roosevelt loyalist who was elected in 1938 for the two remaining years of Royal S. Copeland's Senate term and again in 1940 for six years. Roosevelt preferred Mead, but to the dismay of the president, he could not stop Farley, who campaigned vigorously for Bennett and won the nomination for him at a raucous state party convention in Brooklyn.[20]

To Dubinsky, the Bennett-Farley combination reeked of clubhouse politics, which neither he nor Alex Rose and the right wing of the American Labor Party would endorse.[21] Sidney Hillman, who was recovering from a heart attack, preferred to follow the lead of Roosevelt in this matter. Prior to the state convention, Farley had elicited from a reluctant Roosevelt a pledge to endorse Bennett if he were chosen to oppose the Republican Thomas E. Dewey. After Bennett's nomination by the Democrats, the president urged Hillman to persuade the Labor Party to fall in line.[22]

Dubinsky and Rose would not cooperate. Instead they offered the Labor Party nomination to Adolf Berle, but he declined, causing them to turn to Manhattan lawyer Dean Alfange, who accepted. Of Greek ancestry, though born in Turkey, Alfange had immigrated to the United States in his infancy. An early leader of the ALP, he was closely associated with immigrant groups. As Alfange would later recall, his 1942 campaign was financed mainly by the ILGWU, organized by "chief strategist" Alex Rose, and run to achieve two objectives sought by Dubinsky: "to punish the Democrats who refused to nominate a liberal for Governor and discredit the left wing of the ALP headed by Congressman Vito Marcantonio." "Defeat Farley by defeating Bennett," Dubinsky urged the voters on the eve of the election in a radio address.

On Election Day, November 3, Alfange received 10 percent of the vote, more than either he or Dubinsky had expected. Dewey won a 675,000-vote victory over Bennett as Alfange polled over 400,000 in running third. Dubinsky claimed the result proved "beyond any doubt" that the Labor Party was "the true political voice of labor in New York State."[23]

In fact, the Democrats were humiliated, with Bennett receiving nearly 500,000 votes less than Lehman had in 1938, and the ALP vote about the same as then. Even without Alfange in the race, Bennett would have lost. By polling nearly 18 percent of the New York City vote and 10 percent in the state, the ALP demonstrated that it could retain its following, even without Sidney Hillman and the Amalgamated.[24] As the GEB of the ILGWU later reported, Hillman and the ACWA "walked out of the ALP" in 1942.[25] They chose to follow Roosevelt rather than Dubinsky and Rose.

Recovered from the Great Depression and tired of the ideology and rhetoric of the previous decade, Americans voted Republican in greater numbers than at any time since the heyday of Herbert Hoover. The classic coalition of northern liberals and southern conservatives, which had begun to break down in 1938, was still deteriorating. Moreover, with a war economy providing work and high wages, relatively few Americans would tolerate labor militancy, especially if it threatened the war effort. At heart a member of the Roosevelt administration, Hillman continued to protect what to him seemed its best interests. A strategist whose conception of power realities extended beyond New York, he embraced the wartime alliance with the Soviet Union as well as the American Communist Party.

Dubinsky, by contrast, was unambiguous about the Soviet Union and Communism. Unlike his counterpart at the ACWA, the ILGWU president could not at the same time be pro-Soviet and anti-Communist. With unresolved conflicts between its left and right wings and its leading personalities, the American Labor Party would soon split into two distinct organizations.

As a founder and treasurer of the Jewish Labor Committee, Dubinsky remained closely attuned to the unfolding tragedy of European Jewry. With the JLC, he followed what Gus Tyler has called a "triple R" policy of "rescue, relief and resistance" to Nazism and Fascism.[26] In 1939 the Soviets had arrested two leading Polish Bundists, Henryk Erlich and Victor Alter, accusing them of plotting anti-Soviet sabotage on behalf of Polish intelligence. Six months later, in May 1940, a worse fate seemed to await thousands of others, Socialists and labor leaders who had fled from Germany, Italy, and Poland and found refuge in France. An invasion of France appeared imminent. On May 22, the JLC received an urgent call for help from the American Jewish Joint Distribution Committee in Paris, which reported that its personnel had to leave that city to avoid capture by the Germans. Alarmed by this prospect, the JLC sought to rescue the refugees by petitioning the State Department to give them visas. Recognizing the influence of the American Federation of Labor, Dubinsky "persuaded [William] Green to join" the JLC in its appeal. On July 2, 1940, Green led a delegation that met with Assistant Secretary of State Breckinridge Long, who agreed to accept a list of refugees. Prepared by the JLC, the list that was presented contained "more than 1,200 names." As regular immigration visas were unobtainable, the refugees were to be issued visitors' visas on an emergency basis, one per family. After the war, recipients would have to return home. Eventually, according to historian Gail Malmgreen, "the State Department issued more than 800 visas, leading to the rescue of more than 1,500 people."[27]

The ILGWU maintained close relations with numerous relief agencies. In 1941 it asked each member for the voluntary donation of a half day's wages to be distributed among eleven organizations. By September, $305,000 had been raised, the primary beneficiaries being the Joint Distribution Committee and the British War Sufferers, which received $75,000 and $50,000, respectively. The JLC was third with $35,000. By the end of the year, ILG-ers had donated $320,000.[28]

Through the JLC, Dubinsky kept abreast of the horrors being inflicted on the Jews. In September 1942 he learned of "the expulsion of thousands of Jews from the now-occupied France" and their shipment to concentration camps in Poland. At the same time the JLC sought to raise "at least $15,000 for the underground struggle" to aid the Polish ghettos. By December 1942, $10,300 in cash had been sent, coordinated with the Polish government-in-exile in London and channeled through the Polish embassy in Moscow. Cash for Russian war relief at this time approached $39,000, including $15,000 from the ILGWU transferred to the American Red Cross.[29] Jewish Labor Committee efforts in Russia would ultimately result in the rescue and passage to the United States of "300 labor leaders, writers and teachers" who had fled from the Nazis.[30]

Tensions between Hillman and Dubinsky escalated in May 1943 when Dubinsky, at a convention of the Workmen's Circle, sharply criticized the Soviet Union. Its ire provoked, the Communist *Morning Freiheit* accused him of "conspiring" to overthrow the Russian government.[31] With primary elections approaching, the left-wing controlled New York county executive committee of the American Labor Party attacked "those who seek to disrupt the United Nations through slander of our great fighting ally, the Soviet Union." Dubinsky replied by accusing the Communists of employing "Trojan horse tactics" to gain control of the ALP.[32]

Since 1938 the ALP had experienced primary fights, but in 1943 the left wing finally sensed that it could take full command. Eugene P. Connolly, the New York county secretary of the party, said the fight was "to remove the deadening influence of a handful of willful men headed by David Dubinsky and aided by the so-called Social Democratic Federation. . . . We intend to forge the American Labor Party into a genuine win-the-war party."[33]

The Left found a leader in Sidney Hillman, who early in July founded a new CIO Political Action Committee, which he would chair. A consequence of the poor Democratic showing in the 1942 elections, this committee was a means for labor to pool its resources on behalf of the president. With primaries scheduled for August 10, Hillman proposed restructuring the ALP so that it would come into control of the state's trade unions. He called for all unions to be invited to join the party, with each represented on committees and taxed on a per capita basis according to the size of its membership. The weight of each union's vote on policy matters would depend on how much tax it paid. If adopted, this plan would shift control of the party from the right-wing labor leaders in the AFL to the left-wingers in the CIO. Charging that the ALP's state leadership was a dictatorship run by Dubinsky and Rose, the Left endorsed Hillman's proposal.[34]

Though the plan had handed the left-wingers a potent issue, when the votes were tallied their success was not apparent. The results were inconclusive, with Brooklyn in particular hanging in the balance. Nevertheless, both sides claimed victory. Dubinsky even twitted Hillman. "I trust you are not too greatly distressed over the defeat suffered by the Communists," he wrote. "They surely cannot blame you for it. I have a feeling, though, they will before long."[35]

A week later, things looked different, when the Board of Elections certified the election of the Brooklyn committeemen, which seemed to indicate that the left wing had won a majority. At a tumultuous meeting of the Kings (Brooklyn) County ALP on August 30, for the purpose of electing county officers, John Gelo, the incumbent chairman, and other right-wing leaders violated parliamentary procedure and miscounted votes in order to retain control of the county committee. After the meeting, the leftists obtained a court order for a supervised election, which they won in October, leaving only the Bronx and state committees of the ALP under right-wing control.[36]

Initially slow to respond to Hillman's proposal, the right-wing state leadership took until the end of August to express its emphatic rejection. The ILGWU's *Justice* said the plan would eliminate Progressives who were not affiliated with labor unions from the party's governance, return to the organization Communist-run or tainted unions as well as the Amalgamated, and assist Hillman's Political Action Committee, which cared only for Roosevelt's 1944 reelection campaign and rejected "permanent labor political parties."[37]

As Dubinsky's relations with Hillman deteriorated, those with John L. Lewis remarkably improved as the latter revived interest in CIO-AFL unity. In January 1942, Lewis, in a letter to Green, linked labor peace to the nation's "war economy," and proposed talks to resolve labor's "major internal problem." Setting aside past differences, Dubinsky embraced the idea, calling it "of the utmost importance to the labor movement and to the country as such." Moreover, in the first face-to-face meeting between the two men since 1937, Dubinsky discussed the proposal with Lewis.

Franklin D. Roosevelt and Philip Murray did not share Dubinsky's enthusiasm. The president, Dubinsky discovered, was interested in limiting wage increases rather than healing the labor movement. As for Murray, he was siding with CIO left-wingers who were currently unsympathetic to Lewis, and his opposition was enough to abort the idea.

Lewis remained undaunted. In January 1943 he attempted to take his United Mine Workers back into the AFL but failed when Federation members cited problems of jurisdictional overlap. Then, in May and June, he again aroused the ire of FDR. Lewis refused to accept the "Little Steel Formula" of 1942, calling instead for a 15 percent wage increase consistent with a proportionate increase in the cost of living. In defiance of the White House, he called a nationwide strike. In response, FDR ordered Secretary of the Interior Harold Ickes to take over the coal mines. Then came a second strike, and this time a presidential threat to draft the miners into the military, but only the threat of a third strike produced a settlement, which gave the miners a slight advance over the "Little Steel" level. Dubinsky and Rose sympathized with Lewis as he stood up to Roosevelt. Exerting their influence, they prevented the ALP from chastising him, and the ILGWU newspaper applauded the bid of the United Mine Workers for readmission to the American Federation of Labor.[38]

For two years Dubinsky had been ready to lead the ILGWU out of the ALP. In November 1943 he again presented his case to the General Executive Board, complaining that the Communists in the party had attacked him with "special ferocity" and were widening their "foothold" in the organization financed by its right wing. Only Charles Zimmerman offered serious opposition to the suggestion. Zimmerman called it inadvisable

"to surrender the political field completely to the communists" and suggested strengthening the party's internal resistance to them. He found no
followers.[39]

The union made its decision at the end of 1943, with a primary to elect
members of the State Executive Committee of the ALP three months
away. At a conference attended by about sixty leaders, Alex Rose reported that the state officers unanimously opposed fighting a battle that
would certainly be lost. High school social studies teacher Ben Davidson,
a representative of Queens County, urged "a different approach." He advised entering the primaries "for the purpose of establishing and laying
the basis, for a new political party." They would "organize and educate
the genuine progressive democratic, as against the Communist left wing
forces, and raise the battle cry of democracy against Communist totalitarianism." After Davidson spoke, Dubinsky took the floor. "I think this
man Davidson has an idea," he said. "And I think we ought to think
about it." At Dubinsky's suggestion, the meeting was then adjourned.[40]

Before meeting again, the right-wingers sought counsel at City Hall
and the White House. Then the Communists announced that they were
abandoning their political party status, a move that could only encourage
all party members to throw their energies into the ALP. Still careful not
to tip his hand, Dubinsky restrained the GEB from withdrawing the International.[41] As expected, the state committee rejected the Hillman plan.
Two days later a conference of 1,400 right-wing ALP members at the
Hotel Capitol decided to enter the primary contest, reportedly to fight for
continued control of the party but more truthfully to facilitate the creation of a new organization.[42]

For Hillman, the real issue was national power. Of greater importance
than the ALP, which had outlived its usefulness, were the CIO and its
PAC, which would be instrumental in FDR's election to a fourth term. As
far as the left-wingers in the ALP were concerned, Hillman felt he could
handle them. Regarding the right-wingers, whose withdrawal he seems to
have doubted would actually occur, Hillman had no fears. They had
nowhere to go but behind Roosevelt.[43]

For Dubinsky, who correctly perceived that Hillman's interest in the
ALP had waned and that left-wingers would soon take control, secession
was a means of preserving a labor party. However, much more important
for the moment was the potential impact of the local firestorm on national politics. Roosevelt was indeed concerned about the Communists
and did not want any Communist Party members in top ALP offices.

Adding to the fear of Communists was an attack on the PAC by Representative Martin Dies, chairman of the House Committee on Un-American Activities, who threatened to curtail its activities because it was under their domination. In a rare concession to common sense, the ALP's right-wing leadership denounced this gesture.[44]

Concerned that the Dubinsky–Hillman imbroglio would injure his own 1944 campaign, in February, FDR met with both parties in an effort to resolve it. The president told Dubinsky he was against a third party, while the ILGWU president explained how intolerable it was for him to remain in the ALP. Satisfied that he had made an effective presentation, Dubinsky returned to New York. Roosevelt then met with Hillman and told him he did not want Communists to control the American Labor Party. "I have talked to Sidney Hillman," the president afterward reported to Henry Wallace, "and Hillman has agreed to eliminate all communists from running for office but thinks that David Dubinsky is being unreasonable in wanting to exercise some of his personal prejudices with regard to candidates." Though Dubinsky had support from Berle and Mrs. Roosevelt, Hillman gave FDR the assurance he sought and won him over.[45]

Inevitably, Mayor La Guardia entered the dispute and, six days before the election, proposed a peace plan. "Neither Mr. Hillman nor Mr. Dubinsky wants to see the Communists gain control of the American Labor Party," La Guardia said as he recommended they agree "on a joint slate for the State Executive Committee . . . [consisting of] men and women who have no communistic taint." Hillman swiftly gave his approval, but the right wing was dissatisfied, saying La Guardia's scheme straddled the issues and attempted "to confuse the party's enrolled voters." On the eve of the primary, Dubinsky wrote to the members of the International. "Defeating the Communists in the ALP will complete the job you did when you defeated them in the ILGWU," he told them.[46]

The disaster came as expected. On March 28 the left wing swept to victory with more than 51,000 votes, as opposed to less than 37,000 for their opposition. This majority enabled them to claim 620 of the 750 seats on the State Executive Committee. Moreover, the Left captured the Bronx, the last stronghold of the Right. "The Mayor helped [the left wing]," Dubinsky complained. "He cost us at least 5,000 votes." On the twenty-ninth the right-wing leaders announced their secession from the ALP. The next day Dubinsky added that he would ask the ILGWU to do the same and cease its financial support, which had totaled $532,999.23

through 1943. "Mr. Hillman can act as a front for the Communists; I never did and never will," said Dubinsky as he withdrew.[47]

With these parting shots, the right-wingers created their own organization.[48] The Social Democratic Federation immediately joined the movement to form what would be called the Liberal Party and have the Statue of Liberty as its emblem. At a founding convention on May 19 at the Hotel Roosevelt, Ben Davidson introduced a motion, which David Dubinsky seconded and some 1,100 delegates approved, giving the party life. Its first major goals would be the reelection of Senator Robert F. Wagner, who was among the day's speakers, and President Roosevelt. Following Dubinsky's lead, nine days later the General Executive Board of the ILGWU endorsed the party in its report to the union's twenty-fifth convention in Boston.[49]

At the convention, Dubinsky took the floor, excoriating the ALP and the Communists and alluding to the 1920s, when the ILGWU "was almost wrecked because of Communist domination." Impassioned, he intensified his assault. "We don't talk from books, nor from theory, but from practical experience for which we have paid almost with our lives, with our blood, with the life of our organization. Let John L. Lewis do it. Let Sidney Hillman do it. We will never be a party to a united front!" Without further delay the delegates voted and the ILGWU wed itself to the Liberal Party.[50]

The primary fight, while leading directly to the birth of a new party, placed Dubinsky on the wrong side of Roosevelt. As the ILGWU convention approached, Dubinsky asked Roosevelt for a letter of greetings. The president sent a message that was shorter and less effusive than one sent to Hillman at the ACWA convention.[51]

Through his various affiliations, notably with the Jewish Labor Committee and the American Federation of Labor, Dubinsky plunged directly into the war effort. Whenever the JLC needed money, Benjamin Gebiner recalled, Dubinsky "always came across," the funds coming from the ILGWU general office and locals on whom he leaned for donations. During the first eleven months of 1942, $65,391, which was nearly 80 percent of the JLC's income from trade unions, came from the ILGWU. In 1943 the International conducted a second drive for war relief funds, more than quadrupling the amount raised two years earlier. This time, by asking each member for a day's pay, the yield was nearly $1.4 million, of which the JLC received $50,000.[52] The anti-Fascist Italian-American

Labor Council, founded in December 1941 by Italian American labor leaders and headed by Luigi Antonini, received an equal share. Receiving $25,000 each were "free trade unions" in occupied countries and in Italy and the Italian underground.[53]

During the war years as before, the international situations with which Dubinsky dealt often had a very human quality. On August 20, 1940, apparently as ordered by Josef Stalin, the exiled Leon Trotsky was assassinated in Mexico City. Fifteen weeks later, after the AFL convention at New Orleans, Dubinsky was in the Mexican capital to participate in the inauguration of President Manuel Avila Camacho. There he met Trotsky's widow, Natalia Sedova, who expressed fear for the life of her adolescent grandson. She wanted to take him to safe haven in the United States. A few weeks later, on his return home, Dubinsky met Eleanor Roosevelt at a dinner of the Women's Trade Union League and presented the request. The First Lady approached President Roosevelt and Undersecretary of State Sumner Welles, but neither was inclined to admit the exiles. They remained in Mexico.[54]

Though the Jewish Labor Committee lent its assistance, Dubinsky also failed to bring to the United States Francisco Largo Caballero, a former Socialist prime minister of the Spanish Republic and head of the Spanish Federation of Labor. Caballero had sought refuge in southern France, where he was in the hands of the Nazi-controlled Vichy government. Through Adolf Berle, Dubinsky repeatedly tried to have the State Department arrange his entry to the United States. This effort failed and the Vichy authorities returned him and former war minister Santiago Casares Quiroga to Franco's Spain. Caballero was later sent to the Oranienberg concentration camp in Germany.

Among those for whom Dubinsky and Green attempted to obtain special visas in 1940 were Italian anti-Fascists. The rescue operation was undertaken by the Jewish Labor Committee and the Italian-American Labor Council. Dubinsky provided immediate funds and directed "everything by remote control." The result was an exodus of refugees who went to Marseilles and then via Spain or North Africa to South America, Mexico, or the United States. Though Vanni Montana regarded the effort as "a complete success," it failed to rescue former secretary of the Italian Federation of Labor Bruno Buozzi and former member of the Chamber of Deputies Guido Miglioli, who were arrested. Socialist leader Giuseppe Modigliani had left Italy in 1926. An anti-Fascist exile in Paris, Modigliani kept ahead of the German occupation of France and finally fled to Geneva, where he organized underground activities against Mussolini in Italy.[55]

Beginning with the invasion and occupation of Poland, the Nazis attempted to eliminate Jews entirely from European society. On September 21, 1939, they ordered the concentration of rural Jews in western areas into ghettos within large cities along railroad lines. Piotkow Tribunalski was the site of the first ghetto, followed by Lodz. Behind barbed wire, impoverished and starving, Lodz's Jews lived in one- and two-room apartments that usually had no running water or sewage facilities. By arrangement with Jan Stanczyk, the Polish minister of Labor and Social Welfare, Dubinsky would pay to have food shipped to his relatives who still resided there.[56]

Hitler also transformed Lodz into a thoroughly Germanized administrative capital within the German *Reich*. German became the only officially acceptable language, and between 1939 and 1944 some 80,000 Germans were added by resettlement to the city, which was renamed Litzmannstadt, to honor a German general who had been killed in a battle in its vicinity in 1915.[57]

During the summer of 1941, Hitler decided that the "Final Solution of the Jewish Question" was to be the extermination of all the Jews, and he privately decreed that it be done.[58] On December 7, the day Japanese attacked Pearl Harbor, seven hundred Polish Jews were transported to the village of Chelmo, about thirty miles from Lodz. Transported by the Nazis on the pretext that they were going to work in "the East," they were gassed instead.[59]

The German government shrouded the systematic slaughter of the Jews in secrecy. Reports of killings in Poland, Russia, and Galicia had circulated since July and August 1941, but news of what was happening in eastern Poland was slow to get out. In October, Jan Stanczyk, meeting with a delegation from the Jewish Labor Committee, made no mention of such violence, but in May 1942 the Jewish Labor Bund presented a detailed report of massacres to the Polish government-in-exile in London. By this time, through their closeness to the Bund, Dubinsky and the JLC must also have been aware of what was happening. In July the Swedish government told Washington of more than 280,000 Jews killed by the Germans in territories seized by the Soviets. At this time the Jewish Labor Committee, the American Jewish Congress, and B'nai Brith organized a mass protest meeting at Madison Square Garden.[60]

"Hitler has converted all Poland into a slaughter house," David Dubinsky informed the JLC's national convention in December. With great personal pain, he reported the slaughter of "tens of thousands or our sisters and brothers" in Lodz and the murder of the teachers and their pupils in the ILGWU- and JLC-supported Medem Sanatorium for tubercular children outside Warsaw.[61]

When war broke out in Europe, Dubinsky's interest in the cause of human rights was shared by some of his friends among the AFL hierarchy, notably Matthew Woll. In 1940, Woll addressed the ILGWU convention and expressed a concern for the condition of international labor before the convention. "The only place where there is a free trade union movement is right here in America," he claimed, and "as we go, so shall labor go the world over. And should we lose our liberties, our freedom, should our free trade union organizations be destroyed, then indeed there will be centuries before wage earners the world over will see the light of day."[62]

As early as 1938, the AFL had created the Labor League for Human Rights, Freedom and Democracy, with Woll as president. This organization became the AFL's wartime relief agency and link to similar operations in the United States and Europe. In 1940 its activities included the creation of the American Labor Committee to Aid British Labor, which provided funds for British workers to buy food, clothing, and other essentials they lacked because of German air raids.[63]

Among those whose aversion to totalitarianism matched that of the trade unionists was Raphael Abramovitch, a Russian émigré who was rescued from France through the Jewish Labor Committee's effort of 1940–41. The Menshevik leader's only son had been slain during the Spanish Civil War by the GPU, the Soviet security police. In 1942, Abramovitch drafted a statement of principles to be used by the AFL as the basis for an American Labor Committee on International Affairs. Membership would include figures from the trade union and intellectual communities, who would help America win the war and influence the subsequent peace and reconstruction. Agreeing that such a committee was needed, Green, Woll, and Dubinsky created it, with Dubinsky committing $5,000 from the ILGWU.[64]

The idea of anticipating the postwar world actually resulted in the formation of three committees of labor leaders, each of which included Dubinsky. As for Abramovitch's design, it was enlarged to bring in representatives of the CIO and railway brotherhoods as well as the AFL and intellectuals, and in February 1943 it became the American Labor Conference on International Affairs (ALCIA), with Green and Dubinsky as chairman and vice chairman, respectively. As directed by the AFL's 1942 convention in Toronto, the Executive Council created a Committee on Post-War Planning, chaired by Woll, to recommend Federation policy. Created, according to Green, "to study war and post-war problems and evolve attitudes" on which American and European labor could agree, the short-lived American Labor Conference was the first instance of AFL-CIO cooperation on international policy.[65]

The Conference had no real power, political or otherwise, which made possible the membership of CIO-ers such as Emil Rieve, Louis Hollander, and Clinton Golden in what had originated under AFL auspices.[66] But by May and June 1944, the CIO-ers determined that the ALCIA was "*an AF of L organization in effect, if not so formally,*" and resigned en masse.[67]

The departure of the CIO-ers probably freed the AFL people to proceed with plans of their own. The relief assistance that had been supplied during the war in conjunction with the Jewish Labor Committee and various underground organizations would have to be continued after the defeat of Germany and her allies. Political concerns were even more pressing. Recently returned from Italy, Luigi Antonini had argued at the convention that democratic labor groups must be supported to keep the Communists from overwhelming them and bidding for power. In the fall of 1944 the Federation's leaders obtained the approval of the annual convention to establish a Free Trade Union Committee (FTUC) and a Free Trade Union Fund of one million dollars. Directing the committee would be Woll and Dubinsky, as chairman and vice chairman, respectively, with Green as honorary chairman and George Meany as honorary secretary. Meany had long been associated with Dubinsky. A native New Yorker who grew up in the Bronx, he became a plumber and then head of the plumbers' union and the New York State Federation of Labor. In 1939 he became secretary-treasurer of the AFL. Between George Meany, an Irish Catholic, and the Polish Jew, David Dubinsky, there developed "great mutual respect." Abraham Bluestein, the FTUC's executive secretary, had been executive director of the AFL's Labor League for Human Rights. Early in 1946, Jay Lovestone would succeed him. An activist organization, the FTUC would work to rebuild "free and democratic trade unions" around the world, relying on information supplied by five staff reporters in Europe, Latin America, and Asia. This group would include former Lovestoneite Irving Brown and Henry Ruiz in Europe, Serafino Romualdi in Latin America, and Richard Deverell and Harry Goldberg in Asia.[68]

Their reports would come to FTUC headquarters, located in the ILGWU Building. In 1943, after twenty-one years at 3 West Sixteenth Street, the ILGWU moved its headquarters to the Ford Motor Company Building at 1710 Broadway at Fifty-fourth Street, which it had purchased. The next year Dubinsky established an International Relations Department, with Jay Lovestone as director. Hungry for information, Dubinsky received it from many sources, often through Lovestone.[69]

In 1944 it seemed of secondary significance to Dubinsky that the membership of the International Ladies' Garment Workers' Union had climbed above 300,000, or that the New York and Washington political scenes were even more controversial than usual. The growth of the union, birth of the Liberal Party, and unprecedented fourth-term presidential candidacy, as important as they were, could not deter him from pursuing his international concerns. From his new nerve center, the ILGWU headquarters at 1710 Broadway, he could monitor developments wherever they occurred.

His reach extended to Nazi-occupied Norway. Late in 1943, Haakon Lie of the exiled Norwegian labor federation came to New York and appealed to the Jewish Labor Committee for aid to the "underground movement" in his homeland. Lie sought to borrow funds to reestablish its labor press. The Jewish Labor Committee's Adolph Held cleared Lie's path to David Dubinsky and Sidney Hillman, resulting in a "loan" that "was never paid back." Lie later recalled that Dubinsky and Hillman "were always at logger-heads, but when it came to helping out in Norway there was no 'no.'"[70]

No amount of aid could make conditions tolerable in Poland, but attempts were nevertheless made. Against impossible odds, the inhabitants of the Warsaw Ghetto had risen against the Nazis in the spring of 1943, only to be crushed. Afterward came word of ghetto escapees in hiding and the Zegota, a Polish underground group committed to helping them. The JLC pledged to raise $100,000 for the cause. Dubinsky and the International advanced the first $35,000. Within the two years, from late 1942 to the end of 1944, the JLC sent $350,000 to help Polish Jews in hiding. Much of the money went to the Polish government-in-exile, which relayed it to the Jewish underground in Poland.[71] While sending funds abroad, the JLC joined with other groups in repeated appeals to persuade the U.S. State Department to act to save the lives of Jews under Nazi control. Their proposals included giving Jewish subjects the legal status of prisoners of war and admitting Jewish escapees as refugees.[72]

In helping to finance the anti-Nazi struggle, the generosity of the ILGWU and its members remained exemplary. By 1944 the International had conducted two fundraising drives to aid civilian victims of the war, yielding some $2.2 million, and the General Office had purchased more than $4 million in war bonds. A bond campaign by the Dress Joint Board brought in more than $8 million, which was used to construct four Liberty Ships named for icons of the ILGWU: former presidents Benjamin Schlesinger and Morris Sigman and attorneys Morris Hillquit and Meyer London. Total union contributions during the war well exceeded these figures.[73]

15

Cold War Liberal

In November 1944, Franklin D. Roosevelt savored the sweetness of reelection. He won a fourth term by defeating Republican Thomas Dewey. The infant Liberal Party had performed splendidly, helping FDR carry New York and the nation. In New York, he received 329,235 votes on the Liberal Party and 496,405 on the American Labor Party lines, respectively. His plurality was 316,591.[1]

Overseas, FDR's crusade against totalitarianism also appeared headed for success. Italy, defeated in 1943, had been compelled to declare war on her former allies, Germany and Japan, whose military might was clearly on the wane. Dubinsky could honestly claim that he and the ILGWU were contributors to winning the war. He staunchly supported the commander-in-chief, but perhaps in part because Sidney Hillman was so close to him, he found a friend in the First Lady.

Culturally, Dubinsky was a vestige of the Eastern European Jewish society that Hitler had already largely obliterated. While he shared the Bundists' disdain for religion, he had a traditional attitude toward the role of women in society, as Rose Pesotta sadly discovered. After her marriage, Emma Dubinsky became a homemaker and the dutiful wife of a man who spent long hours "married to the union," whom she affectionately nicknamed "Kid *Geferlach* [dangerous]."[2] An able seamstress, she made many of the clothes she wore and slipcovers for the family's residence in New York and cottage at Unity House.[3] David and Emma had one child, daughter Jean, who graduated from New York University in 1940. Two years later she was married in the family apartment by Mayor La Guardia to Lester Narins, a physician who had enrolled in the U.S. Army. In 1945 she would give birth to a daughter, Ryna, who would be the Dubinskys' only grandchild.[4]

The ILGWU was notorious for its low staff salaries, for which Dubinsky proudly claimed responsibility. He contended that the union's employees should not earn much more than its factory-worker members. Setting an example, he kept his own salary within restraint. Since 1937 he had been earning a very modest (compared to other union presidents) $10,000 per year. A committee of the 1944 ILGWU convention of offered a 50 percent increase, which he declined. However, he was persuaded to accept a 25 percent boost of $2,500.[5]

While he celebrated his proletarian roots, Dubinsky was not ideologically opposed to pursuing the American Dream on Wall Street or acknowledging the connection between the welfare of garment workers and the economic health of their employers. "Trade unionism needs capitalism like a fish needs water," he would say.[6] For his own financial betterment, ILGWU executive secretary Frederick F. Umhey helped him manage an account with Merrill Lynch, Pierce, Fenner and Beane. In 1971 he would estimate that his stocks and bonds were worth $200,000.[7]

The Liberal Party's contribution to Roosevelt's reelection was fresh evidence that Dubinsky had an aptitude for politics as well as trade unionism. With the ILGWU's treasury behind him, he had a political organization that would respond to his will.

The following April, the euphoria of victory turned into deep despair. In February, Franklin Roosevelt had journeyed to Yalta in the Crimea to confer with Winston Churchill and Josef Stalin on the future disposition of the postwar world. On Roosevelt's return to the United States, he appeared worn and haggard. In late March he went for a rest to his retreat at Warm Springs, Georgia. During the afternoon of April 12, a massive cerebral hemorrhage suddenly claimed his life. A few hours later Harry Truman took the oath of office and became President. As he took charge, the American people went into mourning. On April 14, ILG-ers and millions of other Americans took off from work as Roosevelt was laid to rest.[8]

Many liberals openly wondered whether Truman was capable of succeeding the fallen giant. "To me, it looks that [*sic*] the boots are too big for him," Dubinsky observed after a meeting at the White House.[9] Liberals regarded Truman as a corruptible party regular, an ordinary politician who lacked vision, and anything but a New Deal progressive.[10]

Another leadership change occurred in New York City, where Fiorello La Guardia was caught in the crosswinds of change. La Guardia disliked Harry Truman, a feeling the new president reciprocated. Death had recently taken not only Roosevelt but also George Norris of Nebraska, La

Guardia's former Progressive colleague in Congress, and Al Smith. A generation appeared to be passing. Only a quarter of the voters in a straw poll indicated that they supported La Guardia for reelection. On May 7 he began his broadcast with the statement "I am not going to run for Mayor this year."[11]

For the Liberal Party, the mayoral contest proved to be an inauspicious sequel to its electoral debut the previous fall. William O'Dwyer was running again, this time with the support of leftists Michael Quill and Vito Marcantonio and the American Labor Party. To David Dubinsky and Alex Rose, the O'Dwyer combination was utterly unthinkable, as it meant a united front with the Communists as well as underworld elements led by gangster Frank Costello, who were reportedly in active support. Rather than back O'Dwyer, the Liberal leaders preferred a Republican, the highly capable Newbold Morris, president of the City Council, but they decided that he had no chance of winning. Instead they settled for Judge Jonah J. Goldstein of the Court of General Sessions, a Democrat, who also was acceptable to Thomas E. Dewey.

In a rare difference of opinion with Dubinsky, Eleanor Roosevelt thought he was making a mistake that would affect future elections. "I know you are fighting the communists," she told him, "but I think you would fight them more satisfactorily if you and Mr. Hillman were together in the same organization and not weakening each other by being separated." Accordingly, she endorsed O'Dwyer, while the Liberals and Republicans stuck with Goldstein.[12] Backed by La Guardia, Newbold Morris ran as the "No Deal" candidate, but neither candidate could come close to O'Dwyer, who received nearly 700,000 votes more than the runner-up Goldstein. The ALP line gave O'Dwyer about 258,000 votes, significantly less than the 435,000 La Guardia had received in 1941. By giving the lackluster Goldstein more than 120,000 votes, the Liberals confirmed the impression made in their debut that they were a force in New York politics.[13]

Hillman had been elected state chairman of the American Labor Party when the right-wingers seceded, and in that capacity he backed O'Dwyer. Yet during the campaign even he had seemed uneasy about its left-wing component, led by Marcantonio. Acting to distance the CIO from the ALP, Hillman established a Political Action Committee of the New York State CIO Industrial Council. Politically the state CIO would now operate through its own committee, not the ALP, about which many other CIO-ers likewise had qualms.[14]

Early in 1946, with Harry Truman nearing the end of his first year in office, relations between the West and Soviet Russia began to chill. In a speech at Fulton, Missouri, Winston Churchill noted the existence of an "Iron Curtain" across Eastern Europe. Meanwhile, the American Communist Party had already shifted to the left. In June 1945 the more militant William Z. Foster replaced Earl Browder as its leader. A few months earlier, evidence had surfaced of Soviet espionage. *Amerasia*, a journal run by editors with Communist Party connections, was found to be in possession of classified U.S. government materials, and in August, Elizabeth Bentley, an American spy for the Soviet Union, disclosed her activity to the Federal Bureau of Investigation.[15]

In these early days of the Cold War, Sidney Hillman was determined not to overreact to signs that indicated cooperation with the Communists at home and abroad might no longer be possible. Still, he would find it difficult to turn back. In October 1945 he became a vice chairman of the World Federation of Trade Unions (WFTU), an organization he had just helped found.[16] Created by fifty-three labor bodies from around the world, including the CIO and Soviet trade unions, the WFTU succeeded the now-defunct International Confederation of Trade Unions. Unwilling to cooperate with the Soviets, the AFL remained apart.

A man with recurrent coronary problems, Hillman had suffered a major heart attack in 1942 and three lesser ones afterward. On July 10, 1946, a fourth took his life at age fifty-nine while he was at his cottage at Point Lookout, Long Island.[17] As Gus Tyler later recalled, David Dubinsky did not attend the funeral. On the day it took place, Dubinsky was at his office. "He wore a shiny black suit and dark tie and was spiffed up for some public occasion." "What's up?" Tyler asked. "Hillman's funeral," he replied. "I'm waiting for them to call." There was no call and Dubinsky remained away.[18] The jealousy and competition that had soured their relationship for a decade would not have kept Dubinsky from attending, nor would their differences over with the Communists. But the president of the ILGWU expected the honor of an invitation. Its absence did not prevent him from sending condolence messages to Bessie Hillman and the Amalgamated, or *Justice* from printing a front-page editorial eulogizing Hillman as "one of the ablest men on the contemporary labor scene." Dubinsky's personal statement on Hillman emphasized his great contribution "to the welfare of the workers in the men's clothing industry."[19]

· · ·

By 1946, Dubinsky had established himself as both a political broker and a power within the American Federation of Labor. As early as 1943, William Green had attempted to restore his seat on the Executive Council. The resignation of Edward J. Gainor of the Letter Carriers had created a vacancy, which Green attempted to fill with Dubinsky, but another Letter Carrier, William C. Doherty, easily won election. Dubinsky received a single vote, probably from Green. In 1945 the death of the Hotel and Restaurant Employees' Edward E. Flore created another vacancy, which John L. Lewis seemed slated to fill. Independent from the CIO since 1942, Lewis now appeared ready to return to the AFL, with a seat on the EC as a precondition. However, he decided to remain independent a while longer, and Dubinsky was elected to the body from which he had resigned in 1936.[20]

His membership on both the AFL's Free Trade Union Committee and the Executive Council completed Dubinsky's return to grace within the House of Labor. As victory in the war became ever more visible, the membership of the International exceeded 320,000, and its total assets approached $10 million. From 1944 to 1947 it gave various organizations at home and abroad more than $345,000.[21] As the primary agent of this benefaction, Dubinsky commanded much respect.

At the same time, in 1946 he and other liberal admirers of Roosevelt became increasingly convinced of the inadequacy of Harry Truman. Responsive to his critics, in September 1945, Truman had asked Congress for a revival of progressivism in the spirit of the New Deal. He sought measures such as the extension of Social Security and wartime price controls that were anathema to conservative Republicans and Southern Democrats in Congress.

Instead of the postwar depression that many people had feared, inflation gripped the postwar economy. As prices rose in 1946, workers sought higher wages, with numerous strikes resulting. Struggling to end a nationwide railroad strike, Truman seized the railroads, only to incur the wrath of organized labor. Now reviled by liberals as well as conservatives, Truman helplessly observed the Republicans capture control of the Senate and House for the first time since 1928 in the fall elections. Among the new congressional Republicans were California's Richard Milhous Nixon in the House and Wisconsin's Joseph R. McCarthy in the Senate. A House Democrat among the many Republicans was the twenty-nine-year-old John Fitzgerald Kennedy of Massachusetts.[22]

. . .

As Truman sought to cope with Congress and the economy, Dubinsky resumed his war with the Communists, who persisted within some ILGWU unions, including Cutters' Local 10 and the Cloak Operators' Local 117. The election of Isidore Nagler as manager of Local 10 in 1939 had not intimidated the left-wingers. Under the "Rank and File" label, these dissidents strongly supported Hillman over Dubinsky during the battle for control of the American Labor Party. Outspoken in their criticism of the administration of Local 10, which included charges of tyrannical rule and ballot corruption, the dissidents published and distributed much literature, only to find it used as evidence against them during the 1944 union election campaign. Accused of having violated the Local 10 and ILGWU constitutions by defaming both organizations and their officers, seven alleged "Communists" had their union membership rights suspended for periods ranging from two to five years. Until 1947 the radicals fought, unsuccessfully, to be reinstated, first by following union grievance procedures and then by going to court.[23] The greater story was that the ILGWU's epic struggle between Left and Right had become a characteristic of the postwar world.

Another factor in postwar union politics was former servicemen. Of the 8,463 ILG-ers in the armed forces, 135 had died; after demobilization, 4,697 veterans were reinstated in the union. By 1947 another 3,963, who had not previously been ILG-ers, became members.[24] Several veterans' organizations were on hand to welcome the returnees and advance their special interests. To the 8,660 ILGWU veterans, the American Veterans Committee (AVC) had particular appeal. Organized in 1943 by Gilbert Harrison and other liberals, the AVC shared the political sentiments of organized labor.

In 1946 the AVC was possibly headed too far to the left. With the group's first constitutional convention scheduled to convene at Des Moines in June, its moderate leaders feared a Communist takeover. National planning committee members Charles G. Bolte and Oren Root Jr. sought help from the ILGWU, meeting with David Dubinsky, Jay Lovestone, and the Dress Joint Board's Murray Gross. A liberal Republican who had organized Willkie Clubs in the 1940 presidential campaign, Root was now concerned that Communist veterans, who already ran the AVC's New York operation, might gain control of the national apparatus. Adding embarrassment to the situation, from the rival, conservative American Legion came a public warning that the AVC was "under Communist influences."

Root persuaded Dubinsky to help by reminding him of his own and the International's past struggles. The ILGWU president then called in recently returned veteran Gus Tyler, the educational director of Local 91, and instructed him to join the AVC and "get rid of" the Communists. Tyler did his job. He contacted such key people as the United Automobile Workers' Walter Reuther, the Steel Workers' Meyer Bernstein, and Minnesota lawyer Orville Freeman. As Tyler recalls, he organized his forces, including former members of the Young Communist League, to do such things as spread rumors about the Communists and infiltrate their Progressive Caucus in order to inform on them. Attending the convention as delegates, Tyler and Gross were present for the rout of the leftists. The AVC gathering barred from membership persons whose only military service had been as volunteers for Loyalist Spain and elected Bolte national chairman and Harrison vice chairman. In November, the AVC would adopt a loyalty oath that was a prelude to the removal of left-wing leaders.[25]

No observer could have been more satisfied with the rescue of the committee than David Dubinsky. A classic example of how to defeat the Communists, the effort also pleased AVC executive Franklin D. Roosevelt Jr. After the convention, the Committee sought to raise money to expand beyond its current level of about 70,000 members. With photographers present in Dubinsky's office, the ILGWU became the first labor organization to contribute to this campaign as Dubinsky handed Root and Roosevelt a check for $5,000.[26]

In combating Communists, Walter Reuther had not always been a firm ally. A Socialist and admirer of the Soviet Union during the 1930s, he had been an organizer of the sit-down strike of the United Automobile Workers at General Motors in 1936–37. Amenable to Popular Front policies, Reuther collaborated with the Communists in the UAW, but after 1938 he broke with them as well as the Socialists. So severe was the factional warfare in the UAW that it destroyed any trace of unity within the union, which then split into a large group loyal to the CIO and a much smaller one leaning toward the AFL. In 1939, each side held a convention. Engineered by Walter Reuther and Philip Murray, the UAW-CIO group proposed the 240-pound, poker-playing and tobacco-chewing R. J. Thomas for the union presidency. As prearranged, the victorious Thomas made Reuther director of the General Motors Department. When Reuther assumed his new position he continued the rightward drift that had earlier

David Dubinsky, 1912. *Harry Rubenstein, ILGWU, UNITE Archives, Kheel Center, Cornell University.*

Dubinsky (located at the top left, leaning against the tree) and friends on the New Jersey Palisades, c. 1915. *Harry Rubenstein, ILGWU, UNITE Archives, Kheel Center, Cornell University.*

Dubinsky, 1928. "This is the portrait of the greatest father in the *world* . . . Jeannette Dubinsky." *Photographer unknown, UNITE Archives, Kheel Center, Cornell University.*

Dubinsky and Benjamin Schlesinger at Bryant Hall, New York City, 1929. *Photographer unknown, ILGWU, UNITE Archives, Kheel Center, Cornell University.*

Dubinsky and Jay Lovestone at a rally, 1930s. *Photographer Unknown, Jay Lovestone Collection, Envelope A, Hoover Institution Archives.*

Dubinsky, Sidney Hillman, and Jacob Potofsky (l. to r.) at Atlantic City, 1935. *Harry Rubenstein, ILGWU, UNITE Archives, Kheel Center, Cornell University.*

Dubinsky and John L. Lewis at the ILGWU Convention, 1937. *Photographer unknown, UNITE Archives, Kheel Center, Cornell University.*

Dubinsky and President Franklin D. Roosevelt at a command performance of *Pins and Needles* at the White House, 1938. *Photographer unknown, UNITE Archives, Kheel Center, Cornell University.*

Dubinsky and William Green at the return of
the American Federation of Labor charter,
1940. *Photographer unknown, UNITE Archives,
Kheel Center, Cornell University.*

John L. Lewis, Dubin-
sky, and William
Green (l. to. r.) at a
Dubinsky testimonial
dinner, 1947. *Photog-
rapher unknown, UNITE
Archives, Kheel Center,
Cornell University.*

Dubinsky and Walter Reuther.
*Photographer unknown, UNITE
Archives, Kheel Center, Cornell
University.*

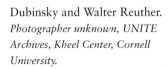

The Dubinskys and Meanys en route to Europe, 1955. *Photographer unknown, UNITE Archives, Kheel Center, Cornell University.*

Shelley Appleton, Emma Dubinsky, Ryna Appleton, Jean Appleton, and DD (l. to r.), 1959. *Photographer unknown, UNITE Archives, Kheel Center, Cornell University.*

Dubinsky and John F. Kennedy at the Kennedy presidential campaign rally in the Garment Center, New York City, 1960. *Burton Berinsky, ILGWU, UNITE Archives, Kheel Center, Cornell University.*

Dubinsky, John F. Kennedy, Alex Rose, and John Childs (l. to. r.), 1960. *Photographer unknown, UNITE Archives, Kheel Center, Cornell University.*

DD at the observance by
the ILGWU of the fiftieth
anniversary of the Triangle
Shirtwaist Fire, 1961. *Burton Berinsky, ILGWU,
UNITE Archives, Kheel Center, Cornell University.*

President John F. Kennedy and DD at the dedication of the Penn Station South houses,
1962. *Martin Leifer, UNITE Archives, Kheel Center, Cornell University.*

President Lyndon B. Johnson helping Dubinsky into his coat, 1966. *Yoichi Okamoto, LBJ Library.*

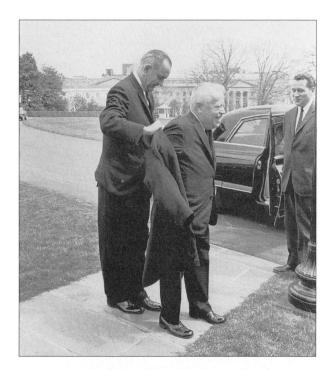

David Dubinsky. *Jerry Soalt, ILGWU, UNITE Archives, Kheel Center, Cornell University.*

separated him from his more radical allies. Increasingly he had aligned himself with New Deal Democrats. In 1939, with the outbreak of war in Europe, he strongly supported the Roosevelt administration's defense and preparedness policies, to the further dismay of the Communists in the UAW. After Pearl Harbor, he was a staunch contributor to the war effort.[27]

Respectful of a no-strike pledge by organized labor during the war, the UAW called no walkouts. However, the defeat of Japan in August 1945 lifted the restraint, and pressure built for substantial wage increases. A government report in October claimed that American industry could afford 24 percent increases and still enjoy prewar profit levels. That month the Auto Workers struck General Motors in a bid for a boost of 30 percent without a corresponding increase in the price of cars. On November 21, after GM offered 10 percent, Reuther called a strike, pulling out 175,000 workers in ninety-five plants.[28]

As the Auto Workers entered the second month of their walkout, they received financial aid from several sources, but most came from UAW members who were not on strike and other CIO-ers. Late in January a coalition of AFL and CIO leaders formed the United Labor Committee to Aid the UAW-GM Strikers. Asked by Reuther for financial assistance, committee member David Dubinsky solicited nearly $87,000 from ILGWU members. On March 10, the strike ended when the UAW settled for an 18.5 percent increase, the same that the Electrical Workers, Steel Workers, and Rubber Workers had just accepted to end disputes of their own.[29]

Dubinsky's help infuriated the left wing of the UAW. In 1946, in order to gain the presidency, Walter Reuther shifted to the right, winning the support of Dubinsky. On the eve of the 1946 UAW convention, Dubinsky sent Charles Zimmerman to various Auto Workers locals with a promise of ILGWU money to induce them to elect Reuther delegates.[30] In a hard-fought election for the presidency, Reuther then beat incumbent R. J. Thomas by a scant 124 votes. After the convention, the press revealed that CIO president Philip Murray had complained to his Executive Council that "the money bags of John L. Lewis and David Dubinsky" were "open to anybody who will split the CIO." When Dubinsky then objected to these "slanderous remarks," Murray replied that the ILG-er's "childish, idiotic blasphemy" was "not worthy of attention."[31]

This election marked an important shift, one that saw the anti-Communism of AFL-ers such as Dubinsky, Meany, and Woll gain increasing acceptance in liberal and labor circles. Reuther was a powerful CIO presence. At least regarding Communism, the gap between the labor federations seemed to lessen.

In January 1947, Dubinsky, Reuther, and the American Veterans Committee's Charles Bolte again joined to fight the Communist enemy, now as founders of Americans for Democratic Action (ADA). This group had originated as the Union for Democratic Action (UDA), founded in 1941 by ILGWU member Murray Gross and theologian Reinhold Niebuhr as an internationalist, anti-Communist coalition of labor leaders and intellectuals. The UDA group favored resistance to Hitler while in pursuit of democratic reform. Thus it opposed both Norman Thomas, whose pacifism had steered the Socialist Party toward isolationism, and the Soviet Union, whose designs it distrusted. It denied membership to Communists.[32]

As if to justify the suspicion of their behavior, the Russians imposed a tight grip on Eastern Europe and refused to cooperate with the United States in the new United Nations on human rights and atomic energy concerns,[33] while Communist sympathizers remained active in the United States. Harry Truman's removal of Secretary of Commerce Henry Wallace produced shock waves on the left. The president's action followed a speech by Wallace at Madison Square Garden on September 12. Departing from administration foreign policy, Wallace urged the United States to accept Soviet dominance in Eastern Europe and to reduce British influence over American foreign policy. Under pressure from Secretary of State James F. Byrnes, Republican Senator Arthur Vandenberg, and presidential adviser Bernard Baruch, Truman asked Wallace to resign. Vowing to "fight for peace," Wallace marshaled his supporters, and on December 30 they founded the Progressive Citizens of America.[34]

This event added urgency to an initiative already begun within the Union for Democratic Action. Spurred also by low finances, its leaders decided to transform it from a New York–based organization into a national body that could more readily attract funds from traditional New Deal Democratic sources.

Toward this end, Niebuhr and James Loeb Jr. recruited an organizational core. By the aftermath of the disastrous November elections, their group included Eleanor Roosevelt, Franklin D. Roosevelt Jr., Charles Bolte, James Wechsler, Walter Reuther and David Dubinsky. The latter already belonged to UDA. As UDA chairman, Niebuhr invited 130 liberals to a conference in Washington on January 4, where the conferees founded Americans for Democratic Action. To set up the structure of ADA, they formed an organizing committee of twenty-five, including Dubinsky, Reuther, and Loeb, who became secretary-treasurer. Dubinsky would subsequently become a member of the subcommittee on finance. "We reject any association with Communists or sympathizers with Communism in the United States as completely as we reject any association with Fascists or their sympathizers," the conferees declared.[35]

On January 27, Dubinsky reported on the Washington meeting of ADA to the General Executive Board of the ILGWU. He had attended, he said, only "as an observer because he had little faith in loosely [organized] former liberal groupings." This conference, however, "very much impressed" him because its "program . . . was substantially the same as that of the Liberal Party." Dubinsky thought most of the conferees "would have voted for a third party," but such was not ADA's intention, and if the issue were raised there would have been opposition. "The organization would, for the present, function with the existing parties." His sole complaint about ADA "was that it did not include liberal Republicans." Otherwise, "it deserved every possible support."[36]

With characteristic enthusiasm, Dubinsky solicited that support.[37] A strong argument for such backing in the spring of 1947 was that ADA favored President Truman's foreign policy, especially aid for Greece and Turkey to prevent them from falling under Communist control.[38] In June, Dubinsky sent his own check for one hundred dollars. Five months later, he helped Hubert Humphrey and the Minnesota chapter of ADA. Planning a race for the U.S. Senate, Humphrey found himself trying to wrest control of the coalition Democratic-Farmer Labor Party of Minnesota from a well-financed Communist Party. "The Commies are very much on the move," he reported to Dubinsky. Considerable energy, bolstered by an ILGWU contribution of one thousand dollars, nevertheless carried the Humphreyites to victory.[39]

The Republican comeback of 1946 virtually guaranteed that the Eightieth Congress would make major amendments to the Wagner Act of 1935.[40] As President Truman had recently vetoed the anti-union Case Bill passed by the Seventy-ninth Congress, he loomed as an obstacle to the enactment of a new law. Nevertheless, Robert A. Taft of Ohio in the Senate and Fred Hartley of New Jersey in the House of Representatives sponsored bills that challenged him and the labor movement by fundamentally changing federal labor policy. The National Labor Relations Board now would serve unions, workers, and businesses impartially, with the three parties enjoying equal rights. Employers could even persuade their employees to cast off a union, which the NLRB could decertify. As for strikes, they would come under new restrictions, including "cooling off periods" to delay them under certain circumstances. Jurisdictional strikes and secondary boycotts would be illegal, as would the closed shop. The union shop would survive, but under Section 14(b) states might pass "right-to-work" laws to subvert it by outlawing union membership as a condition of employment. The Taft and Hartley bills also banned union contributions to political campaigns and required union officials to sign affidavits denying they were Communists.[41]

The most serious legislative attack in years, it stunned organized labor, including the International. Of particular concern to the ILGWU was a provision to outlaw industry-wide collective bargaining and return the United States, as Dubinsky wired Taft, "to the lamentable period when the 'law of the jungle' predominated in labor-employer relations."[42] Three weeks later Dubinsky appeared in person before Taft's Senate Committee on Labor and Public Welfare. Along with industry-wide bargaining, he defended three other endangered areas—the closed shop, organizational strikes, and union welfare funds—and called the proposed legislation "a body blow to our democracy."[43]

The Republican majority in Congress would not be deterred. As the bills moved toward passage, the AFL nevertheless established a $1.5 million publicity campaign headed by Woll, Dubinsky, and Harrison to defeat it. At Dubinsky's suggestion, the AFL Executive Council approved an emergency tax on Federation members to finance extensive newspaper and radio advertising. Though labor's effort could not block the legislation, it was not a total failure. Industry-wide collective bargaining survived, as did union health and welfare agreements negotiated with employers before January 1946. All ILGWU funds, therefore, would remain valid. By early June, with passage of an omnibus bill certain, the most the AFL could do was appeal to President Truman for a veto.[44]

On June 4, New York City's unions issued their own appeal through a "Veto Day" rally at Madison Square Garden. Inside the packed arena, Dubinsky denounced the bill as "a monstrous piece of legislation" fathered by the National Association of Manufacturers and mothered by "a combination of reactionary Republicans and southern Democrats," who, "like the Bourbons of old," never learned or forgot anything.[45]

Yet victory would be theirs. Five days later the Taft-Hartley Act, or Labor Management Relations Act of 1947, passed Congress. On Friday, June 20, Truman vetoed it, explaining that it contained "seeds of discord which would plague this nation for years to come" and that it "would go far toward weakening our trade union movement." The House Republican leadership called for an override vote, which passed by 331 to 83. After a weekend to consider their votes, the members of the Senate also overrode, 68 to 25.[46]

David Dubinsky's attitude toward Taft-Hartley was not nearly as critical in private as in public. In a conversation with reporter Fred Woltman of the *New York World-Telegram,* Dubinsky said he favored the closed shop but did not regard it as the day's most urgent issue. Moreover, he confided in Woltman that he himself had "no use for the tightly closed unions where jobs are open only to sons and grandsons of members and where the union maintains a complete monopoly." In fact, he argued that there should be room for dissenters against unionism. Within the International, he noted, Mennonite religious dissenters enjoyed exemption from certain union obligations at variance with their faith. Their union dues, which they paid to their church for forwarding to the ILGWU, did not support strikes. The closed shop issue, Dubinsky maintained, "apart from industries with monopolistic unions," was "a minor problem" where labor–management stability already existed.[47]

To Dubinsky and the ILGWU, the Taft-Hartley Act's anti-Communist affidavit was also tolerable. The Communists were indeed villainous, and, after all, they were concentrated more in CIO than AFL unions. But Dubinsky knew another way to deal with them. His argument was that democratic trade unions should be strengthened rather than weakened in order to defeat the Communists. In May 1947, Dubinsky had declared in an article in the *New York Times Magazine* that "every anti-union law passed by Congress becomes a trump card in the hands of the Communists. . . . Nearsighted 'regulators' of trade unionism . . . are the best pals the Communists could wish for this country."[48]

When Congress overrode Truman's veto, the ILGWU was in convention in Cleveland. Dubinsky used the occasion to denounce the new legislation, but in listing its objectionable features, he did not mention the non-Communist affidavit.[49]

For nearly three decades, David Dubinsky had been among those who warned the labor movement and American society of the evils of Communism. In 1947 it appeared as though the public was at last taking this alarm seriously. No longer a Lower East Side Socialist leader of the Jewish labor movement, Dubinsky now had a broader audience and could speak with authority on preserving and promoting "the democratic way of life." As the conservative, middle-class clientele of the *Saturday Evening Post* read, he was "labor's most successful communist fighter."[50]

Dubinsky used this success to overcome resistance on the ILGWU's General Executive Board to an increase in the per capita tax on the rank and file. When objections were raised, he announced that he would not seek reelection to the presidency. He was then age fifty-five and had served fifteen years in office. This statement was made in Cleveland on June 15, 1947, the eve of the ILGWU convention. However, four days later, he advised the GEB that he had changed his mind. His initial decision, he explained, had been for reasons of health and administration. He was distressed over what he regarded as excessive decentralization of the International, which made it more difficult to administer.

By threatening to retire, Dubinsky achieved results. He compelled a reconsideration of the tax question, which produced a compromise solution. The GEB would study the International's financial condition and recommend a tax boost "not to exceed $5."[51]

While Dubinsky continued to dominate the internal affairs of the ILGWU, he benefited from the counsel of Gus Tyler in dealing with the world of politics. The articulate, politically astute Tyler had advised Dubinsky to establish a full-time political department in the International, but not until September 1947 was the action taken. To punish the congressmen who had voted for the Taft-Hartley Act, the AFL created Labor's Educational and Political League, soon renamed Labor's League for Political Education. Following the AFL's lead, the ILGWU's GEB authorized the establishment of a political department to be supported by a $500,000 fund from ILGWU member contributions. Tyler was the obvious choice to head this operation, and Dubinsky advised him, "You got a good *pisk* [big mouth], use it!" Tyler proved to be an invaluable aide to Humphrey as well as Dubinsky and regularly represented the latter at meetings of the executive committee of ADA.[52]

The year 1948 promised to be critical in American politics. The Republican steamroller of 1946 seemed ready to repeat its performance in the presidential election. The White House would have its first Republican occupant since Herbert Hoover.

In seeking the support of New Deal Democrats, Truman established a distinctive presidency, featuring a foreign policy aimed at the "containment" of international Communism and a domestic program determined to expand the social insurance of his predecessor and protect the civil rights of black Americans. Each agenda provoked a reaction: from the left, that the United States threatened the security of the Soviet Union and world peace, and from the right, that the administration endangered the social system of the American South.

As early as June 1946, addressing a convention of the Hatters' Union, David Dubinsky had suggested that "only an independent labor party is the solution" to the dilemma faced by anti-Communist liberals. He was not pleased with Truman, suspecting his attitude toward labor, or with Henry Wallace, whom he called "the darling of the fellow travelers." Nevertheless, he did not see a national labor party as an imminent development. At the Liberal Party's second convention, which met ten days later, Dubinsky advised a realistic approach. "I am for a third party," he said, "but I am not one of those who believe that a third party can be built by dreams. I am speaking as a labor leader, and trade unionists cannot be theoretical, but must be practical."[53]

Oddly enough, this hint of independent political action came as Truman began to look more acceptable. In March, the president made it very clear that he was prepared to block Soviet expansionism. The British, who had long been the policemen of the eastern Mediterranean, informed Truman that they could no longer play that role. They confessed their inability to protect Greece from internal Communist subversion or Turkey from external Soviet pressure. Truman then made it a matter of principle to counteract such threats. In keeping with this new "Truman Doctrine," he urged a joint session of Congress to defend the Greeks and Turks with $400 million in loans.

The reaction to Truman's speech was mixed but for the most part positive. Henry Wallace led the dissenters. He forecast that "American loans for military purposes" would not stop change, and that an America that opposed change would "become the most hated nation in the world."[54] William Green had no such qualms. He and Dubinsky immediately joined those who rallied around Truman. Once again Dubinsky became an object of left-wing vilification. On this occasion, for example, he was accused of consorting with "red-baiting Hitlerites." "From time to time we receive mail from ignorant boors," Dubinsky replied to his critic. "We have added your name to that file."[55]

Truman's stand on Greece and Turkey, followed by his Taft-Hartley veto, won him many new admirers but not necessarily support for a full presidential term. Dubinsky made the veto a prerequisite for labor's support of Truman in 1948, but in the event of an override, he said, "organized labor will be passive . . . since both parties would then be equally responsible" for the measure's enactment. By June 1947, Dubinsky had also lost his enthusiasm for a labor party. Support for a third party now came mainly from Henry Wallace and the Communist Left, rendering the idea unacceptable to most anti-Communists.[56]

Among Wallace's people, the founding of a third party of their own appeared to be inevitable as prospects for his remaining within the Democratic Party steadily dimmed. By creating Americans for Democratic Action, with strong New Deal representation headed by Eleanor Roosevelt and labor membership headed by Dubinsky and Reuther, the anti-Communist Left preempted much of the traditional liberal Democratic coalition. This configuration posed a problem for Philip Murray, who was a vice president of Wallace's Progressive Citizens of America, which was closely intertwined with the CIO's Political Action Committee. Moreover, the president of the CIO's United Auto Workers, Walter Reuther, was a founder of ADA. Hoping to preclude internal conflict between PCA and ADA advocates, Murray withdrew from the PCA and urged the CIO to separate itself from both organizations.

In June 1947, Secretary of State George C. Marshall proposed U.S. economic assistance to Europe, where the situation was grim and both France and Italy were in danger of falling under Communist control. To hasten recovery and impart political and social stability, Marshall made his offer, which was similar to a plan of reconstruction Henry Wallace had proposed. Not surprisingly, therefore, Wallace's initial reaction was positive, but that of the Soviets was negative; they declined to participate. Though their rejection of the proposal displeased the former vice president, he soon followed suit and suggested that the plan's adoption would further exacerbate relations between Russia and the West.[57]

The Marshall Plan was another Truman administration initiative around which Dubinsky and his AFL cohorts could rally. Harry Truman may not have been another FDR, but he had fought valiantly to slay Taft-Hartley and was doing his best to counteract the Soviet threat to Europe. Nevertheless, by the end of 1947 he had not yet instilled enough confidence in his political leadership to persuade most observers that he could win the next presidential election. Among liberals in particular, the idea of finding another Democratic nominee was very attractive.[58]

Those liberals who admired Henry Wallace had no such problem. On December 29 he announced that he would "run as an independent candidate for President of the United States in 1948." Under the banner of a "New Party" to be formed, his candidacy seemed certain to draw voters from the Democratic ticket, making it virtually impossible for Truman, or perhaps any Democrat, to defeat the Republicans.[59] For the moment, though, it created a schism within the American Labor Party, which rushed to endorse it. The Amalgamated Clothing Workers of America, led since Hillman's death by Jacob S. Potofsky, opposed the idea of a third-party candidacy. Closely aligned with CIO policy, and supportive of Truman on Taft-Hartley and the Marshall Plan, the ACWA withdrew from the ALP.[60]

With Wallace in the race, speculation among Democrats turned to an alternative to Truman.[61] In March 1948, Dubinsky could not believe the Democrats would nominate Truman. Rather than take chances, though, he suggested that ADA might take "private, not public" steps to oppose it. Ever the pragmatist, he understood that open opposition could result in ADA's serious loss of influence if Truman were nominated. In addition, once Truman was chosen, ADA would have no recourse but to support him. Walter Reuther was less cautious. Fearful of the catastrophic effects of a Truman nomination, he urged an open ADA campaign against it. Reuther favored liberal Supreme Court Justice William O. Douglas or war hero Dwight D. Eisenhower. Dubinsky also leaned toward Eisenhower, despite knowing nothing of the general's politics and being uncertain that even he could be elected. Dubinsky doubted that *any* Democrat could win.

In April, ADA adopted a statement in favor of Eisenhower or Douglas, asserting that Eisenhower's patient and firm personality would be "indispensable to our dealings with the Russians" and that Douglas was "a tested liberal" who had helped FDR forge the New Deal. Despite this interest, neither the general nor the justice was interested in running for president.[62]

When Truman was nominated, with Senator Alben W. Barkley of Kentucky as his running mate, the convention witnessed a threat to Democratic unity, but not from the party's liberal wing. The party adopted a solid civil rights plank, designed largely by Hubert Humphrey. In protest,

Governor J. Strom Thurmond of South Carolina led a walkout by South-ern delegates. Thurmond and Governor Fielding Wright of Mississippi went on, respectively, to become the presidential and vice presidential nominees of a new States' Rights, or "Dixiecrat," Party. At the end of July the Wallace people, in convention at Shibe Park, Philadelphia, finally nominated their hero for president. Thus divided into separate parties, three Democrats prepared to contest the presidency with Thomas E. Dewey, who was again the Republicans' choice, now running with Gov-ernor Earl Warren of California.

With the election campaign gaining momentum, Dubinsky moved de-cisively to aid Truman, first by mobilizing the International. Only one vote on the General Executive Board opposed an endorsement of Truman and Barkley on the basis of the Democrats' positions on civil rights, Taft-Hartley, housing, inflation, and price controls. The board rejected the Wallace candidacy "as an irresponsible adventure controlled by the Com-munist Party [and] as a maneuver to split the liberal and independent vote. . . . We've got to go into this campaign to win," Dubinsky said. "Elections are never certain; we don't concede victory for the Republi-cans." With his purpose thus stated, he announced a campaign of politi-cal action. Among other things, the ILGWU would sponsor four national radio broadcasts and hold several mass meetings. To get around the Taft-Hartley Act, which banned the use of union funds for political activity, Dubinsky urged each ILGWU member to donate two dollars.[63]

Scarcely had the International endorsed Truman and Barkley than the Liberal Party did the same. They demanded the repeal of the Taft-Hart-ley Act and staunchly supported the administration's anti-Soviet foreign policy, setting the stage for an endorsement,[64] which came on August 31. As president of the Liberals' Trade Union Council, Charles Zimmerman explained the party's action. He decried both the congressional record of the Republicans and clearly visible Communist support for the Progres-sives. Along with this endorsement, the AFL and CIO offered theirs.[65]

Organized labor's blessing boosted Truman's chances but could not dispel the impression that he would lose in November. Hailed as "the champion of the common man," Wallace identified himself with Roo-sevelt and campaigned with Vito Marcantonio, the hero of the American Labor Party and left-wing New Yorkers. With defeat evidently facing Truman, perhaps only the brave, or foolhardy, strenuously labored in his behalf. In New York, the ILGWU and the Liberal Party seized the initia-tive to provide such service. True to its pledge, the International sponsored four radio programs. On October 21, Truman himself appeared on the third broadcast, speaking from the White House. He outlined a comprehensive agenda that included an end to Taft-Hartley, an increase in the minimum wage from forty to not less than seventy-five cents an hour, an extension of Social Security as well as increased benefits, an expansion of national health care, federal aid for education, slum clearance and affordable housing, and relief from inflation.

On October 28, the president visited New York City. At 4 p.m. he arrived at Grand Central Station. Then he made his way to a tumultuous ILGWU greeting on Seventh Avenue, followed by a huge ACWA rally at Union Square. After 10 p.m. the Liberals welcomed him at Madison Square Garden. On "every seat" was a copy of *Justice* with a page-one exhortation: "ELECT TRUMAN." Before the 16,000 in attendance, Dubinsky delivered a resounding speech in which he cited Truman's veto of Taft-Hartley. Dubinsky noted that Truman was "responsible for the fact that the United States was the first nation to grant de facto recognition to Israel." In addition to praising the president, Dubinsky castigated Henry Wallace, whom he said confused "the Common Man with the Cominform."[66]

Henry Wallace also championed Israel, questioning the sincerity of both Truman's and Dewey's professed support for the new state, which was besieged by its Arab neighbors. While Truman and the Liberals filled Madison Square Garden, the Progressive nominee argued his case before an audience of 5,000 at a meeting sponsored by the American Jewish Congress at the Manhattan Center.[67] As much as Wallace's people tried, they could not match the publicity Truman and the Liberals received that day.

On Election Day a miracle occurred. The American people kept Truman in the White House and returned control of Congress to the Democrats. With twenty-eight states and 303 electoral votes, Truman bested Dewey, who captured sixteen states and 189 electoral votes. Dixiecrat Thurmond took four states, all in the South, and 39 electoral votes. Wallace polled about as many votes as Thurmond but failed to dent the Electoral College. His 508,000 votes in New York, though, deprived Truman of its forty-seven electors. Dewey won the Empire State by fewer than 50,000 votes. New Yorkers gave Truman nearly 227,000 votes, 8 percent of his total in the state, on the Liberal line.[68]

In the successes of Truman and the Democrats in Congress, euphoric leaders of organized labor saw a reaffirmation of American liberalism and hope for the repeal of Taft-Hartley. The latter, George Meany declared, was the first item on his own agenda. Dubinsky, too, looked forward to repeal, along with a host of other advances in such areas as public housing, Social Security, civil rights, the minimum wage, and "a stable world peace without appeasement."[69]

The ILGWU headquarters at 1710 Broadway was also a center for international news. It was an address to which Varian Fry sent information he gathered as executive director of the American Labor Conference on International Affairs and Jay Lovestone's workplace as executive secretary of the Free Trade Union Committee, with his salary and office overhead expenses covered by the union.[70] It was also where David Dubinsky received a report three weeks after the unconditional surrender of Germany that the German labor movement was in imminent danger of Communist domination. Informed by an exiled German Social Democratic leader that such a calamity might occur, Fry urged "immediate and effective action" by the AFL to prevent it.[71] In November, Lovestone told Dubinsky that German Communists had "an inside track" with General Frank McSherry of the American Military Government and had "managed to control labor policy in Bavaria."[72]

Later reports from Germany confirmed the struggle for control of its workers, as well as the apparent indifference of American occupation authorities to the Communist threat there. In April 1946, Charles Zimmerman reported on a trip he had made to Scandinavia, France, Poland, and Germany on behalf of the Jewish Labor Committee. His view of the German situation was that the Communists were moving forward aggressively while the Social Democrats languished. Zimmerman noted that in the Russian zone of the divided Germany the Communist labor people were receiving five times the amount of newsprint that the Socialists were getting to put across their message.[73]

A fear that Communism would stifle the recovery of democratic trade unionism in Germany also pervaded a group of German Socialists in the United States. Prominent within this group was Martin Plettl, who had fled to the United States in 1933 and had his German citizenship revoked the next year. A key figure in spurring the AFL to act against Nazism in 1934, Plettl waged his own war against Hitler as head of the *Deutscher Freiheitsbund* (League of Free Germans), based in New York. Accordingly, he enjoyed the friendship and support of David Dubinsky. With the approval of Dubinsky and William Green, Plettl and other exiled Social

Democrats founded the German Labor Delegation (GLD) in 1939. Apolitical but also anti-Communist, the GLD published a newspaper, the *Neue Volks Zeitung,* and claimed to represent the German labor movement. Though it had only about ten members, the GLD survived the war, anticipating the revival of German trade unions.[74]

As early as the summer of 1946, the GLD feared that conditions in Germany might abort such a rebirth. With food and other necessities in short supply, a strange phenomenon was occurring, Helmut Wickel of the GLD reported to Dubinsky. "Russian 'social engineers'" were skillfully exploiting growing popular dissatisfaction, while American, British and French authorities did nothing to deter it. The result was that the traditionally anti-Russian Germans were beginning to regard their occupiers from the East "as the 'lesser evil.'" In September, the GLD began a campaign for help from the American labor movement with a plea to Dubinsky.

The ILGWU president was pleased to report that the Executive Council of the AFL had recently adopted a relief plan. Each month a different international union would send a package of food and other essentials, valued at five thousand dollars.[75]

In addition to the GLD in New York, Jay Lovestone kept Dubinsky abreast of developments in Germany, using such sources of information as FTUC operatives Irving Brown and Henry Rutz. Also in Germany were two GLD members, Max Breuer and Rudolph Katz. In the fall of 1946, Breuer became mayor of Hamburg and Katz, the editor of the *Neue Volks Zeitung.* Both men served as FTUC informants.[76]

Largely through Local 89, the Italian Dressmakers' Union, the ILGWU kept abreast of developments in Italy. At the outbreak of the war, Luigi Antonini, Vanni Montana, and others of the local concentrated on the rescue of anti-Fascists.[77] They kept in contact with such exiles as Giuseppe Modigliani and Ignazio Silone in Switzerland and the Resistance movement within Italy itself. Antonini sent Silone "several thousands of dollars donated by the ILGWU and the Italian-American Labor Council," which he headed. Involved was a staunch anti-Communist and former general counsel to the Congress of Industrial Organizations, Arthur J. Goldberg who was now an intelligence officer for the Office of Strategic Services, established by President Roosevelt in 1941.[78]

In July 1943 the Italian landscape changed dramatically. American, British, and Canadian troops landed in Sicily and were on the verge of capturing it. Facing imminent defeat, Benito Mussolini's Fascist council rebelled against his leadership, forcing him to resign. However, a fortnight later German forces rescued Mussolini, who announced the creation of a new Fascist party allied with the Germans, who now occupied Rome. As Mussolini struggled to survive, American forces intensified their assault on the mainland, seizing Naples and advancing toward Rome.

As the Germans clung to the Eternal City, Italian trade unionists planned for the future. Christian Democrats, Communists, and Socialists, who had set aside differences in order to fight Fascism, secretly regrouped. It remained to be seen whether the three parties could continue to act in harmony once the war finally ended. During the Fascist era, the majority of experienced labor leaders had gone to prison or into exile or had been eliminated in other ways. In November 1943, Serafino Romualdi feared the consequences. "Demagogues, political agitators, or professional trouble makers will try to take advantage of the freedom to organize" for personal or political purposes, he observed.[79]

Seven months later, as German forces fled Rome and British and American troops advanced toward the city, the anti-Fascist labor coalition took form. On June 3, 1944, the parties signed the Pact of Rome, creating the *Confederazione Generale Italiana del Lavoro* (the CGIL, or Italian Federation of Labor).

Sir Walter Citrine, secretary of Britain's Trades Union Congress, suggested that an Anglo-American delegation visit Italy to assist the CGIL to restore the Italian labor movement. David Dubinsky was now suspicious of the man who had once helped him found the AFL's Labor Chest to fight Fascism. He regarded Citrine as too sympathetic to the Soviets. Citrine was planning an international conference of unionists to reorganize the International Federation of Trade Unions on a "United Front" basis. To be held in London, the meeting would include Soviet trade unions. In dissent, William Green and the American Federation of Labor declined to participate with Communist organizations. Citing the AFL's stand, the 1944 ILGWU convention endorsed nonparticipation and urged "the earliest re-establishment of free trade unions in all liberated lands." In September, Citrine would be a founder of the World Federation of Trade Unions, thereby prompting the AFL to establish its own Free Trade Union Committee two months later.

Though the AFL boycotted the United Front meeting in London, Green accepted Citrine's invitation to participate in an Anglo-American labor delegation to Italy, and even proposed Dubinsky as its head. The ILGWU president, however, deferred to Luigi Antonini, who was selected.[80]

As August ended, Antonini went to Italy, but no doubt disappointed Dubinsky and Green by giving his approval to the United Front concept and the Pact of Rome. The key to the coalition of Communists, Socialists, and Christian Democrats was "unity" among the anti-Fascists. The Communists "repeatedly" pledged, Antonini wrote Green, that they intended to "fight for democracy" and "endeavor to maintain the labor movement independent from the exigencies of political parties sponsoring it." He assured Dubinsky that "all non-Communist elements" of the coalition were "fully aware of the dangers" of cooperation with the Communists.[81]

The Italian Socialists had entered the coalition in a significantly weakened state. In retreat, the Nazis had murdered their leader, Bruno Buozzi, leaving them under the direction of Pietro Nenni. Unlike the slain Buozzi, Nenni favored collaboration with the Communists, whose leadership and organization remained intact. As early as January 1945, they demonstrated their strength by dominating the first national congress of the CGIL.[82]

Indeed, the CGIL began to mirror Communist Party policy, which was decidedly not revolutionary. Though inflation and a tight job market plagued Italian workers, the CGIL held them in check, resisting strikes, maintaining stability, and winning friends for the Communist Party. As Communist trade unions added members, they enrolled them in the party. At the 1946 congress of the CGIL, the Communists were in the majority.[83]

Socialist leader Pietro Nenni still supported collaboration and seriously considered merger with the Communists. Most Socialists followed this direction, but a moderate wing of the party, headed by Giuseppe Saragat, rejected it and seceded. In January 1947 they created the *Partito Socialista dei Lavoratori Italiani* (PSLI), the Socialist Party. Though the PSLI accounted for little more than 2 percent of the delegates to the CGIL congress in 1947, it nevertheless had influence, which included representation in the cabinet of the Christian Democratic premier Alcide De Gasperi.

As premier since 1945, De Gasperi had enjoyed the economic and political support of the United States, becoming a stable ally in the Cold War with the Soviets. If the Communists, aided by the left-wing Socialists, were to triumph in the April 1948 general elections, this bond would be severed. Meanwhile, the Communists used the trade unions to attempt to discredit the De Gasperi government by destabilizing the economy through strikes and slowdowns affecting all of Italy.[84]

In January 1947, Premier De Gasperi visited the United States seeking economic aid. While in New York he received a warm reception from ILGWU and garment industry leaders.[85] Six months later the ILGWU convention gave a warm welcome to two representatives of Italy's Socialist Party, Matteo Matteotti, the son of murdered anti-Fascist martyr Giacomo Matteotti, and Giuseppi Saragat. Each addressed the ILGWU convention, pleading for economic and political assistance. Dubinsky and Antonini, in response, reaffirmed their support for Italy. Dubinsky noted that the ILGWU had already sent much money to the Socialists and was prepared to provide a loan of an additional $150,000.

Dubinsky's remarks at the convention belied his dissatisfaction with the progress of the anti-Communist cause and the expenditure of U.S. aid in Italy. The primary recipient, the PSLI, was reluctant to stand alongside the Christian Democrats against the Communists, and the money was not going to break the grip of the CGIL on the labor movement. Exercising his power of the purse, the ILGWU president directed Antonini to have Saragat put money into organizing. In 1947 the Italian-American Labor Council sent $150,000, including $100,000 of ILGWU funds, to Italy.[86]

As the Italian election neared, the Cold War became ever more frigid. The Soviets rejected the Marshall Plan and created a new propaganda agency, the Cominform. In Czechoslovakia, the Communists seized power in a coup d'état. The United States now looked with great apprehension toward Italy, whose elections on April 18 would determine whether De Gasperi's Christian Democrats could keep the Communists from taking control. With 48.9 percent of the vote, the De Gasperi's party captured 306 of the 574 seats in the Chamber of Deputies. Though a Communist takeover was averted, Italian politics remained otherwise unsettled. It would take until April 1950, and the creation of the politically independent *Confederazione Italiana Sindacati Lavoratori* (CISL, or the Italian Confederation of Trade Unions), for stability to be established.[87] From 1947 to 1949, various ILGWU organizations sent about $700,000 to Italy to produce such a result.[88]

Three months after De Gasperi's victory, Dubinsky and Antonini arrived in Rome, en route to Mondello, Sicily. About a week before their arrival, the CGIL had declared a general strike after workers throughout Italy had taken to the streets to protest an attempt to assassinate Communist Party general secretary Palmiro Togliatti. The result was violent repression by the government and an excuse for Catholics to abandon the CGIL. In the midst of this turmoil, the Americans met with CGIL dissidents, pledging support for all anti-Communists. On July 23, accompanied by their wives, Dubinsky, Antonini, Jay Lovestone, and Irving Brown received a private audience with Pope Pius XII, who discussed the Communist threat and commended the ILGWU for its contributions to democracy and the Italian people. As the visitors prepared to leave, Dubinsky sought words to respond to the warmth of the audience they had received: "Father, you did a grand job in the Italian elections," he reportedly said. On reflection after the papal audience, Dubinsky suspected that his remark had been out of order and needed reassurance that it had not been disrespectful.[89]

Returning to the United States, Dubinsky reported on September 8 that Italy's economic reconstruction was progressing very well, with a government that was "stable and . . . facing intelligently and capably the Communist issue." A few days later that government awarded him and Antonini the "Star of Italian Solidarity" for their assistance in the rebuilding.[90]

At the end of the war, French labor as well as Italian emerged from German occupation committed to unity, and drew Dubinsky's attention. France's *Confederation Generale du Travail* (CGT), the Confederation of Labor, claimed 5.4 million members, but in December 1945, Irving Brown informed Matthew Woll that two-thirds of its leadership was Communist, and that the Communist Party had gained "control of the most strategic national unions."[91]

Communists were also participating in France's government, which was founded on an unstable coalition with Socialists and Catholics. As the economy was chaotic, with food in short supply, the Communists were in a position to gain even greater power. In a "Confidential Memorandum" to Dubinsky, Varian Fry, executive director of the American Labor Conference on International Affairs, urged an American loan to France. French Socialist leader and former premier Leon Blum then arrived in the United States with a request for aid, received a warm reception, and returned to France with an ILGWU contribution of $50,000.[92]

Under Irving Brown's direction, the AFL moved to weaken the Communist position in the CGT by organizing an opposition faction, the *Force Ouvriere* (FO), headed by a former Resistance fighter, Robert

Bethereau, who in turn persuaded Socialist Leon Jouhaux to assume leadership. In April 1946, at the CGT's convention, the FO tried but failed to remove the Communists. Operating from the sidelines, Brown then moved to lure non-Communist unions from the CGT by converting the FO into a separate labor central. He created a parallel confederation with AFL funding that soon amounted to "$5,000 every three weeks."[93]

Le Populaire was one of the most important beneficiaries of ILGWU assistance. Edited by Leon Blum, it was the newspaper of France's Socialist Party. Late in 1947, Brown wrote Dubinsky that the publication was "in dire need of immediate financial aid" in order to survive. "I arranged with the Jewish Labor Committee to send . . . without delay, $10,000," Dubinsky replied. "In a few months, the Committee will transmit $15,000 more." On April 2 the ILGWU sent that sum to the JLC.[94]

By the end of April *Le Populaire*'s coffers were empty again, and massive internal cost-cutting and fundraising among socialists were needed to keep it running. Nevertheless, in June it was still alive, with a grateful Blum privately praising Dubinsky as the "one we always turn to in a difficult time."[95] As anticipated the Communist-controlled labor confederation accused the *Force Ouvriere* of receiving American financial subsidies. The FO's leadership denied the charge, claiming that arrangements for American labor organizations to help their French brethren had fallen through.[96] In truth, through the Free Trade Union Committee, the AFL was deeply committed to providing such aid. On July 30, 1948, Dubinsky and George Harrison met with Leon Jouhaux in London. The two AFL-ers "agreed to immediately advance $5,000 from the funds of the Free Trade Union Committee" and to recommend an AFL loan of "an additional $25,000."[97] In Paris two weeks later, Dubinsky donated $5,000 of ILGWU funds to the *Force Ouvriere*.[98] During this summer David Dubinsky made yet another significant contribution to the French scene, the establishment of a vocational school under the auspices of the Organization for Rehabilitation through Training (ORT), an agency founded during the 1920s to assist Jewish communities in Europe. At least since 1946, Dubinsky had been interested in sponsoring such a school and was involved in negotiations to purchase a site with money contributed by ILGWU members. On July 15, 1948, at Montreuil, he spoke at the school's dedication. By 1950 the International had contributed some $300,000 to the economic and social revitalization of France.[99]

ILGWU foreign policy remained coordinated with AFL policy. At the end of the war, most Free Trade Union Committee decision making was in the hands of Dubinsky and Matthew Woll. George Meany's role increased with time, as did that of Jay Lovestone. As a member of the AFL Executive Council for the second time, Dubinsky wielded substantial influence. With Lovestone nearby and fellow New Yorker George Meany supportive, Dubinsky promoted anti-Communism and internationalism. In 1946, as an AFL representative, with Matthew Woll, to the Economic and Social Council of the United Nations, he presented a labor "Bill of Rights," and the AFL convention unanimously adopted an ILGWU resolution to establish an international relations department. Moreover, William Green appointed him, with Meany, Woll, and Robert Watt, to a new Trade Union Advisory Committee on International Labor Affairs to work with Assistant Secretary of Labor David A. Morse.[100]

On October 5, 1947, the Soviet Union denounced the Marshall Plan, or European Recovery Program, as a "direct threat to the sovereignty of the nations of Europe." The next day the AFL's sixty-fifth convention opened at San Francisco, affording the Federation the opportunity to help implement the program. As though on cue, the ILGWU delegation introduced a resolution, which passed unanimously, calling for a conference of the sixteen European nations that had already pledged their cooperation with the American initiative.[101]

The CIO as well as the AFL reacted enthusiastically to the Marshall Plan. Rather than kill chances for European unions to rally around it, Moscow's rejection seemed to increase them. Both the CIO and the plan's foremost European proponent, the British Trades Union Congress (TUC), endorsed the idea of an international conference to make it a success. On the AFL side, Irving Brown moved in the same direction, lining up support among Belgian, Dutch, and other non-WFTU unionists. At the TUC's insistence, the conference was called for London early in March 1948. This step displeased Dubinsky, who believed that the AFL had been slighted in arranging the gathering at which it would receive only "observer" status. Accordingly, he told Meany his schedule would not permit his attendance. As the conference was much too important to boycott, the AFL did send representatives, Brown and Director of Organization Frank Fenton, who attended as regular delegates. Twenty-six labor organizations from fifteen countries were represented, with German trade unions participating in such a conference for the first time since 1933, and the AFL and CIO were there as equals, which also was significant. The conference endorsed the Marshall Plan, established administrative machinery to guarantee that European labor would have a role in its implementation, and scheduled a second meeting in London for July.[102]

Selected as AFL delegates in July were David Dubinsky, George Harrison and Irving Brown. Jay Lovestone would serve as secretary and Henry Rutz as observer. On July 27, Dubinsky arrived in London. Perhaps because the TUC still had ties to the WFTU and Britain had a Labor government, its delegates "stressed that Britain needed certain materials and that the British aim was to get, with the aid of ERP [European Recovery Program], a balanced economy rather than a rise in the standard of living in the immediate future." In short, there was no urgency about economic recovery or apparent concern about Communist exploitation of continued distress. American Ambassador-at-Large W. Averell Harriman took up the cause, as did Dubinsky, who noted the need to "beat back the attacks of the Communists and other enemies of world reconstruction and freedom." After considerable negotiation the conferees agreed. The policy statement that emerged after much negotiation lacked "vigor and fire," in Lovestone's words.[103] "They [the British] have something in their throats—the so-called 'World Federation of Trade Unions'—which they cannot swallow but which they are unable to disgorge," Dubinsky later explained. Nevertheless, he felt the conference laid "the foundation for more effective West European trade union action in behalf of the ERP."[104]

Yet another stop, Berlin, awaited Dubinsky before he could return home. On the invitation of General Lucius D. Clay, the military governor of the U.S. occupation zone in Germany and commander of American troops in Europe, he flew to the German capital accompanied by Harrison, Lovestone, and Rutz. They found a city in crisis. Despairing over negotiations with the Soviets on the future of Germany, the Western powers had begun to consolidate their zones and create a West German state. In anger the Soviets quit the Allied Control Council supervising Berlin and, on April 1, began to obstruct Western access to the city's French, British, and American zones of occupation. Late in June 1948 they severed all such commerce between Berlin and West Germany, posing the prospect of starvation. Determined not to abandon the city to the Soviets, the Americans and British flew supplies to the American zone for 321 days and broke the blockade. The establishment of two separate German republics occurred immediately afterward, in May 1949.

In the midst of the Soviet blockade the AFL delegation arrived in Berlin. As Lovestone reported afterward, it was a fateful moment for German labor. "If the Communists were to grab control of Germany's reviving trade movement, they would dominate the country," resulting in Russian mastery over Germany and "the entire continent. . . . Such hegemony would spell the end of the European Recovery Program and all prospects for international reconstruction, harmony, and democracy."

To prevent such a disaster, non-Communist trade unions organized as the *Unabhangige Gewerkschafts Opposition* (UGO), or Independent Trade Union Opposition, which would require the forthright assistance of the American military authorities. The unions in UGO vowed to remain apart from party politics.[105] So that the UGO would thrive as the representative of West German labor, Dubinsky and Harrison met with General Clay and advised him of its requests and those of the AFL. Clay agreed that the democratic unions would be involved in administering the European Recovery Program in Germany, and the military authorities would scrutinize the wishes of German employers' associations before granting them. In addition, frozen wages would be permitted to rise to compensate for sharply increased prices, and trade union property seized by the Nazis would be returned. However, he rejected a request by the AFL-ers that Germany's coal and steel industries be socialized rather than returned to their "still anti-democratic" former owners.[106]

Within days of the Dubinsky-Harrison visit, the democratic German trade unionists severed remaining ties with the FDGB. In 1949 they formed the *Deutsche Gewerkschaftsbund* (DGB), or German Federation of Trade Unions, within the new Federal German Republic. The threat that the Communists would dominate the West German labor movement had ended.[107]

In 1948, the World Federation of Trade Unions, already under strong Communist influence, had struggled to deal with the Marshall Plan. Arthur Deakin of Great Britain, Evert Kupers of the Netherlands, and James Carey of the United States favored it, while Communist members of the WFTU Executive Committee denounced it as a device to enslave Europe. As the rift widened, the AFL Executive Council urged the non-Communist unions to leave the organization. Early in 1949, despite signs that the WFTU was on the verge of disintegration, the Communist opposition to the plan became, if anything, even stronger. As compromise was impossible, the Netherlands Federation of Labor, CIO, and TUC withdrew from the federation, leaving its remnants to the French and Italian Communists and their Asian and African radical allies.[108]

With the WFTU in tatters, non-Communist labor was prepared to create its own organization. In March 1949 a British delegation in Wash-

234 I Cold War Liberal

ington urged the AFL and CIO to move in that direction. Without any hesitancy the Free Trade Union Committee agreed to the request and, over William Green's objections, decided to include the CIO.[109]

At the end of November, 256 delegates from fifty nations assembled in London and founded the International Confederation of Free Trade Unions (ICFTU). The AFL representation included Dubinsky, along with Green, Meany, and Woll. Walter Reuther led the CIO delegation and authored a "Manifesto to the Workers of the World," a declaration based on the ideals "Bread," "Freedom," and "Peace." To Dubinsky's great delight, "the AFL and CIO acted as a unit," which "placed them in the position of leadership at this Conference and Congress." Through the efforts of the Americans, Brussels rather than London was selected as the site for the permanent headquarters of the ICFTU, and Italy received representation on its Executive Committee. In cooperating to found the ICFTU, the AFL and CIO delegations demonstrated a unity the significance of which, as Jay Lovestone observed, "cannot be exaggerated."[110]

Lovestone's own role at this time was of enormous importance. An examination of his correspondence reveals his great influence on Dubinsky, Meany, the AFL, and eventually the AFL-CIO as the head of its International Affairs Department. In the early days of the Cold War, the clever but acerbic Lovestone, working out of ILGWU headquarters, lent frequent, articulate expression to Dubinsky's anti-Communism. A deft ghostwriter, Lovestone helped transform the ILGWU president into American labor's leading spokesman on the Soviet threat. From 1947 to 1953 his fingerprints were on a host of articles under Dubinsky's name in such publications as the *New York Times Magazine,* the *Saturday Evening Post,* and *Foreign Affairs.*[111]

Lovestone served as a clearinghouse for information on the global activities of the Communists. He had a network of informants who provided him, along with factual material, gossip that might be used for personal purposes. With the advent of the Central Intelligence Agency in 1947, Lovestone found a patron. As revealed by former CIA agent Thomas Braden twenty years later, he approached the agency for funds that he and Irving Brown could use to subsidize the anti-Communist unions in France and Italy during the struggle for the control of the labor movements of those countries. Lovestone paid those unions, according to Braden, "nearly two million dollars annually."[112]

In his autobiography, Dubinsky discusses the relationship between the Free Trade Union Committee and the Central Intelligence Agency. He insists that the FTUC resisted intrusions into its affairs by the latter. The FTUC, he reports, told General Walter Bedell Smith, director of the CIA, "to keep hands off."[113] Yet, though Dubinsky claimed that the connection between the CIA and FTUC was minimal, it appears to have been significant. In June 1948 the National Security Council created the Office of Policy Coordination (OPC) to engage in clandestine activities. Headed by Frank G. Wisner, a former intelligence officer with the Office of Strategic Services during World War II, the OPC was the channel through which the CIA financed FTUC activities in Europe for more than two decades, beginning with "the American effort in the 1948 Italian elections." Altogether, "many millions of dollars changed hands." In the Italian operation the FTUC contributed only "a paltry $4,000" of its own funds because of involvements elsewhere in Europe but also "raised about a million dollars from business and labor," much of it from American firms with significant interests in Italy. Altogether, from 1945 to 1950 the FTUC spent $750,000 "in Italy alone" to fight Communism. Total FTUC expenditures during this period were "over two million dollars." At a high-level meeting on November 24, 1950, Lovestone and Dubinsky estimated the CIA's contribution to their committee for the year thus far as "approximately $200,000."[114]

Enthralled with clandestine operations, Lovestone passed the funds for the Italian elections through Switzerland en route to Italy. CIA counterspy James J. Angleton "ran" Lovestone "from 1955 on" and paid him "to send the CIA information on trade union matters in the United States, Europe, Africa, and Latin America." The "JX Reports" was Angleton's code name for the Lovestone reports, which, though "voluminous" in nature, ultimately yielded little important information.[115]

The FTUC was linked to the CIA, but David Dubinsky had misgivings. He regarded the agency as irresponsible and instinctively sought to break the connection. Whatever his personal feelings, though, as the treasurer of the FTUC he was inextricably tied. In the record of the November 1950 meeting he is identified as "Mr. Garment Worker." Other participants are similarly disguised, such as Jay Lovestone ("Mr. Intellectual"), George Meany ("Mr. Plumber"), Matthew Woll ("Mr. Photographer"), and Walter Bedell Smith ("Mr. Soldier"). Still, the FTUC did not become the handmaiden of the agency. Dubinsky, Lovestone, and the other AFL operatives were too independent-minded to permit anything of the sort to happen. They had concerns about funding, which the CIA did not provide on a regular basis, and they sought full control over their own activities, which the CIA would not allow. The AFL-ers had mobilized their resources to fight Communism long before the agency was created. Dubinsky, Meany, Woll, Lovestone, and Brown were not people who required CIA seminars to comprehend the evil within the Kremlin.[116]

David Dubinsky was proud to have joined the General Jewish Workers' Union, or Bund, when he was only fifteen and a member of the bakers' union in Lodz. With its blend of secularism, socialism, and cultural nationalism, the Bund appealed to him, offering ideological direction as well as camaraderie.[117]

As a Bundist, Dubinsky shunned Zionism, but he stopped short of rejecting it outright. As the head of the ILGWU, in which Zionism flourished alongside other beliefs, and as a Jew whose Old World roots were ravaged by the Nazi Holocaust, he tempered his opposition. He knew that the Jewish culture of his youth had largely disappeared and on that basis recognized that the Jewish people must consider a future in other lands. Therefore, Palestine, the Zionists' desired homeland, whose Jewish settlement the ILGWU had long encouraged and whose Jewish labor movement it had supported, began to loom as a distinct possibility. In the tide of postwar history, including that of his union, Dubinsky supported the creation of a Jewish state.

The Zionist movement had grown significantly since 1917, when British foreign secretary Arthur James Balfour wrote Lord Rothschild that Britain viewed "with favour the establishment in Palestine of a national home for the Jewish people" and would do whatever it could "to facilitate the achievement of this object."[118] After the First World War, Palestine became a British mandate under the new League of Nations, but all the land east of the Jordan River was separated and called Transjordan, leaving less than one-fourth of the original territory, between the Jordan and the Mediterranean Sea, open to Jewish settlement.[119]

Though the ILGWU was anything but a bastion of Zionism, its Boston convention in 1918 endorsed Balfour's principles. Two years later the International lauded the British Labour Party for its "tireless moral support . . . to make the dream of the Jewish nation a reality."[120] As Jewish immigrants made their way to Palestine after the war, a labor movement began to form. To prevent destructive rivalry among the disparate trade unions, in December 1920 *Histadrut,* the General Federation of Jewish Labor, was founded.[121]

Through land purchases and reclamation, Jews gradually transformed Palestine into a more viable place to start a new life. Yet money remained a problem, as did growing fear and hostility on the part of the Palestinian Arabs in the face of a rapidly rising Jewish population. Beginning in 1923, *Histadrut* waged annual fundraising campaigns aimed at American Jewish labor. Non-Zionists contributed to these campaigns, as did non-Jews, but it was impossible to separate Zionist ideology from the solicitations. Accordingly, while being supportive financially the non-Zionists, including those within the ILGWU, witnessed an erosion of their own ideological position. "Everyone should consider it his sacred duty to help. The bitter cry of the afflicted Jews of Palestine calls to you, and you must hear and help them," Dubinsky pleaded.[122]

During the 1930s, Jewish emigration from Europe to Palestine became more necessary and numerous. As Hitler consolidated his power and the Great Depression threw millions out of work, the immigration to the United States dwindled. Early in 1937 three ILGWU vice presidents visited Palestine, surveyed the labor scene, and afterward recommended continued strong support. The International then sent $20,500 to *Histadrut* over the next three years.[123]

In 1922, only five years after the Balfour Declaration, the British qualified their commitment to a Jewish national home by suggesting that the extent of Jewish immigration be related to Palestine's economic capacity. Eight years later, they imposed restrictions according to the state of the economy, and in particular Arab unemployment. An Arab rebellion followed in 1936, along with two European events in 1938: the *Anschluss,* German union with Austria, and *Kristallnacht,* "The Night of Broken Glass." In the face of this mounting pressure on Germany's Jews, on May 17, 1939, Britain issued a White Paper intended to end Jewish immigration to Palestine by setting a maximum of 75,000 immigrants over five years. Arab approval would be required for any additional admission of Jews afterward, thereby maintaining the two-to-one Arab-to-Jew population ratio and preventing the creation of a Jewish state.[124]

The timing of the White Paper both followed and preceded disasters. In August came the Nazi-Soviet pact, only a week before the German invasion of Poland and the outbreak of the Second World War. If respected, the new restrictions meant destruction for those Jews who sought safety in Palestine. An alternative was *Aliyah Bet,* illegal immigration. Zionist agencies smuggled into Palestine 16,500 of the 50,000 Jews who arrived between September 1939 and May 1945.[125]

Through the Second World War, *Histadrut* was involved with the U.S. labor movement in European rescue efforts. "In these hours of darkness it is good to know that there is close contact reaching out over oceans between those in position to act and save," appreciative *Histadrut* leaders wired Dubinsky in June 1943.[126] By January 1945, with a postwar world in sight, Dubinsky could look forward to the erection of a trade school in Haifa, financed in good part by the ILGWU.[127]

The British electorate regarded 1945 as a propitious time to change their leadership and ousted the coalition government of Winston Churchill in favor of the Labour Party and Clement Attlee. The Labourites had endorsed the Balfour Declaration from the beginning.[128] Jews therefore expected them, as the party in power, to keep their word. At the Potsdam Conference in August, Foreign Secretary Ernest Bevin received a note from President Truman expressing American concern over Palestine and opposition to the 1939 White Paper. Later in the month, Truman further intervened by forwarding to the British a recommendation that 100,000 Jewish refugees, or displaced persons, in Germany be admitted immediately into Palestine. Contending that it was not in the best interests of the Jews and that the Arabs also had to be considered, the British refused to act on the recommendation.[129]

American Jews were stunned. At the behest of Freda Kirchwey, editor of *The Nation*, Dubinsky cabled Attlee denouncing the White Paper and requesting him to admit the 100,000 displaced Jews and create the "necessary machinery" to fulfill the Balfour Declaration. In response, Bevin created an Anglo-American Committee of Inquiry to study the Jewish refugee situation. The committee's report recommended admitting the 100,000 but not forming a Jewish state. Circumventing the recommendation, the British called for the United States to play a financial and military role in a comprehensive settlement.[130]

By July 1946 the greater problem of Palestine seemed farther than ever from resolution. Under pressure from within the ILGWU, Dubinsky cabled Attlee to adopt a "policy of conciliation and cooperation."[131] In November, Bevin was in New York and invited Dubinsky and Matthew Woll to meet with him at his suite in the Waldorf-Astoria Hotel. They discussed opening up the United States, which had unfilled immigration quota places, as well as Palestine to displaced persons. Only a few weeks earlier the AFL's annual convention in Chicago had adopted a resolution introduced by the ILGWU in favor of the "immediate entry" of displaced persons into the United States.[132] Dubinsky and Woll also suggested the partitioning of Palestine into Jewish and Arab states.[133]

For "an open Non-Zionist" (the description put forward by Israel Mereminski of *Histadrut*) such as Dubinsky to lobby on behalf of Jewish settlement in the Middle East was extraordinary. Perhaps even more unusual was his acceptance of partition.[134] On September 1, 1947, a United Nations Special Committee on Palestine recommended partitioning the region into Jewish, Arab, and Jerusalem states bound to each other by an economic union. Accepting the proposal, Dubinsky enlisted the support of William Green and the AFL, while the GEB of the ILGWU appealed to Britain's Labour government.[135] The AFL responded by adopting two convention resolutions: an ILGWU-sponsored statement urging the United States to admit 400,000 displaced persons and a United Hatters, Cap and Millinery Workers plea to partition Palestine.[136]

The British, however, reluctant to antagonize the Arabs, rejected the recommendation, deciding instead to end their mandate and withdraw their forces. Harry Truman had favored a unitary Palestine but was willing to consider partition, a strong case for which was made by Eddie Jacobson, his former business partner. The president was persuaded. Intensive lobbying to win support then followed in the UN General Assembly. On November 29, 1947, the campaign succeeded by a vote of thirty-three to thirteen, with ten states abstaining.[137]

Louis Nelson, the anti-Zionist manager-secretary of Local 155, the Knitgoods Workers' Union, viewed this development with great dismay and resented the apparent commitment of Dubinsky and other leaders of the Jewish Labor Committee to the cause of Jewish statehood. On December 3, Nelson resigned as vice chairman of the JLC, accusing it of having "deviated from it's [sic] original program." He wrote Dubinsky that the JLC was moving toward an alliance "with political forces which are chauvinistic and nationalistic."[138]

Nelson's resignation came on the eve of a dinner at the Hotel Astor in New York in honor of Zionist leader Dr. Chaim Weizmann to raise one million dollars for *Histadrut*. Dubinsky, who was one of many speakers, first praised Weizmann as a person who aimed for "the liberation and the elevation of the Jewish common man" and was "the undisputed Zionist leader." Then he explained his and the ILGWU's views on the Jews and Palestine. He said that Weizmann recognized that Palestine was "not large enough, in territory or in resources, to take in the entire Jewish people or even a majority of it" and therefore emphasized "the *Yishuv* [the Jewish community in Palestine] as a spiritual center." As such, it "would unite the Jews wherever they may live, as a cultural and moral force, while affording a homeland to a minority of the Jewish people." Dubinsky said that the ILGWU had assisted *Histadrut* "not merely because it was originally founded by Jewish workers, but chiefly because we are a part of the American and worldwide free labor movement."[139]

In Dubinsky's reply to Nelson, he conceded that his remarks at the *Histadrut* dinner "marked a departure from views" he had previously "held on the question of Palestine." Moreover, he elaborated on his shift, making even more explicit his evident embrace of Zionism, citing the dictates of union leadership and changing times:

> I have never been a Zionist, as you know, but there are large and important elements within our organization who are devoted to that cause and I would consider it a violation of my duty as President to place my personal views above those of the organization and to commit the organization to those personal views.

Dubinsky said he was sensitive to "the realities of accomplished events." He noted that Palestine was "now recognized as a Jewish state" with "the largest Jewish population of any other country outside Russia and the United States."[140]

This optimism was premature. Partition was unacceptable to numerous American Jews, Arabs, and the U.S. State Department; meanwhile, in Palestine, anti-Jewish violence escalated. Chances for implementation appeared remote. On March 1, 1948, 35,000 garment workers demanded quick action at a demonstration organized by the Cloak Joint Board at Manhattan Center. Rather than heed this and similar calls, the United States shocked the Zionists on the nineteenth by suggesting the establishment of a UN trusteeship over all of Palestine. This proposal only generated additional controversy as Palestine grew in turbulence and the British prepared to depart on May 15. In the meantime, on April 14, more than 50,000 AFL and CIO unionists renewed the call for partition at a Yankee Stadium demonstration presided over by Local 35's Joseph Breslaw.[141]

Acting without an international accord, on the eve of the British departure the Zionists proclaimed the State of Israel. Against the wishes of his State Department, Truman immediately recognized the new state, but conflict accompanied its birth. Israel's Arab neighbors then invaded from all sides, only to be driven back in defeat. As the Arabs attacked Israel, Dubinsky sent congratulations to first president Chaim Weizmann, expressing a "fervent hope" for imminent peace" and an Israel that would "thrive as a vigorous democracy with freedom and social justice for all."[142]

Weizmann's new government quickly turned to Dubinsky for financial aid. A few days after Israel's founding, future prime minister Golda Myerson (known as Golda Meir) journeyed to the United States as its emissary to obtain funds for arms and the resettlement of Jewish refugees. Meeting with Dubinsky, she requested a loan of $1,000,000, and on June 25 a check was issued. In December the note was repaid and a new loan of $500,000 was requested and approved. Simultaneous with the initial loan, the ILGWU donated $220,000 to *Histadrut* and $150,000 to the United Jewish Appeal.[143]

As Israel took shape, the possibility arose of Communist designs on it. James G. McDonald, who represented the United States in Israel, urged Dubinsky or his "most intelligent and most trusted associate" to investigate in person. Accordingly, Dubinsky sent Charles Zimmerman, who concluded that the Communists were "somewhat of a problem" but not very dangerous. Zimmerman's tour of the country took him to Haifa and the ILGWU's trade school. Israeli life, Zimmerman reported, was "very difficult," largely because of high prices and numerous shortages.[144]

So severe was the housing crisis that *Histadrut* and Israeli housing and financial agencies asked Zimmerman to help obtain private American funds to alleviate it. The result was a plan to construct 8,000 homes by raising $10 million through bond sales. On January 20, 1950, Dubinsky, Zimmerman, and the Amalgamated's Jacob Potofsky were among the incorporators of the Amun-Israeli Housing Corporation, which had a board of directors that included twenty-two business leaders.[145] Over the next sixteen years the corporation fell short of its goal but nevertheless sold bonds worth nearly $6 million, which was sufficient to house 2,000 families.[146]

The International's close ally, the Jewish Labor Committee, which had fought Nazism since 1934, continued after 1945 to deal with the continuing consequences of that disease, especially displaced persons. Among the latter were children who were ill, whose parents had perished in concentration camps, or whose families were unable to support them. The JLC raised funds to sustain more than 1,000 such children in institutions in Poland, France, Belgium, Italy, Romania, and Sweden, and in private homes. To help these children and others in Palestine, in 1946 the JLC began a Child Adoption Program through which any individual or group could, for $300, "adopt" a child, that is, provide food, clothes, toys, and gifts for a year. In 1947, ILG-ers flocked to participate. By 1948, ILGWU groups, led by Local 22 with 100 children, had "adopted" 535 children.[147]

At this time the International also came to the aid of displaced adults. In June, Congress had passed the Displaced Persons Act to admit 205,000 immigrants into the United States. A discriminatory law, it declared as eligible only those persons who had entered displaced persons' camps in Germany, Austria, and Italy as of December 22, 1945, deliberately and effectively excluding many Jews who arrived later. Additionally, it required a job and place of residence as prerequisites for a visa. A Displaced Persons Commission would administer the law.[148] The JLC obtained from the commission an allocation of 500 persons whose relocation would be the committee's responsibility. On learning of this quota, Dubinsky asked JLC executive secretary Jacob Pat to assign it entirely to the ILGWU. The immigrants, experienced or not, would live and work across the nation, apportioned among ILGWU locals.[149]

In 1945, Franklin Roosevelt passed from the scene, but the needle-trades union president who had also been first elected in 1932 was in his prime. Communists continued to maintain a presence in the International, but they were more of an annoyance than a threat. The primary Communist challenge to labor and democracy was overseas. As a liberal Cold War warrior, Dubinsky attacked Moscow and its supporters. Ever the pragmatist, in the aftermath of the Holocaust he abandoned anti-Zionism, permitting the International's traditional ties to Jewish labor in Palestine to lead him to endorse and defend a new Jewish state.

16

Labor Statesman

Seventeen years after taking the helm of the ILGWU, David Dubinsky became the subject of two major magazine articles. "Little David, the Giant," *Time* magazine called him in 1949, as it claimed that his union, "once dominated by Communists," was "now the pillar of the anti-Communist Left" and, "despite the heaviest hand in management in all U.S. industry," enjoyed unequaled "popularity with its employers." Samuel Lubell's "Dictator in Sheep's Clothing" described Dubinsky as "the key figure in a world-flung campaign to halt communist infiltration in trade unions," which has given "the democracies a weapon against Soviet totalitarianism."[1] On the occasion of his sixtieth birthday in 1952, Abe Raskin would call Dubinsky a "Labor Statesman."[2]

Dubinsky's presidency entered its third decade with no end in sight. He was still both president and secretary-treasurer, and only loud but ineffectual left-wingers in scattered locals opposed him. In local elections held in New York City early in 1947, "rank-and-file" dissidents received only 11.5 percent of the vote and failed to elect any convention delegates or union officers.[3]

Acutely aware of public relations and "money honest," Dubinsky supervised the regular publication of the ILGWU's financial reports without converting its treasury into his personal resource. Mindful of the union's near-bankruptcy in the 1920s, he tightly controlled expenditures and made low wages into an almost sacred tradition. His own $15,600-per-year salary in 1949 became a kind of benchmark. As Samuel Lubell noted, Dubinsky treated himself to "flamboyant $7.50 neckties" and "invariably" picked up restaurant checks, "leaving fat tips." For ILG-ers he proudly maintained a *knippel,* or "knot," in which were reserve funds that had been squirreled away for times of need. Aware of Dubinsky's lifestyle, especially his $190-per-month rented penthouse residence, and the attractive quarters occupied by union officers and assistants whose necessity was questionable, ILGWU staff members complained about the low pay they received. William Ross of the Northeast Department attributed the problem to personality. He regarded Dubinsky as a "very cold," "extremely formal" person who had "a low opinion of people who worked for the Union, as if they were given charity when in fact they were being given a job." And for all of Dubinsky's well-publicized fiscal integrity, donations to outside organizations sometimes disappeared from public view. For example, substantial amounts of the money donated to such organizations as the Jewish Labor Committee and the Italian-American Labor Council quietly were applied to unpublicized political purposes.

ILGWU conventions regularly adopted resolutions in support of democracy and civil rights. Yet it was these triennial gatherings, rather than more democratic general elections, that dutifully reelected the president and a virtually static General Executive Board, which as of 1949 still had only one female member—Jennie Matyas, a Dubinsky loyalist—and no blacks or Hispanics.[4]

Traditionally, no ILGWU local had been more sensitive to civil rights than Local 22. Under Charles Zimmerman's management, this policy continued through the war. After 1945, northward migration boosted black and Puerto Rican membership to 30 percent by 1952. Though the solicitousness of the local remained unchanged, its rank-and-file group complained that black dressmakers were not receiving an equitable share of available work and were laboring long workdays for low piece-rate wages. Rather than investigate and possibly remedy the causes of such criticism, ILGWU practice was to deny its validity and denounce it as Communist-inspired.[5]

Perhaps Dubinsky's problem was age and complacency. At mid-century he was fifty-eight and a leader of the American labor movement, heading the ILGWU, a "good union" whose fortunate members enjoyed a "country club" vacation resort, Unity House.[6] Moreover, the International's membership was still growing, to 400,010 by 1950. Yet, since 1932 its basic structure had changed little. Across America was a traditional pattern of ILGWU fiefdoms and local agreements with varying provisions, all linked to the center of power in New York—namely, Dubinsky.[7] Also resistant to change was racketeering, which continued to thrive on the garment industry's intense competitiveness and dependence on credit and trucking. Detecting transgressors was not easy. When complaints of corruption reached Dubinsky, he passed them on to Schlesinger for investigation.[8]

Criminal violence was another enduring tradition in the garment industry. In 1948 a decision by the New York Dress Joint Board of the ILGWU to wage an organization drive brought violence back into the headlines. The reason for the drive was that some 250 jobbers were operating unorganized shops that produced 16.5 percent of the dresses in the New York area. From its beginning in mid-September, the drive encountered violence. On September 20, several thugs entered the Dress Joint Board offices at 218 West Fortieth Street and assaulted three organizers. Within the same week as this attack, thugs, several of whom belonged to the Seafarers' International Union, used lead pipes to beat up pickets on West Thirty-fifth Street. The Dress Joint Board shut down 2,500 shops, and 40,000 unionists packed Thirty-fifth Street from Seventh to Ninth Avenues after 3 p.m. on the twenty-eighth to protest these outrages, but nothing came of it.[9] The organization drive continued into the spring of 1949, when the violence became fatal. On May 8, ILGWU organizer William Lurye participated in a raid that left several nonunion-made dresses slashed in a garment center loft. At 3:45 p.m. the next day, Lurye stepped into a telephone booth in the lobby of a Garment District loft building at 224 West Thirty-fifth Street. Before he could make a call, two men with knives stabbed him. At 4:00 a.m. the next day, in nearby St. Vincent's Hospital, he died, leaving four children and a wife who suffered from tuberculosis. One hundred policemen were asked to find the murderers while the ILGWU posted a reward of $25,000 for their conviction and planned a massive funeral procession for May 12. That day Lurye lay in state at Manhattan Center as David Dubinsky told his mourners, "Little did we think that in 1949 we would have to sacrifice a man. What a mistake that employer made! The union will not permit it, no matter what the police department or the district attorney want to do."[10] More than a year later Benedicto Macri, who had a financial interest in the firm whose dresses had been destroyed, surrendered to newspaper columnist Walter Winchell after having fled prosecution and was subsequently indicted for the murder. At Macri's trial, two eyewitnesses mysteriously failed to identify him, resulting in his acquittal.[11]

Charles Zimmerman was among those who expressed outrage over the killing of Lurye. A decade later he, too, would fall victim to violent crime for the second time in his career. The setting now was a dressmakers' campaign to organize ten nonunion shops in New York and Pennsylvania. In

February 1959, three thugs beat Sol Greene, who co-directed the drive, near his home in New Jersey. Four months later Zimmerman was attacked: an assailant bashed the back of his head with a blackjack while he was in Miami for the ILGWU's triennial convention.[12]

Perhaps the most durable of the unsavory elements that plagued the International was its own Cloak and Dress Drivers, Local 102. Between 1945 and 1950 the truckers' local won wage increases in each of its three branches—regular trucking, packing, and mail-order shipping—and boosted its membership. For the first time, under the management of Samuel Berger, it obtained a written contract in the regular trucking branch.[13] Notwithstanding these achievements, it remained a problem child Dubinsky preferred to supervise rather than see independent or under another parent body, such as the International Brotherhood of Teamsters, which claimed jurisdictional rights to it.[14]

As Emil Schlesinger described him, "Samuel Berger was a bad character" who had disreputable associates, including John Dioguardi, known as Johnny Dio, and Chicago insurance man Paul Dorfman. Berger "was intimately connected" with the former, "who was a powerful racket figure in the coat and suit industry and in the garment industry in general."[15]

In 1950, Berger and Dio were partners in a flower shop in Manhattan, but they had something more important in mind. Despite Berger's leadership of Local 102 of the ILGWU, he obtained through Paul Dorfman a United Auto Workers Local 102–AFL charter, which he passed on to Dio. Dubinsky, who claimed he learned of Berger's role only when he "read about it in the newspapers at the end of 1951 or the beginning of 1952," asked Berger to explain the transaction. The latter replied that he had helped Dio out of "friendship." Though this explanation was weak and the Berger-Dio combination unsavory, Dubinsky only "reprimanded" the manager, without removing him from office. In 1957, after invoking the Fifth Amendment in federal grand jury testimony, Berger finally resigned. Dubinsky, asked why he had not removed Berger years earlier, explained that if he had, his successor at Local 102 would soon afterward have been "carried out feet first."[16]

As organized workers grew to an unprecedented 35.5 percent of the workforce in 1955, anti-union forces in business and government counterattacked. With the major federations under strong anti-Communist direction by this time, it was harder to smear unions as dangerously radical, but they cultivated the perception that the labor movement was too strong, as well as corrupt, and therefore must be reduced in size.

At the center of an industry in which gangsterism was rife, Dubinsky had traditionally fought a war on two fronts. On one side were the racketeers, who refused to disappear, and on the other were labor's enemies, who accused him of corruption. Foremost among the latter was the Hearst publishing empire's right-wing columnist Westbrook Pegler, who told a congressional subcommittee in 1949 that "despots, criminals and Communists" controlled America's unions.[17] Pegler's criticism of Dubinsky continued for many years and extended to the latter's activities on behalf of the AFL's Free Trade Union Committee. He wrote that the earnings of garment workers were being used "to build a Marxian Dubinsky empire in Europe." Assisting Dubinsky to promote a "revolutionary Marxian movement" were his "acknowledged agents," Jay Lovestone and Irving Brown.[18]

More than Pegler's wild-eyed attacks, corruption had indeed emerged as a major problem for organized labor. A New York City Crime Commission, established late in 1951, uncovered an "invasion" of the New York labor movement "of gangsters and racketeers in greater numbers than at any time since the repeal of Prohibition."[19] Appalled at the evident failure of the AFL's Executive Committee to notice these developments, the *New Jersey Labor Herald* called for Federation "housecleaning" before a "Congressional snooping committee" examined "the mess festering in certain of our local and international unions."

Upset over this piece, George Meany sent a copy of it to Dubinsky. What bothered the AFL secretary-treasurer was that its author seemed not to know that the Executive Council had no responsibility for the behavior of local union officers, as "each international union in the A. F. of L. is completely autonomous." In brief, Meany said the Executive Council could not "interfere with the affairs" of AFL affiliates.[20]

Dubinsky read Meany's case against intervention but had not forgotten the AFL convention of 1940. In May 1952, he brought the issue of corruption before the Executive Council. The occasion was a report by A. H. Raskin, headed "Worst Invasion by Gangsters since '33 Vexes Unions Here," that had appeared in April on the first page of the *New York Times*. Citing this account and others, Dubinsky reminded the EC that in 1940 it had agreed "to apply all of its influence to procure such action" as to "correct" abuses. Although the AFL could not discipline unions that were destroying its "good name," Dubinsky continued, it could tell them that they belonged to the labor movement and that everyone paid for their misdeeds.

Of concern to the assembled vice presidents at the moment were the Waste Material Handlers' Union No. 20467 of Chicago, the Automobile Workers of New York, and the Distillery Workers. These unions had either issued or received illegal charters and required investigation. To perform this task, the EC unanimously appointed a committee consisting of Meany, Dubinsky, and William McFetridge, president of the Building Service Employees' International Union.[21]

In the next few months the committee gathered evidence. Attention focused on locals set up by the Jewelry Workers and the Distillery Workers' International, as well as the United Automobile Workers and its local under John Dioguardi. By the time of the AFL convention in September, the Jewelry Workers were compelled to withdraw two charters and the Distillery Workers one. At least some action was taken.[22]

A very ill William Green presided over the AFL's September 1952 convention. Green was suffering from heart disease and was noticeably declining. In November, two shocking events occurred. The Republicans regained the presidency for the first time since Herbert Hoover when Dwight D. Eisenhower defeated Democrat Adlai E. Stevenson, and a fatal heart attack felled CIO president Philip Murray at age sixty-six. On November 20, eleven days after Murray's death, the seventy-nine-year-old Green also suffered a heart attack, which took his life the next day. George Meany automatically became acting president before the Executive Council elected him to the office on the twenty-fifth.[23]

After a month in his new job, Meany received a letter from Dubinsky on union corruption. Describing the problem as "more acute today than it ever was," Dubinsky recalled Resolution 32 that the ILGWU had introduced at New Orleans in 1940 and asked if Meany thought it had authorized the EC to deal with the current and future situations.[24] The new AFL president replied two weeks later, noting that the EC had never been asked to implement the 1940 resolution but saying that he believed the decision had indeed empowered action against corruption. In particular, there was a widely publicized "situation" to be corrected on the New York waterfront, which he would call to the attention of the Council at its next meeting.[25]

The problem concerned the International Longshoremen's Association (ILA). Hearings held by the New York State Crime Commission in December had revealed it to be involved with racketeering and exploitation of longshoremen. Through the notorious "shape-up" system of hiring, the union controlled the lives of the longshoremen. Under pressure from the press, as well as Dubinsky, to abandon the "local autonomy" doctrine and eliminate the racketeering, Meany and the Executive Council demanded widespread reform. EC meetings in Miami at the end of January 1953 produced, on February 3, an extraordinary document, a letter ordering the ILA to cleanse itself or lose its affiliation.[26]

President Joseph Ryan of the ILA responded to the AFL thrust with a lengthy defense of his union. He noted that officers were forbidden to accept bribes and agreed that criminals should not hold union offices, but he denied that there was a lack of democracy in the ILA and accused its critics of bias. The recalcitrance remained unchanged to the eve of the AFL convention in late September, when an exasperated George Meany recommended expulsion, which was voted by the EC. Perhaps fearing that the ILGWU might become liable to expulsion, Dubinsky abstained. He later explained that he felt that only "the crooks" would benefit from expulsion, which he thus regarded as "self-defeating." The convention voted to expel.[27] The Federation chartered a new union, the International Brotherhood of Longshoremen (IBL), committing $200,000 to a campaign to recruit the old ILA membership. Six years of struggle ensued, and some cleansing of the waterfront occurred. However, the ILA overcame the challenge of the IBL and in 1959 returned to a merged AFL-CIO.[28]

What mattered most about the 1948 presidential election was Harry Truman's upset victory, for which organized labor rightfully claimed a share of the credit. The more than $84,000 raised by the ILGWU for the Liberal Party had not been sufficient to win New York but at least contributed to the national success.[29] Apparently having established themselves permanently, the Liberals saw their membership increase by 21 percent within the next year, to 112,859.[30]

Though Dubinsky, backed by the financially responsive ILGWU, stood alongside Alex Rose as co-chief of the Liberal Party, it was the milliner who navigated it through the political waters. "When it comes to politics," Dubinsky told A. H. Raskin, "Alex is a genius. Nobody can match him."[31] "Alex was the political brains, and David was the engine," the Rev. Donald S. Harrington would recall; "David usually deferred to Alex."[32]

According to Jordan A. Schwarz, Adolf Berle's biographer, "Wielding the balance of power between the major parties was the Liberals' sole raison d'etre."[33] Still, it is fair to recall the more idealistic motivation of much of the leadership. Intellectuals such as John Dewey, James Kilpatrick, and James T. Shotwell founded and led the party in the belief that it was an alternative to reactionary Republicans, machine-controlled Democrats, and pro-Communist American Laborites. Rose regarded the Liberals' leadership as primarily "a coalition of intellectuals and progressive trade unionists, each influencing the other; the intellectuals on purity of ideals, the trade unionists on the art of pragmatism."[34] Dubinsky felt that it mattered little if candidates the Liberals endorsed were Democrats or Republicans. What counted was whether they subscribed to Liberal beliefs.[35]

This disregard for party affiliation surfaced as early as 1949, in New York's municipal and statewide elections. In the city, Democrat William O'Dwyer was running for a second term as mayor. O'Dwyer, with his Tammany Hall machine and underworld connections, represented what Dubinsky had traditionally found most repugnant about the Democrats. The Liberals and Republicans settled on the moderate Newbold Morris, who as an Independent in 1945 had received only 18 percent of the vote. Morris became a classic "sacrificial lamb."

On the state level there was a special election to complete the U.S. Senate term of Robert F. Wagner, whose failing health had caused him to resign on June 28. After his appointment by Governor Dewey to take Wagner's place on an interim basis, international lawyer John Foster Dulles became the Republican nominee for the fall election.[36] Herbert H. Lehman was an old friend of Dubinsky and the ILGWU. As governor he had helped save the International, but in 1946 he had run for the Senate from New York without Dubinsky's support.[37] In the wake of Wagner's resignation, Bronx Democratic boss Ed Flynn asked Lehman to make a second senatorial race. He ran against Dulles with both Democratic and Liberal endorsements. On Election Day, Lehman won by fewer than 200,000 votes. The 420,000 he received on the Liberal line clearly made the difference.[38]

By heading their ticket with the Republican Morris as well as the Democrat Lehman, the Liberals had broken ranks with traditional friends and allies in labor and politics and thus boldly asserted the independence of their party. The AFL's Central Trades and Labor Council endorsed O'Dwyer, as did George Meany. Max Zaritsky of the United Hatters, Cap and Millinery Workers led a committee of fifteen members of the Liberal Party's Trade Union Council, including AFL- and CIO-ers, for the mayor.

The Amalgamated's Jacob Potofsky said he would vote for O'Dwyer because he was "pro-labor" and called Morris a "rock ribbed Republican."[39]

The mayor's labor supporters even included the heads of two ILGWU locals, Louis Nelson of the Local 155 Knitgoods Workers and Luigi Antonini of the Italian Dressmakers, who could not back a Republican. As first vice president of the ILGWU and possessor of a weekly radio program, Antonini was influential, which irked Dubinsky.[40]

After the election, Dubinsky had much to celebrate in addition to Lehman's victory. In Manhattan the Liberals helped the Democrats make Robert F. Wagner Jr. an easy winner of the borough presidency. Impressed with this show of strength, columnist Walter Winchell urged the Democrats to appreciate that "the Liberal Party holds the balance of power in New York State."[41] Dubinsky pointed out to Antonini that the Liberals' vote had for the first time surpassed that of the American Labor Party, making them "the third party" in New York City and "the second party in the Bronx," having bested the Republicans there.[42]

Mayor O'Dwyer had been a reluctant candidate for reelection. Physically exhausted after two years at City Hall, in February 1948 he had been hospitalized with a heart condition. A month after defeating Morris, a "breakdown" returned him to the hospital; he resigned in August 1950 in order to take the ambassadorship to Mexico.[43]

O'Dwyer's resignation elevated City Council president Vincent Impellitteri to acting mayor. Loyal to the Democratic Party but undistinguished, Impellitteri appeared to be only a temporary occupant of City Hall. However, he wanted to complete O'Dwyer's term and resisted pressure to step aside. Eventually a Democratic-Liberal slate was agreed on, including Judge Ferdinand Pecora for mayor, Lehman for a full Senate term, and Congressman Walter Lynch for governor. Lynch had a liberal New Deal background, but his problem was his proximity to and identification with boss Ed Flynn, which would prove costly. In November, Lehman easily won reelection over Lieutenant Governor Joseph Hanley, but Thomas E. Dewey trounced Lynch, and Impellitteri successfully exploited his independence and bested Pecora.[44]

William O'Dwyer's resignation had been splendidly timed, for a congressional investigation of urban corruption was around the corner. In 1956, Estes Kefauver of Tennessee chaired the Senate Special Investigating Committee on Organized Crime, which held public hearings on racketeering in major cities across the country. In New York, O'Dwyer testified about his conduct as district attorney. More significant, ultimately, was the committee's verdict on his mayoral administration—that it had failed to attack widespread racketeering and even interfered with investigations. No charges were brought against the former mayor, but some of his staff members eventually were jailed.[45] The nationally televised Kefauver Crime Committee hearings made celebrities of its chairman, who would soon afterward become a Democratic presidential contender, and its chief counsel, Rudolph Halley, who would enter New York City politics.[46]

After the disastrous alliance with Tammany Hall in 1950, the Liberals distanced themselves from the Democratic machine in the next year's race for City Council president. Joseph T. Sharkey, the acting president and a regular Democrat, was seeking election to the office. To oppose him, the Liberal leadership first considered Republican representative Jacob K. Javits, but talks between Liberal and Republican leaders over him broke down.[47] Led by Alex Rose, the Liberals next turned to Halley, who was a known foe of Tammany Hall. Halley agreed to run, and the Liberals chose him while they continued to seek Republican participation in a "clean government" coalition. Halley went on to an overwhelming victory, defeating his Democratic and Republican opponents by more than 163,000 and 221,000 votes, respectively.[48]

Dubinsky was elated. The Liberals had for the first time selected their own candidate to oppose the Democrats and Republicans for the highest contested citywide office, and he had won. At a party victory luncheon in December, Dubinsky boasted of the Liberals' successes since 1949—Lehman, Wagner, and now Halley—and predicted that Halley would succeed Impellitteri as mayor.[49]

Political prospects on the national level were much less optimistic. There a beleaguered Harry Truman was leaving the White House while his administration was under siege for scandals involving his associates, allegations of "softness" toward Communism, and a frustrating, unpopular war in Korea. The Republicans nominated the renowned general Dwight D. Eisenhower to retake the presidency for them for the first time in two decades.

The Democrats knew they needed a strong candidate if they hoped to defeat Eisenhower. The list of Democratic contenders was long, headed by Kefauver and Mutual Security administrator W. Averell Harriman of New York. On the sidelines was Governor Adlai E. Stevenson of Illinois. A person of conservative, even elitist inclinations, Stevenson nevertheless attracted Liberals on the basis of his positions on spending for public schools and welfare services and his state's Fair Employment Practices Commission. Moreover, in 1951 he had defended the right of blacks to move into East Cicero by sending the National Guard to suppress rioters who sought to prevent them.[50] Despite this appeal and the fact that he was governor of a large, Midwestern state, Stevenson hesitated to run. Invited by Berle to address the Liberal Party in late May 1952, Stevenson declined, apparently unmoved by the argument that Liberal support was essential to carry New York State in November.[51]

At the July 1952 Democratic convention in Chicago, the New York delegation, headed by Herbert Lehman, favored Harriman. As the top vote-getter in the Democratic primaries, Senator Estes Kefauver led on the first two ballots, but on the third the delegates turned to Stevenson and drafted him.

In Chicago to observe was a Liberal contingent consisting of Dubinsky, Rose, and Berle. Dubinsky and Rose initially favored Harriman, and Berle preferred Senator Paul Douglas of Illinois, but all finally welcomed the choice of Stevenson. Then came the question of his running mate, and the strong possibility loomed that Stevenson would select a Southerner. As Kefauver's campaign had been both aggressive and bitter, the Tennessean had in effect removed himself from consideration. Dubinsky and Rose realized this fact of politics, but, as Berle observed, they "steamed themselves up to the point where they really wanted Kefauver for Vice-President." What they feared was the front-runner, Senator John J. Sparkman of Alabama, who had voted incorrectly on civil rights. When word then came that Sparkman was already the choice, Dubinsky said "he could not go along and . . . the Liberal Party ought not to nominate Stevenson."[52]

The very next day Dubinsky reported on the convention to the New York members of the General Executive Board of the ILGWU, and, amazingly, the problem seemed to have become minor. The Democrats joined "the best" of both the North and South, he said, noting that Liberals and labor were dissatisfied with "the best of the South." However, he "favored all-out support of the Democratic Party ticket and a decisive defeat of the Republicans in November." Citing the need to continue the New and Fair Deals, the board members voiced their agreement.[53] On August 28, Adlai Stevenson was present as the Liberals nominated him and Sparkman.[54]

Only a miracle could have prevented an Eisenhower landslide in 1952. He was the overwhelming choice in New York and the nation, defeating

254 | *Labor Statesman*

Stevenson by nearly 850,000 votes in the Empire State. In the Senate race, Republican incumbent Irving M. Ives easily overcame Democrat John Cashmore, but on the Liberal line George S. Counts polled 490,000 votes, 70,000 more than Stevenson, which was the most ever received by a Liberal nominee. Therefore, the Liberal Party again demonstrated vitality despite some internal grumbling that the organization was "virtually a dictatorship" run by Dubinsky and Rose.[55]

The Liberals' next challenge occurred in the 1953 mayoralty race, with Rudolph Halley as the Liberal nominee.[56] Vincent Impellitteri would not yield City Hall without a struggle, but Carmine DeSapio and Ed Flynn combined forces to back a stronger candidate, Robert F. Wagner Jr. In a Democratic primary election, Wagner handily defeated Impellitteri and independent Democrat Robert S. Blaikie.[57]

When the campaign began, the opposition depicted Halley as the servile instrument of Dubinsky. In an appearance on television, Republican candidate Harold Riegelman charged that his Liberal rival was "in the vest pocket of a labor czar who is the unquestioned boss of a single great union and [who] now aspires through his stooge, Mr. Halley, to be the unquestioned boss of all the people of New York." Without joining in the attack, Wagner nevertheless asserted his own independence of bossism by claiming that he was less beholden to party leaders than was Halley. Riegelman then declared that the Liberal Party was "a one-man dictatorship, whose life-blood is the money and membership supplied almost entirely by the members of one union . . . and its satellite, the Hatters Union operated by Alex Rose." Moreover, he ominously wondered what would happen to the city's other unions and municipal employees if Dubinsky should come to power through a Halley election.[58]

At an AFL dinner in St. Louis on September 22, former president Harry Truman said he "never" took part in local politics. In New York four days later, Truman endorsed Wagner. At a Four Freedoms dinner that evening Dubinsky asked Truman about his apparent change of mind. "After all," Truman replied, "I'm an active Democrat." Unfazed, Dubinsky countered with "I remember another occasion when you spoke differently" and added, "But who am I to question the wisdom of an ex-President?"[59]

As a well-known officeholder with an illustrious name, who held the Democratic nomination in a largely Democratic city, Wagner easily deflected the attacks that questioned his independence of Tammany Hall.[60] It was obviously too late in the campaign for Halley and Dubinsky to part company, but privately Dubinsky was distressed to see the Halley campaign was foundering. The Liberal nominee "was supposed to be the sure winner," but in November he received 468,392 votes, finishing third behind 1,021,488 for Wagner and 661,410 for Riegelman. So distressing were these numbers that they provoked criticism from within the ILGWU and compelled Dubinsky to consider terminating the union's financial backing of the Liberal Party.[61]

Not surprisingly, discontent was also present within the party. Founder John L. Childs suggested to Ben Davidson that "new forces should be brought into the leadership," while state chairman Berle took a hard look at the party's health. He saw that the Liberals possessed a "hard core" membership of "about 400,000," which was "a powerful factor in coalition, but insufficient to take power." Therefore, Berle concluded, the Liberals could not "do more than shift the balance from one side to another." As it had previously acted mainly with Democrats, the party appeared headed toward an alliance with the Democratic Party and serving "as a pressure group" on it. Scripps-Howard's *New York World-Telegram and Sun* said that "Halley's miserable showing" was "proof that the Liberal party is pretty well washed up as union boss Dave Dubinsky's personal party."[62]

Gloom hung over the Liberal leadership for several months.[63] Whether the party would continue seemed to depend on the next election, the 1954 gubernatorial contest, which coincided with the party's tenth anniversary. On May 26, at the Liberals' annual dinner, Dubinsky offered a historical perspective. He recalled the founding of the American Labor Party and how that organization had "fallen into Communist hands, [and] had to be isolated and ultimately destroyed." He said the Liberals "dared to do the unpopular and to attempt the impossible," but "we can honestly say that we succeeded in our undertakings." Next he expressed great pride in his party as an "openly anti-Communist" "instrument" for trade unionists and went on to note the party's major political contests, losses as well as wins. However, when it came to forecasting the future, he stopped short. Citing a rise of conservatism in the nation and lack of "sentiment for a third party movement," he confessed that the Liberals had "not attracted great new forces" and had in effect become "a party of quality" rather than quantity.[64]

Dubinsky was indeed distressed. "I am about to make a very important decision and I wanted to prepare the way," he wrote Harry Lang the next day. "If I do go through with my decision, I don't want people to say

I gave no warning."[65] On June 8, at a special meeting of the Liberals' state policy committee, he was more explicit and direct. As Ben Davidson noted, Dubinsky "laid it on the line," challenging the party to do more for itself or face the possibility of death from a withdrawal of ILGWU financial support.[66]

Ironically, the energy required to revitalize the Liberal Party came from the Democrats. Thomas E. Dewey was retiring after three terms, thus permitting the Democrats to run a candidate for governor against a nonincumbent. Eager to exploit this opportunity, Democratic Party leader Carmine DeSapio considered potential candidates, among them Averell Harriman, who was indeed interested in the governorship, possibly as a prelude to a White House race in 1956.

In early June, Harriman invited Alex Rose to lunch. The two met at the Prince George Hotel, where the wealthy diplomat asked the unionist–party leader for his support. Rose told Harriman that he would pass his request on to the Liberals, who also admired Franklin Roosevelt Jr. and Robert Wagner Jr. After the luncheon, the Harriman candidacy began to look more viable. A Liberal Party voter study indicated that Roosevelt could not win and Wagner withdrew himself from contention. Rather than lose with Roosevelt, DeSapio and Rose settled on Harriman. Roosevelt would receive the second spot on the ticket, the attorney generalship.

Running against Irving M. Ives, Harriman had an unexpectedly difficult contest and won by a slim majority of 11,125 votes. Roosevelt did even worse. The only loser on the statewide ticket, he was defeated by Jacob Javits, who received heavy support from New York City's Jewish voters.[67]

Of the more than five million votes cast for governor, 264,093 were on the Liberal line for Harriman. In this gubernatorial contest, the narrowest in New York's history, the Liberal vote was indeed critical. *Justice* called Harriman's success "A Liberal Victory."[68]

Seen more realistically, it was clear that this election was orchestrated primarily by DeSapio and the Democrats, and that the Liberals demonstrated relatively little independence. Reportedly, the Democrats were exerting pressure to overhaul the Liberal leadership in order to bring the party more directly under their control. Even Berle, who indeed intended to retire from the state chairmanship, thought Dubinsky would step down as first vice chairman.[69]

This expectation proved premature. With Harriman as governor, neither Dubinsky nor Rose was ready to relinquish power. Personal relations between Harriman and the Liberal leaders were excellent, and the latter expected state jobs for "about ten top Liberal Party people."[70]

Though the outlook for patronage seemed promising, the fact remained that the appeal of the Liberals to the voters had steadily dwindled. From a peak membership of 118,454 in 1949, the party's ranks afterward declined to only 66,608 in 1954. Its strength in New York City, which had been its overwhelming source of membership, was also waning.[71]

17

Riding High at Home and Abroad

In his prime at mid-century, David Dubinsky's interests and influence extended to both labor and politics on the national and international levels. In May 1953 he could boast that the ILGWU, his power source, had a membership of 430,830, a network of 504 locals, collective-bargaining agreements covering 11,500 shops, retirement protection for 338,000 members, and fifteen union health centers, with an another two about to open.[1]

He also took pride in the ILGWU Training Institute (ITI), known as the "workers' West Point." An outgrowth of ILGWU convention resolutions dating back to 1916, it was to Gus Tyler "a cross between a Marine boot camp, a theologic[al] seminary, and a Dale Carnegie course on 'how to make friends and influence people.'"[2] In other words, it was a training program for union leadership.

The program came into being after various attempts at officer training, including scholarships to Brookwood Labor College in the 1930s and Harvard Trade Union Fellowships and an in-house Officers' Qualification Course during the next decade. As Dubinsky acknowledged in 1947, the old Socialist and radical reservoirs of leadership had evaporated, and new leaders were not coming from the shops. He would later blame the largely female composition of the ILGWU membership: "80 to 85 percent of our members were women, many of whom left the shops when they got married."[3]

More truthfully, Dubinsky did not believe women were suited for such work. "Women cannot serve . . . as business agents and organizers, particularly outside of the metropolitan areas where you have to travel at night and be away from home," he told Abe Raskin. In addition, he said, women "sometimes . . . have children, have to take care of a husband—they could be active in a locality but where traveling is involved, it is a real problem."[4]

Another problem he noted was a change in the character of the labor force. Immigrant parents, who had once looked to the garment industry to provide their children with trade skills and jobs, now shunned factory work, and the older immigrant groups, who "were material for officers," had been replaced by "the negro [sic] people and Puerto Ricans." Moreover, it now required "more knowledge, more education, more intelligence to be an officer than it did in the olden days."[5]

Therefore, assuming that the newcomers would not become union leaders, Dubinsky decided to recruit people from outside the shops to attend "a training school for organizers" at the union's general headquarters, with the avowed goal of drawing young people "into union activity and service."[6] Evidently the non-Jews, who made up 46.1 percent of the ILGWU membership in 1948, and especially the blacks and Puerto Ricans, who were nearly a third of the membership of Local 22 and significantly represented in other locals as well,[7] were not smart enough to become organizers. On May 1, 1950, eleven months later, the tuition-free institute opened with a class of thirty-seven students to follow the year-long program.[8]

Over the next eleven years, the ITI offered both day and evening instruction and produced 308 graduates, of whom the International employed 148, or 48.1 percent, in 1962. A victim of its own success, the program filled the gap in staff personnel that had existed in 1950, making future placement difficult, and was therefore suspended after the graduation of the class of 1961.[9]

"The Training Institute," Dubinsky later recalled, "was a good idea that went sour." It bothered him that many graduates preferred careers in government and business over working for the union.[10] Probably more important was what happened to several graduates who remained with the ILGWU and became "the spearhead of a movement to organize a union within our union." Late in 1960 they and other staff members founded the Federation of Union Representatives (FOUR) to serve as their collective-bargaining agent. He regarded this union as a personal affront and vehemently opposed its bid for certification. A battle then followed, during which the Training Institute became a casualty. In the future the ILGWU would exercise greater caution in the recruitment and development of officers.[11]

During the 1950s, ideological dissidence among ILGWU officers in California persisted despite pressure from the Dubinsky administration to compel compliance with the non-Communist affidavit of the Taft-Hartley Act. In February 1950, Jennie Matyas, vice president of the San Francisco Joint Board, complained to Dubinsky that while there were "no out and out commies" in her city's ILGWU leadership, candidates for union office took the Taft-Hartley oath but followed the Communist party line.[12]

Despite Matyas's concern, Los Angeles rather than San Francisco was the main trouble spot on the West Coast. Five Los Angeles left-wingers had been removed from office. The 1950 ILGWU convention overwhelmingly endorsed the offensive, but further changes remained to be made. At last Dubinsky stepped in "to clear up the situation once and for all." In October he shifted former Communist Isidor Stenzor from the Cloak Joint Board in New York to manage the Los Angeles Cloak Joint Board, and Ohio regional director Hyman D. Langer from Cleveland to direct the Pacific Coast operations of the ILGWU.[13]

Instead of collapsing, the left-wingers in Los Angeles continued to assert themselves as a dissident force through the decade. In November 1961, Dubinsky and the General Executive Board again intervened, adopting their own non-Communist affidavit to be signed by candidates in 1962 Los Angeles union local and convention elections. "I am not now and have not been a member of the Communist Party during the last five years," the statement read, along with a pledge that if elected the signer would "carry out all decisions and policies" of ILGWU conventions and the GEB. Thus fortified, the administration forces swept the elections and reported to the 1962 Atlantic City convention that unity had returned to City of Angels.[14] The Los Angeles struggle was the last major battle of the ILGWU's civil war with communism. In 1953, following the rout of the Democrats in the 1952 elections, Senator Joseph McCarthy and his allies were in their prime. As a veteran anti-Communist, Dubinsky was in demand, and he authored "How I Handled the Reds in My Union" for the *Saturday Evening Post* and "Instead of the McCarthy Method" for the *New York Times Magazine*.[15]

In opening the 1953 ILGWU convention in Chicago, Dubinsky proudly noted that the ILGWU had "been fighting Communism and Communists since 1918," when "it wasn't fashionable," as "a matter of conviction." The McCarthyites, whom he called "the self-appointed apostles of anti-Communism who adopt Communist tactics in fighting Communism," he said aided the Soviets "by cheapening this fight and by making a political football out of the Communist issue." Following Dubinsky's lead, the convention resolved its opposition to McCarthyism as well as to Communism and called for the establishment of a presidential commission to study Communist subversion.[16] In the next year Dubinsky supported such anti-Communist organizations as Freedom House and the American Committee for Cultural Freedom, as well as a recall movement in Wisconsin in their efforts to combat McCarthy.[17]

When George Meany and Walter Reuther succeeded to the presidencies of the AFL and CIO, the goal of labor unity finally became visible. They could end the impasse that had plagued William Green and Philip Murray. Meany and Reuther recognized the negative implications for labor of the Republicans' return to power in Washington.[18] At a lunch meeting in January 1953 at the Statler Hotel in Washington, D.C., the two new presidents decided to reactivate the Joint AFL-CIO Unity Committee, which might at the outset address the chronic problem of raiding. By June a subcommittee had come up with a no-raiding agreement, which both federations unanimously approved at their fall conventions.[19]

Changes within the two federations brought them to a more common ground. Since the CIO's inception, AFL-ers had condemned it as Communist-infiltrated. In 1950 things changed as the CIO ousted eleven left-wing unions. After much criticism for inaction against racketeering, the AFL expelled the International Longshoremen's Association, perhaps signifying a new attitude in that regard. Though the demise of the World Federation of Trade Unions and the founding of the International Confederation of Trade Unions did not resolve all foreign policy differences, there was a new similarity of goals.[20]

As a member of the Joint Unity Committee, the ILGWU president returned to the forefront of the quest for labor peace. As close as ever to George Meany, his "favorite gin rummy partner," Dubinsky also maintained good relations with Walter Reuther and Arthur J. Goldberg, the general counsel for both the CIO and the Steel Workers.[21]

From the beginning of the current campaign for unity Meany led the way, supported by a less enthusiastic Reuther. Al Hayes of the Machinists and Harry Bates of the Bricklayers, as well as Dubinsky, stood out as other strongly supportive AFL-ers. On the CIO side, Goldberg, the Amalgamated's Jacob Potofsky, and O. A. Knight of the Oil, Chemical and Atomic Workers were outstanding advocates of the cause.[22]

The no-raiding agreement was a major breakthrough. However, because the unions rather than the federations had been the principal jurisdictional warriors, ratification by the individual autonomous unions themselves was necessary before it could become effective. On June 9, 1954, 65 of the AFL's 110 unions and 29 of the CIO's 32 unions exchanged signatures, and in a joint statement Meany and Reuther declared the existence of a "cease-fire" during which other problems might be solved and a merger of their federations brought about.[23]

Eager to see that outcome, Dubinsky moved to implement the no-raiding pact within his own union. As various locals of the International were in the midst of jurisdictional fights across the country, he sent them copies of it. The ILG-ers had to understand that the agreement was aimed at preventing future disputes rather than resolving past ones.[24]

As the federation presidents had anticipated, the pact served as a truce during which further progress was made, and another dozen AFL unions and one CIO union agreed not to raid. On October 15, the Unity Committee unanimously recommended merger and authorized the presidents "to appoint a joint subcommittee to draft a detailed plan." On February 10, 1955, the Executive Council gave its unanimous approval to the subcommittee's plan, with its CIO counterpart scheduled to meet and act two weeks later. A joint convention in December would consummate the marriage.[25] Dubinsky called it "an event of tremendous historical significance."[26]

As the merger took shape, it was hard to argue that the ILGWU represented anything but the best in American unionism. The press regularly praised its president for his honesty and anti-Communism. Critics said he was a political "boss," but the Liberal Party was the voice of anti-Communist workers and intellectuals in New York State, who revered the New and Fair Deals and helped put Herbert Lehman in the U.S. Senate and W. Averell Harriman in the governor's mansion in Albany.

The ILGWU also continued its tradition of social unionism. Though the Amalgamated Clothing Workers had been the trade-union pioneer in cooperative housing, during the 1950s the International caught up. In 1949 and 1950, Congress had enacted legislation to promote the construction of low-cost housing. Conservative pressure prevented the inclusion of assistance for middle-income housing through cooperatives and other non-profit organizations. Not covered, therefore, were families with incomes too high for public housing and too low to afford the private sector. Incensed at what they regarded as capitulation to the real estate lobby, ILGWU delegates at their 1950 convention passed nine resolutions on public housing.[27]

These resolutions coincided with plans that Abraham Kazan, the president of the Amalgamated Housing Corporation, had for the Lower East Side of Manhattan. Kazan, who had already built three housing developments—one in the Bronx and two in Manhattan—for the Amalgamated Clothing Workers, approached ACWA president Jacob Potofsky with plans for a fourth, to run north from Grand Street along the East River in an area known as Corlears Hook. It would be built by a new United Housing Foundation, which Kazan and others had created to use union funds to produce workers' cooperatives. Potofsky, however, refused to endorse the scheme. "Kazan, what do you want—to build over the whole city?" he asked. "Interest other people. I've got a problem." The "problem" happened to be money, which Potofsky would not commit to a huge mortgage. Kazan turned to Dubinsky and the ILGWU. "All right. . . . What will it mean? Will you handle it?" the ILGWU president asked, to which Kazan replied, "Yes, I'll follow through." In March 1951, Kazan described the project to the New York members of the ILGWU General Executive Board, who agreed to have the International sponsor it.[28]

The Lower East Side houses would cost $20 million, to be financed by private institutions and the federal government. Included was a mortgage of $15 million, to be insured by the Federal Housing Authority (FHA). The GEB authorized the ILGWU to supply the entire amount, despite the reluctance of Executive Secretary Fred Umhey, who thought it mistaken "for the union to invest in long-term mortgages which were not liquid, if it could be avoided." What did appear avoidable was ILGWU coverage of the full loan, as the Bowery Savings Bank offered to provide $7.5 million, half the total. Therefore, pending approval of the plan by the Federal Housing Authority, the financing would be equally shared.

The parties awaited the FHA's approval, which was slow in coming. Among other things, the FHA wanted guarantees that Kazan's proposed budget was sufficient to complete construction. Nearly a year passed, and as it did, the economic climate changed. The Bowery withdrew its offer.

Kazan then sought a replacement institution but, finding none, again turned for help to Dubinsky, who was attending an AFL Executive Council meeting in Miami. To the developer's great relief, the ILGWU president "agreed to take the entire loan." Believing the investment to be sound, and understanding that builders had submitted inflated cost estimates that the FHA accepted, Dubinsky decided to save an estimated $1 million and move ahead without the agency's insurance. Meanwhile, Kazan and Umhey continued to negotiate with the bankers, who finally relented and reclaimed their share.[29]

On November 21, 1953, a groundbreaking ceremony was held "in the midst of vast rubble" at the Grand Street site. "We have wiped out the sweatshop. Now we return to wipe out the slum," Dubinsky said. Giving credit where it was due, he generously complimented the Bowery Savings Bank "for having come forward with the necessary mortgage."[30]

Construction progressed well, despite protests from community activists who complained of its displacement of 878 mainly Puerto Rican families. Heralded as a major cooperative venture, the project had too much powerful support to be stopped, and on October 22, 1955, four buildings designed to house 1,668 families were dedicated. On hand to praise the project, known as the ILGWU Cooperative Village, were such notables as George Meany, Eleanor Roosevelt, Mayor Wagner, and Senators Lehman and Ives. "These buildings represent what free labor can accomplish," the AFL president said.[31]

As the Cooperative Village took shape, overseas events also occupied Dubinsky's mind. The international labor movement and Israel remained major concerns, and Jay Lovestone continued to serve as his chief lieutenant in the war with Communism. In 1949, the founding conference of the International Confederation of Free Trade Unions had placed its headquarters in Brussels and elected Joachim H. Oldenbroek of the Dutch Transport Workers' Federation its general secretary. The next summer, after making an initial request through Lovestone, Oldenbroek persuaded Dubinsky to have the ILGWU lend the ICFTU $50,000 to construct a housing project in the Belgian capital.[32]

When the United Nations was founded, William Green had appointed Dubinsky and Matthew Woll to serve as consultants from the AFL to the UN Economic and Social Council. With the advent of the ICFTU, they became consultants from that body as the AFL stepped aside. Jacob Potofsky and Michael Ross were consultants from the CIO.[33]

In the summer of 1951, Dubinsky was looking forward to another European trip. He would go to Milan as the head of a six-person ILGWU contingent within the AFL delegation to the Second World Congress of the ICFTU, beginning July 4.[34] However, before leaving for Europe, Dubinsky ventured upstate to Bard College at Annandale-on-Hudson to receive an extraordinary award, especially to one who had come from Lodz to the Lower East Side, with little formal education in Europe. On June 16 an honorary Doctor of Laws degree was conferred on him, and he was cited for, among other things, having "fought skillfully and implacably against exploitation in every form" and "opened to others doors of opportunity and education."[35]

On June 18, Dubinsky left New York by airplane for Paris, where he spent a week before going on to Lake Como for a few days and then to Milan. He found an ICFTU less united than it had been at its founding two years earlier in London. Officially the ICFTU seemed determined to break with Communist unions, particularly in France and Italy. However, beneath the surface there was disquiet. The CIO's newly appointed director of European operations, Victor Reuther, was inclined to move in a manner less strident than that favored by the AFL and the overwhelming majority of the three hundred delegates present. Reuther had little use for the belligerent anti-Communism of the AFL's chief anti-Communist strategist, Jay Lovestone, who was on the ILGWU delegation, and the feeling was mutual. As Dubinsky saw things, the CIO was seeking "to push itself to the forefront" of the ICFTU and was impeding the anti-Communist intervention in the Italian labor movement that the AFL had begun.

The Italian question at Milan concerned the *Confederazione Italiana Sindacati Lavoratori* (CISL), dominated by the Catholic trade unionists and the *Unione Italiana del Lavoro* (UIL), a smaller group of Social Democrats. The UIL had been organized in March 1950, a month before the CISL, and refused to follow the leadership of the confederation and its leader, Giulio Pastore. In contrast, the AFL supported the CISL, the sole Italian labor group affiliated with the ICFTU, as a reliable, anti-Communist solution to Italy's labor problems.

At Milan, the UIL applied for membership. The AFL delegates, including the ILGWU members, opposed the move, insisting on a UIL merger with the CISL rather than parallel representation. By contrast, the CIO-ers present, such as Jacob Potofsky and Arthur Goldberg, supported the UIL position and urged collaboration between the two Italian groups, believing that both were democratic and capable of working together. To resolve this and other differences, the American delegates met in a caucus led by Matthew Woll. On most matters, the CIO-ers yielded to the AFL, but the ICFTU admitted the UIL.[36]

As the AFL's relations with the CIO tentatively improved, its differences with the ICFTU increased. In November 1951, the ICFTU's Executive Board took several actions that greatly displeased George Meany, who was in attendance. When the ICFTU was founded, the British and American trade unionists agreed to keep it from domination by a big power. Regardless of this understanding, however, the Executive Board elected Sir Vincent Tewson of the British Trades Union Congress to succeed Paul Finet as president. In addition, the Second World Congress, with American approval, had approved of admitting the anti-Communist Australian Workers Union (AWU), but only after the Australian Council of Trade Unions (ACTU) was affiliated. However, at the November meeting, the ACTU objected to the admission of the AWU. Reneging on the earlier accord, the Executive Board then excluded the Australian Workers Union. To Meany's dismay, the Executive Board also failed to act properly relative to Yugoslavia. He proposed that the ICFTU "condemn" the country's "anti-democratic regime . . . and demand the re-establishment of free trade unions and the liberation of those now imprisoned for this principle." Parliamentary tactics kept this motion from even being discussed.[37]

In May, Meany declared that the AFL would boycott meetings of the ICFTU until it satisfactorily addressed his complaints. The AFL Executive Council reaffirmed this position, as did an editorial in *Justice*, which also decried the breach, calling the ICFTU "free labor's most potent bulwark against communism." Meany was determined to make the ICFTU more hard-line anti-Communist, which included removing Tewson, whom the AFL regarded as weak on Communism, from the presidency. In pursuit of these goals, he ended the AFL boycott and in July 1953 attended the Third World Congress at Stockholm. There he pushed through some structural changes, which included more than doubling the size of the Executive Board. Tewson declined to run for reelection and was succeeded by the secretary-general of the International Transport Workers Federation, Omer Becu of Belgium, who, according to Joseph Goulden, Meany's biographer, "was a close friend of both Lovestone and Dave Dubinsky." Becu's election, delegate Lovestone reported to Dubinsky, "was a big victory for the A. F. of L."[38]

Immersed in Liberal Party as well as ILGWU affairs in 1953, Dubinsky had not gone to Stockholm. To his opponents on the left, he was a sinister figure who, with Lovestone and Irving Brown and support from the CIA, "put into execution . . . the Dubinsky foreign policy for America."[39]

The following May, Dubinsky headed for Europe again, sailing from New York with Emma and the Meanys aboard the *Queen Mary* to attend the Fourth World Congress of the ICFTU in Vienna. On May 20, five days after the signing of the Austrian State Treaty, which ended the postwar division of Austria into occupation zones and created a neutral, independent state, the meeting began. As at the previous congresses, the AFL delegation promoted the cause of anti-Communism and again achieved some success. On May 5, the Federal Republic of Germany had come into being, a sovereign state that the next day joined the North Atlantic Treaty Organization (NATO). With the new state's establishment, the West German Trade Union Federation reversed its previous position and declared itself in favor of armament and participation in the fight against "Soviet tyranny."[40]

After Vienna, Dubinsky visited Israel as the guest of *Histadrut* and followed a hectic itinerary that included addressing trade unionists at Haifa, visiting collective farms, and being honored at a luncheon hosted by Premier Moshe Sharett. On behalf of Radio Liberation, a station operated by refugees from the Soviet Union, Dubinsky broadcast a message to Soviet workers. He recounted his own immigrant experience and the progress organized American labor, notably the ILGWU, had made since the days of the sweatshop. His next stop was Rome, where he met with Giulio Pastore. Then it was off to Mondello, Sicily, to appear at the seventh commencement exercises at the Franklin Delano Roosevelt School of Maritime Trades, which had been constructed with ILGWU money for the vocational training of Italian war orphans. Six weeks after his departure, Dubinsky returned to New York.[41]

The interest of the ILGWU in foreign working conditions was a tradition with roots in the earliest days of the union. With genuine regard for all workers as brethren, the International had regularly expressed compassion for underpaid and overworked laborers overseas, as it had for those in the United States and Canada. Through the 1940s it was evident that exploitation at home also constituted a threat to the higher standards of employment achieved by organized labor. Goods produced by the unorganized enjoyed price and profit advantages over union-made items. Employers whose shops were unionized often became "runaways," relocating their operations in locales friendlier to business, notably the American South. Goods from abroad were not yet a serious problem.

At mid-century the International noticed a change. Between 1939 and 1952, exports of women's clothing had nearly tripled, but imports rose much more sharply—increasing more than sevenfold in the same period. The ratio of exports to imports, which had been 3.15:1 in 1939, dropped to 1.24:1 by 1952. The GEB of the ILGWU attributed this decline to a lack of aggressiveness in promotion on the part of American women's wear producers.[42]

As Gus Tyler would write, the system of "outside" production was undergoing transformation. Traditionally, the term referred to apparel manufactured beyond the premises of a jobber, by an outside contractor. Now it began to mean "beyond the United States," and its initial impact was on the Neckwear Workers, Local 142. "Scarf manufacturers . . . , faced by a withering competition from Japan, . . . turned to importing," resulting in a decline in employment in New York's scarf shops—from 1,400 in 1950 to "only about 125" in 1953.[43]

An alarm sounded, but to no apparent effect, as Japanese-made blouses and sweaters followed scarves. Between 1954 and 1955, cotton blouse and shirt imports rose from 189,214 dozen to 4,234,000 dozen, and sweaters from 13,642 to 104,742 dozen. Among the imports was the "one-dollar blouse," bearing a retail price below the cost of domestic wholesale. Of the American firms that imported the blouses, some did so in violation of ILGWU contracts and were compelled to pay monetary damages. Dubinsky rejected unilateral American trade sanctions as a solution to this problem and instead called for a bilateral accord between the United States and Japan to establish a "free and regulated" trading relationship that would benefit Japanese as well as American workers.[44] Despite this plea, the flood of imports continued and also included high-priced goods; the ILGWU faced a threat against which it had no effective defense.

Still, it could do battle as in the past against cheap domestic labor. In concert with the AFL, the International supported a movement to raise the federal minimum wage from 75 cents, where it had been set in 1949, to $1.25 per hour. The need for a boost was especially great in the South, where low wages and hostility to the ILGWU and other unions went hand in hand. As President Eisenhower favored an increase in the federal minimum to 90 cents, it was clear that some revision would follow. However, an intensive national campaign, which included the International, the

Amalgamated, and the CIO Textile Workers' Union, and an appearance by Dubinsky in April 1955 before the Labor Subcommittee of the Senate Committee on Public Welfare could not persuade Congress to pass the higher amount. In June, Congress settled on $1.00, to take effect in 1956.[45]

Another major problem was the wage differential between workers on the U.S. mainland and those in Puerto Rico. The Wages and Hours Act of 1938 had set a 40-cents-per-hour and forty-hour standard for the mainland but nothing for the island, where a wage board would soon recommend rates. In 1940, as one of the first members of that board, Dubinsky discovered wages of people making corsets and brassieres as low as 5 cents an hour. In 1954, with the rate now at 33 cents, he again served, and a board recommendation raised the wage to 55 cents. Dubinsky, aided by George Meany and the AFL, urged a statutory minimum wage for the commonwealth to keep pace with whatever increase might be obtained for the mainland.

In July 1955, as a bill providing for the mainland but not the island moved toward passage, the ILGWU held a mass meeting of Puerto Rican workers near Union Square. Accompanied by Hipolito Marcano, president of the Puerto Rican Federation of Labor, Dubinsky denounced those who opposed coverage for Puerto Rico as "inhuman and un-American." The rally generated heat, but the bill nevertheless passed without the island's inclusion. Undaunted by this setback, in January 1956 the ILGWU obtained a four-year collective-bargaining agreement that gave 75 percent of Puerto Rico's 4,000 brassiere workers a 15-cent-an-hour increase.[46]

Despite the shadow, these were good times for Dubinsky. The ILGWU was at peak membership and prestige; Wagner and Harriman were in charge of New York city and state government; the AFL and CIO were finally at peace; and the Communist threat to workers at home evidently was under control. From the construction of houses in New York to vocational schools abroad, the International continued to epitomize social unionism. In 1957, Dubinsky would celebrate his sixty-fifth birthday and twenty-fifth year as ILGWU president; but given his unabated energy and extensive activities, retirement was not on the horizon.

18

Trouble on Seventh Avenue

The nearly 1,100 ILG-ers were unusually festive. Coming together at Atlantic City on May 23, 1950, for the International's twenty-seventh triennial convention, they also celebrated the union's fiftieth birthday. At this "Golden Jubilee" the delegates witnessed the premiere showing of *With These Hands,* a motion picture based on the history of the union, and received copies of *ILGWU News-History, 1900–1950,* a book of reprints of news articles, photographs, and cartoons.[1]

As part of the celebration the delegates sought to honor their president for the past eighteen years, David Dubinsky. After he rejected a proposal to raise his $15,600 annual salary by $10,000, they approved a weekly increase of $50. Additionally, they directed the GEB "to find a place of relaxation" where he would "have an opportunity for rest away from the turmoil of his busy and active life and . . . enjoy his leisure moments."[2]

Four years later he found his hideaway, "3 hours by car" from New York, which he rented with an option to buy. Consistent with the convention resolution, in November 1955 the International purchased the house for nearly $35,000, including renovations. Though Dubinsky did not hold the deed, in August 1956 he reported to Harry Lang "that the Dubinskys are now the proud owners of a home of their own in Hampton Bays, Long Island." "Beautifully located on a Bay and not far from the ocean, we bought an old house and renovated it so that it is livable and comfortable."[3]

June 1957 marked the twenty-fifth anniversary of Dubinsky's presidency, and on June 13 a thousand ILG-ers and their friends paid tribute to him at Madison Square Garden on what was called DD Day.[4] Four days later, the General Executive Board met at Unity House, where Dubinsky discussed two more serious developments. Democrat John Mc-Clellan of Tennessee had become chairman of the Senate Permanent Subcommittee on Investigations, which was investigating corruption within trade unions. Moreover, the Executive Council of the AFL-CIO had recently approved several codes of ethical conduct. Drafted by the Ethical Practices Committee, to which he belonged, the codes covered conflicts of interest, racketeering, health and welfare funds, and local union charters. The GEB approved them and created a committee to recommend even "more stringent codes of ethics" for the International.

Though the codes were no problem, Luigi Antonini had some qualms about Dubinsky. Antonini alleged that meetings of ILGWU officers that he had recently called tended to put everyone under suspicion. Turning the tables on the president, he questioned the gift house in Hampton Bays.

Dubinsky defended the meetings as "a genuine service to the union" because they "alerted those few in the union who were under suspicion" and called it "wholly proper for the union to purchase a summer home for its President." Recent events, however, made it necessary to be certain the transaction appeared proper. In Washington, the McClellan Committee had already exposed the Teamsters' practice of buying houses for their presidents. Dave Beck, the incumbent Teamster president, had sold his home, built with supposedly "borrowed" Teamster funds, to his union for $163,215 and then received free use of it. Dubinsky declared that he did not want an "unreasonable parallel" to be drawn with the Teamsters' "utterly improper and unethical" situation and therefore would "repay the union" for his house at the rate of $5,000 a year.[5] The GEB accepted this offer, and in August 1960 the purchase was completed.[6]

Along with his own residences, Dubinsky continued to be interested in housing for others. Regarded as a success upon its dedication, the Cooperative Village sparked additional ILGWU real estate activity both at home and abroad. Such investment, Dubinsky felt, benefited the union's health and welfare funds as well as the occupants of the new homes. In 1956 and 1957 the International committed $40 million to house U.S. military veterans and Air Force families.[7] Also in 1957, after having cooperated with Nelson Rockefeller to build houses in Israel, the ILGWU combined with him to purchase mortgages in San Juan, Puerto Rico, to the extent of $2,600,000. The Rockefeller family would construct a community named for Puerto Rican labor leader Santiago Iglesias that would consist of 400 homes, 250 of which were to be available to the recently organized ILGWU members, who would have first choice. At a groundbreaking ceremony, Dubinsky said the International looked "to a better way of life in general, . . . and better housing means better living."[8]

This vision included additional housing for New York. The Cooperative Village had attracted "thousands" of applicants who could not be accommodated. Only a quarter of the units initially allocated went to ILGWU members because they had been too slow to respond to the initial offering. In January 1956, the possibility of a second project arose when Robert Moses, the chairman of Mayor Wagner's Committee on Slum Clearance, reported that the New York Building Trades Council was interested in investing pension and welfare funds in cooperative housing. In May the International's convention in Atlantic City enthusiastically endorsed the idea.[9]

What Moses had in mind was a project on Manhattan's East Side, between Third and Lexington Avenues and Twenty-third and Twenty-seventh Streets. He mentioned it to Abraham Kazan, who then discussed it with some of the directors of the United Housing Foundation (UHF), including the ILGWU's Charles Zimmerman. It was Zimmerman's idea, which Kazan and the other directors accepted, that the project be "a 'walk to work' job" on the West Side instead of the East, because most garment shops were located in that area. The UHF selected a site bounded by Twenty-third and Twenty-ninth Streets and Seventh and Eighth Avenues, in Manhattan's Chelsea section. At Zimmerman's suggestion, Kazan approached Dubinsky, who obtained his board's approval to cover not more than $20 million of a loan of $30 million to build 2,820 apartments.[10] In March 1959, the New York City Board of Estimate approved the project, but the completion of financial arrangements took another two years. At last, in addition to the ILGWU, the Chemical Bank New York Trust Company, Dry Dock Savings Bank, and the New York State Teachers' Retirement Fund backed the project. In the meantime, work began on the development that came to be referred to as Penn Station South.[11]

On May 19, 1962, a proud David Dubinsky beamed as the president of the United States, John F. Kennedy, participated in a dedication ceremony. Speaking in ninety-nine-degree heat, Kennedy jokingly protested the "sweatshop conditions" under which he was working. In the company of Nelson Rockefeller, Robert Wagner, Eleanor Roosevelt, and thousands of garment workers, Kennedy then praised the International and its president and asked that other unions imitate its example. It was a day to remember.[12]

. . .

In 1958, New York's dressmakers went on strike for the first time since 1933. Their walkout was a startling sign that all was not well on Seventh Avenue, despite the ILGWU's high membership, visibility, and ostensible prosperity. The International had "always boasted," *Justice* editor Leon Stein recalled, that collective bargaining had "worked," as evidenced by the absence of costly stoppages.[13] However, on March 5, 105,000 dressmakers from "approximately two thousand shops" in New York and six neighboring states indeed left their places, jolting an industry "which then produced approximately one hundred million dresses a year, 72% of all domestic dress production."[14]

The conflict originated in Pennsylvania, a state popular with garment manufacturers who escaped from New York City unionized working conditions but enjoyed the advantages of proximity. Unlike those who fled to the South, employers in Pennsylvania paid low wages *and* had their goods trucked inexpensively into the nearby New York market. The organized workers in the Keystone State in effect competed with their brothers and sisters in New York. The depressed conditions most likely resulted from poor contract enforcement. A 1956 study had revealed that the wage level in Wilkes Barre exceeded that of nonunion Dallas, Texas, by "only two cents an hour." Dubinsky demanded action. The result was a campaign to educate shop stewards and the membership and to pressure employers to pay settled rates.[15]

Employers resisted the ILGWU thrust, and by the end of April 1957 walkouts idled "close to 70 shops." Urged on by union leaders at mass rallies, the ILGWU members negotiated contracts with 75 percent of the struck employers. Equally determined not to yield, in late October the contractors who made up the Pennsylvania Garment Manufacturers Association conducted a three-day lockout of its workers and seceded from its parent group, the United Popular Dress Association, which also in effect severed its commitment to the New York Dress Joint Board agreement. Seventy New York–based jobbers then said they, too, would remain apart. The secessionist Pennsylvania contractors and jobbers had thus served notice that they wanted separate and inferior conditions in their shops. Challenged by this adamant defense of a two-tier structure separating Pennsylvania from New York and threatening the control and stability represented by the industry-wide agreement, the General Executive Board of the ILGWU authorized a strike of the New York dress industry.[16]

With this authorization in hand, the International negotiated with the divided employers. On January 31, 1958, when the contract expired, the parties extended it for a month, but no renewal resulted. With a walkout imminent, Dubinsky assured Robert Wagner that the competitiveness of New York industry was at stake and asked that Herbert Lehman and dress industry impartial chairman Harry Uviller serve as mediators. On March 5 the strike began, followed two days later by their appointment. Led by Dress Joint Board manager Julius Hochman, at 4 a.m. on March 9 the International obtained an agreement, but not with the secessionists. The accord provided for, among other things, an 8 percent wage increase, holiday and overtime pay for pieceworkers, a Severance Fund, and a union label to be sewn in all garments.

The holdout Pennsylvania contractors and jobbers took several weeks longer to settle. In April, Dubinsky went to Pennsylvania to rally his troops. Though acts of violence sometimes greeted the strikers, they persevered and all but a handful of the holdouts signed up. The next year, probable mob revenge victimized two ILGWU workers. In February 1959, Sol Greene, the assistant general manager of the Dress Joint Board, was beaten by three assailants outside his Tenafly, New Jersey home, and in May, Charles Zimmerman, who had succeeded Julius Hochman as general manager of the Dress Joint Council and the Dress Joint Board, was blackjacked by a hoodlum in Miami after the ILGWU convention in that city.[17]

Of the eleven left-wing unions expelled by the CIO in 1949, only the International Fur and Leather Workers Union (IFLWU) was directed by an avowed Communist (and longtime adversary of David Dubinsky), Ben Gold, the former secretary of the Needle Trade Workers' Industrial Union. Highly popular and a skilled collective bargainer, Gold had been president of the IFLWU since its creation in 1939 and was also a member of the national committee of the Communist Party of the United States. However, in 1950, with IFLWU locals on the defensive against raids by CIO unions, he declared that he had resigned from the party and then signed the non-Communist Taft-Hartley affidavit. Gold and his union defended themselves on this basis until 1954, when a federal court convicted him of perjury, as no resignation had occurred. Congress's outlawing of the Communist Party in the same year made it clear that the IFLWU would not be permitted to participate in elections conducted by the National Labor Relations Board. Under such pressure Gold resigned as president in October 1954 and was succeeded by the non-Communist director of operations in the Midwest, Abe Feinglass. Presumably the IFLWU could now find safe haven with an AFL or CIO union. Ironically, it turned to the AFL's Amalgamated Meat Cutters and Butcher Workmen of North America, which had been vying with it for the right to represent 1,500 workers in Massachusetts. In agreeing to take the Fur and Leather Workers, the Meat Cutters demanded that all officers sign the Taft-Hartley affidavit and that Gold and Irving Potash, his Communist lieutenant, forever be prohibited from holding union office.[18] The apparent surrender of the IFLWU was not an entirely independent gesture. In its weakened condition, the union could only obey the orders that the Communist Party issued to it and other labor organizations at this time. As Dubinsky noted in 1955, "the Communist Party, for reasons of its own, instructed some of its people not to put up a fight."[19]

Distrustful as usual when Communists were involved, Dubinsky found fault with the reported merger terms. It was important, he wrote Meany, to deal with the "cardinal problem of Communist domination" of the IFLWU's executive board and most affiliates.[20] Moreover, according to Max Federman, who led an anti-Communist opposition group within the union, Feinglass was "a double A-1 Communist and much worse than Gold."[21] Jay Lovestone reminded Meany that, in 1949, Feinglass opposed the expulsion of Communists from the CIO.[22] Not surprisingly, therefore, in December 1954, the AFL Executive Council unanimously disapproved the proposed merger.[23]

Dubinsky's concern was that Patrick E. Gorman, the Meat Cutters' secretary-treasurer, was insufficiently concerned about the Communist menace posed by the Fur and Leather Workers. According to Ben Gold's *Memoirs,* Gorman was indeed hoping to shelter the IFLWU.[24] Whatever his initial intentions, Gorman quickly learned that a merger without AFL approval would mean expulsion from the Federation. Rather than take the fateful step, he first met with the AFL Executive Council in Chicago and Dubinsky in New York. As the experienced combatant with Gold and other Communists in the needle trades, the ILGWU president was Meany's logical choice to instruct Gorman as to how to make the merger acceptable. Gorman soon began the "decommunizing" of the Fur and Leather Workers, including the removal of eleven IFLWU officers in New York and four in Canada.[25]

The purge continued into the fall. On October 25, the AFL vice presidents at last withdrew their objection to the merger. "Be assured that we shall continue to fight Reds wherever we find them," Gorman and Meat Cutters' president Earl W. Jimerson afterward wrote Dubinsky.[26]

When the AFL expelled the Longshoremen in 1953, it at last signaled its readiness to take decisive action against unsavory elements within its ranks. Also that year, a congressional subcommittee investigated Teamster activities in the Detroit area and afterward recommended a "thorough study of so-called welfare and pension funds" in order to draft legislation to safeguard them.[27]

Mindful of the need for additional AFL action, George Meany brought a statement on the funds before the Executive Council for its approval. The Teamsters' Dave Beck said he objected to "any statement" because he felt his union alone was under scrutiny. Defending Meany, Dubinsky argued that the labor movement in general was under attack. The EC adopted an amended statement that praised AFL affiliates that had already tightened their fund administration and urged others to adopt "uniform standards and procedures."[28]

As a union president whose own affiliates managed two dozen funds, Dubinsky argued for effective self-regulation in an article in the July 1954 issue of the *American Federationist*. Unless such action was implemented, Dubinsky warned, the labor movement would find itself targeted by its enemies for "punitive legislation directed against labor as a whole."[29] He took this position well aware that conditions within the International itself were far from perfect.[30]

With the CIO merger drawing near, Meany placed Dubinsky at the head of a committee on welfare funds. However, major actions would have to await the First Constitutional Convention of the merged AFL-CIO in December 1955.[31] The constitution authorized the creation of a Committee on Ethical Practices to help the Executive Council keep the Federation free of corruption.[32]

Before the month was over, Meany announced that such a committee had been formed. The chairman was President Albert J. Hayes of the International Association of Machinists, and Presidents George Harrison of the Railway Clerks, Joseph Curran of the National Maritime Union, Jacob Potofsky of the Amalgamated, and David Dubinsky of the International were members. A few months after the committee's formation, the Federation was under additional pressure to act against racketeering. At 3 a.m., April 5, newspaper columnist and radio commentator Victor Riesel concluded a broadcast in which he condemned a local of the International Union of Operating Engineers. An hour later, as he and two others emerged from Lindy's restaurant, a thug threw sulfuric acid in his face, permanently blinding him.

Riesel and Dubinsky were old friends. Along with a distaste for racketeering, Riesel shared an ILGWU heritage. Nathan Riesel, his father, had been a founder of the Bonnaz Workers' Union and business agent of Local 66, Embroidery Workers, who often took Victor to union meetings. On hearing of the acid attack, Dubinsky called it a "shameful occurrence," and the GEB of the International posted a $10,000 reward for the arrest and conviction of the assailant. On July 28, Abe Telvi, the alleged perpetrator, was found shot to death on Mulberry Street.[33]

"Labor racketeering takes the spotlight," *Fortune* magazine announced in May, noting that federal investigators were looking into New York's garment and food-processing industries, and that the allies of the former head of the Operating Engineers Union, Joseph Fay, who had been convicted for extortion, were moving to control his union. It reported with obvious relish that Teamster vice president James R. Hoffa "was driving hard to form a teamster-longshore combination that would give him absolute rule over the movement of goods in and out" of New York City.[34] When asked if charges of "widespread union racketeering" were justified, Hoffa denied there was racketeering in the Teamsters union.[35] Hoffa's reassurances notwithstanding, Governor Harriman and Mayor Wagner met in July with Dubinsky, Potofsky, and Harrison of the Ethical Practices Committee to coordinate efforts to cleanse the city.[36]

By July the AFL-CIO Executive Council had already begun to empower its Committee on Ethical Practices by authorizing it to investigate Federation affiliates and asking it to "develop principles and guidelines" to keep the organization "free from all corrupt influences."[37] In August the committee issued reports on the Distillery, Laundry, and Allied Industrial Workers unions, concluding that racketeers might be running them. On this basis, the EC unanimously agreed to compel the Distillery Workers to "show cause" why its Federation membership should not be suspended and formally to investigate the others.[38]

At the month's end, the EC adopted a code of conduct with regard to the issuance of local union charters. In January 1957 three more codes followed, on "health and welfare plan administration," on "racketeers, crooks, Communists and fascists," and on "conflicts of interest in the investment and business interests of union officials."[39] In May the EC adopted two final codes, on "financial practices of unions" and on "union democratic processes."[40]

With the adoption of these codes, organized labor at last made eradicating racketeers a major priority, something that Dubinsky had sought since 1940. "What a change," he observed. "Now the crooks have to hide, not the honest men. We have the tools to do the job and we will not stop until we do it."[41] "We must not wait for the verdict of courts," he told the United Auto Workers. "We must act wherever we find and we are convinced that a man is not honest and abuses the trust placed in him." Government, he added, also had to take action. Ignoring labor's traditional aversion to such intervention, he called for legislation to compel unions to report all their funds, not just those related to health and welfare.[42]

Unfortunately for Dubinsky and the AFL-CIO, this call to arms came when the American labor movement was already under siege. Beginning in January 1957, as McClellan's Senate committee conducted hearings, corrupt labor leaders and racketeers made fresh headlines. After McClellan reported that Dave Beck had possibly "misappropriated over $320,000 in [Teamsters] union funds" and had demonstrated "flagrant disregard and disrespect for honest and reputable Unionism and for the best interests and welfare of the laboring people of this country," George Meany called the EC into session. Backed by Dubinsky, he persuaded the body to agree to file charges of misconduct against Beck and direct the Ethical Practices Committee to investigate the Teamsters.[43]

At the heart of Dubinsky's dilemma, as always, was his frustration over out-of-control criminal elements within the International, notably its Truckers Local 102. Also clear is that, in addition to legislation, Dubinsky had long sought help from the Federal Bureau of Investigation. As early as May 1952, he had reported the beginning of mob infiltration of the ILGWU to the FBI and expressed a complete lack of confidence in the ability of either the New York police or the Department of Justice. An informant reported that the "only people he had confidence in Washington were those in the FBI."[44] Eventually Dubinsky requested and received the Bureau's assistance.[45]

The manager of Local 102 and an associate of mobster Johnny Dio, Samuel Berger, was a source of continuing embarrassment. Aware that Dubinsky would at last move against him, after he invoked the Fifth Amendment's protection against self-incrimination before a federal grand jury in February 1957, Berger submitted a letter of resignation.[46] Dubinsky regarded it as right for a union officer to use the Fifth Amendment "to protect his union" but not to avoid "questions . . . on matters affecting his faithfulness to the union trust." In January 1957 the AFL Executive Council adopted a policy statement on the matter, maintaining that a union official had "no right to continue to hold office" if he invoked the Fifth Amendment "for his personal protection and to avoid scrutiny by proper legislative committees, law enforcement agencies or other public bodies into alleged corruption on his part."[47]

The following July the McClellan Committee inquired into Dio's UAW-AFL charter. Samuel Zakman, a former UAW-AFL official, was the witness. Senator Barry Goldwater of Arizona asked if the ILGWU president had known of the charter when Berger helped Dio obtain it. Zakman replied that he did not think Dubinsky was aware of it at the time. McClellan then said it was his understanding that Dubinsky learned about the document "about a year later," and General Counsel Robert F. Kennedy noted that Dubinsky had publicly reprimanded Berger as soon as he heard about it.[48]

The next day saw an additional challenge. Lester Washburn, the former president of the UAW-AFL, which had since become the Allied Industrial Workers, testified that in 1950, Dio had been employed by the ILGWU in Roanoke, Virginia, to help organize an especially resistant factory. The committee also heard that Dubinsky had urged Washburn to oust Dio from the UAW, but what made headlines was that the racketeer had served as an ILGWU "agent."[49] A week later a livid Dubinsky vigorously denied that he either knew or employed Dio. In a sworn affidavit sent to McClellan, Dubinsky noted that the Roanoke shop in question had actually been organized by the ILGWU in 1945, and that Dio "was on the firm's payroll and not ours."[50] The controversial Dio, who had two weeks earlier been convicted on bribery and conspiracy charges, spent two hours before the McClellan Committee. He revealed little other than an ability to invoke the Fifth Amendment 140 times, including in response to whether he had ever worked for Dubinsky.[51]

Without presenting tangible evidence of ILGWU corruption, the McClellan Committee hearings nevertheless raised enough suspicions to tarnish the image of the union and its president. Berger's relationship with Dio, Dubinsky's failure to oust the former from the managership of Local 102, and the allegation that Dio had worked for the International generated headlines unbecoming a member of the AFL-CIO Ethical Practices Committee.

In March, Dave Beck had cited the Fifth Amendment more than two hundred times while testifying before the committee.[52] Seven weeks later, on May 20, the AFL-CIO Executive Council determined that he had used Teamsters funds "for his own personal gain and profit" and voted unanimously to terminate his AFL-CIO vice presidency and Council membership.[53] Teamsters vice president James R. Hoffa followed Beck to McClellan's witness stand but did not "take the Fifth." He relied on his own shrewdness.[54] Nevertheless, as the hearings continued, evidence mounted that he had indulged in financial skulduggery, racketeering, and violence and had demonstrated disdain for union democracy. In October, undeterred by these revelations or pressure from George Meany to change their leadership, the Teamsters elected Hoffa to succeed Beck as president, and the Executive Council suspended the union from the AFL-CIO. Little more than a month later, at the AFL-CIO convention in Atlantic City, the delegates voted four-to-one for the Teamsters' expulsion.[55]

In committee and on the convention floor, Dubinsky voted for expulsion, backing George Meany, who favored this method of discipline. Personally, Dubinsky regarded it as inequitable, because, as he later explained, it exiled the entire Teamsters membership. He would have preferred to undermine racketeers by amending the AFL-CIO constitution to prohibit them, as the AFL constitution had Communists, from sitting as convention delegates. His vote to expel, Dubinsky explained, kept him from appearing to champion "the cause of Dave Beck or Jimmy Hoffa or any other labor renegade."[56]

The mobilization of the AFL-CIO against racketeering was a major victory for Meany and Dubinsky but clearly not the end of the road to reform. Early in 1958, President Dwight D. Eisenhower proposed to Congress that a new federal agency be established to investigate union finances, elections, and measures to ensure union democracy. In fear of "big brother," Meany doubted the wisdom of such intervention. In contrast, Dubinsky, addressing the executive board of the Retail Clerks International Union, praised the idea and forecast that organized labor would eventually welcome such investigative machinery.[57] Meanwhile, within the ILGWU, the General Executive Board tightened its own rules of conduct.[58] In December 1959 the GEB addressed the matter of employer gifts to union officers, business agents, and organizers and their purchase of goods at wholesale prices. It declared such gifts to be "contrary to the ethical practices of the ILGWU."[59]

While the AFL-CIO pursued its campaign against corruption, Congress, influenced by the McClellan Committee hearings, moved inevitably toward new legislation. In June 1959, economist J. F. Bell wrote that it was "crystal clear that union membership must be protected from its own leadership."[60]

In 1957, Democratic senator John Fitzgerald Kennedy of Massachusetts chaired the U.S. Senate's Labor Subcommittee. In 1958 he cosponsored, with Republican senator Irving M. Ives of New York, a bipartisan labor reform bill. This measure easily cleared the Senate but died in the House, a victim of mainly Republican and business, but also some labor, opposition.[61]

In 1959, Kennedy reintroduced his bill in the Senate, with Sam Ervin of North Carolina as cosponsor. With Taft-Hartley amendments unsatisfactory to the AFL-CIO, this version placated business. However, it also exempted the construction and garment industries from restrictions on secondary boycotts. An ILGWU "educational campaign" did much to accomplish this feat. At the suggestion of ILGWU political director Gus Tyler, Dubinsky agreed to send a "goil" to Washington to represent the union. The person chosen was Evelyn Dubrow, who had directed Americans for Democratic Action in New Jersey before becoming Tyler's assistant in 1956. In Washington, Dubrow lobbied with Dubinsky to keep Congress from outlawing one of the International's most important weapons. By working through jobbers to organize contractors or through contractors to organize jobbers, the union restricted subcontracting. Without this restriction, the ILGWU warned, the sweatshop would return. ILGWU lobbyists won the support of such key senators as Democrats John F. Kennedy and John McClellan and Republicans Jacob Javits and Barry Goldwater. "I don't want to see the garment workers go back into the sweatshop," said McClellan.

The final version of the bill was largely unsympathetic to organized labor. It tightly regulated internal union operations and gave union members a "bill of rights" to protect them from their leaders. Kennedy, who had presidential ambitions, found it politically perilous. On the eve of passage, he quietly withdrew his name from it. Dubinsky regarded it from a different perspective. He proudly reminded the ILGWU's General Executive Board "that he was the first leader in the labor movement to favor the adoption of labor legislation." Known as the Landrum-Griffin Act, the bill became law in September 1959.[62]

. . .

In New York, the ILGWU's political machinery operated through the Liberals, but outside the state it directly endorsed liberal Democrats. Gus Tyler's Political Department functioned as a nationwide control center. In good times—for example, after the 1954 congressional and gubernatorial elections—the International could claim some credit; the Republicans lost control of both the House of Representatives and the Senate.[63] If David Dubinsky was not a kingmaker, neither was he a court jester. His union had raised more than $200,000 in contributions for the 1954 congressional campaign.[64] An experienced political warrior, he commanded and received respect.

Despite Averell Harriman's slim gubernatorial victory in 1954, the governor hoped to win the Democratic presidential nomination in 1956. His dream was to form a coalition of northern liberals, labor people, and urban politicians, most notably New York boss Carmine DeSapio, to boost him as the true heir of the New Deal.[65]

Harriman addressed the ILGWU's Atlantic City convention in May. He said the Liberal and Democratic parties were "one and the same thing in New York State" and denounced President Eisenhower as "the prisoner of big business."[66] Harriman stroked the Liberals even though Alex Rose had already told him they favored Adlai Stevenson.[67]

After Estes Kefauver unexpectedly bested Stevenson in the March Minnesota primary, he won a major victory in California in June. Harriman nevertheless remained hopeful.[68] After the California primary, Dubinsky addressed the convention of Rose's United Hatters', Cap and Millinery Workers' International Union. To Rose's "utter surprise," Dubinsky discussed the situation on the West Coast, where division continued between Stevenson and Harriman backers. He told the Harriman people that as Stevenson was "the leading candidate among the Democrats," they should not "continue to divide the ranks of liberalism" and "had better stop the nonsense."

These remarks greatly "embarrassed" Rose, who feared that Harriman would feel the convention had "deliberately upstaged" him. Minor surgery had kept the governor from hearing Dubinsky's speech in person. When he afterward discovered what was said, he was very perturbed and accepted an invitation from Rose to address the convention the next day. He arrived to "a standing ovation," offered a rebuttal, and praised Dubinsky as "a great man" and "friend" who had pioneered the fight against Communism. Then he pledged to attend the Chicago convention as a fighter for "the principles of Franklin Roosevelt and Harry Truman."

In an obviously defiant mood, he tossed a hat to the delegates, proclaiming that it was "in the ring."[69]

Harriman was in the race, but without much support other than from DeSapio and the New York delegation. The five Liberal Party delegates backed Stevenson, as did Eleanor Roosevelt. On the first ballot the inevitable occurred: Stevenson trounced Harriman. Kefauver then defeated John F. Kennedy and three others for the second spot. As expected afterward, the Stevenson-Kefauver ticket failed to topple Eisenhower.[70]

The Liberal Party's nomination of Stevenson (twice), Wagner, and Harriman erased any remaining doubt as to its direction. Though Dubinsky remained personally distrustful of Tammany Hall, collaboration with the Democrats made sense in view of their reputable candidates and the absence of independent alternatives. In 1957 the pattern continued when Mayor Wagner as the Democratic-Liberal nominee won reelection over Republican businessman Robert Christenberry.[71]

In January 1958 the Liberals proposed an ambitious twenty-one-point program calling for significant increases in state spending on low- and middle-income housing, a boost in unemployment insurance, and the outlawing of discrimination in private housing.[72] The party hoped this program would help reelect the friendly, if not scintillating, incumbent governor, W. Averell Harriman.

They stayed with Harriman despite the presence of Carmine DeSapio and Tammany Hall behind him. This loyalty was tested when the Republicans chose Nelson Rockefeller to challenge him in November. Rockefeller was a "good" Republican who had collaborated with Dubinsky on financing housing in Israel and Puerto Rico, and Liberal Party leaders studiously refrained from criticizing him personally. The Republican nominee was a crowd pleaser who received the endorsement of the liberal *New York Post.*

Dubinsky, Rose, and Liberal Party state chairman Adolf A. Berle Jr. hoped to assert some independence in the senatorial contest. At the Democrats' convention in Buffalo, DeSapio pushed through the choice of Frank Hogan for senator and the host city's boss, Peter Crotty, for attorney general. It was classic machine politics, but Dubinsky felt an independent Senate candidate would in effect hand the election to the Republicans, and in any case no one was available. Nevertheless, the Liberals made a statement against bossism by selecting lawyer Edward Goodell to run against incumbent attorney general Louis Lefkowitz.[73]

As expected, Rockefeller easily defeated Harriman, winning by 550,000 votes and carrying almost the entire Republican ticket with him. The party's success in New York was especially gratifying because in 1958 its nationwide prospects were handicapped by several factors, including an economic recession and a conflict-of-interest scandal involving presidential assistant Sherman Adams. Only in New York and Arizona, where Barry Goldwater was resoundingly reelected to the Senate, did the Republicans dramatically defy the Democratic tide that ensued.[74]

With Rockefeller as Harriman's successor, few Liberal tears were shed. The new governor was at home in the company of the supposed political opposition. After the 1958 dress strike, the ILGWU aggressively promoted a newly designed, industry-wide union label. Ever the astute publicist, Dubinsky assembled Nelson Rockefeller, Herbert Lehman, Robert Wagner, and various union and industry figures for a public sewing of the first label into a garment. Surrounded by the dignitaries, Mrs. Rockefeller sewed in the label.[75]

In 1959, Dubinsky had met with yet another wealthy politician, John F. Kennedy. The occasion was a summertime breakfast at Kennedy's residence in Georgetown, to which Dubinsky and Alex Rose were invited. At this gathering, Kennedy told the labor leaders that he wanted them to line up support within the AFL-CIO and the Democratic Party for a presidential race in 1960. Presumably the Liberal Party would influence the Democrats' choice of convention delegates.[76]

In 1960, Dubinsky believed that Kennedy, whom he called "my boy," was the best bet for the Democrats to reclaim the White House from the Republicans. Within the labor movement there was some support for either Minnesota's stalwart liberal senator Hubert Humphrey or Adlai Stevenson, who was not averse to a third presidential race. But the Massachusetts senator gained the support of such other labor influentials as George Meany, Walter Reuther, and lawyer Arthur Goldberg, Kennedy's main envoy to the labor movement. Aided by Alex Rose in particular, he worked on Meany and the AFL-CIO hierarchy. Accordingly, though the AFL-CIO was officially neutral early in 1960, Meany, Reuther, and most labor delegates to the Democratic national convention favored Kennedy for the nomination. Many backed him out of fear of an unacceptable alternative, Lyndon B. Johnson of Texas, the majority leader of the Senate, whose labor record Meany regarded as "horrible."[77]

During the primary campaign, Kennedy seemed to overcome the question of his Catholicism. He defeated Humphrey in heavily Protestant

West Virginia and won the Democratic nomination on the first ballot. Next came the matter of a vice presidential running mate. In May, Alex Rose had recommended Humphrey, and Kennedy later approached the Minnesota senator, but he declined to run despite pressure from several sources, including labor leaders Dubinsky, Rose, Goldberg, and Joseph Keenan.[78]

George Meany's preference for the second slot was Senator Henry Jackson of Washington, but on July 14, Kennedy telephoned to say he had chosen Johnson. The reason, Kennedy explained, was to carry the South and "balance the Catholic thing." Meany told Kennedy what he thought of Johnson's labor record but added that he would not begin a floor fight over his nomination.[79] Across the continent from the Los Angeles convention, as Dubinsky later remembered, he received a call from Arthur Goldberg, from Reuther's hotel suite. Goldberg informed Dubinsky that Rose, Reuther, and Meany were unhappy with Johnson. "They're crazy! Dubinsky retorted. "It's a winning ticket." "Go out and convince your friends," Goldberg replied. "I will. I'll try," Dubinsky said.

Wasting no time, Dubinsky called his three disgruntled friends, beginning with Rose. "Alex, this is a winning ticket," he said. "You have no problem with me," Rose replied. "Dave Dubinsky thinks that this is the smartest thing that could ever have happened. It's wonderful! It's great!" Leonard Woodcock of the United Auto Workers remembered him saying.

Next came Reuther, who was preparing a statement against Johnson. Dubinsky advised him to "keep calm" and not rush any statements. The UAW leader stopped dictating. Meany was third, and Dubinsky reached him at the hotel swimming pool, but he gave Dubinsky "a cold shoulder," refusing to be swayed. That evening Reuther blocked any statement that might have been issued by the Executive Council, leaving Meany obviously displeased.[80] Dubinsky's calls to support the ticket did not go unnoticed by Lyndon Johnson. Evidently informed of them by Goldberg, Johnson was enormously appreciative. Dubinsky would come to regard the Texan as "a close, hardy, intimate, sincere friend."[81]

Again the ILGWU committed its resources to a presidential campaign, this time against the Republican ticket of Vice President Richard M. Nixon and former ambassador to the United Nations Henry Cabot Lodge Jr. Financed by more than $289,000 in members' contributions, the ILGWU Campaign Committee promoted voter registration and advertised on radio, on television, and in newspapers. On October 27 the campaign reached its climax with a massive garment center rally on Seventh

Avenue, attended by an estimated 250,000 spectators. John Kennedy was the main speaker, along with Herbert Lehman, Robert Wagner, and numerous stage and screen personalities. Twelve days later Kennedy was narrowly elected, with 303 electoral votes to Nixon's 219. Most gratifying to Dubinsky, Kennedy's total included 45 electoral votes from New York. The 406,176 popular votes he received on the Liberal Party line exceeded the margin by which he won the state by 22,510, which suggested to some Liberals that they had elected him.[82]

With a Democrat again headed for the White House, Dubinsky and Rose sought to influence the appointment of the next secretary of labor. They preferred Goldberg, as did Kennedy, but the president-elect also wanted Meany to recommend him. The problem here was that the building trades unions, fearing that Goldberg might turn the Landrum-Griffin Act against them, were opposed. Determined to have Goldberg, Kennedy asked Meany to temper the opposition within labor, and Dubinsky and Rose applied "fierce pressure" in his behalf. At last Meany yielded, and to Dubinsky's delight, Kennedy appointed Goldberg.[83] At the outset of the new administration, Kennedy established a President's Advisory Committee on Labor-Management Policy to study wage-and-price stability, automation, worker productivity, and dispute resolution. Quite naturally, Goldberg recommended that Kennedy make Dubinsky a member.[84]

The solid support they showed for Kennedy placed the Liberals in an excellent position to influence the 1961 New York City mayoralty contest, in which Robert Wagner was seeking reelection. Wagner's image was that of a well-meaning public servant too weak to extricate himself from Carmine DeSapio and the Tammany Hall Democratic machine. The mayor knew the time had come to break with this organization. He had a friend and confidant in Alex Rose, whose party had backed him for the Senate in 1956 and for reelection in 1957. Moreover, Rose's Liberals had strong support among Jewish voters, which might be essential if the Republicans fielded a Jewish mayoral candidate in 1961. As Wagner moved toward a separation from DeSapio, he had assurance from Rose of a Liberal nomination even if he should be denied one by the Democrats.[85]

Apart from Wagner, within the Democratic Party a significant reform movement had been developing. As the 1961 contest approached, the reformers could count among their supporters Eleanor Roosevelt, Herbert Lehman, and Thomas Finletter. Mrs. Roosevelt had despised DeSapio at least since 1954, when he gave the gubernatorial nomination to Harriman, keeping it from Franklin Roosevelt Jr., and 1956, when he backed Harriman over Stevenson for president. The reformers set up a New York Committee for Democratic Voters aimed at toppling him.[86] In February, Wagner finally broke with DeSapio, demanding he step down as Tammany leader. On June 23, Wagner announced his candidacy. Keeping his pledge, Rose, along with Dubinsky, sought the Liberal line for him, but at a meeting of the party's policy committee at the Park-Sheraton Hotel, another contender appeared: Stuart Scheftel, whom Wagner had appointed to a housing board, wanted the honor. Scheftel and his followers complained that Rose and Dubinsky were themselves bosses. Moreover, as the decision would be by hand vote, ILGWU members would be fearful of voting for him because Dubinsky would see and then punish them. Ridiculing the complaint, Dubinsky said he would shut his eyes, which he did, as well as turn his back. Yet as columnist Murray Kempton commented afterward, it made no difference, as "everyone knows Dubinsky has eyes in the back of his head." Visible or not to Dubinsky, 28 voted for Scheftel, as opposed to 378 for Wagner.[87]

The candidate of the Democratic Party regulars, Arthur Levitt, entered the mayoral race a week after Wagner's announcement. As usual, the ILGWU mobilized its resources. Thirty-five managers of locals and joint boards endorsed Wagner, and *Justice* hailed the "Fight against Bossism." In the September 7 Democratic primary the contest was decided, with Wagner winning citywide, while in Greenwich Village reformer James S. Lanigan was elected assembly district leader, deposing DeSapio as head of Tammany Hall. In November, Wagner went on to an easy victory.[88]

That organized labor took delight in John F. Kennedy's presidency was evident from its outset. In a brief but eloquent inaugural address, he called on Americans to defend freedom and dedicate themselves anew to national greatness. *Justice* commented that it was evident that "the achievement of world peace and of domestic prosperity" constituted for Kennedy "a single problem" and reported that he had sent Congress drafts of bills to provide medical care for the aged and an increase in the federal minimum wage from $1.00 to $1.25 per hour over a three-year period.[89]

In an instant the ILGWU machinery started up, supervised by Gus Tyler in New York and Evelyn Dubrow in Washington. Dubrow devised a schedule for ILGWU lobbying activity across the country.[90] On assignment from the White House, Dubinsky approached two local Republicans: James P. Mitchell, a secretary of labor under Eisenhower, who was running for the New Jersey governorship, and Nelson Rockefeller. It was hoped that both would publicly support the higher wage, while Rockefeller would "privately" persuade two Republican congressmen to back it. According to Dubinsky, Rockefeller, mindful of his position as governor and sensitive to party criticism, agreed to the quiet conversations but not a public statement, while Mitchell consented to the latter. Coming forward from behind the scenes, on April 11, 1960, Dubinsky argued before the House Labor Committee for an increase in the Puerto Rican minimum wage simultaneous to the one for the U.S. mainland.[91]

In March 1961 the House adopted a version of the bill, followed by the Senate the next month. After bargaining and reconciliation in conference, on May 3 both houses passed it. The minimum wage for previously covered workers would rise to $1.25 per hour in 1963, while that for some 3.6 million new workers would reach it two years later. Workers in Puerto Rico and the Virgin Islands would also receive adjustments. With Dubinsky and a coterie of AFL-CIO, administration, and congressional figures as witnesses, Kennedy added his signature.[92]

ILGWU satisfaction with the Kennedy administration also extended to the courts. Ever since 1924, when New York's Battle Commission had recommended that the garment industry limit the contractors employed by jobbers as a means of protecting working conditions, manufacturers had legally challenged such arrangements. During the Eisenhower presidency, in April 1955, the Federal Trade Commission took up the issue, complaining that ILGWU jobber-contractor agreements in California tended "unduly to hinder competition, restrain trade, and create a monopoly in women's sportswear." In December 1957, after extensive hearings, the FTC upheld the ILGWU position, finding the agreements did not restrain trade or create a monopoly. Despite this ruling, in March 1959, Attorney General Herbert Brownell brought suit against Charles Kreindler, the manager of ILGWU Local 25, and others for alleged restraint of trade in the blouse industry. The indictment achieved special attention as it included mention of racketeer Harry Strasser, who had nothing to do with Kreindler or the ILGWU but figured prominently in the Justice Department press release announcing it.[93]

The indictment did not go unanswered. Pledging its support to the International, the AFL-CIO Executive Council termed it "an attack upon the historic and hard-won protection of the entire labor movement." Addressing the 1959 ILGWU convention in Miami Beach, Dubinsky noted that the indictment was criminal rather than civil and charged that the ILGWU was given "different treatment" because of what it represented as a "progressive union," the name of whose president "happens to be David Dubinsky."[94]

The Eisenhower Justice Department kept the indictment alive into and through the 1960 presidential campaign. The ILGWU regarded the matter as strictly political, and when Kennedy was elected there was an expectation that the new Democratic administration would drop it.[95] Even though John Kennedy's younger brother Robert had become attorney general, the indictment persisted. However, in January 1962 the Kennedy Justice Department abandoned its criminal prosecution in favor of a civil suit in the matter. Noting the significance of this action, Dubinsky declared that it would permit "a test in a civil forum rather than bring a sensational criminal case." ILGWU contracts, he declared, aimed "not to restrict competition" but "to put an end to sub-standard labor conditions."[96]

Less than three months later a third Kennedy brother made political headlines: thirty-year-old Edward Moore ("Ted") Kennedy announced his candidacy for his brother John's U.S. Senate seat. Though Ted was but an assistant district attorney in Suffolk County, Massachusetts, he would have been an easy choice for a Senate nomination, if not for the presence of another Democrat with a prominent relative. Edward McCormack, the attorney general of Massachusetts and nephew of John McCormack, the speaker of the U.S. House of Representatives, was also a candidate. A primary election in September, which promised to be intense, would decide the contest.[97]

Relations between key ILGWU officials and both sides were amicable. Manager of the Boston Joint Board Philip Kramer was a close, personal friend of John McCormack, while both Sol Chaikin, now assistant director of the Northeast Department, and Dubinsky were close to the Kennedys. Early in 1962, Ted Kennedy called Chaikin and requested support. He told the ILGWU director that three Boston-area labor leaders, including Kramer, were raising money for newspaper advertisements to attack him and back McCormack. An alarmed Chaikin took the matter to Dubinsky.

Ted also did his part, and Robert Kennedy decided to have Arthur Goldberg, regarded as "the House Jew," call Dubinsky. After introducing himself as "Ted Kennedy's business agent," Goldberg requested ILGWU support for him. Easily persuaded by his friend, Dubinsky called Kramer. He told the ILGWU vice president to "do nothing" further in the campaign, explaining that he would make the decision on whom to support in Massachusetts. Dubinsky then sent Chaikin to Boston to recruit trade unionists, especially ILGWU members, for Kennedy. Meeting at Springfield, state ILGWU leaders gave Ted their endorsement.[98] In September, Kennedy won the primary in a vote of 559,303 to 257,403 and then went on to an easy victory in the general election.[99]

The ILGWU endorsement by itself did not elect Ted Kennedy to the U.S. Senate, but it is reasonable to suggest that the Kennedy family appreciated the assistance and acted accordingly. Fourteen months after the election, the Justice Department moved to dismiss the blouse industry antitrust indictment, declaring that a review of the evidence indicated there was no case against the International. In April 1964, federal judge Edward Weinfeld agreed, and both Herbert Brownell's criminal case and Robert Kennedy's civil suit were dismissed.[100]

Dubinsky's support for Ted Kennedy should not have surprised anyone, in view of his fondness for John Kennedy, to whom he "felt a deep sense of loyalty."[101] While the blouse matter was pending, and without Justice Department interference, the ILGWU negotiated its first national collective-bargaining agreements. In March 1961 it came to terms with Bobbie Brooks, the largest women's clothing manufacturer in the nation with thirty-seven factories in twelve states, and in February 1962 the International duplicated the feat with an agreement with Majestic Specialties, which had a dozen plants in six states.[102] A few days after the conclusion of the Majestic pact, Arthur Goldberg presented a letter of greeting from John Kennedy to Hugh Gaitskell, the head of England's Labour Party, at a luncheon in his honor. Kennedy's message contained kind words for Dubinsky as well, hailing him as a "long term personal friend" and praising him as "a true member of the new frontier."[103]

In May there were additional demonstrations of mutual admiration. On successive days, Kennedy helped dedicate the Penn Station South cooperative houses and received forty-fifth birthday greetings from ILGWU and other retirees at a massive rally at Madison Square Garden for health care legislation for the aged. At the end of month, the ILGWU convention at Atlantic City extended its good wishes.[104] On November 20, 1963, the president signed legislation to create a silver medal to commemorate the fiftieth anniversary of the Union Health Center. This was the last bill he would ever approve. Two days later he was assassinated in Dallas.[105]

Though Dubinsky enjoyed what may be regarded as a personal relationship with all the Democratic presidents since Franklin Roosevelt, he was closest to John Kennedy's successor, Lyndon Johnson. For the Texan he had fond recollections that began in 1938, when Johnson was a New Deal congressman. Dubinsky "buttonholed" Congressman Johnson, and then Senate Majority Leader Johnson two decades later, to support minimum-wage legislation, each time receiving considerable sympathy. In 1939 the ILGWU had donated $2,000 to Maury Maverick, a liberal congressman who was running for mayor of San Antonio. Maverick converted Dubinsky's check into silver dollars that he distributed to pay the poll taxes of his supporters. On the eve of the contest, Maverick's opponent charged that ILGWU "gold" had been brought in to elect him. Though the allegation failed to defeat Maverick, he was later indicted for improperly using union contributions. Subsequently, by explaining that all he had done was obtain Yankee money to make it possible for poor Southerners to vote, Maverick was acquitted, leaving Johnson and Dubinsky with a good story to tell.[106]

After his nomination for the vice presidency, Johnson had several occasions on which to tell ILGWU members this story and others. Though he was suspicious of New York liberals, during the 1960 campaign he appeared before the Trade Union Council of the Liberal Party. After a lavish introduction by Dubinsky, Johnson attacked sweatshops and inequality and defended his record on Social Security, housing, and education, to the resounding approval of the four hundred liberals in the audience.[107] In May 1962, the ILGWU convention at Atlantic City gave him a similar reception.[108]

During the fall of 1963, disturbed by reports that Kennedy was about to drop Johnson from the 1964 reelection ticket, Dubinsky and Rose decided to give him "a lift" and invited him back to New York. On October 15 the vice president attended a morning meeting with trade-union leaders that was followed by two tours of the Garment District, with Dubinsky serving as guide.

When Johnson sought election to the presidency in 1964, his relations with Dubinsky could not have been closer. In February, both were at the Hotel Fontainebleau in Miami Beach. Johnson was there to address a hundred-dollar-a-plate Democratic fundraising dinner while Dubinsky would serve as master of ceremonies at the annual meeting of the National Coat and Suit Industry Recovery Board. Early in the evening, Dubinsky telephoned the president to ask if he might discuss "an important matter" with him. Johnson called him up to his room and, while shaving and changing into formal attire, chatted with Dubinsky. After the president spoke, he sought a place to relax and found his way, with his wife and two daughters, to the gathering of the labor management group, where they were cordially received.[109]

On June 6, accompanied by Senator Hubert Humphrey, the president participated in the fiftieth anniversary celebration of the ILGWU Union Health Center. He dedicated a plaque at the facility, addressed an overflow crowd at the High School of Fashion Industries, lunched at the headquarters of Local 23–25, and greeted well-wishers along Seventh Avenue and Twenty-fourth Street.[110]

With Humphrey as his running mate, Johnson ran hard to be an elected president. Senator Barry Goldwater, Arizona's conservative stalwart, opposed him. The ILGWU established a campaign committee to solicit donations and in New York City organized an Apparel Industries Committee to Elect Lyndon B. Johnson, headed by Abraham Schrader. Campaign donations would exceed $400,000.[111]

Ironically, in 1964 the ILGWU campaign umbrella covered Robert F. Kennedy as well as Lyndon Johnson. On the eve of the Democratic National Convention, Kennedy resigned as U.S. attorney general to enter the New York Senate race. Aside from meeting the state's residency requirement, which was not difficult, what Kennedy had to do was build support among local leaders, in particular those of the Liberal Party and Reform Democrats, some of whom feared that Kennedy was an anti-Johnson influence and thus divisive.

There were few potential rivals. Robert Wagner, who might have been the leading contender, had recently lost his wife and, as his son later recalled, lacked "the real passion to run." UN Ambassador Adlai Stevenson, the early favorite of the Liberals, was undecided. One evening the ambassador met with Dubinsky, Rose, and Wagner upstairs at Wagner's residence. From outside their room, Dubinsky could be heard yelling at Stevenson while "pounding" on a table: "You can never make up your mind, what's wrong with you?" By contrast, Arthur Schlesinger Jr. breakfasted with Rose at the Hotel Astor on behalf of Kennedy and departed with an understanding that Rose "thought he might manage to bring the Liberal party around." When Wagner endorsed Kennedy, both the Democrats and the Liberals fell in line, and he became their nominee.[112]

On October 15 the Liberal Party brought Kennedy and Johnson together at a Madison Square Garden rally. Though this event was itself an extravaganza, it served also as a prelude to the traditional garment center rally of the ILGWU two weeks later on Seventh Avenue. This gathering featured Humphrey, standing in for Johnson, and Kennedy. As ticker tape fell, a waving sign said, "Sew it up for Lyndon." "Please behave," master of ceremonies Dubinsky told the crowd. "This is the greatest rally in the history of America—my estimate a quarter of a million people—we got to be orderly." Police estimates put the number at "between 50,000 and 100,000." On November 3, Election Day, a plurality of 15.6 million votes kept Johnson in the White House, and a margin of 650,000 votes elected Robert Kennedy to the Senate.[113]

Barry Goldwater's nomination for the presidency had meant to many moderate and liberal Republicans that their party had been captured by its extreme right wing. Republican John Vliet Lindsay, who had represented New York City's Seventeenth, or "Silk Stocking," Congressional District since 1959, had broken ranks and not endorsed Goldwater. At age forty-three his political potential remained very much alive, and in 1965 the question was to which office he might turn. Republicans Nelson Rockefeller and Jacob Javits were in the Governor's Mansion and U.S. Senate, respectively, while Robert Kennedy was at the beginning of his six-year senatorial term and hardly an inviting political target.

Early in June, the possibility of City Hall suddenly appeared. A tearful Robert Wagner announced that he would keep a promise not to run again that he had made to his wife, Susan, who had died in March. With Wagner headed for retirement, his friend and ally Alex Rose was now free to entertain suitors for the affections of the Liberal Party. Robert Price, Lindsay's campaign director, was first on line.[114]

Before deciding on Lindsay, the Liberals had to interview him, but hernia surgery at Beth Israel Hospital kept Dubinsky from being present. On June 19, Louis Stulberg and Charles Zimmerman represented the ILGWU on the subcommittee that met with the congressman. He told the Liberals he would never use the mayor's office "to promote the interests of the Republican Party." Moreover, he said he favored collective bargaining, repeal of the right-to-work section of the Taft-Hartley Act, national minimum wage of $1.50, cooperative housing, free tuition in the city colleges of New York, and a host of other positions supported by his interviewers.[115]

The Liberal Party, which had not offered the electorate an exciting candidate since Rudolph Halley in 1951, and which had not proven attractive to New York's growing African American and Puerto Rican population, nor to young Democratic Reformers, saw Lindsay as a godsend. On June 28 the Liberals met in convention at the Hotel Astor and overwhelmingly endorsed him.[116]

Two ILGWU vice presidents took exception to him. Though Luigi Antonini was home with health problems, in an "open letter," which was read to the conference, he nominated Democratic City Council president Paul R. Screvane. "The election of a republican as Mayor of New York City would be construed," Antonini said, "as a setback for the democratic and liberal administration of our great President Lyndon B. Johnson."[117] Israel Breslow, who had managed Local 22 since 1958, charged that the Liberal Party leadership had "made a mistake." "Isn't it possible that Alex Rose could make a mistake, or even David Dubinsky?" At this point Dubinsky rose and replied angrily, "Is this the way I was teaching you for so many years, for a quarter of a century, I was teaching you? Is this the way I was teaching you?" Turning to the press, Dubinsky gave assurance that neither Breslow "or anyone else" would be fired for their opposition to Lindsay.[118]

This balm failed to soothe Breslow, who two weeks later wrote a long letter in Yiddish to Dubinsky. In it Breslow extolled Dubinsky as a teacher from whom he was continuing to learn. However, in conclusion he observed what "wise men" had said, "If you embarrass someone publicly, it's a big sin."

After receiving this letter, Dubinsky asked Hannah Haskel to invite Breslow to meet with him at his office. As Breslow arrived, Haskel warned him to "be careful," as the president was "in a very bad mood." When the vice president entered Dubinsky's office, he discovered how correct she had been. A furious Dubinsky immediately began to castigate him. "What do you mean, you come to a public meeting, a public convention, and you criticize your president?" With Breslow seated, Dubinsky then walked around the office, simultaneously yelling and banging a yardstick on a table until it broke. His tirade lasted between fifteen and twenty minutes. When Dubinsky finally tired and sat down, Breslow expressed his great reverence and respect for him as president and reminded him of their mutual opposition to the Communists in the American Labor Party. He had firmly supported the Liberal Party, he added, but then he denied that it was "a crime" to differ with Rose and Dubinsky. "Show me a constitutional provision in the ILG constitution," he added, "which prohibits me of speaking out politically." With the discussion now "subdued," Breslow compelled Dubinsky to concede that in his eight years as

Local 22's manager there had never been a complaint about his administration. The meeting ended with the two men walking out of the office together; Dubinsky's left hand was on Breslow's shoulder. They shook hands as they parted. Haskel then asked Breslow what had happened: "What are you, a magician?" "We had a very friendly political discussion," he replied.[119]

As a "Fusion" candidate on the Republican as well as Liberal lines, Lindsay won the election by 1,167,000 votes. The 293,000 votes he gained as a Liberal made the difference. As interpreted by the Liberals, this was a victory over bossism—in other words, the Democratic machine.[120]

Dubinsky later recalled the personal significance of this contest. The dissent from within the ILGWU on his choice of Lindsay "was one of a number of things" that made him "start thinking about resigning as president." It disappointed him "that the union was no longer a united force politically." Though the opposition to Lindsay also came from Lyndon Johnson, Hubert Humphrey, and George Meany, he had clearly not anticipated and was then shaken by the sharp public criticism voiced by Antonini and Breslow.[121]

Open dissent by ILGWU vice presidents was unheard of in the decade after mid-century. But time was against its aging leader. In 1962, as Dubinsky celebrated his seventieth birthday and thirtieth anniversary as president, criticism was very much in the air. From outside the International came complaints that it was guilty of racial discrimination, while within there were demands for recognition of a staff union. To Dubinsky in 1965, accustomed to fealty and wearied by these controversies, the flap over Lindsay by supposedly loyal lieutenants may indeed have been a sign that retirement was imminent.

19

End of an Era

In 1957, Max Danish wrote, Dubinsky was "not overly worried about his successor" and had not designated a "crown prince" to follow him. Even after twenty-five years in office, age had "scarcely begun to affect him." Still, Danish noted that Dubinsky's "closest aide" for the past decade had been Louis Stulberg, the executive vice president of the ILGWU. In January 1955 executive secretary Frederick F. Umhey had died, but Dubinsky left his position vacant for more than a year until he finally redesigned it with responsibilities that had formerly been his own and appointed Stulberg to occupy it.[1]

Like Dubinsky, Stulberg had come from Poland, where he had been born on April 14, 1901. The son of a coal dealer, at age three he migrated to Toronto, where he later attended school and worked as a junior dress cutter. In 1915 he joined the International. Four years later he moved to Chicago. While working in the garment industry, he completed high school and attended the University of Chicago for a year. Afterward he played professional baseball for two years, as a shortstop for the Memphis Chicks. In 1924 he became an ILGWU organizer in Toledo until moving to New York in 1927 and a long career as an officer first of Local 10 and then of Local 62. Elected to the General Executive Board in 1947, he attracted the attention of Dubinsky, who began to assign him tasks pertaining to the General Office.[2] In 1956, when Dubinsky made him executive vice president, it was with a "promise," his wife late recalled, that he would become president the next year. Three years later, conceding that his dual responsibilities as president and general secretary-treasurer were too great, Dubinsky recommended Stulberg for the latter post, to which he was then elected. As the heir apparent, he anticipated only a brief wait before assuming the ILGWU throne.[3]

. . .

The 1960s began with the organization Stulberg longed to lead seemingly in good health. Its total membership, though down slightly from a high of 445,093 in 1956, was still more than 442,000, and the nation's economy seemed strong. Retail sales of women's and children's clothing, which had totaled slightly less than $13.7 million in 1958, increased in the next three years to $14.9 million.

In 1962 the General Executive Board of the ILGWU adopted a "favorable" outlook "for the immediate future"[4] but also noted the growing problem of imported garments from low-wage countries, "a 'runaway shop' situation on a global scale." In 1947, wearing apparel valued at $55.6 million was imported; in 1961 the value was $131.3 million. Even more alarming, $60.8 million of knitwear was imported in 1961, as compared to $5.6 million in 1947.[5]

As imports rose, garment industry wages, unionization, and employment fell. Domestic manufacturers offered little sympathy.[6] Rejecting this attitude, the ILGWU acted directly against imports. The Dress Joint Council negotiated contracts that prohibited the importation of garments.[7] From 1959 to 1961 the union petitioned Congress and the White House to prevent trade concessions to foreign apparel and textile producers. In response to reports of excessive exports from Hong Kong, in January 1960 the GEB requested the U.S. Tariff Commission institute tight restrictions instead of relying on voluntary restraint.[8] In May 1961, President Kennedy presented a program that emphasized a need for international accords to deal with these goods. Within the same year, and again in 1963, Japan negotiated bilateral trade agreements that authorized increases in both U.S. apparel exports and Japanese imports.[9]

During the 1950s, as the flow of imports became heavier, garment production also shifted from the New York Metropolitan Region to nearby Pennsylvania. And New York's labor force was still changing, with African Americans and Latin Americans replacing Jews and Italians. In addition, physical problems, such as inadequate and expensive loft space and intense traffic congestion that impeded trucking, plagued the New York City garment center. Also significant was the chronic racketeering problem, affecting the shipment of goods, and, finally, state taxes, which other locations did not levy.[10]

Of the 100,000 New York City manufacturing jobs lost in the 1950s, 70,000 were in apparel.[11] Between 1956 and 1959, ILGWU Local 22 alone lost 1,208 members.[12] By 1961 there was an employment drop in the New York dress industry of 31.5 percent in Manhattan and 17.5 percent in New York State compared with 1953.[13]

Late in 1961, Judy Bond, Inc. made its contribution to the decline. One of New York's most prominent blouse manufacturers, Judy Bond was legally bound to the ILGWU through a contract with the National Association of Blouse Manufacturers. On December 11, with the contract due to expire on the thirty-first, the firm notified the ILGWU that it had withdrawn from the Association and was therefore not obligated to respect any future agreement between the Association and the International.

Recent financial losses, the company explained, compelled a drastic change in its operations. Henceforth it would manufacture in Brewton, Alabama, in a recently purchased shop currently affiliated with another union, the United Garment Workers. The truth was that the company had already been having its manufacturing "done in the South, in shops not under Union agreement with the I.L.G.W.U.," and it intended to do the same in the future. In January, members of ILGWU Local 25, the Blouse and Waistmakers Union, found themselves locked out of Judy Bond's warehouse and shipping department in Manhattan. Without hesitation, the union declared the company on strike.[14]

The ILGWU campaigned against Judy Bond along several fronts. The United Garment Workers' contract with the Brewton Manufacturing Company, which Judy Bond had purchased, was due to expire in June 1962. Dubinsky requested President Joseph McGurdy of the UGW refrain from renegotiating a contract with the new "runaway firm." Rejecting this plea, the UGW entered into a new agreement in January, only to be condemned by the AFL-CIO Executive Council, which also authorized ILGWU organizing at Brewton. Before the National Labor Relations Board, the ILGWU accused Judy Bond and the UGW of collusion. Agreeing with the International, the NLRB ordered them to cease their practices and rehire with back pay ten workers who had been fired at Brewton. In a nationwide campaign, the ILGWU advised consumers, "Don't Buy Judy Bond." Continually defeated in the courts between 1962 and 1966, Judy Bond wound up facing judgments totaling $230,000, including $75,000 in back pay for 727 workers abandoned in New York.[15]

Though the Judy Bond campaign succeeded, during the 1960s the women's garment industry was in an uncertain state. An expanding national economy boosted garment-industry employment between 1961 and 1966, but apparel-industry unemployment remained well above the level for manufacturing in general, and the dollar value of women's and children's imports rose 29 percent between 1964 and 1967. ILGWU membership fluctuated, standing at 446,856 at the end of 1965 and rising to 455,164 a year later but slipping to 451,192 two years later making for a net gain of 8,874 since 1964.[16]

David Dubinsky was proud of what he would describe in his autobiography as the ILGWU's "outstanding civil rights record and . . . promotion and practice of racial equality." On the occasion of the twenty-fifth anniversary of Dubinsky's presidency of the International, Channing H. Tobias, chairman of the board of the National Association for the Advancement of Colored People, wrote that black workers knew he had "fought well for the principles of social and economic democracy in the manufacturing plants of the nation's garment industry and for a truly democratic America."[17]

As 1958, began relations between the AFL-CIO and the NAACP became tense. Herbert Hill, the white Jewish labor secretary of the Association, asked the Federation to withdraw from participation in a forthcoming conference of the President's Committee on Government Contracts because many of the corporations involved blatantly violated the antidiscrimination clause in their contracts with the U.S. government. Citing the Federation's commitment to cooperate with the committee, Boris Shishkin, the director of its civil rights department, rejected the request.[18]

Both Hill and NAACP executive secretary Roy Wilkins continued to pursue the problem of discriminating government contractors, but the labor secretary also challenged the AFL-CIO itself. "I strongly believe," he wrote Charles Zimmerman, who chaired the Federation's civil rights committee, "that the AFL-CIO must now begin a direct frontal attack against segregated locals, exclusion practices and separate lines of progression based upon race in collective bargaining agreements." In December 1958, the NAACP provided Shishkin with affidavits from black workers and a detailed memorandum on discriminatory union practices.[19]

Zimmerman had long been identified with racial equality in the workplace, but neither he nor the Federation was prepared to yield to the NAACP. In November 1958, speaking at a civil rights conference in Chicago, he demonstrated no awareness of discrimination within the AFL-CIO and instead denounced acts of intolerance elsewhere.[20]

Herbert Hill had thus far refrained from criticizing the ILGWU, but in October 1958 things changed. An article in a *New York Herald Tribune* series critical of the ILGWU quoted him as saying that "every garment employer knows that he cannot cheat on the I.L.G. contract to discriminate against a Negro." By contrast, toward members of the newer ethnic groups the ILGWU had adopted a "white man's burden" state of mind. "Twenty years ago," Hill added, "the I.L.G.W.U. played a decisive role in bringing thousands of Negroes into the organized labor movement, on the basis of equal treatment in the shop and full membership within the union," but now "the status of Negroes in the I.L.G.W.U. indicates that Negroes are largely concentrated in the low-paid unskilled job classifications."[21]

Hill's observations "shocked" the General Executive Board of the ILGWU, which denied that the International had ever brought blacks into the factories in the past or was currently assigning them to job classifications. "Our union is not the *hiring* or *placement* agency in the industry," Stulberg wrote Wilkins. Hill, he alleged, had knowingly misinformed the newspaper relative to industry hiring and placement, thereby committing "an act of malice."[22]

It took three months for Wilkins to reply to Stulberg's letter, because when it arrived he was on vacation and it was misplaced. In March 1959 he discovered it and replied, emphasizing the "friendly" relationship between his organization and the International but also supporting Hill. Though he conceded that the ILGWU was not a hiring agency, he contended that it had "a great deal to say about the fortunes" of garment employees. Wilkins also said he would gladly meet with the ILGWU to resolve any civil rights problems, while noting that in the past the NAACP had been "rebuffed" when it attempted to address "allegations of unfair treatment in the union."[23]

On March 18, Wilkins and Hill had amicably discussed "mutual problems" and agreed on future cooperation with AFL-CIO vice president A. Philip Randolph of the Brotherhood of Sleeping Car Porters and with George Meany.[24] Between his meeting with Meany and belated reply to Stulberg, Wilkins thus managed, for the moment, to restore peace.

In July, Hill again asked for specific action.[25] Instead of compliance came a rebuke. In September, Zimmerman, at the National Urban League Conference in Washington, called the *Herald Tribune* articles "totally distorted."[26] His main message was that a split had occurred between the AFL-CIO and the NAACP.[27]

In December the *Pittsburgh Courier,* the nation's largest-circulation black newspaper, identified another area of friction. "Negro and labor leaders," *Courier* managing editor Harold L. Keith reported, "are on the 'brink' of outright war between themselves" over civil rights. The "chief architects" of the war, according to Keith, were Zimmerman, Hill, and the Jewish Labor Committee's national director, Emanuel Muravchik. The conflict would involve the JLC, the NAACP, and a new group founded by A. Philip Randolph to deal with union discrimination, the Negro American Labor Council.[28]

Muravchik, Wilkins, and the National Urban League's Lester Granger all denied that any such conflict existed. Wilkins wrote Keith that the originator of the story "was either badly informed, or was trying desperately to stir up intergroup strife on the lowest level by inventing a 'Jewish-Negro' conflict."[29]

The real conflict was between the NAACP and the AFL-CIO. In January, Hill issued "Racism within Organized Labor: A Report of Five Years of the AFL-CIO, 1955–1960," which concluded that the Federation had not eliminated "the broad pattern of racial discrimination and segregation in many important affiliated unions."[30]

Charles Zimmerman remained the chief spokesman for the Federation's record and a visible proponent of civil rights.[31] While he engaged in this activity, he was also general manager of the Dressmakers' Joint Council, ILGWU. In February 1961, citing time-consuming ILGWU duties, he resigned as chairman of the AFL-CIO civil rights committee. George Meany said Zimmerman "got tired of being hit over the head."[32]

"Our Negro and Spanish-speaking members," Zimmerman had observed in 1952, "constitute an important and increasing part of our union membership."[33] Despite their prominence, they constituted a low-wage workforce in part because the ILGWU restrained itself from aggressively pursuing higher pay in order to save jobs in New York City. In the 1960s the ILGWU would fight successfully to keep New York City from adopting a $1.50-per-hour minimum wage.[34]

Another factor was discrimination. In 1953, Local 22's former education director, Will Herberg, noted that race prejudice was "regarded as a high crime in the union ethic" but was "by no means absent from the shops." With regard to a lack of upward mobility for blacks and Latin Americans, he said there was a "'job ceiling' . . . set just above the semi-skilled level." In 1977, Maida Springer Kemp, who had been the

ILGWU's first black business agent, would recall "that black people, or Spanish were excluded . . . on the basis of race" from working on the better lines. Later she would say, "If you were white, you got a chance. But if you were Negro, you didn't get a chance. It was very hard."[35]

It did not take long for the newer ethnic groups within the ILGWU to challenge the leadership. Ernest Holmes was a black veteran of the Korean War and civil rights sit-ins in Georgia. On April 7, 1961, after eight months' employment, he was fired from his job as an assistant cutter at Primrose Foundations on West Twenty-third Street. Holmes had worked in the cutting department, at first laying and stretching materials and then operating an electric cutter. After a month's employment, he sought membership in ILGWU Cutters' Union, Local 10, with whom the company was under contract. Several fruitless visits to the union's offices convinced him that he was a victim of delaying tactics. Therefore, he complained to the State Commission for Human Rights that Primrose and Local 10 had discriminated against him on the basis of race. Three days later he was dismissed.[36]

With help from the NAACP's labor secretary Herbert Hill and attorney Jawn Sandifer, Holmes pressed his complaint. Emil Schlesinger represented the union but was immediately undermined by Manager Moe Falikman of Local 10, who called the charge of discrimination absurd and declined to offer a proper, fully documented reply.

After a fifteen-month investigation by Commissioner Ruperto Ruiz, on June 28, 1962, the State Commission issued its rulings. It dismissed the complaint against Primrose Foundations but found that there was "probable cause" to believe Holmes's allegations of bias against Local 10, which it ordered to arrange his employment at a union rate on a level commensurate with his skill and to admit him to union membership if he did satisfactory work.

Applauding the decision, the NAACP said its own investigations revealed the local had only twenty-three black members. Falikman said the report revealed "a complete lack of understanding of the cutting craft." Furthermore, he claimed there were "several hundred Negro and Puerto Rican members in Local 10 . . . in various branches of the garment industry."[37] When Dubinsky read about the decision in the *New York Times,* he went into a "total rage" and then "gave hell" to Falikman.[38]

Local 10 appealed Ruperto Ruiz's decision.[39] Emil Schlesinger, representing the union,[40] claimed he had additional information and sought to have Ruiz reopen his investigation and hold an open hearing, at which time the union would be exonerated. On September 14, Ruiz complied with Schlesinger's request. However, using the excuse that he distrusted Ruiz and his handling of information provided him, the ILGWU attorney waited five months, until February 1963, to produce lists of blacks and Puerto Ricans in Local 10.[41] The ILGWU position was that Local 10 had several hundred black members; in October 1962, Harry Fleischman of the National Labor Service of the American Jewish Committee stated it when he wrote, "There are currently some 200 Negro and Spanish-speaking cutters in Local 10." During Ruiz's investigation, Hill had "offered to withdraw his complaint" if the union would produce their names and addresses or indicate where they were employed. In a letter to Fleischman, Hill reviewed the commissioner's attempts to gain information. ILGWU staffer Will Chasan read this account and told Charles Zimmerman that it was "on the whole, probably an accurate summary, and it exposes the awful idiocy of the way this situation was handled."[42]

While Ruiz awaited the data from Schlesinger, Local 10 offered to find Holmes a job and admit him to the union. He then informed Ruiz in writing that he had decided to decline the ILGWU offer in favor of the "better job" he had found for himself, and to withdraw his complaint. As NAACP attorney Robert L. Carter informed Roy Wilkins, "That was supposed to end the matter," but Schlesinger was still demanding that Local 10 be "vindicated." In other words, though Holmes had withdrawn, the NAACP could not extricate itself.[43]

Carter now thought it was risky for the NAACP to continue its participation. He advised Wilkins that the Association faced "the possibility that the ILGWU may well disprove all the charges which have been made against it by us through Herbie Hill. This could make our faces look red as well as the Commission's." "We have to participate," Wilkins replied. "The ILGWU figures, while disproving lily-whiteism, are far from strong enough to prove no discrimination."[44]

In April, Schlesinger won another victory. State Supreme Court justice Thomas Aurelio ordered an "expeditious hearing" to decide the case. The hearings began on May 15. In the audience with their membership books were about two hundred black and Spanish-speaking ILGWU members ready to testify for the union, but such an opportunity never arose. Ernest Holmes was the only person to testify, and his appearance was disastrous. Under cross-examination by Schlesinger, he proved contradictory and forgetful. The next day attorney Henry Spitz approached Schlesinger and requested a settlement. On May 17, the third day, the Commission dropped its charges in a stipulation agreement in which Local 10 agreed to admit all applicants without discrimination on the basis of "race, creed, color, or national origin" and consented to assist Holmes "to become a qualified cutter and to gain admission to the membership in the Union." In an affidavit accompanying the agreement, Moe Falikman swore that as of May 1963 a "spot check" of the Local 10 membership revealed "103 Negro members and 149 Puerto Rican and Spanish speaking members." The total membership of the local as of December 31, 1962, was 7,343. "As far as I am concerned," Schlesinger wrote Louis Stulberg, "Mr. Spitz . . . unconditionally surrendered." The NAACP interpreted the agreement as a victory for its side. "Local 10 was forced to open its doors and the ILGWU is very careful about racial issues," Hill would recall.[45]

In the aftermath of the agreement, the State Commission for Human Rights monitored the employment record of Ernest Holmes and Local 10's efforts to assist and offer him membership. As of August 1963, the union had helped him obtain one position from which he was dismissed on account of his "slowness," another that he declined, and a third that he was holding thanks to union intervention with his employer. He was still learning the cutting trade and therefore ineligible for union membership.[46] Holmes applied for membership in Local 10 in December 1964 and was admitted the same day. Unemployed at the time, he received additional help from Local 10, which found him another job in February. In April 1965, four years after Ernest Holmes had filed his complaint, the National Labor Relations Board, with whom the charges had also been filed, announced that the case was closed.[47]

Though Ruperto Ruiz's initial ruling would be upset, its issuance triggered an investigation of the ILGWU by Congressman Adam Clayton Powell Jr. of Harlem and his House Committee on Education and Labor. The pastor of the Abyssinian Baptist Church, in 1941, Powell had become the first black person elected to the New York City Council and three years later successfully sought to become "the first Negro Congressman in the United States from the East."[48] A civil rights activist since the 1930s, Powell also leaned to the political left, even extending into ILGWU politics. In 1944 the "People's Committee" he chaired urged black dressmakers to support the insurgent "Rank and File" faction in Local 22 elections.[49] Closely associated with the American Labor Party in the late 1940s, Powell was held suspect by the leadership of the Liberal

Party. "Powell, as you know," Executive Director Ben Davidson wrote to Dubinsky, Rose, and Berle in February 1950, "has played ball again and again with the Commies, with the ALP and with [Vito] Marcantonio." Gus Tyler shared this aversion to the congressman, reminding Dubinsky of his "close association with the ALP."[50]

Powell frequently made headlines through marital and tax problems as well as politics but remained a staunch proponent of civil rights. During the 1950s he added the "Powell Amendment" to proposed federal grant legislation to deny funds to schools, hospitals, and housing projects that practiced racial segregation or discrimination. The 1956 ILGWU convention endorsed it as applied to education,[51] but with Eisenhower against it, the Powell Amendment cleared only the House of Representatives.[52]

Immediately after Commissioner Ruiz's ruling on Holmes, Powell created a subcommittee chaired by Congressman Herbert Zelenko of Washington Heights to investigate corruption as well as discrimination on the part of the ILGWU. In A. H. Raskin's words, Dubinsky regarded this inquiry as the instrument of a "racist mountebank" who was retaliating against him for his refusal to provide "election funds."[53] As Powell had always won election and reelection without ILGWU support, this allegation seems unsound. He more likely acted at the behest of the NAACP, whose labor secretary was his special consultant. Evelyn Dubrow, the ILGWU's lobbyist, felt that Herbert Hill "sold Adam Clayton Powell a bill of goods."[54]

As August 3, 1962, the first day of hearings, approached, it was clear that, with the exception of Zelenko, the International would not face a hostile subcommittee. (Though Local 10's Moe Falikman had been assisting Chairman Zelenko's campaign to represent a newly formed Twentieth District, the Liberal Party was leaning to Congressman William Fitts Ryan, whom it eventually endorsed.)[55] Intense ILGWU lobbying was succeeding; the other subcommittee members were sympathetic to the union, including Democrats James Roosevelt of California and John Dent of Pennsylvania and Republicans Carroll D. Kearns of Pennsylvania and Robert P. Griffin of Michigan. Kearns "admired" Dubinsky and wanted "to help" fight Powell,[56] and both Kearns and Griffin wanted "to prove" their friendliness toward labor.[57]

The hearings initially ran for two days, August 3 and 4, in closed session and produced no fireworks. Subcommittee investigators leaked word that the next round, beginning on August 17 and featuring open testimony, would be different.[58]

Excitement developed on the second day when, as special consultant to the subcommittee, Herbert Hill took the stand. His testimony consisted of a fourteen-page report that charged the ILGWU practiced "*de facto* discrimination" against blacks and Puerto Ricans, who were "relegated to second-class membership." "For all practical purposes," the report declared, "Locals 10, 60 and 89 are 'lily-white' and Negro and Puerto Rican workers are limited to membership in Local 22 and . . . 60A, which is the 'Jim Crow' auxiliary of Local 60."[59] Hill had just begun to read when he came under attack from the members of the subcommittee, including Zelenko, who protested that he had not seen the report beforehand. His reading was interrupted several times, and the committee compelled him to delete sections considered to be opinionated. Only in edited form would the document be entered into the record of the hearing.

Though Hill was thus constrained, Charles Zimmerman contended that the hearings were biased. Taking the stand after the NAACP representative, he lashed out at Zelenko, who the previous day had said on television that the subcommittee already had evidence of discrimination by the ILGWU. "I just won't permit you to try to frame our union," he shouted, shaking his finger at Zelenko. "Our union has a history of fighting discrimination. What are you trying to do—crucify us?"[60]

After five days' adjournment, on August 23, Florence Rice, a black woman, told of how blacks and Puerto Ricans in the Knitgood Workers' Local 155 had "been subject to discrimination in many subtle forms," which the union's business agents overlooked or condoned. She said that white employees were better paid than blacks and Puerto Ricans for the same piecework jobs, were the first to be taught to operate new machinery, and were the first to be called back after layoffs.[61]

The next day Dubinsky took the stand, with thirty black and Puerto Rican ILGWU members and officers on hand to lend support. Before answering questions, Dubinsky plunged into a defense of himself and his union that was autobiographical, historical, comprehensive, and audacious, yielding no ground to their critics. On ethnic group members as union officers, he declared, "I'll be damned if I will support this idea of professional Negroes, professional Jews, and professional Italians or anyone else that should be a manager or president because he belongs to this race or he belongs to the other race." He insisted that the ILGWU was "a union that does not discriminate," that the Local 102 situation was a "problem" that the International would "try to meet" and "have to meet," and that the statement Hill (not mentioned by name) read was "untruthful, irresponsible, gross exaggeration, unfair, imagination and . . . done in a spirit of revenge."

Three and a half hours later Dubinsky concluded his testimony, only to resume for another two hours on September 21 in Washington. Again he faced questions about discrimination and corruption and even about expenditures to promote the union label. With thirty-one ILGWU witnesses waiting to testify, "the subcommittee recessed, subject to recall." Additional hearings were never held.[62]

"Dubinsky Rebuffs Bias Charge at Congressional Unit's Hearing," *Justice* shouted after his initial testimony. Again he appeared to have rescued the International.[63] Yet, with the Holmes case about to be reopened and relations between the ILGWU and the NAACP adversarial, the union's image on civil rights was tarnished, and the "natural alliance" between blacks and Jews that had existed since the founding of the NAACP in 1909 was badly strained.[64]

Behind the scenes the heat was intense. To subcommittee counsel Livingston Wingate, Hill described Dubinsky as "the one-man dictator" who ran the ILGWU "as if it were his personal property."[65] Union counsel Elias Lieberman discovered that the NAACP staffer had led the Socialist Workers Party in New York City during the 1940s and referred to him as "Comrade Hill."[66] When, early in September, Hill distributed a copy of his unedited testimony of August 16 to members of Congress, Dubinsky protested to Zelenko that his consultant had turned the congressional investigation into a "platform through which a staff member may vent his personal spite."[67] Four days later Hill resigned as committee consultant, citing "the introduction of personalities," which "obscured" the investigation of the ILGWU's "racial discrimination and denial of democratic rights."[68]

Hill's steadfast pursuit of the ILGWU continued, prompting the Board of Directors of the NAACP to adopt a resolution in October calling on the committee "to pursue a vigorous and thoroughgoing investigation" of the union.[69] Charles Zimmerman then resigned from the Board of Trustees of the NAACP Legal Defense and Educational Fund. Citing Hill's influence, Zimmerman accused the Association of having "driven a wedge between the Negro community and the labor movement."[70]

The adoption of the resolution prompted Dubinsky to go on the attack. He discovered that the vote on it was taken late in an NAACP board meeting originally attended by thirty-six members, "only twelve" of whom were present to discuss the matter and vote on it. Dubinsky wrote to Herbert Lehman, who had missed the meeting, that the action was taken "in accordance with known Communist tactics, engineered by its Trotzkyite [*sic*] labor secretary." The problem now, Dubinsky concluded, was not "with an individual"; it involved "the organization itself." Lehman immediately disassociated himself from the resolution.[71]

Inevitably, the controversy touched upon local politics. Herbert Zelenko, whom the Liberals had rejected for the Twentieth Congressional District nomination, was denied Democratic endorsement as well. On September 6, with ILGWU support, William Fitts Ryan resoundingly defeated him in a Democratic primary contest. In November, Ryan won the seat, but Mae Watts, the union's candidate against Adam Clayton Powell, was trounced.[72]

By the middle of October, the feud between the ILGWU and the NAACP was threatening to get out of hand. On one side were white-led labor organizations, such as the AFL-CIO and the Jewish Labor Committee. On the other were black unionists, the black press, and various civil rights advocates, including actors Ossie Davis and Ruby Dee.[73] Frank R. Crosswaith and A. Philip Randolph were exceptions. In September, Crosswaith had issued a statement on behalf of the Negro Labor Committee in praise of Dubinsky and the ILGWU. The next month the Greater New York Chapter of Randolph's Negro American Labor Council distributed a circular that bitterly denounced the ILGWU. Informed of this document by Dubinsky, Randolph vehemently repudiated it. Writing to Dubinsky, he declared that he did not regard him, "Zimmerman or the ILGWU to be anti-Negro." Randolph then conveyed this point to Wilkins, who he hoped would meet with Dubinsky.[74]

George Field, Harry Fleischman, and Lester Granger added their voices for reconciliation. Field, the founder and executive secretary of Freedom House, sought to arrange a meeting between Dubinsky and Wilkins; Fleischman wanted NAACP representatives visit garment shops to observe black and Puerto Rican members of Local 10 on the job; and Granger of the National Urban League advocated an end to what he termed a "family fight."[75]

Field's initiative succeeded. Wilkins and Dubinsky were eager to talk and met three times before the end of 1962. At their first encounter, much of the discussion concerned Hill, whose dismissal Dubinsky demanded, offering a decade of ILGWU financial support for the NAACP as an inducement. Offended, Wilkins told Dubinsky he was interested in the garment industry rather than NAACP staff problems and began to leave the room. Dubinsky, realizing he had blundered, then apologized and asked that the conversation resume.[76]

During their second meeting, Wilkins defended and Dubinsky attacked the NAACP resolution on the International. The NAACP leader also challenged Dubinsky, who claimed ignorance, by inquiring into a problem the ILGWU had not been able to conceal, concerning the ILGWU wing of the Workmen's Circle Home for the Aged in the Bronx.[77]

In February 1959, Dubinsky had announced that the ILGWU would finance the construction of this structure, which would accommodate "all" retirees of the union, "without any discrimination," including those who did not belong to the Workmen's Circle. They would pay their way according to their means. Dedicated in June 1961, the seven-story building with seventy-five rooms and 150 beds cost the International $1.3 million. The project indeed seemed promising, but in the fall Dubinsky and the home's administrators came into conflict over eligibility for admission: the Workmen's Circle refused to admit gentile ILGWU members. Of 170 applicants, there were initially six Italians, one black, and two others who might have been Polish or Russian. Three would withdraw, reducing the total to six.

As the International was then embroiled in the Holmes case, it no doubt wanted to avoid a second charge of discrimination. With this consideration in mind, Dubinsky separated the union from the operation of the home, instructing ILGWU members on its board of directors to withdraw. Equally resolute, the Workmen's Circle refused to yield, arguing that the admission of gentiles to the Jewish institution would create dietary, social, and cultural problems. Rejecting this contention and the home's failure to process any applications from gentiles, on November 16, Dubinsky demanded that the processing of all ILGWU applications be suspended. By April 1962, with the suspension still in effect, "only twenty" ILGWU members had been admitted, and another nineteen were awaiting action.[78]

When Wilkins asked Dubinsky about the Workmen's Circle Home, he noted that no black ILGWU members resided there. In fact, he cited a problem that had already been acknowledged but was as yet unresolved. It was a more conciliatory, and probably embarrassed, Dubinsky who was now ready to consider other concerns of the NAACP as well as this one. In particular, he agreed to add blacks to the ILGWU staff and support the removal of provisions from the union's constitution that he contended had been used to keep out Communists but had also kept blacks and Puerto Ricans from advancement into the hierarchy. Wilkins agreed to refrain from publicly attacking the International while these concerns were addressed. So that the ILGWU would not appear to capitulate to the NAACP, Dubinsky sought time to make the necessary changes.[79]

By the end of 1962, Wilkins feared that the conflict would injure the NAACP as well as the ILGWU. Feeling that the Association's campaign had become too personal, he directed his labor secretary to refrain from public discussion. But Hill continued to make news by lambasting the ILGWU at a meeting of the NAACP Chelsea–Greenwich Village Branch.[80] Also troubling Wilkins was what he regarded as the poor taste of the attacks by the *Pittsburgh Courier*.[81] What probably frustrated the NAACP leader most was his belief as late as January 1963 that Hill had not made an ironclad case against the ILGWU relative to size of its black and Puerto Rican membership. "You don't have any figures to refute the ILGWU figures and percentages," he complained to Hill, "but still you maintain these are wrong."[82]

At their third conference Dubinsky and Wilkins agreed to a peace settlement. Each would prepare a position paper to serve as a basis for a joint statement.[83] Though peace appeared imminent, by March, ten weeks after the conference, Dubinsky was annoyed that he had not heard anything from Wilkins.[84]

While he waited, the ILGWU's racial policies were debated in the periodicals. In mid-1962, Hill had fired the first shot by presenting his congressional testimony in the journal *New Politics*. In reply, Gus Tyler turned up the heat, calling Hill's indictment "an anonymous smear," which he defined as "the great mark of McCarthyism, of the anti-Semite, of the white racist, of the bigot." In December, Paul Jacobs made things even hotter with his article in *Harper's*, deriding Dubinsky's leadership of the ILGWU.[85] More temperately, sociologist Daniel Bell and Shelley Appleton, an ILGWU vice president who had married Dubinsky's daughter Jean in 1953, traded differences early in 1963 in the *New Leader*.[86]

While awaiting a statement from the NAACP, the ILGWU again made a public commitment to the cause of civil rights. Under the leadership of Local 62 manager Matthew Schoenwald, Dubinsky's nephew, in August "about 60 shops" and more than one thousand people participated in the historic "March on Washington." The ILGWU contingent marched twenty abreast from the foot of the Washington Monument to the Lincoln Memorial, where the Reverend Dr. Martin Luther King Jr. delivered a stirring address.[87] On November 26, Dr. King again spoke on civil rights, this time at the annual dinner of Freedom House at New York's Waldorf-Astoria Hotel—but now in sorrow, as President John F. Kennedy had been slain in Dallas four days earlier. On the dais at this dinner was David Dubinsky, and he received "a laudatory reference" that evening from none other than Roy Wilkins.[88] Though Dubinsky welcomed the gesture by Wilkins, he did not feel it closed the rift between the ILGWU and the NAACP. The statement by Wilkins was still outstanding, and the Association had never rescinded its resolution in condemnation of the International. As far as the NAACP leader was concerned, he was ready to make peace. "I *do not* want things kept alive and will see to this in the future," he wrote Zimmerman in September 1964.[89]

Also unresolved was the Workmen's Circle Home dilemma. Despite considerable personal diplomacy, Dubinsky had not been able to persuade its managers to admit gentiles to the ILGWU wing. After an impasse of more than two years, in September 1963 the GEB at last appointed a three-man committee "to make a final effort to resolve the problems." This effort "proved fruitless." Finally, in April 1965, the GEB unanimously condemned "the attitude of the Old Age Home as discriminatory against ILGWU members" and "decided to sever its relations" with the institution.[90]

The timing of this decision is intriguing, because it was made only a month before the opening of the thirty-second annual convention of the ILGWU at Miami Beach. Dubinsky had extended an invitation to Roy Wilkins to address the gathering. After an introduction by Dubinsky, Wilkins spoke at length about blacks in relation to the national economy and the labor movement. Alluding to the recent differences between the International and the Association, he reported that after "detailed and lengthy discussion," Dubinsky, Zimmerman, and he had "discovered that neither of us was as bad as had been pictured." "We are friends of the NAACP and the NAACP is a friend of ours," Dubinsky responded as the feud at last subsided.[91]

At least since 1932, there had been little doubt that the ILGWU was "Dubinsky's union." Uncontested triennial elections from that date into the 1960s demonstrated his complete control. As its savior from Communism and bankruptcy, who then made it the epitome of social unionism and a political force for nearly three decades, he did appear to be indistinguishable from the union itself. Never mind the white-collar officers and blue-collar shop workers whose time, talent, and money had sustained the operation. What the world saw through his superb cultivation of public relations was the ILGWU as his family, which it was in a very real sense.

Therefore, consider Dubinsky's chagrin when, late in 1960, members of the "family" organized a union of organizers, business agents, and staff members. Instead of regarding their bid to employ collective bargaining as a means to ameliorate their condition, he viewed their action as a bid "to demand recognition from me as if the union were my personal possession." Moreover, he added, the union was "not a business" and they were not "mere employees of the corporation" but "missionaries out to convert the unorganized and defending the interests of the membership they represent."[92] As though these adversaries were Communists, Dubinsky vowed to defeat them, and the image of the ILGWU was further tarnished.

In 1960, they were indeed underpaid. Even the highest salaries were relatively low, with the president receiving $550 per week and the general secretary-treasurer $400. Down the line, local managers averaged only $136.50, business agents $118.00, and organizers $82.75.[93]

The Wagner Act of 1935 guaranteed labor's right to organize and bargain collectively, but it took sixteen years for the staff of a labor union to exercise that option. Staff members of the Air Line Pilots Association took this action and won an initial judgment from the National Labor Relations Board that, legally, the ALPA was an "employer," which made them "employees" with organizational rights. After four years of litigation the NLRB reversed itself, citing the nonprofit nature of labor unions as the basis for a ruling that as a class they were not employers over whom it had jurisdiction. The question finally reached the Supreme Court, which, in 1957, upheld the original decision; the NLRB had jurisdiction when unions were employers, and staff members could organize. Lest there be another reversal, in 1959 the Landrum-Griffin Act gave that right legislative reinforcement.[94] Such activity also was occurring even within the national structure of the AFL-CIO organization. In May 1958, organizers for the Federation won a six-month fight for recognition, and in September 1960, a union of field workers followed suit.[95]

These developments did not go unnoticed by staff members of the ILGWU. By the fall of 1959, ILGWU members in Pennsylvania, Maryland, New York, and Massachusetts were planning to form a union. A steering committee planned "a national meeting" in New York City for

December 1960, when staffers would be in the city for an ILGWU Legislative Conference and a Northeast Department Christmas party. On December 3, at a final planning session in Washington, December 11 was set
as the date for the founding meeting, and Federation of Union Representatives was adopted as the name of the new organization. Chaired by
Constantine "Gus" Sedares of the International's Eastern Region, who
had been fired two days earlier, a group of twenty-five ILGWU organizers met and "adopted a temporary constitution and a statement of principles." Though Sedares might have been regarded as a radical, the
twenty-two male and three female founders of the union, which would be
known as FOUR, represented no particular political, demographic, or
racial tendencies. As far as Marvin Rogoff of the Northeast Department,
who was elected temporary secretary-treasurer, was concerned, they
reflected only the ILGWU staff.[96]

Once FOUR as founded, the next step was to ask Dubinsky for recognition. On December 18, Sedares, Rogoff, William Karker, Winifred
Lippman, and Martin Waxman sent Dubinsky a telegram. They requested recognition to represent "all field staff employees listed as organizers on the ILGWU general staff" and threatened "to petition the National Labor Relations Board for a representation election" if they did not
"receive a favorable reply . . . during the week of December 18 1960."[97]

At eight o'clock the next morning, Rogoff telephoned David Gingold
at home and advised him of the message, only to be told a committee
should have gone to Dubinsky. Gingold insisted that he should "have
tried to work within the ILGWU and not through an outside Union,"
which would be "forming a power bloc to influence policy, just as the
Communists did in the 1920s." His group, Rogoff maintained, was "interested only in wages and working conditions and it seemed peculiar" to
call it "a power bloc" as its president, Sedares, "had already been fired."
Gingold replied that Sedares had only been reassigned, but when Rogoff
assured him that he had indeed been discharged, the manager explained
that the leader of FOUR had "crazy ideas."[98]

When Dubinsky received the telegram and digested its contents, he
replied to the managers of Northeast Department locals and districts instead of its authors. At a meeting of the managers on Friday, December
23, he termed the message "an ultimatum," devised behind his back and
without his knowledge.[99] In the absence of a direct reply, on December
27, FOUR petitioned the NLRB for an election.[100]

The next day Sedares and Rogoff wrote to Dubinsky with a request for a face-to-face meeting, which they hoped would produce a settlement. In reply, Dubinsky stated that only the General Executive Board, which would meet at the end of January, could grant recognition, but he would nevertheless meet with them. On January 9 they met at Dubinsky's office, and the ILGWU president complained about the "ultimatum" in the telegram and the involvement of the NLRB. However, he also made an offer. If FOUR would agree to delay the NLRB hearing, which had been scheduled for January 17, he would direct ILGWU managers to refrain from attacking those who supported the new group. The ILGWU would not recognize Sedares as a representative of FOUR because he was no longer employed, but his dismissal would be reviewed. Pressure on members of FOUR was indeed being applied. One charge was that it pandered to latent anti-Semitism. Aware of the counterattack in progress, Sedares and Rogoff accepted Dubinsky's offer. Four days before this meeting, the International had already asked the NLRB for a postponement of the hearing.[101]

Dubinsky regarded the advent of FOUR as a "deep personal affront." Sol Chaikin, now assistant director of the Northeast Department, was equally hostile. He saw Sedares and his cohorts as politically motivated conspirators who disguised their intentions in collective-bargaining rhetoric. Nevertheless, many ILGWU members sympathized with the staff, regarding them not as policy makers but as underpaid employees who "wanted to be treated properly," "young kids who wanted to get ahead" rather than be errand boys. ILGWU counsel Morris Glushien thought they had a right to organize and said as much to Dubinsky, but with little or no effect. As counsel for the International at the first NLRB hearing, Glushien had an "emotionally wrenching" experience in which he felt he was on the wrong side. He then stepped aside as others, briefly Julius Topol and then Emil Schlesinger, represented the ILGWU before the labor board.[102]

Keeping his promise, Dubinsky directed ILGWU regional directors not to harass members of the "union within our union," while also denying knowledge of discrimination.[103] In addition, he appointed a committee of the General Executive Board to hear Sedares's appeal of his discharge. On January 16 and 23 the committee of three, headed by Julius Hochman, heard witnesses for both sides testify more than ten hours. Edward Kramer, director of the Eastern Region, cited a history of erratic behavior at several job assignments. Kramer said Sedares had displayed a violent temper, spent union funds without authorization, disappeared "from his assignment for long periods of time," been "abusive, discourteous and insolent to office workers," and generally "created dissension and bad feelings." Sedares denied many of the allegations, especially concerning his attitude. His witnesses and written statements by others that he submitted attested to his character and ability as an organizer. However, on January 26 the review committee reported that he had performed unsatisfactorily and received a deserved discharge.[104]

On January 31, the General Executive Board deliberated whether to recognize FOUR. As Sedares had been barred from attending because he was no longer a staff member, Rogoff also absented himself. Therefore, lesser personalities—Martin Waxman, J. W. Mitchell, and Bernard Cohen—appeared, but only as ILGWU staff members with grievances, not as official representatives of FOUR. On no other basis would Dubinsky permit their attendance.

To their dismay, the GEB unanimously upheld the dismissal of Sedares and refused to recognize their union. Still, Dubinsky suggested a possible concession. If the NLRB were to regard its approval of the AFL-CIO's Field Representatives Federation as a precedent, he would accept collective bargaining for staff organizers. The GEB then prepared a statement in support of this position, noting that organizers had "only minimal impact on the shaping of union policy." As for business agents, the statement said they had "directorial" duties and were "the embodiment of the union," which meant they should not organize. If they bargained collectively with the ILGWU, they "would in effect be sitting on both sides of the bargaining table." In sum, without mentioning FOUR by name, the GEB rejected its bid; however, five members also opposed an exception for organizers. As an obvious alternative to collective bargaining, the board set up a review committee to consider personnel grievances and suggestions and afterward to recommend measures pertaining to wages and other issues.[105]

In February, in three days of NLRB hearings, the union was referred to as the "employer" and its organizers and business agents as "employees." But even organizers, Louis Stulberg testified, were "definitely not employees, but staff officers."[106] The war had begun, and Dubinsky was prepared for a long fight. The "union within a union," he told Northeast Department managers, would be recognized only "over his dead body." Meanwhile, the review committee would investigate the question of wage increases. He would fight on indefinitely, going if necessary to the Supreme Court.[107]

Meanwhile, there was retribution. ILGWU officers in such cities as Atlanta and Chicago assembled their staffs and condemned those who had joined FOUR. Food allowances had been reduced, scheduled wage increases delayed, and jobs threatened or eliminated. Including Sedares, twenty-nine staffers would be terminated by October 19, 1961.[108]

Firm in their belief that they had "an inherent right" to bargain collectively, Sedares and Rogoff appealed to George Meany to "develop a policy" to cover relations between staff organizations and international unions. Reluctant to contradict Dubinsky and displeased that the Field Representatives Federation had taken root within the AFL-CIO, Meany endorsed the ILGWU position.[109] Yet, even as he prepared to file a brief with the NLRB in support of the International, Thomas E. Harris, its author, advised him that the union would "lose the case" and, along with the labor movement, "get some bad publicity." Harris told Meany the ILGWU organizers and business agents had "much less independence and responsibility and much closer supervision than AFL-CIO organizers." Moreover, the business agents were only appointed rather than elected officers.[110]

While the NLRB deliberated, Dubinsky aired his views in *Justice*.[111] To many in the labor movement, he was simply fighting the tide. Proponent of union democracy Herman Benson commented that the advent of FOUR had "not initiated any trend"; it was merely a "sign of what has already begun."[112] Staff unionism had spread to organizers for the International Union of Electrical Workers without opposition.[113] In his column in the *New York Post* and a subsequent personal letter, Murray Kempton taunted Dubinsky for defying what he had previously championed—unionism.[114] While Dubinsky was considering Kempton's criticism, FOUR filed charges of unfair labor practices with the NLRB. In particular, it alleged that Sedares and Michael Gross, an ILGWU educational director in Pennsylvania, had been fired for their organizational activities.[115] Two weeks later, on April 14, a unanimous NLRB rejected the ILGWU's arguments against recognition and ordered the holding of a representation election within thirty days.[116]

The board then scheduled the election for Friday, May 12, to be held at its regional offices in thirteen cities.[117] Without delay, Dubinsky took to the mails. Already in receipt of copies of the letters of resignation of fifty-five members of FOUR, he sent each of these people a note accompanied by one of their letters and excerpts from others.[118] The GEB followed this letter with one of its own to all staffers, urging them to "close ranks, unite our house, [and] settle our inequities and grievances through ILGWU channels." Five days later Dubinsky sent them a personal note.[119] Reporting to Dubinsky on the Midwest Department, Director Morris Bialis assured him that "things are brightening up." Inquiries by Bialis revealed eleven of his staffers in favor of the ILGWU, two probably all right, and only two "definitely for FOUR."[120]

"It has been a harrowing experience," Rogoff confided to a supporter. "Not that we didn't expect opposition, vindictiveness, intimidation, pressures—but the sheer depravity of the opposition amazes me," he wrote. Disheartened by "the cowardice among the high and low in the ILG," he wondered, "if only the ILG would see the fantastic human resources it has!"[121] On behalf of FOUR, representatives of six other union staff organizations sent an appeal to ILGWU staffers.[122]

In the *Post*, Murray Kempton again assailed Dubinsky, acknowledging his "great tactical skill" but noting that it was "always easier to break a union than to organize one."[123] The next day a letter to the editor from the venerable Socialist Norman Thomas appeared in the *Herald Tribune*. Thomas warned that by turning "against the right of its own employees to organize," a "great union" would "not further the organization of the large mass of the unorganized."[124]

The representation election was held as scheduled but failed to decide the contest. The balloting yielded 115 votes for FOUR and 100 against it, but another 33 were challenged, 24 by FOUR and 9 by the NLRB. Also in dispute was the conduct of the International in the representation process. Responding to two separate complaints by FOUR, in June the labor board issued its own *Consolidating Complaint* that the ILGWU had unfairly interfered with organizing activities.[125]

"It seems . . . that we will eventually win," Rogoff speculated, but he also feared that the ILGWU would persist in taking the dispute "to the ends of the globe."[126] In June 1961, nobody could foresee the full extent of the litigation that lay ahead.[127]

As the two sides prepared themselves for protracted conflict, Dubinsky interpreted the struggle as though it were a new civil war. Though he did not publicly brand the leaders of FOUR as Communists, he and the GEB described them in language reminiscent of the conflict of the 1920s. The GEB statement of January 30, 1961, included a contention that, more than any other, would explain the vehemence of the ILGWU position, namely, that the staff union "inevitably must evolve into a factional caucus directed at control and determination of union policy for its own special and private interests." In September 1962, Dubinsky would describe FOUR as "a political faction."[128]

For the moment, the representation election required resolution. After studying the lists presented, the regional director of the NLRB upheld twenty-six challenges and recommended that FOUR be certified on the basis of a majority of 115 to 107. Contesting this decision, the ILGWU complained about nineteen of FOUR's challenges. Finally, in June 1962, the NLRB declared that FOUR had won by a margin of 115 to 113, and in August certified it as a collective-bargaining representative.[129]

In defiance of the NLRB ruling, the ILGWU steadfastly refused to concede defeat and instead looked to the courts for eventual vindication. Clearly in no hurry to resolve the dispute, Dubinsky advised the GEB in March 1963 that the matter would "probably take another year or year and a half" to "reach the courts."[130]

The U.S. Court of Appeals for the Second Circuit issued a ruling in November 1964, setting aside most of the charges of unfair labor practices and deferring a determination on certification because ten ballots FOUR had challenged, which the ILGWU wanted admitted, were still outstanding. Accordingly, the court ordered them counted. On April 5, 1965, instead of providing a final count, the NLRB announced that they had been "lost" and called for a new election. However, at this point neither side wanted anything of the sort. In light of the time that had passed since the original election and the ILGWU's "intimidation and harassment" of its supporters, FOUR argued, a complete rerun "would be a travesty of justice." Also citing the elapsed time, along with union turnover since then and the disruption that would be caused, the ILGWU likewise stood in opposition. In addition, it asked that that the case and charges against it be dismissed. On September 14 the Court of Appeals issued an order to that effect to the NLRB, which, on October 1, complied. In May 1966 the NLRB formally closed the case.[131]

Dubinsky won this war, but at considerable cost to all concerned: the ILGWU, the members of FOUR, the labor movement, and himself. The energy the International expended was disproportionate to the threat the staff union represented, and the publicity it received was largely negative, calling into question the sincerity of his commitment to collective bargaining. This dispute, along with the civil rights controversy, ultimately concerned power. Opposed to sharing it with the newer ethnic groups seeking job equity or with staff members seeking improved working conditions, Dubinsky fought them. When these controversies were resolved, the victorious Dubinsky decided to retire.[132]

In 1959, when David Dubinsky recommended Louis Stulberg for the position of general secretary-treasurer, a sense of change was clearly in the air. On the eve of Stulberg's appointment Dubinsky had created a new position, assistant to the president, to which a highly capable thirty-six-year-old attorney with sixteen years of service to the ILGWU, Wilbur Daniels, was appointed.

While Stulberg waited his turn to take the helm, talk of succession included other names, most prominently Shelley Appleton and Gus Tyler. Appleton was a native New Yorker who had attended New York University and New York University Law School before serving in the U.S. Air Force during the Second World War. An organizer for the ILGWU in 1941 and 1942, he returned to the union after the war as business agent, then assistant manager, and finally manager of the Office and Distribution Employees, Local 99. In 1959 he became manager of the Skirtmakers, Local 23. Three years later he rose to an ILGWU vice presidency.[133] As he climbed the ILGWU ladder, he married Jean Dubinsky, whose previous marriage to Dr. Lester Narins had ended in divorce but produced a daughter, Ryna, who remained with her mother.[134]

Intelligent, competent, and knowledgeable about the women's garment industry, Appleton had undoubtedly earned his place on the General Executive Board. Moreover, he had friends who might assist if he had higher aspirations, especially Edward Kramer and Douglas Levin, the general managers of the ILGWU's Eastern Region and Local 99, respectively. In addition, his very capable wife wanted him to become president. His liabilities included opposition to a continuation of Dubinsky's rule through his son-in-law and some doubts as to his work ethic.[135]

The quintessential social unionist, Gus Tyler stood apart from those ILGWU officers who tended to the business of collective bargaining. Distant from the factory floor, he was the "house intellectual" and more, a political thinker and strategist, an educator, and an articulate spokesman for progressivism. Neither a confidant of Dubinsky nor an aspirant to be his successor, Tyler did not appear to be presidential timber.

Not until Dubinsky abruptly elevated him. In March 1963 the president announce to the GEB that he had long sought a replacement for Wilbur Daniels, who had resigned as his assistant in 1961. Dubinsky then revealed that Gus Tyler accepted an offer to take the job, with a new title, "assistant president." Dubinsky told the GEB members, "I am giving you someone you will be proud of." Then Dubinsky looked to his own future. With a broad grin he said, "I'm not getting any younger, but I am getting older." "Conventions designate successors," he noted, but further added, "I wanted someone they could look up to." As *Women's Wear Daily* reported the next morning, "The appointment raised speculation whether Mr. Dubinsky was grooming his own successor," and the magazine quoted an anonymous "union official" who regarded the appointment as "significant" because Tyler "has a great future in the union and may play a key role in it."

Louis Stulberg was angered and upset by the announcement. Characteristically, he maintained his composure but advised Tyler that he would never be president because he lacked a union behind him. In other words, Stulberg said, Tyler's title did not mean much.[136] What mattered was that Dubinsky was contemplating retirement.[137] Left with little choice but to wait, Stulberg remained a loyal lieutenant, hiding his emotions. An efficient, uncharismatic aide, he understood that Dubinsky would not have countenanced an assertive, highly visible personality alongside him as secretary-treasurer. Dubinsky demanded both loyalty and a low profile, which Stulberg provided.[138]

He labored in Dubinsky's shadow, often treated more like a "troubleshooter" or "flunky" than a respected colleague. And Dubinsky was not above humiliating him in the presence of other people.[139] Despite Tyler's title, Stulberg remained first in line, which may in part account for his treatment. Dubinsky put him in position but, according to Tyler, regretted having placed him there because he did not want him to become president. Dubinsky favored Appleton.[140] "My husband loved him [Dubinsky] very dearly. . . . I hated him," Mrs. Bebe Stulberg would later recall.[141]

Accompanying the interest in Dubinsky's retirement was concern over the numerous retirement funds that protected the 440,000 ILGWU members. Since the establishment of the Cloak Workers' Retirement Fund in 1943, financed by a 3 percent payroll tax, 25,331 ILGWU members had retired with benefits through 1958.[142] Yet, as the fund concept spread, there was a noticeable lack of coordination. Along the East Coast it became evident as early as 1952 that there existed a "helter-skelter situation," where some employers would turn over funds to ILGWU affiliates or depart-ments while others were retaining their contributions until the establishment of a centralized fund. To deal with this disorder, in December 1952, Dubinsky called fifteen employer and fifteen ILGWU representatives in the Eastern Region to meet with him. At his suggestion, an Eastern Region Retirement Fund was created, with him as chairman.[143]

Within the next few years the Eastern Region Fund grew dramatically, and the financial and administrative advantages of merged funds prompted the creation of additional ones in the Midwest and Southwest.[144] However, with the funds' proliferation came concerns regarding their solvency. At the 1956 ILGWU convention, Dubinsky noted that in certain branches of the garment industry there were "few new members" and "old members retiring in large numbers." To prevent failures, the convention accepted his recommendation that the minimum employer contribution be 2 percent and that the forty-two funds then in existence become only one.[145]

Despite this decision, the number of funds grew, reaching 57 by 1962. Nevertheless, Dubinsky continued to promote consolidation.[146] Two years later the Internal Revenue Service agreed that the tax-exempt status of the ILGWU's individual funds could be extended to a single fund. The Eastern Region Retirement Fund would become the ILGWU National Retirement Fund, merging what were now forty-one funds into one, and begin operations under that name on January 1, 1965.[147] Dubinsky called this merger "a major landmark in the pursuit of social justice under the union label."[148]

Another goal concerned collective bargaining in an age of technological change and corporate growth and diversification. Seeking to raise capital with which to finance expansion, encourage mergers, or simply generate higher profits, numerous American businesses during the 1950s had issued stock and become public corporations. In 1950 only eighteen women's garment firms sold stock to the public, but by February 1962 the number had advanced to sixty-five. Merger and acquisition also posed a potential threat to the small businesses that had traditionally dominated the industry. Giant firms with diverse product lines and operations extending over vast expanses of territory made difficult collective-bargaining partners.

The ILGWU had entered into an agreement with Bobbie Brooks in 1961, followed by one with Majestic Specialties the next year, but a systematic, institutional means of dealing with such firms remained to be devised. For the time being, new vice president Shelley Appleton would administer the two agreements, while a committee headed by Charles Zimmerman studied the matter.[149] In 1965 a new Master Agreements Department resulted, with Wilbur Daniels, back with the ILGWU, as its director.[150]

The year 1966 found Dubinsky weary with success after having spent much of the previous few years withstanding challenges in the areas of antitrust, civil rights, and staff unionism. While defending his policies, he had also solidified worker pensions by establishing the ILGWU National Retirement Fund and strengthened the International's contract negotiating hand by creating the Master Agreements Department. In a daring political thrust, the Liberal Party had made Republican John Lindsay mayor of New York.

Now he was ready to retire. March 16 was the date and the Hotel Americana the place for a meeting of the General Executive Board. On hand by invitation were lawyers Elias Lieberman and Emil and Abraham Schlesinger and journalists Irving Vogel, A. H. Raskin, James Wechsler, Victor Riesel, and Harry Berlfein. Absent was Emma Dubinsky, who had the previous day returned home following a hospitalization. After a long introductory statement by Dubinsky, Gus Tyler read a letter of resignation addressed to the board. Prepared by Tyler, the letter reviewed Dubinsky's career with the ILGWU from its beginning in 1911 through the controversies and achievements of the 1960s. "Now, with no major problems of an emergency nature confronting our union," the letter said, "I feel justified in turning again to personal considerations. I have decided to retire and hereby submit . . . my resignation as President." Furthermore, Dubinsky requested that as he planned to leave for a European vacation "within a month," his retirement begin April 12 and a successor be elected "immediately."[151]

As the stunned audience contemplated the significance of these remarks, Stulberg took the floor. Advised in advance of what was coming, he said that "this house fell on me last week." After praising Dubinsky as "one of the greatest presidents of a labor union in this century," Stulberg proposed that a committee of seven, plus Luigi Antonini in an ex officio capacity, be formed "to persuade" him "to postpone his decision." The GEB acceded to this request, but Dubinsky then pleaded with the board "to comply with my wishes now."[152]

Two days later the committee issued its report, but before it was read Dubinsky again took the floor. This time he launched an impassioned denunciation of those who the previous year had fought him over the Lindsay nomination. He contended that ILGWU members had "a right to disagree" but not "to come out and show the world that we are divided and split." He was "a success," he continued, because there was "unity in our ranks." "Yes, we fought racketeering, we fought communism, we fought enemies. We fought chiselling employers. But *we did not fight internally,* even when we had disagreements." Therefore, he issued his "parting words": "Maintain unity."[153]

The committee report followed. As Dubinsky could not be induced to change his decision, the committee recommended accepting it. However, he had agreed to have his resignation take effect June 15, the anniversary of his presidency, and hopefully he would now accept the title "Honorary President." Without hesitation, Dubinsky announced that he was "glad to accept."[154]

After hearing the text of a letter from George Meany to Dubinsky and remarks by Stulberg, the GEB considered the committee's two remaining recommendations, on the president and the general secretary-treasurer, both of which were unanimous. As everyone expected, Stulberg was the presidential choice, but the second recommendation came as a surprise, at least to Dubinsky. During the committee's deliberations, Stulberg had sent the committee a message advising it that though Shelley Appleton was the logical choice for the position, his wife worked for a bank that held ILGWU deposits. Such connections precluded his appointment. Unable to recommend Appleton or anyone else at the moment, the committee asked that the decision be postponed to the next GEB meeting, and that in the meantime Stulberg continue to occupy the position.

Tyler, who read the recommendations to the GEB, sat next to Dubinsky. From this vantage point he witnessed an incredible sight. When the outgoing president heard the statement on secretary-treasurer, he yelled for thirty seconds, only "no words came out." He screamed "like a stuck pig" because "he knew" Appleton would not be named.[155]

Dubinsky's reaction appeared to confirm a rumor then in circulation. Stulberg was reputed to have conspired with Dubinsky to make his son-in-law secretary-treasurer after he became president, thereby placing him next in the line of succession. Stulberg had reneged. "He [Dubinsky] thought he had a deal," Tyler later recalled.[156] Dr. Donald S. Harrington, who became state chairman of the Liberal Party in 1966, shared this interpretation. Harrington recalled that after his retirement Dubinsky gave a "very strong impression" on the matter. He intimated that he had expectations regarding Appleton.[157]

Not everyone felt a deal had been in place, or would acknowledge it. Stulberg repeatedly issued denials, to such people as his wife, Wilbur Daniels, and E. Howard Molisani, the manager of ILGWU Local 48. Daniels, who was very close to the new president, could not believe that Dubinsky would have made such an important arrangement in private, without a record or witnesses. Nevertheless, Daniels sensed that Appleton had expectations of becoming general secretary-treasurer as late as March 1973, when the honor finally went to Sol C. Chaikin.[158]

What, then, actually happened? It appears that in Dubinsky's mind, but not Stulberg's, there was an understanding rather than a firm agreement, perhaps confirmed by a wink or a handshake. An arrangement may have been the price of the presidency for which Stulberg waited while enduring the speculation, spread by Dubinsky, that Tyler was next in line.[159] By making Stulberg wait until he was age sixty-five and in declining health before becoming president, Bebe Stulberg later recalled, Dubinsky "took nine years from his life."[160] Nevertheless, it is clear that Dubinsky underestimated Stulberg, who immediately made independence of his predecessor a hallmark of his administration. Without flamboyance, he would assert himself and take the ILGWU in new directions while Dubinsky watched with dismay from the sidelines. The greater the gap between old and new, the less the chance for Appleton to obtain the coveted position.

Despite the elaborate explanation Dubinsky offered in his farewell address, his retirement appears to have been based on two primary factors: his perceived incapacity to continue in office and the effect of a series of controversies, beginning with the labor racketeering investigations of the 1950s and culminating in the endorsement of John Lindsay for mayor. Dubinsky was progressively wounded by the McClellan Committee's attack on his integrity, the NAACP's challenge to his position on civil rights, FOUR's demand for staff unionism, and, finally, the senior ILGWU officers' public opposition to Lindsay.

In October, he confided privately to Harry Lang. "The work and responsibilities were becoming too much for me," he wrote, observing also that he had "been thinking of retirement for several years" before he actually stepped down. As for his decision to retire, it was made "in September, 1965," at the time of the opposition to Lindsay. "On the possibility that Lindsay might be defeated," Dubinsky continued, "I concluded that I had given the union the best I had and that it was now time to retire." Lindsay's victory reinforced the decision; "it came to my mind that if I wished to quit, it would be better to quit while I was 'plus' rather than when I was 'minus.'"[161]

With a touch of defiance and the taste of victory, Dubinsky thus ended his presidency and an era he defined. After thirty-four years, the ILGWU no longer was "his" union, but with characteristic energy he was determined to remain active and influential in labor and politics. Another kind of era had begun.

20 | Honorary President

David Dubinsky had much cause for satisfaction with his retirement speech. Designed to come as a surprise, even to most ILGWU insiders, it clearly explained his departure from office as a logical step after overcoming the union's adversaries and strengthening its foundation. It was a proclamation of victory.

Now he would have more time for his family and himself. "You will have to concede," he later told the GEB, "that I did not have a life. I had a union life. I don't want to die in my boots. I'm not waiting for the free funeral that you will give me." That evening, while sitting in a café with Emma Dubinsky and Shelley Appleton, he added, "For 45 years I slept with the union—ask Emma." "I thought you slept with me," she replied, with characteristic wit. "Stop kidding—you know how many times I got up in the middle of the night and walked around because of some union problem and couldn't get back to sleep," he then said. "Yes I know," she replied once more, "and then I'd make you lie down and the phone would ring at 7 and you know, I was always surprised, you always sounded so wide awake."[1]

Emma indeed wanted her husband to spend more time home with her. Though she was a fine cook and hostess who often accompanied her husband on overseas trips and did splendid volunteer work for the Organization for Rehabilitation through Training, she did not pursue an independent career. She also refrained from interfering in her husband's union activities, and with David relations often were strained, no doubt exacerbated by his late hours at the office. She required his presence and comfort, especially as she had taken ill with cancer at least a year before his retirement.[2]

Despite this personal crisis, Dubinsky could not separate himself entirely from union service. While anticipating his own retirement, he thought of the rank-and-file ILGWU retirees. On March 15, the eve of his resignation, he had told the GEB of hardship among many who were in-eligible to receive retirement benefits. Along with financial assistance, recreational and cultural activities, he believed, would benefit the needy retirees. The next day the board voted to establish an ILGWU Special As-sistance Fund to be financed mostly from the collection of liquidated damages, monies paid by employers for violating collective-bargaining agreements, and managed by a new Retiree Service Department under an appointed administrator.[3]

At Stulberg's urging, Dubinsky agreed to be that person, as an un-salaried volunteer with a weekly expense allowance, an office, and con-tinued use of his ILGWU-owned automobile.[4] Rather than occupy an office at ILGWU headquarters, Dubinsky persuaded Stulberg to rent space above a Chinese restaurant owned by his friend Sou Chan on West Fifty-second Street. Dubinsky chose that location, he said, to indicate to his successor that he did not want to interfere with his presidency.[5]

Of the 46,000 ILGWU retirees in 1968, 27,000 resided in the New York City area. Many required direct personal assistance to cope with everyday living. In March 1967, under Title III of the Older Americans Act of 1965, the ILGWU established a Friendly Visiting Program. Ad-ministered by the Retiree Service Department, 78 percent of its funds were provided by the federal government and New York State and 22 per-cent by the International. Under the direction of a social worker, Friendly Visitors, all of whom who were themselves retirees, visited senior citizens at home and frequently helped them gain access to medical treatment or insurance coverage through Medicare and Medicaid. In cooperation with New York State, the program was soon extended to include visits to old age and nursing homes. In 1970, 23,893 of the 27,000 New York retirees received at least one home visit.[6]

The new job gave Dubinsky great satisfaction.[7] Interested in opera and music since his youth, he made such cultural fare central to the activities of the Retiree Service Department. In 1967 it produced a revival of *Pins and Needles,* a highly successful musical revue featuring garment work-ers that the ILGWU had first presented thirty years earlier, and two con-certs conducted by Leopold Stokowski at Carnegie Hall. The next year featured a concert series at the High School of Fashion Industries, fol-lowed in 1969 by concerts at the Lincoln Center for the Performing Arts.[8]

On June 14, 1966, the ILGWU hosted what Stulberg had intended to be a farewell dinner for Dubinsky in the Grand Ballroom of the Hotel Astor. However, Dubinsky agreed to the affair only if the honoree were

Stulberg, whom he would install. Vice President Hubert Humphrey was the featured speaker. Dubinsky could not resist touting the Minnesotan, an honorary ILGWU member in Minneapolis, for the presidency in 1968. "We are with you all the way," Dubinsky told him.[9]

The next day Louis Stulberg took charge of the ILGWU, with Dubinsky now an observer at General Executive Board meetings. His attendance at these sessions resulted in some less-than-pleasant experiences. The man who had dominated the GEB for decades, often humiliating individual members in the process, now sat at the end of the head table. Made to feel small, he was treated with coldness and dislike, an object for retribution. Yet he did not complain; he sat quietly.[10]

This animosity even became public. In the Yiddish-language daily the *Day-Morning Journal,* Herman Morgenstern reported that Stulberg intended to encourage individual expression and initiatives within the ILGWU, marking a clear departure from Dubinsky's style of administration. Deeply offended, Dubinsky called Morgenstern's account "meddlesome and hypocritical" and suggested that he should have added:

> I have all these years written friendly articles about the International under the leadership of David Dubinsky only because he terrorized the union's leaders and me as a writer. However, now that he is no longer president, the leaders are free to do as they please, and I am free to write as I please. What I wrote until now was not true, but the present article expresses the real truth.[11]

As for Stulberg, Dubinsky refused to "believe for a moment that [he] ... had any part" in the account. Dubinsky had confronted Stulberg, who assured him of his continued loyalty.[12] Stulberg spoke this way while also making it clear that the ILGWU no longer was "Dubinsky's union."[13]

At the Liberal Party there was no change in leadership. Alex Rose continued to serve as chief strategist, assisted by Dubinsky and financially supported by the ILGWU. Together they remained respected political operatives. Early in 1966, Robert Kennedy, whom New Yorkers had elected to the U.S. Senate in 1964, moved to gain control of the Democratic Party in Manhattan. Kennedy intervened in a surrogate court primary election. Careful to touch base with Liberals as well as Reform Democrats, he consulted with Rose and Dubinsky as his candidate, Arthur Silverman, went on to win the contest. More directly, Rose gave a Seventeenth Congressional District nomination to Jerome Wilson, which helped him win the Democratic nomination for that position over attorney Peter Berle, Adolf's son. The elder Berle sensed that this "spectacular act of dirtiness . . . precipitated a crisis in the ILGWU with Stulberg and perhaps also Dubinsky."[14]

The 1966 New York race for governor involved even greater complications. Republican Nelson Rockefeller was still the incumbent. In running for a third term, Rockefeller would certainly face Frank O'Connor, the regular Democratic president of the New York City Council. As Queens district attorney in 1965, O'Connor had deferred to Comptroller Abraham Beame in the mayoral race in exchange for a promised gubernatorial nomination the next year.[15] With that choice assured, the question remaining was whether the Liberals would follow suit.

According to Dubinsky, in August the Democrat paid Alex Rose two visits to win over the Liberals, but at a policy committee meeting back in May, none but Louis Stulberg and Gus Tyler had favored O'Connor.[16] The Republican governor might have been an alternative, but, unlike John Lindsay, he was too much of a party regular for whom there was "little love." If the Liberals opted for their own choice, however, they might draw sufficient votes from O'Connor to reelect Rockefeller anyway.[17]

The Liberal line on O'Connor was that he was not only boss-dominated but too conservative as well. As a state senator, he had favored subjecting welfare recipients to a two-year residency requirement and, even worse, sponsored legislation that might have destroyed the Liberal Party. His bill would have prohibited the Liberals and others from nominating candidates whose registration was with other parties.[18]

These allegations had substance, but what really mattered was that Alex Rose did not want him. Rose regarded him as a tool of Democratic county leaders Charles Buckley and Stanley Steingut, of the Bronx and Brooklyn respectively, and rejected him outright. As for Dubinsky, he did what was customary and followed his leader, despite a midnight call from Lyndon Johnson. For at least thirty minutes the president gave Dubinsky "a miserable time" as he argued to no avail for a Liberal endorsement of O'Connor.[19]

On August 8 the Liberals' policy committee also followed Rose and decided to seek their own candidate if the Democrats went forward with O'Connor. Stulberg, who attended the committee's meeting, was not enthralled with O'Connor or any of the other Democratic possibilities, including Nassau County executive Eugene Nickerson, businessman Howard Samuels, and Franklin D. Roosevelt Jr. Based on Stulberg's report, a meeting of ILGWU managers agreed that another candidate should be found if O'Connor were nominated.[20] On August 22 the Liberal Party announced that it would seek an independent candidate.[21]

It took less than a week for a familiar figure to emerge as front-runner. On August 26, Franklin D. Roosevelt Jr., who had pursued the Democratic nomination, stepped aside in favor of O'Connor.[22] Alex Rose considered Roosevelt for the Liberal nomination, which the party's twenty-six-member policy committee would have to ratify.

Though Roosevelt possessed a famous name and considerable intelligence, and had been a Liberal nominee for Congress in 1949 and state attorney general in 1954, his designation was far from certain. He won the House race but served without distinction, and his defeat by Jacob Javits in the attorney general contest made him the only loser at the top of the combined Democratic-Liberal ticket. As if to tarnish his image even further, after his loss he represented Rafael Trujillo, the dictator of the Dominican Republic. Finally, he was known to have had a drinking problem.[23]

The last of these no longer was true, but Roosevelt's reputation was none too impressive. To George Field, "his selection would be like an announcement of the bankruptcy of the Liberal Party."[24] Even Rose, who had helped block Roosevelt's bid for a gubernatorial nomination in 1954, was not an enthusiastic supporter. However, in 1966, he could not abide O'Connor. Furthermore, he wanted a proven vote-getter to outpoll the candidate of the four-year-old Conservative Party and thus permit the Liberals to retain line C on New York State's ballot. Accordingly, Rose recruited support from among the Liberal Party hierarchy, including Dubinsky, state chairman Donald Harrington, and black civil rights leader James Farmer, the former director of the Congress of Racial Equality, who was himself a possible nominee. As Harrington recalled, Dubinsky remained in the background of this maneuvering.[25]

Nevertheless, on September 8 at the Liberals' nominating convention at the Americana Hotel, he was not hard to find. During the morning, Dubinsky was at a meeting of the ILGWU's General Executive Board. In an impassioned statement, he asked the board not to abandon the Liberal Party. After lunch he left for New York to be on hand for the nomination. The Liberals' policy committee had decided on Roosevelt by a vote of 19 to 4, with three abstentions. The votes of the four ILGWU members were divided. Only Dubinsky backed Roosevelt. Stulberg and Gus Tyler voted against him, and Charles Zimmerman abstained. The convention delegates then gave Roosevelt 209 votes to 33 for Farmer, with twelve abstentions. Roosevelt was thus nominated, and posing "conspicuously" with him afterward was Dubinsky.[26]

Louis Stulberg, who had remained at Unity House, was not pleased with what had been happening. On September 6, James Wechsler reported in the *New York Post* that "Frank O'Connor's dream of any serious stop-Roosevelt upsurge at the Liberal enclave perished quietly during a closed-door meeting" of the GEB the previous day. "The heralded clash between pro-Roosevelt David Dubinsky and his successor, Louis Stulberg, ended in amicable accord on the prospective Roosevelt candidacy." Angrily, Stulberg prepared a statement that the board approved in refutation of Wechsler's report; the GEB, it said, had not acted in an open or closed session on the gubernatorial campaign. "Although the ILGWU has not taken an official position," Stulberg's statement concluded, "I am certain that the ILGWU will continue its traditional support of the Liberal Party." Three additional words in the draft version, "and its candidates," were deleted from the final version.

The next day, immediately following Dubinsky's speech, Stulberg issued a statement of his own. As the divided policy committee vote had been reported in the press, he felt obliged to discuss the nomination and called for unity.[27] In a press interview a few days later, Stulberg became more open and explicit. O'Connor, Roosevelt, and Rockefeller, he said, were "all equally bad." "I felt they ought to nominate a real liberal for the Liberal Party," Stulberg said. As for the ILGWU's financial support of the Liberal Party, which had normally covered about a third of its expenses, it suddenly seemed to vanish. "I don't expect we'll spend any great amount of money for the Governorship," he added, while noting that most funds would be spent on congressional contests.[28]

Many key ILGWU members fell in line with Stulberg. "We follow the lead of our president," declared Matthew Schoenwald, the manager of the Undergarment and Negligee Workers and a vice chairman of the Queens Liberal Party. Moe Falikman announced that the executive board of the Cutters Union had "unanimously decided not to participate actively in the state campaign." It appeared to matter little that Schoenwald was Dubinsky's nephew or that the Cutters had been his local.[29]

The major story, of course, was that Stulberg had broken with Dubinsky. While refraining from public criticism, Stulberg nevertheless took his stand. As James Wechsler saw things, Stulberg had "quickly and defiantly turned his back on his sponsor; Stulberg is not a headline name without Dubinsky as his target." Yet Dubinsky seemed "to have taken unaccustomed vows of silence" and "issued no reply."[30] "Oh, my God," Wilbur Daniels said when he read Wechsler's column. "It's almost like a declaration of war." Daniels had no doubt that Wechsler had been influenced by Dubinsky.[31]

Though Murray Kempton interpreted Stulberg's recalcitrant position as unsurprising retribution for decades of abuse by Dubinsky, Daniels, who was much attuned to the new ILGWU leader's thinking, saw it differently. Stulberg, according to Daniels, felt the Liberal Party had become Alex Rose's "personal power base" and as such was not beneficial to the International. Furthermore, Stulberg's "guts" were with the Democratic Party, with which he sought improved relations.[32]

By repudiating O'Connor, the Liberals virtually gave the governorship to the Republicans. Nevertheless, they refused to hand the Republicans control of the New York State Constitutional Convention. In November the state's voters had authorized the holding of a convention in 1967. The task in 1966 was to elect 186 delegates, 3 from each senatorial district and 15 at large. For both the Liberals and Democrats, collaboration on the at-large delegates was the best chance, they thought, to prevent Republican domination. Accordingly, they agreed on bipartisan slates of candidates for those seats. The Liberals would include eight Democrats on their slate, while the Democrats would have three Liberals on theirs. Consequently, in September, Donald Harrington, Alex Rose, and David Dubinsky would be nominated on the Democratic as well as Liberal convention tickets.[33]

Though the Liberals fraternized with the Democrats over the convention, they could not make peace among themselves over the gubernatorial race. Similarly, the ILGWU remained divided. Stulberg and Rose became the subjects of special press attention, and discord continued among the ILGWU locals. The *World Journal Tribune* reported that Stulberg was intent on demonstrating to Rose that he was "president of the ILG." Leaders of the ILGWU squabbled in public over Roosevelt. Louis Nelson said Roosevelt did not deserve organized labor's support, while Murray Gross and Luigi Antonini defended him.[34]

As the controversy continued, Dubinsky and Stulberg avoided public criticism of one another. At the Liberals' annual dinner, for example, Dubinsky reviewed their party's history, explained his opposition to O'Connor, and praised Roosevelt.[35] Privately, he and Walter Reuther exchanged harsh words. In a letter to Dubinsky, Reuther charged that the Roosevelt nomination had created a "clear, apparent and unfortunate" division in the ranks of the labor movement in the state. Taking this criticism personally, Dubinsky replied that there had to be "some significance" to the fact that for "the first time . . . a majority of unions [in New York State] have given their endorsement to a Republican candidate."[36]

As if Reuther's attack were not sufficiently annoying, Dubinsky could not have been thrilled to read Victor Riesel's report on Lyndon Johnson. The president, Riesel said, desired "to develop personal and political relations with Stulberg" because of his "swift repudiation of Roosevelt."[37]

Frank O'Connor received strong backing from Robert Kennedy, while Franklin Roosevelt attacked "bossism"; but on November 8, Election Day, neither came close to Nelson Rockefeller. The Republican incumbent won a third consecutive term by about 400,000 votes over O'Connor. In an upset, Dr. Paul L. Adams, the Conservative nominee, ran third, receiving 510,023 votes, which was 2,789 more than cast for Roosevelt. The Liberals would be displaced from line C. With regard to the constitutional convention, the politics of collaboration succeeded as the Democrats won control by a margin of 102 to 84. Included in their majority were Dubinsky, Rose, and Harrington, the at-large Liberals.[38]

The successful convention strategy was small consolation for the failure of the Liberal ticket. On a personal level, the defeat could only have injured David Dubinsky. Roosevelt's candidacy and subsequent poor showing called into question Dubinsky's political acumen, tested his relationship with Lyndon Johnson, and gave Louis Stulberg a grand opportunity to establish his own political identity. Five days before the election, Johnson had approved packaging legislation; as was customary, the president gave out pens used in his signing. Among the recipients was Evelyn Dubrow, but a few moments after handing one to her, he gave her a second. "This is for David," LBJ said to the ILGWU lobbyist, "but tell him it's not for the Liberal Party." As Victor Riesel reported this quip, he also announced that a "new labor shadow cabinet was born," with Stulberg as the "new leader" who "apparently will speak for the New York labor-liberal coalition from now on."[39] Much perturbed by this claim, Dubinsky confronted its likely source, the ILGWU president, who denied his complicity.[40]

Regardless of Dubinsky's concerns, Stulberg more openly than ever criticized the Roosevelt nomination and the man who had engineered it,

Alex Rose. The Liberals had not intended to elect Rockefeller, he said, "but you add O'Connor's and Roosevelt's figures and they're higher than Rockefeller's."[41] He considered challenging Rose's domination of the Liberal Party but held off because such a move would be defeated by Dubinsky and other Rose stalwarts on the party policy committee.[42]

Meanwhile, Stulberg encouraged insurgency within Liberal ranks. In June 1968, the contest was decided. The leadership group headed by Harrington, Rose, and Davidson overwhelmingly won primary elections, which had never been held before, for party positions. In addition, Rose's choice for the Liberals' New York senatorial nomination, Republican incumbent Jacob K. Javits, easily defeated the insurgents' Murray Baron, a former New York County Liberal chairman. Eleven days later, Stulberg failed to win reelection as a party vice chairman. In November, Javits won a third senatorial term over Democrat Paul O'Dwyer and Conservative James Buckley.[43]

In 1969, Stulberg at last separated himself and the ILGWU from the Liberal Party. The occasion was John Lindsay's bid for reelection after a turbulent term in office, during which crime, racial tension, poor labor relations, and other problems upset the equanimity of New York City. Committed to liberalism, with Lindsay as its local avatar, Rose again arranged his endorsement by the Liberals. Dubinsky, as usual, concurred, regarding Lindsay as "the most liberal, the most intelligent and sincerely dedicated of all the candidates." Among the Democrats ready to reclaim control of City Hall was a former occupant, Robert Wagner. With Wagner available, Stulberg seized the opportunity to leave the Liberal Party. In May, the GEB formally disaffiliated the International as it endorsed its old friend. Wagner subsequently lost his bid for the Democratic nomination to Comptroller Mario Procaccino, who in November was defeated by Lindsay, but for the ILGWU there was additional evidence that the Dubinsky era had ended.[44]

As Stulberg demonstrated that he was president in fact as well as name of the ILGWU, he also made it clear that he was not a "caretaker president" who was paving the way for the succession of his predecessor's son-in-law, Shelley Appleton.[45] In effect emphasizing this point, Stulberg followed the precedent set by Dubinsky as president and retained the position of general secretary-treasurer. Perhaps to demonstrate that all was harmonious as well as normal in the International, the GEB implemented a resolution of the 1965 convention. With Stulberg's obvious approval, it decided on an "appropriate celebration" of Dubinsky's seventy-fifth birthday, which would occur on February 22, 1967: the GEB resolved to establish the David Dubinsky Foundation. Over a period of twelve years, $1 million in grants would be awarded "to causes and institutions in line with the traditional objectives of the ILGWU." Present for the resolution's unanimous adoption, Dubinsky "expressed his heartfelt gratitude."[46]

When Stulberg criticized the Liberal leaders, he hoped not only to overthrow them but also to bring their party closer to Lyndon Johnson and the Democrats.[47] A cause of growing separation was Johnson's conduct of the war in Vietnam. Since 1965 the United States had been sending increasing numbers of troops to defend South Vietnam against Communist guerrillas and regular military units from North Vietnam. In that year, faced with the prospect of Communist victory, Lyndon Johnson escalated the U.S. military commitment, triggering vigorous protests at home and abroad. Critics charged that the United States had intervened in a civil war and demanded that its forces be withdrawn. David Dubinsky thought otherwise. Consistent with a resolution of the AFL-CIO Executive Council in March 1965, he urged the ILGWU convention in May "to rally to the support of the President."[48]

Stulberg shared this position. In May 1967, when Americans for Democratic Action's National Board adopted a resolution expressing an intention to support a peace candidate in the 1968 election, Gus Tyler waged a campaign to have it upset.[49] While ADA bitterly debated Vietnam, Stulberg and the GEB reaffirmed their support for Johnson.[50] In February 1968, ADA endorsed a peace candidate, Eugene McCarthy, a Democratic senator from Minnesota. Two days later Stulberg notified ADA national chairman John Kenneth Galbraith that he was "herewith resigning as a board member" and that the ILGWU was "officially withdrawing its affiliation and all forms of support."[51] Dubinsky did not resign. He remained with ADA, he said, because he expected there would "be an opportunity to rectify the present A.D.A. decision at a forthcoming A.D.A. convention after President Johnson has been renominated, as he undoubtedly will be."[52]

Though the ILGWU presidency was behind Dubinsky, he did not think retirement automatically excluded him from continued participation in AFL-CIO affairs. Accordingly, he was displeased to discover that Stulberg believed otherwise. The first sign of this difference of opinion occurred in July 1967. On the thirteenth, without Dubinsky present, the GEB met in Chicago and elected a delegation of ten persons, headed by Stulberg, to represent the International at the AFL-CIO convention in Bal Harbour, Florida, in December. With the exception of Louis Nelson, who abstained from voting, the vice presidents in attendance had unanimously accepted Stulberg's recommendation that Dubinsky's name be omitted from the delegation.[53]

In a telephone conversation the next day, Luigi Antonini reported this action to the former president, who mulled it over. On the sixteenth, a kidney stone sent Dubinsky to New York Hospital, where he had additional time to consider what had happened. Finally, on the twenty-fifth, he exploded, sending blistering letters to Antonini and Stulberg. To Antonini he expressed shock that as chairman of the nominating committee he had not given him advance notice, nor opposed the omission of his name at the meeting.[54] "With deep disappointment," Dubinsky wrote Stulberg that his action was "shocking and inexplicable." Moreover, he said, never had such treatment been meted out to a member of the Executive Council who had voluntarily retired.[55]

Antonini's reply was conciliatory. He noted that he had indeed "reminded" his committee that when Dubinsky retired he had clearly indicated his intention "to represent our Union in the AFL-CIO." However, Antonini's committee and Stulberg "took the position that *a retired Officer constitutionally could not be elected a delegate to the AFL-CIO.*" "I made an appeal to all of them," Antonini explained, "to pause for a few moments and ponder on the moral damage such a decision could cause to our Union, but to no avail." What he could likewise not comprehend was "the complete change of atmosphere in the General Executive Board," all of whom Dubinsky had "raised and promoted."[56]

Coldly and curtly, Stulberg replied, three weeks later, "I believe there are some inaccuracies in your letter. In my judgment, the Board acted responsibly in this matter." "Of course," Stulberg added, he was "always available . . . to discuss the matter candidly and frankly" with Dubinsky.[57]

In December, Dubinsky ignored the slight and attended the AFL-CIO convention. It was a gratifying experience. After Paul Hall of the Seafarers' Union nominated him, he was reelected to the Executive Council. The ILGWU delegates, showing "little enthusiasm over the election," "did not stand up and cheer." Their choice for the seat Dubinsky retained had been Louis Stulberg.[58]

From April to September 1967, courtesy of the voters of New York State, the retired president occupied a seat in Albany at the constitutional convention. The major controversy before them concerned Article 11,

Section 3 of the New York State Constitution. Incorporated into the constitution in 1894, this article, the so-called Blaine Amendment, prohibited either direct or indirect state assistance to parochial schools. Its opponents regarded it as an anti-Catholic measure.[59] The ban remained intact until 1938, when it was amended to permit the use of state funds for the purpose of busing parochial school pupils. Never had a concerted move been made to repeal it altogether. However, in 1967, New York Assembly speaker Anthony J. Travia, Democrat of Brooklyn, led such an effort despite much opposition, especially from Protestant and Jewish groups.[60]

Dubinsky took this issue most seriously, doing background research on it well before the convention opened.[61] He decided, along with Rose and Harrington, that the controversial article should be retained. At the outset of the convention, Donald Harrington introduced a resolution to that effect and later presented it in a speech that warned that repeal or amendment of the article would lead to "the decline and possible death of . . . the American public school."[62]

While the foes of state aid argued on the basis of separation of church and state, Travia and the Democrats alleged that the ban discriminated against pupils in private religious schools. On August 15, Harrington's proposal came to a vote and was defeated by 130 to 48, a sure sign that the convention favored repeal. Four days later Governor Rockefeller ended his silence on the issue and called for aid to parochial schools. However, Rockefeller urged that the issue be separated from the proposed constitution on the ballot that would be presented to the voters. In taking this position, Rockefeller supported Republican leaders Earl W. Brydges and Perry B. Duryea Jr. in opposition to Travia, who urged but one vote on the entire package. Practically speaking, the Republicans argued that the presence of repeal might doom the document in November. On this question and none other during the convention, the Liberals sided with the Republicans. As the convention drew to a close, the Republican proposal failed. Next came the question of whether the constitution as a whole should go to the voters. Rather than have the convention end in deadlock after six months, the Liberals joined with the Democrats to support it, and the document cleared the convention with the required minimum of 94 votes for, as opposed to 81 against.[63]

Though the school aid question was time-consuming, at the convention Dubinsky devoted much more effort to protecting the rights of labor. In June, as a member of the Committee on Labor, Civil Service and Public Pensions, he spoke at length on the history of labor in the United

States, noting that New York State had already enacted its own versions of the federal Norris-La Guardia and Wagner Acts. His plea was that the principles embedded within this legislation be incorporated into the new state constitution. As related by Emil Schlesinger, a fellow convention delegate advised Dubinsky that such material would be out of place and take up too much space. Moreover, the delegate said, the best constitution ever was written by Moses in ten sentences. Dubinsky replied, "But where are you going to find such a writer?"[64] Though he achieved no major breakthroughs in this area, the final document did preserve labor's right to organize and bargain collectively and the right of workers to join unions regardless of "race, color, creed or national origin."[65]

After the convention, Dubinsky conceded that "the proposed constitution is an improvement over the old one." However, the "one package" decision of the convention disturbed him. The repeal of the Blaine Amendment, he complained, "upset the balance."[66] Therefore, he intended "to vote 'No' on the 'package.'"[67] On Election Day most voters did likewise, defeating the constitution by a margin of nearly three to one and "about 1.8 million votes."[68]

As Dubinsky passed his seventy-fifth birthday, forgetfulness made its appearance but could not prevent him from retaining his affiliations in labor and politics. Often he would sit and enjoy an event without actively participating in it.[69] With Stulberg now in firm control of the ILGWU and Rose leading a Liberal Party without ILGWU financial support, Dubinsky's influence waned. For a person who had been married to his union, a greater degree of family life had become possible. Nevertheless, he would confess, "I cannot pretend that I found retirement a pleasure."[70]

By contrast, Dubinsky must have found some gratification from the first ILGWU convention he attended as a former president. At Atlantic City in May 1968, after a gracious introduction by Stulberg and a standing ovation, he addressed the delegates. He spoke for more than an hour, recalling his and the International's struggles and successes since 1920. In conclusion he said, "I am David Dubinsky, the same Dubinsky that I was 50 years ago, 40 years ago, 30 years ago, 20 years ago. I will continue to believe in the same principles and be devoted to and serve the cause of the labor movement." Six days later, as the proceedings were ending, he installed the ILGWU's newly elected officers.[71]

On both the national and international stages in 1968, few things appeared to go well. Assurances from the Johnson administration that the war in Vietnam was proceeding according to plan disintegrated in the aftermath of a bloody Communist offensive during the month of Tet, the Vietnamese lunar new year. The shock of this assault destroyed the administration's credibility at home, leading in March to a stunning showing by Eugene McCarthy in New Hampshire's Democratic presidential primary election, Robert Kennedy's entry into the race, and, finally, Lyndon Johnson's withdrawal. April began with an eruption of violence in the United States. A racist former convict assassinated Dr. Martin Luther King Jr. in Memphis, precipitating riots and destruction in more than one hundred cities. Two months later, after having just won California's Democratic primary, Kennedy was killed in Los Angeles by an Arab who resented his support for Israel. Late in August, the Democrats nominated Hubert Humphrey for president in a Chicago convention hall surrounded by antiwar protestors. This chaos seemed to ensure Republican nominee Richard Nixon an easy victory in November.

Along with millions of other Americans, Dubinsky watched in horror as this scenario developed, but he must have been encouraged when, in October, Americans for Democratic Action endorsed Humphrey, who had altered his position on Vietnam.[72] In a demonstration of his support for Humphrey, Dubinsky participated first in a "Cyclists for Humphrey" rally in Central Park and then the traditional garment center rally for Democratic nominees on Seventh Avenue.[73] But the late rush to Humphrey's side by voters across the country was insufficient to pull him through, and Nixon was elected by a slim margin.

Despite this debacle, Dubinsky remained interested in politics; but age was taking its toll. Still the first vice chairman of the Liberals, he watched with dismay the next year as they and the Democrats nominated his longtime friend Arthur J. Goldberg to wrest the New York governorship from Nelson Rockefeller. As a former secretary of labor, associate justice of the U.S. Supreme Court, and ambassador to the United Nations, Goldberg had the right credentials for the office. Yet as a politician he was out of his element. On the campaign trail Goldberg projected pomposity. "His profile is not as strong as his character. For casting purposes, he doesn't make a good candidate for Governor. But I suspect he will make a good Governor," Gus Tyler observed. As anticipated, Goldberg failed to generate excitement and Rockefeller won a fourth term.[74]

Arthur Goldberg may not have been a strong gubernatorial candidate, but he was a good friend of David Dubinsky, and as such, in the 1970s he

was concerned to see the latter suffer from an "advanced form" of senil-
ity. Near Washington Square Park one day, Goldberg met Dubinsky, who
could not recognize him.[75] Every February for a decade, Dubinsky had
gone to Miami for meetings of the AFL-CIO Executive Council. While
there, his colleagues had celebrated his birthday with him. However, in
1972, as his eightieth birthday approached, he decided he "did not want
any hypocritical celebrations" and thus "declined all offers for parties."
Sadly, his "only celebration" was dinner with his family at a new restaurant in the Fifth Avenue Hotel where he resided.[76] Two days later, he was
mugged a block from the hotel. While Dubinsky was en route to a deli-
catessen to purchase a quart of milk for Emma, a young thug punched
him and took his wallet, containing ninety dollars. Luckily uninjured,
Dubinsky proceeded to buy the milk on credit. "I couldn't forgive myself
for not putting up a better fight, even if I had been hurt," he commented
afterward.[77]

Well before reaching eighty, Dubinsky thought of shedding his non-
ILGWU responsibilities. At the 1969 AFL-CIO convention he did not
seek reelection to the Executive Council, which subsequently elected him
to the position of vice president emeritus.[78] Also in 1969, Dubinsky, in
collaboration with A. H. Raskin, had accepted an offer to write the autobiography that Simon and Schuster published in 1977.[79] Three years
later he attempted to resign as first vice chairman of the Liberal Party,
only to find that the party leaders "just wouldn't hear of it."[80] In October 1979 the Liberals honored him at their annual dinner. Missing from
this event was Alex Rose, who had died three years earlier.[81]

David Dubinsky's final years were not happy ones. After sixty years of
marriage, on December 25, 1974, Emma died of a stroke at age eighty.[82]
After her death, he continued to decline. "Physically, he appears well, but
his mental state is deteriorating. I see him from time to time; I try to believe he recognizes me, but I think it is just wishful thinking. That's how
it is!" a dismayed Hannah Haskel wrote to a niece of his in Israel in November 1981.[83] Six months later Haskel reported that Dubinsky had spoken to her, but she "could not make out what he wanted to convey."[84]
Moreover, "his physical condition is deteriorating." On September 17,
1982, in his ninetieth year, David Dubinsky died. After undergoing hip
surgery at St. Vincent's Hospital in New York, "he contracted a virus and
lapsed into semi-consciousness from which he did not recover."[85]

Dubinsky's passing did not mean the end of his dream. "The important thing," he noted in his autobiography, "is that the union goes on."[86]

And it did. Stulberg led it until his own retirement for health reasons in 1975, when Sol C. Chaikin took over. In 1986, Chaikin stepped down to be succeeded by Jay Mazur, an alumnus of the ILGWU Training Institute.[87] As the ILGWU approached its ninety-fifth birthday, Dubinsky became the sixth inductee into the U.S. Department of Labor's National Labor Hall of Fame. On that occasion, Mazur hailed him as the "distillation" of social unionism, a "spirit" that continued to be a powerful force within the International.[88] A year later, in 1995, the ILGWU, its membership shrinking as a result of foreign imports, merged with the Amalgamated Clothing and Textile Workers Union to form UNITE, the Union of Needletrades, Industrial and Textile Employees. The new union, with Jay Mazur as its first president, began with 350,000 members and a commitment to traditions established by David Dubinsky and Sidney Hillman. "We do not live in the past but the past lives with us," Mazur observed.[89]

Notes

NOTES TO CHAPTER I

1. Personal interview with Matthew Schoenwald, 1 May 1984.

2. Ezra Mendelsohn, *Class Struggle in the Pale: The Formative Years of the Jewish Workers' Movement in Tsarist Russia* (Cambridge, Eng.: Cambridge University Press, 1970), 7.

3. Shimson Leib Kirshenboim, "Lodz," *Encyclopedia Judaica*, 1971 ed., *s.v.*; Joseph Thon, "Lodz," *The Universal Jewish Encyclopedia*, 1942 ed., *s.v.*

4. Samuel Milman, "The Beginnings of the Jewish Proletariat in Lodz," *Our Lodz*, no. 3 (September 1954), 62.

5. A. Tenenbaum-Arazi, *Lodz* (Buenos Aires: Union Central Israelita Polaca, 1956), 187.

6. Waclaw Solski, "The Schooling of David Dubinsky," *Commentary*, August 1949, 139–140.

7. Mendelsohn, *Class Struggle in the Pale*, 113n.

8. Ibid., 138n.; Nathan Weinstock, *Le pain de misere: histoire du movement ouvrier juif en Europe* (Paris: Editions la Decouverte, 1984), 144–145.

9. A. H. Raskin interviews with David Dubinsky and others for *David Dubinsky: A Life with Labor* (MS, n.d.), cass. 1, pp. 7–8, ILGWU Archives (now known as the UNITE Archives), Kheel Center for Labor-Management Documentation and Archives, Martin P. Catherwood Library, Cornell University, Ithaca, N.Y.

10. David Dubinsky and A. H. Raskin, *David Dubinsky: A Life with Labor* (New York: Simon and Schuster, 1977), 18–19.

11. Personal interview with Helen Novarsky, 10 September 1987.

12. Dubinsky and Raskin, *David Dubinsky*, 20.

13. Solski, "Schooling of David Dubinsky," 139.

14. Dubinsky and Raskin, *David Dubinsky*, 21–22.

15. Mendelsohn, *Class Struggle in the Pale*, 89; Solski, "Schooling of David Dubinsky," 140; Max Danish, *The World of David Dubinsky* (Cleveland: World Publishing Company, 1957), 16.

16. Bernard K. Johnpoll, *The Politics of Futility: The General Jewish Workers Bund of Poland, 1917–1943* (Ithaca, N.Y.: Cornell University Press, 1967), 33.

17. Ibid., 32.

18. Ibid.

19. Raphael R. Abramovitch, "The Jewish Socialist Movement in Russia and Poland (1897–1919)," in *The Jewish People Past and Present*, vol. 2 (New York: Jewish Encyclopedic Handbooks, 1948), 376–378; A. Tschermerinsky, "Lodz in 1905," *Lodzer Almanak*, Lodzer Branch 324, Workmen's Circle (New York: n.p., n.d.), 59–61; Nora Levin, *While Messiah Tarried: Jewish Socialist Movements, 1871–1917* (New York: Schocken Books, 1977), 322–323.

20. Tschermerinsky, "Lodz in 1905," 59–61; Levin, *While Messiah Tarried*, 322–323.

21. Raskin interviews, cass. 1, pp. 15–16.

22. Levin, *While Messiah Tarried*, 258;

Abramovitch, "Jewish Socialist Movement in Russia and Poland," 369; Jonathan Frankel, *Prophecy and Politics: Socialism, Nationalism, and the Russian Jews, 1862–1917* (Cambridge, Eng.: Cambridge University Press, 1981), 207–208.

23. Johnpoll, *Politics of Futility*, 25.

24. Solski, "Schooling of David Dubinsky," 140; Dubinsky and Raskin, *David Dubinsky*, 22; J. C. Rich, "David Dubinsky: The Young Years," *Labor History*, special supplement, 9 (Spring 1968), 8–9; interview with Helen Novarsky, 10 September 1987.

25. Dubinsky and Raskin, *David Dubinsky*, 22–24; Raskin interviews, cass. 1, pp. 18, 20–22.

26. J. S. Hertz, *The History of the Jewish Labor Bund in Lodz* (New York: Farlag Unser Tsait, 1958), 210.

27. David Dubinsky, "Testimony before Special Subcommittee #19 on Puerto Rico," MS, 9 January [?] 1956, 6, David Dubinsky Correspondence, ILGWU Archives; hereafter cited as DD Corr.

28. Ibid., 6–7; Solski, "Schooling of David Dubinsky," 141–142.

29. Raskin interviews, cass. 1, pp. 24–28l; Dubinsky and Raskin, *David Dubinsky*, 26–27.

30. Solski, "Schooling of David Dubinsky," 140, 144–146; Dubinsky and Raskin, *David Dubinsky*, 30–37; Daniels interview with Dubinsky, 11–14; Jacob Kalmus to David Dubinsky, 30 August 1979; Dubinsky to Kalmus, 12 September 1979; and Dubinsky to M. Poznanski, 23 April 1958, all in DD Corr.

31. Telephone interviews with Joseph Gotteiner, 20 October and 8 December 1987.

32. Danish, *World of David Dubinsky*, 20; Dubinsky and Raskin, *David Dubinsky*, 37; Solski, "Schooling of David Dubinsky," 146.

33. "List or Manifest of Alien Passengers for the United States Immigration Officer at Port of Arrival . . . S.S. Lapland Sailing from Antwerp Decbr 24th 1910 Arriving at Port of New York Jany 3 1911," National Archives, Washington, D.C.

NOTES TO CHAPTER 2

1. Raskin interviews, cass. 2, p. 24.

2. Ibid., cass. 2, pp. 25–27; cass. 3, pp. 1–2; Dubinsky and Raskin, *David Dubinsky*, pp. 38–40

3. Dubinsky and Raskin, *David Dubinsky*, 43.

4. Robert D. Parmet, *Labor and Immigration in Industrial America* (Boston: Twayne Publishers, 1981), 110–111; James Oneal, *A History of the Amalgamated Ladies' Garment Cutters' Union Local 10* (New York: Local 10, 1927), 11–129.

5. Regular Minutes of the Executive Board, Local 10, Amalgamated Ladies' Garment Cutters' Union, 1 June 1911, ILGWU Archives.

6. Local 10 Minutes, Membership Meetings, 12 June 1911, ILGWU Archives.

7. Ibid., 29 June 1911.

8. Ibid., 13 July 1911; Oneal, *History of Local 10*, 431.

9. Parmet, *Labor and Immigration in Industrial America*, 107–113.

10. Ibid., 113–114.

11. Danish, *World of David Dubinsky*, 37.

12. Leon Stein, *The Triangle Fire* (New York: Carroll and Graf, 1985), *passim*; Gus Tyler, *Look for the Union Label: A History of the International Ladies' Garment Workers' Union* (Armonk, N.Y.: M. E. Sharpe, 1995), 88–89.

13. Dubinsky and Raskin, *David Dubinsky*, 40–41.

14. Ibid., 40; Gerald Sorin, *The Prophetic Minority: American Jewish Immigrant Radicals, 1880–1920* (Bloomington: Indiana University Press, 1985), 85.

15. Socialist Party Membership Roll Book, reel 2634, p. 147, Socialist Party Papers, New York State, 1906–1912, Tamiment Library, New York University.

16. Interviews with Charles S. Zimmerman, 5 November 1975, vol. 1, pp. 126–127, ILGWU Archives; Raskin interviews,

cass. 3, p. 6; Ronald Sanders, *The Downtown Jews: Portraits of an Immigrant Generation* (New York: Harper and Row, 1969), 256–271.

17. Raskin interviews, cass. 3, pp. 6–8; personal interview with Morris S. Novik, 30 May 1985, 5, ILGWU Archives; Zalmon Scher, "David Dubinsky—The 'Boss' and Warm Jew," *Der Wecker*, September 1965, 20.

18. Zimmerman interview, 5 November 1975, vol. 1, pp. 126–127; Louis Waldman, *Labor Lawyer* (New York: E. P. Dutton and Company, 1945), 49, 107–109.

19. Judd L. Teller, *Strangers and Natives: The Evolution of the American Jew from 1921 to the Present* (New York: Delacorte Press, 1968), 51–53; Nahma Sandrow, *Vagabond Stars: A World History of the Yiddish Theater* (New York: Harper and Row, 1977), 301–302; Dubinsky and Raskin, *David Dubinsky*, 39, 54; Danish, *World of David Dubinsky*, 35; Daniels interview with Dubinsky, 1–2; interview with Abraham Kazan, 30 September 1967, 53, Oral History Research Office, Columbia University.

20. Danish, *World of David Dubinsky*, 35.

21. Daniels interview with Dubinsky, 1; Danish, *World of David Dubinsky*, 35–36; Dubinsky and Raskin, *David Dubinsky*, 54–55; Raskin interviews, cass. 4, pp. 4–5; interview with Helen Novarsky. This biographer has been unable to confirm the date and place of Dubinsky's wedding. They do not appear in any full biography or biographical listing. In 1987, before granting me an interview, daughter Jean Appleton requested a written list of specific questions. Among those I submitted was "Exactly when and where did the marriage of David and Emma take place?" Mrs. Appleton did not reply and afterward declined to be interviewed. More recently, at my request, the New York City Municipal Archives conducted a search for their wedding "in Brooklyn in 1914 or 15" and reported that the names David Dubinsky and Emma Goldberg are not in their records. This lack of corroboration casts strong doubt on Dubinsky's account. Author to Shelley Appleton, 8 September 1987, and to New York City Municipal Archives, 16 February 2000; Kenneth R. Cobb to the author, 5 April 2000, in possession of the author.

22. Benjamin Stolberg, *Tailor's Progress: The Story of a Famous Union and the Men Who Made It* (Garden City, N.Y.: Doubleday Doran, 1944), 48–58.

23. Robert Asher, "Jewish Unions and the American Federation of Labor Power Structure, 1903–1935," *American Jewish Historical Quarterly*, 65 (March 1976), 214–227; Parmet, *Labor and Immigration in Industrial America*, 146–159.

24. Scher, "David Dubinsky," 20.

25. Oneal, *History of Local 10*, 434.

26. Interview with Louis Painkin, ca. 1968, 4, Irving Howe Collection, YIVO Institute for Jewish Research, Center for Jewish History, New York, N.Y.

27. Oneal, *History of Local 10*, 187–188.

28. Ibid., 48; Harry Haskel, *A Leader of the Garment Workers: The Biography of Isidore Nagler* (New York: Amalgamated Ladies' Garment Workers' Union, Local 10, ILGWU, 1950), 41; interview with Louis Painkin, 6.

29. Danish, *World of David Dubinsky*, 34.

30. Dubinsky and Raskin, *David Dubinsky*, 49.

31. Interview with Morris Novik, 30 May 1985, p. 5; Bernard Bellush to the author, 27 October 1987.

32. Arthur Liebman, *Jews and the Left* (New York: John Wiley and Sons, 1979), 422.

33. Raskin interviews, cass. 4, pp. 5–8; Harry Rogoff, *An East Side Epic: The Life and Work of Meyer London* (New York: Vanguard Press, 1930), 159–165; Ronald Sanders, *The High Walls of Jerusalem* (New York: Holt, Rinehart and Winston, 1983), 612–613; Stephen J. Whitfield, *Scott Nearing: Apostle of American Radicalism* (New York: Columbia University Press, 1974), 93, 110.

34. Report of Election Board [n.d.] of Election held 28 December 1918, Local 10 Minutes, Membership Meetings; Report of Election Board, 3 January 1920, of Election held 27 December 1919, Minutes of the Local 10 Executive Board, 3 January 1920, Local 10 Executive Board Minutes, ILGWU Archives.

35. Oneal, *History of Local 10,* 277–279.

36. Local 10 Minutes, Membership Meetings, 22 March 1920; 29 November 1920; 27 December 1920; Oneal, *History of Local 10,* 434, 436–439.

37. Stolberg, *Tailor's Progress,* 109–110.

38. Interview with Charles Zimmerman, 5 November 1975, vol. 1, pp. 133–134, ILGWU Archives; interview with Charles Zimmerman, 13 November 1964, pp. 22–25, YIVO Institute; Melech Epstein, *Jewish Labor in U.S.A., 1882–1952* (2 vols.; New York: Trade Union Sponsoring Committee, 1950–1953), vol. 2, pp. 130–131.

39. Parmet, *Labor and Immigration in Industrial America,* 68–69.

40. Theodore Draper, *The Roots of American Communism* (New York: Viking Press, 1957), 314–318, 320–322; Theodore Draper, *American Communism and Soviet Russia: The Formative Period* (New York: Vintage Books, 1986), 155–157; William Z. Foster, *History of the Communist Party of the United States* (New York: International Publishers, 1952), 184–185.

41. Louis Levine, *The Women's Garment Workers: A History of the International Ladies' Garment Workers' Union* (New York: B. W. Huebsch, 1924), 354–356; Stanley Nadel, "Reds versus Pinks: A Civil War in the International Ladies Garment Workers Union," *New York History,* 66 (January 1985): 54–55.

42. Raskin interviews, cass. 4, pp. 9–10.

43. Melech Epstein, *The Jew and Communism, 1919–1941* (New York: Trade Union Sponsoring Committee, 1959), 71–71.

44. Raskin interviews, cass. 4, p. 10.

45. Draper, *American Communism and Soviet Russia,* 17–28; Nathan Glazer, *The Social Basis of American Communism* (Westport, Conn.: Greenwood Press, 1974), 38–39.

46. Oneal, *History of Local 10,* 301–304.

47. Ibid., p. 284; Levine, *Women's Garment Workers,* 342–349; J. Joseph Huthmacher, *Senator Robert F. Wagner and the Rise of Urban Liberalism* (New York: Atheneum, 1968), 47–48.

48. Oneal, *History of Local 10,* 285–286; Local 10 Minutes, Membership Meetings, 24 December 1921; Haskel, *Leader of the Garment Workers,* 49; *Justice,* 23 December 1921; Dubinsky and Raskin, *David Dubinsky,* 52.

49. David Dubinsky, "'I Remember . . .' —A Personal Memoir," *Fiftieth Anniversary Celebration, 1902–1952, Amalgamated Ladies Garment Cutters' Union, Local 10, ILGWU, Carnegie Hall, October 5, 1952* (n.d., n.p.), 12–13; Local 10 Minutes, Membership Meetings, 29 August 1921; Haskel, *Leader of the Garment Workers,* 49–50.

50. Melech Epstein, *Portraits of Eleven* (Detroit: Wayne State University Press, 1965), 237–238.

51. International Ladies' Garment Workers' Union (ILGWU), *Report and Proceedings,* Seventh Convention, 1906, 36.

52. J. M. Budish and George Soule, *The New Unionism in the Clothing Industry* (New York: Harcourt, Brace and Howe, 1920), 46n.; Hyman Berman, "Era of the Protocol: A Chapter in the History of the International Ladies' Garment Workers' Union, 1919–1916" (Ph.D. diss., Columbia University, 1956), 24.

53. Will Herberg, "The Jewish Labor Movement in the United States," *American Jewish Year Book,* 53 (1952): 53–54; Charles S. Zimmerman, "Changes in the Jewish Labor Movement in the United States," MS, 21 February 1952; English translation of article written for *Jewish Daily Forward),* 4–5, DD Corr.; Humbert S. Nelli, *From Immigrants to Ethnics: The Italian Americans* (New York: Oxford Uni-

versity Press, 1983), 160; J. B. S. Hardman, "The Jewish Labor Movement in the United States: Jewish and Non-Jewish Influences," *American Jewish Historical Quarterly*, 52 (December 1962): 104; Herman Feldman, *Racial Factors in American Industry* (New York: Harper and Brothers, 1931), 221.

54. ILGWU, *Report and Proceedings*, Sixteenth Convention, 1922, 3, 7–8.

55. Ibid., 16, 18, 39–41.

56. Ibid., 27–28, 35–37, 47–51.

57. Ibid., 175.

58. Ibid., 193–199, 206; Haskel, *Leader of the Garment Workers*, 72–73.

59. Interview with Charles Kreindler, 2 August 1965, 5, YIVO Institute.

60. David Gurowsky, "Factional Disputes within the ILGWU, 1919–1928" (Ph.D. diss., State University of New York at Binghamton, 1978), 84, 92–93.

61. Jowl Seidman, *The Needle Trades* (New York: Farrar and Rinehart, 1942), 159; Nadel, "Reds versus Pinks," 50, 50n., 55–56; Dubinsky and Raskin, *David Dubinsky*, 88; interview with Charles S. Zimmerman, 13 November 1964, 22; and 11 December 1964, 53, YIVO Institute.

62. Raskin interviews, cass. 4, pp. 17–18.

63. Epstein, *Jewish Labor*, vol. 2, pp. 372–373

64. Stolberg, *Tailor's Progress*, 116–117.

65. Telephone interview with Emil Schlesinger, 1 March 1988.

66. Minutes of the General Executive Board (GEB), ILGWU, 8 January 8 1923, 1–12, ILGWU Archives.

67. Ibid., 28–29; Epstein, *Jewish Labor*, vol. 2, p. 129; Stolberg, *Tailor's Progress*, 117; Dubinsky and Raskin, *David Dubinsky*, 60.

68. Dubinsky and Raskin, *David Dubinsky*, 61.

69. Minutes of the GEB, 8 January 1923, 29–30.

70. Dubinsky and Raskin, *David Dubinsky*, 61.

71. Ibid.; Minutes of the Executive Board of Local 10, 8 March 1923; inter-

view with Emil Schlesinger, 29 August 1974, ILGWU Archives; Danish, *World of David Dubinsky*, 48.

72. Epstein, *Jewish Labor*, vol. 2, p. 129; ILGWU, *Report of the General Executive Board to the Seventeenth Convention . . . 1924*, 12–13.

73. Minutes of the GEB, 26 March 1923, 7, 9–10.

74. Ibid., 28–29.

75. Minutes of the GEB, 25 September 1923, 1–7; and 17 October 1923, 1–3; ILGWU, *Report of the GEB*, Seventeenth Convention, 1924, 131–132, 135.

76. Minutes of the GEB, ILGWU, 10 October 1923, 1; 17 October 1923, 8, 13, 21–30, 43–44, 46–50; and 10 December 1923, 7–9; Gurowsky, "Factional Disputes within the ILGWU," 118–119; Minutes of the Executive Board of Local 10, 6 December 1923, vol. 13, p. 2; Stolberg, *Tailor's Progress*, 123–124; ILGWU, *Report of the GEB*, Seventeenth Convention, 1924, 136–137.

77. ILGWU, *Report of the GEB*, Seventeenth Convention, 1924, 137; William Z. Foster to Morris Sigman, 23 October 1923, Morris Sigman Correspondence, ILGWU Archives; Gurowsky, "Factional Disputes within the ILGWU," 119–120.

78. Minutes of the GEB, ILGWU, 10 December 1923, 4.

NOTES TO CHAPTER 3

1. Minutes of the Executive Board of Local 10, 3 January 1924.

2. Minutes of the GEB, 9 January 1924, 1.

3. ILGWU, *Report and Proceedings*, Seventeenth Convention, 1924, 5, 36–44, 51–56, 64–67, 99–105, 126–128; "Report on the Convention of the I.L.G.W.U." (MS, n.d.), 1, Charles Zimmerman Correspondence, ILGWU Archives; *Justice*, 16 May 1924.

4. ILGWU, *Report and Proceedings*, Seventeenth Convention, 1924, 36–48.

5. Ibid., 103–104.

6. Danish, *World of David Dubinsky*,

49; Dubinsky and Raskin, *David Dubinsky,* 89; "Report on the Convention of the I.L.G.W.U.," 2; *Justice,* 16 May 1924.

7. ILGWU, *Report of the GEB,* Eighteenth Convention, 1925, 8–10; Morris Sigman to Samuel Gompers, 3 June 1924, Sigman Correspondence; Haskel, *Leader of the Garment Workers,* 82–83; Danish, *World of David Dubinsky,* 49–50.

8. ILGWU, *Report and Proceedings,* Seventeenth Convention, 1924, 207–209.

9. Minutes of the Executive Board of Local 10, 22 May 1924.

10. ILGWU, *Report of the GEB,* Eighteenth Convention, 1925, 18 – 19; Gurowsky, "Factional Disputes within the ILGWU," 143–146; Haskel, *Leader of the Garment Workers,* 83–85.

11. Gurowsky, "Factional Disputes within the ILGWU," 147–148.

12. "Report of the National Committee, Needle Trades Section, T.U.E.L. for the Month of October" (MS, n.d.), p. 1, Bund Archives, YIVO Institute.

13. Minutes of the Executive Board of Local 10, 7 August 1924.

14. Minutes of the Executive Board of Local 10, 18 August 1924; 25 August 1924.

15. Dubinsky, "'I Remember . . . ,'" 12; *Justice,* 22 August 1924; Minutes of the Executive Board of Local 10, 25 August 1924.

16. Dubinsky, "'I Remember . . . ,'" 12; Minutes of the Executive Board of Local 10, 21 August 1924; Oneal, *History of Local 10,* 312; Minutes of the GEB, 26 September 1924, 33; Local 10 Minutes, Membership Meetings, 25 August 1924.

17. Oneal, *History of Local 10,* 313–314; Minutes of the Executive Board of Local 10, 4 December 1924; Local 10 Minutes, Membership Meetings, 27 December 1924, 8; *Justice,* 30 January 1925.

18. Celia S. Heller, *On the Edge of Destruction: Jews of Poland between the Two World Wars* (New York: Schocken Books, 1980), 69–74, 98–109.

19. *Justice,* 13 February 1925.

20. Minutes of the Executive Board of Local 10, 25 June 1924 and 1 July 1924; *Justice,* 22 May 1925, 8; and 24 July 1925,

3; Dubinsky and Raskin, *David Dubinsky,* 64; U.S. Department of State, Passport No. 4847, issued 16 March 1925, DD Corr.

21. ILGWU, *Report and Proceedings,* Eighteenth Convention, 1925, 43–44; Stolberg, *Tailor's Progress,* 126; Nadel, "Reds versus Pinks," 60–61.

22. *Daily Worker,* 31 March 1925; Epstein, *Jewish Labor,* vol. 2, p. 138.

23. Epstein, *Jewish Labor,* vol. 2, p. 138; Dubinsky and Raskin, *David Dubinsky,* 64.

24. ILGWU, *Report of the GEB,* Eighteenth Convention, 1925, 45–47; *Justice,* 19 June 1925; *Daily Worker,* 13 June 1925.

25. *Daily Worker,* 23 June 1925.

26. *Daily Worker,* 26 June 1925.

27. Epstein, *Jewish Labor,* vol. 2, pp. 138–139.

28. Local 10 Minutes, Membership Meetings, 29 June 1925; Oneal, *History of Local 10,* 315–316.

29. Local 10 Minutes, Membership Meetings, 13 July 1925; "Statement by Morris Sigman . . . July 14, 1925," Sigman Correspondence; Oneal, *History of Local 10,* 316–317.

30. *New York World,* 15 July 1925.

31. Minutes of the GEB, 27 July 1925, 1–3.

32. *Justice,* 7 August 1925.

33. *Justice,* 28 August 1925; Local 10 Minutes, Membership Meetings, 28 August 1925.

34. *Justice,* 14 August 1925.

35. *Justice,* 21 August 1925.

36. *Justice,* 31 July 1925; Morris Sigman, press release, 1 August 1925, with photocopy of E. R. Browder to Workers' Party Branches in New York, 24 April 1925, Sigman Correspondence.

37. Statements by Morris Sigman, undated and 14, 17, 18, and 19 August 1925, Sigman Correspondence; *New York Times,* 15 August 1925.

38. Statements by Morris Sigman, 20 and 21 August 1925, Sigman Correspondence; Minutes of the GEB, 28 August 1925; *New York Herald Tribune,* 21 August 1925.

39. Minutes of the Membership Meeting

of Local 10, 24 August [*sic.*—31 August] 1925; Epstein, *Jewish Labor,* vol. 2, pp. 139–140; Nadel, "Reds versus Pinks," 63.

40. Minutes of the GEB, 28 August 1925, 1–6; Morris Sigman to M. J. Ashbes, 31 August 1925, Sigman Correspondence; *Justice,* 4 September 1925.

41. Local 10 Minutes, Membership Meetings, 31 August 1925; *Justice,* 4 September 1925.

42. Sholem Shally to Morris Sigman, 2 September 1925, with resolutions adopted 29 September 1925 attached, Sigman Correspondence.

43. "Shop Chairman Meeting, Wednesday, September 2, 1925" (MS), pp. 1–25, Sigman Correspondence; David Dubinsky to Editor, *New York Times,* 3 September 1925, DD Corr.; *Justice,* 11 September 1925.

44. Minutes of the GEB, 9–13 September 1925, 2; Local 10 Minutes, Membership Meetings, 14 September 1925; *Justice,* 18 September 1925.

45. *Justice,* 25 September and 2 October 1925; L. Hyman, L. Hurwitz, and S. Shally, "The Official Peace Agreement" (MS [September 1925]), Miscellaneous Collections, and C. E. Ruthenberg to Rose Wortis, 16 September 1925, Zimmerman Correspondence, ILGWU Archives.

46. "Shop Chairman Meeting, Held Thursday, September 24, 1925" (MS, n.d.), 19–20, 30–31; *Justice,* 9 October 1925, 2.

47. ILGWU, *Report of the GEB,* Eighteenth Convention, 1925, 172.

48. Local 10 Minutes, Membership Meetings, 12 October 1925; *Justice,* 16 October 1925.

49. Minutes of the Good and Welfare Meeting of Local 10, 17 October 1925; Oneal, *History of Local 10,* 322–324.

50. Local 10 Minutes, Membership Meetings, 26 October 1925; Minutes of the GEB, 7 November 1925, 1; *Justice,* 30 October and 6, 13, and 20 November 1925; Oneal, *History of Local 10,* 323–325.

51. *Justice,* 13 November 1925.

52. Local 10 Minutes, Membership Meetings, 23 November 1925.

53. Interview with Charles S. Zimmerman, 14 November 1976, vol. 3, p. 360, Interviews with Charles S. Zimmerman, ILGWU Archives; Dubinsky and Raskin, *David Dubinsky,* 94.

54. ILGWU, *Report and Proceedings,* Eighteenth Convention, 1925, 1.

55. Ibid., 17–22; *Justice,* 11 December 1925; *Philadelphia Inquirer,* 3 December 1925.

56. ILGWU, *Report and Proceedings,* Eighteenth Convention, 1925, 24–25.

57. Ibid., 209, 232, 262–264; Dubinsky and Raskin, *David Dubinsky,* 96; interview with Charles S. Zimmerman, 14 October 1976, vol. 3, pp. 362–363; *Justice,* 8 January 1926.

58. ILGWU, *Report and Proceedings,* Eighteenth Convention, 1925, 309–311; Julius Hochman, as quoted by Charles S. Zimmerman, in interview with Charles S. Zimmerman, 14 October 1976, vol. 3, pp. 363–364.

59. ILGWU, *Report and Proceedings,* Eighteenth Convention, 1925, 328–333; *Justice,* 25 December 1925.

60. ILGWU, *Report and Proceedings,* Eighteenth Convention, 1925, 337–339, 355; Dubinsky and Raskin, *David Dubinsky,* 96–97; Local 10 Minutes, Membership Meetings, 11 January 1926.

61. Minutes of the GEB, 18 December 1925, 1.

62. Local 10 Minutes, Membership Meetings, 18 December 1925; *Justice,* 25 December 1925.

63. Charles A. Zappia, "Unionism and the Italian American Worker: The Politics of Anti-Communism in the International Ladies' Garment Workers' Union in New York City, 1900–1925," in Rocco Caporale (ed.), *The Italian Americans through the Generations* (Staten Island, N.Y.: American Italian Historical Association, 1986), 82–86.

64. Fannia Cohn to Florence C. Thorne, 24 June 1926, Fannia Cohn Papers, New York Public Library.

65. Draper, *American Communism and Soviet Russia,* 222.

66. Minutes of the GEB, 5 January 1926, 1–2.

67. Ibid., 13.

68. Minutes of the GEB, ILGWU, 26 April 1926, 52–54; Pistol License number 21379, granted by the Police Department, City of New York, to David Dubinsky, 17 March 1926, DD Corr.; Danish, World of David Dubinsky, 56.

69. Stolberg, Tailor's Progress, 136; Local 10 Minutes, Membership Meetings, 24 May 1926; Justice, 21 May 1926.

70. Benjamin Gitlow, I Confess (New York: E. P. Dutton, 1940), 357.

71. Ibid., 358; Epstein, Jew and Communism, 119.

72. James Robert Prickett, "Communists and the Communist Issue in the American Labor Movement, 1920–1950" (Ph.D. diss., University of California at Los Angeles, 1975), 81–82.

73. Irving Howe and Lewis Coser, The American Communist Party: A Critical History (1919–1957) (Boston: Beacon Press, 1957), 239–241.

74. Gitlow, I Confess, 359–360; Stolberg, Tailor's Progress, 136–137.

75. Justice, 18 June 1926; interview with Charles S. Zimmerman, 8 November 1976, vol. 3, pp. 378, 380; Oneal, History of Local 10, 366.

76. Interview with Charles S. Zimmerman, 8 November 1976, vol. 3, pp. 374–375; Minutes of the Membership Meeting of Local 10, 14 June 1926.

77. Morris Sigman to William Green, 18 June 1926, Sigman Correspondence.

78. Minutes of the GEB, 23 June 1926, Sigman Correspondence.

79. Local 10 Minutes, Membership Meetings, 28 June 1926; Justice, 25 June and 2 July 1926.

80. Local 10 Minutes, Membership Meetings, 28 June 1926; Justice, 2 July 1926.

81. William Green to Morris Sigman, 28 June 1926, and "Resolution Adopted at the Madison Square Garden Meeting" [29 June 1926], Sigman Correspondence; Freiheit, 30 June 1926; Jack Hardy, The Clothing Workers (New York: International Publishers, 1935), 45; Oneal, History of Local 10, 361–362, ILGWU, Report of the GEB, Nineteenth Convention, 1928, 57.

82. Justice, 9 July 1926.

83. Ibid.; Executive Board and Committee of Twenty-five to Members of Local 10, 3 July 1926, Zimmerman Correspondence.

84. Minutes of the Mass Meeting of Striking Cloak, Suit and Reefer Cutters, 7 July 1926, appended to the Local 10 Minutes, Membership Meetings, 28 June 1926; Justice, 9 July 1926.

85. Justice, 16 July 1926.

86. Statement by Morris Sigman, 4 August 1926, Sigman Correspondence.

87. Morris Sigman and Louis Hyman to Al Smith, 26 August 1926, Sigman Correspondence; ILGWU, Report of the GEB, Nineteenth Convention, 1928, 72.

88. Al Smith to the International Ladies' Garment Workers' Union, 28 August 1926, Sigman Correspondence.

89. Statement by the ILGWU [31 August 1926], Sigman Correspondence; Freiheit, 1 September 1926.

90. Stolberg, Tailor's Progress, 137, 141.

91. Ibid., 141; ILGWU, Report of the GEB, Nineteenth Convention, 1928, 69–70; Epstein, Jewish Labor, vol. 2, pp. 145–146.

92. Interview with Charles S. Zimmerman, 8 November 1976, vol. 3, pp. 397–398; Epstein, Jewish Labor, vol. 2, pp. 145–146.

93. ILGWU, Report of the GEB, Nineteenth Convention, 1928, p. 73; Justice, 10 and 17 September and 1 October 1926; Minutes of the Executive Board of Local 10, 16 September 1926.

94. Statement by International Ladies' Garment Workers' Union, 14 September 1926, Sigman Correspondence.

95. Justice, 17 September 1926.

96. Local 10 Minutes, Membership Meetings, 27 September 1926; Justice, 24 September and 1 October 1926.

97. Hardy, Clothing Workers, 47; Min-

utes of the Local 10 Executive Board, 16 September 1926; Minutes of the GEB, 30 November 1926, 11–12, 32.

98. Interview with Charles S. Zimmerman, 8 November 1976, vol. 3, pp. 400–401.

99. Statement by ILGWU, 18 October 1926, Sigman Correspondence; *New York Times,* 12 November 1926; *Justice,* 19 November 1926.

100. ILGWU, *Report of the GEB,* Nineteenth Convention, 1928, 77–90; "Statement to the Membership of the International Ladies' Garment Workers' Union," November 1926, Sigman Correspondence; "Statement of Executive Committee of the Cloakmakers' General Strike Committee," 18 November 1926, New York Dress Joint Board Records, ILGWU Archives; Minutes of the GEB, 30 November 1926, 11–34; Louis Hyman, Joseph Boruchowitz, and Charles Zimmerman, "Report on the General Strike in the Cloak Industry of New York to the General Executive Board," November 1926, 1–10, Isidor Stenzor Collection, ILGWU Archives; *Justice,* 3 and 10 December 1926.

101. Minutes of the GEB, 13 December 1926, 1–9; ILGWU, *Report of the GEB,* Nineteenth Convention, 1928, 90–101; *Justice,* 10, 17 December 1926.

102. *The Cutter,* December 1926, 1.

103. Local 10 Minutes, Membership Meetings, 27 December 1926.

104. ILGWU, *Report of the GEB,* Nineteenth Convention, 1928, 108–115; Stolberg, *Tailor's Progress,* 142.

105. Sam Schultz et al., n.d., to David Dubinsky, Miscellaneous Collections, ILGWU Archives; Gurowsky, "Factional Disputes within the ILGWU," 278.

106. ILGWU, *Report of the GEB,* Nineteenth Convention, 1928, 104–105; Stolberg, *Tailor's Progress,* 142–143; Epstein, *Jewish Labor,* vol. 2, pp. 147–148; *Justice,* 31 December 1926; *The Cutter,* 7 January 1927.

107. Benjamin Stolberg, "The Collapse of the Needle Trades," *The Nation,* 4 May 1927, 499.

108. David Dubinsky to Charles Jaffee, 24 January 1927, DD Corr.

109. Local 10 Minutes, Membership Meetings, 31 January 1927.

110. Local 10 Minutes, Membership Meetings, 14 and 28 February and 14 March 1927.

111. Minutes of the GEB, 12–14 February 1927, 5, 9, 12–16; and 2 March 1927, 1–4.

112. Local 10 Minutes, Membership Meetings, 1 April 1927.

113. Ibid.

114. Local 10 Minutes, Membership Meetings, 13 and 27 June 1927; *Justice,* 17 June 1927 and 1 July 1927.

115. Local 10 Minutes, Membership Meetings, 9 May 1927.

116. *The Cutter,* 9 May 1927.

117. *The Cutter,* 17 June 1927.

118. ILGWU, *Report of the GEB,* Nineteenth Convention, 1928, 271–275.

119. Rose Wortis, "Struggle in Ladies Garment Union Is Reaching Climax," *Labor Unity,* 1 October 1927, 2; "The International Ladies Garment Workers Union" (MS [February 1928]), 7, Daniel Bell Collection, Tamiment Library, New York University.

120. ILGWU, *Report of the GEB,* Nineteenth Convention, 1928, 319.

121. Local 10 Minutes, Membership Meetings, 28 November 1927.

122. ILGWU, *Report of the GEB,* Nineteenth Convention, 1928, 319.

123. Local 10 Minutes, Membership Meetings, 19 December 1927.

NOTES TO CHAPTER 4

1. *Justice,* 23 December 1927.

2. Ibid.

3. *Justice,* 30 December 1927; Epstein, *Jewish Labor,* vol. 2, pp. 153–154.

4. Minutes of the GEB, 25 January 1928, 7–8, 57.

5. Minutes of the National Executive Committee of the Trade Union Educational League, 21 January 1928, Zimmerman Correspondence, ILGWU Archives.

6. Dubinsky and Raskin, *David Dubinsky,* 71–72.

7. ILGWU, *Report of the GEB,* Nineteenth Convention, 1928, 150–152.

8. Leonard Schapiro, *The Communist Party of the Soviet Union* (New York: Vintage Books, 1964), 286–308.

9. Draper, *American Communism and Soviet Russia,* 282–290.

10. Stolberg, *Tailor's Progress,* 149; Dubinsky and Raskin, *David Dubinsky,* 71–72.

11. Statement by Louis Hyman, 7 May 1928, and Louis Hyman and Joseph Levin to ILGWU Convention, 8 May 8 1928, ILGWU Research Department Records, ILGWU Archives.

12. ILGWU, *Report and Proceedings,* Nineteenth Convention, 1928, 8–9, 25, 39, 146–152.

13. Ibid., 9–10, 59–63, 81–88.

14. Ibid., 110–111, 113–114, 117–120; Epstein, *Jewish Labor,* vol. 2, p. 154.

15. Dubinsky and Raskin, *David Dubinsky,* 73–74.

16. ILGWU, *Report and Proceedings,* Nineteenth Convention, 1928, 104–108, 115–124, 179–187.

17. Benjamin Schlesinger to David Dubinsky, 27 August 1928, DD Corr.; interview with Emil Schlesinger, 28 August 1974, 57.

18. ILGWU, *Report of the GEB,* Twentieth Convention, 1929, 9.

19. Ibid., 83; ILGWU, *Report of the GEB,* Nineteenth Convention, 1928, 22, 90.

20. Minutes of the GEB, 25 June 1928, 25–27.

21. Schlesinger to Dubinsky, 27 August 1928.

22. ILGWU, *Report and Proceedings,* Nineteenth Convention, 1928, 44–45, 187–189; ILGWU, Report of the GEB, Twentieth Convention, 1929, 12–22; Minutes of the GEB, 22 October 1928, 8–8a, 57, with "Report of Special Committee" attached following 8; Stolberg, *Tailor's Progress,* 150.

23. Minutes of the GEB, 22 October 1928, 37–53, 58.

24. Hardy, *Clothing Workers,* 51–52; "Resolution Adopted at the Mass Meeting of Cloakmakers and Dressmakers held on Wednesday, May the 16th 1928," ILGWU Research Department Collection, ILGWU Archives.

25. "Report of the Activities of the National Organization Committee" [October 1928], Bund Archives, YIVO Institute.

26. *Dressmakers Bulletin,* 7 December 1928.

27. Benjamin Schlesinger to Max Danish, 26 November 1928; Schlesinger to M. J. Keough, 5 December 1928; and Keough to Schlesinger, 7 December 1928, Benjamin Schlesinger Records, ILGWU Archives; Minutes of the GEB, 20 December 1928, 1–3.

28. Local 10 Minutes, Membership Meetings, 14 January 1929; ILGWU, *Report of the GEB,* Twentieth Convention, 1929, 30–31; Haskel, *Leader of the Garment Workers,* 129; *Justice,* 25 January 1929 and 8 and 22 February 1929; Minutes of the GEB, April 10, 1929, 2, 9.

29. *Justice,* 11 January 1929.

30. Ibid.; Hardy, *Clothing Workers,* 53–54; Harvey Klehr, *The Heyday of American Communism* (New York: Basic Books, 1984), 38; Robert J. Alexander, *The Right Opposition: The Lovestoneites and the International Communist Opposition of the 1930s* (Westport, Conn.: Greenwood Press, 1981), 43.

31. Julius Katz to Dr. Katz, 20 February 1929, Schlesinger Records; telephone interview with Emil Schlesinger, 1 March 1988.

32. Epstein, *Profiles of Eleven,* 244–245.

33. Morris Sigman to Harry Greenberg, 14 January 1929, 10 and 11 February 1929, and 6 March 1929, Miscellaneous Collections.

34. William W. Weinstone to All Trade Union Fractions et al., 31 January 1929 (flyer), Zimmerman Correspondence, ILGWU Archives.

35. Weinstone to Comrades Litwin and Bydarian, 5 February 1929, Zimmerman Correspondence.

36. *Justice,* 8 and 22 February 1929; Local 10 Minutes, Membership Meetings, 11 February 1929.

37. *Justice,* 11 and 25 January 1929.

38. *Justice,* 22 February 1929; Minutes of the GEB, 15 March 1929, p. 1; Danish, *World of David Dubinsky,* 62; Dubinsky and Raskin, *David Dubinsky,* 74–75.

39. *Justice,* 12 April 1929; Minutes of the GEB, 15 March 1929, 1; and 10 April 1929, 9, 50; Minutes of the Executive Board of Local 10, 18 April 1929.

40. David Dubinsky to Benjamin Schlesinger, 23 and 29 April 1929, Schlesinger Correspondence.

41. Dubinsky and Raskin, *David Dubinsky,* 76–77.

42. Local 10 Minutes, Membership Meetings, 13 and 27 May 1929; *Justice,* 10 and 24 May 1929 and 7 June 1929.

43. David Dubinsky to William Green, 24 May 1929, and Green to Dubinsky, 11 June 1929, in Minutes of the GEB, 12 June 1929, 5–7; Dubinsky to Israel Rosenberg, 10 June 1929, DD Corr.

44. *Justice,* 19 July 1929; Haskel, *Leader of the Garment Workers,* 132–135; Local 10 Minutes, Membership Meetings, 29 July 1929; B. C. Vladeck to David Dubinsky, 18 July 1929, and Dubinsky to Benjamin Schlesinger, 6 September 1929, DD Corr.; ILGWU, *Report of the GEB,* Twentieth Convention, 1929, 44–57.

45. *Justice,* 19 July 1929.

46. *Justice,* 2 August 1929; Minutes of the GEB, 5 August 1929, 5.

47. *Justice,* 27 September 1929.

48. *Justice,* 16 August 1929; Local 10 Minutes, Membership Meetings, 12 August 1929.

49. ILGWU, *Report of the GEB,* Twentieth Convention, 1929, 36–37; *Justice,* 13 September 1929.

50. *Justice,* 25 October 1929.

51. ILGWU, *Report of the GEB,* Twentieth Convention, 1929, 5.

52. Ibid., 20–23, 144–145, 164–165, 185–186.

53. Ibid., 186–191; Dubinsky and Raskin, *David Dubinsky,* 79.

54. David Dubinsky to Executive Board, Local 10, 16 December 1929, DD Corr.; Local 10 Minutes, Membership Meetings, 23 December 1929; *Justice,* 20 December 1929; Minutes of the GEB, 19 March 1930, 6.

NOTES TO CHAPTER 5

1. John Kenneth Galbraith, *The Great Crash, 1929* (Boston: Houghton Mifflin, 1961), 103–116.

2. Brookings Institution, *The Recovery Problem in the United States* (Washington, D.C.: Brookings Institution, 1936), 563; Robert S. McElvaine, *The Great Depression* (New York: Times Books, 1984), 75.

3. Julia Saparoff Brown, "Factors Affecting Union Strength: A Case Study of the International Ladies' Garment Workers' Union, 1900–1940" (Ph.D. diss., Yale University, 1942), 72; ILGWU, *Report of the GEB,* Twenty-first Convention, 1932, 7–8, 19–20.

4. Julia Saparoff Brown, "Union Size as a Function of Intra-Union Conflict," *Human Relations,* 9 (1956): 80; ILGWU, *Financial and Statistical Report,* April 1, 1947 to March 31, 1950, Twenty-seventh Convention, 1950, 51.

5. Robert Laurentz, "Racial/Ethnic Conflict in the New York City Garment Industry, 1933–1980" (Ph.D. diss., State University of New York at Binghamton, 1980), 91–93, 199; Abraham I. Shiplacoff (per Frank Crosswaith) to Fannia M. Cohn, 18 July 1927, Cohn Papers; "Colored Members Attention," notice of meeting to be held on 9 December 1928, Local 22 Records; *Justice,* 27 September 1929.

6. Herberg, "Jewish Labor Movement in the United States," 53–54; Zimmerman, "Changes in the Jewish Labor Movement in the United States."

7. ILGWU, *Report of the GEB,* Twenty-first Convention, 1932, 7–8.

8. *Justice,* 17 January 1930; Local 10 Minutes, Membership Meetings, 13 January 1930; Morris Sigman to David Dubinsky, 19 January and 11 February 1930; Du-

binsky to Sigman, 19 February 1930; and Abraham Baroff to Dubinsky, 2 February 1930, DD Corr.; Dubinsky and Raskin, *David Dubinsky,* 80; Danish, *World of David Dubinsky,* 66.

9. Abraham Plotkin to David Dubinsky, 13 and 17 February 1930; Dubinsky to Plotkin, 17 February 1930; and Jacob Mencoff et al. to Benjamin Schlesinger, 16 February 1930, DD Corr.; ILGWU, *Report of the GEB,* Twenty-first Convention, 1932, 61–62.

10. Plotkin et al. to Dubinsky, 22 February 1930, DD Corr.; Dubinsky to Schlesinger, 29 March 1930, Schlesinger Records.

11. ILGWU, *Report and Proceedings,* Twentieth Convention, 1929, 126; Minutes of the GEB, 19 March 1930, 26–27; Local 10 Minutes, Membership Meetings, 31 March 1930; *Justice,* 11 April 1930; Haskel, *Leader of the Garment Workers,* 140; David Dubinsky and Salvatore Ninfo to Benjamin Schlesinger, 3 April 1930, Schlesinger Records.

12. Minutes of the GEB, 19 March 1930, 34; *Justice,* 16 May 1930 and 23 and 27 June 1930; David Dubinsky to Abraham Baroff, 22 May 1930, and Dubinsky to Morris Sigman, 22 May 1930, DD Corr.

13. E. C. Davison to Abraham Baroff, 6 July 1930; David Dubinsky to Davison, 11 July 1930; Davison to Dubinsky, 25 July 1930 and 5 August 1931; and Dubinsky to Davison, 11 September 1931, DD Corr.

14. *Justice,* 25 July 1930 and 12 and 16 September 1930.

15. *Justice,* 10 and 24 October 1930.

16. Minutes of the GEB, 13 October 1930, 7.

17. Benjamin Schlesinger to Pauline Newman, 26 August 1930, Local Managers' Correspondence, ILGWU Archives.

18. *Justice,* 5 and 19 December 1930; interview with Emil Schlesinger, 29 August 1974, 98.

19. Minutes of the GEB, New York Members, 29 December 1930, 3.

20. *Justice,* 2, 16, and 30 January 1930;

and 20 February 1930; Minutes of the GEB, 10 February 1931, 1, 24, 33.

21. Bezalel Dobnievski to David Dubinsky, 24 March 1931; Lazer Dobniewski to David Dubinsky, 10 May 1931; and Application for Personal Loan, National City Bank of New York [9 April 1931], DD Corr.

22. David Dubinsky to J. L. Fine, 25 May 1931; Dubinsky to Eve and Moshe Novarski, 11 September 1931, DD Corr.

23. David Dubinsky to Joseph Spielman, 6 March 1931, Local 22 Records, ILGWU Archives; Minutes of the GEB, 10 February 1931, 16, and 14 May 1931, 15; *Justice,* 20 March, May, and June 1931.

24. David Dubinsky to Gustave Eisner, 28 May and 27 August 1931, DD Corr.; interview with Helen Novarsky, 10 September 1987; ILGWU, *Report of the GEB,* Twenty-first Convention, 1932, 96.

25. Telephone interview with Joseph Gotteiner, 20 October 1987.

26. Warsaw *Naye Folkstaitung,* 26 June 1931; *Justice,* August 1931.

27. *Justice,* September 1931; *New York Times,* 13 August and 6 September 1931; David Dubinsky to Mr. Bograchev, 26 September 1931, DD Corr.; Danish, *World of David Dubinsky,* 66–67.

28. Hannah Haskel and Salvatore Ninfo to David Dubinsky, 20 July 1931, DD Corr.; ILGWU, *Report of the GEB,* Twenty-first Convention, 1932, 89.

29. *New York Times,* 13 August 1931; *Justice,* September 1931; Dubinsky and Raskin, *David Dubinsky,* 189; Daniels interview with David Dubinsky, 1–8.

30. David Dubinsky to Bezalel Dobnievski, 11 September 1931, DD Corr.

31. Minutes of the GEB, 18 August 1931, 1–2.

32. Minutes of the GEB, 9 September 1931, 1–3; *Justice,* November 1931.

33. Minutes of the GEB, 22 December 1931, 1.

34. Minutes of the GEB, 26 October 1931, 6, 31; 19 November 1931, 1–3; 14 December 1931, 1–7; and 22 December

1931, 1–4; *Women's Wear Daily,* 7 December 1931.

35. Minutes of the GEB, 26 October 1931, 4; *Justice,* February 1932.

36. ILGWU, *Report of the GEB,* Twenty-first Convention, 1932, 26–31; *Justice,* March 1932.

37. Alexander, *Right Opposition,* 15–18; Draper, *American Communism and Soviet Russia,* 380–441; Harry J. Ausmus, *Will Herberg: From Right to Right* (Chapel Hill: University of North Carolina Press, 1987), 8–10; Bertram D. Wolfe, *A Life in Two Centuries* (New York: Stein and Day, 1981), 476–552; Stephen F. Cohen, *Bukharin and the Bolshevik Revolution: A Political Biography* (New York: Alfred A. Knopf, 1973), 270–336; Dubinsky and Raskin, *David Dubinsky,* 105–106; Ted Morgan, *A Covert Life: Jay Lovestone, Communist, Anti-Communist, and Spymaster* (New York: Random House, 1999), 84–110; ILGWU, *Report and Proceedings,* Twenty-first Convention, 1932, 262.

38. Personal interview with Israel Breslow, 4 April 1985.

39. Interview with Charles S. Zimmerman, 30 March 1977, 564–566; Dubinsky and Raskin, *David Dubinsky,* 105.

40. ILGWU, *Report and Proceedings,* Twenty-first Convention, 1932, 1.

41. Dubinsky and Raskin, *David Dubinsky,* 105–106.

42. Benjamin Gitlow to Charles S. Zimmerman, 2 May 1932, and Gitlow to Zimmerman, n.d., Zimmerman Correspondence.

43. ILGWU, *Report and Proceedings,* Twenty-first Convention, 1932, 216–221.

44. Ibid., 17–25, 221–225; Dubinsky and Raskin, *David Dubinsky,* 106–107.

45. "To the Delegates of the I.L.G.W.U.," statement attached to Charles Zimmerman to David Dubinsky, 11 May 1932, Zimmerman Correspondence.

46. Interview with Israel Breslow, 4 April 1985.

47. Dubinsky and Raskin, *David Dubinsky,* 106–107.

48. Report by Benjamin Gitlow, 2, attached to Gitlow to Zimmerman, n.d., Zimmerman Correspondence; Zimmerman interviews, vol. 3, p. 431; Jenna Weissman Joselit, *Our Gang: Jewish Crime and the New York Jewish Community, 1900–1940* (Bloomington: Indiana University Press, 1983), 122–129.

49. Report by Gitlow, 2.

50. Interview with Emil Schlesinger, 29 August 1974, 125–128; telephone interview with Emil Schlesinger, 1 March 1988.

51. Report by Gitlow, 2–3.

52. Interviews with Emil Schlesinger, 8 and 9 May 1968, 34–35, YIVO Institute; interview with Emil Schlesinger, 29 August 1974, 128–130, 137–138.

53. Report by Gitlow, 3.

54. ILGWU, *Report and Proceedings,* Twenty-first Convention, 1932, 311–312; Dubinsky and Raskin, *David Dubinsky,* 107–109.

55. Interview with Emil Schlesinger, 29 August 1974, 138–143.

56. ILGWU, *Report and Proceedings,* Twenty-first Convention, 1932, 316–321; interviews with Emil Schlesinger, 8 and 9 May 1968, 35–37.

57. Interview with Emil Schlesinger, 29 August 1974, 132.

58. David Dubinsky and Salvatore Ninfo, "At the Bier of Benjamin Schlesinger," *Justice,* June 1932, 2.

59. Minutes of the GEB, 13 June 1932, 1–8.

60. Dubinsky and Raskin, *David Dubinsky,* 83, 325.

61. Telephone interview with Emil Schlesinger, 1 March 1988.

62. Interview with David Gingold, 28 August 1974, ILGWU Archives.

NOTES TO CHAPTER 6

1. Dubinsky and Raskin, *David Dubinsky,* 189.

2. ILGWU, *Financial Report,* 1 April 1932 to 30 April 1934, Twenty-second Convention, 1934, 6, 19.

3. Raskin interviews, cass. 31, p. 22.

4. Interview with David Dubinsky, 25 June 1974, 6, ILGWU Archives.

5. Ibid., 5–6; David Dubinsky to Abraham Baroff, 6 September 1932, DD Corr.; Minutes of the GEB, New York Members, ILGWU, 9 September 1932, 1–2; 22 September 1932, 1; and 6 December 1932, 1; ILGWU, *Report of the GEB,* Twenty-second Convention, 1934, 161–162.

6. Interview with David Gingold, 28 August 1974, 144–145.

7. Dubinsky to Fine, 27 June and 22 August 1932; Fine to Dubinsky, 12 and 20 July 1932 and 19 August 1932; Sigmund Haiman to Dubinsky, 5 July 1932; Dubinsky to Haiman, 11 July 1932; Charles Kreindler to Dubinsky, 20 July 1932; Dubinsky to Kreindler, 21 July 1932, DD Corr.

8. Herbert Harris, "America's Best Union," *Current History,* January 1938, 54.

9. Minutes of the GEB, 3 October 1932, 40.

10. ILGWU, *Financial Report,* 1 April 1932 to 30 April 1934, 15.

11. Minutes of the GEB, 3 October 1932, 37; David Dubinsky to Max Bluestein, 28 November 1932, DD Corr.; *Justice,* December 1932.

12. ILGWU, *Report of the GEB,* Twenty-first Convention, 1932, 26; ILGWU, *Report of the GEB,* Twenty-second Convention, 1934, 50.

13. ILGWU, *Report of the GEB,* Twenty-second Convention, 1934, 17–22; Minutes of the GEB, 3 October 1932, 1–9; Haskel, *Leader of the Garment Workers,* 162–167.

14. Irving Bernstein, *A Caring Society: The New Deal, the Worker, and the Great Depression* (Boston: Houghton Mifflin Company, 1985), 18.

15. James MacGregor Burns, *Roosevelt: The Lion and the Fox* (New York: Harcourt, Brace and Company, 1956), 163–164.

16. Minutes of the GEB, 10 January 1933, 8; Minutes of the GEB, New York Members, 19 January 1933, 1.

17. Minutes of the GEB, New York Members, 22 September 1932, 2–3; Minutes of the GEB, 3 October 1932, 26, 34; Max Bluestein to Charles S. Zimmerman, 2 September 1932, Zimmerman Correspondence; ILGWU, *Report of the GEB,* Twenty-second Convention, 1934, 51; Dubinsky and Raskin, *David Dubinsky,* 109.

18. David Dubinsky to Charles M. Schwartzberg, 6 December 1932, and Schwartzberg to Dubinsky, 19 December 1932 (two letters), DD Corr.

19. Minutes of the GEB, New York Members, 6 December 1932, 1.

20. William E. Leuchtenburg, *Franklin D. Roosevelt and the New Deal, 1932–1940* (New York: Harper and Row, 1963), 41–66.

21. David Dubinsky to Edward J. Flynn, 21 December 1932, ILGWU Archives; Dubinsky to Herbert H. Lehman, 21 December 1932, Herbert H. Lehman Papers, Columbia University; "The Reminiscences of Herbert H. Lehman," 197–198, Oral History Research Office, Columbia University.

22. Matthew Josephson, *Sidney Hillman: Statesman of American Labor* (Garden City, N.Y.: Doubleday & Company, 1952), 360–361; George Martin, *Madam Secretary: Frances Perkins* (Boston: Houghton Mifflin Company, 1976), 251–256.

23. David Dubinsky to William Green, 29 April 1933, and Dubinsky to Frances Perkins, 29 April 1933, DD Corr.; Craig Phelan, *William Green: Biography of a Labor Leader* (Albany: State University of New York Press, 1989), 61–62; Frances Perkins, *The Roosevelt I Knew* (New York: Harper and Row, 1964), 192–196; Martin, *Madam Secretary,* 260–269.

24. Steven Fraser, "Sidney Hillman: Labor's Machiavelli," in Melvyn Dubofsky and Warren Van Tyne (eds.), *Labor Leaders in America* (Urbana: University of Illinois Press, 1987), 208–218; Parmet, *Labor and Immigration in Industrial America,* 121–124.

25. Josephson, *Sidney Hillman,* 361–362; *New York Times,* 28 May 1933.

26. ILGWU, *Report of the GEB,*

Twenty-second Convention, 1934, 164–165; Raskin interviews, cass. 6, 1–4, 20–21, 25, 38–39; "The Reminiscences of Jacob S. Potofsky," 282–283, 670, and "The Reminiscences of Boris Shishkin," 617, Oral History Research Office, Columbia University; interviews with Gus Tyler, 28 April 1984, and Henoch Mendelsund, 25 September 1984; Josephson, *Sidney Hillman,* 363–364.

27. Minutes of the GEB, 4 April 1933, 21–22.

28. ILGWU, *Report of the GEB,* Twenty-second Convention, 1934, 26–27; Raskin interviews, cass. 6, p. 5; *New York Times,* 20 July 1933; Norma Fain Pratt, *Morris Hillquit: A Political History of an American Jewish Socialist* (Westport, Conn.: Greenwood Press, 1979), 242–243; David Dubinsky to Morris Hillquit, 11 August 1933, Morris Hillquit Papers (microfilm edition), State Historical Society of Wisconsin, Madison, Wisconsin; Haskel, *Leader of the Garment Workers,* 175.

29. ILGWU, *Report of the GEB,* Twenty-second Convention, 1934, 29–31; Danish, *World of David Dubinsky,* 76–77; *Justice,* 1 and 15 August, 1 September, and 1 October 1933.

30. ILGWU, *Report of the GEB,* Twenty-second Convention, 1934, 72–73; Dubinsky and Raskin, *David Dubinsky,* 109–111; Minutes of the GEB, 7 October 1933, 6; Danish, *World of David Dubinsky,* 75.

31. Nathan Margolis to Editor, *Amsterdam News,* 11 March 1933, Local 22 Records; Charles S. Zimmerman to James H. Hubert, 29 May 1933, Zimmerman Correspondence; Minutes of the GEB, 4 April 1933, 1–2, 11–12; and 24 April 1933, 1–2.

32. Zimmerman, "Changes in the Jewish Labor Movement in the United States," 4–5, 8; *New York American,* 18 August 1933; Danish, *World of David Dubinsky,* 77–78; interview with Charles S. Zimmerman, 29 July 1980, 1225–1226, ILGWU Archives.

33. Minutes of the GEB, ILGWU, 7 October 1933, 1–6, 8.

34. *Needle Worker,* October 1933.

35. In 1934 the officers of Local 9 were removed from office and barred from future office holding for a minimum of two years after their conviction on charges of "acts of disloyalty to the International Union and to the Cloak Joint Board of New York." ILGWU, *Report of the GEB,* Twenty-second Convention, 1934, 47–48.

NOTES TO CHAPTER 7

1. American Federation of Labor, *Report of Proceedings,* Fifty-third Convention, 1933, vi; ILGWU, *Report of the GEB,* Twenty-second Convention, 1934, 161; Minutes of the GEB, 12 March 1934, 28.

2. Stolberg, *Tailor's Progress,* 214–216.

3. ILGWU, *Financial Report, April 1, 1932 to April 30, 1934,* 18–19.

4. Robert Asher, "Jewish Unions and the American Federation of Labor Power Structure, 1903–1935," *American Jewish Historical Quarterly,* 65 (March 1976): 215–227.

5. ILGWU, *Report of the GEB,* Twenty-second Convention, 1934, 162; *New York Times,* 13 and 14 October 1933; American Federation of Labor (AFL), *Report of Proceedings,* Fifty-third Convention, 1933, 141–142, 433–434.

6. Parmet, *Labor and Immigration in Industrial America,* 183–193; John Higham, *Strangers in the Land: Patterns of American Nativism, 1860–1925* (New Brunswick, N.J.: Rutgers University Press, 1955), 300–330; Robert A. Divine, *American Immigration Policy, 1924–1952* (New Haven: Yale University Press, 1957), 78–79; David S. Wyman, *America and the Refugee Crisis, 1938–1941* (New York: Pantheon Books, 1985), 3–4; David Brody, "American Jewry, Refugees and Immigration Restriction (1932–1942)," *Publications of the American Jewish Historical Society,* 45 (June 1956): 220.

7. Moshe R. Gottlieb, *American Anti-Nazi Resistance, 1933–1941: An Historical Analysis* (New York: Ktav Publishing

House, 1982), 15–17; *New York Times,* 23 and 28 March 1933.

8. Gottlieb, *American Anti-Nazi Resistance,* 47–85, 119–121; *New York Times,* 8 and 16 May 1933.

9. George L. Berlin, "The Jewish Labor Committee and American Immigration Policy in the 1930's," in Charles Berlin (ed.), *Studies in Jewish Bibliography History and Literature in Honor of I. Edward Kiev* (New York: Ktav Publishing House, 1971), 46; Minutes of the GEB, 12 March 1934, 10; Gottlieb, *American Anti-Nazi Resistance,* 176–177.

10. *New York Times,* 5 April 1934.

11. Ibid.; Minutes of the GEB, 12 March 1934, 10.

12. *New York Times,* 26 June 1934.

13. ILGWU, *Report of the GEB,* Twenty-second Convention, 1934, 3, 13, 14.

14. Ibid., 1–2; Wilfred Carsel, *A History of the Chicago Ladies' Garment Workers' Union* (Chicago: Normandie House, 1940), 220–221; Minutes of the GEB, 12 March 1934, 36.

15. *Justice,* April 1934.

16. Minutes of the GEB, 12 March 1934, 36; and 9 May 1934, 7; ILGWU, *Report and Proceedings,* Twenty-second Convention, 1934, 223; interview with Morris S. Novik, 18 June 1985, 16, ILGWU Archives.

17. *Women's Wear Daily,* 4 June 1934; ILGWU, *Report and Proceedings,* Twenty-second Convention, 1934, 14.

18. *Report of the Delegation of Local 22 on the 22nd Biennial Convention of the I.L.G.W.U.* (New York: Dressmakers' Union Local 22, ILGWU, 1934), 2.

19. ILGWU, *Report and Proceedings,* Twenty-second Convention, 1934, 10.

20. Ibid., 41, 97, 125; *Report of the Delegation of Local 22,* 2.

21. *Women's Wear Daily,* 4 June 1934.

22. Ibid.; *Women's Wear Daily,* 5 June 1934; ILGWU, *Report and Proceedings,* Twenty-second Convention, 1934, 223–224, 240, 249; *Report of the Delegation of Local 22,* 2–3; *Justice,* October 1934;

David Dubinsky to Charles S. Zimmerman, 10 August and 16 November 1934; unsigned copy of petition from "Colored Members of Local 22" to Dubinsky, 17 July 1934, Zimmerman Correspondence.

23. ILGWU, *Report and Proceedings,* Twenty-second Convention, 1934, 249.

24. Ibid., 250–251, 329–331; *Report of the Delegation of Local 22,* 3; Vanni B. Montana, "The Shambles: Broken Bridges over the Seas" (MS [1977]), 255, ILGWU Archives; *New York Times,* 25 October 1934; *Jewish Daily Forward,* 20 December 1934.

25. David Dubinsky to Moshe Novarski, 24 May 1934, Gustave Eisner to Dubinsky, 10 July 1934 and 15 and 22 August 1934; and Hannah Haskel to Eisner, 22 December 1934, DD Corr.; *Jewish Daily Forward,* 24 August 1934.

26. ILGWU, *Report and Proceedings,* Twenty-second Convention, 1934, 10–12.

27. Ibid., 383–398; Dubinsky and Raskin, *David Dubinsky,* 114–116.

28. ILGWU, *Report and Proceedings,* Twenty-second Convention, 1934, 423–428; Minutes of the GEB, 10 June 1934, 1.

29. Irving Bernstein, *Turbulent Years* (Boston: Houghton Mifflin Company, 1969), 217–218.

30. Ibid., 293; Minutes of the GEB, 16 July 1934, 19; *New York Times,* 22 July 1934; Jennie Matyas, "Jennie Matyas and the I.L.G.W.U." (MS, 1957), 119–120, ILGWU Archives.

31. *New York Times,* 22 July 1934.

32. David Dubinsky to Charles S. Zimmerman, 2 August 1934, Zimmerman Correspondence.

33. *New York Times,* 24 and 26 September 1934; *Justice,* October 1934.

34. Minutes of the GEB, 16 July 1934, 17–19; *Justice,* September 1934.

35. David Dubinsky to Louis Levy, 20 July 1934, DD Corr.

36. Minutes of the GEB, 16 July 1934, 16, and 6 September 1934 (New York Members), 2–4; David Dubinsky to William Green, 18 August 1934, DD Corr.

37. Minutes of the GEB, New York

Members, 6 September 1934, 1–2, including David Dubinsky to All Locals and Joint Boards of Dressmakers Affiliated with the I.L.G.W.U., 29 August 1934; Minutes of the GEB, New York Members Jointly with the GEB of the Amalgamated Clothing Workers, 13 September 1934, 1; *New York Times,* 13 October 1934.

38. Martin Plettl to David Dubinsky, 8 July 1934; Dubinsky to William Green, 27 July and 28 August 1934; Dubinsky to William Green, 23 August 1934; Green to Walter Citrine, 23 August 1934, and Citrine to Green, 24 August 1934; B. C. Vladeck to Dubinsky, 24 September 1934; and Lawrence B. Dunham to Dubinsky, 24 September 1934, DD Corr.; Sir Walter Citrine, K.B.E., "Mr. B. Charney Vladeck: An Appreciation," 1–2, Walter Citrine Collection, London School of Economics (Courtesy of Gail Malmgreen); Lord [Sir Walter McLennan] Citrine, *Men and Work: An Autobiography* (London: Hutchinson, 1964), 305–309.

39. AFL, *Report of Proceedings,* Fifty-fourth Convention, 1934, 433–445, 569–571; *New York Times,* 9 October 1934; William Green to David Dubinsky, 12 November 1934; and Dubinsky to Green, 15 November 1934, DD Corr.; Philip Taft, *The A. F. of L. from the Death of Gompers to the Merger* (New York: Harper and Brothers, 1959), 205.

40. AFL, *Report of Proceedings,* Fifty-fourth Convention, 1934, 573–574; James O. Morris, *Conflict within the AFL: A Study of Craft versus Industrial Unionism, 1901–1938* (Ithaca, N.Y.: Cornell University Press, 1958), 277–278, 278n.; John P. Windmuller, *American Labor and the International Labor Movement, 1940 to 1953* (Ithaca, N.Y.: Institute of International, Industrial and Labor Relations, Cornell University, 1954), 13–14.

41. Robert H. Zieger, *John L. Lewis: Labor Leader* (Boston: Twayne Publishers, 1988), 1–44; Morris, *Conflict within the AFL,* 280–281; AFL, *Report of Proceedings,* Fifty-fourth Convention, 1934, 179, 649–662, 664–668; *New York Times,* 13 October 1934.

42. Morris, *Conflict within the AFL,* 193–196; AFL, *Report of Proceedings,* Fifty-fourth Convention, 1934, 581–598; *New York Times,* 10 October 1934.

NOTES TO CHAPTER 8

1. *New York Times,* 25 October 1934.

2. *Justice,* November 1934.

3. ILGWU, *Report and Proceedings,* Twenty-second Convention, 1934, 319–320; Ben Gold to the General Executive Board of the ILGWU, 6 September 1934, DD Corr.; Minutes of the GEB, 19 November 1934, 2–8; *Justice,* December 1934.

4. William Green and Frank Morrison to the Officers and Members of All Organizations of Labor, 11 September 1934, DD Corr.

5. Minutes of the GEB, 6 September 1934, 8.

6. Levine, *Women's Garment Workers,* 344, 476–478; Raymond and Mary Munts, "Welfare History of the I.L.G.W.U.," *Labor History,* 9, special supplement (Spring 1968): 84; *Commemoration Fiftieth Anniversary First Union Health Center in the United States, Friday June 5–Saturday June 6, 1964* (New York: ILGWU, 1964).

7. ILGWU, *Report of the GEB,* Nineteenth Convention, 1928, 284–285; ILGWU, *Report of the GEB,* Twentieth Convention, 1929, 123.

8. Minutes of the GEB, New York Members, 14 February 1933; George M. Price to David Dubinsky, 25 March 1933, with typed "Medical Department Budget 1933" attached, DD Corr.; Minutes of the GEB, 4 April 1933, 14; ILGWU, *Report of the GEB,* Twenty-second Convention, 1934, 181.

9. ILGWU, *Report of the GEB,* Twenty-third Convention, 1937, 160–161.

10. Levine, *Women's Garment Workers,* 487–488; Stefan Kanfer, *A Summer World* (New York: Farrar, Straus & Giroux, 1989), 80–82.

11. Levine, *Women's Garment Workers,* 492–493; Stolberg, *Tailor's Progress,* 287; Danish, *World of David Dubinsky,* 220;

ILGWU, *Report of the GEB,* Sixteenth Convention, 1922, 88–89; ILGWU, *Report and Proceedings,* Sixteenth Convention, 1922, 67; ILGWU, *Report of the GEB,* Seventeenth Convention, 1924, 124; ILGWU, *Report of the GEB,* Eighteenth Convention, 1925, 153; *Justice,* 24 October and 5 December 1924.

12. ILGWU, *Report of the GEB,* Eighteenth Convention, 1925, 154.

13. ILGWU, *Report of the GEB,* Nineteenth Convention, 1928, 287.

14. *Justice,* September 1934 and 1 July 1935; ILGWU, *Report of the GEB,* Twenty-third Convention, 1937, 164.

15. William Green to David Dubinsky, 29 March 1935, DD Corr.; Minutes of the Meeting of the GEB, New York Members, 29 March 1935, 1.

16. Green to Dubinsky, 28 February 1935, Dubinsky to ILGWU Affiliated Unions and Joint Boards, 7 March 1935, Dubinsky to Green, 7 March 1935, and Dubinsky to Matthew Woll, 7 March 1935, DD Corr.; *New York Times,* 11 March 1935.

17. Dubinsky to Sidney Hillman, 27 March 1935; and Hillman to J. Klahr Huddle, 29 March 1935, Sidney Hillman Correspondence, Kheel Center for Labor-Management Documentation and Archives, Martin P. Catherwood Library, Cornell University, Ithaca, New York; Frederick F. Umhey to Dubinsky, 30 March 1935, Umhey Correspondence.

18. *New York Times,* 14 April 1935; *Justice,* 15 May 1935.

19. *Justice,* 1 May 1935; Frederick F. Umhey to Collector of the Port of New York, 30 April 1935, and David Dubinsky to C. Warwick Perkins, Jr., draft, n.d., Umhey Correspondence; personal interview with Matthew Schoenwald, 1 May 1984.

20. *Justice,* 1 May 1935.

NOTES TO CHAPTER 9

1. *Justice,* 15 February 1935; ILGWU, *Report of the GEB,* Twenty-third Conven-

tion, 1937, 70; Minutes of the GEB, 27 May 1935, 10–11.

2. Rhonda F. Levine, *Class Struggle and the New Deal: Industrial Labor, Industrial Capital, and the State* (Lawrence: University Press of Kansas, 1988), 111.

3. Ibid., 112.

4. Robert H. Zieger, *American Workers, American Unions, 1920–1985* (Baltimore: Johns Hopkins University Press, 1986), 35–36.

5. Jesse Thomas Carpenter, *Competition and Collective Bargaining in the Needle Trades, 1910–1967* (Ithaca, N.Y.: New York State School of Industrial and Labor Relations, Cornell University, 1972), 634–639.

6. *Justice,* 15 February 1935.

7. *New York Times,* 16 February 1935.

8. *New York Times,* 24 May 1935; David Dubinsky to Sidney Hillman, 14 May 1935, with attached "Copy of Call Forwarded to Locals of the International Ladies' Garment Workers' Union in Cities Outside of New York," Hillman Correspondence; Minutes of the GEB, New York Members, 13 May 1935, 1; *Justice,* 1 June 1935.

9. *New York Times,* 28 May 1935.

10. Harry A. Millis and Emily Clark Brown, *From the Wagner Act to Taft-Hartley: A Study of National Labor Policy and Labor Relations* (Chicago: University of Chicago Press, 1950), 28–29.

11. *Justice,* 15 June and 1 and 15 July 1935; *Morning Freiheit,* 26 June 1935; Danish, *World of David Dubinsky,* 91.

12. Herbert H. Lehman to David Dubinsky, 27 June and 1 and 17 July 1935; Dubinsky to Lehman, 2 and 10 July 1935; Dubinsky to William Green, 8 July 1935; Green to Dubinsky, 11 July 1935, DD Corr.

13. Joselit, *Our Gang,* 120–122; Josephson, *Sidney Hillman,* 333–339; Albert Fried, *The Rise and Fall of the Jewish Gangster in America* (New York: Holt, Rinehart and Winston, 1980), 161–162.

14. Emil Schlesinger, "Transcript on Racketeering" (MS, n.d.), 5–6, ILGWU Archives.

15. Richard Norton Smith, *Thomas E. Dewey and His Times* (New York: Simon and Schuster, 1982), 112–117, 133–135, 149–150; Nevins, *Herbert H. Lehman and His Era,* 179–181.

16. *Justice,* 15 August 1935; Taft, *A. F. of L. from the Death of Gompers to the Merger,* 424.

17. Schlesinger, "Transcript on Racketeering," 1.

18. Interview with Vanni B. Montana, 19 March 1987.

19. Schlesinger, "Transcript on Racketeering," 1–2; Raskin interviews, cass. 33, pp. 2–5.

20. Telephone interview with Emil Schlesinger, 1 March 1988; Schlesinger, "Transcript on Racketeering," 1–2; Raskin Interviews, cass. 33, pp. 2–5.

21. Schlesinger, "Transcript on Racketeering," 3.

22. Raskin interviews, cass. 33, p. 5.

23. Schlesinger, "Transcript on Racketeering," 3.

24. Ibid., 4; telephone interview with Schlesinger, 1 March 1988.

25. Schlesinger, "Transcript on Racketeering," 4.

26. Ibid., 5; Philip V. Cannistraro, "Luigi Antonini and the Italian Anti-Fascist Movement in the United States, 1940–1943," *Journal of American Ethnic History,* 5 (Fall 1985): 24–25, 41–443.

28. David A. Shannon, *The Socialist Party of America* (Chicago: Quadrangle Books, 1967), 211–217; Lewis Waldman, *Labor Lawyer* (New York: E. P. Dutton and Company, 1945), 193–207; Pratt, *Morris Hillquit,* 235–242.

29. Irving Howe, *World of Our Fathers* (New York: Harcourt Brace Jovanovich, 1976), 349; Shannon, *Socialist Party of America,* 237–242; Klehr, *Heyday of American Communism,* 98–102.

30. Dubinsky to Norman Thomas, 22 May 1935; Dubinsky to Matthew Woll, 22 May 1935; and Woll to Dubinsky, 24 May 1935, DD Corr.

31. Thomas to Dubinsky, 27 September 1935; and Dubinsky to Thomas, 3 October 1935, DD Corr.

NOTES TO CHAPTER 10

1. Minutes of the Meeting of the Executive Council of the American Federation of Labor, 29 January to 14 February 1935 (microfilm edition), 222; Melvyn A. Dubofsky and Warren Van Tine, *John L. Lewis: A Biography* (New York: Quadrangle, 1977), 210–212.

2. *New York Times,* 16 and 17 October 1935; *Justice,* 1 November 1935; AFL, *Report of Proceedings,* Fifty-fifth Convention, 1935, vi, 521–542, 552–575; Dubofsky and Van Tine, *John L. Lewis,* 217–220; Morris, *Conflict within the AFL,* 204–209.

3. Minutes of the Executive Council (EC), AFL, 5 to 21 October 1935, 109; Roger Keeran, *The Communist Party and the Auto Workers' Unions* (Bloomington: Indiana University Press, 1980), 137; Wyndham Mortimer, *Organize! My Life as a Union Man* (Boston: Beacon Press, 1971), 88–89; Harvey A. Levenstein, *Communism, Anticommunism and the CIO* (Westport, Conn.: Greenwood Press, 1981), 43.

4. AFL, *Report of Proceedings,* Fifty-fifth Convention, 1935, 726–727; Dubofsky and Van Tine, *John L. Lewis,* 220; *New York Times,* 19 October 1935.

5. John Brophy, *A Miner's Life,* ed. John O. P. Hall (Madison: University of Wisconsin Press, 1964), 253–254; "The Reminiscences of John Brophy," Oral History Research Office, Columbia University, 1957, 561–562; Dubinsky and Raskin, *David Dubinsky,* 221; Bernstein, *Turbulent Years,* 394–395.

6. "Minutes of Meeting of Committee of Industrial Organization Washington, D.C., November 9, 1935," 1–3, DD Corr.; Dubofsky and Van Tine, *John L. Lewis,* 222.

7. Morris, *Conflict within the AFL,* 216n.

8. Dubinsky and Raskin, *David Dubinsky,* 222.

9. David Dubinsky to John Brophy, 11 December 1935; and Brophy to Dubinsky, 16 December 1935, DD Corr.

10. Charles P. Howard to Dubinsky, 11 November 1935; and Dubinsky to Howard, 18 November 1935, DD Corr.; Meeting of the GEB, New York Members, 12 November 1935, 1.

11. William Green to Dubinsky, 23 November 1935, DD Corr.

12. John L. Lewis to Green, 23 November 1935 (copy), attached to Green to Dubinsky, 26 November 1935, DD Corr.; Dubofsky and Van Tine, *John L. Lewis*, 224.

13. Dubinsky and Raskin, *David Dubinsky*, 22; Lewis to Dubinsky, 25 November 1935, DD Corr.

14. Asher, "Jewish Unions and the American Federation of Labor Power Structure," 222; Philip Taft, "Dubinsky and the Labor Movement," *Labor History*, special supplement, 9 (Spring 1968): 29.

15. Interview with Henoch Mendelsund, 25 September 1984.

16. Oral History interview with Katherine Pollack Ellickson, 4 May 1979, 5, AFL-CIO Merger Interviews, George Meany Center for Labor Studies, George Meany Memorial Archives.

17. Taft, "Dubinsky and the Labor Movement," 30–31.

18. Asher, "Jewish Unions and the American Federation of Labor Power Structure," 222–226.

19. Minutes of the GEB, New York Members, 12 November 1935, 1.

20. Minutes of the GEB, 2 December 1935, 65–68.

21. Interview with Henoch Mendelsund, 26 September 1984; "The Reminiscences of Boris Shishkin," Oral History Research Office, Columbia University, 1959, 617; "The Reminiscences of Benjamin Stolberg," Oral History Research Office, Columbia University, 1950, 17.

22. Matyas, "Jennie Matyas and the I.L.G.W.U.," 292–293.

23. Minutes of the Committee for Industrial Organization (CIO), 9 December 1935, 1–2, DD Corr.

24. David Dubinsky to William Green, 11 December 1935, DD Corr.

25. Dubinsky to Andrew Conley, 6 January 1936, DD Corr.

26. Minutes of the EC, AFL, 15–29 January 1936, 104–105, 117; Dubinsky to John L. Lewis, 24 January 1936; Lewis to Dubinsky, 27 January 1936; "Statement by President Dubinsky" [24 January 1936]; and William Green to Dubinsky, 7 February 1936, with American Federation of Labor Press Statement, 23 January 1936, all in DD Corr.; *Justice*, 1 February 1936; Bernstein, *Turbulent Years*, 407–409.

27. Hannah Haskel to John Brophy, 12 February 1936, DD Corr.; *Justice*, 15 February 1936.

28. Dressmakers' General Strike Bulletins, 8–13 February 1936, Herman Wolf Collection, Archives of Labor History and Urban Affairs, Wayne State University, Detroit, Michigan; *Justice*, 15 February 1936.

29. Green to Dubinsky, 4 and 7 February 1936; and Dubinsky to Green, 8 and 14 February 1936, DD Corr.

30. Homer Martin to Dubinsky, 14 February 1936, DD Corr.

31. William Beedie to Members of Local 18609, Radio Factory Workers Union, A. F. of L., 15 February 1936, DD Corr.

32. *New York Times*, 21 February 1936; John L. Lewis et al., to Officers and Members of State Federations of Labor, City Central Labor Unions, and Directly Affiliated Local Trade and Federal Labor Unions, 25 February 1936, DD Corr.

33. Lewis to Charles P. Howard, 22 February 1936 (copy), enclosed with William Green to David Dubinsky, 24 February 1936, DD Corr.

34. Alan Brinkley, *Voices of Protest: Huey Long, Father Coughlin, and the Great Depression* (New York: Vintage Books, 1983), 72–73, 179, 222–226, 255–256.

35. George Wolfskill, *The Revolt of the Conservatives: A History of the American Liberty League, 1934–1940* (Boston: Houghton Mifflin Company, 1962), 20–36.

36. Harry Fleischman, *Norman Thomas:*

A *Biography* (New York: W. W. Norton and Company, 1964), 190.

37. Ibid., 108; W. A. Swanberg, *Norman Thomas: The Last Idealist* (New York: Charles Scribner's Sons, 1976), 190.

38. Murray B. Seidler, *Norman Thomas: Respectable Rebel* (2d ed.; Syracuse, N.Y.: Syracuse University Press, 1967), 160; *New York Times*, 4 April 1936.

39. Joseph C. Goulden, *Meany: The Un-challenged Strong Man of American Labor* (New York: Atheneum, 1972), 61.

40. *New York Times*, 2, 4, and 10 April 1936; Steven Fraser, *Labor Will Rule: Sidney Hillman and the Rise of American Labor* (New York: Free Press, 1991), 356; Dubinsky and Raskin, *David Dubinsky*, 262–263; Dubofsky and Van Tine, *John L. Lewis*, 249.

41. *Jewish Daily Forward*, 11 April 1936; *New York Times*, 12 April 1936; *Daily Worker*, 13 April 1936.

42. *New York Herald Tribune*, 23 April 1936; *New York Sun*, 23 April 1936; *Socialist Call*, 2 May 1936; *Daily Worker*, 13 April 1936.

43. Minutes of the GEB, 22 May 1936, 69–71.

44. *New York Times*, 30 November 1932; interview with Jacob Potofsky by Kenneth Waltzer, 13 November 1968, 1, Jacob Potofsky Oral History Interviews, Kheel Center for Labor-Management Documentation and Archives, Martin P. Catherwood Library, Cornell University.

45. "The Reminiscences of Edward J. Flynn," 20–21, Oral History Research Office, Columbia University, 1950.

46. Ibid., 21.

47. "The Reminiscences of Frances Perkins," vol. 7, 225, Oral History Research Office, Columbia University, 1955–1961.

48. Thomas Kessner, *Fiorello H. La Guardia and the Making of Modern New York* (New York: McGraw-Hill Publishing Company, 1989), 408.

49. Raskin interviews, cass. 46, pp. 1–7; Fraser, *Labor Will Rule*, 363; Dubinsky and Raskin, *David Dubinsky*, 265.

50. Raskin interviews, cass. 45, pp. 14–15; Dubinsky and Raskin, *David Dubinsky*, 265–266; Kenneth Waltzer, "The American Labor Party" (Ph.D. diss., Harvard University, 1977), 78.

51. Raskin interviews, cass. 7, pp. 8, 10; Flynn, "Reminiscences," 21; Jordan A. Schwarz, *Liberal: Adolf A. Berle and the Vision of an American Era* (New York: Free Press, 1987), 102.

52. Fraser, *Labor Will Rule*, 360–362; Seidler, *Norman Thomas*, 190; Waltzer, "American Labor Party," 79–80.

53. Raskin interviews, cass. 45, pp. 11, 15; Fraser, *Labor Will Rule*, 364; *New York Times*, 17 July 1936; *Justice*, 1 August 1936; Minutes of the Executive Board of Labor's Non-Partisan League of New York State, 20 July 1936, Antonini Papers, ILGWU Archives.

54. Minutes of the EC, AFL, 5–20 May 1936, 444–46; William Green to David Dubinsky, 2 and 13 March 1936, DD Corr.; Phelan, *William Green*, 135–136; Dubofsky and Van Tine, *John L. Lewis*, 234–238; Danish, *World of David Dubinsky*, 110.

55. Meeting of the GEB, New York Members, 17 April 1936, 2–3.

56. *New York Times*, 24 April 1936.

57. Meeting of the GEB, ILGWU, 28 August 1936, 15; ILGWU, *Report of the GEB*, Twenty-third Convention, 1937, 194.

58. Minutes of the EC, AFL, 5–20 May 1936, 80; ILGWU, *Report of the GEB*, Twenty-third Convention, 1937, 200; Morris, *Conflict within the AFL*, 226.

59. Meeting of the GEB, 22 May 1936, 67.

60. Ibid., 64–66; Morris, *Conflict within the AFL*, 229–230, 230n; *Justice*, 15 June 1936.

61. William Green to David Dubinsky, 20 and 24 June 1936; and Dubinsky to Green, 30 June 1936 (two letters), DD Corr.; Dubinsky to George M. Harrison, 1 June 1936, in Meeting of the GEB, New York Members, 26 June 1936, 2–3.

62. John P. Frey to Members of AFL Executive Council, 15 July 1936, and William Green to John L. Lewis, 16 July 1936

(copies), DD Corr.; Meeting of the GEB, New York Members, 24 July 1936, 2–3; Morris, *Conflict within the AFL,* 228.

63. Meeting of the CIO, 21 July 1936, 1–2, including copy of John L. Lewis to William Green, 21 July 1936, DD Corr.; Meeting of the GEB, 24 July 1936, 4–7; *Justice,* 1 August 1936.

64. Meeting of the GEB, New York Members, 24 July 1936, 7–8; Meeting of the GEB, ILGWU, New York Members, 4 August 1936, 1.

65. *New York Times,* 5 August 1936.

66. *New York Times,* 6 August 1936; Bernstein, *Turbulent Years,* 421–422; Morris, *Conflict within the AFL,* 236, 236n.–237n.; Minutes of the EC, AFL, 5 August 1936, 46–63.

67. William Green to David Dubinsky, 6 August 1936; Meeting of the CIO, 10 August 1936, 1–3; Dubinsky to John Brophy, 20 and 24 August 1936, DD Corr.

68. Minutes of the EC, AFL, 8–15 July 1936, 188–190, 194–195; Dubinsky to Green, 28 August 1936; and Dubinsky to Israel Feinberg, 29 August 1936, DD Corr.; Meeting of the GEB, 28 August 1936, 4–15, with undated statement by Isidore Nagler attached; Haskel, *Leader of the Garment Workers,* 231–234.

69. Dubinsky to Green, 1 September 1936, DD Corr.

70. Dubinsky to All ILGWU Locals and Joint Boards, 2 September 1936, DD Corr.

71. Green to Dubinsky, 2 September 1936, DD Corr.

72. Charles S. Zimmerman to Green, 4 September 1936, and Green to Zimmerman, 4 September 1936 (copies); Dubinsky to Green, 4 September 1936, all in DD Corr.

73. *Justice,* 15 September 1936.

74. *New York Times,* 5 August 1936; Minutes of the GEB, New York Members, 4 August 1936, 2–3.

75. Dubinsky and Raskin, *David Dubinsky,* 267–268; Epstein, *Jew and Communism,* 307, 416; ILGWU, Report of the GEB, Twenty-third Convention, 1937, 185;

Local 10 Minutes, Membership Meetings, 19 August 1936, 2.

76. Allen Guttmann, *The Wound in the Heart: America and the Spanish Civil War* (New York: Free Press of Glencoe, 1962), 53–67.

77. W. A. Swanberg, *Citizen Hearst: A Biography of William Randolph Hearst* (New York: Charles Scribner's Sons, 1961), 472–475.

78. *New York American,* 8 August 1936, quoted in research memorandum, Max D. Danish Collection, ILGWU Archives.

79. *New York Times,* 18 September 1936.

80. *New York Times,* 24 September 1936; Arthur M. Schlesinger Jr., *The Politics of Upheaval* (Boston: Houghton Mifflin Company, 1960), 619.

81. "Dubinsky, Zaritsky and Hillman Are for Roosevelt" newspaper advertisement (n.d.), DD Corr.; Epstein, *Jew and Communism,* 269.

82. *New York Times,* 12 and 15 September 1936; Charles J. Tull, *Father Coughlin and the New Deal* (Syracuse: Syracuse University Press, 1965), 147; Sheldon Marcus, *Father Coughlin: The Tumultuous Life of the Priest of the Little Flower* (Boston: Little, Brown and Company, 1973), 132; ILGWU, *The 'Dubinsky Issue' in the 1936 Campaign* (New York: ILGWU, 1936), 8.

83. *New York Times,* 14, 21, and 24 September 1936; ILGWU Press Release, 30 October 1936.

84. *New York Times,* 25 and 28 September 1936.

85. Dubinsky and Raskin, *David Dubinsky,* 267.

86. David Dubinsky to George W. Alger, 28 December 1936, DD Corr.

87. Dubinsky and Raskin, *David Dubinsky,* 207; David Dubinsky to Elinore Herrick, 14 September 1936; Dubinsky to ILGWU Members, 31 October 1936; Dubinsky to Charles S. Zimmerman, 8 October 1936; Herrick to Dubinsky, 5 October 1936; and Dubinsky to James A. Farley, 26 October 1936, all in DD Corr.; Herrick to

Sidney Hillman, 13 September and 20 October 1936, ACWA Records; David Dubinsky, "Address at American Labor Party Rally, October 27, 1936," DD Corr.

88. Hamilton Fish Armstrong to Dubinsky, 5 November 1936, DD Corr.

89. Waltzer, "American Labor Party," 95–96.

NOTES TO CHAPTER 11

1. U.S. Circuit Court of Appeals, Eighth District, No. 13019, *Donnelly Garment Company . . . vs. David Dubinsky et al.,* and No. 13020, *Lorraine Smith et al. . . . vs. David Dubinsky et al., Abstract of Record,* filed 28 December 1944, 3658–3660; David Dubinsky to Marion Burns, 26 June 1933, and Abraham Plotkin to Dubinsky, 15 and 20 August 1933, DD Corr.; *Justice,* 1 August, 1 September, and December 1933; ILGWU, *Report of the GEB,* Twenty-second Convention, 1934, 104–105.

2. ILGWU, *Report of the GEB,* Twenty-second Convention, 1934, 105; *Justice,* April 1934.

3. Minutes of the GEB, 12 March 1934, 27; Dubinsky and Raskin, *David Dubinsky,* 171–172; *New York Times,* 14 December 1933 and 9 September 1944; Lee Meriwether, *Jim Reed: "Senatorial Immortal"* (Webster Groves, Mo.: International Mark Twain Society, 1948), 222–224, 241–242.

4. ILGWU, *Report of the GEB,* Twenty-second Convention, 1934, 106; Minutes of the GEB, 12 March 1934, 32–33; *Justice,* April 1934; U.S. National Labor Relations Board (NLRB), *In the Matter of Donnelly Garment Company and International Ladies' Garment Workers' Union: Decision and Order* (Case No. C-1382, 6 March 1940), 15

5. Wave Tobin to Donnelly Garment Company, 9 March 1937; and Jane Palmer to Meyer Perlstein, 22 March 1937, DD Corr.; NLRB, *In the Matter of Donnelly,* 15–30, 33–34; *Justice,* 15 March 1937; Minutes of the GEB, 5 April 1937, 3.

6. *Justice,* 1 August 1938; ILGWU, *Report of the GEB,* Twenty-third Convention, 1937, 234–237.

7. ILGWU, *Report of the GEB,* Twenty-third Convention, 1937, 269; Kansas City *Missouri Democrat,* 14 May 1937.

8. ILGWU, *Report of the GEB,* Twenty-third Convention, 1937, 269–270.

9. District Court of the United States for the Western Division of the Western District of Missouri, *Judgment Findings of Fact and Conclusions of Law, Donnelly Garment Company vs. International Ladies' Garment Workers' Union* [27 April 1939], 8.

10. Meyer Perlstein to David Dubinsky, 6 and 8 July 1937; Dubinsky to Perlstein, 8 July 1937; and Jay Lovestone to Dubinsky, 21 July 1937, all in DD Corr.; Dubinsky and Raskin, *David Dubinsky,* 177.

11. Perlstein to Dubinsky, 8 July 1937, DD Corr.; *Justice,* 15 July 1937.

12. *Justice,* 15 October 1937.

13. Frank P. Walsh to David Dubinsky, 31 December 1937 (letter and telegram); and Merrill E. Otis to Jacob Billikopf, 8 January 1938, DD Corr.

14. Minutes of the GEB, 10 November 1938, 30; ILGWU, *Report of the GEB,* Twenty-fourth Convention, 1940, 95–96.

15. ILGWU, *Report of the GEB,* Thirty-fourth Convention, 1971, 131.

16. Taft, "Dubinsky and the Labor Movement," 30–31; Dubofsky and Van Tine, *John L. Lewis,* 242–243.

17. James B. Carey, "The Reminiscences of James B. Carey," 85–86, Oral History Research Office, Columbia University, 1960.

18. Dubofsky and Van Tine, *John L. Lewis,* 242–243; Shishkin, "Reminiscences of Boris Shishkin," 809–810; Epstein, *Jewish Labor,* vol. 2, 180–182.

19. *New York Times,* 6 October 1936; Taft, *A. F. of L. from the Death of Gompers to the Merger,* 181.

20. *New York Times,* 5 and 17 October 1936; Minutes of the GEB, 9 November 1936, 3.

21. *New York Times,* 7 October 1936.

22. *New York Times,* 8 October 1936.

23. Minutes of the GEB, 9 November 1936, 3; AFL, Minutes of the Executive

Council, 8–21 October 1936, 45–50, George Meany Memorial Archives.

24. *New York Times,* 9 October 1936.

25. AFL, Minutes of the Executive Council, 8–21 October 1936, 51–62, 63–64, 122–127.

26. David Dubinsky to John L. Lewis, 16 and 17 October 1936, Hillman Correspondence; *New York Times,* 17 and 20 October 1936; Bernstein, *Turbulent Years,* 525; Dubofsky and Van Tine, *John L. Lewis,* 243.

27. "I am convinced that Lewis does not want peace established in the labor movement," Dubinsky wrote after the GEB meeting. Dubinsky to Israel Feinberg, 12 November 1936, DD Corr.; *New York Times,* 26 October 1936; AFL-CIO Oral History interview with Charles S. Zimmerman, 8 March 1979, 5–6, courtesy of Mrs. Rose Zimmerman; Raskin interviews, cass. 40, pp. 9–11; ILGWU, Minutes of the GEB, 9 November 1936, 3–9.

28. Dubofsky and Van Tine, *John L. Lewis,* 243–244.

29. Zieger, *John L. Lewis,* 89.

30. AFL-CIO interview with Charles S. Zimmerman, 5–6.

31. AFL, *Report of Proceedings,* Fifty-sixth Convention, 1936, 503–517, 552–553; Taft, *A. F. of L. from the Death of Gompers to the Merger,* 186; Minutes of the GEB, 5 January 1937, 70, with editorial from Jewish edition of *Justice,* December 1936, translated into English, attached; *New York Times,* 24 November 1936.

32. *New York Times,* 25 and 26 November 1936; *Justice,* 1 December 1936.

33. George L. Berry to David Dubinsky, 8 and 21 December 1936 and 7 January 1937; Berry to George M. Harrison, 8 December 1936 and 7 January 1937; Harrison to Berry, 14 and 30 December 1936; and Dubinsky to Berry, 15 December 1936, all in DD Corr.; Minutes of the GEB, 5 January 1937, 70–71.

NOTES TO CHAPTER 12

1. *Position of the International Ladies'* *Garment Workers' Union in Relation to the CIO and AFL, 1934–1938,* 30–31; William Green to AFL Officers and Members, 24 February 1937; David Dubinsky to Israel Feinberg, 12 March 1937; and Dubinsky to Samuel Kraisman, 12 March 1937, all in DD Corr.

2. ILGWU, *Report of the GEB,* Twenty-third Convention, 1937, 194–219; Minutes of the GEB, 5 April 1937, 3.

3. Bernstein, *Turbulent Years,* 783; Klehr, *Heyday of American Communism,* 228.

4. Klehr, *Heyday of American Communism,* 167–206; Earl Browder, *The People's Front* (New York: International Publishers, 1938), 66.

5. Earl Browder, *Communism in the United States* (New York: International Publishers, 1935), 196.

6. Klehr, *Heyday of American Communism,* 223–231; Len De Caux, *Labor Radical: From the Wobblies to CIO, a Personal History* (Boston: Beacon Press, 1971), 219–220; Brophy, *Miner's Life,* 258–261; Bert Cochran, *Labor and Communism: The Conflict That Shaped American Unions* (Princeton, N.J.: Princeton University Press, 1977), 95, 345–347.

7. Sidney Fine, *Sit-Down: The General Motors Strike of 1936–1937* (Ann Arbor: University of Michigan Press, 1969), 1–13, 121–177, 266–312; Sidney Fine, *Frank Murphy: The New Deal Years* (Chicago: University of Chicago Press, 1979), 289–325; Henry Kraus, *The Many and the Few: A Chronicle of the Dynamic Auto Workers* (2d ed.; Urbana: University of Illinois Press, 1985), 86–145.

8. Bernstein, *Turbulent Years,* 551–554.

9. Ibid., 554–569; Dubinsky and Raskin, *David Dubinsky,* 240–242; interview with David Dubinsky by Henoch Mendelsund, 24 July 1974, 74, ILGWU Archives; Alexander, *Right Opposition,* 56–57.

10. Personal interview with Victor G. Reuther, 26 August 1986; Jay Lovestone to David Dubinsky, 19 March 1937 and 9 September 1937, DD Corr.; Alexander,

Right Opposition, 57; Victor G. Reuther, *The Brothers Reuther and the Story of the UAW: A Memoir* (Boston: Houghton Mifflin Company, 1976), 183 – 184; Cochran, *Labor and Communism,* 131–133; Fine, *Sit-Down,* 328–329; Keeran, *Communist Party and the Auto Workers' Union,* 188.

11. United Automobile Workers of America, *Proceedings,* Second Convention, 1937, 21–22; Walter Galenson, *The CIO Challenge to the AFL: A History of the American Labor Movement, 1935–1941* (Cambridge, Mass.: Harvard University Press, 1950), 156–157.

12. Interview with Victor G. Reuther, 26 August 1986; Irving Howe and B. J. Widdick, *The UAW and Walter Reuther* (New York: Random House, 1949), 264–265, tells this story with slightly different details but labels it as "probably apocryphal." Reuther related Dubinsky's remarks to this interviewer without any doubt that he made them.

13. Waltzer, "American Labor Party," 123–124; Kenneth Waltzer, "The Party and the Polling Place: American Communism and an American Labor Party in the 1930s," *Radical History Review,* 23 (Spring 1980): 116; Warren Moscow, *Politics in the Empire State* (Westport, Conn.: Greenwood Press, 1979), 108.

14. Transcript of interview with Jacob Potofsky by Kenneth Waltzer, 13 November 1968, 2, Jacob Potofsky Oral History Interviews, Columbia University.

15. Minutes of the GEB, 5 January 1937, 9, 72.

16. Ibid., 73; Dubinsky and Raskin, *David Dubinsky,* 269.

17. Minutes of the GEB, 22 November 1917, 33–34.

18. Charles Garrett, *The La Guardia Years: Machine and Reform Politics in New York City* (New Brunswick, N.J.: Rutgers University Press, 1961), 259.

19. Kessner, *Fiorello H. La Guardia and the Making of Modern New York,* 410–414.

20. Ibid., 415–417.

21. *New York Herald Tribune,* 29 October 1937.
22. Ibid.
23. Kessner, *Fiorello H. La Guardia and the Making of Modern New York,* 365.
24. Smith, *Thomas E. Dewey and His Times,* 227–231; Schwarz, *Liberal,* 290.
25. *New York Times,* 4 November 1937; *Justice,* 15 November 1937; Waltzer, "American Labor Party," 117–118; Smith, *Thomas E. Dewey and His Times,* 239; Kessner, *Fiorello H. La Guardia and the Making of Modern New York,* 419.
26. Waltzer, "American Labor Party," 125–128; telephone interview with George Field, 16 April 1987; Waldman, *Labor Lawyer,* 289–290; Epstein, *Jew and Communism,* 303–304.
27. ILGWU, *Report of the GEB,* Twenty-third Convention, 1937, 194–219.
28. Minutes of the GEB, 5 April 1937, 3.
29. ILGWU, *Report and Proceedings,* Twenty-third Convention, 1937, 444–446.
30. Ibid., 146–155, 293–303, 356–360, 390–391, 438; *Justice,* 1 June 1937.
31. David Dubinsky to Matthew Woll, 19 May 1937, DD Corr.
32. *A.F.L. vs. C.I.O.: The Record* (Washington, D.C.: American Federation of Labor, 1939), 44–51. AFL, *Report of Proceedings,* Fifty-seventh Convention, 1937, 377–417; Morris, *Conflict within the AFL,* 255.
33. Josephson, *Sidney Hillman,* 416–417.
34. Ibid., 417–418.
35. Minutes of the GEB, 5 April 1937, 6.
36. ILGWU, *Report of the GEB,* Twenty-third Convention, 1937, 131–132.
37. Minutes of the GEB, 29 April 1937, 1–3; Dubinsky to Sidney Hillman, 28 April 1937, and Dubinsky to John L. Lewis, 28 April 1937, DD Corr.
38. ILGWU, *Report of the GEB,* Twenty-third Convention, 1937, 300, 356–360.
39. *New York Times,* 19 May 1937.
40. Dubinsky to Woll, 19 May 1937.
41. Minutes of the GEB, 21 June 1937, 16.

42. David Dubinsky to Sidney Hillman, 24 August 1937 (copy), Zimmerman Records; Minutes of the GEB, New York Members, 2 September 1937, 1–4, and 7 October 1937, 2; agreement dated 14 December 1937 between the ILGWU and the TWOC, attached to Minutes of the GEB, 23 May 1938, following p. 22.

43. David Dubinsky to William Green, 9 and 18 June 1937; Nathan Solomon to Green, 12 June 1937; and Green to Dubinsky, 14 June 1937, all in DD Corr.; Minutes of the GEB, 21 June 1937, 3–6; ILGWU, *Report of the GEB,* Twenty-third Convention, 1937, 69.

44. Minutes of the GEB, 21 June 1937, 6.

45. Rose Pesotta, *Bread Upon the Waters,* ed. John Nicholas Beffel (New York: Dodd, Mead and Company, 1944), 278–304; ILGWU, *Report of the GEB,* Twenty-fourth Convention, 1940, 85–86.

46. Dubinsky to William Green, 30 June 1937, in ILGWU press release of the same date; and Green to Dubinsky, 2 July 1937, DD Corr.

47. "AFL-CIO Conflicts," memorandum attached to Dubinsky to John Brophy, 27 July 1937; and Elias Reisberg to William Green, 30 July 1937, DD Corr.

48. Benjamin Stolberg, *The Story of the CIO* (New York: Viking Press, 1938), 28, 28n.

49. ILGWU, *Report of Proceedings,* Twenty-third Convention, 1937, 405–412; Klehr, *Heyday of American Communism,* 243.

50. *Does the CIO Seek to Promote Red Revolution?* (Boston: Industrial Defense Association, Inc., [1937]), attached to Philip Kramer to Dubinsky, 7 July 1937, DD Corr.

51. *Chicago Tribune,* 28 August and 24 September 1937; Dubinsky to Editor, *Chicago Tribune,* 17 September 1937, DD Corr.

52. *New York Sun,* 2 September 1937; *New York Times,* 3 September 1937.

53. *New York Times,* 4 September 1937.

54. Dubinsky to Israel Feinberg, 29 September 1937, DD Corr.

55. *New York Times,* 5 October 1937.

56. AFL, *Report of Proceedings,* Fifty-seventh Convention, 1937, 377–417; *New York Times,* 12 October 1937.

57. "Statement by David Dubinsky," 12 October 1937; speeches by Philip Murray and David Dubinsky, 12 October 1937; Harvey Fremming to Frank Morrison, 12 and 14 October 1937 (copies); Morrison to Fremming, 14, 15 October 1937 (copies); Philip Murray to Morrison, 16 October 1937 (copy); Morrison to Murray, 17 October 1937 (copy), all in DD Corr.

58. Morris, *Conflict within the AFL,* 257–258.

59. Minutes of the GEB, 22 November 1937, 24.

60. *CIO-AFL Washington Conferences,* Notes (n.d.), DD Corr.; *A.F.L. vs. C.I.O.: The Record,* 55–56

61. Dubinsky and Raskin, *David Dubinsky,* 236.

62. Ibid.; Dubofsky and Van Tine, *John L. Lewis,* 306.

63. Minutes of the GEB, New York Members, 3 January 1938, 1.

64. Ibid., 4–5; "Remarks by Vice-President Zimmerman at meeting of N.Y. Board, January 3, 1938," DD Corr.

65. ILGWU, *Position of the International Ladies' Garment Workers' Union in Relation to the CIO and AFL, 1934–1938,* 49–63; *Chicago Tribune,* 12 and 13 January 1938; *Justice,* 15 January 1938.

66. *New York Herald Tribune,* 13 January 1938.

67. Ibid.; Sol M. Stroock to David Dubinsky, 18 January 1938, DD Corr.

68. Jay Lovestone to David Dubinsky, 5 January 1938, DD Corr.; *Daily Worker,* 14 January 1938.

69. Heywood Broun, "Shoot the Works," *New Republic,* 26 January 1938, 335.

70. "Growing Pains of the CIO," *New Republic,* 26 January 1938, 323–324.

71. T.R.B., "Washington Notes," *New Republic,* 26 January 1938, 336.

72. Amalgamated Clothing Workers of America (ACWA), *Report and Proceedings,*

Twelfth Convention, 1938, 347; Josephson, *Sidney Hillman*, 430.

73. Dubofsky and Van Tine, *John L. Lewis*, 307.

74. Samuel Dickstein to David Dubinsky, 14 January 1938, and Michael Gallagher to Dubinsky, 17 January 1938, DD Corr. Congressman Dickstein commended Dubinsky for warning against Communist "infiltration . . . into our Labor Unions," but in 1938 he became a paid agent for the Soviet People's Commisariat for Internal Affairs (NKVD) in exchange for monthly payments of $1,250. Allen Weinstein and Alexander Vassiliev, *The Haunted Wood: Soviet Espionage in America — The Stalin Era* (New York: Random House, 1999), 142–143.

75. J. W. Buzzell to Dubinsky, 8 March 1938, and Dubinsky to Buzzell, 15 March 1938, DD Corr.

76. Lovestone to Dubinsky, 28 April 1928, and Communist Party, New York State, *Proceedings*, Tenth Convention, 20–23 May 1938 (MS), 4, DD Corr.; *New York Journal-American*, 9 April 1938; *New York Times*, 27 April and 1 May 1938; *Justice*, 5 May 1938; Epstein, *Jew and Communism, 1919–1941*, 342.

77. Alexander, *Right Opposition*, 9–10.

78. "The Reminiscences of Lee Pressman," Oral History Research Office, Columbia University, 1958, 156.

79. Communist Party, New York State, *Proceedings*, Tenth Convention, 2, 5.

80. Interview with Gus Tyler, 28 April 1984.

81. Gus Tyler, "The Intellectual and the ILGWU," in Bernard Rosenberg and Ernest Goldstein (eds.), *Creators and Disturbers: Reminiscences by Jewish Intellectuals of New York* (New York: Columbia University Press, 1982), 169.

82. Klehr, *Heyday of American Communism*, 327–343; Mark Naison, *Communists in Harlem during the Depression* (Urbana: University of Illinois Press, 1983), 154–158.

83. John C. Walter, "Frank R. Crosswaith and the Negro Labor Committee in Harlem, 1925–1939," *Afro-Americans in New York Life and History*, 3 (July 1979): 39–41; John H. Seabrook, "Black and White Unite: The Career of Frank R. Crosswaith" (Ph.D. diss., Rutgers University, 1980), 140–149; ILGWU, *Report and Proceedings*, Twenty-third Convention, 1937, 332–333, 353.

84. Interview with Maida Springer Kemp, 2 July 1984; Laurentz, "Racial/Ethnic Conflict in the New York City Garment Industry," 169–170; Seabrook, "Black and White Unite," 136.

85. Ira Rosenwaike, *Population History of New York City* (Syracuse: Syracuse University Press, 1972), 133; Gilbert Osofsky, *Harlem: The Making of a Ghetto* (New York: Harper Torchbooks, 1968), 130.

86. Charles Lionel Franklin, *The Negro Labor Unionist in New York* (New York: Columbia University Press, 1936), 162–163.

87. Zappia, "Unionism and the Italian American Worker," 86–87.

88. Interview with Gus Tyler, 28 April 1984; Cannistraro, "Luigi Antonini and the Italian Anti-Fascist Movement in the United States," 24–25; Minutes of the GEB, 23 May 1938, 24.

89. Allan S. Haywood to David Dubinsky, 3 January 1938, DD Corr.; *New York Times*, 22 January 1938; *Daily Worker*, 22 January 1938.

90. *New York Herald Tribune*, 26 January 1938.

91. Minutes of the GEB, New York Members, 3 February 1938, 2–3.

92. *Daily Worker*, 26 January 1938.

93. John L. Lewis to Dubinsky, 1 April 1938, DD Corr.; *New York Times*, 11 April 1938.

94. *New York Times*, 13 April 1938.

95. *New York Times*, 13 and 14 April 1938; *United Mine Workers Journal*, 1 May 1938.

96. ILGWU Press Release, "Statement by David Dubinsky, 14 April 1938"; and Dubinsky to Lewis, 14 April 1938, DD Corr.; *New York Times*, 3 May 1938.

97. *New York Times*, 3 May 1938.

98. Ibid.; *Justice,* 1 May and 15 June 1938; Minutes of the GEB, 23 May 1938, 52–53.

99. Dubinsky to Managers of ILGWU Local Unions in New York City, 9 August 1938; and Allan S. Haywood to Dubinsky, 19 August 1938, DD Corr.

100. I. Lutsky to Dubinsky, 8 August 1938, DD Corr.

101. Israel Feinberg to Dubinsky, 31 August 1938, DD Corr.

102. Stolberg, *Story of the CIO,* 153–154.

103. Minutes of the GEB, New York Members, 31 August 1938, 2.

104. Dubinsky to John L. Lewis, 12 August 1938 (copy); Ralph Hetzel, Jr., to Dubinsky, 13 and 19 August 1938; and Special Committee of the General Executive Board of the I.L.G.W.U., "Report of the Special Committee Appointed by General Executive Board of the ILGWU to Seek Reopening of Peace Conferences between the CIO and the AFL," 10 November 1938, 1–3, all in DD Corr.; *New York Post* and *New York World Telegram,* 24 August 1938; *New York Daily Mirror,* 26 August 1938; *Justice,* 15 November 1938.

105. *New York Times,* 18 June 1938; Allan Nevins, *Herbert H. Lehman and His Era* (New York: Charles Scribner's Sons, 1963), 193; *Milwaukee Leader,* 20 June 1938; Robert F. Carter, "Pressure from the Left: The American Labor Party, 1936–1954" (Ph.D. diss., Syracuse University, 1965), 97.

106. Waltzer, "American Labor Party," 123–133.

107. Ibid., 132; Dubinsky to Herbert H. Lehman, 20 July 1937, DD Corr.; *New York Times,* 19 June 1938.

108. Raskin interviews, cass. 46, pp. 9–14; Dubinsky and Raskin, *David Dubinsky,* 270; telephone interview with Emil Schlesinger, 1 March 1988.

109. *New York Times,* 22 and 23 June 1938.

110. *New York Times,* 28 and 29 June and 3 July 1938; Dubinsky to Alex Rose, 2 July 1938, DD Corr.

111. *New York Times,* 6 July and 28 September 1938; Josephson, *Sidney Hillman,* 455.

112. Thomas Corcoran to Marvin McIntyre, 4 September 1938, Roosevelt Papers.

113. Dubinsky to Sidney Hillman, 7 July 1938, DD Corr.

114. *New York Times,* 17 and 18 September 1938; *New York Post,* 17 September 1938; "Statement of Dressmakers Local Union 22, I.L.G.W.U., on the State C.I.O. Conference," 16 September 1938, DD Corr.

115. Dubinsky to Sidney Hillman, 4 October 1938; Herbert H. Lehman to Dubinsky, 4 October 1938, with nominating speech by David Dubinsky for Herbert H. Lehman, 3 October 1938, attached, DD Corr.; Nevins, *Herbert H. Lehman and His Era,* 194–196.

116. ILGWU press release, 6 October 1938; and Dubinsky to Frank Dussault, 21 October 1938, DD Corr.; Minutes of the GEB, 19 October 1938, 1.

117. Ralph Hetzel, Jr., to Dubinsky, 25 October 1938, and Dubinsky to Hetzel, 27 October 1938, DD Corr.

118. Jay Lovestone to Louis Stark, 1 November 1938, DD Corr.

119. Minutes of the GEB, 10 November 1938, 8–11; *Justice,* 15 November 1938; *New York Times,* 17 November 1938.

NOTES TO CHAPTER 13

1. Dubinsky and Raskin, *David Dubinsky,* 157–162.

2. *Position of the International Ladies' Garment Workers' Union in Relation to CIO and AFL,* 81.

3. *Chicago Daily News,* 30 January 1939.

4. *New York Times,* 26 February 1939; ILGWU press release [February 1939], ILGWU Archives; Dubofsky and Van Tine, *John L. Lewis,* 309–312.

5. George Wishnak to David Dubinsky, 19 May 1938 and 19 December 1938, DD Corr.

6. Meeting of the GEB, 22 May 1939, 29–30.

7. *Women's Wear Daily,* 20 and 24 July 1939.

8. *Women's Wear Daily,* 3 and 4 August 1939; *New York Post,* 3 August 1939.

9. *New York Herald Tribune,* 6 August 1939.

10. Harry Greenberg to Sidney Hillman, 11 August 1939, DD Corr.

11. [Gus Tyler], "Digest of Meeting at Labor Club on Bathrobe Situation on the Evening of August 14th [1939], attached to Greenberg to Dubinsky, 17 August 1939; [Dubinsky], undated statement on bathrobe industry dispute, DD Corr.

12. *New York Times,* 22 August 1939; *Women's Wear Daily,* 22 August 1939; *Justice,* 1 September 1939.

13. *New York Herald Tribune,* 22 August 1939; *The Advance,* September 1939.

14. Adolph Held, David Dubinsky, and Joseph Baskin to British Trades Union Congress, 8 August 1939; Dubinsky to Held, 29 August 1939, DD Corr.

15. Meeting of the GEB, 15 November 1939, 17–19; *New York Times,* 19 November 1939.

16. *New York Times,* 20 November 1939; *Daily Worker,* 21 November 1939.

17. Meeting of the GEB, 15 March 1940, 1–2; ILGWU, *Report of the GEB,* Twenty-fourth Convention, 1940, 43–44.

18. *Jewish Daily Forward,* 9 February 1937; Dubinsky to Director of the *Forward,* 9 February 1937, DD Corr.

19. Carter, "Pressure from the Left," 121–122; "Report of State Secretary Alex Rose to the State Committee of the American Labor Party Meeting Held at Hotel Edison January 6th, 1940," 8, DD Corr.

20. Dubinsky to "Friend," 29 March 1940; and Dubinsky, "In Defense of Our Party," 30 March 1940, DD Corr.

21. Meeting of the GEB, 9 April 1940, 1–2; ILGWU, *Report of the GEB,* Twenty-fourth Convention, 1940, 32; Andrew R. Armstrong to Luigi Antonini and Alex Rose, 14 May 1940, DD Corr.

22. Haskel, *Leader of the Garment Workers,* 290–296; Joint Committee for the Election of Isidore Nagler and an Efficient

Progressive Administration, "Damaged Goods in Local 10" (flyer, 1939); *Rank and File Cutter,* election issue, 1939, and Cutters Rank and File Committee, "Vote the Rank and File Ticket" (flyer, 1939), Zimmerman Records; Local 10 Minutes, Membership Meetings, 16, 23, and 30 January 1939; Meeting of the Executive Board of Local 10, 11 January 1939, 1. For additional evidence of radical activity in Local 10, see Albert Afterman Rank and File Caucus Local 10 ILGWU Collection, Robert F. Wagner Labor Archives, New York University.

23. Tenth Assembly District, Communist Party, flyer addressed to "Dressmakers of Local 22," October 1939, DD Corr.; *Daily Worker,* 10 October 1939.

24. *New York Times,* 25 February 1939; ILGWU press release [February 1939]; Dubinsky to J. C. Weber, 10 March 1939, DD Corr.

25. Dubofsky and Van Tine, *John L. Lewis,* 309–312.

26. Meeting of the GEB, 22 May 1939, 8.

27. Meeting of the GEB, 15 November 1939, 27; *Justice,* 1 December 1937.

28. Meeting of the GEB, New York Members, 18 September 1939, 1.

29. Bernstein, *Turbulent Years,* 706–707, 710–711; Minutes of the GEB, 4 June 1940, 1; Oral History interview with Leon Stein, 8 March 1979, 6, AFL-CIO Merger Interviews, George Meany Memorial Archives, Silver Spring, Maryland.

30. Meeting of the EC, AFL, 20 May 1940, 93–96.

31. ILGWU, *Report and Proceedings,* Twenty-fourth Convention, 1940, 183–192.

32. Ibid., 447–457, 531; personal interview with Henoch Mendelsund, 22 January 1985; telephone interview with Gus Tyler, 9 November 1994. The day after the vote Dubinsky reported to the convention that two of the twelve dissenting delegates denied they were Communists. Schlesinger, "Transcript on Racketeering," 29–30; Raskin interviews, cass. 33, pp. 12–13; Stolberg, *Tai-*

lor's Progress, 277–278. Dubinsky and Raskin, *David Dubinsky,* 157–158, alters the account Schlesinger gave when he was interviewed by Raskin.

33. Oral History interview with Leon Stein, 8 March 1979, 5.

34. Cochran, *Labor and Communism,* 143–144; Maurice Isserman, *Which Side Were You On? The American Communist Party during the Second World War* (Middletown, Conn.: Wesleyan University Press, 1982), 74–75; *New York Herald Tribune,* 25 July 1940; *New York World-Telegram,* 26 July 1940; *New York Times,* 1 November 1940; Dubofsky and Van Tine, *John L. Lewis,* 357–361; Dubinsky to Charles Zimmerman, 6 November 1940, Zimmerman Records.

35. At 1 a.m., Thanksgiving Day, Joseph S. Fay, vice president of the International Union of Operating Engineers, expressed his opposition to the ILGWU resolution in a direct, personal way at the bar of the Hotel Roosevelt. He began an altercation in which he pushed Dubinsky's cigar against his face and punched ILGWU executive secretary Fred Umhey. Fay inadvertently publicized the ILGWU cause. *New York Times,* 21 and 22 November 1940 and 19 September 1982; Dubinsky and Raskin, *David Dubinsky,* 159–162.

36. AFL, *Report of Proceedings,* Sixtieth Convention, 1940, 64–65.

37. AFL, *Report of Proceedings,* Sixtieth Convention, 1940, 504–506, 630; *New York Times,* 24, 27, and 29 November 1940; Dubinsky to Zimmerman, 28 December 1943, Zimmerman Records; Raskin interviews, cass. 33, p. 7.

38. CIO, *Daily Proceedings,* Third Constitutional Convention, 1940, 52.

39. Dubofsky and Van Tine, *John L. Lewis,* 369; "The Reminiscences of James B. Carey," 134–135.

NOTES TO CHAPTER 14

1. Roger D. Waldinger, *Through the Eye of the Needle: Immigrants and Enterprise in New York's Garment Trades* (New York:

New York University Press, 1986), 54–56; Roy B. Helfgott, "Women and Children's Apparel," in Max Hall (ed.), *Made in New York* (Cambridge, Mass.: Harvard University Press, 1959), 88–89.

2. Joel Seidman, *The Needle Trades* (New York: Farrar and Rinehart, 1942), 43–44; ILGWU, *Financial and Statistical Report,* 1 April 1937 to 31 March 1940, 38.

3. Seidman, *Needle Trades,* 43.

4. Will Herberg, "Old-Timers and Newcomers: Ethnic Group Relations in a Needle Trades Union," *Jewish Frontier* (November 1953): 26.

5. ILGWU, *Report of the GEB,* Twenty-third Convention, 1937, 333.

6. ILGWU, *Report of Proceedings,* Twenty-fourth Convention, 1940, 340–341.

7. T. Arnold Hill to David Dubinsky, 11 June 1937; Abraham Plotkin to Dubinsky, 14 June 14 1937 (copy); Dubinsky to Hill, 21 June 1937, all in DD Corr.; *Justice,* 1 May, 1 July and 15 July 1937.

8. ILGWU, *Report of Proceedings,* Twenty-fourth Convention, 1940, 376–377.

9. Carter, "Pressure from the Left," 138; *New York Times,* 7 November and 5 December 1940.

10. Waltzer, "American Labor Party," 234–238.

11. Jacob Potofsky to Hyman Blumberg, 19 June 1941, ACWA Papers.

12. *New York Times,* 11, 13, 15, and 28 September 1940.

13. Ibid., 26 June 1941.

14. Ibid., 3 October 1941.

15. Gerald Meyer, "Vito Marcantonio," in Mary Jo Buhle, Paul Buhle, and Harvey Kaye (eds.), *The American Radical* (New York: Routledge, 1994), 271.

16. *New York Times,* 16 November 1941.

17. ILGWU, Minutes of the GEB, New York Members, 25 November 1941, 1–2.

18. ILGWU, Minutes of the GEB, New York Members, 19 December 1941, 1, and 23 December 1941, 1–2.

19. Fulton Lewis Jr., "Clothing Contract Policy" (MS), attached to Hushing to Dubinsky, 5 March 1942; Albert J. Engel, "Were Workers in Factories Making Women's Garments Barred From Bidding on Army Clothing Contracts?" *Congressional Record*, 11 March 1942, A1041–A1042, attached to Hushing to Dubinsky, 12 March 1942, Legislative Department Records, George Meany Memorial Archives; Fraser, *Labor Will Rule*, 488–489; ILGWU, Minutes of the GEB, 15 June 1942, 6.

20. Nevins, *Herbert H. Lehman and His Era*, 22; Moscow, *Politics in the Empire State*, 89–91; John Syrett, "Roosevelt vs. Farley: The New York Gubernatorial Election of 1942," *New York History*, 66 (January 1975): 54–61.

21. Dubinsky and Raskin, *David Dubinsky*, 273.

22. James McGregor Burns, *Roosevelt: The Soldier of Freedom, 1940–1945* (New York: Harcourt Brace Jovanovich, 1970), 277; Fraser, *Labor Will Rule*, 499.

23. Diary of Adolf A. Berle, Jr., 22 and 24 August 1942, Adolf A. Berle, Jr. Papers, Franklin D. Roosevelt Library; *Justice*, 1 September 1942; *New York Times*, 27 October 1989; Dean Alfange, MS enclosed with Alfange to the author, 3 March 1985; Smith, *Thomas E. Dewey and His Times*, 350; ILGWU, *Report of the GEB*, Twenty-fifth Convention, 1944, 20; David Dubinsky, "Radio Address, 11/2/42" and "Statement for The New Leader, 11/4/42," DD Corr.

24. Syrett, "Roosevelt vs. Farley," 78; Waltzer, "American Labor Party," 271; Fraser, *Labor Will Rule*, 499–500.

25. Fraser, *Labor Will Rule*, 499–500; ILGWU, *Report of the GEB*, Twenty-fifth Convention, 1944, 20; Franklin D. Roosevelt to Sidney Hillman, 9 October 1942, and Edwin M. Watson to Roberta C. Barrows, 13 October 1942, Roosevelt Papers.

26. Address by Gus Tyler at Robert F. Wagner Labor Archives, 19 October 1994.

27. Jacob Pat to Dubinsky, 22 May 1940, DD Corr.; Gail Malmgreen, "Labor and the Holocaust: The Jewish Labor Committee and the Anti-Nazi Struggle," *Labor's Heritage*, 3 (October 1991): 24; David S. Wyman, *Paper Walls: America and the Refugee Crisis, 1938–1941* (New York: Pantheon Books, 1985), 138; Meeting of the GEB, 22 July 1940, 8; Dubinsky and Raskin, *David Dubinsky*, 248; William Green to Breckinridge Long, 3 July 1940, in *German-American Trade Union Solidarity in the Struggle against Fascism, 1933–1945: How the American Trade Unions Helped Their Persecuted German Colleagues: A Report* (Washington, D.C.: American Federation of Labor–Congress of Industrial Organizations, [1985]), 32–33.

28. Minutes of the GEB, 15 September 1941, 26–27; *New York Times*, 19 September 1941; ILGWU, *Report of the GEB*, Twenty-fifth Convention, 1944, 16.

29. Pat to Dubinsky, 29 September 1942, and "Conference with Polish Minister of Labor," 24 October 1941, attached to Pat to Dubinsky, 25 October 1941; and Jewish Labor Committee, *Report*, 30 November 1942, 9, all in DD Corr.; David Engel, *In the Shadow of Auschwitz: The Polish Government-in-Exile and the Jews, 1939–1942* (Chapel Hill: University of North Carolina Press, 1987), 125–132.

30. Jacob Pat, "The Jewish Labor Committee and the International Anti-Nazi Resistance Movement," *Labor and Nation*, January–February 1947, 44.

31. *Morning Freiheit*, 5 May 1943.

32. *New York Times*, 15 and 16 May 1943; Address by David Dubinsky, 16 May 1943 (MS), DD Corr.

33. *Daily Worker*, 7 July 1943; *New York Times*, 7 July 1943.

34. *Daily Worker*, 2, 5, and 9 August 1943; *New York Times*, 8 August 1943.

35. Dubinsky to Hillman, 11 August 1943, Hillman Papers; *New York Times*, 11, 12, and 18 August 1943.

36. *New York Times*, 31 August and 12 October 1943; Richard H. Rovere, "Is This Clean Politics?" *The Nation*, 11 September 1943, 306.

37. *Justice*, 1 September 1943.

38. Saul Alinsky, *John L. Lewis: An Unauthorized Biography* (New York: G. P. Putnam's Sons, 1949), 249–250; Dubinsky, Address to Local 22, January 1943 (MS), 45–46, DD Corr.; Meeting of the GEB, New York Members, 15 June 1942, 19, 28; Nelson Lichtenstein, *Labor's War at Home: The CIO in World War II* (New York: Cambridge University Press, 1982), 159–160; *Justice*, 1 and 15 June 1943; Waltzer, "American Labor Party," 285. When Dubinsky met with Lewis early in 1943, he could not miss the opportunity to tease the Mine Workers' president about the Communists' disproportionate influence in the CIO and their attacks on him. "Who was the hunter, John," Dubinsky asked Lewis, "and who was the dog?" John Alsop and Stewart Alsop, "Will the CIO Shake the Communists Loose?" *Saturday Evening Post*, 1 March 1947, 117.

39. Minutes of the GEB, 8 November 1943, 10; Minutes of the GEB, New York Members, 18 November 1943, 1–2.

40. Ben Davidson, "The Reminiscences of Ben Davidson," 84–88, Oral History Research Office, Columbia University, 1979; Donald S. Harrington, "The Reminiscences of Donald Szantho Harrington," 27, Oral History Research Office, Columbia University.

41. *New York Times*, 11 January 1944; Minutes of the GEB, New York Members, 12 January 1944, 4; Fraser, *Labor Will Rule*, 520.

42. "Statement of the Executive Committee of the American Labor Party," 12 January 1944, DD Corr.; *New York Times*, 8, 13, and 15 January 1944; Davidson, "Reminiscences of Ben Davidson," 8.

43. Waltzer, interview with Jacob Potofsky, 13 November 1968, 3.

44. Hyman Blumberg to George Counts and Alex Rose, 24 February 1944, ACWA Records; Fraser, *Labor Will Rule*, 521.

45. Raskin interviews, cass. 7, pp. 1–2; Dubinsky and Raskin, *David Dubinsky*, 274–275; John Morton Blum (ed.), *The Price of Vision: The Diary of Henry Wallace, 1942–46* (Boston: Houghton Mifflin Company, 1973), 305, 309.

46. MS statement issued by Fiorello H. La Guardia, 22 March 1944, and press releases issued by the Liberal and Labor Committee to Safeguard the American Labor Party, 23 and 24 March 1944, DD Corr.; Dubinsky to Members of ILGWU, 27 March 1944, Zimmerman Records, ILGWU Archives; *New York Times*, 23, 25, 26, and 27 March 1944.

47. Liberal-Labor Committee, American Labor Party, "Statement to American Labor Party Voters [March 1944]," and "Statement by David Dubinsky," 29 March 1944, DD Corr.; *New York Times*, 29 and 30 March 1944; ILGWU, *Report of the GEB*, Twenty-fifth Convention, 1944, 20–21.

48. *New York Times*, 8 April 1944.

49. *New York Times*, 1, 4, 15, 19, 20, 21, and 28 May 1944 and 22 December 1991; *Report of the GEB*, Twenty-fifth Convention, 1944, 230, 511–514, 564.

50. ILGWU, *Report and Proceedings*, Twenty-fifth Convention, 1944, 230, 511–514, 564.

51. Dubinsky to Roosevelt, 9 May 1944; J. V. Fitzgerald to William D. Hassett, 17 May 1944; Hassett to David Niles, 18 May 1944; Niles to Hassett, 23 May 1944; Hassett to Isador Lubin, 25 May 1944, Roosevelt Papers, Roosevelt Library; ILGWU, *Report and Proceedings*, Twenty-fifth Convention, 1944, 251.

52. Personal interview with Benjamin A. Gebiner, 28 September 1984; Jewish Labor Committee, *Report*, 30 November 1942, Schedule 1, DD Corr.; ILGWU, *Financial and Statistical Report*, 1 April 1940 to 29 March 1944, 6, 27, 29–33.

53. ILGWU, *Financial and Statistical Report*, 1 April 1940 to 29 March 1944, 33.

54. Victor Serge and Natalia Sedova Trotsky, *The Life and Death of Leon Trotsky*, trans. Arnold J. Pomerans (New York: Basic Books, 1975), 267–269; Dubinsky to Frederick H. Umhey, 4 December 1940; Eleanor Roosevelt to Dubinsky, 17 February 1941; Dubinsky to Eleanor Roosevelt, 1 February 1941; Eleanor Roosevelt to Sumner Welles, 4 February 1941; Welles to

Eleanor Roosevelt, 4 February 1941; and Eleanor to Franklin D. Roosevelt, 11 February 1941, all in Eleanor Roosevelt Papers, Franklin D. Roosevelt Library. Biographer Emil Ludwig likewise petitioned unsuccessfully on behalf of Trotsky's widow. Ludwig to Franklin D. Roosevelt, 27 January 1941; Edwin D. Watson to Ludwig, 19 February 1941; and Franklin D. Roosevelt to Watson, 18 February 1941, all in OF Collection, Roosevelt Library.

55. Jacob Pat to Dubinsky, 18 June and 25 November 1941; Dubinsky to Adolf A. Berle, Jr., 16 and 26 November 1940; Berle to Dubinsky, 27 and 29 March 1940; and Serafino Romualdi to Dubinsky, 25 February 1941, all in DD Corr.; Berle to Dubinsky, 11 January 1941, Berle Papers; Dubinsky to Franklin D. Roosevelt, 17 March 1941, in *German-American Trade Union Solidarity,* 33; Montana, "The Shambles," 304–308; Minutes of the GEB, 16 November 1943; "Rescue of Democratic and Labor Leaders from Nazi Occupation Forces," *Labor and Nation,* January–February 1947, 43; Susan Zucott, *The Italians and the Holocaust* (New York: Basic Books, 1987), 256.

56. Yehuda Bauer, *A History of the Holocaust* (New York: Franklin Watts, 1982), 147–151, 153–154; A. Adamczyk to David Dubinsky, 31 January 1942; Alexander Znamiecki to Dubinsky, 19 March 1942; Dubinsky to Znamiecki, 23 March 1942, and Wladyslaw Malinowski to Dubinsky, 12 April 1942, all in DD Corr.

57. Lucjan Dobroszycki (ed.), *The Chronicle of the Lodz Ghetto, 1941–1944* (New Haven, Conn.: Yale University Press, 1984), xxiii–xxiv.

58. Lucy S. Dawidowicz, *The War against the Jews, 1933–1945* (New York: Holt, Rinehart and Winston, 1975), 129.

59. Ibid., 135–139; Martin Gilbert, *The Holocaust: A History of the Jews of Europe during the Second World War* (New York: Holt, Rinehart and Winston, 1985), 135–139.

60. David Engel, *In the Shadow of Auschwitz: The Polish Government-in-Exile and the Jews, 1939–1942* (Chapel Hill: University of North Carolina Press, 1987), 174–175; David S. Wyman, *The Abandonment of the Jews: America and the Holocaust, 1941–1945* (New York: Pantheon Books, 1984), 19–23, 43–55; Jacob Pat to Dubinsky, 25 October 1941, with attached memorandum of conference with Polish minister of labor, 24 October 1941, and Dubinsky, Address before the National Convention, Jewish Labor Committee, 18 December 1942, DD Corr.; Henry L. Feingold, *The Politics of Rescue: The Roosevelt Administration and the Holocaust, 1938–1945* (New Brunswick, N.J.: Rutgers University Press, 1970), 168–171.

61. David Dubinsky, Address before the National Convention, Jewish Labor Committee, 18 December 1942, 1–2, DD Corr.

62. ILGWU, *Record of Proceedings,* Twenty-fourth Convention, 1940, 262.

63. Roy Godson, *American Labor and European Politics: The AFL as a Transactional Force* (New York: Crane, Russak and Company, 1976), 42; *Justice,* 1 January and 1 March 1941.

64. Epstein, *Jewish Labor,* vol. 2, p. 403; D. B. [Daniel Bell], "Raphael Abramovitch, 1880–1963," *New Leader,* 29 April 1963; Raphael Abramovitch to Dubinsky, 20 May 1942, with draft, "American Labor Committee on International Affairs," attached; Woll to Dubinsky, 30 June 1942, in DD Corr.; Minutes of the GEB, 15 June 1942, 19; Minutes of the GEB, 16 November 1942, 8.

65. Minutes of the GEB, 1 June 1943, 8; *New York Times,* 8 February 1943; Windmuller, *American Labor and the International Labor Movement,* 75; Minutes of the First Meeting, A. F. of L. Committee on Post-War Planning, 12 February 1943, 1, DD Corr.; John Childs, "David Dubinsky and the Work of the A.F.L. Postwar Planning Committee," 1, Jay Lovestone, Collection, ILGWU Archives; Cordell Hull to Dubinsky, April 10, 1943, DD Corr.

66. *The Work of the American Labor Conference on International Affairs* (n.p., [1945]).

67. Emil Rieve to Varian Fry, 8 May 1944; Louis Hollander, Abraham Miller, Irving Abramson, John Green, and J. Raymond Walsh to Fry, n.d.; and Abramson to Fry, 20 June 1944 (all copies), attached to Fry to Dubinsky, 29 June 1944, all in DD Corr.

68. Goulden, *Meany,* 8–15, 62, 66–67, 74–77; Oral History interview with Leon Stein, 8 March 1979, AFL-CIO Merger Interviews, George Meany Memorial Archives; AFL, *Report of Proceedings,* 1944, 520–521, 556–557; *Complete Report of Proceedings, American Federation of Labor Forum on Labor and the Post-War World* (Washington, D.C.: American Federation of Labor, 1944); Windmuller, *American Labor and European Politics,* 76–77; ILGWU, *Record of Proceedings,* Twenty-sixth Convention, 1947, 14; Godson, *American Labor and European Politics,* 35–37; Roy Godson, "The AFL Foreign Policy Making Process from the End of World War II to the Merger," *Labor History,* 16 (Summer 1975): 325–329.

69. Interview with Gus Tyler, 16 November 1994; *Justice,* 15 May 1943. *New York Times,* 1 May 1943; Minutes of the GEB, 1 June 1943, 1; Godson, American Labor and European Politics, 41; interview with E. Howard Molisani, 9 May 1985.

70. Haakon Lie to Adolph Held, 28 October 1943 (copy), attached to Jacob Pat to Dubinsky, 29 October 1943, DD Corr.; interview with Haakon Lie by Morris Weisz, 1 March 1994, 23–24, Association for Diplomatic Studies and Training Labor Diplomacy Oral History Project, courtesy of Morris Weisz; "Accounting of Money Needed by Norwegian Trade Unions," n.d., Jewish Labor Committee Papers, Wagner Labor Archives.

71. Kenneth Waltzer, "American Jewish Labor and Aid to Polish Jews during the Holocaust" (paper presented at the Seventeenth Annual Conference on the Holocaust and the Church Struggle, 8–10 March 1987, Washington, D.C., Wagner Labor Archives), 10–11.

72. Dubinsky to William Green, 24 Au-

gust 1943; Green to Dubinsky, 1 September 1943; Cordell Hull to Adolph Held, 4 December 1943 (copy), attached to Jacob Pat to Dubinsky, 20 December 1943; S. Margoshes, "News and Views," n.d., attached to Leon Dennen to Dubinsky, 7 October 1943; Held to Dubinsky, 4 May 1944, all in DD Corr.

73. ILGWU, *Report of the GEB,* Twenty-fifth Convention, 1944, 16–18.

1. *New York Times,* 9 November 1944; Carter, "Pressure from the Left," 212–213.

2. David Dubinsky to Ryna Appleton, 21 January 1966, DD Corr.

3. Win Booth to Robert T. Elson, 11 August 1949, Daniel Bell Collection, Tamiment Library, New York University.

4. *Justice,* 1 December 1942; David Dubinsky to Chaim Dubinsky, 28 November 1942; Jean and Shelley Appleton to Emma and David Dubinsky, 23 September 1965, DD Corr.

5. Interview with Evelyn Dubrow, 21 August 1976; ILGWU, *Report of Proceedings,* Twenty-fifth Convention, 1944, 490; John S. Martin to Frederick F. Umhey, 27 November 1944, DD Corr.

6. Win Booth to Robert T. Elson, 14 August 1949, Bell Collection.

7. Frederick F. Umhey to William A. Kelly, 26 March and 13 April 1946, Umhey Correspondence, ILGWU Archives; David Dubinsky, Affidavit of Support, 7 April 1971, attached to Dubinsky to U.S. Department of Justice, Immigration and Naturalization Service, 8 April 1971, DD Corr.

8. Harry S. Truman, *Memoirs,* vol. 1: *Year of Decisions* (Garden City, N.Y.: Doubleday and Company, 1955), 2–7; David McCullough, *Truman* (New York: Simon and Schuster, 1992), 353.

9. Raskin interviews, cass. 32, p. 3; Dubinsky to Abraham Plotkin, 13 April 1945, Chicago Joint Board Records, ILGWU Archives.

10. Alonzo L. Hamby, *Beyond the New Deal: Harry S. Truman and American Lib-*

eralism (New York: Columbia University Press, 1973), 54–55.

11. Lawrence Elliott, *Little Flower: The Life and Times of Fiorello La Guardia* (New York: William Morrow and Company, 1983), 238–239; Kessner, *Fiorello H. La Guardia and the Making of Modern New York,* 568–570; Garrett, *La Guardia Years,* 292–293.

12. Moscow, *Politics in the Empire State,* 117–118; "The Reminiscences of Henry Agard Wallace," 4082; Edward J. Flynn, *You're the Boss* (New York: Viking Press, 1947), 222; *New York Times,* 10 August 1945; Eleanor Roosevelt to David Dubinsky, 9 and 24 August 1945; Dubinsky to Eleanor Roosevelt, 27 August 1945, DD Corr.

13. Carter, "Pressure from the Left," 236–239.

14. Ibid., 233–235; Fraser, *Labor Will Rule,* 570.

15. Harvey Klehr and John Earl Haynes, *The American Communist Movement: Storming Heaven Itself* (New York: Twayne Publishers, 1992), 102–105, 107; Fraser Ottanelli, *The Communist Party of the United States: From the Depression to World War II* (New Brunswick, N.J.: Rutgers University Press, 1991), 211–212.

16. Josephson, *Sidney Hillman,* 650–654.

17. Fraser, *Labor Will Rule,* 572–573.

18. *New York Times,* 5 March 1995.

19. Interview with Gus Tyler, 28 April 1984; Minutes of the GEB, 9 September 1946, 7; *Justice,* 15 July 1946.

20. Meeting of the Executive Council, AFL, 18 January 1943, 61–62, 64; and 19 October 1945, 75, 78; Taft, *A. F. of L. from the Death of Gompers to the Merger,* 455–456; *New York Times,* 20 October 1945; *Justice,* 1 November 1945.

21. ILGWU, *Financial and Statistical Report,* 1 April 1944 to 31 March 1947, 24–26, 46.

22. Robert J. Donovan, *Conflict and Crisis: The Presidency of Harry S. Truman, 1945–1948* (New York: W. W. Norton and Company, 1977), 237.

23. *Daily Worker,* 14 January 1944; "Shake-Down Protested to President Dubinsky," "Administration Machine Runs Riot at Meeting," and Arnold Ames, "A Message to the Cutters on the Coming Elections in Local 10," flyers, 1944, and *Rank and File Cutter,* March 1944, Albert Afterman Rank and File Caucus Local 10, ILGWU Collection; Abraham Skolnik and Frank Blumenkrantz to Frederick F. Umhey, 23 January 1947, attached to Skolnik and Blumenkrantz to Dubinsky, same date, and Ernest T. Hammer to Dubinsky, 20 May 1947, DD Corr.; ILGWU, *Report of the GEB,* Twenty-sixth Convention, 1947, 87.

24. ILGWU, *Report of the GEB,* Twenty-sixth Convention, 1947, 26.

25. Jay Lovestone to Dubinsky, 2 April 1946, DD Corr.; interview with Gus Tyler, 16 November 1994; *New York Times,* 10 and 12 May and 15, 16, and 17 June 1946; *Justice,* 1 July 1946; John S. Atlee, "A. V. C. Sets the Pace," *Nation,* 22 June 1946, 740–741; Curtis D. MacDougall, *Gideon's Army,* vol. 1 (3 vols.; New York: Marzani and Munsell, 1965), 124–125.

26. *New York Times,* 30 August 1946; *Justice,* 1 September 1946.

27. John Barnard, *Walter Reuther and the Rise of the Auto Workers* (Boston: Little, Brown and Company, 1983), 54–80; Frank Cormier and William J. Eaton, *Reuther* (Englewood Cliffs, N.J.: Prentice-Hall, 1970), 141–150.

28. Cormier and Eaton, *Reuther,* 220–225; Bert Cochran, *Harry Truman and the Crisis Presidency* (New York: Funk and Wagnalls, 1973), 202–203; Martin Halpern, *UAW Politics in the Cold War Era* (Albany: State University of New York Press, 1988), 86.

29. Minutes of the GEB, 17 December 1945, 37; Walter P. Reuther to David Dubinsky, 25 January 1946, and Dubinsky to ILGWU Affiliates, 1 February 1946, DD Corr.; Dubinsky to Reuther, 15 March 1946, Walter P. Reuther Collection, Archives of Labor History and Urban Affairs, Wayne State University, Detroit, Mich.; ILGWU, *Report of the GEB,*

Twenty-sixth Convention, 1947, 22; Halpern, *UAW Politics in the Cold War Era*, 86–87.

30. Interview with David Dubinsky by Charles Eaton, 25 February 1968, 1, John F. Kennedy Library, Boston, Mass.

31. Ibid.; Levenstein, *Communism, Anticommunism, and the CIO*, 198; Jean Gould and Lorena Hickok, *Walter Reuther: Labor's Rugged Individualist* (New York: Dodd, Mead and Company, 1972), 242–243; *Justice*, 1 April 1946; Dubinsky to Philip Murray, 2 April 1946; Murray to Dubinsky, 5 April 1946; and Dubinsky to R. J. Thomas, 2 April 1946, all in DD Corr; ILGWU, *Report of the GEB*, Twenty-sixth Convention, 1947, 22–23.

32. Mary Sperling McAuliffe, *Crisis on the Left: Cold War Politics and American Liberals, 1947–1954* (Amherst: University of Massachusetts Press, 1978), 5; Steven M. Gillon, *Politics and Vision: The ADA and American Liberalism, 1947–1985* (New York: Oxford University Press, 1987), 9–10; Richard Wightman Fox, *Reinhold Niebuhr: A Biography* (New York: Pantheon Books, 1985), 197–198.

33. Gillon, *Politics and Vision*, 10–13.

34. Ibid., 12–14; Karl M. Schmidt, *Henry A. Wallace: Quixotic Crusade 1948* (Syracuse, N.Y.: Syracuse University Press, 1960), 19–28; McDougall, *Gideon's Army*, vol. 1, pp. 104–117.

35. *New York Times*, 5 and 6 January 1947; Gillon, *Politics and Vision*, 16–18; McDougall, *Gideon's Army*, vol. 1, pp. 121–122; Fox, *Reinhold Niebuhr*, 229–230; Dubinsky to Morris Bialis, 7 January 1947; Wilson Wyatt and Leon Henderson to Dubinsky, 7 January 1947; and Joseph P. Lash to UDA Members, 14 January 1947, all in DD Corr.

36. Minutes of the GEB, 27 January 1947, 6–7.

37. Dubinsky to Bernard M. Baruch, 21 January 1947, and Dubinsky to Jennie Matyas, 5 May 1947, DD Corr.

38. *New York Times*, 31 March 1947; David Dubinsky to Baruch, 8 May 1947, attached to Joseph Rauh to Dubinsky, 12 May 1947, DD Corr.

39. Dubinsky to James Loeb, Jr., 5 June 1947, Hubert H. Humphrey to Dubinsky, 30 October 1947; and Dubinsky to Humphrey, 10 November 1947, all in DD Corr.; Carl Solberg, *Hubert Humphrey: A Biography* (New York: W. W. Norton and Company, 1984), 118.

40. Millis and Brown, *From the Wagner Act to Taft-Hartley*, 271–272.

41. Zieger, *American Workers, American Unions*, 110–111.

42. Dubinsky to Robert A. Taft, 30 January 1947, DD Corr.; Meeting of the GEB, 27 January 1947, 10–11.

43. "Statement of David Dubinsky . . . before the Senate Committee on Labor and Public Welfare, 25 February 1947," Zimmerman Records, ILGWU Archives.

44. Minutes of the GEB, 30 April 1947, 1; Danish, *World of David Dubinsky*, 162–163; Millis and Brown, *From the Wagner Act to Taft-Hartley*, 561–562; William Green to Officers of State Federations of Labor and City Central Bodies, and Green to Harry S. Truman, 7 June 1947, attached to Green to Dubinsky, 10 June 1947, DD Corr.

45. David Dubinsky, "The Taft-Harley Anti-Labor Bill," 4 June 1947, DD Corr.; also in Jay Lovestone Papers, Hoover Institution Archives, Stanford, Calif., Box 339, David Dubinsky Folder.

46. Donovan, *Conflict and Crisis*, 300–303.

47. Fred Woltman, "Memo—David Dubinsky's Reactions to the Meeman Proposals (Confidential)," 8 May 1947, DD Corr.

48. David Dubinsky, "A Warning against Communists in Unions," *New York Times Magazine*, 11 May 1947, 65.

49. ILGWU, *Report and Proceedings*, Twenty-sixth Convention, 1947, 40, 453, 527, 529–532, 685; Minutes of the GEB, 2 September 1947, 3–5; Dubinsky to ILGWU Officers, 20 January 1950, DD Corr.

50. Dubinsky to Ben Hibbs, 19 August 1947, DD Corr.; J. C. Rich, "How the Gar-

ment Unions Licked the Communists," *Saturday Evening Post,* 9 August 1947, 86.

51. Minutes of the GEB, 15 June 1947, 2–3, and 19 June 1947, 1–2; ILGWU, *Report and Proceedings,* Twenty-sixth Convention, 1947, 542–544.

52. Interview with Tyler, 16 November 1994; Minutes of the GEB, 2 September 1947, 15–17; ILGWU, *Report of the GEB,* Twenty-seventh Convention, 1950, 14; Eugenie Anderson to Dubinsky, 27 December 1947, and Humphrey to Dubinsky, 5 January 1948, DD Corr.

53. *New York Times,* 5 and 15 June 1946; *Justice,* 1 July 1946.

54. Joseph M. Jones, *The Fifteen Weeks* (New York: Viking Press, 1955), 17–23; Richard J. Walton, *Henry Wallace, Harry Truman, and the Cold War* (New York: Viking Press, 1976), 147.

55. William Green to Howard Hunter, 10 March 1947; Alexander Karanikas to Dubinsky, 15 March 1947; and Dubinsky to Karanikas, 21 March 1947, DD Corr.

56. "Questions by Eve Curie, Answers by David Dubinsky, . . . ," 6–7, 10 June 1947, attached to Curie to Dubinsky, 14 July 1947, DD Corr.; *New York Times,* 9 July 1947, DD Corr.

57. Schmidt, *Henry A. Wallace,* 28–30; McAuliffe, *Crisis on the Left,* 29; Jones, *Fifteen Weeks,* 31–36, 281–284.

58. Dubinsky and Raskin, *David Dubinsky,* 252, 257; Israel Feinberg to Dubinsky, 24 November 1947; statement of Adolph A. Berle, Jr., attached to Ben Davidson to Dubinsky et al., 24 December 1947, DD Corr.

59. MacDougall, *Gideon's Army,* vol. 1, pp. 284–285; John C. Culver and John Hyde, *American Dreamer: A Life of Henry A. Wallace* (New York: W. W. Norton and Co., 2000), 456–458.

60. Carter, "Pressure from the Left," 325–327.

61. James Loeb, Jr. to Frank W. McCulloch, 9 March 1948; Chester Bowles to Leon Henderson, 5 March 1948, Americans for Democratic Action Papers, State Historical Society of Wisconsin, Madison, Wis. The author thanks Alonzo L. Hamby for sharing these and other ADA documents with him. Alonzo L. Hamby, *Beyond the New Deal: Harry S. Truman and American Liberalism* (New York: Columbia University Press, 1973), 225.

62. James Loeb, Jr., "Memorandum on Conversation with David Dubinsky," 15 March 1948, ADA Papers; "Draft Statement on Political Policy," attached to Charles S. Zimmerman to Dubinsky, 12 April 1948, DD Corr.; Gillon, *Politics and Vision,* 42–47.

63. *New York Times,* 1 September 1948; Minutes of the GEB, 31 August 1948, 1–3.

64. *Justice,* 1 and 15 May 1948.

65. *New York Times,* 2 September 1948.

66. Ibid., 22 and 29 October 1948; *Justice,* 15 October and 1 November 1948; "Address by David Dubinsky . . . October 28, 1948," press release, DD Corr.; "The Participation of the International Ladies Garment Workers Union, Its Political Department, and Its Various Unions in the Liberal Party Election Campaign of 1948" and "Itinerary and Visit of President Truman to New York Oct. 28 and 29," Liberal Party of New York State Papers, New York Public Library.

67. *New York Times,* 29 October 1948.

68. *New York Times,* 4 November 1948; McCullough, *Truman,* 710–711; Hamby, *Beyond the New Deal,* 269.

69. *New York Times,* 4 November 1948.

70. Dubinsky and Raskin, *David Dubinsky,* 251.

71. Varian Fry to Dubinsky, 28 May and 7 June 1945, DD Corr.

72. Alfred Bingham to Murray Gross, 18 November 1945 (copy), attached to Lovestone to Dubinsky, 28 December 1945, DD Corr.

73. Charles S. Zimmerman, "Report on My Trip to European Countries for the Jewish Labor Committee" (MS), 19 April 1946, 7–9, Zimmerman Records, ILGWU Archives.

74. *German-American Trade Union Sol-*

idarity in the Struggle against Fascism, 10–12.

75. Ibid., 40–41; Helmut Wickel to Dubinsky, 5 July 1946, Lovestone Papers, Box 234, Folder 1944–1948 General, 1946, Hoover Archives; Friedrich Stampfer and Alfred Braunthal to Dubinsky, 1 September 1945; Dubinsky to Stampfer, 5 September 1946, DD Corr.

76. Godson, *American Labor and European Politics,* 41; Lovestone to Dubinsky, 10 December 1946, with copies of Rudolph Katz to Dubinsky, 17 November and 2 December 1946, attached; and Lovestone to Dubinsky, 21 January 1947, with copy of Katz to Dubinsky, 4 January 1947, attached, DD Corr.

77. Montana, "The Shambles," 304–309.

78. Ibid., 310–339; Joseph Persico, *Piercing the Reich: The Penetration of Nazi Germany by American Secret Agents during World War II* (New York: Ballantine Books, 1979), 24–25.

79. Joanne Barkan, *Visions of Emancipation: The Italian Workers' Movement since 1945* (New York: Praeger, 1984), 20–21.

80. Daniel L. Horowitz, *The Italian Labor Movement* (Cambridge, Mass.: Harvard University Press, 1963), 186–187; personal interview with Vanni Montana, 19 March 1987; ILGWU, *Report and Proceedings,* Twenty-fifth Convention, 1944, 316, 494–502.

81. Luigi Antonini to Dubinsky, 1 September 1944, attached to Antonini to William Green, 1 September 1944 (copy), DD Corr.

82. Horowitz, *Italian Labor Movement,* 186–198; interview with Montana, 19 March 1987; Barkan, *Visions of Emancipation,* 21; Taft, *A. F. of L. from the Death of Gompers to the Merger,* 395.

83. Horowitz, *Italian Labor Movement,* 202–209; Anthony Carew, *Labour under the Marshall Plan: The Politics of Productivity and the Marketing of Management Science* (Detroit: Wayne State University Press, 1987), 27–28.

84. Horowitz, *Italian Labor Movement,* 210–212; Adolf Sturmthal, *Left of Center: European Labor since World War II* (Urbana: University of Illinois Press, 1983), 89.

85. *Justice,* 15 January 1947; Italian-American Labor Council, "Summary Report 1947," 1, Umhey Correspondence.

86. ILGWU, *Report and Proceedings,* Twenty-sixth Convention, 1947, 387–397; Ronald Filippelli, "Luigi Antonini, the Italian-American Labor Council, and Cold War Politics in Italy, 1943–1949," *Labor History,* 33 (Winter 1992): 116.

87. Horowitz, *Italian Labor Movement,* 213–224.

88. ILGWU, *Report of the GEB,* Twenty-seventh Convention, 1950, 27.

89. *Justice,* 15 December 1948. "You've done a mighty fine job yourself, Father" was Dubinsky's reply according to Victor Riesel, "A Stitch in Time . . . ," *New York Times,* 17 May 1959, sec. 10, p. 6. "Father, you did a great job in the elections" is a later recollection. Dubinsky and Raskin, *David Dubinsky,* 258; Ronald L. Filippelli, *American Labor and Postwar Italy, 1949–1953: A Study of Cold War Politics* (Stanford, Calif.: Stanford University Press, 1989), 142–143, 146–148.

90. *Justice,* 1 and 15 September 1948; *New York Times,* 12 September 1948.

91. Lewis L. Lorwin, *The International Labor Movement: History, Politics, Outlook* (New York: Harper and Brothers, 1953), 245; Irving Brown to Matthew Woll, 10 December 1945, Lovestone Papers, Box 234, Irving Brown Folder, Hoover Archives.

92. Varian Fry to Dubinsky, 27 February 1946, DD Corr.; *Justice,* 1 May 1946; Minutes of the GEB, 29 April 1946, 4.

93. Goulden, *Meany,* 128; ILGWU, *Report of the GEB,* Twenty-seventh Convention, 1950, 28.

94. Irving Brown to Dubinsky, 16 December 1947; Dubinsky to Brown, 7 January 1948; check from ILGWU payable to Jewish Labor Committee, 5 April 1948 (copy), attached to B. Tabachinsky to Dubinsky, 7 April 1948; Hannah Haskel to Brown, 13 May 1948; and Brown to

Haskel, 19 May 1948 (copy), all in Irving Brown Papers, George Meany Memorial Archives

95. Draft of letter by Rene Naegelen, August 1948; Leon Blum to Dubinsky, 16 June 1948, DD Corr.

96. *New York Times,* 31 March 1948.

97. George M. Harrison to William Green, 21 August 1948, DD Corr.

98. Robert Bothereau to Dubinsky, 10 August 1948; Dubinsky to Bothereau, 30 August 1948; and P. Neumayer to Dubinsky, 14 September 1948, DD Corr.; Taft, *A. F. of L. from the Death of Gompers to the Merger,* 394.

99. David Lvovitch and Abraham Alperine to Dubinsky, 3 June 1946; Louis B. Boudin to Dubinsky, 10 January 1947, DD Corr.; *Justice,* 1 August 1948; ILGWU, *Report of the GEB,* Twenty-seventh Convention, 1950, 28.

100. ILGWU, *Report of the GEB,* Twenty-sixth Convention, 1946, 292, 529–530; William Green to Lewis D. Schwellenbach, 13 November 1946 (copy), DD Corr.

101. AFL, *Report of Proceedings,* Sixtysixth Convention, 1947, 36, 474; Taft, *A. F. of L. from the Death of Gompers to the Merger,* 378.

102. Taft, *A. F. of L. from the Death of Gompers to the Merger,* 380–382; Windmuller, *American Labor and the International Labor Movement,* 130–132; Dubinsky to George Meany, 20 February 1948, DD Corr.

103. Itinerary (MS, n.d.), DD Corr.; *Justice,* 15 July and 1 August 1948; "Report by Jay Lovestone. Secretary in Behalf of A. F. of L. Delegation to E. R. P. Trade Union Conference—George Harrison and David Dubinsky—London July 29–30, 1948," 1–6 (MS), DD Corr.

104. *Justice,* 15 September 1948.

105. Jay Lovestone, "Report on Germany . . . in behalf of George Harrison and David Dubinsky . . . ," 1948 (MS), 1, DD Corr.; Lorwin, *International Labor Movement,* 330–331.

106. Lovestone, "Report on Germany," 3.

107. Lorwin, *International Labor Movement,* 250.

108. Ibid. 258–261; Denis MacShane, *International Labour and the Origins of the Cold War* (Oxford: Clarendon Press, 1992), 136–137; Reuther, *Brothers Reuther,* 330–331.

109. Archie Robinson, *George Meany and His Times* (New York: Simon and Schuster, 1981), 138.

110. If the Italians had not been accorded representation, they would have been, Dubinsky noted, "the only important group on the Continent not represented on the Executive," and Italian Communists would have been given "an undeserved issue." Sturmthal, *Left of Center,* 23–24; Dubinsky to Hannah Haskel, 9 December 1949, and Jay Lovestone to Dubinsky, 30 December 1949, DD Corr.

111. David Dubinsky, "A Warning against Communists in Unions," *New York Times Magazine,* 11 May 1947, 7, 61–65; David Dubinsky, "Rift and Realignment in World Labor," *Foreign Affairs,* 27 (January 1949): 232–245; David Dubinsky, "World Labor's New Weapon," *Foreign Affairs,* 28 (April 1950): 451–462; David Dubinsky, "How I Handled the Reds in My Union," *Saturday Evening Post,* 9 May 1953, 31, 145–146; and David Dubinsky, "Instead of the McCarthy Method," *New York Times Magazine,* 26 June 1953, 9, 41–43.

112. George Meany and the *Force Ouvriere* issued immediate denials of this allegation, and Lovestone denied having had any dealings with Braden. Walter Reuther, however, conceded that he had accepted $50,000 from Braden to bolster West German trade unions. Telephone interview with Morris Weisz, 28 August 1995; Thomas W. Braden, "I'm Glad the CIA Is Immoral," *Saturday Evening Post,* 20 May 1967, 10, 12, 14; *New York Times,* 8 and 9 May 1967; James A. Wechsler, "Tangled Web," *New York Post,* 11 May 1967; *John Herling's Labor Letter,* 4 March 1967, 4; "Reuther Explains Use of U.S. Funds to Aid Free Labor Movement in Europe," United Auto Workers Press Release, 7 May 1967,

Reuther Collection, Archives of Labor History and Urban Affairs, Wayne State University.

113. Dubinsky and Raskin, *David Dubinsky,* 259–261.

114. Morgan, *Covert Life,* 196–198; Mario Del Pero "The United States and 'Psychological Warfare' in Italy, 1948–1955," *Journal of American History,* 87 (March 2001): 1309; Filippelli, *American Labor and Postwar Italy,* 132–133; Memorandum, 24 November 1950, Lovestone Papers, Box 528, Carmel Offie Folder, Hoover Archives.

115. Tom Mangold, *Cold Warrior: James Jesus Angleton—The CIA's Master Spy* (New York: Simon and Schuster, 1991), 315.

116. Anthony Carew, "The American Labor Movement in Fizzland: The Free Trade Union Committee and the CIA," *Labor History,* 39 (February 1998): 28–41; personal interview with Morris Weisz, 15 October 1995.

117. Dubinsky and Raskin, *David Dubinsky,* 22; Danish, *World of David Dubinsky,* 272–273.

118. Walter Laqueur, *A History of Zionism* (New York: Holt, Rinehart and Winston, 1972), 198; Ronald Sanders, *The High Walls of Jerusalem: A History of the Balfour Declaration and the Birth of the Jewish Mandate for Palestine* (New York: Holt, Rinehart and Winston, 1984), 606–613.

119. Joan Peters, *From Time Immemorial: The Origins of the Arab-Jewish Conflict over Palestine* (New York: Harper and Row, 1984), 234–239.

120. ILGWU, *Report and Proceedings,* Fifteenth Convention, 1920, 116–117.

121. Laqueur, *History of Zionism,* 306.

122. Samuel Halperin, *The Political World of American Zionism* (Silver Spring, Md.: Information Dynamics, 1985), 60–61; ILGWU, *Report of the GEB,* Twentieth Convention, 1929, 120–121; ILGWU, *Report of the GEB,* Twenty-first Convention, 1932, 88; David Dubinsky and Abraham Baroff to All ILGWU Locals and Members,

3 September 1929, Local 22 Managers' Correspondence, ILGWU Archives; *Justice,* 13, 27 September, 11 and 25 October, and 22 November 1929.

123. ILGWU, *Report of the GEB,* Twenty-third Convention, 1937, 184; ILGWU, *Financial and Statistical Report,* 1 April 1937 to 31 March 1940, 29; Dubinsky to Histadrut, 3 March 1938, DD Corr.

124. Dalia Ofer, *Escaping the Holocaust: Illegal Immigration to the Land of Israel, 1939–1944* (New York: Oxford University Press, 1990), 5–7, 14; Tad Szulc, *The Secret Alliance: The Extraordinary Story of the Rescue of the Jews since World War II* (New York: Farrar, Straus and Giroux, 1991), 6.

125. Ofer, *Escaping the Holocaust,* 318.

126. "The General Federation of Jewish Labor in Palestine—The Histadrut—in Wartime," attached to Israel Mereminski to Abraham Bluestein, 2 February 1944 (copy), attached to Mereminski to Dubinsky, 9 February 1944; Goldie Myerson and David Remex to Dubinsky, 19 June 1943, DD Corr.

127. Ezra Chaikes to Dubinsky, 3 January 1945 and 31 October 1945; Mereminski to Dubinsky, 24 September 1945, 19 October 1945, 20 March 1946, and 1 April 1946; Dubinsky to Mereminski, 20 March 1946; Dubinsky to ILGWU Locals and Joint Boards, 29 March 1946, DD Corr.

128. Allan Bullock, *Ernest Bevin: Foreign Secretary, 1945–1951* (New York: W. W. Norton and Company, 1983), 164.

129. Michael J. Cohen, *Truman and Israel* (Berkeley: University of California Press, 1990), 111–112; Bullock, *Ernest Bevin,* 164, 175.

130. Freda Kirchwey to Dubinsky, 3 October 1945; Dubinsky to Clement Attlee, 6 October 1945; Joseph Sprinzak and Goldie Myerson to Dubinsky, 27 November 1945, DD Corr.; Bullock, *Ernest Bevin,* 175–177, 254–258; Cohen, *Truman and Israel,* 122–130.

131. Bernard Shane to Dubinsky, 27

June 1946; Dubinsky to Attlee, 1 July 1946, DD Corr.

132. Jay Lovestone to Hannah Kreindler, 19 July 1946, Lovestone Papers, Hoover Archives, Box 234, Folder ILGWU '44–'48; *Justice,* 15 November 1946; ILGWU, *Report of the GEB,* Twenty-sixth Convention, 1947, 20–21; AFL, *Summarized Report of Proceedings,* Sixty-fifth Convention, 15 October 1946, 26.

133. Bullock, *Ernest Bevin,* 333–334.

134. Israel Mereminski to Dubinsky, 19 August 1946; Israel Mereminski and Joseph Mereminski to Dubinsky, 16 November 1946, DD Corr.; Minutes of the GEB, 9 September 1946, 6; *New York Times,* 8 August 1946.

135. Minutes of the GEB, 2 September 1947, 6; Dubinsky to Green, 30 September 1947; Green to Dubinsky, 1 October 1947, DD Corr.

136. AFL, *Report of Proceedings,* Sixty-sixth Convention, 1947, 611–617.

137. Cohen, *Truman and Israel,* 149–170; Roger Baldwin to Hannah Haskell [*sic*], 27 November 1947; Matthew Woll to Hugues Le Gallais, 28 November 1947, DD Corr.

138. Louis Nelson to Jacob Pat, 3 December 1947, Local 155 Managers' Records, ILGWU Archives; Nelson to Dubinsky, 3 December 1947, DD Corr.

139. *Justice,* 15 December 1947; Danish, *World of David Dubinsky,* 275–276.

140. Dubinsky to Nelson, 12 December 1947, Local 155 Managers' Records.

141. *Justice,* 15 March and 15 April 1948; Danish, *World of David Dubinsky,* 276–277; "Comments by President Dubinsky for the Demonstration of Cloakmakers of the Joint Board in Manhattan Center, Monday, March 1, 1948" (Yiddish), in New York Cloak Joint Board Records, ILGWU Archives.

142. Walter Isaacson and Evan Thomas, *The Wise Men: Six Friends and the World They Made* (New York: Simon and Schuster, 1986), 451–453; Clark Clifford, with Richard Holbrooke, *Counsel to the President: A Memoir* (New York: Random

House, 1991), 3–25; Dubinsky to Chaim Weizmann, 17 May 1948, and Weizmann to Dubinsky, 20 May 1948, DD Corr.

143. Minutes of the GEB, 7 June 1948, 10; Minutes of the GEB, 21 December 1948, 6; photocopy of check number B1226 for $1,000,000, dated 25 June 1948, signed by David Dubinsky and payable to United Palestine Appeal, DD Corr.; Golda Meir, *My Life* (New York: G. P. Putnam's Sons, 1975), 233–236; Danish, *World of David Dubinsky,* 277; *Justice,* 15 June and 15 December 1948.

144. James G. McDonald to Dubinsky, 1 October 1948, DD Corr.; Minutes of the GEB, 21 December 1948, 13, with attached "Report by Vice-President Charles Zimmerman on His Trip to Israel Submitted to the General Executive Board, December 22nd, 1948," 7–8, 10–11.

145. Dubinsky to Herbert Bayard Swope, 16 February 1950; Charles S. Zimmerman to Dubinsky, 17 February 1950; "Background Information" (MS, n.d.), DD Corr.; ILGWU, *Report of the GEB,* Twenty-seventh Convention, 1950, 27; *New York Times,* 9 March 1950; Danish, *World of David Dubinsky,* 185.

146. Its mission largely accomplished, in 1966 the corporation decided to go out of business. Dubinsky to Joseph Schlossberg, 17 June 1966; unsigned draft of Dubinsky [?] letter, 27 September 1966; "Application of Directors of Amun-Israeli Housing Corporation for Order to Transfer Assets to the Cultural, Medical Help and Assistance Fund of the General Federation of Jewish Labor in Eretz-Israel," 6 June 1967, DD Corr.

147. Jewish Labor Committee, "Ten Years of Child Adoption" (MS, 1957); Malmgreen, "Labor and the Holocaust," 30; ILGWU, *Report and Proceedings,* Twenty-sixth Convention, 1947, 320; *Justice,* 15 July 1948.

148. Leonard Dinnerstein, *America and the Survivors of the Holocaust* (New York: Columbia University Press, 1982), 163–176.

149. Minutes of the GEB, New York

Members, 31 August 1948; Minutes of the GEB, 21 December 1948, 8–9; Joseph Godson to ILGWU, 26 September 1949, DD Corr.

NOTES TO CHAPTER 16

1. "Little David, the Giant," *Time,* 29 August 1949, 12; Samuel Lubell, "Dictator in Sheep's Clothing," *Saturday Evening Post,* 19 November 1949, 19; Harry Crone to David Dubinsky, 27 October 1949, DD Corr.
2. A. H. Raskin, "David Dubinsky: Labor Statesman," *New Leader,* 10 March 1952, 9.
3. *Justice,* 1 April 1947.
4. Lubell, "Dictator in Sheep's Clothing," 21; Dubinsky and Raskin, *David Dubinsky,* 209–210; Win Booth to Robert T. Elson, 13 and 15 August 1949, Bell Collection; interview with William Ross, 1 June 1955, 166, ILGWU Archives; Annelise Orleck, *Common Sense and a Little Fire: Women and Working-Class Politics in the United States, 1900–1935* (Chapel Hill: University of North Carolina Press, 1995), 200.
5. Booth to Elson, 15 August 1949; Hasia Diner, *In the Almost Promised Land: American Jews and Blacks, 1915–1935* (Baltimore: Johns Hopkins University Press, 1995), 216, 221; "Puerto Rican and Negro Members, ILGWU New York City Locals December 1952" (MS), Max D. Danish Collection, ILGWU Archives; Laurentz, "Racial/Ethnic Conflict in the New York City Garment Industry," 218.
6. Victor Riesel, "Garment Workers Country Club," *Survey Graphic,* September 1948, 388–391.
7. ILGWU, *Financial and Statistical Report,* 1 April 1947 to 31 March 1950, 49; Booth to Elson, 15 August 1949.
8. Telephone interview with Emil Schlesinger, 1 March 1988.
9. ILGWU, *Report of the GEB,* Twenty-seventh Convention, 1950, 97–99; *Justice,* 1 October 1948.
10. Minutes of the GEB, New York Mem-

bers, 11 May 1949, 1–2; ILGWU, *Report of the GEB,* Twenty-seventh Convention, 1950, 99–100; *Catholic Worker,* June 1949; Walter Goodman, "Muscling In on Labor," *New Republic,* 30 April 1956, 11–12; Bruce Bliven, "Murder on Thirty-fifth Street," *New Republic,* 20 June 1949, 11–12.
11. *New York Daily Mirror,* 22 June 1949; Goodman, "Muscling In on Labor," 11–12; Julius Hochman to Frank S. Hogan [5 August 1952 (?)], New York Dress Joint Board Records; Minutes of the GEB, ILGWU, 24 March 1952, 10; ILGWU, *Report of the GEB,* Twenty-eighth Convention, 1953, 93–94.
12. Gus Tyler, *Look for the Union Label: A History of the International Ladies' Garment Workers' Union* (Armonk, N.Y.: M. E. Sharpe, 1995), 241; *Justice,* 1 June 1959.
13. ILGWU, *Report of the GEB,* Twenty-sixth Convention, 1947, 186–187; ILGWU, *Report of the GEB,* Twenty-seventh Convention, 1950, 199–200.
14. Dubinsky to John T. Burke, 20 June 1949; Burke to Dubinsky, 27 June 1949; Dubinsky to Daniel J. Tobin, 29 September 1949; Tobin to Dubinsky, 3 October 1949, DD Corr.
15. Schlesinger, "Transcript on Racketeering," 7.
16. Memorandum on John Dioguardi a.k.a. John Dio, 16 January 1952, and "Confidential" report on Samuel Berger, 13 March 1952; and Robert W. Greene to Charles S. Zimmerman, 23 March 1953, DD Corr.; ILGWU, *Report of the GEB,* Twenty-eighth Convention, 1953, 200; *New York Times,* 16 August 1954; affidavit by David Dubinsky, 9 August 1957, attached to Dubinsky to John L. McClellan, 9 August 1957, DD Corr.; Goodman, "Muscling In on Labor," 11; Westbrook Pegler, "Dubinsky Knew About," *New York Journal-American,* 21 February 1957, 25.
17. *New York Daily News,* 8 July 1949; *New York Herald Tribune,* 9 July 1949.
18. *New York Journal-American,* 1 August, 7 and 15 October, and 28 November 1952.

19. *New York Journal-American,* 25 April 1952; *New York Daily Mirror,* 25 April 1952.

20. Goodman, "Muscling In on Labor," 11–12; "AFL Needs Thorough Purging," *New Jersey Labor Herald,* March 1952, attached to George Meany to Dubinsky, 4 April 1952, DD Corr.

21. Minutes of the EC, AFL, 19 May 1952, 65–68, Meany Archives; *New York Times,* 27 May 1952.

22. Minutes of the EC, AFL, 14 August 1952, 51–60, Meany Archives; *New York Herald Tribune,* 16 August 1952; AFL, *Report of the Executive Council,* Seventy-first Convention, 1952, 21; John Hutchinson, *The Imperfect Union: A History of Corruption in American Trade Unions* (New York: E. P. Dutton and Co., 1970), 294–295.

23. Goulden, *Meany,* 178–180.

24. Dubinsky to Meany, 30 December 1952; Raskin interviews, cass. 48, p. 9.

25. Meany to Dubinsky, 15 January 1952, DD Corr.

26. Edward Rosenbaum, "The Expulsion of the International Longshoremen's Association from the American Federation of Labor" (Ph.D. diss., University of Wisconsin, 1954), 513–514 and appendix B, iv–vi.

27. Ibid., 572–603; Hutchinson, *Imperfect Union,* 296–297; Dubinsky and Raskin, *David Dubinsky,* 165; Raskin interviews, cass. 48, p. 9.

28. Goulden, *Meany,* 192–194; Hutchinson, *Imperfect Union,* 297–303; Rosenbaum, "Expulsion of the International Longshoremen's Association from the American Federation of Labor," 651–681.

29. "Report to David Dubinsky from Gus Tyler In Re: ILGWU 1948 Campaign Committee," Appendix C, DD Corr.; Robert T. Elson to Win Booth, 12 August 1949, Bell Collection.

30. "Enrollment Figures of the Liberal Party" (n.d., MS), Liberal Party Papers.

31. A. H. Raskin, "Alex Rose Revisited: Theme Talk" (MS), 4 April 1978, 3, DD Corr.

32. Interview with Donald Harrington by Chris McNickle, 28 September 1988, 2,

Robert F. Wagner Collection, La Guardia-Wagner Archives, La Guardia Community College, New York.

33. Schwarz, *Liberal,* 293.

34. Alex Rose, "Preface" to memoir (MS), 9 July 1976. In possession of Herbert Rose.

35. Oral History interview with Evelyn Dubrow by Alice M. Hoffman, 20 March 1979, 9, Meany Archives.

36. *New York Post,* 14 April 1949; Schwarz, *Liberal,* 293; Nathan Glazer and Daniel P. Moynihan, *Beyond the Melting Pot: The Negroes, Puerto Ricans, Jews, Italians, and Irish of New York City* (2d ed.; Cambridge: MIT Press, 1970), 214; "The Reminiscences of Warren Moscow," Oral History Research Office, Columbia University, 1951, 11; Chris McNickle, *To Be Mayor of New York: Ethnic Politics in the City* (New York: Columbia University Press, 1999), 85.

37. In 1946 the Liberals nominated Teachers College professor George S. Counts for senator. "The Reminiscences of Ludwig Teller," Oral History Research Office, Columbia University, 1963, 267–268.

38. Nevins, *Herbert H. Lehman and His Era,* 308–311; Dubinsky and Raskin, *David Dubinsky,* 288–289.

39. Press releases, Citywide Independent Citizens Committee for the Reelection of O'Dwyer-Joseph-Impellitteri, 22 and 27 September 1949; and Jacob S. Potofsky to Members of ACWA, 26 October 1949, DD Corr.; George Meany to Dubinsky, 2 November 1949, Meany Correspondence, Meany Archives.

40. Press releases (mimeographed), "Leader in Own Union, a Liberal Party Founder, Disputes Dubinsky Claims," 16 October 1949; and "Don't Make a Mistake, says Antonini—Vote Row 'B' for O'Dwyer, Lehman and the 'Fair Deal'" (n.d.), DD Corr; Minutes of the GEB, 14 November 1949, 11–12.

41. McNickle, *To Be Mayor of New York,* 80; *New York Daily Mirror,* 10 November 1949.

42. Dubinsky to Antonini, 9 November 1949, DD Corr.; "The Reminiscences of Newbold Morris," Oral History Research Office, Columbia University, 1950, 71.

43. William O'Dwyer, *Beyond the Golden Door,* ed. Paul O'Dwyer (Jamaica, N.Y.: St. John's University, 1987), 294, 327, 333–338.

44. Warren Moscow, *The Last of the Big-Time Bosses: The Life and Times of Carmine DeSapio and the Rise and Fall of Tammany Hall* (New York: Stein and Day, 1971), 90–91; Smith, *Thomas E. Dewey and His Times,* 565; Salvatore J. La Gumina, *New York at Mid-Century: The Impellitteri Years* (Westport, Conn.: Greenwood Press, 1992), 105–109; *Justice,* 15 September 1950.

45. McNickle, *To Be Mayor of New York,* 83–84; Charles L. Fontenay, *Estes Kefauver: A Biography* (Knoxville: University of Tennessee Press, 1980), 183.

46. *New York Times,* 6 November 1951.

47. Dubinsky and Raskin, *David Dubinsky,* 308–309; McNickle, *To Be Mayor of New York,* 88; "The Reminiscences of Ben Davidson," 308; *New York Times,* 6 June 1951.

48. *New York Times,* 1, 2, and 6 June 1951 and 7 November 1951; La Gumina, *New York at Mid-Century,* 117–130.

49. McNickle, *To Be Mayor of New York,* 88; *New York Times,* 9 December 1951.

50. Gillon, *Politics and Vision,* 83–84.

51. John Bartlow Martin, *Adlai Stevenson of Illinois: The Life of Adlai E. Stevenson* (Garden City, N.Y.: Anchor Press/Doubleday, 1977), 546.

52. Rudy Abramson, *Spanning the Century: The Life of W. Averell Harriman, 1891–1986* (New York: William Morrow and Company, 1992), 497; Nevins, *Herbert H. Lehman and His Era,* 331; Schwarz, *Liberal,* 295; Adolf A. Berle, Diary file, 28 July 1952, 1–10, Berle Papers.

53. Minutes of the GEB, New York Members, 30 July 1952, 2.

54. *Justice,* 15 September 1952; *New York Times,* 5 September 1952; Minutes of the GEB, 2 September 1952, 12.

55. *New York World-Telegram and Sun,* 9 December 1952; Berle to Ben Davidson, 12 November 1952, Liberal Party of New York State Papers, New York Public Library; ILGWU, *Report of the GEB,* Twenty-eighth Convention, 1953, 40.

56. Berle Diary, 23 April 1953, Berle Papers; Beatrice Bishop Berle and Travis Beal Jacobs (eds.), *Navigating the Rapids, 1918–1971: From the Papers of Adolf A. Berle* (New York: Harcourt Brace Jovanovich, 1973), 619; *New York Times,* 30 May 1953, 26 and 27 June 1953, and 1 and 3 July 1953.

57. *New York Times,* 21 and 23 July 1953, 7 August 1953, and 16 and 17 September 1953; interview with Robert F. Wagner by Chris McNickle, 28 March 1988, Robert F. Wagner Collection, La Guardia-Wagner Archives.

58. *New York Times,* 2, 23, and 24 September 1953.

59. *New York Times,* 28 and 29 September 1953; Victor Riesel, "Inside Labor" (mimeographed press release), 3 October 1953, 1, attached to Riesel to Hannah Haskel, 6 October 1953, DD Corr.

60. *New York Times,* 15 October 1953.

61. *New York Times,* 2 October 1953, 4 November 1953; Raskin interviews, cass. 47, pp. 46–47.

62. John L. Childs to Ben Davidson, 19 November 1953, and Adolf A. Berle to Davidson, 17 November 1953, Liberal Party Papers; *New York World-Telegram and Sun,* 4 November 1953.

63. *Justice,* 1 March 1954; Childs to Davidson, 27 April 1954, Liberal Party Papers.

64. "May 25, 1954, DD Address at Liberal Party Dinner, Hotel Commodore" (MS), DD Corr.; *Justice,* 1 June 1954.

65. Dubinsky to Harry Lang, 27 May 1954, DD Corr.

66. Ben Davidson, notes on Dubinsky speech, 8 June 1954, attached to Davidson to Members of State Policy Committee, 2 June 1954, Liberal Party Papers.

67. Alex Rose, "Harriman Campaign—1954" (MS), in possession of Herbert Rose; Moscow, *Last of the Big-Time Bosses*, 122–125; Schwarz, *Liberal*, 296; Abramson, *Spanning the Century*, 505–515; Houston Irvine Flournoy, "The Liberal Party in New York State" (Ph.D. diss., Princeton University, 1956), 165.

68. *Justice*, 15 December 1954; Flournoy, "Liberal Party in New York State," 165.

69. *New York Journal-American*, 23 November 1954; Berle, Diary, 17 November 1954, Berle Papers; Berle and Jacobs, *Navigating the Rapids*, 638.

70. Dubinsky to W. Averell Harriman, 17 December 1954 (copy), DD Corr.; Minutes of the GEB, 21 March 1955, 9.

71. Flournoy, "Liberal Party in New York State," 104–105.

NOTES TO CHAPTER 17

1. ILGWU, *Report and Proceedings*, Twenty-eighth Convention, 1953, 296; David Dubinsky, "A Man and a Union," *New Leader*, 1 June 1953, 13.

2. Tyler, *Look for the Union Label*, 205–206.

3. Ibid., 205; ILGWU, *Report of the GEB*, Twenty-seventh Convention, 1950, 225–226; Dubinsky and Raskin, *David Dubinsky*, 212–213.

4. Raskin interviews, cass. 31, p. 1.

5. Ibid., 1–2.

6. Minutes of the GEB, 6 June 1949, 23–26.

7. Herberg, "Jewish Labor Movement in the United States," 74; "Puerto Rican and Negro Members, ILGWU New York City Locals December 1952."

8. Minutes of the GEB, 17 April 1950, 6; ILGWU, *Report of the GEB*, Twenty-seventh Convention, 1950, 227–228; *New York Herald Tribune*, 2 May 1950.

9. ILGWU, *Report of the GEB*, Thirty-first Convention, 1962, 150–151.

10. Dubinsky and Raskin, *David Dubinsky*, 212–214.

11. Ibid., 214–215; Gus Tyler to Dubinsky, 17 September 1962, DD Corr.

12. Jennie Matyas to Dubinsky, 25 February 1950, DD Corr.

13. Dubinsky to Louis Levy, 6 October 1950, DD Corr.; *Justice*, 15 October 1950; Isidor Stenzor, "Biographical Notes on Over a Half Century of a Stormy but Interesting and Rewarding Life" (MS, Los Angeles, 1974), 32–33, ILGWU Archives.

14. "Resolution Pertaining to 1962 Elections in Los Angeles Cloak and Dress Sportswear Joint Boards, adopted by General Executive Board, ILGWU, on November 22, 1961" (MS), attached to Louis Stulberg to Isidor Stenzor and John Ulene, 4 December 1961; ILGWU, *Report of the GEB*, Thirty-first Convention, 1962, 123–124; ILGWU, *Report and Proceedings*, Thirty-first Convention, 1962, 278–279.

15. David Dubinsky, "How I Handled the Reds in My Union," *Saturday Evening Post*, 9 May 1953, 31, 145–146; and "Instead of the McCarthy Method," *New York Times Magazine*, 26 July 1953, 9, 41–43.

16. ILGWU, *Report and Proceedings*, Twenty-eighth Convention, 1953, 302, 372.

17. George Field to Dubinsky, 5 May 1954; Harry Crone to Dubinsky, 30 September 1954; and Morris Novik to Dubinsky, 28 June 1954, DD Corr.

18. Goulden, *Meany*, 181–184; Arthur J. Goldberg, *AFL-CIO: Labor United* (New York: McGraw-Hill Book Company, 1956), 74–79.

19. Goldberg, *AFL-CIO*, 78–79; AFL, Minutes of the Executive Council, 21 May 1953, Meany Archives.

20. Oral History interviews with Leon Stein, 8 March 1979, 8; A. H. Raskin, 18 April 1979, 4; Henry Fleisher, 4 May 1979, 15; George L.-P. Weaver, number 1, 18 May 1979, 20; and Arthur J. Goldberg, 9 October 1979, 1, 3, AFL-CIO Merger Interviews, Meany Archives; *New York Times*, 2 January 1951.

21. Oral History interviews with Charles S. Zimmerman, 8 May 1979, 2; Leon Stein, 8 March 1979, 9; Jack Conway, 23 May

388 | *Notes to Chapter 17*

1979, 10, and Abe Raskin, 18 April 1979, 7, 24, AFL-CIO Merger Interviews.

22. Oral History interviews with Jack Barbash, 2 and 9 February 1979, 5, 15; Evelyn Dubrow, 20 March 1979 and 23 May 1979, 5; A. J. Hayes, 4 May 1979, 10, AFL-CIO Merger Interviews.

23. Goldberg, *AFL-CIO*, 80–83; *AFL-CIO No-Raiding Agreement* (Washington, D.C.: American Federation of Labor, 1954), 2, 7–11; *Justice*, 15 June 1954; Minutes of the EC, AFL, 9 February 1955, 67, Meany Archives.

24. Minutes of the GEB, 14 September 1955, 7.

25. Minutes of the EC, AFL, 1 February 1955, 67–72; *American Federationist*, March 1955, 3–10.

26. *Justice*, 15 February 1955.

27. ILGWU, Report and Proceedings, Twenty-seventh Convention, 1950, 530–532.

28. Joel Schwartz, *The New York Approach: Robert Moses, Urban Liberals, and the Redevelopment of the Inner City* (Columbus: Ohio State University Press, 1993), 136, 176; Minutes of the GEB, 21 August 1950, 4–5; Minutes of the GEB, New York Members, 15 March 1951; "The Reminiscences of Jacob Samuel Potofsky," 187–189, Oral History Research Office, Columbia University, 1965.

29. Minutes of the GEB, 2 September 1952, 27–28, and 31 August 1953, 30–21; Minutes of the GEB, New York Members, 26 January 1954, 1; 3 February 1954, 1; and 25 May 1954, 1–2; ILGWU, *Report of the GEB*, Twenty-ninth Convention, 1956, 193; "The Reminiscences of Abraham Kazan," 321–325; "The Reminiscences of Jacob Samuel Potofsky," 189–190; Tyler, *Look for the Union Label*, 259.

30. *Justice*, 1 December 1953; Danish, *World of David Dubinsky*, 305–306; Schwartz, *New York Approach*, 136.

31. Schwartz, *New York Approach*, 177; *Justice*, 1 November 1955; Danish, *World of David Dubinsky*, 306–307.

32. J. H. Oldenbroek to Jay Lovestone, 26 April 1950 (copy); Oldenbroek to Du-

binsky, 18 July 1950 and 2 October 1950; and Dubinsky to Oldenbroek, 21 July 1950 (copy), DD Corr.; Minutes of the GEB, 21 August 1950, 3, 22.

33. Dubinsky and Raskin, *David Dubinsky*, 246; Danish, *World of David Dubinsky*, 308–309.

34. William Green and George Meany to Dubinsky, 23 April 1951 (copy), DD Corr.

35. *Justice*, 1 July 1951.

36. "DD—Trip to Europe—1951" (MS) and "Resolution on I.C.F.T.U. Executive Council Meeting November 1951 Adopted by the Executive Council of the A. F. of L. February 2, 1952—Miami Beach, Florida" (MS), 2–3, DD Corr.; Reuther, *Brothers Reuther*, 331, 350; Dubinsky and Raskin, *David Dubinsky*, 256; Minutes of the GEB, 10 September 1951, 12, and 2 September 1952, 5; personal interview with Victor G. Reuther, 26 August 1986; *New York Times*, 5, 10, and 11 July 1951; 15 August 1951; 25 September 1951; and 12 November 1951; Windmuller, *Labor and the International Labor Movement*, 189–190; Taft, *A. F. of L. from the Death of Gompers to the Merger*, 396–397; Filippelli, *American Labor and Postwar Italy*, 193–194.

37. "Resolution on I.C.F.T.U. Executive Council Meeting November 1951," 3–5; Taft, *A. F. of L. from the Death of Gompers to the Merger*, 392–393.

38. Windmuller, *American Labor and the International Labor Movement*, 192–217; *New York World-Telegram and Sun*, 21 May 1952; *Justice*, 1 June 1952; Goulden, *Meany*, 226; Anne Stolt to Dubinsky, 7 July 1953, and Anne Larkin to Dubinsky, 20 July 1953, DD Corr.

39. *Washington Times-Herald*, 20 September 1953.

40. *New York Times*, 6 March 1955; 5, 6, 7, and 10 May 1955; *Justice*, 15 May 1955, 1 June 1955, and 1 August 1955.

41. *Justice*, 15 June 1955 and 1 July 1955; Dubinsky message to Soviet Workers (MS), 25 May 1955; and "David Dubinsky and S. Romualdi at the FDR Institute at Mondello" (translation, MS), DD Corr; Minutes of the GEB, 3 October 1955, 4–5.

42. ILGWU, *Report of the GEB,* Twenty-ninth Convention, 1956, 65.

43. Ibid., 190; Tyler, *Look for the Union Label,* 265.

44. ILGWU, *Report of the GEB,* Twenty-ninth Convention, 1956, 14–15; Dubinsky, policy statement, 31 October 1955, Jay Lovestone Papers, Meany Archives; Tyler, *Look for the Union Label,* 266; Diary of David Gingold, 8 November 1954; 19 and 25 April 1955 and 13 July 1955, ILGWU Archives; Minutes of the GEB, 3 October 1955, 8; *Justice,* 15 November 1955.

45. Minutes of the GEB, 21 March 1955, 6–7; "Statement of David Dubinsky . . . April 20, 1955," Lovestone Papers, Meany Archives; Danish, *World of David Dubinsky,* 232; ILGWU Political Department, "The Campaign to Raise the Minimum Wage, January to July, 1955" (MS, 1955), 1–9, attached to Minutes of the GEB, 3 October 1995.

46. *Justice,* 15 July 1955; Dubinsky to Louis Stulberg, 30 June 1955, Local 62 Managers' Correspondence, ILGWU Archives; ILGWU Political Department, "Campaign to Raise the Minimum Wage," 9–10; Danish, *World of David Dubinsky,* 234–236; Miguel Garriga to Peter M. Mc-Gavin, 22 January 1954; McGavin to Meany, 2 February 1954; Meany to Dubinsky, 4 February 1954; and Dubinsky to Meany, 4 February 1954, Meany Papers; Jay Lovestone to Dubinsky, 19 January 1956, Lovestone Papers, Meany Archives; *Justice,* 1 and 15 January 1956.

NOTES TO CHAPTER 18

1. ILGWU, *Report and Proceedings,* Twenty-seventh Convention, 1950, 254, 320, 509–511; [Max D. Danish and Leon Stein], *ILGWU News-History, 1900–1950* (New York: ILGWU, 1950).

2. ILGWU, *Report and Proceedings,* Twenty-seventh Convention, 1950, 714.

3. MS [June 1957], and Dubinsky to Harry Lang, 7 August 1956, DD Corr.; Deed: Bargain and Sale—Individual, Louis

Berg to 1710 Broadway, dated 7 November 1955 and recorded 14 November 1955, Suffolk County, New York, copy courtesy of Joseph Kissane.

4. Gingold Diaries, 12–18 June 1957, Northeast Department Records, ILGWU Archives; *Justice,* 1 July 1957.

5. Minutes of the GEB, 17 June 1957, 7–9; MS [June 1957], DD Corr.; Hutchinson, *Imperfect Union,* 231; Robert F. Kennedy, *The Enemy Within* (New York: Harper and Row, 1960), 10; John L. Mc-Clellan, *Crime without Punishment* (New York: Duell, Sloan and Pearce, 1962), 14–15.

6. Indenture, between David and Emma Dubinsky and 1710 Broadway, Inc., dated 29 August 1960 and recorded 1 February 1961, Suffolk County, New York, copy courtesy of Joseph Kissane. As then assistant to the president Wilbur Daniels would recall in 1985, "at some point money went from Dubinsky to the union for the house." Personal interview with Wilbur Daniels, 23 May 1985. ILGWU attorney Morris Glushien recalled in 1985 that Dubinsky was not initially aware that the house was taxable as income as a reward for his services; it was "a form of remuneration." Advised by attorney Elias Lieberman, Dubinsky paid taxes after its formal receipt. Personal interview with Morris Glushien, 18 April 1985.

7. *Justice,* 1 May 1957.

8. *New York Times,* 16 May 1957; Danish, *World of David Dubinsky,* 307; ILGWU, *Report of the GEB,* Thirtieth Convention, 1959, 64.

9. ILGWU, *Report of the GEB,* Twenty-ninth Convention, 1956, 194, 303, 453–454.

10. "The Reminiscences of Abraham Kazan," 404–405; Minutes of the GEB, 14 January 1957, 27 and 18 November 1957, 2; ILGWU, *Report of the GEB,* Thirtieth Convention, 1959, 60; Elias Lieberman to William Girden, 8 September 1960, DD Corr.

11. *Justice,* 1 April 1959; "The Reminiscences of Abraham Kazan," 406–420;

Lieberman to Dubinsky, 17 August 1960 and 2 May 1961, and Adolph Held to Dubinsky, 18 April 1961, DD Corr.

12. ILGWU, *Report and Proceedings,* Thirtieth Convention, 1959, 256–257.

13. Personal interview with Leon Stein, 5 June 1984.

14. *New York Times,* 8 March 1958; David Melman, "The Cause and Effect of the ILGWU Dress Industry General Strike of 1958" (master's thesis, Baruch College, City University of New York and New York State School of Industrial and Labor Relations, Cornell University, 1994), 1. The author thanks David Melman for giving him a copy of his thesis.

15. Melman, "Cause and Effect of the . . . General Strike of 1958," 18–19.

16. Ibid., 22; Harry Crone, *35 Northeast: A Short History of the Northeast Department International Ladies' Garment Workers' Union, AFL-CIO Based on the Reminiscences and Diaries of David Gingold and Official ILGWU Records* (New York: Northeast Department, ILGWU, 1970), 102; Minutes of the GEB, 18 November 1957, 10.

17. Melman, "Cause and Effect of the . . . General Strike of 1958," 23–31; Crone, *35 Northeast,* 104–105; Dubinsky and Raskin, *David Dubinsky,* 142–143; Minutes of the GEB, 12 May 1958, 1–7, and 24 August 1959, 1; ILGWU, *Report of the GEB,* Thirtieth Convention, 1959, 121, and *Report of the GEB,* Thirty-first Convention, 1962, 90.

18. Gerald Zahavi, "Fighting Left-Wing Unionism: Voices from the Opposition to the IFLWU in Fulton County, New York," in *The CIO's Left-Led Unions,* ed. Steve Russwurm (New Brunswick, N.J.: Rutgers University Press, 1992), 160; Levenstein, *Communism, Anticommunism, and the CIO,* 324; David Caute, *The Great Fear: The Anti-Communist Purge under Truman and Eisenhower* (New York: Simon and Schuster, 1978), 357.

19. Klehr and Haynes, *American Communist Movement,* 141; Minutes of the GEB, 3 October 1955, 13.

20. Dubinsky to George Meany, 29 November 1954, Meany Papers, Meany Archives.

21. Max Federman to Meany, 29 November 1954, Meany Papers, Meany Archives.

22. Lovestone to Meany, 13 December 1954, Meany Papers, Meany Archives.

23. AFL press release, 15 December 1954, DD Corr.

24. Minutes of the GEB, 22 March 1955; *Women's Wear Daily,* 25 March 1955; Ben Gold, *Memoirs* (New York: William Howard Publishers, n.d.), 185–186.

25. *New York Times,* 27 March 1955 and 10 August 1955; Patrick E. Gorman to Dubinsky, 26 and 27 July 1955 and 16 and 24 August 1955; Dubinsky to Gorman, 26 July 1955, DD Corr.; *Women's Wear Daily,* 15 August 1955; Gold, *Memoirs* 187–188.

26. Earl W. Jimerson and Patrick E. Gorman to Secretaries of Amalgamated Meat Cutters and Butcher Workmen of North America Local Unions, 28 October 1955, DD Corr.

27. *Investigation of Welfare Funds and Racketeering: Report of a Special Subcommittee to the Committee on Education and Labor* (Washington, D.C.: Government Printing Office, 1954), 13.

28. Minutes of the EC, AFL, 9 February 1954, 55–57, Meany Archives.

29. David Dubinsky, "Safeguarding Union Welfare Funds," *American Federationist,* July 1954, 12–13; Danish, *World of David Dubinsky,* 194–195.

30. ILGWU, *Report of the GEB,* Twenty-eighth Convention, 1953, 200; Gingold Diaries, 15–16 June 1954 and 13–16 July 1954.

31. Minutes of the EC, AFL, 2 February 1955, 21; Meany Archives; Danish, *World of David Dubinsky,* 196.

32. AFL-CIO, *Proceedings,* First Constitutional Convention, 1955, 98–99; Hutchinson, *Imperfect Union,* 305, 431.

33. ILGWU, press release, 5 April 1956, DD Corr.; *Justice,* 15 April 1956; *New York Times,* 5 January 1995; ILGWU, *Report of*

the GEB, Twenty-sixth Convention, 1946, 230.

34. "Labor," *Fortune,* May 1956, 215–218. Fay had physically assaulted Dubinsky during the 1940 AFL convention. See chapter 13, note 35.

35. *New York Herald Tribune,* 31 May 1956.

36. Dubinsky to A. J. Hayes, 12 July 1956, DD Corr.

37. Minutes of the Executive Council, AFL-CIO, 6 June 1956, 10–11, Meany Archives.

38. Minutes of the Executive Council, AFL-CIO, 7 August 1956, 4–6; "A Modest Housecleaning," *Fortune,* September 1956, 207–208, 210.

39. Minutes of the Executive Council, AFL-CIO, 27 August 1956, 12, and 31 January 1957, 12, 55–67.

40. Minutes of the Executive Council, AFL-CIO, 20 May 1957, 12, 14, 73–77.

41. *New York Times,* 4 February 1957.

42. *New York Times,* 12 April 1957.

43. Minutes of the Executive Council, AFL-CIO, 29 March 1957, 1–2.

44. Louis B. Nichols to Clyde A. Tolson, 9 May 1952, Federal Bureau of Investigation File 100-222930, obtained via Freedom of Information Act.

45. Nichols to Tolson, 21 March 1957, FBI File 100-222930. The FBI file on Manager Samuel Berger of Local 102 is on microfilm and mainly illegible. Emil P. Moschella to the author, 27 April 1987 and 15 October 1987; Minutes of the GEB, 17 June 1954, 4.

46. ILGWU, *Report of the GEB,* Thirtieth Convention, 1959, 116; unsigned memorandum, 31 July 1957, DD Corr.; Hutchinson, *Imperfect Union,* 312; *New York Daily Compass,* 16 July 1952.

47. Dubinsky and Raskin, *David Dubinsky,* 166; *Justice,* 15 February 1957; Hutchinson, *Imperfect Union,* 435–436.

48. *New York Times,* 1 August 1957; "Select Committee Extracts" (MS, 1957), 1–4, DD Corr.

49. *New York Herald Tribune,* 2 August 1957.

50. Dubinsky to John L. McClellan, 9 August 1957, with sworn affidavit of same date attached; and Wilbur Daniels, "Memorandum of Conversation [with Francis Hensen]," 1 August 1957, DD Corr.; unsigned FBI memorandum, "David Dubinsky," 11 September 1964, 3, FBI File 100-222930; Minutes of the Executive Council, AFL-CIO, 12 August 1957, 1–2, 21–25.

51. *New York Times,* 9 August 1957.

52. Ralph James and Estelle James, *James Hoffa and the Teamsters* (Princeton, N.J.: D. Van Nostrand and Company, 1965), 20; Hutchinson, *Imperfect Union,* 333.

53. Minutes of the Executive Council, AFL-CIO, 20 May 1957, 2–4.

54. James and James, *James Hoffa and the Teamsters,* 20, 22.

55. Goulden, *Meany,* 244–251; Hutchinson, *Imperfect Union,* 337–338.

56. Dubinsky and Raskin, *David Dubinsky,* 167–168.

57. *New York Times,* 30 January 1958; ILGWU, *Report of the GEB,* Thirtieth Convention, 1959, 26.

58. Louis Stulberg to All Affiliates of the I.L.G.W.U., 11 February 1958, DD Corr.

59. Minutes of the GEB, 1 December 1959, 1.

60. J. F. Bell, "Corruption and Union Racketeering," *Current History,* June 1959, 346.

61. Herbert S. Parmet, *Jack: The Struggles of John F. Kennedy* (New York: Dial Press, 1980), 417–433.

62. Ibid., 489–497; personal interview with Evelyn Dubrow, 10 June 1985; interview with Dubrow by Lydia Kleiner, 21 August 1976; Melvyn Dubofsky, *The State and Labor in Modern America* (Chapel Hill: University of North Carolina Press, 1994), 219–221; ILGWU, *Report of the GEB,* Thirty-first Convention, 1962, 20; Minutes of the GEB, 24 August 1959, 4; *New York Times,* 4 September 1959; "Current Documents: Proposed Changes, Labor Legislation," *Current History,* September 1959, 173–179; Alan K. McAdams, *Power and Politics in Labor Legislation* (New York:

Columbia University Press, 1964), 244–265.

63. *Report of the GEB,* Twenty-ninth Convention, 1956, 47.

64. ILGWU, *Financial and Statistical Report,* 1 April 1953 to 31 March 1956, 10, 42–47.

65. Herbert S. Parmet, *The Democrats: The Years after FDR* (New York: Oxford University Press, 1976), 130–131.

66. ILGWU, *Report and Proceedings,* Twenty-ninth Convention, 1956, 338.

67. Alex Rose, "Harriman Campaign—1954" (MS, chapter of unfinished memoir, 8 July 1976), 18, in possession of Herbert Rose, New York, N.Y.

68. Abramson, *Spanning the Century,* 534–536.

69. Ibid., 538; Rose, "Harriman Campaign—1954," 18–21; *Hat Worker,* 15 June 1956.

70. "The Reminiscences of Ben Davidson," 388; Schwarz, *Liberal,* 296–297; Fontenay, *Estes Kefauver,* 263–283.

71. *Justice,* 15 November 1957.

72. *Justice,* 1 February 1958.

73. *Justice,* 1 February 1958 and 1 October 1958; Berle Diary, 29 August 1958; Berle and Jacobs, *Navigating the Rapids,* 688; Minutes of the GEB, 3 September 1958, 2; "The Reminiscences of Ben Davidson," 417–418; Cory Reich, *The Life of Nelson A. Rockefeller: Worlds to Conquer, 1908–1958* (New York: Doubleday, 1996), 740–741; McNickle, *To Be Mayor of New York,* 124–130.

74. McNickle, *To Be Mayor of New York,* 130; *Justice,* 15 November 1958.

75. ILGWU, *Report of the GEB,* Thirtieth Convention, 1959, 96–97; David Dubinsky, "The Problems of Success," advertisement, *New York Times Magazine,* 17 May 1959, 3; Dubinsky and Raskin, *David Dubinsky,* 306.

76. Dubinsky and Raskin, *David Dubinsky,* 290.

77. Ibid., 290–291; Goulden, *Meany,* 299–300; personal interview with Dr. Donald S. Harrington, 1 May 1985; Berle Diary, 28 June 1960; "The Reminiscences of Rev-erend Donald Szantho Harrington," vol. 1, pp. 107, 120, 120, Oral History Research Office, Columbia University, 1983; Oral History interview with Alex Rose, 3 December 1974, by Roberta W. Greene, for the Robert F. Kennedy Oral History Program of the Kennedy Library, 4–6, rough draft with editorial corrections in possession of Herbert Rose; David L. Stebenne, *Arthur J. Goldberg: New Deal Liberal* (New York: Oxford University Press, 1996), 217.

78. Oral History interview with Joseph Keenan, 3 January 1988, John F. Kennedy Library; Oral History interview with Alex Rose by Roberta F. Greene, 3 December 1974, 2; Robert Dallek, *Lone Star Rising: Lyndon Johnson and His Times, 1908–1960* (New York: Oxford University Press, 1991), 574.

79. Goulden, *Meany,* 300–301.

80. Dubinsky and Raskin, *David Dubinsky,* 292–293; interview with Shelley Appleton, 29 May 1984; Nelson Lichtenstein, *The Most Dangerous Man in Detroit: Walter Reuther and the Fate of American Labor* (New York: Basic Books, 1995), 356; Oral History interview with Leonard Woodcock, 27 January 1970, 13, and with Albert Zack, 28 November 1967, 10, Kennedy Library; interview with David Dubinsky, 7 May 1969, Lyndon B. Johnson Library (copy in DD Corr.); Oral History interview with Jack Conway, 23 May 1979, 23–24, AFL-CIO Merger Interviews, Meany Archives.

81. Interview with Dubinsky, 7 May 1969, 12.

82. Minutes of the GEB, 22 August 1960, 15–16; *Justice,* 1 and 15 November 1960; ILGWU, *Report of the GEB,* Thirty-first Convention, 1962, 14–15; Arthur M. Schlesinger Jr. (ed.), *The Coming to Power: Critical Presidential Elections in American History* (New York: Chelsea House, 1972), 521.

83. Stebenne, *Arthur J. Goldberg,* 233–234; Irving Bernstein, *Promises Kept: John F. Kennedy's New Frontier* (New York: Oxford University Press, 1991), 184; Herbert

S. Parmet, *JFK: The Presidency of John F. Kennedy* (New York: Dial Press, 1983), 66; Dubinsky to John F. Kennedy, 15 December 1960, DD Corr.

84. Stebenne, *Arthur J. Goldberg,* 255–256; Minutes of the GEB, 19 June 1961, 7; *Justice,* 16 June 1961.

85. McNickle, *To Be Mayor of New York,* 152–153.

86. Joseph P. Lash, *Eleanor: The Years Alone* (New York: W. W. Norton and Company, 1972), 274–275; Nevins, *Herbert H. Lehman and His Era,* 382; Allida M. Black, *Casting Her Own Shadow: Eleanor Roosevelt and the Shaping of Postwar Liberalism* (New York: Columbia University Press, 1996), 188.

87. McNickle, *To Be Mayor of New York,* 160–161; *Justice,* 1 July 1961; interview with Stuart Scheftel, 30 October 1991 (revised 7 October 1993), 1–2, Robert F. Wagner Collection, La Guardia-Wagner Archives.

88. McNickle, *To Be Mayor of New York,* 163; *Justice,* 1 July 1961, 1 and 15 September 1961, and 15 November 1961; *New York Times,* 12 March 1997.

89. *Justice,* 1 and 15 February 1961.

90. Evelyn Dubrow to Gus Tyler, 3 March 1961, Gus Tyler Records, ILGWU Archives.

91. Dubinsky and Raskin, *David Dubinsky,* 313; Bernstein, *Promises Kept,* 197; ILGWU, *Report of the GEB,* Thirty-first Convention, 1962, 22.

92. Bernstein, *Promises Kept,* 197–198; *Justice,* 15 May 1961; Minutes of the GEB, 19 June 1961, 2; ILGWU, *Report of the GEB,* Thirty-first Convention, 1962, 22.

93. ILGWU, *Report of the GEB,* Twenty-ninth Convention, 1956, 60; ILGWU, *Report and Proceedings,* Thirtieth Convention, 1959, 30–32, 430; personal interview with Sol C. Chaikin, 2 April 1985; personal interview with Morris Glushien, 18 April 1985.

94. Minutes of the Executive Council, AFL-CIO, 21 May 1959, 64; ILGWU, *Report and Proceedings,* Thirtieth Convention, 1959, 258.

95. Interview with Sol C. Chaikin, 2 April 1985.

96. *Justice,* 1 February 1962.

97. James McGregor Burns, *Edward Kennedy and the Camelot Legacy* (New York: W. W. Norton and Company, 1976), 74.

98. Interview with Sol C. Chaikin, 2 April 1985.

99. Burns, *Edward Kennedy and the Camelot Legacy,* 90–96.

100. ILGWU, *Report of the GEB,* Thirty-second Convention, 1965, 34–35.

101. Personal interview with Shelley Appleton, 29 May 1984.

102. ILGWU, *Report of the GEB,* Thirty-first Convention, 1962, 54–55.

103. *Justice,* 1 March 1962.

104. *Justice,* 15 May 1962 and 1–15 June 1962; John F. Kennedy to David Dubinsky, 1 June 1962, Kennedy Library; Dubinsky and Louis Stulberg to Kennedy, 29 May 1962, DD Corr.

105. ILGWU, *Report of the GEB,* Thirty-second Convention, 1965, 30.

106. Interview with David Dubinsky, 7 May 1969, 7–8; *New York Times,* 16 October 1963 and 30 December 1963; Dubinsky and Raskin, *David Dubinsky,* 303.

107. *New York Times,* 30 December 1963.

108. ILGWU, *Report and Proceedings,* Thirty-first Convention, 1962, 244–246.

109. Victor Riesel, "Inside Labor: 50 Minutes in the Personal—and Political— Life of Lyndon Johnson," press release, 3 March 1964, 1–3, attached to Riesel to Dubinsky, 5 March 1964, DD Corr.

110. *Justice,* 15 June 1964; Minutes of the GEB, 8 June 1964, 2.

111. ILGWU, *Report of the GEB,* Thirty-second Convention, 1965, 65; Richard Schwartz to Clerk, House of Representatives, 10 January 1965, Wilbur Daniels Papers, ILGWU Archives.

112. Interview with Robert F. Wagner Jr., 27 December 1991, by Richard K. Lieberman, Robert F. Wagner Collection, La Guardia-Wagner Archives; Arthur Schlesinger Jr., *Robert Kennedy and His*

394 | Notes to Chapter 18

Times (Boston: Houghton Mifflin Company, 1978), 666–668.

113. *New York Times,* 30 October 1964; *Justice,* 15 October–1 November 1964 and 15 November 1964; ILGWU, *Report of the GEB,* Thirty-second Convention, 1965, 66.

114. McNickle, *To Be Mayor of New York,* 187–197.

115. Dubinsky and Raskin, *David Dubinsky,* 309; "Transcript of Conference Held June 19th, 1965 at the Hotel Astor, New York City, with Representative John V. Lindsay and the Liberal Party Sub-Committee" (MS), ILGWU Legal Department Records, Political Department folder, unprocessed collection; Sou Chan to Fred Woltman, 27 May 1965 (copy), attached to Chan to Shelley Appleton, 27 May 1965, DD Corr.

116. *New York Times,* 28 and 29 June 1965.

117. Luigi Antonini, "An Open Letter to the Citywide Conference of the Liberal Party held on Monday, June 28, 1965 at the Astor Hotel, N.Y.C." (MS), ILGWU Local 155 Managers Records.

118. *New York Times,* 29 June 1965; Dubinsky and Raskin, *David Dubinsky,* 309; interview with Israel Breslow, 4 April 1985; interview with Israel Breslow by Henoch Mendelsund, 15 June 1982, 592, ILGWU Archives.

119. Israel Breslow to Dubinsky, 16 July 1965, DD Corr.; interview with Breslow, 4 April 1985; interview with Breslow by Henoch Mendelsund, 15 June 1982, 592–594.

120. *New York Times,* 4 November 1965; Ben Davidson to Liberal Party County and Club Organizations, 15 November 1965, Israel Breslow Papers, in possession of Allen B. Breslow, Bethpage, New York.

121. Dubinsky and Raskin, *David Dubinsky,* 309–310.

NOTES TO CHAPTER 19

1. Danish, *World of David Dubinsky,* 316–318; *New York Times,* 27 January 1955; Minutes of the GEB, 3 April 1956, 9.

2. Danish, *World of David Dubinsky,* 317–318; Gary M. Fink (ed.), *Biographical Dictionary of American Labor Leaders* (Westport, Conn.: Greenwood Press, 1974), 341–342.

3. Stulberg served nine years as president, from 1966 to 1975. He retired for health reasons in 1975 and died two years later, in December 1977, at age seventy-six. Telephone interviews with Bebe Stulberg, 24 March 1985 and 2 December 1994; ILGWU, *Report of Proceedings,* Thirtieth Convention, 1959, 480–481, 496–500.

4. ILGWU, *Report of the GEB,* Thirty-first Convention, 1962, 30–32, 44–45.

5. Ibid., 23–24.

6. Gingold Diaries, 26 March 1959.

7. Minutes of the GEB, 22 August 1960, 17.

8. Minutes of the GEB, 25 January 1960, 22.

9. ILGWU, *Report of the GEB,* Thirty-first Convention, 1962, 25–26; Minutes of the GEB, 9 September 1963; ILGWU, *Report of the GEB,* Thirty-second Convention, 1965, 78–79.

10. Roy B. Helfgott, "Women's and Children's Apparel," in Max Hall (ed.), *Made in New York: Case Studies in Metropolitan Manufacturing* (Cambridge, Mass.: Harvard University Press, 1959), 67–112.

11. U.S. Department of Labor, Bureau of Labor Statistics, Middle Atlantic Regional Office, *Employment, Earnings, and Wages in New York City, 1950–60* (June 1962), 1.

12. Martin Segal, *Wages in the Metropolis: Their Influence on the Location of Industries in the New York Region* (Cambridge, Mass.: Harvard University Press, 1960), 182; "Report of Dressmakers Union Local 22, I.L.G.W.U. to the Executive Board of the International Ladies' Garment Workers' Union, March 2, 1959" (MS), 1. The author thanks Mr. Allen Breslow for giving him a copy of this document.

13. Leon Keyserling, "The New York Dress Industry Problems and Prospects" (MS, November 1963), I-4, ILGWU Archives.

14. Elias Lieberman to Charles Kreindler, 27 December 1961; and memorandum of conference held on 4 January 1962 regarding Local 25 and Judy Bond, Inc., DD Corr.; *Women's Wear Daily,* 10 January 1962.

15. Minutes of the Executive Council, AFL-CIO, 26 April 1962, 31–34, and 3 August 1964, 3–4, 29–31, Meany Archives; *Justice,* 15 July 1962; ILGWU, *Report of the GEB,* Thirty-third Convention, 1968, 111.

16. ILGWU, *Report of the GEB,* Thirty-third Convention, 1968, 10–11, 92–95; ILGWU, *Financial and Statistical Report,* 1 January 1965 to 31 December 1967, 40.

17. Dubinsky and Raskin, *David Dubinsky,* 326; Channing H. Tobias to Louis Stulberg, 4 June 1957, National Association for the Advancement of Colored People (NAACP) Papers, Library of Congress.

18. Herbert Hill to Zimmerman, 8 January 1958, and Boris Shishkin to Hill, 14 January 1958, Zimmerman Records.

19. Hill to Richard M. Nixon, 2 April 1958 (copy), attached to Hill to Zimmerman, 3 April 1958, Zimmerman Records; Hill to Zimmerman, 24 June 1958, and Hill to Shishkin, 16 October, NAACP Papers; Hill to Shishkin, 23 July 1959, Rose Zimmerman Collection.

20. Charles Zimmerman, "Report on the AFL-CIO Civil Rights Program," 8 November 1958 (MS), Rose Zimmerman Collection; Hill to Zimmerman, 20 June 1958 (copy), attached to Hill to Zimmerman, 24 June 1958 (copy), in possession of the author, gift of Rose Zimmerman.

21. *New York Herald Tribune,* 6 October 1958.

22. Minutes of the GEB, 17 November 1958, 15; Louis Stulberg to Roy Wilkins, 28 November 1958, NAACP Papers, and copy in DD Corr.

23. Roy Wilkins to Louis Stulberg, 20 March 1959, DD Corr.

24. NAACP press release, 20 March 1959, "Joint Statement of NAACP Executive Secretary and AFL-CIO President," NAACP Papers.

25. Hill to Shishkin, 23 July 1959, NAACP Papers.

26. "National Urban League Conference September 9, 1959" (MS), 12–15, New York Joint Board Records, ILGWU Archives; *Detroit Free Press,* 14 September 1959.

27. Zimmerman to James E. Turner, 9 October 1959, and J. Carlton Yeldell to Ernest L. Brown, Jr., 19 October 1959, New York Dress Joint Board Records; *Detroit Free Press,* 14 September 1959; *Akron Beacon Journal,* 12 September 1959; *Cleveland Plain Dealer,* 19 September 1959.

28. *Pittsburgh Courier,* 12 December 1959.

29. Emanuel Muravchik to Executive Board of National Trade Union Council, 28 December 1959, with texts of articles from *Pittsburgh Courier,* 12 and 19 December 1959 and *New York Amsterdam News,* 17 December 1959; and Wilkins to Harold L. Keith, 17 December 1959, New York Dress Joint Board Records. See also Herbert Hill, "Labor Unions and the Negro," *Commentary,* December 1959, 479–488.

30. Herbert Hill, "Racism within Organized Labor: A Report of Five Years of the AFL-CIO, 1955–1960" (MS), 1959, NAACP Papers. Privately, Wilkins told Hill he found the report disturbing. The use of "racism" in the title, Wilkins said, "immediately creates an attitude before the text can be concluded." In addition, he questioned the scope and organization of the indictment. Wilkins to Hill, 16 December 1960 [*sic,* 1959], NAACP Papers.

31. Press release, Joint Board of Dress and Waistmakers' Union, ILGWU, AFL-CIO, 10 March 1960, attached to Eunice King to Zimmerman, 12 May 1960; and Zimmerman to Dwight D. Eisenhower, 26 October 1960, attached to Harold R. Tyler, Jr., to Zimmerman, 4 November 1960, New York Dress Joint Board Records.

32. Zimmerman to George Meany, 7 February 1961, and Meany to Zimmerman, 16 March 1961, New York Dress Joint Board Records; AFL-CIO Oral History interview number 1 with Charles S. Zimmer-

man by Miles Galvin, 8 May 1979, 12, Meany Archives.

33. Zimmerman, "Changes in the Jewish Labor Movement in the United States," 9.

34. Helfgott, "Women's and Children's Apparel," 88; Herbert Hill, "Black Workers, Organized Labor, and Title VII of the 1964 Civil Rights Act: Legislative History and Litigation Record," in Herbert Hill and James E. Jones, Jr. (eds.), *Race in America: The Struggle for Equality* (Madison: University of Wisconsin Press, 1993), 297; Segal, *Wages in the Metropolis,* 131; Roger Waldinger, *Still the Promised City? African-Americans and New Immigrants in Postindustrial New York* (Cambridge, Mass.: Harvard University Press, 1996), 149.

35. Herberg, "Old-Timers and New-comers," 26; Oral History interview with Maida Springer Kemp by Elizabeth Balanoff, 4 January 1977, in "The Twentieth Century Trade Union Woman: Vehicle for Social Change" (Sanford, N.C.: Microfilming Corporation of America, 1979); personal interview with Maida Springer Kemp, 2 July 1984.

36. *Ernest Holmes v. Moe Falikman,* Amended Complaint, Case No. C-7580-61, State Commission for Human Rights, 29 March 1963; *New York Herald Tribune,* 2 July 1962; Nancy L. Green, *Ready-to-Wear Ready-to-Work: A Century of Industry and Immigrants in Paris and New York* (Durham: Duke University Press, 1997), 233. Hill filed the complaint on Holmes's behalf. Robert L. Carter to Roy Wilkins, 18 March 1963, NAACP Papers.

37. NAACP press release, 2 July 1962, courtesy of Herbert Hill; Raskin interviews, cass. 21, p. 17; telephone interview with Emil Schlesinger, 1 March 1988; *New York Herald Tribune,* 2 July 1962; *New York Times,* 2 and 3 July 1962; press release, Local 10, ILGWU, 2 July 1962, DD Corr. At one point Falikman claimed that Local 10 had five hundred blacks. Telephone interview with Herbert Hill, 7 April 1992; Hill, "Black Workers, Organized Labor, and Title VII," 298n.; Minutes of the Exec-

utive Board, Local 10, ILGWU, 19 July 1962, 1–8.

38. Telephone interview with Emil Schlesinger, 1 March 1958.

39. Emil Schlesinger to Ruperto Ruiz, 25 July 1962 (copy), attached to Schlesinger to Louis Stulberg, 25 July 1962, ILGWU Legal Department Papers, ILGWU Archives.

40. Raskin interviews, cass. 21, p. 18.

41. Ibid.; Ruiz to Schlesinger, 14 September 1962, attached to Schlesinger to Falikman, 18 September 1962; and Ruiz to Schlesinger, 21 February 1963, Local 10 Records; Minutes of the GEB, 4 March 1963, 10. Hill contends that the during the five-month delay the union "greatly inflated" its minority membership and generated "spurious numbers." Telephone interview with Herbert Hill, 20 January 1998.

42. Harry Fleischman, "Is the ILGWU Biased" (draft of article), 5 November 1962; Hill to Fleischman, 23 October 1962; and Will Chasan to Charles Zimmerman, n.d. [October 1962], Zimmerman Records.

43. Ernest Holmes to Ruiz, 7 February 1963, with notarization, Local 10 Records; Robert L. Carter to Roy Wilkins, 18 March 1963, NAACP Papers.

44. Carter to Wilkins, 26 March 1963, with undated reply by Wilkins at bottom of page, NAACP Papers.

45. ILGWU press release, 30 April 1963; stipulation agreement by State Commission for Human Rights on the complaint of Ernest Holmes, complaint against Moe Falikman, 17 May 1963, DD Corr.; Schlesinger to Louis Stulberg, 21 May 1963, ILGWU Legal Department Records; *Justice,* 1 June 1963; personal interview with Harry Fleischman, 21 September 1994; Herbert Hill to the author, 10 March 1998.

46. Henry Spitz to Local 10, 7 August 1963, Local 10 Records; Schlesinger to State Commission for Human Rights, 14 August 1963, ILGWU Legal Department Records.

47. Schlesinger to George H. Fowler, 9 February 1965; Ivan McLeod to Ernest

Holmes, 9 April 1965; and Schlesinger to Falikman, 13 April 1965, Local 10 Records.

48. Will Haygood, *King of the Cats: The Life and Times of Adam Clayton Powell, Jr.* (Boston: Houghton Mifflin Company, 1993), 82–84, 100–103.

49. *Justice*, 1 March 1944, clipping attached to Adam Clayton Powell, Jr. to "Dear Sister," 9 February 1944, Zimmerman Records.

50. Ben Davidson to Adolf A. Berle, Jr., David Dubinsky and Alex Rose, 21 March 1950, attached to Gus Tyler to Dubinsky, 23 March 1950, DD Corr.; Haygood, *King of the Cats*, 161–162.

51. Herbert S. Parmet, *Eisenhower and the American Crusades* (New York: Macmillan Company, 1972), 442–443; ILGWU, *Report and Proceedings*, Twenty-ninth Convention, 1956, 460–461, 587.

52. Haygood, *King of the Cats*, 217–218.

53. Dubinsky and Raskin, *David Dubinsky*, 15.

54. Personal interview with Herbert Hill, 13 February 1986; personal interview with Evelyn Dubrow, 10 June 1985; Raskin interviews, cass. 21, p. 19.

55. Herbert Zelenko to Leo Schwartz, 13 June 1962, ILGWU Legal Department Records; *New York Times*, 14 August 1962; Liberal Party press release, 14 August 1962, attached to Ben Davidson to Dubinsky, 13 August 1962, appended to Minutes of the GEB, 4 September 1962.

56. David Wells to Louis Stulberg, 17 July 1962, ILGWU Legal Department Records.

57. Dubrow to Schlesinger, n.d. [ca. 1 August 1962], ILGWU Legal Department Records; personal interview with Evelyn Dubrow, 10 June 1985.

58. Powell Committee Hearing Notes, 8 August 1962, ILGWU Legal Department Records; Raskin interviews, cass. 21, p. 20; *New York Amsterdam News*, 4 August 1962.

59. "Testimony of Herbert Hill . . . August 17, 1962" (MS), 2, 9, attached to Min-

utes of the GEB, 4 September 1962; U.S. House Committee on Education and Labor, *Investigation of the Garment Industry: Hearings before the Ad Hoc Subcommittee on Investigation of the Garment Industry*, 87th Cong., 2d sess., 1962 (Washington, D.C.: U.S. Government Printing Office, 1962), 6–67, 108–113.

60. *Investigation of the Garment Industry*, 115–116; *New York Times*, 19 August 1962.

61. *Investigation of the Garment Industry*, 166–168.

62. Ibid., 185–226, 230–266; *New York Times*, 25 August 1962; Raskin interviews, cass. 22, p. 5. According to Hill, "A political deal was made not to continue the investigation." Personal interview with Hill, 13 February 1986.

63. *Justice*, 1 September 1962.

64. Green, *Ready-to-Wear Ready-to-Work*, 235–239; Nancy L. Green, "Blacks, Jews, and the 'Natural Alliance': Labor Cohabitation and the ILGWU," *Jewish Social Studies*, 4 (Fall 1997): 79–104.

65. Hill to Livingston Wingate, 7 August 1962, NAACP Papers.

66. Elias Lieberman to Zimmerman, 31 August 1962, Zimmerman Records.

67. Dubinsky to Herbert Zelenko, 14 September 1962, Zimmerman Records.

68. Hill to Adam Clayton Powell, Jr., 18 September 1962, NAACP Papers.

69. "Resolution on ILGWU by NAACP Board of Directors," 8 October 1962, NAACP Papers.

70. Charles S. Zimmerman, "Statement of Resignation from Board of Trustees of NAACP Legal Defense and Educational Fund," Zimmerman Records.

71. Dubinsky to Herbert H. Lehman, 19 October 1962, Herbert H. Lehman Papers, Columbia University; Lehman to Roy Wilkins, 23 October 1962, attached to Lehman to Dubinsky, 24 October 1962, DD Corr.

72. Minutes of the GEB, 4 September 1962; Haygood, *King of the Cats*, 283; Ossie Davis and Ruby Dee to Hill, 14 November 1962, Hill Collection; Roy Wilkins

to Emanuel Muravchik, 31 October 1962. Another labor group in support of the NAACP, with many Hispanic members, was the Association of Catholic Trade Unionists. Daniel J. Schulder to Hill, 10 November 1962, Hill Collection.

73. See *Justice*, 1 and 15 September 1962 and 1 and 15 October 1962, for the ILGWU position.

74. Negro Labor Committee press release, 19 September 1962, Local 10 Papers; "To All Garment Workers—Congressional Committee Opens Hearing on Exploitation of Workers in Garment Industry" (flyer issued by the Greater New York Chapter of the Negro American Labor Council, August 1962), and A. Philip Randolph to Dubinsky, 20 August 1962, Zimmerman Records; Minutes of the GEB, 4 March 1963, 9; Dubinsky to Randolph, 17 August 1962, attached to Minutes of the GEB, 4 September 1962.

75. George Field to Francis E. Rivers, 19 October 1962, DD Corr.; Harry Fleischman to Hill, 26 October 1962, Zimmerman Records; Minutes of the Executive Committee, Freedom House, 6 November 1962, and Field to Dubinsky, 7 November 1962, Freedom House–George Field Files, Seeley G. Mudd Memorial Library, Princeton University; *New York Amsterdam News*, 10 November 1962.

76. Minutes of the GEB, New York Members, 25 December 1962, 1; Minutes of the GEB, 4 March 1963, 9; telephone interview with Herbert Hill, 12 June 1989 and Personal Interview with Hill, 7 April 1992.

77. Minutes of the GEB, 4 March 1963, 9; telephone interviews with Hill, 12 June 1989 and 7 April 1992; Hill to the author, 10 March 1998.

78. Minutes of the GEB, 23 April 1962, 4; ILGWU, *Report of the GEB*, Thirty-second Convention, 1965, 56–58.

79. Article 8, Section 16 of the ILGWU Constitution prohibited membership clubs, groups, and causes, and Article 3, Section 6 limited eligibility for GEB membership to paid officers of the ILGWU for three years,

who made up a miniscule percentage of all ILGWU members. Herbert Hill, "The ILGWU Today—The Decay of a Labor Union," *New Politics*, 1 (Summer 1962): 10–12; telephone interview with Hill, 7 April 1992.

80. "Chelsea NAACP Meeting November 28, 204 West 4th St." (MS), Zimmerman Records; Wilkins to Muriel Outlaw, 30 November 1962; Wilkins to Hill, 30 November 1962 and 3 December 1962, NAACP Papers.

81. Wilkins to Hill, 18 December 1962, NAACP Papers.

82. Hill to Wilkins, 15 January 1963, and Wilkins to Hill, 28 January 1963, NAACP Papers.

83. Minutes of the GEB, 26 December 1962.

84. Minutes of the GEB, 4 March 1963, 10.

85. Hill, "ILGWU Today," 6–7; Gus Tyler, "The Truth about the ILGWU," *New Politics*, 2 (Fall 1962): 6–17; Paul Jacobs, "David Dubinsky: Why His Throne Is Wobbling," *Harper's*, December 1962, 77. Hill soon returned with "The ILGWU—Fact and Fiction," *New Politics*, 2 (Winter 1963): 7–27.

86. Daniel Bell, "Reflections on the Negro and Labor," *New Leader*, 21 January 1963, 18–20; Shelley Appleton, "The Negro and Labor," *New Leader*, 18 February 1963, 32–35.

87. Personal interview with Matthew Schoenwald, 1 May 1984; *Justice*, 1 and 15 September 1963.

88. *New York Times*, 27 November 1963; telephone interview with George Field, 16 April 1987; Minutes of the GEB, 16 March 1964, 20.

89. Minutes of the GEB, 16 March 1964, 20; Wilkins to Zimmerman, 18 September 1964, NAACP Papers.

90. Minutes of the GEB, 9 September 1963, 22–23, and 12 April 1965, 5; ILGWU, *Report and Proceedings*, Thirty-second Convention, 1965, 58–60, 433–436; personal interview with Benjamin Gebiner, 28 September 1994. The NAACP

felt its involvement in this dispute was critical to the withdrawal of financial support. Hill to the author, 10 March 1998.

91. Field to Dubinsky, 10 March 1965 and 6 May 1965, and Field to Wilkins, 10 May 1965, Freedom House Archives, Seeley G. Mudd Library, Princeton University; ILGWU, *Report and Proceedings,* Thirty-second Convention, 1965, 362–369.

92. Personal interview with Sol C. Chaikin, 12 March 1985.

93. Dubinsky and Raskin, *David Dubinsky,* 214–216.

94. John Henry Stamm, "The Second-Generation Union: A Study of the Unionization of Union Representatives" (D.B.A. diss., Graduate School of Business Administration, Harvard University, 1969), 16–50.

95. "Agreement between AFL-CIO and the Field Representatives Federation, Directly Affiliated Local Union No. 3017," DD Corr.; *New York Post,* 29 December 1960.

96. Stamm, "Second-Generation Union," 66–67; affidavit by Marvin Rogoff, County of Dauphin, State of Pennsylvania, n.d., 1–4, and "Roll Call of Formative Meeting of F.O.U.R. Sunday, December 11, 1960," Marvin Rogoff Collection, Archives of Labor History and Urban Affairs, Wayne State University, Detroit, Michigan; telephone interview with Marvin Rogoff, 21 August 1986; "Declaration of Principles and Purpose of the Federation of Union Representatives (FOUR)," DD Corr.

97. William Karker, Winifred Lippman, Marvin Rogoff, Constantine Sedares, and Martin Waxman to Dubinsky, 18 December 1960, DD Corr.

98. Affidavit by Rogoff, 5; Peter Detlefsen to Gus Sedares, 9 December 1960 (copy), attached to schedule of conferences and telephone calls, 8–24 December 1960, DD Corr.

99. "Statement by President Dubinsky at Meeting of Managers of Northeast Department in ILGWU Council Room, Friday, December 23, 1960—A.M." (MS), DD Corr.

100. *New York Times,* 28 December 1960; *New York Herald Tribune,* 28 December 1960; Sedares and Rogoff to Members of FOUR, 11 January 1961, DD Corr.

101. Sedares and Rogoff to Members of FOUR, 11 January 1961; Morris P. Glushien to Ivan C. McLeod, 4 January 1961; and E. T. Kehrer to Dubinsky, 5 January 1961, DD Corr.; telephone interview with Rogoff, 21 August 1986.

102. Personal interview with Morris Glushien, 21 March 1985; personal interview with Sam Eisenberg, 21 March 1985; personal interview with Sol C. Chaikin, 2 April 1988; personal interview with Wilbur Daniels, 16 April 1985.

103. Stamm, "Second-Generation Union," 70; affidavit by Rogoff, 6.

104. Edward Kramer to Dubinsky, 6 January 1961, DD Corr.; memorandum of meeting of review committee on Constantine Sedares, 16 January 1961; written statements by Ann Addeo, 17 January 1961; Shirley Langman, 22 January 1961; Florence Vaverchak, 21 January 1961; and Pauline Solomon, 21 January 1961; summary of testimony of Joseph Shane and fourteen other witnesses for Sedares, 23 January 1961; and testimony and statements on Sedares, 16 and 23 January 1961, all in ILGWU Legal Department Records.

105. The GEB refused to let Sedares appear as a representative of FOUR. "I also did not go into the meeting," Rogoff said afterward, "since I was there as an officer of FOUR, and the board would not agree to listen to representatives of FOUR." Affidavit by Rogoff, 6–7; Minutes of the GEB, 30 January 1961, 4–5, 15, 17, 22, 31.

106. *New York Post,* 9 February 1961; *New York Herald Tribune,* 11 February 1961.

107. Affidavit by Rogoff, 7; unsigned memorandum [by Dubinsky], 14 February 1961, DD Corr.

108. "Schedule of Terminated Employees From June 1, 1961 to date [19 October 1961]"; and Sedares and Rogoff to Dubinsky, 13 February 1961, DD Corr.; Henry Glasser to Rogoff, 16 February 1961, Baltimore Joint Board Records, ILGWU Archives; *Boston Globe,* 17 February 1961.

109. Sedares and Rogoff to George Meany, 20 February 1961, DD Corr.; *New York Times,* 24 February 1961; *Justice,* 1 March 1961.

110. Thomas E. Harris to Meany, 7 March 1961, ILGWU Legal Department Records.

111. *Justice,* 15 February 1961, 1 March 1961, and 15 April 1961.

112. *New America,* 7 April 1961.

113. *Boston Globe,* 15 and 26 March 1961.

114. *New York Post,* 10 March 1962; Murray Kempton to Dubinsky, 14 March 1961, DD Corr.

115. *New York Times,* 13 March 1961.

116. *New York Times,* 16 April 1961; *Wall Street Journal,* 17 April 1961.

117. Stulberg to ILGWU Vice-Presidents et al., 27 April 1961, ILGWU Legal Department Records.

118. Dubinsky to ILGWU Staff Members, 28 April 1961, with Ruth M. McMurray to Rogoff, 24 February 1961, Dubinsky to McMurray, 28 April 1961, and "Excerpts from a Few Letters of Resignation" attached, DD Corr.

119. Minutes of the GEB, 3 May 1961, 1–3; David Dubinsky, Luigi Antonini and Louis Stulberg to ILGWU Staff Members, 3 May 1961, and Dubinsky to ILGWU Staff Members, 8 May 1961, ILGWU Legal Department Records.

120. Morris Bialis to Dubinsky, 4 May 1961, DD Corr.

121. Rogoff to Sally Parker, 7 May 1961, DD Corr.

122. John Barry et al. to ILGWU Staff Members, 9 May 1961, DD Corr.

123. *New York Post,* 9 May 1961.

124. *New York Herald Tribune,* 11 May 1961; *Justice,* 1 June 1961.

125. Ivan C. McLeod, *Order Consolidating Complaint and Notice of Hearing,* Cases No. 1-CA-78 57-1 and 2-CA-7923, International Ladies' Garment Workers' Union of America, AFL-CIO and Federation of Union Representatives, National Labor Relations Board, Second Region, 22 June 1961; and Ivan C. McLeod, *Report on Objections and Report on Challenged Ballots,* Case No. 2-RC-11158, International Ladies' Garment Workers' Union and Federation of Union Representatives, before the National Labor Relations Board, Second Region, 29 June 1961, 1–3; ILGWU Legal Department Records; Minutes of the GEB, 19 June 1961, 14.

126. Rogoff to Benjamin Magliozzi, 2 June 1961, Rogoff Collection.

127. Rogoff to Joseph M. Guffin, 2 June 1961, Rogoff Collection.

128. Minutes of the GEB, 20 January 1961, 31, and 4 September 1962, 3.

129. Stamm, "Second-Generation Union," 91–93; Ivan C. McLeod, *Regional Director's Report and Certificate of Representative,* Case No. 2-RC-11158, International Ladies' Garment Workers' Union and Federation of Union Representatives, United States National Labor Relations Board, 6 August 1962, ILGWU Legal Department Records; McLeod, *Report on Objections,* 29 June 1961, 2.

130. Minutes of the GEB, 4 March 1963, 5.

131. ILGWU, *Report of the GEB,* Thirty-second Convention, 1965, 54–56; Sanford M. Katz to Ogden W. Mills, 10 June 1965; Emil Schlesinger to Dubinsky, 4 October 1965; Schlesinger to Stulberg, 4 May 1966; and NLRB, *Supplemental Decision and Recommendations,* 27 August 1965, Cases No. 1-CA-8849 and 2-RC-1158, 1–6, ILGWU Legal Department Records; *Justice,* 1 October 1965; *New York Times,* 17 October 1965.

132. Stamm, "Second-Generation Union," 127.

133. *Who's Who in Labor* (New York: Arno Press, 1976), 16.

134. *Justice,* 1 December 1942; wedding announcement, Jean Dubinsky to Lester M. Narins, 3 November 1942, DD Corr.; *New York Times,* 22 January 1968.

135. Confidential personal interview, 21 March 1985; personal interview with Mendelsund, 25 September 1984; telephone interview with Bebe Stulberg, 17 March 1985.

136. Minutes of the GEB, 6 March 1963, 16; *Women's Wear Daily*, 7 March 1963; personal interview with Gus Tyler, 16 November 1994; confidential interviews, 8 and 24 March 1985.

137. Dubinsky to Harry Lang, 11 July 1963, DD Corr.

138. Personal interview with Mendelsund, 25 September 1984.

139. Personal interview with Glushien, 21 March 1985.

140. Personal Interview with Tyler, 6 November 1994; telephone interview with Rogoff, 21 August 1986.

141. Telephone interview with Bebe Stulberg, 17 March 1985.

142. ILGWU, *Report of the GEB*, Twenty-fifth Convention, 1944, 57; ILGWU, *Report of the GEB*, Thirtieth Convention, 1959, 51.

143. ILGWU, *Report of the GEB*, Twenty-eighth Convention, 1953, 205.

144. ILGWU, *Report of the GEB*, Thirtieth Convention, 1959, 52.

145. ILGWU, *Report and Proceedings*, Twenty-ninth Convention, 1956, 264, 485.

146. ILGWU, *Report of the GEB*, Thirty-first Convention, 1962, 213, 349, 352–353.

147. Minutes of the GEB, New York Members, 2 July 1964, 1–2.

148. Dubinsky and Raskin, *David Dubinsky*, 326–327.

149. ILGWU, *Report of the GEB*, Thirty-first Convention, 1962, 52–55; Minutes of the GEB, 23 April 1965, 22.

150. ILGWU, *Report of the GEB*, Thirty-second Convention, 1965, 172, 294. Minutes of the GEB, 23 April 1965, 22.

151. Minutes of the GEB, 14 March 1966, 26–34.

152. Ibid., 34–37.

153. Ibid., 46–50.

154. Ibid., 51–52.

155. Ibid., 57–60; personal interview with Tyler, 16 November 1994.

156. Personal interview with Tyler, 13 October 1994.

157. Personal interview with Dr. Donald S. Harrington, 1 May 1985.

158. Personal interviews with Wilbur Daniels, 16 April 1985, and E. Howard Molisani, 9 May 1985; telephone interview with Bebe Stulberg, 17 March 1985.

159. Personal interview with Tyler, 16 November 1994.

160. Telephone interview with Bebe Stulberg, 2 December 1994.

161. Dubinsky to Harry Lang, 7 October 1966, Harry Lang Correspondence, ILGWU Archives.

NOTES TO CHAPTER 20

1. Minutes of the GEB, 14 March 1966, 31, 36; *New York Post,* 17 March 1966.

2. Personal interview with Virginia Tehas, 11 June 1985; personal interview with Leon Stein, 24 May 1984; telephone interview with Miriam Sluchan, 4 January 1985.

3. Minutes of the GEB, 14 March 1966, 12–13, 19–22; ILGWU, *Report of the GEB,* Thirty-third Convention, 1968, 44; Dubinsky to Jan Peerce, 26 September 1969, DD Corr.

4. Minutes of the GEB, New York Members, 21 June 1966, 1.

5. Ibid.; personal interview with E. Howard Molisani, 9 May 1985; Dubinsky to Harry Lang, 7 October 1966, Harry Lang Correspondence, ILGWU Archives.

6. ILGWU, *Report of the GEB,* Thirty-third Convention, 1968, 45; ILGWU, *Report of the GEB,* Thirty-fourth Convention, 1971, 85; ILGWU, *Report of the GEB,* Thirty-fifth Convention, 1974, 110; "Progress Report on Friendly Visiting Program, March 1, 1967–December 1, 1967 (First Nine Months)" (MS), 1–6, and Zalman Lichtenstein to Dubinsky, "Evaluation of Endeavor and Achievement Outline of Projected Activities for 1976/9" (MS), 2, New York Cloak Joint Board Records.

7. Dubinsky to Peerce, 26 September 1969.

8. Ibid.; Dubinsky to Isaac Stern, 6 October 1970, DD Corr.; ILGWU, *Report of the GEB,* Thirty-third Convention, 1968, 46–47.

9. Dubinsky to ———, 17 May 1966 (draft), Gus Tyler Correspondence, ILGWU Archives; ILGWU, Minutes of the GEB, 5 September 1966, 16; press release, Victor Riesel, "Inside Labor" newspaper column, 16 June 1966, Tyler Correspondence.

10. Personal interview with Morris Glushien, 21 March 1985.

11. *Day-Morning Journal*, 30 September 1966; Dubinsky to Herman Morgenstern, 6 October 1966; Dubinsky to Lang, 7 October 1966, DD Corr.

12. Dubinsky to Lang, 7 October 1966.

13. Dubinsky and Raskin, *David Dubinsky*, 311.

14. *New York Times*, 27 May 1966; Berle Diary, 30 June 1966; Schlesinger, *Robert Kennedy and His Times*, 751; Robert F. Kennedy to Dubinsky, 15 and 24 June 1966, DD Corr.

15. McNickle, *To Be Mayor of New York*, 198; Dubinsky and Raskin, *David Dubinsky*, 311.

16. Dubinsky and Raskin, *David Dubinsky*, 311–313.

17. *New York Times*, 10 August 1966.

18. *New York Times*, 15 August 1966.

19. Personal interview with Dr. Donald S. Harrington, 1 May 1998; Raskin interviews, cass. X–4, p. 18; Dubinsky and Raskin, *David Dubinsky*, 314–315.

20. Meeting of New York Managers, ILGWU, 18 August 1966, 2–3.

21. Liberal Party press release, 22 August 1966, DD Corr.

22. *New York Times*, 2 September 1966.

23. *New York Post*, 6 September 1966; personal interview with Dr. Donald S. Harrington, 1 May 1985.

24. George Field to Dubinsky, 1 September 1966.

25. Personal interview with Dr. Donald S. Harrington, 1 May 1985; *New York Post*, 8 September 1966.

26. *New York Times*, 9 and 13 September 1966; *New York Post*, 6 September 1966; personal interview with Henoch Mendelsund, 25 September 1984; Minutes of the GEB, 5 September 1966, 31–35.

27. *New York Post*, 6 September 1966; Minutes of the GEB, 5 September 1966, 27, 35; "Resolution Adopted at Sept. GEB" (MS), Stulberg Correspondence.

28. *New York Post*, 13 September 1966; *New York Times*, 13 September 1966.

29. *Long Island Press*, 14 September 1966; *Women's Wear Daily*, 21 September 1966.

30. *New York Post*, 14 September 1966.

31. Evelyn Dubrow to Stulberg, 14 September 1966, Stulberg Correspondence.

32. Personal interview with Wilbur Daniels, 10 April 1985.

33. *New York World Journal Tribune*, 14 September 1966; Liberal Party press release, 19 September 1966, DD Corr.

34. *New York World Journal Tribune*, 25 September 1966; *New York Post*, 22 and 24 October 1966; *Our Local 66*, October–November 1966; *Knitgoods Workers' Voice*, October 1966.

35. David Dubinsky, "Text of Remarks at Liberal Party Annual Dinner, October 13, 1966, Americana Hotel, New York City" (MS), Stulberg Correspondence.

36. Walter P. Reuther to Dubinsky, 30 September 1966 and 27 October 1966; Dubinsky to Reuther, 17 October 1966, Reuther Collection, Reuther Archives, Wayne State University.

37. *New York World Journal Tribune*, 24 October 1966.

38. *New York Times*, 10 November 1966 and 16 December 1966; Schlesinger, *Robert Kennedy and His Times*, 754–758.

39. *New York World Journal Tribune*, 10 November 1966.

40. [David Dubinsky], memorandum, 11 November 1966, DD Corr.

41. *Newsday*, 11 November 1966.

42. *New York World Journal Tribune*, 6 December 1966.

43. *New York Times*, 28 April 1968, 19 and 30 June 1968, and 6 November 1968; Jacob K. Javits, with Rafael Steinberg, *Javits: The Autobiography of a Public Man* (Boston: Houghton Mifflin, 1981), 359–360.

44. Dubinsky to John L. Childs, 16 December 1969, DD Corr.; *New York Times*,

10 and 15 May 1969; ILGWU, *Report and Proceedings,* Thirty-fourth Convention, 1971, 48–49; McNickle, *To Be Mayor of New York,* 223–236.

45. *New York Times,* 20 November 1966.

46. ILGWU, *Report and Proceedings,* Thirty-second Convention, 1965, 487, 550; Minutes of the GEB, 30 January 1967, 30–31.

47. Stulberg to Donald Harrington, 18 January 1967, DD Corr.; *New York Daily News,* 6 March 1967.

48. ILGWU, *Report and Proceedings,* Thirty-second Convention, 1965, 77, 226.

49. "ADA Policy Position Adopted at National Board Meeting Statler-Hilton Hotel [Washington, D.C.] May 19–21, 1967" (MS), DD Corr.; Gillon, *Politics and Vision,* 197–198.

50. Minutes of the GEB, 14 December 1967, 24–25.

51. Two other union presidents, I. W. Abel of the United Steelworkers and Joseph A. Beirne of the Communications Workers, also resigned at this time. *New York Times,* 13 February 1968; ILGWU, *Report and Proceedings,* Thirty-third Convention, 1968, 61–63; Stulberg to John Kenneth Galbraith, n.d. (copy), attached to Dubinsky to Tyler, 14 February 1968, DD Corr.

52. Dubinsky to Clifton Daniel, 15 February 1968, DD Corr.; Dubinsky's statement to the press is attached to Dubinsky to Tyler, 14 February 1968, and printed in the *New York Times,* 19 February 1968.

53. Decisions of the GEB, ILGWU, 10–13 July 1967, 1, Wilbur Daniels Correspondence, ILGWU Archives; *New York Times,* 23 August 1967; *Justice,* 15 August 1967; Dubinsky to Stulberg, 25 July 1967, Stulberg Correspondence.

54. Dubinsky to Luigi Antonini, 25 July 1967, DD Corr.

55. Dubinsky to Stulberg, 25 July 1967, Stulberg Corr.

56. Antonini to Dubinsky, 25 July 1967, DD Corr.

57. Stulberg to Dubinsky, 15 August 1957, DD Corr.

58. *Women's Wear Daily,* 12 December 1967; *New York Post,* 2 January 1968; Secretary to Dubinsky [Julie Krisberg] to James Wechsler, 27 December 1967, with text of nominating statement by Paul Hall attached, DD Corr.

59. *New York Times,* 17 February 1970.

60. John Webb Pratt, *Religion, Politics, and Diversity: The Church-State Theme in New York History* (Ithaca, N.Y.: Cornell University Press, 1967), 242–254, 283–288; *New York Times,* 17 February 1970; David Wells to Dubinsky, 23 March 1967, DD Corr.

61. Wells to Dubinsky, 28 February 1967 and 21, 23, and 30 March 1967, DD Corr.

62. Statement by Donald Harrington, 23 May 1967 (MS); statement by Harrington, n.d., attached to Dubinsky to L. Fogelman, 4 October 1967, DD Corr.

63. Dubinsky to William J. Vanden Heuvel, 23 October 1967, DD Corr.; Dubinsky to Fogelman, 4 October 1967; *New York Times,* 16 August 1967 and 20 and 27 September 1967.

64. *Justice,* 15 June 1967; David Dubinsky, speech before New York State Constitutional Convention, 12 June 1967 (MS), DD Corr.; Raskin interviews, cass. 22, pp. 18–19.

65. *New York Times,* 27 September 1967.

66. Dubinsky to Vanden Heuvel, 23 October 1967.

67. Dubinsky to Mary Boyd, 4 October 1967, DD Corr.

68. *New York Times,* 9 November 1967.

69. Personal interview with Dr. Donald S. Harrington, 1 May 1985.

70. Dubinsky and Raskin, *David Dubinsky,* 330.

71. ILGWU, Report and Proceedings, Thirty-third Convention, 1968, 253–256, 427–429.

72. Leon Shull to Officers, National Board and Chapters, Americans for Democratic Action, 6 October 1968, DD Corr.

73. *New York Times,* 21 and 31 October 1968 and 6 November 1968.

74. "The Reminiscences of Ben Davidson," 623–525, 629; "The Reminiscences of Reverend Donald Szantho Harrington," vol. 2, pp. 240–241; Gus Tyler to A. H. Raskin, 19 October 1970, DD Corr.; personal interview with Dr. Donald S. Harrington, 1 May 1985.

75. Telephone interview with Arthur J. Goldberg, 12 June 1985.

76. Sou Chan to Dubinsky, 29 February 1972, and Dubinsky to Chan, 2 March 1972, DD Corr.

77. *New York Times,* 21 February 1972.

78. Press release, "Council Reaffirms Opposition to Carswell for High Court Seat," AFL-CIO News Service, 16 February 1970, DD Corr.

79. Richard Kluger to Dubinsky, 10 July 1969 and 1 August 1969, and "Publishing Agreement . . . 12 November 1969," A. H. Raskin Collection, Columbia University.

80. Harrington to Dubinsky, 18 January 1973, and Dubinsky to Ben Davidson, 25 January 1973, DD Corr.; "The Reminiscences of Ben Davidson," 672.

81. Morris S. Novik to Dubinsky [October 1979], and Menu, Thirty-fifth Annual Liberal Party Dinner, 10 October 1979, DD Corr.; "The Reminiscences of Ben Davidson," 672.

82. *New York Times,* 26 December 1974; *New York Post,* 26 December 1974.

83. Hannah Haskel Kreindler to Broche Kopstein, 19 November 1981, ILGWU Archives. Cited with permission of Hannah Haskel Kreindler.

84. Kreindler to Kopstein, 6 May 1982, ILGWU Archives. Cited with permission of Hannah Haskel Kreindler.

85. Kreindler to Kopstein, 29 September 1982, ILGWU Archives. Cited with permission of Hannah Haskel Kreindler. *New York Times,* 18 September 1982; *Newsday,* 18 September 1982; *Justice,* October 1982.

86. Dubinsky and Raskin, *David Dubinsky,* 331.

87. ILGWU, *Report and Proceedings,* Thirty-six Convention, 1977, 1–9; ILGWU, *Report and Proceedings,* Thirty-ninth Convention, 1986, 369–377; *New York Times,* 15 December 1977 and 7 June 1986.

88. "Labor Hall of Fame Induction of David Dubinsky, Remarks by Jay Mazur, . . . January 21, 1994," 1. Courtesy of Jay Mazur.

89. In 1976 the Amalgamated Clothing Workers of America had merged with the Textile Workers Union of America. *New York Times,* 21 February 1995. In 2004 UNITE merged with HERE, the Hotel Employees and Restaurant Employees Union, creating UNITE HERE. *New York Times,* 26 February 2004; *Women's Wear Daily,* 9 July 2004.

Index

To conserve space, acronyms appearing in the text are used in subheadings. For example: "ACWA" is used as a subheading instead of "Amalgamated Clothing Workers of America." The following acronyms also appear in subheadings: "DD" for David Dubinsky, "NYC" for New York City, and "NYS" for New York State. All acronyms appear as main headings along with their translations.

ILGWU (*Continued*)
dressmakers' strike
(1958), 274; educational
activities, 93; effect of
left-right disputes, 65; exclusion of leftists from
conventions, 31; General
Executive Board (*see* "DD
and" under "ILGWU
General Executive
Board"); ILGWU acting
president, 62–63, 66–80;
ILGWU dual office hold-
ing, 79, 101, 243;
ILGWU Honorary Presi-
dent, 233; ILGWU Local
89, 41; ILGWU presi-
dency, 78–79, 82, 101;
ILGWU secretary-trea-
surer, 65, 79, 101;
ILGWU vice presidency,
26; ILGWU–ACWA dis-
pute, 180; ILGWU's fi-
nances, 107, 243, 321;
ILGWU's reaffiliation
with the AFL, 183–185;
indictment of ILGWU for
restraint of trade, 289;
married to the union,
326, 338; minimum
wages, 87–88, 287–288,
291; organizational dri-
ves, 68–69; Philadelphia
(1925), 38–41; research
department, 93; resigna-
tion as president, 295;
Retirees Service Depart-
ment, 327; retirement,
218, 319, 320–325, 338;
Schlesinger's election as
ILGWU president, 59,
75–78; settlement com-
mittee, 43; social union-
ism, 1, 341; strengthening
ILGWU, 63; succession,
296, 319–320; weakening
NTWIU, 63; Workmen's
Circle Home for the
Aged, 309
– Democratic Party, 282

– dissent in, 295
– dual unionism, 93
– "Dubinsky's union," 80,
311–312, 325
– dues, 32–33, 54, 71–72,
77
– economic conditions: in
1920s, 23–24, 32, 66;
Great Depression of the
1930s, 66–67, 81, 193;
postwar years, 210; sub-
standard employment
conditions, 58, 143
– educational activities, 93,
258–259, 273
– Federation of Union Representatives (FOUR),
312–319
– finances: ALP, 198–199;
anti-fascist efforts, 107;
anti-Nazi efforts, 205;
bankruptcy threat, 57;
bond issuance, 60, 71;
charitable contributions,
61–62, 210; cloakmakers'
strike (1926), 41, 43,
45–46, 49; collection of
liquidated damages, 327;
congressional races
(1954), 282; DD and,
107, 243, 321; expense
cutting, 83; financial relief, 59–60; following
1928 convention, 57;
Force Ouvriere, 230;
Franklin Delano Roo-
sevelt School of Maritime
Trades, 267; French revi-
talization, 230; FTUC,
224; Haifa trade school,
238; health care costs,
109; *Histadrut*, 237, 241;
Humphrey's Minnesota
campaign (1947), 215;
ILGWU Special Assis-
tance Fund, 327; indebt-
edness, 69–70, 71–72,
82–83; Italian-American
Labor Council, 244; Ital-
ian trade unions, 228;

JLC, 199–200, 230, 242,
244; *knippel* ("knot"),
243; *Le Populaire*, 230;
Liberal Party, 256, 328,
331; loans to, 69; missed
payments, 78; penny
pinching, 107; pension
funds, 276, 320–322,
326–327; per capita pay-
ments to AFL, 82, 95; per
capita tax, 218; personal
underwriting of loans to
the union, 92; Polish un-
derground, 204; prosper-
ity, 188; real estate invest-
ments, 271; refusal of locals to pay dues, 71–72;
relief agencies, 194; re-
tirement funds, 276,
320–322, 326–327;
salaries for staff/officers,
71, 85, 206–207, 243,
244, 270; San Antonio
mayoral election (1939),
291; support for ALP,
156; TWOC, 161; US
presidential race (1960),
285–286
– first woman organizer,
109
– *Force Ouvriere*, 230
– founding, 18
– FTUC, 224
– Gompers and, 14, 18–19,
94
– headquarters, 204, 224
– healthcare for workers,
108–109, 216, 258
– Hill and, 300, 303, 306,
310
– *Histadrut*, 237, 240, 241
– housing, 262–264,
271–272
– Humphrey and, 215, 292,
328
– IAM, 69, 83
– IFTU, 104
– *ILGWU News-History*,
270
– imported goods, 268, 297

121, 123, 124–125, 126,
132, 141, 146, 149,
165–167, 170, 172–173,
177, 196, 374n38; Foster
and, 154; Green and, 87,
149–150, 182–183, 196;
Hutcheson and, 123;
ILGWU convention
(1937), 158, 160; industrial unionism, 105, 123;
isolationism, 190; Labor's
Non-Partisan League,
129, 151; Murray and,
133, 187; Nagler and,
150; NIRA extension,
115; organization of the
steel industry, 128,
132–133; Roosevelt
(Franklin D.) and, 151,
179, 182, 186, 196;
SWOC, 132–133; UMW,
129; Vice Presidency of
U.S., 186; Willkie and, 186
Liberal Party: 1950 New
York elections, 251;
ADA, 215; African Americans, 293; Berle (Adolph)
and, 255, 256; chairman,
323; Davidson and, 199,
255; DD and, 199, 207,
249–250, 252, 256, 328,
330, 340; decline, 257,
283; Democratic Party,
255–256, 335, 337; endorsements, 2, 250;
Farmer and, 330–331; finances, 256, 328, 331;
first own candidate, 252;
founding, 199; Harriman
and, 257; Harrington
and, 323; ILGWU, 199,
249, 256, 328, 331, 334;
intellectuals, 250, 262;
Johnson (Lyndon) and,
335; Lindsay and, 294;
membership, 249, 257;
NYC City Council elections (1951), 252; NYC
mayoral race (1945), 208;
NYC mayoral race

(1953), 254–255; NYC
mayoral race (1961), 286;
NYC mayoral race
(1965), 293–294; NYC
mayoral race (1969), 334;
NYC municipal elections
(1949), 250–251; NYS
Constitutional Convention (1967), 332, 337;
NYS gubernatorial race
(1954), 255; NYS gubernatorial race (1966),
329–333; NYS senatorial
race (1949), 250; NYS
senatorial race (1952),
254; NYS senatorial race
(1958), 283; NYS senatorial race (1964), 292; O'-
Connor and, 329; Powell
and, 304–305; Puerto Ricans, 293; raison d'etre,
249–250; Republican
Party, 252, 337; Riegelman and, 254; Roosevelt
(Franklin D., Jr.) and,
256, 330–331; Rose and,
249–250, 332; Schwarz
on, 249–250; Stevenson
and, 253, 292; Stulberg
(Louis) and, 334–335;
Taft-Hartley Act, 222;
Trade Union Council,
222; US presidential race
(1944), 206; US presidential race (1948), 222–223;
US presidential race
(1956), 282–283; US
presidential race (1960),
284, 286, 291; US presidential race (1964),
292–293; as a voice, 262;
Wagner (Robert F.) and,
199; Wagner (Robert F.,
Jr.) and, 256; Zelenko
and, 308; Zimmerman
and, 222
Liberals, 207, 210,
213–214, 219, 220, 221
Lie, Haakon, 204
Lieberman, Elias, 307, 322

Lindsay, John V., 2, 3,
293–295, 322, 323,
324–325, 334
Lippman, Winifred, 313
Lodge, Henry Cabot, 285
Lodz (Russia, later Poland),
4, 7, 70, 201
Loeb, James, Jr., 214–215
London, Meyer, 16–17, 20,
205
Long, Breckinridge,
193–194
Long, Huey P., 128
Los Angeles, 68, 172
Los Angeles Trade Union
Conference, 172
Lovestone, Jay: 1948 TUC
meeting, 232; American
Veterans Committee, 211;
Becu and, 266; Braden
and, 234; Brown (Irving)
and, 225; Bukharin and,
72; Central Intelligence
Agency, 234–236; Communist International, 168;
DD and, 2, 155, 168,
225, 234, 264; Feinglass
and, 275; FTUC, 224,
231; ILGWU International Relations Department, 204; ILGWU participation in Committee
for Industrial Organization, 176; influence, 234;
informants, 225; Katz
and, 225; to leftists, 267;
Meany and, 234, 275;
"Mr. Intellectual," 235;
Nelson (Louis) and, 168;
office space, 224; Pegler
and, 247; Pius XII and,
229; Reuther (Victor)
and, 265; subsidies to European trade unions,
234–235, 381n112;
WFTU, 232; *Workers
Age*, 186; Workers'
(Communist) Party, 72;
Zimmerman and, 72,
155, 168

About the Author

Robert D. Parmet is Professor of History at York College of The City University of New York. He is also the author of *Labor and Immigration in Industrial America* and co-author of *American Nativism, 1830–1860*.